T0181484

Lecture Notes in Computer Science 12761

More information about this subseries at http://www.springer.com/series/7407

Heike Jagode · Hartwig Anzt ·
Hatem Ltaief · Piotr Luszczek (Eds.)

High Performance Computing

ISC High Performance Digital 2021 International Workshops
Frankfurt am Main, Germany, June 24 – July 2, 2021
Revised Selected Papers

Springer

Editors
Heike Jagode 🄳
University of Tennessee at Knoxville
Knowville, TN, USA

Hartwig Anzt 🄳
Karlsruhe Institute of Technology
Karlsruhe, Baden-Württemberg, Germany

Hatem Ltaief 🄳
King Abdullah University of Science
and Technology
Thuwal, Saudi Arabia

Piotr Luszczek 🄳
University of Tennessee System
Knoxville, TN, USA

ISSN 0302-9743   ISSN 1611-3349 (electronic)
Lecture Notes in Computer Science
ISBN 978-3-030-90538-5   ISBN 978-3-030-90539-2 (eBook)
https://doi.org/10.1007/978-3-030-90539-2

LNCS Sublibrary: SL1 – Theoretical Computer Science and General Issues

This Springer imprint is published by the registered company Springer Nature Switzerland AG
The registered company address is: Gewerbestrasse 11, 6330 Cham, Switzerland

Preface

The ISC High Performance 2021 conference was planned to be held in Frankfurt, Germany. Due to the severe impact of COVID-19 and the travel restrictions, the 36th edition of ISC was rescheduled to be conducted online as ISC 2021 Digital during June 24 – July 2, 2021.

In the organization and realization of this second fully virtual edition of the conference series, the organizing team around Martin Schultz (TU Munich) heavily benefited from the lessons learned during ISC 2020 Digital and the countless virtual meetings everyone had experienced throughout the past year. The steep learning curve and thorough preparation to cater to the needs of HPC enthusiasts manifested in 2,051 attendees from 51 countries.

Like in previous years, ISC 2021 Digital was accompanied by the ISC High Performance workshop series. Being under the assumption that 2021 would bring back in-person meetings we, Heike Jagode and Hartwig Anzt as the ISC 2020 Digital Workshop Chair and Deputy Chair, respectively, committed to remain in our positions for the ISC 2021 edition. To make up for the virtual realization of the 2020 workshops, all 23 workshops accepted for ISC 2020 were allowed to roll over to the 2021 edition without a new call for workshop proposals. In the end, 19 workshops used that opportunity, even though the plans for an in-person meeting had to be postponed again. This extremely strong outcome reveals a significant interest and commitment of the workshop organizers, and we gratefully acknowledge their strong contributions to ISC 2021 Digital.

Like in the previous edition, the ISC workshops were composed of workshops with and without proceedings. While we had 12 workshops with proceedings, only the following nine workshops decided to publish their papers in this year's proceedings:

- Second International Workshop on the Application of Machine Learning Techniques to Computational Fluid Dynamics and Solid Mechanics Simulations and Analysis
- HPC-IODC: HPC I/O in the Data Center Workshop
- Compiler-assisted Correctness Checking and Performance Optimization for HPC
- Machine Learning on HPC Systems
- 4th International Workshop on Interoperability of Supercomputing and Cloud Technologies
- 2nd International Workshop on Monitoring and Operational Data Analytics
- 16th Workshop on Virtualization in High-Performance Cloud Computing
- Deep Learning on Supercomputers
- 5th International Workshop on In Situ Visualization

We, Hatem Ltaief and Piotr Luszczek, teamed up as Proceedings Chair and Deputy Chair, respectively, and managed the organization of the workshops' proceedings. Given all of these challenges, the quality of this year's ISC workshops proceedings is remarkable. In total, we have 35 high-quality papers that all underwent thorough reviews. Each chapter of the book contains the accepted and revised papers for one of the workshops. For some workshops, an additional preface describes the review process and provides a summary of the outcome.

For a second time we hope that, perhaps next year, we will be able to once again host the ISC High Performance workshops in person. Until then, we want to thank our workshops committee members, organizers of workshops, and all contributors and attendees of the ISC Digital 2021 workshops, and we are proud to present the latest findings on topics related to research, development, and the application of large-scale, high-performance systems.

August 2021   Heike Jagode
                                                              Hartwig Anzt
                                                              Hatem Ltaief
                                                              Piotr Luszczek

Organization

Workshops Chairs

Heike Jagode   University of Tennessee, USA
Hartwig Anzt   Karlsruhe Institute of Technology, Germany,
         and University of Tennessee, USA

Workshops Committee

Emmanuel Agullo	Inria, France
Hartwig Anzt	Karlsruhe Institute of Technology, Germany, and University of Tennessee, USA
Richard Barrett	Sandia National Laboratories, USA
Roy Campbell	Department of Defense, USA
Florina Ciorba	University of Basel, Switzerland
Anthony Danalis	University of Tennessee, USA
Manuel F. Dolz	Universitat Jaume I, Spain
Nick Forrington	Arm, USA
Karl Fuerlinger	Ludwig Maximilian University Munich, Germany
Judit Gimenez Lucas	Barcelona Supercomputing Center, Spain
Thomas Gruber	University of Erlangen-Nuremberg, Germany
Joachim Hein	Lund University, Sweden
David Henty	University of Edinburgh, UK
Marc-Andre Hermanns	RWTH Aachen University, Germany
Kevin Huck	University of Oregon, USA
Sascha Hunold	TU Wien, Austria
Heike Jagode	University of Tennessee, USA
Eileen Kuehn	Karlsruhe Institute of Technology, Germany
Diana Moise	HPE, Switzerland
Tapasya Patki	Lawrence Livermore National Laboratory, USA
Jelena Pjesivac-Grbovic	Verily Life Sciences and Google, USA
Philip Roth	Oak Ridge National Laboratory, USA
Ana Lucia Varbanescu	University of Amsterdam, The Netherlands

Proceedings Chairs

Hatem Ltaief   KAUST, Saudi Arabia
Piotr Luszczek   University of Tennessee, USA

Contents

**Fourth International Workshop on Interoperability
of Supercomputing and Cloud Technologies**

**Second International Workshop on Monitoring and Operational
Data Analytics**

**Sixteenth Workshop on Virtualization in High–Performance
Cloud Computing**

Second International Workshop on the Application of Machine Learning Techniques to Computational Fluid Dynamics and Solid Mechanics Simulations and Analysis

Second International Workshop on the Application of Machine Learning Techniques to Computational Fluid Dynamics and Solid Mechanics Simulations and Analysis

1 Background and Description

The Second International Workshop on the Application of Machine Learning Techniques to Computational Fluid Dynamics and Solid Mechanics Simulations and Analysis (CFDML), co-located with ISC High Performance 2021 Digital, was held online on July 2nd, 2021. It followed the first successful workshop[1] organized at ISC 2020. The event was designed to stimulate research at the confluence of computational fluid dynamics (CFD), solid mechanics, and machine learning (ML), by providing a venue to exchange new ideas and discuss new challenges and emerging opportunities. The workshop was also an opportunity to expose a rapidly emerging field to a broader research community.

The workshop solicited papers on all aspects of CFD and solid mechanics where ML plays a significant role or enables the solution of complex problems. Topics of interest included physics-based modeling with the main focus on fluid physics, such as reduced modeling for dimensionality reduction and the Reynolds-averaged Navier-Stokes (RANS) turbulence modeling, shape and topology optimization in solids, prediction of aeroacoustics, uncertainty quantification and reliability analysis, reinforcement learning for the design of active/passive flow control, and ML approaches that enable or enhance any of the above techniques. All submitted manuscripts were peer reviewed by three program committee members using a single-blind process. Submissions were evaluated on originality, technical strength, significance, quality of presentation, and interest and relevance to the workshop. Ten papers were selected for workshop presentation and inclusion in the proceedings. Authors were asked to revise their papers based on the feedback of the program committee members.

2 Workshop Summary

The workshop started with a brief overview by the organizing committee followed by a live keynote presentation delivered by George Em Karniadakis. Authors of all accepted papers were asked to record videos of their presentations, which were posted together with PowerPoint slides on the workshop's website[2] prior to the event. On the day of the workshop, all presenters and attendees connected to a Zoom channel for an on-line four-hour long series of presentations and Q&A sessions. Pre-recorded presentations

---

[1] http://www.ncsa.illinois.edu/enabling/data/deep_learning/news/cfdml20.

[2] http://www.ncsa.illinois.edu/enabling/data/deep_learning/news/cfdml21.

were played, and the attendees asked questions and discussed the results. This session was attended by over 30 participants.

2.1 Keynote

The keynote session was chaired by Eloisa Bentivegna from IBM Research Europe, UK. Professor George Em Karniadakis, the invited keynote speaker of the CFDML 2021, presented a new approach to developing a data-driven, learning-based framework for simulating fluid flows and discovering hidden physics from noisy data. He introduced a Physics constrained deep learning approach based on neural networks (PINNs) and generative adversarial networks (GANs). Unlike other approaches that rely on big data, the proposed method "learns" from small data by exploiting the information provided by the physical conservation laws, which are used to obtain informative priors or regularize the neural networks. He demonstrated the power of PINNs for several inverse problems, including multi-fidelity modeling in monitoring ocean acidification levels in the Massachusetts Bay. He also introduced new NNs that learn functionals and nonlinear operators from functions and corresponding responses for system identification, the so-called DeepONet. He demonstrated that DeepONet could learn various explicit operators such as integrals, Laplace transforms, fractional Laplacians, and implicit operators representing deterministic and stochastic differential equations. More generally, DeepONet can even learn multiscale operators spanning across many scales and be trained by diverse data sources simultaneously. Finally, professor Karniadakis illustrated DeepONet's outstanding achievements with numerical experiments of electroconvection and hypersonic boundary layers.

2.2 Research Papers

Research papers were organized into three sessions, with time for Q&A at the end of each session.

2.2.1 Session 1: Fluid Mechanics with Turbulence, Reduced Models, and Machine Learning

The session was chaired by Ashley Scillitoe from the Alan Turing Institute, UK. This session examined the application of machine learning to reduced order modelling and turbulence modelling in fluid mechanics. In their paper titled "Nonlinear mode decomposition and reduced-order modeling for three-dimensional cylinder flow by distributed learning on Fugaku", Ando et al. use a convolutional neural network (CNN) to decompose a three-dimensional cylinder flow into reduced order modes. A long short-term memory (LSTM) network is then used to predict the time evolution of the latent vector. Although there is room for improvement regarding the reconstruction accuracy, the training process used here is particularly notable, with up to 10,500 CPU nodes used in a distributed manner. The training of such models serves to demonstrate the potential for training complex deep learning models on existing CPU clusters.

In the next paper, "Reconstruction of mixture fraction statistics of turbulent jet flows with deep learning", Gauding and Bode use a generative adversarial network

(GAN) for super-resolution of turbulent flows. They show that the mixture fraction field of a planar turbulent jet flow can be recovered from coarse-grained data with good accuracy. In other words, the GAN is able to reconstruct small-scale turbulent structures from relatively low-resolution large eddy simulations, allowing for significant computational cost savings. Of particular note is the physics-informed nature of the loss function, with gradient and continuity terms added to ensure accuracy of the scalar dissipation rate, as well as enforce the continuity equation.

In "Reservoir computing in reduced order modeling for chaotic dynamical systems", Carvalho et al. presented their work using a recurrent neural network (RNN) to predict the evolutionary state of chaotical systems. A reservoir computing network is used; a class of RNN which has attracted attention in recent years as a lower training cost solution for a number of applications, mainly for modelling complex time series systems. The RNN is combined with space-only proper orthogonal decomposition (POD) in order to build a reduced order model (ROM) that produces sequential short-term forecasts of pollution dispersion over the continental USA region. In comparison to the first paper, where a CNN was used to perform mode decomposition, this work shows how deep learning methods can also be combined with a mode decomposition technique.

Finally, in "A data-driven wall-shear stress model for LES using gradient boosting decision trees", Radhakrishnan et al. use the well-known XGBoost algorithm to construct a wall-shear stress model for use in large eddy simulations. The resulting model is able to emulate the behavior of an algebraic equilibrium wall model, giving good skin friction predictions for equilibrium flows. Unsurprisingly, since the model was trained on equilibrium flows, the model performs less well on a wall-mounted test case where strong turbulent non-equilibrium effects are present. This leaves the door open for the development of more advanced machine learning augmented wall-shear stress models in the future.

2.2.2 Session 2: Novel Methods Development in Machine Learning and Fluid Simulation

The session was chaired by Alberto Costa Nogueira Junior from IBM Research in Brazil, Brazil. This session covered three of the accepted papers. In the first presentation, "Lettuce: PyTorch-based Lattice Boltzmann" by Bedrunka et al., the presenter introduced a PyTorch-based LBM code with a threefold aim: a) enabling GPU accelerated calculations with minimal source code; b) facilitating rapid prototyping of LBM models; and c) enabling the integration of LBM simulations with PyTorch's deep learning and automatic differentiation facility. The authors demonstrated the code capabilities through a baseline example by combining ML with LBM where a model was trained on a doubly periodic shear layer and then transferred to a decaying turbulence flow. Results also showed PyTorch's automatic differentiation features in flow control and optimization.

In "Novel DNNs for stiff ODEs with applications to chemically reacting flows", Brown et al. introduced a new Deep Neural Network to approximate stiff ODEs. Numerical experiments designed to assess this model showed that it is helpful to account for the physical properties of species while designing DNNs. Results also indicated that the proposed approach generalizes well.

In "Machine-learning-based control of perturbed and heated channel flows" by Rüttgers et al. the authors proposed a reinforcement learning algorithm coupled to a thermal lattice-Boltzmann method to control flow through a 2D heated channel narrowed by a bump. The thermal lattice-Boltzmann method was validated for a fully developed isothermal channel flow. Numerical results indicated that the presented method was a valid approach for avoiding expensive parameter space explorations and promises to be effective in supporting shape optimizations for complex configurations.

2.2.3   Session 3: Confluence of Machine Learning and Fluid Simulation Applications

The session was chaired by Charalambos Chrysostomou from the Cyprus Institute, Cyprus. The first presentation of the session was entitled "Physics informed machine learning for fluid-structure interaction" by Yan et al. This work presented a physics-informed neural network (PINN) framework that fuses physical principles and labeled data for fluid-structure interaction (FSI) problems. The presented results indicate the great potential of machine learning for FSI simulations.

In the second presentation, "Film cooling prediction and optimization based on deconvolution neural network" by Wang et al., the authors demonstrated a theoretic model based on Deconvolutional Neural Network (Deconv NN) to model the non-linear and high-dimensional mapping between coolant jet parameters and the surface temperature distribution. The results of the optimization show that the film cooling effectiveness has been successfully improved with QE 7.35% when compared with the reference.

In "Turbomachinery blade surrogate modeling using deep learning" by Luo et al. the authors presented the feasibility of convolutional neural network techniques for aerodynamic performance evaluation. The proposed CNN method was shown to automatically detect essential features and effectively estimate the pressure loss and deviation much faster than a CFD solver.

Organizing Committee

Volodymyr Kindratenko	National Center for Supercomputing Applications, USA
Eloisa Bentivegna	IBM Research Europe, UK
Andreas Lintermann	Jülich Supercomputing Centre, Germany
Charalambos Chrysostomou	The Cyprus Institute, Cyprus
Jiahuan Cui	Zhejiang University, China
Ashley Scillitoe	The Alan Turing Institute, UK
Morris Riedel	University of Iceland, Iceland
Jenia Jitsev	Jülich Supercomputing Centre, Forschungszentrum Jülich, Germany
Seid Koric	National Center for Supercomputing Applications, USA

Shirui Luo   National Center for Supercomputing Applications,
                                        USA
Jeyan Thiyagalingam   Science and Technology Facilities Council, UK
Alberto Costa Nogueira Junior   IBM Research Brazil, Brazil
Nikos Savva   The Cyprus Institute, Cyprus

Machine-Learning-Based Control of Perturbed and Heated Channel Flows

Mario Rüttgers[1,2,3(✉)] ⓘ, Moritz Waldmann[1,3] ⓘ, Wolfgang Schröder[1,3] ⓘ,
and Andreas Lintermann[2,3] ⓘ

[1] Institute of Aerodynamics and Chair of Fluid Mechanics, RWTH Aachen
University, Wüllnerstraße 5a, 52062 Aachen, Germany
m.ruettgers@aia.rwth-aachen.de
[2] Jülich Supercomputing Centre, Forschungszentrum Jülich GmbH,
Wilhelm-Johnen-Straße, 52425 Jülich, Germany
[3] Jülich Aachen Research Alliance Center for Simulation and Data Science,
RWTH Aachen University and Forschungszentrum Jülich, Seffenter Weg 23,
52074 Aachen, Germany

Abstract. A reinforcement learning algorithm is coupled to a thermal
lattice-Boltzmann method to control flow through a two-dimensional
heated channel narrowed by a bump. The algorithm is allowed to change
the disturbance factor of the bump and receives feedback in terms of
the pressure loss and temperature increase between the inflow and outflow region of the channel. It is trained to modify the bump such that
both fluid mechanical properties are rated equally important. After a
modification, a new simulation is initialized using the modified geometry
and the flow field computed in the previous run. The thermal lattice-
Boltzmann method is validated for a fully developed isothermal channel flow. After 265 simulations, the trained algorithm predicts an averaged disturbance factor that deviates by less than 1% from the reference
solution obtained from 3,400 numerical simulations using a parameter
sweep over the disturbance factor. The error is reduced to less than
0.1% after 1,450 simulations. A comparison of the temperature, pressure, and streamwise velocity distributions of the reference solution with
the solution after 1,450 simulations along the line of the maximum velocity component in streamwise direction shows only negligible differences.
The presented method is hence a valid method for avoiding expensive
parameter space explorations and promises to be effective in supporting shape optimizations for more complex configurations, e.g., in finding
optimal nasal cavity shapes.

Keywords: Reinforcement learning · Proximal policy optimization ·
Thermal lattice-Boltzmann · Flow control

M. Rüttgers and M. Waldmann—Authors contributed equally.

The original version of this chapter was revised: this chapter not an open access publication. It has now been converted to open access under a CC BY 4.0 license and the
copyright holder updated to 'The Author(s)'. The correction to this chapter is available
at https://doi.org/10.1007/978-3-030-90539-2_37

© The Author(s) 2021, corrected publication 2022
H. Jagode et al. (Eds.): ISC High Performance 2021 Workshops, LNCS 12761, pp. 7–22, 2021.
https://doi.org/10.1007/978-3-030-90539-2_1

1 Introduction

A deviated septum is a common rhinological pathology, which may cause narrowed upper airway passages blocking the inhaled air. Frequently, removing tissue to widen the nasal airway is a popular surgical intervention to alleviate a patient's complaints. The treatment is known as septoplasty. Unfortunately, patients are often unsatisfied with the outcome of such surgical treatments. In [22], it is reported that only 68.0% of patients experience improved nasal breathing and only 55.9% are satisfied after a septoplasty. To increase the success rate of the surgery, a method is required that suggests shape modifications while maintaining two of the main functionalities of the nose: (i) supplying the lung comfortably with air and (ii) ensuring that the incoming air is sufficiently heated up before entering the lungs.

These two functionalities can be evaluated from a fluid mechanics point of view [9,10,12,14,25]. At inspiration, the human diaphragm has to provide sufficient energy in the form of negative pressure to drive a flow. This flow experiences a pressure loss due to complex anatomical structures causing flow separation, recirculation zones etc. Comfortable breathing is thus characterized by only a small pressure loss and a small amount of work the diaphragm has to perform. While a narrowed nasal passage increases the pressure loss, it favors the ability to heat up the air due to the higher heat transfer in the vicinity of the wall. That is, considering these two functionalities, a balanced solution needs to be found with a low pressure loss while maintaining a high temperature increase. Hence, a major challenge for a surgeon is to find a suitable shape of the nasal channels that controls the flow in such a way that a compromise between the pressure loss and the temperature increase is found.

Recently, *reinforcement learning* (RL) techniques have shown great potential to control flow in different applications [3,19,24]. The main concept behind RL is shown in Figure 1. An agent is trained to interact with an environment. It therefore performs an action that changes the state of the environment and receives feedback from the environment in terms of an observation. An observation may include all information of a state or only a fraction. Subsequent to an action, the state is evaluated with respect to a pre-defined criterion. The agent is then rewarded, depending on its performance in relation to this criterion.

Novati et al. [17] study the swimming kinematics of a leading and a following fish. They use a *deep Q network* (DQN) to derive an energy efficient swimming strategy of the follower. Verma et al. [23] extend the problem from two fishes to a swarm of fishes and improve the algorithm by using recurrent neural networks with *long-short term memory* (LSTM) layers. They report collective energy savings by an efficient use of the wake generated by other swimmers. In [16], an agent of a *trust region policy optimization* (TRPO) algorithm controls the interaction of several fluid jets with rigid bodies. Instead of extracting observations directly from the flow field, a convolutional autoencoder is used to extract low-dimensional features. In [19], an agent of a *proximal policy optimization* (PPO) algorithm is successfully trained to reduce the cylinder drag in a two-dimensional flow by injecting air at the two minimum pressure locations on the cylinder

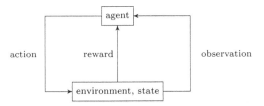

Fig. 1. Interaction between an agent and its environment in an RL algorithm.

contour in an irrotational freestream flow. The PPO algorithm has the stability and reliability of trust region methods. It is easy to implement and tune [21], and has been successfully used in previous flow control applications [19,20]. It is therefore also used in this study. In [24], wing-like shapes are generated by an *asynchronous advantage actor critic* (A3C) algorithm that considers aerodynamic properties while optimizing the shapes. In these examples, numerical flow simulations are employed to determine the change in an environment after an action. RL algorithms are, however, also used in experimental fluid dynamics. Gueniat et al. [4] apply a *Q learning* strategy to reduce the drag of a cylinder by blowing and suction. In [3], an agent learns to reduce the cylinder drag force by controlling the rotation speed of two smaller cylinders that are located downstream of a main cylinder.

In the present study, a PPO-based RL agent is trained to find the previously described compromise between the pressure loss and the temperature distribution. To simplify the complex shape of a nasal cavity, a two-dimensional channel case is considered. The septum deviation is modeled by a bump that narrows the channel. The agent controls the flow by changing the size of the bump. Feedback on an action is delivered in terms of the aforementioned two fluid mechanical properties, computed by a numerical flow simulation. For the simulation, the *thermal lattice-Boltzmann* (TLB) solver of the m-AIA code [11] (formerly know as *Zonal Flow Solver* - ZFS) is employed. The code is developed by the Institute of Aerodynamics and Chair of Fluid Mechanics, RWTH Aachen University. In various studies, the TLB method of m-AIA is successfully used to analyze the fluid mechanical properties of human respiration [9,10,12,14,25]. When the agent changes the bump, the TLB reads the updated geometry and restarts the simulation based on the flow field computed in the previous run. To reduce the degrees of freedom, the agent is only allowed to scale the bump size. Note that investigating a generic two-dimensional channel flow is the first step to applying such methods to more complex cases such as the three-dimensional respiratory flow. The method will be extended to such cases in the future.

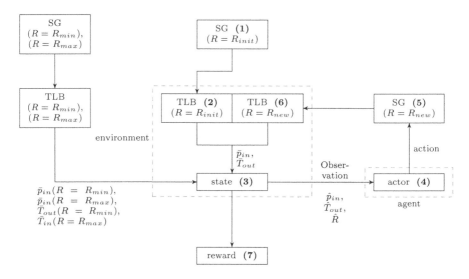

Fig. 2. Processing chain coupling the PPO RL method to `m-AIA`. Individual steps of the algorithm described in the text are colored blue. (Color figure online)

The manuscript is structured as follows. Sect. 2 presents the computational methods. This includes explanations on the channel flow setup, the TLB method, the boundary conditions, and the RL algorithm. In Sect. 3, a grid refinement study of the TLB method is conducted and results of the trained agent are reported. A summary and conclusions are given together with an outlook in Sect. 4.

2   Numerical Methods

The shape of the bump in the channel is automatically modified using a PPO algorithm, which is coupled to `m-AIA`. The coupled approach follows the numerical processing chain depicted in Fig. 2. The individual components of this chain are explained in more detail in the following.

Section 2.1 explains the computational setup and how the channel domain is generated by an automated *shape generator* (SG). Subsequently, Sect. 2.2 introduces the TLB method and the relevant boundary conditions. Finally, Sect. 2.3 describes the PPO algorithm and specifies the role of each component of the processing chain.

2.1   Computational Domain and Shape Generator

A sketch of the computational domain of the channel with the streamwise and wall-normal directions x and y is shown in Fig. 3. It is characterized by the

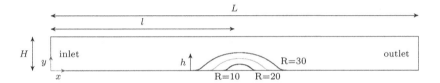

Fig. 3. Two-dimensional channel case setup and examples of the bump for three disturbance factors.

channel height $H = 20$, the channel length $L = 10H$, and a bump at the lower wall. The bump contour **B** is computed by transforming the bump function

$$b(i) = e^{\left(\frac{1}{(\frac{i}{100})^2 - 1}\right)}, \qquad i = \mathbb{Z} \in [-99; 99] \tag{1}$$

into the coordinate system of the channel. That is, the bump function $b(i)$ is multiplied by the disturbance factor $R = h \cdot e$. The control variable i is multiplied by $R/100$ and shifted in horizontal direction by adding the shift factor l, i.e.,

$$\mathbf{B} = \begin{pmatrix} B_x(i) \\ B_y(i) \end{pmatrix} = \begin{pmatrix} \frac{R}{100}i + l \\ R \cdot b(i) \end{pmatrix}. \tag{2}$$

Figure 3 shows examples of the bump for $R = 10$, $R = 20$, and $R = 30$. For $R = 0$ the bump vanishes. The agent changes the size of the bump by varying the quantity R.

The REYNOLDS number Re_{ch} of the flow is based on the channel height H, the kinematic viscosity ν, and the bulk velocity $\bar{v}$. It is set to $Re_{ch} = 100$. The flow reaches its maximum velocity v_{max} at the smallest cross section of the channel. Obviously, for increasing R, v_{max} also increases. The TLB is due to its derivation limited to quasi-incompressible flows at small MACH numbers $Ma = v_{max}/c_s \ll 1$, where c_s is the speed of sound. To avoid reaching the incompressibility limits of the TLB, a maximum disturbance factor of $R_{max} = 33$ is chosen to guarantee numerically stable and valid simulations.

As illustrated in Fig. 2, the SG automatically generates the channel surface as a function of R. The output is handed to the TLB method for the computation of the corresponding flow field.

2.2 Thermal Lattice-Boltzmann Method

The TLB operates on hierarchical unstructured Cartesian meshes, which are generated using a massively parallel grid generator [13]. Starting with an initial square cell that covers the entire geometry, the mesh is created by iteratively refining the initial cell and all subsequent generated cells. The refinement splits each cell into four equally-sized child cells. At every iteration, cells located outside of the geometry are deleted and parent-child relations are stored. This procedure is repeated until the maximum refinement level is reached. Subsequently, cells marked for local grid refinement are refined similarly. The hierarchy is represented by a quad-tree.

The TLB method is a highly parallelizable algorithm, which is well suited for efficiently simulating complex flows in intricate geometries [11,15]. It solves the discrete formulation of the Boltzmann equation [6]

$$f_i(\mathbf{r} + \boldsymbol{\xi}_i \cdot \delta t, t + \delta t) = f_i(\mathbf{r}, t) + \frac{1}{\tau_f} \cdot (f_i^{eq}(\mathbf{r}, t) - f_i(\mathbf{r}, t)), \tag{3}$$

where $\mathbf{r}$ is the location vector, t and δt denote the time and the time increment, $\boldsymbol{\xi}_i$ is the vector of the discrete molecule velocity in the direction $i \in \{0, \ldots, 8\}$, and f_i is the corresponding discrete *particle probability distribution function* (PPDF). Furthermore, the relaxation time is formulated as $\tau_f = \nu/c_s^2$. The discrete Maxwellian distribution functions f_i^{eq} are given by

$$f_i^{eq}(\mathbf{r}, t) = \rho \cdot t_p \cdot \left(1 + \frac{\mathbf{v} \cdot \boldsymbol{\xi}_i}{c_s^2} + \frac{\mathbf{v} \cdot \mathbf{v}}{2c_s^2} \left(\frac{\boldsymbol{\xi}_i \cdot \boldsymbol{\xi}_i}{c_s^2} - \delta \right) \right), \tag{4}$$

where ρ is the fluid density, $\mathbf{v}$ is the macroscopic velocity vector, δ is the Kronecker delta, and t_p is a direction-dependent coefficient. The discretization model chosen for the two-dimensional simulations conducted in this study is the well known D2Q9 model [18].

To solve the decoupled energy equation, a passive scalar transport equation of the temperature T is used. That is, a second set of PPDFs $g(\mathbf{r}, t)$ describing the diffusion and convection of the temperature is solved on the same lattice. The thermal PPDFs are calculated using [9]

$$g_i(\boldsymbol{r} + \boldsymbol{\xi}_i \cdot \delta t, t + \delta t) = g_i(r, t) + \frac{1}{\tau_t} \cdot (g_i^{eq}(r, t) - g_i(r, t)), \tag{5}$$

where $\tau_t = \alpha/c_s^2$ is the thermal relaxation based on the thermal conductivity α and c_s. The equilibrium distribution functions g_i^{eq} are defined similarly to f_i^{eq} by

$$g_i^{eq}(\boldsymbol{r}, t) = T \cdot t_p \cdot \left(1 + \frac{\mathbf{v} \cdot \boldsymbol{\xi}_i}{c_s^2} + \frac{\mathbf{v} \cdot \mathbf{v}}{2c_s^2} \left(\frac{\boldsymbol{\xi}_i \cdot \boldsymbol{\xi}_i}{c_s^2} - \delta \right) \right), \tag{6}$$

where $\mathbf{v}$ is the macroscopic velocity vector calculated from the moments of the PPDFs $f_i(\boldsymbol{r}, t)$, i.e. by solving

$$\rho = \sum_{i=0}^{8} f_i(\boldsymbol{r}, t) \tag{7}$$

$$\rho \mathbf{v} = \sum_{i=0}^{8} \boldsymbol{\xi}_i \cdot f_i(\boldsymbol{r}, t). \tag{8}$$

The temperature is obtained from the moments of the PPDFs $g_i(\boldsymbol{r}, t)$

$$T = \sum_{i=0}^{8} g_i(\boldsymbol{r}, t) \tag{9}$$

and the pressure is calculated using the equation of state for an ideal gas

$$p = \rho \cdot c_s^2. \tag{10}$$

At the inlet, the velocity profile of a fully developed channel flow is prescribed, the density is extrapolated from the inner cells, and the temperature is set to unity. Additionally, a constant pressure is prescribed at the outlet of the channel. Here, the velocity and the temperature are extrapolated from the inner cells. The wall boundary conditions are based on a second-order accurate interpolated bounce-back scheme for the velocity [1] and an isothermal wall scheme for the temperature [8].

2.3   Proximal Policy Algorithm

Before the training is started, the SG creates surfaces with $R = R_{min}$ and $R = R_{max}$, and the corresponding flow fields are computed with the TLB method. From these results, the area-averaged pressures and temperatures at the in- and outlets are calculated according to

$$\bar{p}_{\{in,out\}} = \frac{1}{N} \sum_{n=0}^{N} p_{\{in,out\}}(n) \tag{11}$$

$$\bar{T}_{\{in,out\}} = \frac{1}{N} \sum_{n=0}^{N} T_{\{in,out\}}(n), \tag{12}$$

where $n = 0, \dots, N$ is the running index of the cells in the y-direction at the in- or outlets and $p_{\{in,out\}}(n)$ and $T_{\{in,out\}}(n)$ are the pressure and the temperature at cell n, c.f. Figure 2. In the training of the PPO algorithm, these quantities are used to calculate the area-averaged normalized pressure at the inlet and area-averaged normalized temperature at the outlet

$$\hat{p}_{in} = \frac{\bar{p}_{in}(R) - \bar{p}_{in}(R_{min})}{\bar{p}_{in}(R_{max}) - \bar{p}_{in}(R_{min})} \tag{13}$$

$$\hat{T}_{out} = \frac{\bar{T}_{out}(R) - \bar{T}_{out}(R_{min})}{\bar{T}_{out}(R_{max}) - \bar{T}_{out}(R_{min})}. \tag{14}$$

Two phases take turns in the training. In the first phase, a batch, the agent interacts with the environment. A batch is composed of $E = 3$ episodes. In each episode, the agent performs $W = 10$ interactions, yielding a total number of $K = 30$ interactions per batch. The workflow of the first phase is shown in Fig. 2. Its starting point is step (1), where a surface is created by the SG with $R_{init} = 10$. In step (2), the flow field is computed for this surface. The state s is then complemented with $\hat{p}_{in}$, $\hat{T}_{out}$, and $\hat{R}$ in step (3), where $\hat{R} = (R - R_{min})/(R_{max} - R_{min})$. The complete information of s is passed as an observation to the agent.

The actor network uses the observation as input in step (4). The input layer is followed by two fully connected layers with 64 neurons each, and a final layer with a single neuron. The two fully connected layers have *rectified linear unit* (ReLU) activation functions. The final layer has a tanh activation function, mapping the output to the interval $[-1; 1]$. The output then functions as a mean to generate a Gaussian normal distribution with a standard deviation of $\sigma = 0.5$.

From this distribution, the normalized action a is sampled close to the mean of the distribution. The action in form of a change of the disturbance factor ΔR is computed by $\Delta R = \beta a$, with $\beta = 3$ to avoid relatively large changes of the disturbance factor and guarantee numerically stable simulations. The new disturbance factor is then determined by $R_{new} = R + \Delta R$. If the new disturbance factor exceeds R_{min} or R_{max}, an episode ends.

In step (5), the SG generates a new surface with the current disturbance factor. Subsequent to creating the surface, new flow properties are computed using the TLB method in step (6), which restarts from the results of the previous flow field. With these properties, a reward r is calculated in step (7). The agent is rewarded according to a pre-defined criterion. With the criterion of the current case the agent is trained to change R such that the pressure loss and the temperature gain between the inlet and outlet are rated equally important.

Note that an equal consideration of both properties is not the only existing criterion definition. In case of a septoplasty, surgeons might weight the properties according to their preferences. The current criterion is expressed by the following reward function

$$r = \frac{(\mu - ||\hat{p}_{in} - 1| - \hat{T}_{out}|)^{\kappa}}{\mu^{\kappa}}, \tag{15}$$

where $\mu = 2$ is the theoretical maximum of the second term of the numerator, keeping the reward positive. The reward is scaled by an exponent κ and normalized by μ^{κ}. The exponent must be chosen such that high weights are assigned on higher rewards, but at the same the gradients between lower rewards are not too small. A preliminary study revealed an exponent of $\kappa = 5$ to function best with the current setup.

If the agent exceeds R_{min} or R_{max}, it is punished with $r = 0$. If the agent stays within R_{min} and R_{max}, and reaches a target zone of $||\hat{p}_{in} - 1| - \hat{T}_{out}| \leq \lambda$, an episode is stopped. In case of surgical interventions, surgeons could specify λ depending on their tolerance. Here, a target zone of $\lambda = 0.1$ is chosen. If the agent is not interrupted, the processing chain continues with step (4) and progresses until an episode ends. To assess long-term rewards, for each interaction in an episode, the rewards-to-go r_{tg} are computed by

$$r_{tg}(w) = \sum_{j=w}^{W} \gamma^{j-w} r(j). \tag{16}$$

The discount factor γ weights late rewards in an episode. The higher γ, the more weight is assigned to rewards received at later interactions. Here, a discount factor of $\gamma = 0.95$ is used [2]. For each interaction, r_{tg} and the probabilities of a normalized action a_{prob} are collected.

In the second phase, actor and critic networks are trained based on the collected data from the first phase. The critic network differs from the actor network at the final layer, where it has a linear activation. The output of the critic network is the value V. Before actor and critic losses can be computed, the advantage estimates A are calculated for all interactions of a batch by

$$A = r_{tg} - V. \tag{17}$$

The actor loss is determined by the loss function

$$L_{act} = \frac{1}{K} \sum_{k=0}^{K} - \min\left(\frac{a_{prob}(k)}{a_{prob}^{tr}(k)} A(k), clip(\frac{a_{prob}(k)}{a_{prob}^{tr}(k)}, 1 - \epsilon, 1 + \epsilon)A(k)\right), \tag{18}$$

where $a_{prob}^{tr}(k)$ is the probability of an action at interaction k that is predicted while training the actor network. In the *clip*-function, the probability ratio is clipped at $1 \pm \epsilon$, depending on whether $A(k)$ is positive or negative. A clipping parameter of $\epsilon = 0.2$ is applied [21]. The critic loss is computed by

$$L_{crit} = \frac{1}{K} \sum_{k=0}^{K} (V^{tr}(k) - r_{tg}(k))^2, \tag{19}$$

where V^{tr} is predicted while training the critic network. After each batch, the network updates are repeated five times. Weights are updated by an *adaptive moments* (ADAM) optimizer [7]. The ADAM optimizer adjusts the learning rate LR by considering an exponentially decaying average of gradients in the previous update steps. The learning rate is initialized with $LR = 0.005$.

3 Results

In this section, the numerical methods introduced in Sect. 2 are employed to investigate the flow through a channel constricted by a bump, cf. Fig. 3. Before the corresponding results of the performance of the RL algorithm are presented in Sect. 3.2, the simulation method is validated using a generic test cases in the subsequent Sect. 3.1.

3.1 Validation of the Simulation Method

For validation purposes, a two-dimensional fully developed isothermal channel flow is simulated. The TLB approach was already validated by Lintermann et al. in [12].

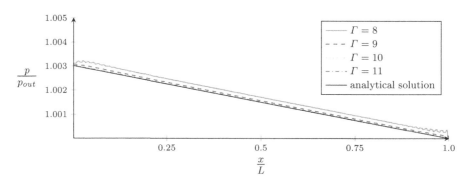

Fig. 4. Pressure distribution along the centerline of the channel for several refinement levels $\Gamma \in \{8, \ldots, 11\}$ at $Re_{ch} = 100$. Additionally, the analytical solution is given.

The calculated pressure loss of the fully developed channel flow is compared to the analytical solution given by

$$\Delta p = \frac{8 v_{max} \rho \nu L}{H^2} = 12 \frac{\bar{v}^2 \rho}{Re_{ch}} \frac{L}{H}, \tag{20}$$

with the density ρ, the maximum channel velocity magnitude $v_{max} = (3/2)\bar{v}$, and the channel length L. The solution is derived from the well-known Hagen-Poiseuille law [5]. The channel geometry equals the geometry shown in Fig. 3 with $R = 0$. The REYNOLDS number is again set to $Re_{ch} = 100$. The boundary conditions at the inlet, the outlet, and the channel walls are set according to the description in Sect. 2.2. The pressure distributions along the centerline of the channel, obtained from flow simulations, are plotted for different mesh refinement levels against the analytical solution in Fig. 4. For refinement level $\Gamma = 8$, the channel is resolved by 256×26 cells. The number of cells per direction doubles with each refinement level increase. At the maximum considered level $\Gamma = 11$, the channel is resolved by $2{,}048 \times 208$ cells. Figure 4 shows that the pressure gradient in the middle of the computational domain remains the same for all refinement levels. However, near the in- and the outlets, the pressure curves differ slightly. In these areas, only simulations with a refinement level of $\Gamma \geq 10$ produce sufficiently accurate results. Therefore, a uniform refined mesh at refinement level $\Gamma = 10$ is chosen to test the performance of the RL algorithm, see Sect. 3.2.

3.2   Comparison of Simulative and RL-Based Results

Simulations are conducted on 2 nodes with 24 cores per node on the supercomputer CLAIX at RWTH Aachen University. In simulations at the beginning of an episode around 3 min are needed to reach a solution that is independent from the initial condition. After that, the simulations time is reduced to 90 s, since simulations can be restarted from previous results and therefore reach such a solution faster. Training time for the actor and critic networks are negligible compared to the simulation time.

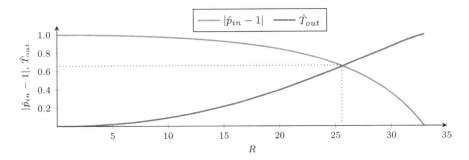

Fig. 5. Temperature and pressure development of the channel flow for different disturbance factors R of the bump.

To analyze the behavior of the RL algorithm, a number of $3,400$ simulations are conducted, in which the disturbance factor of the bump is continuously increased from $R = R_{min}$ to $R = R_{max}$ in steps of 0.01, to achieve an accuracy of two decimal places. For each simulation, the pressure in the form of $|\hat{p}_{in} - 1|$ and the temperature $\hat{T}_{out}$ are evaluated. Figure 5 shows that both graphs cut each other for a simulated disturbance factor of $R_{ref} = 25.58$. At this location, $|\hat{p}_{in} - 1|$ and $\hat{T}_{out}$ have the same value which perfectly fulfills the criterion formulated in Eq. (15). The corresponding results are therefore defined as the reference solution.

The temperature, the static pressure, and the velocity distributions for $R = 20$, R_{ref}, and $R = 30$ are shown in Fig. 6. On the one hand, it is obvious from Fig. 6a that the temperature increases in the vicinity of the bump, especially in its wake region. While the increase is upstream of the bump lower, the temperature towards the outlet, downstream of the bump, increases stronger. In case of R_{ref}, the average temperature at the outlet $\hat{T}_{out}$ reaches $98.63\ \%$ of the wall temperature. On the other hand, a strong drop of the pressure due to the acceleration of the flow in the constricted region is visible in Fig. 6b. With an increasing bump size, the inlet pressure is raised, i.e., a maximum inlet pressure is obtained at $R = 30$. Large velocities are observed in the constricted region, see Fig. 6c. Consequently, the maximum streamwise velocity components are also found at $R = 30$. For all configurations a recirculation zone with negative streamwise velocities is observed, indicating flow separation. The zone increases with larger bump sizes.

The performance of the agent that uses the processing chain from Fig. 2 is evaluated in terms of the averaged disturbance factor at each batch

$$\hat{R}_t(b) = \frac{1}{E_t(b)} \sum_{b=0}^{E_t(b)} R_t, \qquad (21)$$

where R_t is the target disturbance factor in case the target zone is reached in an episode, and $E_t(b)$ is the number of episodes in which the target zone has been reached from the beginning of the training until batch b. Figure 7 shows $\hat{R}_t(b)$

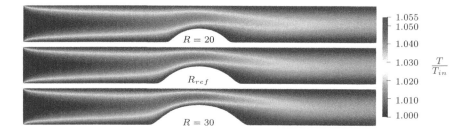

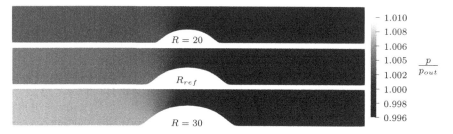

(a) Temperature T normalized by the inflow temperature T_{in}.

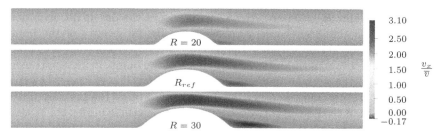

(b) Static pressure p normalized by the pressure at the outlet p_{out}.

(c) Streamwise velocity v_x normalized by the bulk velocity $\bar{v}$.

Fig. 6. Simulation results for three channel geometries with $R \in \{20, R_{ref}, 30\}$, where $R_{ref} = 25.58$.

and the error of $\hat{R}_t(b)$ in relation to R_{ref}. At batch 6, after 177 simulations, the agent hits the target zone for the first time at $\hat{R}_t(6) = 24.62$, yielding an error of 3.7%. After 265 simulations in 10 batches, the error remains below an acceptable error of 1.0% for the rest of the training. The averaged disturbance factor is $R_t(10) = 25.32$. At 69 batches, or $1,450$ simulations, an averaged disturbance factor of $R_t(69) = 25.61$ misses R_{ref} by less than only 0.1%. From here on the error remains below 0.1% for the rest of the training.

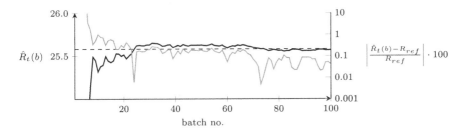

Fig. 7. Averaged disturbance factor from the beginning of the training to each batch $\hat{R}_t(b)$ (black) and relative error of $\hat{R}_t(b)$ to R_{ref} (red) for 100 batches. The dashed black line represents R_{ref}. (Color figure online)

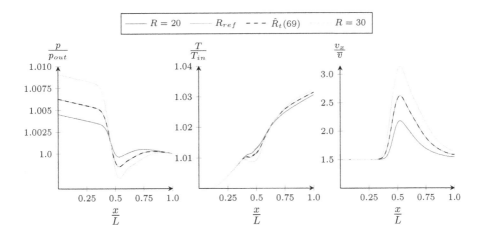

(a) Normalized pressure (l.), temperature (c.), and streamwise velocity (r.) distributions along the lines shown in Fig. 8b.

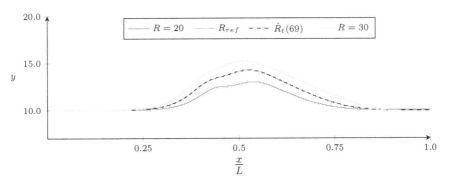

(b) Lines following the maximum streamwise velocity component.

Fig. 8. Quantitative results for different $R \in \{20, R_{ref}, \hat{R}_t(69), 30\}$.

A further quantitative analysis is performed by comparing the distributions of the static pressure, the temperature, and the streamwise velocity along the line with the maximum streamwise velocity component for $R \in \{20, R_{ref}, \hat{R}_t(69), 30\}$. The results are depicted in Fig. 8a and the corresponding lines in Fig. 8b. Plots of all fluid mechanical properties for the reference solution and the RL-based method show an almost perfect alignment proving the RL-based processing chain to be a valid alternative to using a brute-force parameter sweeping.

4   Summary, Conclusion, and Outlook

A PPO algorithm is combined with a TLB simulation method to change the shape of a heated narrowed channel, while considering the pressure loss and temperature difference between the inflow and outflow region. The algorithm controls the flow by changing the disturbance factor of a bump. It is capable of finding a target disturbance factor that weights both fluid mechanical properties equally. Averaging the target factor over multiple tries yields a deviation from the reference disturbance factor, which is determined iteratively with 3,400 numerical simulations, of less than 1.0% after 265 simulations in 10 batches, and less than 0.1 % after 1,450 simulations in 69 batches. A comparison of the temperature, pressure, and streamwise velocity distributions between the predicted and the reference solutions along the line of the maximum velocity component in streamwise direction shows only negligible differences.

Surgical interventions in rhinology often include the removal of anatomical structures. Such removals influence the capability to breathe comfortably. Ideally, the pressure loss and the heating capability of a nasal cavity are balanced such that respiration is energy efficient and the air reaches body temperature.

The current results build the foundation for applying RL algorithms to shape optimization problems in rhinology. To close the gap between the simplified channel flow and a nasal cavity flow, the method will be extended to more complex flow configurations such as two-dimensional domains with multiple bumps or three-dimensional geometries like a stenotic pipe. The increase of the domain complexity will lead to enlarged action and state spaces, and variations of the actor and critic networks can be investigated. Furthermore, the PPO algorithm will be compared with other RL algorithms. It is the ultimate vision, to develop a tool that assists surgeons in their decision making process.

Acknowledgments. The research leading to these results has been conducted in the CoE RAISE project, which receives funding from the European Union's Horizon 2020 – Research and Innovation Framework Programme H2020-INFRAEDI-2019-1 under grant agreement no. 951733. The training of the RL algorithm has been performed on two nodes of the CLAIX HPC system at RWTH Aachen University. Each node is equipped with two Intel Xeon Platinum 8160 Processors "SkyLake", clocked at $2.1GHz$, with 24 cores each and 192 GB main memory per node. The authors gratefully acknowledge the computing time granted by the JARA Vergabegremium and provided on the JARA Partition part of the supercomputer CLAIX at RWTH Aachen University. This work was performed as part of the Helmholtz School for Data Science in Life, Earth and Energy (HDS-LEE).

References

1. Bouzidi, M., Firdaouss, M., Lallemand, P.: Momentum transfer of a Boltzmann-lattice fluid with boundaries. Phys. Fluids **13**(11), 3452–3459 (2001). https://doi.org/10.1063/1.1399290
2. Fakoor, R., Chaudhari, P., Smola, A.J.: P3O: olicy-on policy-off policy optimization. In: Adams, R.P., Gogate, V. (eds.) Proceedings of the 35th Uncertainty in Artificial Intelligence Conference. Proceedings of Machine Learning Research, vol. 115, pp. 1017–1027. PMLR, 22–25 July 2020
3. Fan, D., Yang, L., Triantafyllou, M., Karniadakis, G.: Reinforcement learning for active flow control in experiments, March 2020
4. Guéniat, F., Mathelin, L., Hussaini, M.Y.: A statistical learning strategy for closed-loop control of fluid flows. Theor. Comput. Fluid Dyn. **30**(6), 497–510 (2016). https://doi.org/10.1007/s00162-016-0392-y
5. Hagenbach, E.: Über die bestimmung der zähigkeit einer flüssigkeit durch den ausfluss aus röhren. Poggendorf's Annalen der Physik und Chemie **108**, 385–426 (1860)
6. He, X., Luo, L.S.: Theory of the lattice Boltzmann method: from the Boltzmann equation to the lattice Boltzmann equation. Phys. Rev. E **56**(6), 6811–6817 (1997). https://doi.org/10.1103/PhysRevE.56.6811
7. Kingma, D.P., Ba, J.: Adam: A method for stochastic optimization (2014)
8. Li, L., Mei, R., Klausner, J.F.: Boundary conditions for thermal lattice Bboltzmann equation method. J. Comput. Phys. **237**, 366–395 (2013). https://doi.org/10.1016/j.jcp.2012.11.027
9. Lintermann, A., Meinke, M., Schröder, W.: Investigations of the inspiration and heating capability of the human nasal cavity based on a lattice-Boltzmann method. In: Proceedings of the ECCOMAS Thematic International Conference on Simulation and Modeling of Biological Flows (SIMBIO 2011), Brussels, Belgium (2011)
10. Lintermann, A., Meinke, M., Schröder, W.: Investigations of nasal cavity flows based on a lattice-Boltzmann method. In: Resch, M., Wang, X., Bez, W., Focht, E., Kobayashi, H., Roller, S. (eds.) High Performance Computing on Vector Systems 2011, pp. 143–158. Springer, Heidelberg (2012). https://doi.org/10.1007/978-3-642-22244-3
11. Lintermann, A., Meinke, M., Schröder, W.: Zonal Flow Solver (ZFS): a highly efficient multi-physics simulation framework. Int. J. Comput. Fluid Dyn. 1–28 (2020). https://doi.org/10.1080/10618562.2020.1742328
12. Lintermann, A., Meinke, M., Schröder, W.: Fluid mechanics based classification of the respiratory efficiency of several nasal cavities. Comput. Biol. Med. **43**(11), 1833–1852 (2013). https://doi.org/10.1016/j.compbiomed.2013.09.003
13. Lintermann, A., Schlimpert, S., Grimmen, J., Günther, C., Meinke, M., Schröder, W.: Massively parallel grid generation on HPC systems. Comput. Methods Appl. Mech. Eng. **277**, 131–153 (2014). https://doi.org/10.1016/j.cma.2014.04.009
14. Lintermann, A., Schröder, W.: A hierarchical numerical journey through the nasal cavity: from nose-like models to real anatomies. Flow, Turbul. Combust. **102**(1), 89–116 (2017). https://doi.org/10.1007/s10494-017-9876-0
15. Lintermann, A., Schröder, W.: Lattice–Boltzmann simulations for complex geometries on high-performance computers. CEAS Aeronaut. J. **11**(3), 745–766 (2020). https://doi.org/10.1007/s13272-020-00450-1
16. Ma, P., Tian, Y., Pan, Z., Ren, B., Manocha, D.: Fluid directed rigid body control using deep reinforcement learning. ACM Trans. Graph. **37**(4), 1–11 (2018). https://doi.org/10.1145/3197517.3201334

17. Novati, G., Verma, S., Alexeev, D., Rossinelli, D., van Rees, W.M., Koumoutsakos, P.: Synchronisation through learning for two self-propelled swimmers. Bioinspiration Biomimetics **12**, 3 (2017)
18. Qian, Y.H., D'Humières, D., Lallemand, P.: Lattice BGK models for Navier-stokes equation. Europhys. Lett. (EPL) **6**, 479–484 (1992). https://doi.org/10.1209/0295-5075/17/6/001
19. Rabault, J., Kuchta, M., Jensen, A., Réglade, U., Cerardi, N.: Artificial neural networks trained through deep reinforcement learning discover control strategies for active flow control. J. Fluid Mech. **865**, 281–302 (2019). https://doi.org/10.1017/jfm.2019.62
20. Rabault, J., Kuhnle, A.: Accelerating deep reinforcement learning strategies of flow control through a multi-environment approach. Phys. Fluids **31**, 094105 (2019). https://doi.org/10.1063/1.5116415
21. Schulman, J., Wolski, F., Dhariwal, P., Radford, A., Klimov, O.: Proximal policy optimization algorithms, July 2017
22. Toyserkani, N., Frisch, T.: Are too many septal deviations operated on? A retrospective patient's satisfaction questionnaire with 11 years follow-up. Rhinology **50**, 185–190 (2012). https://doi.org/10.4193/Rhino11.218
23. Verma, S., Novati, G., Koumoutsakos, P.: Efficient collective swimming by harnessing vortices through deep reinforcement learning. Proc. Natl. Acad. Sci. **115**(23), 5849–5854 (2018). https://doi.org/10.1073/pnas.1800923115
24. Viquerat, J., Rabault, J., Kuhnle, A., Ghraieb, H., Hachem, E.: Direct shape optimization through deep reinforcement learning, August 2019. https://doi.org/10.13140/RG.2.2.19572.50566
25. Waldmann, M., Lintermann, A., Choi, Y.J., Schröder, W.: Analysis of the effects of MARME treatment on respiratory flow using the lattice-Boltzmann method. In: Dillmann, A., Heller, G., Krämer, E., Wagner, C., Tropea, C., Jakirlić, S. (eds.) DGLR 2018. NNFMMD, vol. 142, pp. 853–863. Springer, Cham (2020). https://doi.org/10.1007/978-3-030-25253-3_80

Novel DNNs for Stiff ODEs
with Applications to Chemically
Reacting Flows

Thomas S. Brown[1,3(✉)], Harbir Antil[3], Rainald Löhner[1], Fumiya Togashi[2],
and Deepanshu Verma[3]

[1] Center for Computational Fluid Dynamics, College of Science,
George Mason University, Fairfax, VA 22030-4444, USA
{tbrown62,rlohner}@gmu.edu
[2] Applied Simulations, Inc., 1211 Pine Hill Road, McLean, VA 22101, USA
[3] Center for Mathematics and Artificial Intelligence (CMAI), College of Science,
George Mason University, Fairfax, VA 22030-4444, USA
{hantil,dverma2}@gmu.edu

Abstract. Chemically reacting flows are common in engineering, such
as hypersonic flow, combustion, explosions, manufacturing processes and
environmental assessments. For combustion, the number of reactions can
be significant (over 100) and due to the very large CPU requirements of
chemical reactions (over 99%) a large number of flow and combustion
problems are presently beyond the capabilities of even the largest supercomputers.

Motivated by this, novel Deep Neural Networks (DNNs) are introduced to approximate stiff ODEs. Two approaches are compared, i.e.,
either learn the solution or the derivative of the solution to these ODEs.
These DNNs are applied to multiple species and reactions common in
chemically reacting flows. Experimental results show that it is helpful to
account for the physical properties of species while designing DNNs. The
proposed approach is shown to generalize well.

1 Introduction

Chemically reacting flows are common in many fields of engineering, such as
hypersonic flow, combustion, explosions, manufacturing processes, and environmental assessments [4,17,28,30]. For hydrocarbon combustion and explosions
the numbers of species and reactions can reach into hundreds and thousands
respectively. Even with so-called reduced models [12,15,18,20,29,31], which try
to keep the main species and reactions while neglecting those that are not important, typically over 100 reactions need to be updated. An expedient (and widely
used) way to compute flows with chemical reactions is to separate the advection
and diffusion of species from the actual reactions, see for example [27,33]. In this

This work was supported by the Defense Threat Reduction Agency (DTRA) under
contract HDTRA1-15-1-0068. Jacqueline Bell served as the technical monitor.

© Springer Nature Switzerland AG 2021
H. Jagode et al. (Eds.): ISC High Performance 2021 Workshops, LNCS 12761, pp. 23–39, 2021.
https://doi.org/10.1007/978-3-030-90539-2_2

way, the vastly different timescales of the reactants can be treated in a separate, stiff ODE solver. Such chemical reaction solvers take the given species u^{n-1} at the $n - 1^{\text{th}}$ time step and desired timestep δt and update the species to u^n. In terms of a 'black box solver' this implies either:

$$u^n = Chem_1(\delta t, u^{n-1}), \tag{1}$$

or

$$\frac{u^n - u^{n-1}}{\delta t} = Chem_2(u^{n-1}), \tag{2}$$

where $Chem_1$ stands for the ODE integrator of chemical reactions and $Chem_2$ is the right-hand side of the system. This is the formulation to solve the system of ODEs numerically using the standard Euler method. Compared to a typical 'cold' flow case, the presence of these chemical reactions implies an increase of computing requirements that can exceed factors of 1:100, i.e. 2 orders of magnitude. This makes many of these flow simulations so expensive that entire classes of problems have been sidelined, waiting for faster computers to be developed in years to come. The goal here is to replace the 'black box' solvers (equivalently the functions $Chem_1$ and $Chem_2$) given in (1) and (2) by novel, robust Deep Neural Networks (DNNs) without sacrificing accuracy.

The list of references on using DNNs in computational fluid dynamics (CFD) is growing fast, see for example, [9,19]. However, the results on using DNNs in chemical kinetics are scarce. A popular approach to solve PDEs and ODEs is through the use of so-called Physics-Informed Neural Networks (PINNs) [6,24]. The goal of PINNs is to minimize the PDE/ODE residual by using a neural network as a PDE/ODE solution Ansatz. The inputs to the network are space-time variables (x, t) and all the derivatives are computed using automatic differentiation. See [11] for an example of a PINN for stiff ODE systems where the only input is time.

The approach presented here fundamentally differs from the aforementioned approaches. Instead of *Physics-Informed-Neural-Networks*, the goal is to pursue *Learn-from-Physics/Chemistry*. For instance in (1) and (2), DNNs will be used to learn $Chem_1$ and $Chem_2$ from a given dataset coming from physics/chemistry simulations. Such an approach to learn $Chem_1$ has also been considered recently in [21,22,26] where the authors employ an architecture that is motivated by standard feed forward networks. The authors of [32] consider a similar problem, but use an autoencoder, which is a type of DNN used to reduce the dimension of the system. Notice that the proposed approach will allow for the chemical reactions described by (1) and (2) to start at any point in time without knowing a reference time. The latter is crucial for the application under consideration.

The DNNs used in this paper have been motivated by the Residual Neural Network (ResNet) architecture. ResNets have been introduced in [2,10,25] in the context of data/image classification, see also [1] for parameterized PDEs and [8] where the (related) so-called Neural ODE Nets [5] have been used to solve stiff ODEs. The ResNet architecture is known to overcome the vanishing gradient problem, which has been further analyzed using fractional order derivatives in

[2]. The key feature of a ResNet is that in the continuum limit, it becomes an optimization problem constrained by an ODE. Such a continuous representation further enables the analysis of the stability of the network using nonlinear ODE theory. In addition, standard approaches from optimization, such as the Lagrangian approach can be used to derive the sensitivities with respect to the unknown weights and biases.

The main novelties in the DNNs presented in this work are the following:

- These networks allow for learning both the solution (see (1)) and difference quotients (see (2)). A similar approach to learn the solution in the context of parameterized PDEs has been recently considered in [1].
- Motivated by chemically reacting flows, the goal is to create networks that can learn multiple reactions propagating multiple species. To accomplish this task, parallel ResNets are constructed where the data corresponding to multiple quantities is used as input for each network but the output is only a single species. Similar approaches for chemical kinetics can be found in [22,26], where the authors use standard feed forward networks.
- The proposed DNNs are applied to non-trivial chemically reacting flows. Experimental results show that it is helpful to know the underlying properties of the species while designing the networks.

The remainder of the paper is organized as follows: In Sect. 2, the DNNs used to approximate systems of type (1) and (2) are introduced, and training strategies are discussed. Section 3 provides some information on the implementation of the method. Several experimental results are discussed in Sect. 4. Additional information on the data being used in the experiments is provided in Appendix A.

2   Deep Residual Neural Networks

2.1   Problem Formulation

Consider an input-to-output map

$$u \mapsto S(u),$$

where S could be $Chem_1$ or $Chem_2$ in (1) and (2), respectively. The goal is to learn an approximation $\widehat{S}$ of S using Deep Neural Networks (DNNs). In particular, the proposed DNNs are motivated by Deep Residual Neural Networks (ResNets). See [2,25] for examples of ResNets for classification problems and [1] for an application to parameterized PDEs.

Given a training dataset $\{(u^n, S(u^n))\}_{n=0}^{N-1}$, the DNN approximation $\widehat{S}$ of S is given by the output of the DNN (ResNet)

$$\begin{cases} y_1 = \tau\sigma(K_0 y_0 + b_0), \\ y_\ell = y_{\ell-1} + \tau\sigma(K_{\ell-1} y_{\ell-1} + b_{\ell-1}), & 1 < \ell \leq L-1, \\ y_L = K_{L-1} y_{L-1}, \end{cases} \qquad (3)$$

i.e., $\widehat{S}(u) = y_L$. Here $\tau > 0$ is a given parameter called the skip connection parameter. The number of layers (depth of the network) is denoted by L. Layer 0 is referred to as the input layer, layers 1 through $L - 1$ as hidden layers and layer L as the output layer.

The nonlinear function σ denotes an activation function. This work considers a differentiable version of the well-known ReLU activation function. This differentiability is accomplished by locally smoothing ReLU near the 'kink'. The learning problem is a constrained optimization problem which requires minimizing a loss function subject to constraints (3). An efficient and mathematically rigorous way to solve this problem is by using the adjoint method [1–3]. The latter requires differentiability of σ with respect to its arguments. This is the main reason behind considering a differentiable version of ReLU. In particular, σ is taken to be a smooth quadratic approximation of the ReLU function, i.e.,

$$\sigma(x) = \begin{cases} \max\{0, x\} & |x| > \varepsilon, \\ \frac{1}{4\varepsilon}x^2 + \frac{1}{2}x + \frac{\varepsilon}{4} & |x| \leq \varepsilon. \end{cases}$$

Figure 1 (left) shows that $\sigma(x)$ is a good approximation of ReLU. Here, and in the experiments below, ε is taken to be 0.1. This is not the only choice for activation function. In fact, some experiments (not included in this brief report) have been conducted using hyperbolic tangent as the activation function.

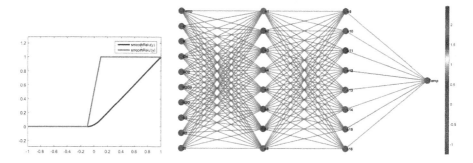

Fig. 1. Left: Smooth ReLU and its derivative for $\varepsilon = 0.1$. Right: Example of a typical Deep ResNet used in the experiments.

The quantities $\{K_\ell\}_{\ell=0}^{L-1}, \{b_\ell\}_{\ell=0}^{L-2}$ denote the weights and biases, i.e. the parameters that need to be determined. In this setting K_ℓ is a matrix and b_ℓ is a vector, together they introduce an affine transformation. If $y_\ell \in \mathbb{R}^{n_\ell}$ for $\ell = 0, \ldots, L$, then $K_\ell \in \mathbb{R}^{n_{\ell+1} \times n_\ell}$ and $b_\ell \in \mathbb{R}^{n_{\ell+1}}$. The dimension n_ℓ is also referred to as the width of the ℓ-th layer. Notice that for $0 < \ell < L$ in (3), it is assumed that $n_\ell = n_{\ell+1}$, but this can be easily generalized, see [25]. Nevertheless, in the current setup the dimension of the input y_0 and output y_L can be different.

An example of a typical DNN is shown in Fig. 1 (right) with depth 3, width 8, input dimension 10, and output dimension 1. The values of the weights are given by the color of the lines connecting the neurons, the values of the biases are given by the color of the neurons, and the color of the input layer has been set to zero.

The question remains of how to compute the weights $\{K_\ell\}_{\ell=0}^{L-1}$ and biases $\{b_\ell\}_{\ell=0}^{L-2}$ in order to obtain a good approximation $\widehat{S}$ of S. Following [2, 25], these weights are computed by solving

$$\min_{\{K_\ell\}_{\ell=1}^{L-1},\{b_\ell\}_{\ell=0}^{L-2}} \left\{ J(K_\ell, b_\ell) := \frac{1}{2N} \sum_{n=0}^{N-1} \|y_L^n - S(u^n)\|^2 \right\} \quad \text{subject to constraints} \quad (3),$$
$$(4)$$

where $y_L^n = \widehat{S}(u^n)$, that is, y_0 in (3) is taken to be the training data $\{u^n\}_{n=0}^{N-1}$. The problem (4) is a constrained optimization problem. To solve this problem, the gradient of J with respect to K_ℓ and b_ℓ needs to be evaluated. This requires introducing the so-called adjoint equation (also known as back-propagation in machine learning literature). See [1, 2, 25] for complete details. Having obtained the gradient, an approximate Hessian is computed via the BFGS routine. Both the gradient and the approximate Hessian are used to solve the minimization problem.

2.2   Proposed Approach and Applications

As stated earlier, the goal is to replace $Chem_1$ and $Chem_2$ in (1) and (2), respectively by DNNs. The continuous ODE is given by

$$\frac{du}{dt}(t) = S(u(t)), \quad u(0) = u_0. \tag{5}$$

The simplest time discretization of (5) is given by

$$\frac{u^n - u^{n-1}}{\delta t} = S(u^{n-1}), \quad u^0 = u_0, \tag{6}$$

for $n = 1, \ldots, N$. At first, the right-hand-side of (6) is approximated. This is referred to as the *first approach*. In this case, the training data (input and output) is $\left\{ \left(u^{n-1}, \frac{u^n - u^{n-1}}{\delta t} \right) \right\}_{n=1}^{N}$. In the *second approach*, the map to be approximated is $u^{n+1} = S(u^n)$, i.e., the setting of (1). Here S marches u forward in time with time increments given by δt. The training data for this approach is given by $\{(u^{n-1}, u^n)\}_{n=1}^{N}$.

Scaling. The training data in the examples below has been computed using CHEMKIN [13]. Before training the networks, the data is scaled in the following manner: For a data set $\{x_j\}_{j=0}^{N}$, each entry x_i is scaled as

$$\widehat{x}_i := \frac{x_i - \min_j x_j}{\max_j x_j - \min_j x_j}, \tag{7}$$

so that the resulting data set $\{\hat{x}_j\}_{j=1}^N$ lies in the interval $[0,1]$. Given that chemical reactions follow an exponential Arrhenius-type law, a logarithmic scaling was also tried. This implies performing the above scaling on the dataset $\{\log x_j\}$ instead of $\{x_j\}$.

Architecture. For the DNNs implemented below, the input dimension will always be given by

$$
n_0 = \underset{\text{(temperature)}}{1} + \underset{\text{(\# of species)}}{M} + \underset{\text{(time increment, } \delta t)}{1} = M + 2.
$$

The output dimension is $n_L = M + 1$, which corresponds to temperature plus the number of species.

Rather than using a single DNN to approximate the entire solution map S, in many cases a parallel ResNet architecture is implemented in which a separate ResNet is created to correspond to each desired output. With this structure the output dimension for each ResNet is 1, but there are $M+1$ ResNets implemented in parallel. The inputs to all of the parallel ResNets are the same, and so the parallel architecture can also be thought of as a single large ResNet (with $n_L = M + 1$) that is not fully connected.

The choice to use parallel ResNets was motivated by the work reported in [22,26]. Previous results coming from a single ResNet had difficulties learning the different species, suggesting that larger, more robust networks were needed. Rather than attempt to train a large single network, which could lead to memory limitations and larger training times, the choice was made to use parallel networks. These parallel networks are significantly advantageous as each of them have fewer unknowns in comparison to a large single network. Additionally, they can be (and are) trained in parallel, thus significantly cutting the training times.

Loss Function and Training. In the case of a parallel ResNet architecture, each parallel network is associated to a separate loss function. The same form of the loss function is used for each network. Letting $\theta^{(i)}$ represent the concatenation of all weight and bias parameters associated to the i-th parallel network, the loss function takes the form

$$
\frac{1}{2N} \sum_{n=0}^{N-1} \|y_L^{(i)} - S(u^n)^{(i)}\|_2^2 + \frac{\lambda}{2} \left(\|\theta^{(i)}\|_1 + \|\theta^{(i)}\|_2^2 \right), \qquad i = 1, \ldots, M+1. \quad (8)
$$

In other words, the process of training each network is the process of finding the parameters $\theta^{(i)}$ which minimize the mean squared error between the network output and the training data, while also using both ℓ^1 and ℓ^2 regularizations to penalize the size of the parameters. As indicated in Sect. 2, a gradient based method (BFGS in particular) is used to solve the constrained optimization problem.

Validation. DNNs are trained with validation data in order to overcome the overfitting issue. The validation data is a subset of the training data that is not used to compute the weights and biases. Instead, a separate loss function is formed that computes the mean squared error between the ResNet output and the validation data. This is a way to test how the ResNet performs on unseen data during the training process itself. If the validation error increases, the training continues for a certain number of additional iterations, called the *patience*. During this time, if the validation error decreases to a new minimum, the patience resets to zero and training continues. If the validation error does not attain a new minimum and the full number of patience iterations is reached, then the training process is terminated.

Testing. After training and validation comes the testing phase in which the DNN approximations are used to carry out time marching. Using the *first approach* (see above) this involves implementing an Euler time-stepping commonly used to numerically solve ODEs, with the usual right-hand-side of the ODE replaced by the DNN output, that is,

$$\widehat{u}^n = \widehat{u}^{n-1} + \delta t \widehat{S}(\widehat{u}^{n-1}) \qquad n = 1, \dots, N, \tag{9}$$

where $\widehat{u}^0 = u^0$ is known data. For the *second approach*, results are tested by using the following update step $\widehat{u}^n = \widehat{S}(\widehat{u}^{n-1})$ for $n = 1, \dots, N$, where again $\widehat{u}^0 = u^0$ is known.

Application. The above methods are applied to a system of ODEs that model hydrogen-oxygen reaction. In particular, the reduced hydrogen-air reaction model with 8 species and 18 reactions [23] is used. This model is simpler than the hydrocarbon reaction model mentioned in Sect. 1. However, it can still capture several essential key features. These stiff systems are typically solved using an implicit time-stepping method to handle the chemistry, for example in CHEMKIN, while the fluid advection is handled separately with an explicit method. The examples in this work are only concerned with replacing the implicit chemistry solver with neural networks with the goal of finding a method that lowers the computational expense without sacrificing accuracy. Since this work represents a first step in this direction, a relatively simple model is used. More complicated DNNs which can handle over 100 reactions will be part of future work.

3 Implementation

To start, the *second approach* was implemented in Keras [7] using stochastic gradient descent. Libraries such as Keras have proven to be highly successful for classification problems, but their success in physics based modeling is still limited. Initially, it was observed that the results produced by using Keras were unable to capture the 'pulse' in chemical reactions. After gaining access to some of the Keras code, and seeing some improvement, the results were still highly inconsistent. For example, when running the same experiment multiple times, with the same hyperparameters, different solutions were obtained. Such an inconsistency may not be critical for classification problems (for example [14,16]), but it is critical for ODE/PDE problems. Implementation through Keras was abandoned as further customization of the code proved to be a daunting task.

The DNN implementation used in this paper was carried out in MATLAB and a BFGS routine with an Armijo line-search was used to solve the optimization problem. Unlike many neural network software packages, this code uses the framework and closely resembles code that is used to solve optimal control problems.

4   Results

In this section a variety of results are presented that represent different approaches and architectures. The results will be grouped together by the type of data that was used to train the networks. Further details on the training data are provided in Appendix A. The loss function is as given in (8) with $\lambda = 1e - 7$, the skip connection parameter (in (3)) $\tau = 2/(L-1)$, where L is the depth of the network, and a constant time increment of $\delta t = 1e - 7$. Unless otherwise specified, all training data was scaled by the method outlined in (7). All of the results presented below were achieved by using the MATLAB implementation of the ResNets described above. The blue curves in the plots below represent 'true solution' (data generated using CHEMKIN), while the dashed red curves represent DNN output.

4.1   Training with a Single Data Set

As a "proof of concept" example, to show that this approach is feasible, a single ResNet was trained using the *first approach* on data corresponding to temperature, 8 species, and δt. In Fig. 2, the results from a ResNet with depth 9 and width 15 are shown. For this experiment only ℓ^2 regularization has been used in the loss function. After being trained, the training data was used again to test the network, and these results can be seen in the left plots of Fig. 2. The initial condition from the training data was marched forward in time as described in (9), and the results are shown on the right of Fig. 2 compared with the actual u.

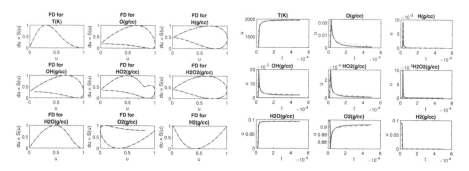

Fig. 2. A comparison between the actual du/dt and the learned difference quotient (left 9 plots) and the results of marching in time as in (9) (right 9 plots) using a Deep ResNet of depth 9 and width 15.

4.2   Training Data Sets with Varying Equivalence Ratio And fixed Initial Temperature

Experimental results showed that while a single ResNet was able to handle data corresponding to a single initial condition, it struggled with data containing multiple initial conditions. To improve results, the parallel ResNet structure described in Sect. 2.2 was created. The parallel DNNs were trained on a data set containing multiple initial conditions with the same initial temperature but varying equivalence ratio (see Appendix A). Figure 3 shows the results for ResNets trained on this data without the use of validation data. Each ResNet has depth 4 and width 10. For this result, the testing data was a subset of the training data, and so these plots do not represent a generalization of the networks to unseen data. Figure 4 shows the result of an experiment trained with a configuration of data subsets from the same data set as Fig. 3, (see Appendix A for specific details). Additionally, validation data was implemented during training with a patience of 250 iterations. The ResNets used for this experiment have varying depths (3 to 5) but a fixed width of 10. The plots in Fig. 4 are the result of testing the DNNs on data that was not used in training. For these results mass conservation is also implemented in the sense that the sum of the densities of the 8 species is adjusted at the end of each update step (9) to be equal to that of the previous step. Specifically the quantities related to species (temperature excluded) are adjusted as

$$(\widetilde{u}^n)^{(i)} = \frac{(\widehat{u}^n)^{(i)}}{\sum_{j=1}^{8}(\widehat{u}^n)^{(j)}}.$$

In the data that is used for these experiments, the sum of the species densities is fixed at 1. This is the only experiment presented in this work in which mass conservation is enforced.

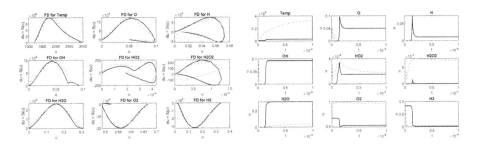

Fig. 3. A comparison between the actual du/dt and the learned difference quotient (left 9 plots), and the results of marching in time as in (9) (right 9 plots) using parallel Deep ResNets of depth 4 and width 10.

The next result uses the *second approach* described in Sect. 2.2, in which the ResNets are trained to learn the next time step rather than the right-hand-side

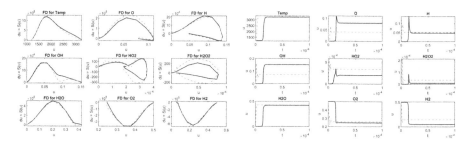

Fig. 4. A comparison between the actual du/dt and the learned difference quotient (left 9 plots), and the results of marching in time as in (9) (right 9 plots) using parallel Deep ResNets of different depths and width 10, trained with validation data with patience of 250 iterations.

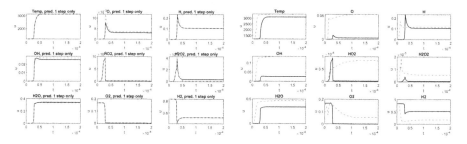

Fig. 5. Results from using parallel ResNets to predict a single step (left 9 plots) and marching in time from an initial condition (9 right plots) using DNNs with a depth of 7 and a width of 50.

of the ODE. For the results shown in Fig. 5 parallel ResNets of depth 7 and width 50 were used. These ResNets were trained using validation data with a patience of 400. For the nine subplots on the left side of Fig. 5, the ResNets are being used to predict only a single timestep. In other words, the red dashed curves are produced by plotting $\widehat{u}^{n+1} = \widehat{S}(u^n)$ for all n where u^n comes from known data. The right nine subplots show $\widehat{u}^{n+1} = \widehat{S}(\widehat{u}^n)$ where only u^0 is from known data. The plots on the left are included as evidence that the networks are close to learning the correct curves. The accumulation and propagation of errors when the quantities are marched in time can significantly affect the accuracy of the results as shown in the right plots. The results shown in Fig. 5 come from data on which the ResNets were not trained.

In Fig. 6, results are displayed in which the training data was log-scaled (i.e. where $\log x_i$ is used rather than x_i in (7)). The ResNets used for these results all have depth 9 and width 20 and were trained using validation data with a patience of 400 iterations. The plots in Fig. 6 were created using the same data set that was used to create the curves in Fig. 5. From these results, and many others not shown here, it is unclear if log-scaling provides any improvement in accuracy.

4.3   Grouping Training Data Based on Equivalence Ratio

For the next results the training data is split into three groups: fuel lean (equivalence ratio ≤ 0.1), fuel balanced (equivalence ratio between 0.1 and 2), and fuel rich (equivalence ratio >2). See Appendix A for more details on these data sets. The results of an experiment using the second approach, where a different group of parallel ResNets is trained for each of the fuel-based data sets, are presented in Fig. 7. In other words, there are 9 plots corresponding to results from ResNets trained only on fuel lean data sets, 9 plots for ResNets trained only on fuel balanced data sets, and 9 plots for ResNets trained only on fuel rich data sets. All ResNets have a depth of 6 and width of 30 and were trained using validation data with a patience of 400 iterations. Furthermore, these plots are presented with a logarithmically scaled x-axis, as for some of the data the reactions happen very quickly. All of the plots in Fig. 7 show results of marching in time given only an initial condition from known data that was not seen by the networks during training. These results show that the ResNets trained on fuel-based grouping is more successful than the previous attempts.

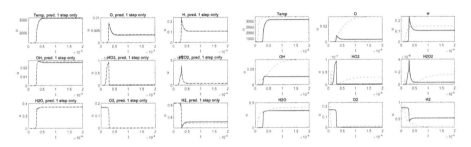

Fig. 6. Predicting a single timestep (left 9 plots) and marching in time (right 9 plots) from ResNets trained on log-scaled data. The ResNets used here have a depth of 9 and a width of 20, and were trained with validation data with patience of 400 iterations.

4.4   Training Data Sets with Varying Initial Temperatures, but Fixed Equivalence Ratio

For all of the results shown in Figs. 3 through 7 the ResNets were trained on data sets where the equivalence ratio was varied and there were at most two different initial temperatures (see Appendix A for more details). For this final result, parallel ResNets were trained on data sets that had initial conditions with the same equivalence ratio, but different initial temperatures. The results of an experiment using DNNs trained on this data can be seen in Fig. 8. The 9 plots on the left show results from ResNets with a depth of 6 and width of 30. On the right, the results came from ResNets with different depths (3 to 8) all with width 30. All of the ResNets were trained with validation data with patience of 400 iterations.

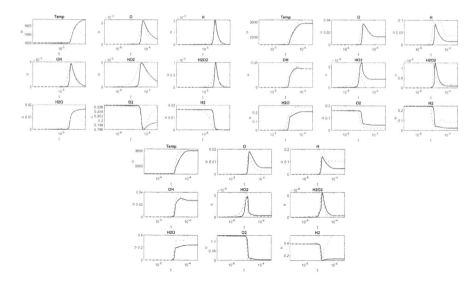

Fig. 7. Results from marching initial conditions forward in time using ResNets trained on fuel lean data (top left), fuel balanced (top right), and fuel rich (bottom) data sets. The ResNets used have a depth of 6 and a width of 30, and were trained with validation data with patience of 400 iterations.

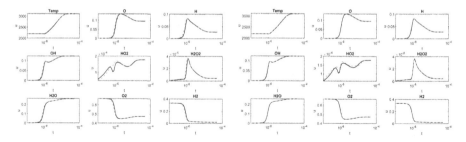

Fig. 8. Results from ResNets trained on data that varies the initial temperature. The plots on the left were produced from ResNets with a depth of 6 and a width of 30, and were trained with validation data with patience of 400 iterations. The plots on the right came from ResNets with varying depths all with a width of 30, and were trained with validation data with patience of 400 iterations. All plots show the results of marching in time (known data in blue, ResNet results in red). (Color figure online)

5   Conclusions and Future Directions

A number of ResNet based approaches to approximate the stiff ODEs arising in chemical kinetics were developed. The experiments presented indicate that when the equivalence ratio is fixed and initial temperature is varied (this case has been considered in [21,26]), the proposed DNNs can (almost) perfectly generalize to unseen data. This capacity for generalization deteriorates, however, when the initial temperature is kept fixed and the equivalence ratio is varied. In order to overcome this issue, the training data was separated into fuel lean, fuel balanced, and fuel rich based on the equivalence ratio. This approach has led to encouraging results.

There are several questions that are currently being investigated:

- All DNNs are dependent on the quality of training data. The data used for experiments reported here were generated using CHEMKIN. In view of the high dimensionality of the data, and the nature of chemical reactions (large periods of inactivity followed by a sudden reaction followed by a convergence to a steady state), quality criteria need to be developed to make sure redundant data is avoided.
- It will be interesting to see if further dividing the training data based on equivalence ratio is helpful.
- The usefulness of training with noisy data is also being explored. For some classification problems, this approach is known to increase the robustness of ResNets.
- It is of interest to see how the proposed approach generalizes to more reactions and species.

Acknowledgements. This work was supported by the Defense Threat Reduction Agency (DTRA) under contract HDTRA1-15-1-0068. Jacqueline Bell served as the technical monitor.

It is a pleasure to acknowledge a number of fruitful discussions with Drs. Adam Moses, Alisha J. Sharma and Ryan F. Johnson from the Naval Research Laboratory that lead to several improvements in the techniques discussed in this paper.

A   Description of the Training Data Sets

In this appendix the data sets that were used to train the DNNs and create the plots presented above are described in more detail. Specifically, information about the number of points, the equivalence ratio, and initial temperature of the individual data sets is provided. For the results in Fig. 2, a single ResNet was trained with a set containing data from a single initial condition. This set has 4,999 points, and the initial condition has equivalence ratio 0.1 and initial temperature 1,200K. Once the network was trained on this data, it was tested with the same initial point from the set on which it was trained.

The parallel ResNets used to produce the plots in Figs. 3 through 6 were trained on a data set with subsets that correspond to 9 different initial conditions, all with initial temperature 1,200 K. The data is described further in Table 1, where the subsets are numbered for convenient reference. This set also contains the data used to create Fig. 2 (set 3). After being trained on this entire data set, the ResNets that were used for the results in Fig. 3 were then tested on set 5, and therefore these results do not reflect the ResNets generalizing to unseen data.

The subsets of data described in Table 1 are of different sizes. For the results in Fig. 4 the differences in sizes was compensated by training with copies of the smaller sets. Specifically, the ResNets were trained with set 1, two copies of sets 3 and 9, and eight copies of sets 5 and 7. The ResNets were then tested by using the initial condition from set 6, and these are the results that are shown in Fig. 4. To train the ResNets that produced the results in Figs. 5 and 6 a single copy of sets 1, 3, 5, 7, and 9 from Table 1 was used. The trained networks were then tested on set 8. The difference between these two experiments are the architecture of the ResNets and the way that the training data was scaled prior to training. Also, as opposed to the experiments represented by Figs. 3 and 4, the experiments that resulted in Figs. 5 and 6 use the *second approach*, where the ResNets are being trained to learn the next timestep of the data. To create the training data in this situation, the same data is used as both components (input and output). This results in size of each subset being reduced by one, because there is no next timestep to learn at the final time.

Table 1. Description of the training data used to produce Figs. 3 through Fig. 6.

Set	1	2	3	4	5	6	7	8	9
Number of points	8,000	6,000	4,999	1,999	999	999	999	1,999	3,999
Equivalence ratio	0.01	0.05	0.1	0.25	0.5	1	2	5	10
Initial temperature	1,200	1,200	1,200	1,200	1,200	1,200	1,200	1,200	1,200

In Table 2 the data sets that have been separated into fuel lean, balanced, and rich sets are described. The first thing to notice about this data is that it contains the data sets from Table 1, where here the number of points is one less for the same reason described above. This data was used to create the results shown in Fig. 7. The ResNets trained on fuel lean sets (top left set of 9 plots) were trained with subsets 1, 3, 4, 6, and 9, and then tested with the initial condition from set 8. The ResNets trained on the fuel balanced sets were trained on subsets 1, 3, 5, 7, 9, and 12, and subsequently tested with the initial condition from set 11. Finally the networks trained on fuel rich sets were trained with subsets 1, 2, 3, 5, and 7, and then tested with the initial condition from set 4.

Table 2. Description of the training data with fuel-based grouping that was used for the results in Fig. 7.

Fuel lean sets									
Set	1	2	3	4	5	6	7	8	9
Number of points	7,999	5,999	4,998	4,999	4,999	4,999	4,999	4,999	4,999
Equivalence ratio	0.01	0.05	0.1	0.01	0.02	0.04	0.06	0.08	0.1
Initial temperature	1,200	1,200	1,200	1,500	1,500	1,500	1,500	1,500	1,500

Fuel balanced sets											
Set	1	2	3	4	5	6	7	8	9	10	11	12
Number of points	1,998	998	998	998	4,999	4,999	4,999	4,999	4,999	4,999	4,999	4,999
Equivalence ratio	0.25	0.5	1	2	0.2	0.4	0.5	0.75	0.9	1	1.5	2
Initial temperature	1,200	1,200	1,200	1,200	1,500	1,500	1,500	1,500	1,500	1,500	1,500	1,500

Fuel rich sets							
Set	1	2	3	4	5	6	7
Number of points	1,998	3,998	4,999	4,999	4,999	4,999	4,999
Equivalence ratio	5	10	2.5	3	3.5	4.5	5
Initial temperature	1,200	1,200	1,500	1,500	1,500	1,500	1,500

For the experiments that produced the plots in Fig. 8, the training data consists of 13 subsets. Each subset has 499 points and an equivalence ratio of 1. Furthermore, each subset has a different initial temperature beginning with 1,200 K and increasing by increments of 100 K to 2,400 K. For the experiment shown in Fig. 8, the ResNets were trained with the sets corresponding to initial temperatures 1,200 K, 1,500 K, 1,800 K, 2,100 K, and 2,400 K. The trained ResNets were then tested using the initial condition with temperature 2,200K.

References

1. Antil, H., Elman, H.C., Onwunta, A., Verma, D.: Novel deep neural networks for solving bayesian statistical inverse. arXiv preprint arXiv:2102.03974 (2021)
2. Antil, H., Khatri, R., Löhner, R.L., Verma, D.: Fractional deep neural network via constrained optimization. Mach. Learn. Sci. Technol. **2**(1), 015003 (2020). http://iopscience.iop.org/10.1088/2632-2153/aba8e7
3. Antil, H., Kouri, D.P., Lacasse, M.-D., Ridzal, D. (eds.): Frontiers in PDE-Constrained Optimization. TIVMA, vol. 163. Springer, New York (2018). https://doi.org/10.1007/978-1-4939-8636-1Papers based on the workshop held at the Institute for Mathematics and its Applications, Minneapolis, MN, 6–10 June 2016
4. Camelli, F., Löhner, R.: Assessing maximum possible damage for contaminant release events. Eng. Comput. **21**(7), 748–760 (2004)
5. Chen, R.T.Q., Rubanova, Y., Bettencourt, J., Duvenaud, D.K.: Neural ordinary differential equations. In: Bengio, S., Wallach, H., Larochelle, H., Grauman, K., Cesa-Bianchi, N., Garnett, R. (eds.) Advances in Neural Information Processing Systems, vol. 31. Curran Associates, Inc. (2018). https://proceedings.neurips.cc/paper/2018/file/69386f6bb1dfed68692a24c8686939b9-Paper.pdf
6. Cheng, C., Zhang, G.T.: Deep learning method based on physics informed neural network with resnet block for solving fluid flow problems. Water **13**(4), 423 (2021). https://doi.org/10.3390/w13040423. https://www.mdpi.com/2073-4441/13/4/423
7. Chollet, F., et al.: Keras (2015). https://keras.io

8. Ghosh, A., Behl, H.S., Dupont, E., Torr, P.H.S., Namboodiri, V.: Steer: Simple temporal regularization for neural odes. arXiv preprint arXiv:2006.10711 (2020)
9. Grimberg, S.J., Farhat, C.: Hyperreduction of CFD Models of Turbulent Flows using a Machine Learning Approach (2020–0363). https://doi.org/10.2514/6.2020-0363, https://arc.aiaa.org/doi/abs/10.2514/6.2020-0363
10. He, K., Zhang, X., Ren, S., Sun, J.: Deep residual learning for image recognition. In: 2016 IEEE Conference on Computer Vision and Pattern Recognition (CVPR), pp. 770–778 (2016). https://doi.org/10.1109/CVPR.2016.90
11. Ji, W., Qiu, W., Shi, Z., Pan, S., Deng, S.: Stiff-pinn: Physics-informed neural network for stiff chemical kinetics. arXiv preprint arXiv:2011.04520 (2020)
12. Keck, J.C.: Rate-controlled constrained-equilibrium theory of chemical reactions in complex systems. Prog. Energy Combust. Sci. **16**(2), 125–154 (1990)
13. Kee, R.J., et al.: Chemkin collection, release 3.6 (2000)
14. Krizhevsky, A., Sutskever, I., Hinton, G.E.: ImageNet classification with deep convolutional neural networks. Commun. ACM **60**(6), 84–90 (2017)
15. Lam, S.H., Goussis, D.A.: The CSP method for simplifying kinetics. Int. J. Chem. Kinet. **26**(4), 461–486 (1994)
16. Lecun, Y., Bottou, L., Bengio, Y., Haffner, P.: Gradient-based learning applied to document recognition. Proc. IEEE **86**(11), 2278–2324 (1998). https://doi.org/10.1109/5.726791
17. Löhner, R., Camelli, F.: Optimal placement of sensors for contaminant detection based on detailed 3D CFD simulations. Eng. Comput. **22**(3), 260–273 (2005)
18. Lu, T., Law, C.: A directed relation graph method for mechanism reduction. Proc. Combust. Instit. **30**, 1333–1341 (2005). https://doi.org/10.1016/j.proci.2004.08.145
19. Lye, K.O., Mishra, S., Ray, D.: Deep learning observables in computational fluid dynamics. J. Comput. Phys. **410**, 109339 (2020)
20. Maas, U., Pope, S.: Simplifying chemical kinetics: intrinsic low-dimensional manifolds in composition space. Combust. Flame **88**(3), 239–264 (1992)
21. Owoyele, O., Pal, P.: Chemnode: A neural ordinary differential equations approach for chemical kinetics solvers. arXiv preprint arXiv:2101.04749 (2021)
22. Peng, W.Y., Pinkowski, N.H.: Efficient and accurate time-integration of combustion chemical kinetics using artificial neural networks (2017)
23. Petersen, E.L., Hanson, R.K.: Reduced kinetics mechanisms for ram accelerator combustion. J. Propul. Power **15**(4), 591–600 (1999)
24. Raissi, M., Perdikaris, P., Karniadakis, G.E.: Physics-informed neural networks: a deep learning framework for solving forward and inverse problems involving nonlinear partial differential equations. J. Comput. Phys. **378**, 686–707 (2019). https://doi.org/10.1007/978-3-030-44992-6_14
25. Ruthotto, L., Haber, E.: Deep neural networks motivated by partial differential equations. J. Math. Imaging Vis. **62**(3), 352–364 (2020). https://doi.org/10.1007/s10851-019-00903-1
26. Sharma, A.J., Johnson, R.F., Kessler, D.A., Moses, A.: Deep learning for scalable chemical kinetics. In: AIAA Scitech 2020 Forum (2020–0181). https://doi.org/10.2514/6.2020-0181, https://arc.aiaa.org/doi/abs/10.2514/6.2020-0181
27. Sportisse, B.: An analysis of operator splitting techniques in the stiff case. J. Comput. Phys. **161**(1), 140–168 (2000)
28. Stück, A., Camelli, F.F., Löhner, R.: Adjoint-based design of shock mitigation devices. Int. J. Numer. Methods Fluids **64**(4), 443–472 (2010)
29. Sun, W., Chen, Z., Gou, X., Ju, Y.: A path flux analysis method for the reduction of detailed chemical kinetic mechanisms. Combust. Flame **157**(7), 1298–1307 (2010)

30. Togashi, F., Löhner, R., Tsuboi, N.: Numerical simulation of h2/air detonation using detailed reaction models. In: 44th AIAA Aerospace Sciences Meeting and Exhibit (2006–954). https://doi.org/10.2514/6.2006-954, https://arc.aiaa.org/doi/abs/10.2514/6.2006-954
31. Vajda, S., Valko, P., Turányi, T.: Principal component analysis of kinetic models. Int. J. Chem. Kinet. **17**, 55–81 (2004). https://doi.org/10.1002/kin.550170107
32. Zhang, P., Sankaran, R., Stoyanov, M., Lebrun-Grandie, D., Finney, C.E.: Reduced Models for Chemical Kinetics derived from Parallel Ensemble Simulations of Stirred Reactors. https://doi.org/10.2514/6.2020-0177, https://arc.aiaa.org/doi/abs/10.2514/6.2020-0177
33. Ziegler, J.L., Deiterding, R., Shepherd, J.E., Pullin, D.: An adaptive high-order hybrid scheme for compressive, viscous flows with detailed chemistry. J. Comput. Phys. **230**(20), 7598–7630 (2011)

Lettuce: PyTorch-Based Lattice Boltzmann Framework

Mario Christopher Bedrunka[1,2] , Dominik Wilde[1,2] , Martin Kliemank[2],
Dirk Reith[2,3] , Holger Foysi[1] , and Andreas Krämer[4(✉)]

[1] Department of Mechanical Engineering, University of Siegen,
Paul-Bonatz-Straße 9-11, 57076 Siegen-Weidenau, Germany
[2] Institute of Technology, Resource and Energy-efficient Engineering (TREE),
Bonn-Rhein-Sieg University of Applied Sciences, Grantham-Allee 20,
53757 Sankt Augustin, Germany
[3] Fraunhofer Institute for Algorithms and Scientific Computing (SCAI),
Schloss Birlinghoven, 53754 Sankt Augustin, Germany
[4] Department of Mathematics and Computer Science, Freie Universität Berlin,
Arnimallee 6, 14195 Berlin, Germany
andreas.kraemer@fu-berlin.de

Abstract. The lattice Boltzmann method (LBM) is an efficient simulation technique for computational fluid mechanics and beyond. It is based on a simple stream-and-collide algorithm on Cartesian grids, which is easily compatible with modern machine learning architectures. While it is becoming increasingly clear that deep learning can provide a decisive stimulus for classical simulation techniques, recent studies have not addressed possible connections between machine learning and LBM. Here, we introduce *Lettuce*, a *PyTorch*-based LBM code with a threefold aim. *Lettuce* enables GPU accelerated calculations with minimal source code, facilitates rapid prototyping of LBM models, and enables integrating LBM simulations with *PyTorch*'s deep learning and automatic differentiation facility. As a proof of concept for combining machine learning with the LBM, a neural collision model is developed, trained on a doubly periodic shear layer and then transferred to a different flow, a decaying turbulence. We also exemplify the added benefit of *PyTorch*'s automatic differentiation framework in flow control and optimization. To this end, the spectrum of a forced isotropic turbulence is maintained without further constraining the velocity field. The source code is freely available from https://github.com/lettucecfd/lettuce.

Keywords: Lattice Boltzmann method · Pytorch · Machine learning · Neural networks · Automatic differentiation · Computational fluid dynamics · Flow control

1 Introduction

Innovations are more important than ever in the face of global challenges such as climate change and pandemics. Bridging the gap from basic understanding to

© Springer Nature Switzerland AG 2021
H. Jagode et al. (Eds.): ISC High Performance 2021 Workshops, LNCS 12761, pp. 40–55, 2021.
https://doi.org/10.1007/978-3-030-90539-2_3

technological solutions often requires physical models in some stages of development. Such models can predict aspects of global warming or the spread of viruses based on fluid dynamics, for example [8,9,32]. However, the models' equations, usually in the form of partial differential equations (PDEs), require efficient solution approaches due to their complexity. By using numerical methods, computers solve these PDEs, which are discretized in space and time. Even though great care is taken, numerical errors inevitably occur during discretization, where the truncation error usually depends on grid and time step size. Hence, large resolutions are necessary if high accuracy is required, especially if modeling is reduced as much as possible, e.g., during direct numerical simulations (DNS). When DNS are computationally intractable, alternatives like the well-known Reynolds averaged Navier-Stokes equations (RANS) or large-eddy simulation (LES) are routinely used. These approaches require expressing unresolved or unclosed terms through known quantities [36,42]. Parameters involved in these modeling approaches are often not optimally determined or change for different flows. For this purpose, machine learning (ML) in fluid dynamics is a rapidly evolving research field that enables new impulses to tackle such problems and provide interesting new approaches to the modeling problem. The benefit of ML approaches in computational fluid dynamics (CFD) simulations has been demonstrated in various recent studies [10,19,39,40]. A successful use of machine learning in combination with well-known Navier-Stokes solvers was recently shown by Kochkov et al. [19]. They introduced learned forcing terms into PDE solvers, thereby reaching the same accuracy as a classical solver at 8-10x finer resolution.

When integrating machine learning into numerical algorithms, it can be beneficial to resort to simulation methods whose mathematical structure is easily compatible with neural networks. The present work shows that a highly suitable CFD approach for this purpose is the lattice Boltzmann method [21,27] (LBM), which is particularly competitive in the fields of transient, turbulent, or multiphase fluid dynamics. The LBM is a second order accurate simulation method that exhibits similar performance as classical finite difference schemes [41]. In contrast to classical solvers, it involves a linear streaming of particle distribution functions on a regular grid and a local collision step. Despite its successful application to many fluid problems, recent studies have only scarcely addressed possible combinations of ML and LBM. As a prototypical approach, Hennigh [15] has demonstrated the potential of ML-driven flow prediction based on LBM. He compressed flow fields onto coarser grids using convolutional autoencoders and learned the propagation of the latent representations, which can then be decoded back onto the fine grid. This approach, however, has limited transferability as it is primarily data-informed and does not encode the underlying physics. Furthermore, Rüttgers et al. [33] have applied deep learning methods to the lattice Boltzmann method to predict the sound pressure level caused by objects. They introduced an encoder-decoder convolutional neural network and discussed various learning parameters to accurately forecast the acoustic fields. To the best of our knowledge, no further ML-enhanced LBM methods were proposed.

Although the mathematics and physics behind the LBM are ambitious, the implementation is relatively simple. This allows beginners to quickly set up simple test cases in one or two dimensions with popular scripting languages like Matlab or Python. However, when switching to three dimensions, the algorithmic and computational complexity of simulations severely limits such prototypical implementations. More efficient simulations in compiled languages usually rely on optimized software packages and require initial training to simulate complex flows. This is particularly true for GPU-accelerated codes, which enhance performance [26,29] but defy fast implementation.

Both the lack of machine learning studies in the context of LBM and the code complexity of 3D implementations motivate an LBM framework that allows ease of use, despite extensive built-in functionality for machine learning algorithms. For this purpose, the software package *Lettuce* has been developed based on the open-source machine learning framework *PyTorch* [31]. *PyTorch* implements optimized numerical operations on CPUs and GPUs, which can easily be accessed via Python instructions. Internally, those operations are vectorized using efficient backends such as BLAS/LAPACK and highly optimized CUDA code. By resorting to those efficient *PyTorch* core routines, the LBM code remains maintainable and lean, which will be demonstrated throughout this article. Furthermore, the *Lettuce* framework can seamlessly integrate *PyTorch*'s machine learning modules into the fluid dynamics solver and thereby provide a substantial contribution to future work in this area.

Lettuce is meant to complement existing optimized codes like the well-known LBM frameworks OpenLB [17], Palabos [25], waLBerla [1,14], and others [28,30,38]. It intends to bridge the gap between scripting language codes for local machines and highly optimized codes based on compiled programming languages that run efficiently on computer clusters, too. With an off-the-shelf GPU, *Lettuce* can simulate fairly complex three-dimensional problems even on a local workstation with 24 GB of GPU memory. Independent of machine learning research, this also enables rapid prototyping of general methodological extensions for the lattice Boltzmann method.

This short paper is structured as follows. Section 2 presents an overview of the software functionalities and briefly describes the LBM and its implementation. Section 3 shows simple examples of coupling the LBM with machine learning, demonstrates the use of *PyTorch*'s automatic differentiation capabilities in CFD simulations, and provides a computational benchmark. Section 4 presents a summary and conclusions. Scripts for all simulations in this paper are accessible on https://github.com/lettucecfd/lettuce-paper.

2   Software Description

2.1   Software Functionalities

The lattice Boltzmann method (LBM) is based on the kinetic theory of gases, concretely a discretized version of the BGK-Boltzmann equation. It evolves a discrete particle distribution function $f_i(\mathbf{x}, t)$ according to the lattice Boltzmann equation

$$f_i(\mathbf{x} + \mathbf{c}_i \delta_t, t + \delta_t) = f_i(\mathbf{x}, t) + \Omega_i(\boldsymbol{f}(\mathbf{x}, t)), \tag{1}$$

where δ_t and $\mathbf{c}_i$ denote the time step and discrete particle velocities, respectively. At its core, the LBM involves two operations. First, the so-called streaming step shifts the particle distributions $f_i(\mathbf{x}, t)$ to the neighboring nodes along the trajectories $\mathbf{c}_i$. Second, the collision step introduces interactions between the particles on each node. Among the various collision models available in the literature, $\Omega(\boldsymbol{f})$ is selected based on considerations such as asymptotic behavior, accuracy, memory usage and stability. The most commonly used collision operator is the Bhatnagar-Gross-Krook model:

$$\Omega_i(\boldsymbol{f}) = -\frac{f_i - f_i^{\mathrm{eq}}}{\tau} \tag{2}$$

This operator describes the relaxation of the particle distribution function towards an equilibrium distribution influenced by a single relaxation parameter τ. The equilibrium distribution is given by

$$f_i^{\mathrm{eq}}(\mathbf{x}, t) = w_i \rho \left(1 + \frac{\mathbf{u} \cdot \mathbf{c}_i}{c_s^2} + \frac{(\mathbf{u} \cdot \mathbf{c}_i)^2}{2c_s^4} - \frac{\mathbf{u} \cdot \mathbf{u}}{2c_s^2}\right), \tag{3}$$

where w_i and c_s are the lattice weights and speed of sound, respectively. The density ρ and fluid velocity $\mathbf{u}$ are obtained as

$$\rho(\mathbf{x}, t) = \sum_i f_i(\mathbf{x}, t) \qquad \text{and} \qquad \rho\mathbf{u}(\mathbf{x}, t) = \sum_i \mathbf{c}_i f_i(\mathbf{x}, t). \tag{4}$$

Lettuce is equipped with a variety of frequently used collision models, such as the Bhatnagar-Grook-Krook (BGK) model [2], multi-relaxation time collision models [7,22], the two-relaxation time model [13], the regularized model [23] and entropic two-relaxation time models by Karlin, Bösch and Chikatamarla (KBC) [18]. For the latter, implementations are rare in open software packages. Many of these collision models are implemented in a stencil- and dimension-independent manner.

2.2   Code Example

After *Lettuce* is installed, the user can run simulations with minimal code. The following example demonstrates a lean executable Python script that simulates a three-dimensional Taylor-Green vortex (TGV3D), one of several flows provided in the library. The *Lettuce* library contains various boundary conditions, forcing and initialization schemes, thus covering a wide range of setups. After importing *Lettuce*, the stencil and the hardware are selected. Then, the flow, collision model, and streaming step are chosen and run through the Simulation class.

```
import lettuce as lt
lattice = lt.Lattice(stencil=lt.D3Q27, device='cuda') #or 'cpu'
flow = lt.TaylorGreenVortex3D(
    resolution=256,
    reynolds_number=1600,
    mach_number=0.05,
    lattice=lattice)
collision = lt.BGKCollision(
    lattice=lattice,
    tau=flow.units.relaxation_parameter_lu)
streaming = lt.StandardStreaming(lattice)
simulation = lt.Simulation(
    flow=flow,
    lattice=lattice,
    collision=collision,
    streaming=streaming)
simulation.step(num_steps=10000)
```

Lettuce provides various observables that can be reported during the simulation (e.g. kinetic energy, enstrophy, energy spectrum). These observables can be added easily to the Simulation class and exported for further analysis as follows:

```
energy = lt.IncompressibleKineticEnergy(lattice, flow)
simulation.reporters.append(
    lt.ObservableReporter(energy, interval=10,))
simulation.reporters.append(
    lt.VTKReporter(
        lattice,
        flow,
        interval=10,
        filename_base="./output"))
```

Besides, *Lettuce* comes with a VTK-reporter based on the PyEVTK library [16]. This reporter exports velocity components and pressure, which both can then be visualized by third-party software. An example is given in Fig. 1, which shows the isosurfaces of the three-dimensional Taylor-Green vortex simulation from the code snippet above.

Fig. 1. Q-criterion isosurfaces of a three-dimensional Taylor-Green Vortex at time step $t = 5000$, 7000 and 10000 colored by streamwise velocity. The Reynolds number and grid resolution were 1600 and 256^3, respectively. (Color figure online)

Figure 2 shows the energy dissipation that is obtained from the kinetic energy k by calculating $-dk/dt$ ($=\nu\langle\epsilon\rangle$ in isotropic turbulence) using finite differences. That way it includes numerical dissipation effects and spurious contributions from LBM, too. The data is compared to the reference taken from Brachet [3], who used a spectral code with a resolution of 256^3 grid points. The dissipation, $-dk/dt$, shows excellent agreement with the reference data up to a Reynolds number of 1600. For Reynolds numbers of $Re = 3000$ and higher the maximum dissipation rate deviates slightly due to under-resolution.

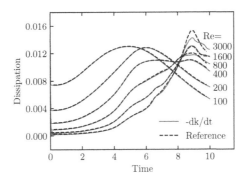

Fig. 2. Energy dissipation rate $\epsilon(t) = -dk/dt$ of a three-dimensional Taylor-Green-Vortex using the BGK collision model. Reference is taken from Brachet [3].

3   Advanced Functionalities

3.1   Machine Learning

The collision model constitutes the core of the LBM as it determines the macro-scopic system of PDEs and thereby encodes the solver's physics. It has long been known that the choice of collision model for a given PDE is ambiguous, which is related to the discrepancy between the number of degrees of freedom (discrete distribution functions) and macroscopic variables of interest. For example, the standard D2Q9 stencil uses nine degrees of freedom per lattice node to encode six physically relevant moments (density, momentum, and stress tensor). The remaining degrees of freedom (represented by higher-order moments or cumulants) are usually propagated in a way that offers certain numerical advantages such as improved stability [18, 20, 23] or accuracy [12].

In the following, we want to exploit this ambiguity to define neural collision operators as a more accurate alternative to classical collision models. For this purpose, we define a collision model that relaxes the moments m_i towards their respective equilibria m_i^{eq} by individual relaxation rates $\mathbf{S} = \text{diag}(\tau_0, \tau_1, ..., \tau_{Q-1})$, where Q is the number of discrete velocities per grid point. A transformation matrix $\mathbf{M}$ (according to Dellar [7]) maps the distribution function $\boldsymbol{f}$ to the moments $\mathbf{m} = \mathbf{M}\boldsymbol{f} = (\rho, \rho\mathbf{u}, \mathbf{\Pi}, \mathcal{N}, \boldsymbol{\mathcal{J}})^T$, where ρ is the density, $\mathbf{u} = (u, v)$ is the fluid velocity, $\mathbf{\Pi}$ is the momentum flux, and $\mathcal{N}$ and $\boldsymbol{\mathcal{J}} = (\mathcal{J}_0, \mathcal{J}_1)$ are non-hydrodynamic moments. These moments are relaxed towards the moment equilibrium $\mathbf{m}^{\text{eq}} = \mathbf{M}\boldsymbol{f}^{\text{eq}}$ with the relaxation rates given by $\mathbf{S}$:

$$\Omega(\boldsymbol{f}) = -\mathbf{M}^{-1}\mathbf{S}^{-1}(\mathbf{M}\boldsymbol{f} - \mathbf{m}^{\text{eq}}). \tag{5}$$

The relaxation rates for the conserved moments ρ and $\rho\mathbf{u}$ have no effect and are thus set to unity. Since the shear relaxation rates are related to the kinematic viscosity ν, they are set to $\tau_n = \nu c_s^{-2}\delta_t^{-1} + 0.5$, $n = 3, 4, 5$, which recovers the Navier-Stokes equations in the weakly compressible regime. A neural network provides the relaxation rates τ_n, $n = 6, 7, 8$, for the higher moments. For this purpose, a shallow network with one hidden layer and 530 parameters is introduced to keep the computational cost feasible. The network determines the higher-order relaxation rates based on local moments and is optimized to reproduce a finer-resolved reference simulation. Moreover, we want to ensure that the collision operator is stable. For this purpose, an exponential function is applied to the output $\tilde{\tau}_n$ of the neural network: $\tau_n = \exp(\tilde{\tau}_n) + 0.5$, $n = 6, 7, 8$. This operation renders the output larger than 0.5, which prevents excessive over-relaxation. The relaxation parameters are not upper bounded as $\tau_n \to \infty$ yields the identity and is usually uncritical in terms of stability.

Training data was generated by simulating a doubly periodic shear layer at a Reynolds number of 5000 on a domain of size 128^2 using the BGK model [4]. The shear layer provides both large gradients and smooth areas which need to be detected. Most relevant engineering flows have features that are locally present in shear layer turbulence, such that good performance of a model in this setup will likely transfer to other flows. Instead, training with isotropic flows only would likely hamper transferability.

Depending on the information contained in the local moments, the network should adjust the local relaxation parameters. The training procedure optimizes the network parameters ϑ to minimize the discrepancy between a low-resolution and a high-resolution simulation. Therefore, the discrete distributions from the training trajectory are mapped onto a coarser grid with 64^2 grid points. Batches of short simulations with the neural collision model are started from each snapshot. After 100 simulation steps, the flow fields are compared with the finer-resolved reference simulation based on energy E, vorticity ω, and velocity u, which are all computed on the coarse grid. The mean-squared error (MSE) of these quantities from the reference are minimized using the Adam optimizer and the loss function

$$L(t; \vartheta) = w_u \sum_i^N \text{MSE}\left(u(\mathbf{x}_i, t; \vartheta), \tilde{u}(\mathbf{x}_i, t)\right)$$

$$+ w_\omega \sum_i^N \text{MSE}\left(\omega(\mathbf{x}_i, t; \vartheta), \tilde{\omega}(\mathbf{x}_i, t)\right) \tag{6}$$

$$+ w_E \, \text{MSE}\left(E(t; \vartheta), \tilde{E}(t)\right),$$

where N is the number of grid points. The weights are hyperparameters that were selected as $w_u := 0.6$, $w_\omega := w_E := 0.2$. This choice emphasizes the optimization of dissipation effects, which are critical in under-resolved turbulence. Such flows exhibit large gradients that occur intermittently, leading to locally under-resolved spatial structures. Therefore, the model has to strike a balance between retaining the physical structures on small scales and adding numerical dissipation for stabilization.

The fluid velocity is the most natural target as it directly measures numerical errors. The kinetic energy tracks the dissipation globally but does not resolve the spatial heterogeneity. In contrast, including the vorticity as a target stresses the finest resolved structures; the enstrophy, i.e., the integral over the vorticity magnitude, measures the viscous shear stresses that induce dissipation. In homogeneous turbulence, it peaks at high wave numbers around the Kolmogorov scale. Consequently, optimizing the loss function (6) deliberately targets the dissipation occurring on small scales. A detailed hyperparameter optimization, the inclusion of other target properties, and the incorporation of multiple flows with different boundary conditions in the training set will likely further improve the model. These next steps as well as a systematic study of transferability are beyond the scope of this proof-of-concept and will be left for future work.

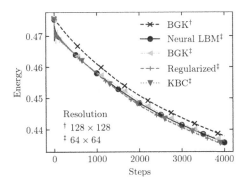

Fig. 3. Comparison of the kinetic energy evolution of various collision models for the doubly periodic shear layer at $Re = 5000$.

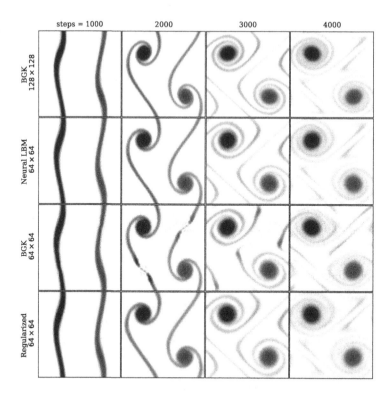

Fig. 4. Evolution of vorticity fields for a doubly periodic shear layer flow for Reynolds number 5000 using several collision models [4].

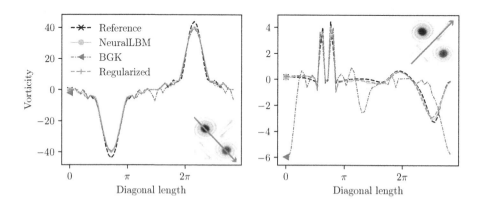

Fig. 5. Vorticity along a diagonal line for a doubly periodic shear layer flow after 4000 steps for Reynolds number 5000.

Turning to results, Fig. 3 compares the evolution of kinetic energy for the doubly periodic shear layer. Several collision models were used for this assessment. In the beginning, the energy of the lower-resolved simulations dropped due to under-resolution. Then, all collision models produced similar energies. However, the vorticity fields depicted in Fig. 4 clearly show that the simulation using the BGK operator can no longer capture the vortices from the finer-resolved reference simulation. In contrast, the neural collision model accurately reproduces these structures, as shown in more detail in Fig. 5 by the vorticity along the diagonals. The improvement compared to the BGK operator becomes clear while still providing less dissipation than the regularized model.

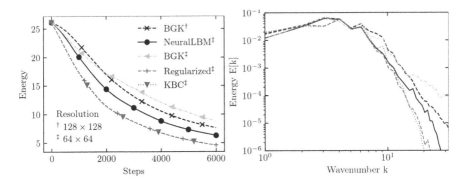

Fig. 6. Enstrophy evolution (*left*) and energy spectrum (*right*) of an isotropic decaying turbulence at Reynolds number 30000. Colors and line types are equal for both plots. (Color figure online)

The crucial question is whether the optimized network is transferable to other flows. Figure 6 shows the vorticity evolution and energy spectrum for an isotropic decaying turbulence simulation at a Reynolds number of 30000 [37]. Although trained on a different flow, the neural collision model reproduced the vortex field far better, while other collision models were either unstable or overly dissipative, as shown in Fig. 7. The BGK model was not able to handle the high Reynolds number and introduced unphysical small-scale oscillations. These numerical artefacts are visible in the energy spectrum, revealing a lot of unphysical energy accumulated at high wavenumbers. By contrast, the KBC and regularized collision models are more dissipative at larger wavenumbers, resulting in much faster energy and enstrophy decay. In comparison to these baseline models, the ML-enhanced simulation produced the best match with the reference simulation. This example demonstrates generalization capabilities and the potential benefit of using collision models based on neural networks.

A promising future direction of research is to target the current limitations of the LBM, including high Mach number compressible flows. These flows require higher-order moments so that current compressible LBMs usually resort to larger stencils [6,11,24,43], off-lattice streaming [5,43,44], or non-local collision models

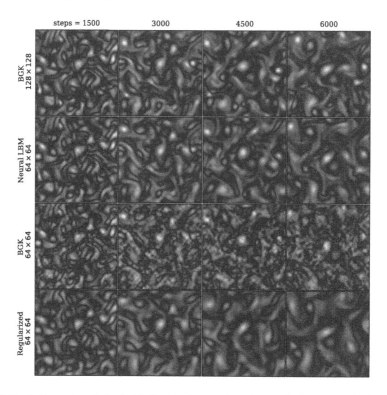

Fig. 7. Evolution of vorticity fields for a isotropic decaying turbulence flow for Reynolds number 30000 using several collision models.

[34,35] that introduce additional numerical approximations. In this application, neural collisions could help reduce numerical errors and advance the state of the art.

3.2   Flow Control Through Automatic Differentiation

The availability of an automatic differentiation framework within a CFD simulation engine has additional advantages (besides machine learning). *PyTorch* provides analytic derivatives for all numerical operations, which is, for example, useful in flow control and optimization.

As a demonstration of these capabilities, forced isotropic turbulence is simulated, i.e., the energy spectrum is maintained throughout the simulation using a forcing term as detailed below. A cost functional R is introduced as the relative deviation of the instantaneous spectrum $\sigma(\mathbf{u})$ from the target spectrum σ_0 with a cutoff at $c := 2 \cdot 10^{-5}$. R is defined as

$$R(\boldsymbol{u}) = \| \ln \max(\sigma(\boldsymbol{u}), c) - \ln \max(\sigma_0, c) \|_2^2,$$

where the logarithm and maximum are taken elementwise.

To incorporate this restraint into the simulation, the equilibrium distribution $f^{eq}(\rho, \mathbf{u} + \Delta\mathbf{u})$ is expanded around a velocity that is locally shifted by a forcing term $\Delta\mathbf{u} := -\kappa \cdot \nabla_{\mathbf{u}} R$ with a force constant $\kappa = 5 \cdot 10^{-5}$. Computing the gradient requires differentiating through various numeric operations, including a Fast Fourier Transform, which is easily done within *PyTorch* due to the automatic differentiation facility.

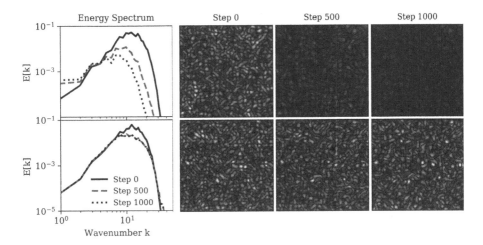

Fig. 8. Energy spectrum $E[k]$ (left column) and evolution of vorticity fields in isotropic turbulence. Upper row: free simulation; lower row: restrained simulation.

Figure 8 shows the vorticity fields and energy spectrum for a simulation at a resolution of 128^2 grid points with $Re = 2000$ and $Ma = 0.1$. While the unrestrained simulation decays, the restrained simulation maintains the spectrum after an initial adjustment phase took place, starting from the artificial initialization field. This example shows that complicated forces are easily incorporated into simulations through automatic differentiation. This feature can be useful in many other applications.

3.3   Benchmark

Lettuce attains a satisfactory performance due to the GPU operations provided by *PyTorch*. The optimized backend code enables fast CUDA-driven simulations on both cluster GPUs and even standard GPUs for workstations. We evaluated the performance of *Lettuce* by simulating a Taylor-Green vortex in both 2D (D2Q9) and 3D (D3Q19). The results are compared for both an NVIDIA Tesla V100 and an NVIDIA RTX2070S in single and double precision. Figure 9 compares the performance in MLUPS (Million Lattice Updates Per Second) for different resolutions.

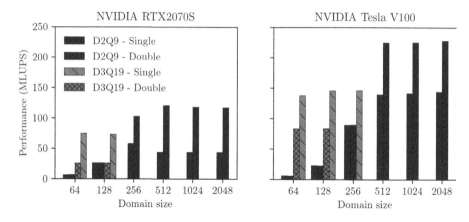

Fig. 9. Performance of Lettuce for simulating a Taylor-Green vortex.

With increasing domain size $64^2; 128^2; 256^2; 512^2$, the simulation speed increases to 140 MLUPS in two dimensions and 83 MLUPS in three dimensions using an NVIDIA Tesla V100 in double precision. The simulation speed increases by over 60% to 75% when calculations are performed in single precision. Using an off-the-shelve NVIDIA RTX2070S, the computational efficiency was lower, as expected. Performance peaked at 58 MLUPS using a domain size of 256^2 in two dimensions. For higher resolutions, the performance decreased to 44 MLUPS. By using single precision, the performance can be increased by 180% for higher resolutions. This comparison shows that even on a commercially available consumer-grade GPU high-performance simulations can be performed in an acceptable time. Further speedups will be obtained by implementing custom C++ and CUDA extensions, for which *PyTorch* offers a modular and well-documented interface. Such extensions as well as a distributed multi-GPU implementation through `torch.distributed` are natural enhancements that are currently in progress.

4   Conclusion

We have introduced *Lettuce*, a *PyTorch*-based lattice Boltzmann code that bridges lattice Boltzmann simulations and machine learning. We have demonstrated how simulations can be set up and run with minimal use of source code. This eases code development significantly and flattens the learning curve for beginners. Scientists and engineers can run GPU-accelerated three-dimensional simulations even on local workstations, which benefits rapid prototyping of lattice Boltzmann models. Besides machine learning routines, the framework supports automatic differentiation for flow control and optimization. As an example, a forced isotropic turbulence simulation was run with a maintained energy spectrum. Furthermore, we have defined a neural collision model to demonstrate the benefits of incorporating neural networks into the lattice Boltzmann method.

The presented results indicate that neural collision models can outperform traditional collision operators and reduce numerical errors, which motivates further research in this direction.

References

1. Bauer, M., et al.: waLBerla: a block-structured high-performance framework for multiphysics simulations. Comput. Math. with Appl. **81**, 478–501 (2021)
2. Bhatnagar, P.L., Gross, E.P., Krook, M.: A model for collision processes in gases. I. Small amplitude processes in charged and neutral one-component systems. Phys. Rev. **94**(3), 511–525 (1954)
3. Brachet, M.E., Meiron, D.I., Orszag, S.A., Nickel, B., Morf, R.H., Frisch, U.: Small-scale structure of the Taylor-green vortex. J. Fluid Mech. **130**, 411–452 (1983)
4. Brown, D.L.: Performance of under-resolved two-dimensional incompressible flow simulations. J. Comput. Phys. **122**(1), 165–183 (1995)
5. Chen, T., Wen, X., Wang, L.P., Guo, Z., Wang, J., Chen, S.: Simulation of three-dimensional compressible decaying isotropic turbulence using a redesigned discrete unified gas kinetic scheme. Phys. Fluids **32**(12), 125104 (2020)
6. Coreixas, C., Latt, J.: Compressible lattice Boltzmann methods with adaptive velocity stencils: an interpolation-free formulation. Phys. Fluids **32**(11), 116102 (2020)
7. Dellar, P.J.: Incompressible limits of lattice Boltzmann equations using multiple relaxation times. J. Comput. Phys. **190**(2), 351–370 (2003)
8. Diwan, S.S., Ravichandran, S., Govindarajan, R., Narasimha, R.: Understanding transmission dynamics of Covid-19-type infections by direct numerical simulations of cough/sneeze flows. Trans. Indian Natl. Acad. Eng. **5**, 255–261 (2020)
9. Fabregat, A., Gisbert, F., Vernet, A., Dutta, S., Mittal, K., Pallarès, J.: Direct numerical simulation of the turbulent flow generated during a violent expiratory event. Phys. Fluids **33**(3), 035122 (2021)
10. Font, B., Weymouth, G.D., Nguyen, V.T., Tutty, O.R.: Deep learning of the spanwise-averaged Navier-Stokes equations. J. Comput. Phys. **434**, 110199 (2021)
11. Frapolli, N., Chikatamarla, S.S., Karlin, I.V.: Entropic lattice Boltzmann model for compressible flows. Phys. Rev. E Stat. Nonlinear Soft Matter Phys. **92**(6), 061301 (2015)
12. Geier, M., Pasquali, A., Schönherr, M.: Parametrization of the cumulant lattice Boltzmann method for fourth order accurate diffusion. Part I: Derivation and validation. J. Comput. Phys. **348**, 862–888 (2017)
13. Ginzburg, I., Verhaeghe, F., D'Humières, D.: Two-relaxation-time Lattice Boltzmann scheme: about parametrization, velocity, pressure and mixed boundary conditions. Commun. Comput. Phys. **3**(2), 427–478 (2008)
14. Godenschwager, C., Schornbaum, F., Bauer, M., Köstler, H., Rüde, U.: A framework for hybrid parallel flow simulations with a trillion cells in complex geometries. In: Proceedings of the International Conference for High Performance Computing, Networking, Storage and Analysis - SC 2013, New York, NY, USA, pp. 1–12. ACM Press (2013)
15. Hennigh, O.: Lat-Net: compressing lattice Boltzmann flow simulations using deep neural networks. arXiv preprint arXiv:1705.09036 (2017)
16. Herrera, P.: pyevtk 1.2.0. PyPI (2021). https://pypi.org/project/pyevtk/

17. Heuveline, V., Krause, M.J.: OpenLB: towards an efficient parallel open source library for lattice Boltzmann fluid flow simulations. In: International Workshop on State-of-the-Art in Scientific and Parallel Computing, PARA, vol. 9 (2010)
18. Karlin, I.V., Bösch, F., Chikatamarla, S.: Gibbs' principle for the lattice-kinetic theory of fluid dynamics. Phys. Rev. E Stat. Nonlinear Soft Matter Phys. **90**(3), 1–5 (2014)
19. Kochkov, D., Smith, J.A., Alieva, A., Wang, Q., Brenner, M.P., Hoyer, S.: Machine learning accelerated computational fluid dynamics. Proc. Nat. Acad. Sci. **118**(21), e2101784118 (2021).
20. Krämer, A., Wilde, D., Küllmer, K., Reith, D., Foysi, H.: Pseudoentropic derivation of the regularized lattice Boltzmann method. Phys. Rev. E **100**(2), 023302 (2019)
21. Krüger, T., Kusumaatmaja, H., Kuzmin, A., Shardt, O., Silva, G., Viggen, E.M.: The Lattice Boltzmann Method: Principles and Practice. Springer, Heidelberg (2017)
22. Lallemand, P., Luo, L.S.: Theory of the lattice Boltzmann method: dispersion, dissipation, isotropy, Galilean invariance, and stability. Phys. Rev. E Stat. Phys. Plasmas Fluids Relat. Interdiscip. Top. **61**(6), 6546–6562 (2000)
23. Latt, J., Chopard, B.: Lattice Boltzmann method with regularized pre-collision distribution functions. Math. Comput. Simul. **72**(2–6), 165–168 (2006)
24. Latt, J., Coreixas, C., Beny, J., Parmigiani, A.: Efficient supersonic flow simulations using lattice Boltzmann methods based on numerical equilibria. Philos. Trans. R. Soc. A Math. Phys. Eng. Sci. **378**(2175), 20190559 (2020)
25. Latt, J., et al.: Palabos: parallel lattice Boltzmann solver. Comput. Math. Appl. **81**, 334–350 (2021)
26. Lenz, S., et al.: Towards real-time simulation of turbulent air flow over a resolved urban canopy using the cumulant lattice Boltzmann method on a GPGPU. J. Wind Eng. Ind. Aerodyn. **189**, 151–162 (2019)
27. McNamara, G.R., Zanetti, G.: Use of the Boltzmann equation to simulate lattice-gas automata. Phys. Rev. Lett. **61**(20), 2332–2335 (1988)
28. Mora, P., Morra, G., Yuen, D.A.: A concise python implementation of the lattice Boltzmann method on HPC for geo-fluid flow. Geophys. J. Int. **220**(1), 682–702 (2020)
29. Obrecht, C., Kuznik, F., Tourancheau, B., Roux, J.J.: Scalable lattice Boltzmann solvers for CUDA GPU clusters. Parallel Comput. **39**(6), 259–270 (2013)
30. Pastewka, L., Greiner, A.: HPC with python: an MPI-parallel implementation of the lattice Boltzmann method. In: Proceedings of the 5th bwHPC Symposium (2019)
31. Paszke, A., et al.: PyTorch: an imperative style, high-performance deep learning library. In: Wallach, H., Larochelle, H., Beygelzimer, A., D'Alché-Buc, F., Fox, E., Garnett, R. (eds.) Advances in Neural Information Processing Systems 32, pp. 8024–8035. Curran Associates, Inc. (2019)
32. Porté-Agel, F., Bastankhah, M., Shamsoddin, S.: Wind-turbine and wind-farm flows: a review. Boundary Layer Meteorol. **174**(1), 1–59 (2020)
33. Rüttgers, M., Koh, S.-R., Jitsev, J., Schröder, W., Lintermann, A.: Prediction of acoustic fields using a lattice-Boltzmann method and deep learning. In: Jagode, H., Anzt, H., Juckeland, G., Ltaief, H. (eds.) ISC High Performance 2020. LNCS, vol. 12321, pp. 81–101. Springer, Cham (2020)
34. Saadat, M.H., Hosseini, S.A., Dorschner, B., Karlin, I.V.: Extended lattice Boltzmann model for gas dynamics. Phys. Fluids **33**(4), 046104 (2021)

35. Saadat, M.H., Bösch, F., Karlin, I.V.: Lattice Boltzmann model for compressible flows on standard lattices: variable Prandtl number and adiabatic exponent. Phys. Rev. E **99**(1), 013306 (2019)

36. Sagaut, P.: Large Eddy Simulation for Incompressible Flows. An Introduction. Springer, Heidelberg (2006)

37. Samtaney, R., Pullin, D.I., Kosović, B.: Direct numerical simulation of decaying compressible turbulence and shocklet statistics. Phys. Fluids **13**(5), 1415–1430 (2001)

38. Schmieschek, S., et al.: LB3D: a parallel implementation of the lattice-Boltzmann method for simulation of interacting amphiphilic fluids. Comput. Phys. Commun. **217**, 149–161 (2017)

39. Brunton, S.L., Noack, B.R., Koumoutsakos, P.: Machine learning for fluid mechanics. Annu. Rev. Fluid Mech. **52**, 477–508 (2020)

40. Um, K., Fei, Y.R., Holl, P., Brand, R., Thuerey, N.: Solver-in-the-loop: learning from differentiable physics to interact with iterative PDE-solvers. In: 34th Conference on Neural Information Processing Systems (NeurIPS 2020), Vancouver, Canada, vol. 1, no. c, pp. 1–37 (2020)

41. Wichmann, K.R., Kronbichler, M., Löhner, R., Wall, W.A.: A runtime based comparison of highly tuned lattice Boltzmann and finite difference solvers. Int. J. High Perform. Comput. Appl. (2021).

42. Wilcox, D.C.: Turbulence Modeling for CFD. DCW Industries, CA (1993)

43. Wilde, D., Krämer, A., Bedrunka, M., Reith, D., Foysi, H.: Cubature rules for weakly and fully compressible off-lattice Boltzmann methods. J. Comput. Sci. **51**, 101355 (2021)

44. Wilde, D., Krämer, A., Reith, D., Foysi, H.: Semi-Lagrangian lattice Boltzmann method for compressible flows. Phys. Rev. E **101**(5), 53306 (2020)

Reservoir Computing in Reduced Order Modeling for Chaotic Dynamical Systems

Alberto C. Nogueira Jr.[1]([✉]), Felipe C. T. Carvalho[2], João Lucas S. Almeida[1],
Andres Codas[1], Eloisa Bentivegna[3], and Campbell D. Watson[4]

[1] IBM Research Brasil, 13186-900 Hortolandia, SP, Brazil
`albercn@br.ibm.com`
[2] School of Mechanical Engineering, State University of Campinas,
Campinas 13083-860, SP, Brazil
[3] IBM Research Europe, WA4 4AD Warrington, UK
[4] IBM Research,Yorktown Heights, New York 10598, NY, USA
`https://www.research.ibm.com/labs/brazil/`

Abstract. The mathematical concept of chaos was introduced by
Edward Lorenz in the early 1960s while attempting to represent atmospheric convection through a two-dimensional fluid flow with an imposed
temperature difference in the vertical direction. Since then, chaotic
dynamical systems are accepted as the foundation of the meteorological sciences and represent an indispensable testbed for weather and climate forecasting tools. Operational weather forecasting platforms rely on
costly partial differential equations (PDE)-based models that run continuously on high performance computing architectures. Machine learning
(ML)-based low-dimensional surrogate models can be viewed as a cost-
effective solution for such high-fidelity simulation platforms. In this work,
we propose an ML method based on Reservoir Computing - Echo State
Neural Network (RC-ESN) to accurately predict evolutionary states of
chaotic systems. We start with the baseline Lorenz-63 and 96 systems
and show that RC-ESN is extremely effective in consistently predicting
time series using Pearson's cross correlation similarity measure. RC-ESN
can accurately forecast Lorenz systems for many Lyapunov time units
into the future. In a practical numerical example, we applied RC-ESN
combined with space-only proper orthogonal decomposition (POD) to
build a reduced order model (ROM) that produces sequential short-term
forecasts of pollution dispersion over the continental USA region. We use
GEOS-CF simulated data to assess our RC-ESN ROM. Numerical experiments show reasonable results for such a highly complex atmospheric
pollution system.

Keywords: Machine learning · Reservoir computing · Reduced order
modeling · Chaotic systems.

1 Introduction

Reduced order models (ROMs) are a classical method used to capture the principal features of a dynamical system and leverage them to accelerate model

H. Jagode et al. (Eds.): ISC High Performance 2021 Workshops, LNCS 12761, pp. 56–72, 2021.
https://doi.org/10.1007/978-3-030-90539-2_4

evaluation, as well as gain physical insight into the key effects that govern its evolution. Building a ROM usually entails a subspace projection, which yields a spectrum of principal modes, combined with the ability to evolve these modes forward in time. Many novel approaches have been investigated recently to accomplish the second task; in particular, ODE integrators based on machine-learning tools are growing in popularity [3,5,7,9].

As many of the applications of interest (such as turbulence in fluid dynamics, or financial time series prediction) involve a degree of chaoticity, the main challenge these approaches have to address is how to maintain solution accuracy in the long term, as measured by the prediction horizon. This problem couples the two apparently unrelated tasks of mode decomposition and mode evolution, as certain decompositions may be inherently more amenable to accurate long-term integration. In particular, schemes that are efficient at capturing both spatial and temporal dynamics, as opposed to spatial information alone, appear to lead to longer prediction horizons [10,18].

In [4], some of the authors applied a combination of Proper Orthogonal Decomposition (POD) and two well-known ANN architectures, namely, Dense Neural Networks and LSTM, to build a surrogate model of lacustrine circulation. Tests of this scheme performed on a benchmark, the Lorenz 63 system, showed that both architectures could achieve reasonable accuracy in the short term, considering exclusively the training data set, but started diverging from the reference solution after less than ten Lyapunov units. In this work, we present a refinement of the ML components of [4] replacing the previous mentioned ANN architectures by RC-ESN, which enable much longer accurate evolutions for Lorenz systems. We also apply such an approach to a realistic dataset obtained from the GEOS Composition Forecasting (GEOS-CF) system developed by NASA[1], which simulates the dispersion of passive scalar atmospheric pollutants over the continental United States.

2 Dimensionality Reduction with POD

As in [4], we aim at building a dynamical system emulator which is compact and light, although as accurate as possible. In this way, we follow the previous standard approach to reduce dimensionality of the input data used for training the ROM by applying POD technique [19]. POD identifies the set of orthonormal modes that captures the highest variance in the data and then performs a projection onto this modes to recover time-dependent coefficients. The inner product between time coefficients and modes yields the ROM's approximation of the dynamical system as

$$Q_{rb}(\mathbf{x}, t) = \overline{q}(\mathbf{x}) + q'(\mathbf{x}, t) = \overline{q}(\mathbf{x}) + \sum_{i=1}^{L} c_i(t)\psi_i(\mathbf{x}) \qquad (1)$$

---

[1] https://fluid.nccs.nasa.gov/cf/classic_geos_cf/.

where $\overline{q}$ and q' are mean and fluctuating quantities that split the approximation Q_{rb}, ψ_i is a generic eigenmode obtained through POD with its respective time coefficient $c_i(t)$ computed by a suitable ANN, and L is the dimension of the reduced space.

Assuming that the input data is the time evolution of states

$$\mathbf{Q} = [\mathbf{Q}_1, \dots, \mathbf{Q}_N] \in \mathbb{R}^{M \times N},$$

where M is the number of grid points times the number of state variables and N is the number of snapshots, POD provides the following state approximation in matrix form

$$\mathbf{Q}_{rb} = \overline{\mathbf{q}} + \boldsymbol{\Phi}\mathbf{C} \quad \text{with} \quad \boldsymbol{\Phi} \in \mathbb{R}^{M \times L}, \ \mathbf{C} \in \mathbb{R}^{L \times N}, \tag{2}$$

where $\overline{\mathbf{q}}$ is the temporal mean of the state variables vector, $\boldsymbol{\Phi} = [\boldsymbol{\Psi}_1, \dots, \boldsymbol{\Psi}_L]$ is the matrix of L truncated eigenmodes, and $\mathbf{C} = [\mathbf{c}_1, \dots, \mathbf{c}_N]$ is the matrix of projected vector temporal coefficients with $\mathbf{c}_i \in \mathbb{R}^L$. We choose the reduced order dimension L based on the energy content of each eigenmode. We calculate the percentage of the energy preserved in the reduced order model by summing the truncated eigenvalues corresponding to the highest energetic eigenmodes and divide it by the sum of all eigenvalues.

3   Reservoir Computing - Echo State Neural Network

RC-ESNs [2,3] are considered a subclass of the Recurrent Neural Network (RNN) family. The RC algorithms have attracted attention in recent years as a lower training-cost solution for a number of applications, mainly for modelling complex time series systems [2,3,13]. The most interesting feature of RC algorithms is their versatility, both in architecture and in the fitting process.

The classical RC-ESN architecture can be represented as an operator $\mathcal{E}$: $\mathcal{X} \subseteq \mathbb{R}^{n_i} \to \mathcal{Y} \subseteq \mathbb{R}^{n_o}$, in which n_i is the number of features of the input space and n_o the number of features of the output or target space. The operator $\mathcal{E}$ is composed of three stages or layers, namely input-to-reservoir, reservoir and reservoir-to-output [3].

The first layer of the RC-ESN is a matrix operator $\mathbf{W}_{in}$ of size $D \times n_i$ which maps the input to the intermediate neurons space $\mathcal{R}$, called hidden space. Let $\mathbf{x} = \mathbf{x}(t)$ and $\mathbf{y} = \mathbf{y}(t)$ be time series such that $\mathbf{x} \in \mathcal{X}$ and $\mathbf{y} \in \mathcal{Y}$, with $\mathbf{x}$ and $\mathbf{y}$ being the input and output vectors of the RC-ESN architecture, respectively. The relationship between the input space $\mathcal{X}$ and the hidden space $\mathcal{R}$ is shown below

$$\mathbf{r}(t + \Delta t) = (1 - \beta)\tanh(\mathbf{A}\mathbf{r}(t) + \mathbf{W}_{in}\mathbf{x}(t)) + \beta\mathbf{r}(t) \tag{3}$$

where β is the leaking rate parameter, which is commonly set as zero.

The hidden space vector $\mathbf{r}$ is modified according to a nonlinear transformation $\mathcal{T} : \mathcal{R} \to \mathcal{R}$ (cf. Appendix A for details), resulting in a transformed vector $\tilde{\mathbf{r}}$. This operation is essential to achieve accurate predictions [3]. Then, the output vector is computed as follows

$$\mathbf{y}(t + \Delta t) = \mathbf{W}_{out}\tilde{\mathbf{r}}(t + \Delta t) \tag{4}$$

The reservoir hidden vector $\mathbf{r}$ is constructed with a set of D neurons or cells. The D cells are sparsely connected via an adjacency matrix $\mathbf{A}$ of size $D \times D$, filled with a random distribution in the interval $[-\sigma, \sigma]$ [3], in which σ is a modeling hyperparameter. The spectral radius of matrix $\mathbf{A}$ influences the model echo state property (ESP), which affects the model capability to describe a given dynamical system. This parameter is set by scaling matrix $\mathbf{A}$ and, usually, is smaller than one. However, according to [20] the spectral radius can be larger than one and still retain the ESP, if the driving input is sufficiently strong. The spectral radius is another RC-ESN modeling hyperparameter [12]. In the neural network's last layer, a matrix operator $\mathbf{W}_{out}$ of size $n_o \times D$ maps the transformed hidden space into the output.

An important characteristic of the RC-ESN architecture is that the matrices $\mathbf{W}_{in}$ and $\mathbf{A}$ are fixed and just $\mathbf{W}_{out}$ is updated to construct the final model. In order to fit the model and get the $\mathbf{W}_{out}$ matrix, we solve a minimization problem of the form

$$\mathbf{W}_{out} = \text{argmin}_{\mathbf{W}_{out}} ||\mathbf{W}_{out}\tilde{\mathbf{r}}(t) - \mathbf{y}(t)||_2 + \alpha ||\mathbf{W}_{out}||_2 \tag{5}$$

where $||\cdot||_2$ denotes the L^2-norm and α is the penalty of the ridge regularization term.

In [3], the authors proposed to solve an algebraic linear system to find the loss function's minimum in Eq. 5 with a single shot (cf. Appendix B for details). A diagram of the RC-ESN architecture can be seen in Fig. 1.

Compared to other recurrent neural network (RNN) approaches such as LSTM, GRU, and Unitary cells, RC-ESN is noticeably less expensive from the computational viewpoint since it does not rely on any gradient-descent boosted algorithm. Such a feature speeds up the training times. According to [17], RC-ESN tends to overfit more easily than its RNN competitors due to their validation-based early stopping and regularization techniques which are not workable for RC architectures. However, RC-ESN is well known for its excellent forecasting capacity capturing most of the relevant features of the underlying dynamical systems.

RC-ESN also compares favorably with Expectation-Maximization (EM) procedures: in [11], the forecasting error for two EM variants (as well as other reference methods) are illustrated. Where results can be visually compared, RC-ESN appears to have twice to three times as large a prediction horizon in dimensions 0 and 1, and to perform somewhat better in dimension 2. It has to be noted, however, that the results in [11] correspond to a *noisy* Lorenz 63 system.

In this work we use an RC-ESN architecture to train and predict the time series associated to two discrete chaotic dynamical systems, namely, Lorenz 63 and 96, and a spatiotemporal system that tracks passive scalar pollutants transported by the atmosphere.

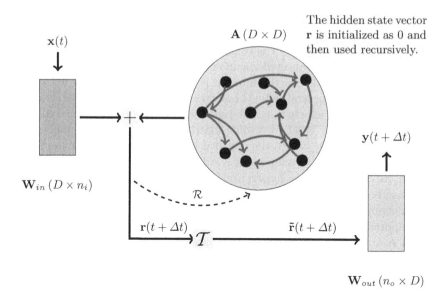

Fig. 1. Schematic of the RC-ESN architecture.

4 Network Training Parallelism

As the latent space dimension increases, it becomes harder and harder to get a global ML model that describes an entire set of features in time. For realistic chaotic models such as those describing atmospheric circulation or pollution dispersion, representative ROMs can still need hundreds of dimensions to perform satisfactorily. In this way, we adopted the parallel training strategy proposed in [18], in which the time series are modeled in sub-groups, each one using a dedicated architecture.

This approach resembles computational parallelism as each sub-model can be trained independently, just sharing data and not model parameters or structures. Such an approach can be applied for different regression network architectures (Echo-State networks, LSTMs, Dense networks, etc.), with no *a priori* restriction regarding the choices of the parametric values. It also enables the construction of heterogeneous pools of sub-models.

5 Numerical Results

In this section, we assess the effectiveness of the proposed ESN-RC method via three examples: forecasting the Lorenz-63 and 96 systems, and the dispersion of pollutant passive scalar over the continental USA region. Since Lorenz systems are discrete models in space they do not require dimensionality reduction, and therefore allow us to focus on improving the ANN component of our previous study [4]. These systems are also suitable emulators of the atmospheric chaotic behavior and represent a relevant test case to check RC-ESN forecast capabilities before tackling more realistic use cases.

5.1 Lorenz 63

The Lorenz 63 system consists of the following set of ODEs:

$$\frac{dX}{dt} = \sigma(Y - X), \tag{6}$$

$$\frac{dY}{dt} = X(\rho - Z) - Y, \tag{7}$$

$$\frac{dZ}{dt} = XY - \beta Z. \tag{8}$$

This system was designed to represent atmospheric convection through a two dimensional fluid flow of uniform depth with an imposed temperature difference in the vertical direction by Edward Lorenz in 1963.

Each one of these ODEs in the coordinates x, y and z represents a time series. This system is numerically integrated to feed the training and testing steps of the RC-ESN forecasting model. We fixed the number of reservoirs in all experiments to 1 and performed a hyper-parameter optimization using the library Optuna [1] to find the best fit RC-ESN that predicts the system's chaotic regime. We assessed the similarity between the predicted and the reference time series through the Pearson's cross correlation coefficient [14]. The physical parameters of the Lorenz 63 system in nondimensional form were set as $\rho = 28.0$, $\sigma = 10.0$, $\beta = 8/3$, $T = 80.0$, $dt = 0.01$. Differently from [4], we did not assess the forecasting generalization to steady state solutions of Lorenz 63's deterministic regimes. Our goal is to evaluate the applicability of the proposed RC-ESN to more complex chaotic systems such as pollution dispersion.

In order to compare the forecasting capabilities of different dynamical systems, we standardized time in terms of model time units (MTU) [3].

The best hyper-parameter configuration based on an unseen testing dataset for this particular experiment can be found in Table 1. We generated a dataset with 80MTU, where we used the first 60MTU for training and the last 20MTU for testing.

Table 1. Lorenz 63 RC-ESN parameters set up.

Leaking rate	Reservoir size	Sparse density	Spectral radius	α regularizer	Activation function
0.2212	828×828	0.5770	1.3498	1.2848×10^{-5}	tanh

Figure 2 shows plots of the discrete variables compared to the reference values over time, along with the absolute errors. We observe that the RC-ESN can remarkably capture the trends of all variables x, y and z for as long as 12.5 MTUs which corresponds to 11.8 Lyapunov time units[2]. It is worth noting that the RC-ESN approach can also maintain the time-series topology for longer forecasting which is one of the most important criteria in chaotic systems identification [11].

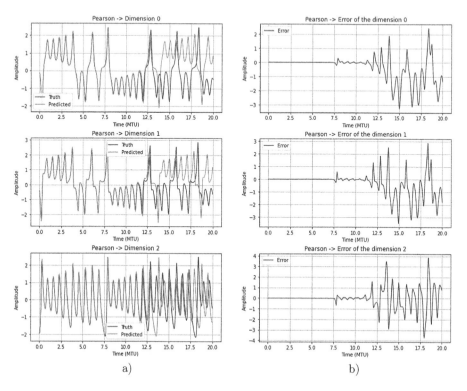

a) b)

Fig. 2. Lorenz 63 system: a) X, Y, Z true and predicted; b) $Error(X) = X^{true} - X^{pred}$, $Error(Y) = Y^{true} - Y^{pred}$, $Error(Z) = Z^{true} - Z^{pred}$.

5.2 Lorenz 96

In this work, we consider a modified version of the multi-scale Lorenz 96 system proposed in [16], which can be set out as follows

$$\frac{dX_k}{dt} = X_{k-1}\left(X_{k+1} - X_{k-2}\right) + F - \frac{hc}{b}\Sigma_j Y_{j,k} \; , \tag{9}$$

$$\frac{dY_{j,k}}{dt} = -c\,b\,Y_{j+1,k}\left(Y_{j+2,k} - Y_{j-1,k}\right) - c\,Y_{j,k} + \frac{hc}{b}X_k - \frac{he}{d}\Sigma_i Z_{i,j,k} \; , \tag{10}$$

$$\frac{dZ_{i,j,k}}{dt} = e\,d\,Z_{i-1,j,k}\left(Z_{i+1,j,k} - Z_{i-2,j,k}\right) - g\,e\,Z_{i,j,k} + \frac{he}{d}Y_{j,k} \; . \tag{11}$$

---

[2] Lyapunov time unit is computed based on the reciprocal of the maximum Lyapunov exponent. Like the largest eigenvalue of a given matrix, the largest Lyapunov exponent is responsible for the dominant behavior of a system.

These coupled nonlinear ODEs are a 3-tier extension of the original Lorenz 63 model. As emphasized in [3], this improved model can capture the multi-scale chaotic variability of weather and climate systems making it a more challenging experiment towards realistic scenarios. As in the previous example, the numerical experiments kept the number of reservoirs fixed at 1, the hyper-parameter optimization was performed by the Optuna library, and we applied Pearson's cross correlation metric to evaluate the model's performance.

We followed the same setup proposed in [3] fixing $F = 20$ and $b = c = d = e = g = 10$ and $h = 1$ with $i, j, k = 1, \ldots, 8$. The system evolved for $T = 24$ nondimensional time units with $dt = 0.01$. Although the system's ODEs are coupled, we used only the evolution of X_k to generate the training dataset of our surrogate model. We obtained the reference X_k time series using a forth order five stages explicit Runge-Kutta sheme. We considered only unsteady solutions of Lorenz 96 to evaluate the forecasting capability of the RC-ESN.

The best hyper-parameter configuration based on an unseen testing dataset for this particular experiment can be found in Table 2. We generated a dataset with 24MTU, where we used the first 18MTU for training and the last 6MTU for testing.

Table 2. Lorenz 96 RC-ESN parameters set up.

Leaking rate	Reservoir size	Sparse density	Spectral radius	α regularizer	Activation function
0.0726	2633×2633	0.4928	1.5266	1.2830×10^{-5}	tanh

Figs. 3 and 4 show plots of the first set of modified Lorenz 96's discrete variables $X_k, k = 1, \ldots, 8$ compared to the reference values over time, along with the absolute errors. We can observe that the RC-ESN performed even better in this more sophisticated system capturing the trends of all variables X_k for as long as 5.01 MTUs which corresponds to an astonishing 22.7 Lyapunov time units.

During the numerical experiments we observed that as the training dataset size increased, the RC-ESN performance also increased until a certain limit where we could not observe any further performance gain. That threshold varied depending on the system being modeled. For instance, Lorenz 63 used a 60MTU training dataset while Lorenz 96 only 18MTU. The smaller training dataset in the later case reduced the RC-ESN's training cost significantly.

As both Lorenz 63 and 96 baseline examples showed previously develop stationary time series, we can be led to conclude that RC-ESN is effective only in cases where time series fluctuate along with a constant value. That is not necessarily true. Although the best way to cope with any time series is to "stationarize" it first by decoupling it into its essential characteristics like linear trend and seasonal qualities and then add them back to recover the original time series shape, there is no constraint for successfully applying the RC-ESN technique for more general time series like those appearing in stock prices prediction [15], for instance.

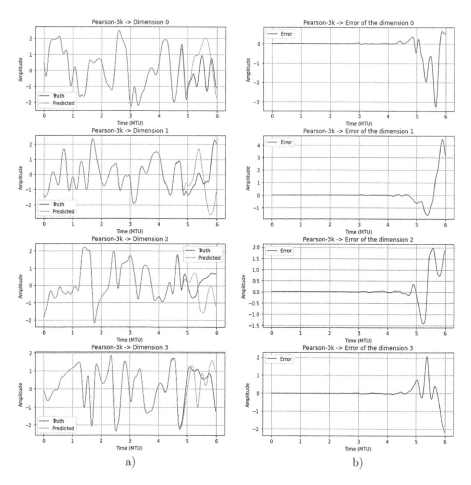

Fig. 3. Lorenz 96 system: a) $X_k, k = 1, \ldots, 4$ true and predicted; b) $Error(X_k) = X_k^{true} - X_k^{pred}, k = 1, \ldots, 4$.

5.3   Atmospheric Dispersion of a Pollutant Passive Scalar

Atmospheric dispersion models are one of the most common classes of air quality models. Dispersion models vary in complexity and are used to understand or predict the dispersion of pollutants across a range of spatial scales. Global predictions are provided by computationally-intensive models such as the GEOS-CF system developed by NASA, which simulates the interactions among global atmospheric transport, surface emissions, chemical processes, and wet and dry deposition. Ozone is one such pollutant simulated by the GEOS-CF system which, near ground level, is a respiratory hazard for humans and damaging to vegetation and ecosystems.

Truncated POD Reconstruction Skills. In this section, we assess the POD method's skill in representing the correct spatial correlation of the ozone (O_3)

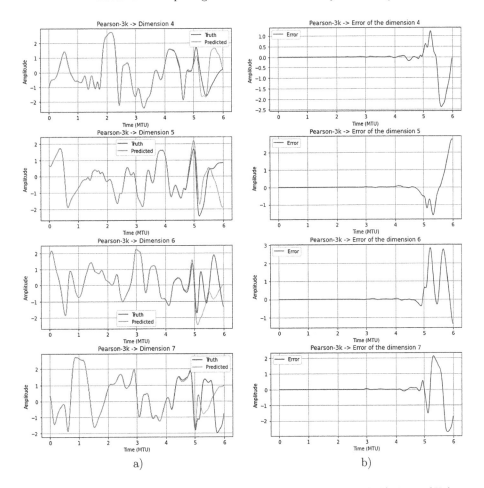

Fig. 4. Lorenz 96 system: a) $X_k, k = 5, \ldots, 8$ true and predicted; b) $Error(X_k) = X_k^{true} - X_k^{pred}, k = 5, \ldots, 8$.

pollutant dispersion structures simulated by the GEOS-CF. We compare the approximate field reconstruction given by a truncated number of POD modes, namely, 200 eigenmodes, with a subset of the GEOS-CF dataset, which was not considered while building the POD modes. This process is analogous to the well-known machine learning practice of splitting the original dataset into training and validation subsets.

The top plot of Fig. 5 shows the ozone distribution in the atmosphere over the continental USA region for the last snapshot of the GEOS-CF validation subset. The middle plot shows the truncated POD reconstruction of the same passive scalar field with 200 eigenmodes and the bottom plot displays the pointwise error between the two previous field maps. We notice that the largest errors are scattered on relatively small spots over the entire domain and kept under 15.0%. Such error drops to 7.4% if computed with the L_2-norm. Although 200 modes seem not to be a sufficient dimension reduction, we should bear in mind that the original dynamical system has 24,000 dimensions. Furthermore, the pollution dynamics have very complex coherent structures and wave patterns that can not be captured by just a few spatial correlated modes [8].

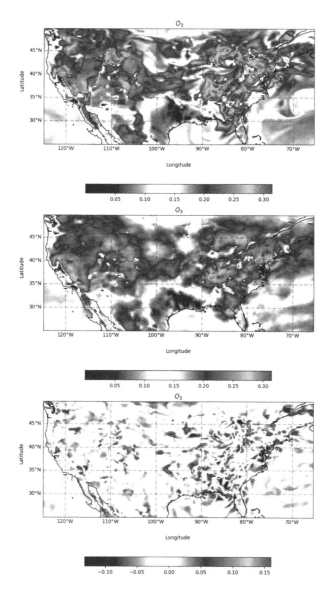

Fig. 5. Pollutant distribution over the continental USA surface. From top to bottom: ground truth O_3 concentration in parts per billion normalized within the interval $[0, 1]$, POD reconstruction with 200 dimensions, and pointwise error measure.

Energy Spectrum Analysis. As each of the POD eigenmodes preserves some energy content of the original dynamical system, we expect that we can extract meaningful information about the underlying flow field transporting the passive scalar pollutant if we look at the energy decaying rate between consecutive eigenmodes.

We compute the cumulative energy E associated to a given number N_m of eigenmodes and then compute the difference between consecutive cumulative energies as $E(N_m) - E(N_{m-1})$. We increase the number of modes in powers of 2 as $N_m = 2^m$; $m = 2, \ldots, 10$. Figure 6 plots the cumulative energy differences as a function of the number of eigenmodes in log-log scale. Such an approach allows the visualization of the energy decaying rate (or energy spectrum) of sequences of consecutive eigenmodes with decreasing energy content. Interestingly, this plot shows close similarities with the Kolmogorov energy spectrum of turbulent flows. It suggests that the turbulent nature of the underlying atmospheric flow transporting a passive scalar species can be captured by the POD method.

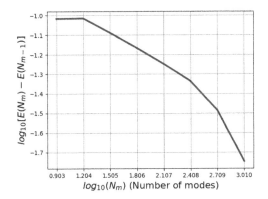

Fig. 6. POD eigenmode energy cascade as a function of the number of modes for the GEOS-CF dataset.

RC-ESN ROM for Pollution Dispersion. In the following, we discuss the numerical experiment designed to assess our RC-ESN ROM applied to a practical pollution dispersion problem. We attempted to predict the O_3 concentration values over the entire USA surface for a time horizon of about 44 hours ahead.

The GEOS-CF dataset provided training data with 1-hour output resolution for a 6-month span. We used the O_3 chemical concentration as the training and target variable in supervised learning, ignoring any forcing variables such as the underlying atmospheric field velocities. We took the last 44 snapshots of the input data corresponding to 1% of the entire training dataset for testing purposes. We justify this choice by the need of quite long training samples to capture all the features embedded in a high complex system such as the atmospheric pollution dispersion.

We started by applying POD to the training dataset, keeping 200 eigenmodes for approximation which preserve 99% of the reference system's total energy.

Then, we recovered the corresponding time series coefficients (cf. Equation 1) by projecting the training dataset onto the eigenmodes. The recovered time coefficients were used as input for the RC-ESN time series predictor. The neural network was trained using a parallel algorithm as described in Sect. 4 with 5 subgroups of time series, 40 time series per sub-group, and 10 time series for each left and right interface layers between adjacent subgroups.

We performed hyper-parameter optimization of the neural network architecture using two libraries in sequence, Optuna, for the initial search and NOMAD [6] for a more tuned search. Table 3 shows the optimum hyperparameters selection for RC-ESN ROM.

Table 3. RC-ESN best hyperparameters configuration for the pollution ROM.

Leaking rate	Reservoir size	Sparse density	Spectral radius	α regularizer	Activation function
0.0000	$10\,000 \times 10\,000$	3.0000	0.6938	1×10^{-5}	tanh

Figure 7 shows the plots of the first 6 temporal coefficients of the RC-ESN ROM corresponding to the first 6 POD eigenmodes of O_3 concentration. In these plots, orange lines represent the ground truth values and blue lines the ROM approximate values for the 44-h forecasting horizon. We observe from these plots that the time series are fairly predicted for the first most energetic eigenmodes. However, we should notice that we adopted an LSTM-like approach to training the RC-ESN predictor as the dynamical system revealed too stiff to accommodate an optimal fit for all 200 time series simultaneously. In this way, we used ground truth inputs to feed the neural network at each advancing time step in the testing phase. Thus, the proposed RC-ESN ROM is a one-shot predictor rather than a long-term dynamical system surrogate.

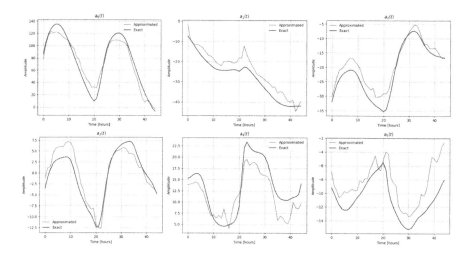

Fig. 7. First 6 RC-ESN ROM time series corresponding to the first 6 POD eigenmodes.

Figure 8 shows the comparison between the ground truth O_3 distribution over the USA continental region and the RC-ESN ROM reconstructed values for the same region (cf. top and middle plots). The bottom plot shows the pointwise error between those two concentration field maps. We observe that the reconstructed values are smoother than the reference ones and pointwise error is not so confined

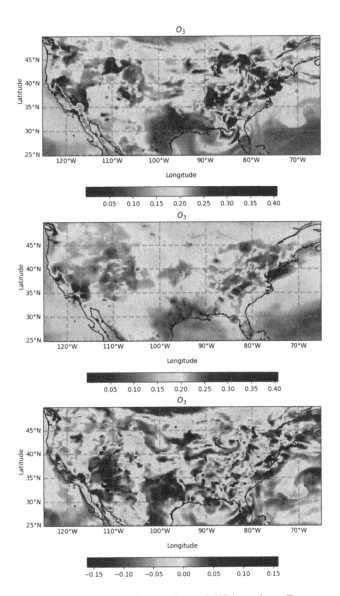

Fig. 8. Pollutant distribution over the continental USA surface. From top to bottom: ground truth O_3 concentration in parts per billion normalized within the interval $[0, 1]$, RC-ESN ROM reconstruction with 200 dimensions, and pointwise error measure.

as in the reconstructed POD modes alone (cf. Figure 5). We notice that the largest errors are kept slightly above 15.0% and the equivalent L_2-norm of the error achieves 14.8%.

6   Discussion and Conclusions

In this work, we developed a data-driven reduced order model (ROM) applying RC-ESN as a time series predictor and space-only POD to build the best spatial-correlated modes describing the dynamics of a pollution dispersion system over the continental USA surface.

To assess the RC-ESN skills in forecasting time series, we also considered two baseline chaotic systems, namely, Lorenz 63 and 96, which can simplistically describe the atmosphere dynamics. The RC-ESN architecture showed remarkable results specially for the modified multi-scale Lorenz 96 system which produced accurate forecasting for 22.7 Lyapunov time units before diverging from the reference solution. The atmospheric pollution dispersion RC-ESN ROM showed fair results for the target 44-hours forecast of the O_3 concentration over the USA surface with pointwise errors slightly above 15%. However, we should notice that the lack of an exogenous wind velocity forcing, together with the need for a high number of modes to preserve most of the energy of the underlying dynamical system, prevented the RC-ESN ROM from succeeding in long term predictions. It is well known that any RNN architecture has severe limitations to fit too many time series simultaneously, even with a parallel training scheme in the latent space. That's why we chose an LSTM-like approach for the RC-ESN model in which we fed ground truth inputs into the neural network to drive predictions at each time step. Strictly speaking, our model is a short-term predictor. Regarding the parallel training approach of the ROM time coefficients, we essentially kept the same algorithm proposed in [18]. Thus, we confirmed that RC-ESN in the reduced-order latent space is not as successful as in the full-order space dynamics as claimed by those authors. A possible explanation for this undesired performance might be related to the loss of neighboring spatial connections among the time series after dimensionality reduction by the POD method.

As a next step, we want to test the skills of the spectral POD (SPOD) [10] method to reduce dimensionality and describe the atmospheric pollution system with higher fidelity since SPOD produces eigenmodes from a cross-spectral density matrix which guarantees optimality and space-time coherence properties for statistically stationary flows. A better space-time representation in terms of a reduced basis potentially requires fewer eigenmodes, increasing the neural network training process's effectiveness significantly.

Acknowledgement. EB acknowledges a UKRI Future Leaders Fellowship for support through the grant MR/T041862/1. FCTC acknowledges the São Paulo Research Foundation (FAPESP) for support through the grant #2019/14597-5.

A   Non Linear Transformation in RC-ESN Hidden Space

Following the same approach proposed in [3], we defined three options for the nonlinear transformations $\mathcal{T}$:

$$
\begin{aligned}
\mathcal{T}_1 : \quad & \tilde{r}_{ij} = r_{i,j}, && \text{if} \quad \mathrm{mod}\,(j,2) = 0 \\
& \tilde{r}_{ij} = r_{i,j}^2, && \text{if} \quad \mathrm{mod}\,(j,2) \neq 0 \\
\mathcal{T}_2 : \quad & \tilde{r}_{ij} = r_{i,j}, && \text{if} \quad \mathrm{mod}\,(j,2) = 0 \\
& \tilde{r}_{ij} = r_{i,j-1}\, r_{i,j-2}, && \text{if} \quad \mathrm{mod}\,(j,2) \neq 0 \text{ and } j > 1 \\
\mathcal{T}_3 : \quad & \tilde{r}_{ij} = r_{i,j}, && \text{if} \quad \mathrm{mod}\,(j,2) = 0 \\
& \tilde{r}_{ij} = r_{i,j-1}\, r_{i,j+1}, && \text{if} \quad \mathrm{mod}\,(j,2) \neq 0 \text{ and } j > 1
\end{aligned}
$$

B   Single Shot RC-ESN Loss Function Minimization

The least-squares problem stated in Eq. 5 aims at finding the *reservoir-to-output* matrix $\mathbf{W}_{out} \in \mathbb{R}^{n_i \times D}$. We can equivalently solve that problem by writing the following linear system [2]:

$$
\mathbf{W}_{out} = \mathbf{X}\tilde{\mathbf{R}}^T(\tilde{\mathbf{R}}\tilde{\mathbf{R}}^T + \alpha\mathbf{I}), \tag{12}
$$

where $\mathbf{X} \in \mathbb{R}^{n_i \times N}$ is the matrix that stacks every input data $\mathbf{x}(t)$ shifted by one time step for all N time steps, and $\tilde{\mathbf{R}} \in \mathbb{R}^{D \times N}$ is the matrix that stacks every corresponding $\mathcal{T}$-transformed hidden states $\tilde{\mathbf{r}}(t)$. The parameter α is the ridge regularization, and $\mathbf{I}$ is the identity matrix.

References

1. Akiba, T., Sano, S., Yanase, T., Ohta, T., Koyama, M.: Optuna: a next-generation hyperparameter optimization framework. In: Proceedings of the 25rd ACM SIGKDD International Conference on Knowledge Discovery and Data Mining (2019)
2. Bollt, E.: On explaining the surprising success of reservoir computing forecaster of chaos? the universal machine learning dynamical system with contrasts to VAR and DMD (2020). arXiv:2008.06530
3. Chattopadhyay, A., Hassanzadeh, P., Subramanian, D.: Data-driven prediction of a multi-scale Lorenz 96 chaotic system using deep learning methods: reservoir computing, ANN, and RNN-LSTM. Nonlinear Process. Geophys. **27**, 373–389 (2020). https://doi.org/10.5194/npg-27-373-2020
4. Costa Nogueira, A., de Sousa Almeida, J.L., Auger, G., Watson, C.D.: Reduced order modeling of dynamical systems using artificial neural networks applied to water circulation. In: Jagode, H., Anzt, H., Juckeland, G., Ltaief, H. (eds.) High Performance Computing, pp. 116–136. Springer International Publishing, Cham (2020)
5. Gao, Z., Liu, Q., Hesthaven, J.S., Wang, B.S., Don, W.S., Wen, X.: Non-intrusive reduced order modeling of convection dominated flows using artificial neural networks with application to Rayleigh-Taylor instability. Commun. Comput. Phys. **30**(1), 97–123 (2021)

6. Le Digabel, S.: Algorithm 909: Nomad: Nonlinear optimization with the mads algorithm. ACM Trans. Math. Softw. **37**(4), 1–15 (2011). https://doi.org/10.1145/1916461.1916468

7. Lee, K., Carlberg, K.: Model reduction of dynamical systems on nonlinear manifolds using deep convolutional autoencoders. J. Comput. Phys. (2019). https://doi.org/10.1016/j.jcp.2019.108973

8. Mendible, A., Brunton, S.L., Aravkin, A.Y., Lowrie, W., Kutz, J.N.: Dimensionality Reduction and Reduced Order Modeling for Traveling Wave Physics (2020). arXiv e-prints arXiv:1911.00565v2

9. Mohan, A., Gaitonde, D.: A deep learning based approach to reduced order modeling for turbulent flow control using LSTM neural networks (2018). arXiv:1804.09269

10. Nekkanti, A., Schmidt, O.T.: Frequency-time analysis, low-rank reconstruction and denoising of turbulent flows using SPOD (2020). arXiv e-prints arXiv:2011.03644

11. Nguyen, D., Ouala, S., Drumetz, L., Fablet, R.: EM-like Learning Chaotic Dynamics from Noisy and Partial Observations (2019). arXiv e-prints arXiv:1903.10335

12. Ozturk, M.C., Xu, D., Principe, J.C.: Analysis and design of echo state networks. Neural Comput. **19**(1), 111–138 (2007)

13. Pathak, J., Hunt, B., Girvan, M., Lu, Z., Ott, E.: Model-free prediction of large spatiotemporally chaotic systems from data: a reservoir computing approach. Phys. Rev. Lett. **120**, 024102 (2018)

14. Pearson, K.: Note on regression and inheritance in the case of two parents. Proc. R. Soc. London. **58**, 240–242 (1895)

15. Stewart, M.: Predicting stock prices with echo state networks. Towards Data Science (2019). https://towardsdatascience.com/predicting-stock-prices-with-echo-state-networks-f910809d23d4

16. Thornes, T., Düben, P., Palmer, T.: On the use of scale-dependent precision in earth system modelling. Q. J. R. Meteorol. Soc. **143**, 897–908 (2017). https://doi.org/10.1002/qj.2974

17. Vlachas, P.R., Byeon, W., Wan, Z.Y., Sapsis, T.P., Koumoutsakos, P.: Data-driven forecasting of high-dimensional chaotic systems with long short-term memory networks. Proc. R. Soc. A Math. Phys. Eng. Sci. **474**(2213), 20170844 (2018). https://doi.org/10.1098/rspa.2017.0844

18. Vlachas, P.R., et al.: Backpropagation Algorithms and Reservoir Computing in Recurrent Neural Networks for the Forecasting of Complex Spatiotemporal Dynamics (2019). arXiv e-prints arXiv:1910.05266

19. Wang, Q., Ripamonti, N., Hesthaven, J.: Recurrent neural network closure of parametric pod-galerkin reduced-order models based on the mori-zwanzig formalism (2020). https://doi.org/10.1016/j.jcp.2020.109402

20. Yildiz, I.B., Jaeger, H., Kiebel, S.J.: Re-visiting the echo state property. Neural Netw. **35**, 1–9 (2012)

Film Cooling Prediction and Optimization
Based on Deconvolution Neural Network

Yaning Wang[1,2], Shirui Luo[3], Wen Wang[1,2], Guocheng Tao[1,2], Xinshuai Zhang[1],
and Jiahuan Cui[1,2(✉)]

[1] School of Aeronautics and Astronautics, Zhejiang University, Hangzhou, China
jiahuancui@intl.zju.edu.cn
[2] ZJUI Institute, Zhejiang University, Haining, China
[3] University of Illinois at Urbana-Champaign, Urbana, USA

Abstract. For film cooling in high pressure turbines, it is vital to predict the temperature distribution on the blade surface downstream of the cooling hole. This temperature distribution depends on the interaction between the hot mainstream and the coolant jet. Deep learning techniques have been widely applied in predicting physical problems such as complex fluids dynamics. A theoretic model based on Deconvolutional Neural Network (Deconv NN) was developed to model the non-linear and high-dimensional mapping between coolant jet parameters and the surface temperature distribution. Computational Fluid Dynamics (CFD) was utilized to provide data for the training models. The input of the model includes blowing ratio, density ratio, hole inclination angle and hole diameters etc. Comparison against different methods and data set size for accuracy is conducted and the result shows that the Deconv NN is capable of predicting film cooling effectiveness on the surface in validation group with quoted error (QE) less than 0.62%. With rigorous testing and validation, it is found that the predicted results are in good agreement with results from CFD. At the end, the Sparrow Search Algorithm (SSA) is applied to optimize coolant jet parameters using the validated neural networks. The results of the optimization show that the film cooling effectiveness has been successfully improved with QE 7.35% when compared with the reference case.

Keywords: Film cooling prediction · Deep learning · Surrogate model · Deconvolution neural network

1 Introduction

The inlet temperature of the high-pressure turbine keeps increasing to improve the thermal efficiency and power output. Currently the inlet temperature in the most advanced gas turbine is far beyond the melting point of material [1]. Therefore, high performance cooling technologies are needed to protect the blade from high temperature and excessive thermal stresses and extend its service lifetime. Film cooling is one of the most critical cooling techniques for turbine blades [2]. Coolant is ejected into the mainstream through discrete holes drilled on blades and forms a relatively cold film covering the

© Springer Nature Switzerland AG 2021
H. Jagode et al. (Eds.): ISC High Performance 2021 Workshops, LNCS 12761, pp. 73–91, 2021.
https://doi.org/10.1007/978-3-030-90539-2_5

blade external surface. This cold film is effectively preventing blades from contacting high temperature flow in the mainstream [3, 4].

Film cooling is basically a jet in crossflow. It is difficult to calculate various vortex structures generated by the interaction between the coolant jet and the main flow [5–7]. In fact, the cooling effectiveness is highly dependent on the coolant jet parameters. Thus, predicting the film cooling effectiveness and optimizing the film-cooling parameters is necessary to achieve higher cooling performance [8]. These parameters can be broadly classified into two categories: geometry parameters and fluid dynamic parameters. The former includes hole shape [9–11], inclination angle [12, 13], compound angle orientation [14], length to diameter ratio of the hole (L/d) [15] and surface curvature [16]; while the latter includes density ratio (dr) [9, 17, 18], blowing ratio (br) [18, 19], mainstream turbulence level [20], and the jet velocity profile [21].

Conventionally, CFD is used to predict the temperature distribution downstream of the coolant hole. Past studies have shown that CFD is able to acquire accurate results of film cooling [1]. However, it is still relatively time consuming and computationally expensive, especially for optimization tasks where a large number of simulations are required [22]. Moreover, extensive works have been conducted using the surrogate-based optimization methods [23–25]. Many semi-empirical correlations based on these parameters have been proposed to predict film-cooling effectiveness. Nevertheless, the accuracy of these correlations is difficult to maintain due to the nonlinearity of three-dimensional flows [26]. Therefore, it is desirable to develop a surrogate model, which can calculate film-cooling effectiveness faster and more accurate than the conventional CFD method and semi-empirical correlation, respectively.

More recently, with the rapid development in the field of data science, machine learning has attracted attention in various fields including fluid mechanics [27–31]. According to the "Universal approximation theorem" [32], a feed-forward neural network is capable of building an accurate mapping between two carefully designed subsets. Meanwhile, the prediction of the temperature distribution based on neural networks could be achieved in only a few seconds.

In the field of predicting film-cooling effectiveness, Wang et al. [33] applied least square support vector machine (LS-SVM) to predict the lateral averaged adiabatic film-cooling effectiveness on a flat plate surface downstream of a row of cylindrical holes. Milani et al. [34, 35] utilizes a random forest method to predict the turbulent diffusivity in the film cooling flows on gas turbine blades. Ma et al. [36] proposed a method of using U-net to predict the mixing characteristics between coolant film and hot gases in a rocket combustion chamber with different inlet flow conditions. Yang et al. established modified Convolutional Neural Network (CNN) [37, 38] and Conditional Generative Adversarial Networks (CGAN) based on CNN [39] to directly predict the film cooling effectiveness distribution on the wall. CNN is one of the most effective networks applied to the analysis of visual imagery [40]. Commonly, the input of CNN is image and the output is the extracted features of the input image. The previous studies of the Yang et al. [37–39] used the hole location conditions as the input image. By convolution calculation, the local features were extracted from the input image and converted into a temperature image.

However, low dimensional variables such as the film cooling parameters could only be fed into the neural network in additional separated image layers as color blocks [41], while the major input images are the surface geometry or other high dimensional information [22, 42, 43]. For the film cooling optimization, it is vital to extract flow field information using only a few film cooling parameters. Therefore, more advanced deep learning methods are demanded to directly predict the film cooling effectiveness and dimensionless temperature distribution based on film cooling parameters.

The present study utilized an advanced deep learning method to predict the film cooling effectiveness only using a few film cooling parameters. A Deconv NN algorithm was adopted to regression the film cooling effectiveness distribution on the wall as a function of the film cooling parameters. A series of CFD simulations was conducted to provide the training data. Comparisons with different deep learning methods and data set size are presented and analyzed. Eventually, an optimization algorithm is deployed to determine the best geometrical and aerodynamical parameters.

2 Methodology and Data Acquisition

The film cooling optimization consists of the modules of the geometry generation, the mesh automatic generation, the CFD simulation, the surrogate model and the optimizer. In the present study, the surrogate-based film cooling parameters optimization framework based on Deconv NN is proposed. As shown in Fig. 1, deconvolution calculation is implemented to construct a surrogate model for the film cooling optimization and the data acquisition is running in parallel on a high-performance computer.

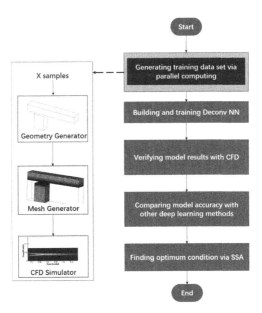

Fig. 1. Flowchart for the current study

2.1 Test Case Configuration

Data acquisition is vital for a high-performance deep learning model. The film cooling geometries in present study were defined by several geometrical and fluid dynamic parameters. In previous studies, it was found that density ratio, blowing ratio, hole inclination angle, and hole diameters are important in film cooling performance [37, 38]. Accordingly, these parameters are considered as the mainly research variables.

A brief description of the computational domains, and the reference geometry are presented below. As Fig. 2 shown, the hole diameter of the reference geometry is $d_0 = 12.5$ mm and the hole incline angle of the reference geometry is $\theta = 35°$. The dimension of the mainstream inflow chamber is $39d_0 \times 6d_0 \times 5d_0$, and the dimension of the coolant feeding chamber is $8d_0 \times 6d_0 \times 11.5d_0$. The distance between the mainstream inlet and the center (x_0) of the hole exit is $13d_0$. Here, x_1 is the x coord of the hole exit. And the hole length is $3.8d_0$. These variables would keep same while the hole incline angle θ and the hole diameter d varied as shown in Table 1.

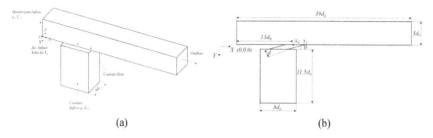

(a)   (b)

Fig. 2. Computational domain of a coolant jet ejecting into mainstream

Table 1. Geometry parameters

Variables	Amount	Range	Delta
d/(mm)	9	10.5–14.5	0.5
θ/(degree)	9	15–55	5

2.2 Computational Setups

In order to acquire representative temperature distribution downstream of the coolant jet, the computational domain in Fig. 2 is used in the current study. The geometry was generated automatically using script. The fluid is assumed as incompressible ideal gas for both the mainstream flow and coolant flow.

As for boundary conditions, fixed velocity is adopted for both mainstream inflow and coolant inflow and the outlet pressure is set as the atmospheric pressure at sea level. All the walls are set as adiabatic and no-slip walls. As for aerodynamic parameters, the density ratio dr depends on the ratio of the mainstream inflow temperature to the coolant inflow temperature, while the blowing ratio br depends on the ratio of the product of mainstream inflow temperature and velocity to the product of coolant inflow temperature and velocity, as in Eqs. 1 and 2. respectively.

$$dr = \frac{\rho_j}{\rho_\infty} = \frac{T_j}{T_\infty} \tag{1}$$

where T_∞ is the mainstream inflow temperature and T_j is the jet temperature, ρ_∞ is the mainstream inflow density and ρ_j is the jet density.

$$br = \frac{\rho_j U_j}{\rho_\infty U_\infty} \tag{2}$$

where U_∞ is the mainstream inflow velocity and U_j is the jet velocity.

As both the aerodynamic parameters (dr and br) could be affected by changing the inflow temperature. Therefore, dr is controlled only by changing the mainstream inflow temperature, while br is modified both by the jet velocity and the value of dr. Specific variables are given in Table 2. And the value of jet velocity would change under different br and dr.

Table 2. Aerodynamic parameters

Variables	Amount	Value	T_j/k	T_∞/k	U_j/(m/s)	U_∞/(m/s)
dr	3	1.1	263	289	---	
		1.2	263	313	---	
		1.3	263	342	---	
br	3	0.5	---		---	20
		1.0	---		---	20
		1.5	---		---	20

Based on the number of the parameters involved in this study, there are 729 (=9 × 9 × 3 × 3) cases in total. The computational cost of the all the cases was about 1500 wall-clock hours (around 2 h for each case) using 56 CPU cores. Meanwhile a subset of the cases is obtained with 225 cases (=5 × 5 × 3 × 3). For the subset, the value of the hole incline angle includes 15°, 25°, 35°, 45°, 55° and the value of the hole diameters includes 10.5 mm, 11.5 mm, 12.5 mm, 13.5 mm, 14.5 mm; whereas the value of dr and br are kept the same.

In order to evaluate the film cooling effectiveness, the dimensionless temperature T^* is introduced, which is defined as

$$T^* = \frac{T - T_j}{T_\infty - T_j} \tag{3}$$

where T_∞ is the mainstream inflow temperature, T_j is the jet temperature, and T is the adiabatic wall temperature. Film cooling effectiveness η is given by

$$\eta = \frac{T_\infty - T}{T_\infty - T_j} = 1 - T^* \tag{4}$$

It is noted that the dimensionless temperature T^* and the film cooling effectiveness η are dependent variables.

All the cases are performed using Fluent® 18.0 software. Following many other studies [36, 37, 42, 45], Reynolds-Averaged Navier-Stokes (RANS) is employed to provide the training dataset. To evaluate the accuracy for different turbulence models, validatation is carried out against the Large Eddy Simulation (LES) data of Wang et al. [1] and the experiment data of Ito et al. [16] and Sinha et al. [18]. To directly compare the performance of these methods, mean absolute error (MAE) is introduced to compare the absolute differences between the results of different turbulence models and LES result, which is defined as

$$MAE = \frac{1}{m} \sum_i^m |a_i - y_i| \tag{5}$$

where m denotes the total number of sampling points in Fig. 3(a), a is the data from RANS and y is the data from LES.

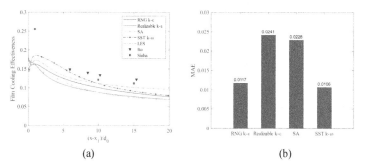

(a)   (b)

Fig. 3. Comparison between RANS, LES and experiments: (a) the lateral averaged film cooling efficiency; (b) the mean absolute difference between RANS and LES

The validation is based on the reference case ($d = 12.5$ mm, $\theta = 35°$, $dr = 1.2$, $br = 1.0$) as in Fig. 2. Figure 3(a) shows the lateral-averaged film cooling efficiency downstream of the cooling hole prediced using different numerical mehtods. The experiemtal data is also superimposed. Here, x_1 is the x coord of the hole exit. Figure 3(b) shows the MAE between RANS and LES results. It is clear that the accuracy of SST k-ω model and RNG k-ε model is relatively higher. In the current study, the RNG k-ε model is adopted.

Grid independent study is conducted for the reference case as shown in Fig. 4, where the film cooling efficiencies at the central line with different mesh sizes are presented. As the results of mesh size of 6 million and 7.5 million almost overlap, all the CFD data used for the training and validation in the current study are based on the 6 million mesh size.

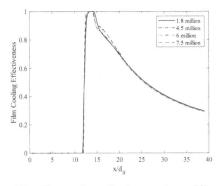

Fig. 4. Central line film cooling effectiveness from different mesh size

3   Deconvolution Modeling and Validation

3.1   Generation of Data Samples

Data pre-processing and preparation are the first step for deep learning approaches. The most effective cooling region is located immediately the downstream of cooling hole. The simulation domain on the wall $(x > x_0)$ is chosen as the learning domain, whose length is $26\,d_0$ and width is $6\,d_0$. The information of dr, br, d, θ is converted into a four-dimension matrix I_i as the input of the model. Here, the sum of dimensionless temperature and film cooling effectiveness is equal 1. Therefore, predicting the dimensionless temperature is essentially the same thing as predicting film cooling effectiveness. Also, the information of the dimensionless temperature distribution on the wall $(x > x_0)$ is interpolated into a matrix $O(x)$ whose shape is [64,256]. An example of data samples is shown in Fig. 5.

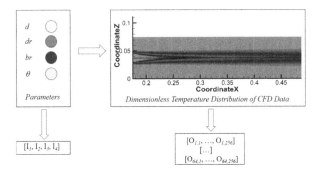

Fig. 5. Input data and learning target

3.2 Selection on Network Structure

The deep learning method presented here was inspired by both the Multilayer Perceptron (MLP) and deconvolution Neural Networks [44]. Deconvolution is also named as transposed convolution, which is essentially a special convolution calculation. Different from normal convolution, the transposed convolution increased the size of the output by sparse zero padding. Convolution neural network is one of the most popular deep learning methods for the analysis of visual imagery. By convolution calculation, the feature map could be extracted from the original images. One of the major advantages of convolution is that it can achieve weight-sharing and the total number of training parameters decreased rapidly compared to MLP. To achieve weight-sharing, the kernel size is set as $k \times k$, and the channel of the kernel is set as q. The convolution is executed based on this kernel. For MLP, the number of neurons for the first layer is set as m, and the number of neurons for the second layer is set as n, so there is $m \times n$ parameters needs to be trained in MLP. Obviously, with the number of neurons increasing, the number of parameters increases exponentially. However, the number of parameters for CNN between two layers equals to $k \times k \times q$, which is the product of the kernel's size and the number of the channel. It would not change with the increasing of the number of neurons for every layer.

Direct feeding of the four-dimensional input into the deconvolutional neural networks needs many layers to convert the input to the final output. To improve computational effectiveness, the first two layer used full connected layers to convert the four-dimensional input into the 256-dimensional vector. After that, deconvolution layers were deployed. The schematic of Deconv NN in this paper is shown in Fig. 6.

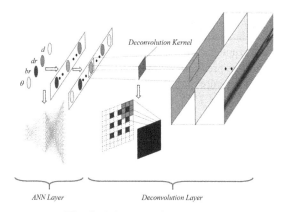

Fig. 6. Schematic of Deconv NN

3.3 Training and Validation of the Deconv NN

In Deconv NN, the input information I_i propagates from the front to the back; whereas the weighted and bias operations and activation are conducted between adjacent layers.

To train the Deconv NN, mean squared error (MSE) for the dimensionless temperature filed downstream of the cooling hole is introduced as the loss function.

$$MSE = \frac{1}{m} \sum_{i}^{m} (a_i - y_i)^2 \tag{6}$$

where m denotes the total number of output neurons, a is the data of the output layer and y is original target data.

In order to minimize the loss, parameters of weights and bias need to be updated iteratively using back propagation algorithm, where the Adam algorithm for gradient decent is adopted. The initial learning rate is set at 0.01 and it is reduced to one tenth of the original value every 150 iterations. The total number of epochs is set as 600. More detailed architecture of Deconv NN is shown in Fig. 7. Firstly, the input data including d, θ, dr and br is introduced into the architecture as the first layer. After two full-connected layers, the original data is transferred into a data list composed of 256 neurons. At the same time, the data list is reshaped into a matrix whose size is $1 \times 1 \times 256$ and then the matrix is fed into the deconvolutional neural networks. After 8 deconvolutional layers, output data is obtained. Including the input layer and output layer, the architecture consists of 11 layers.

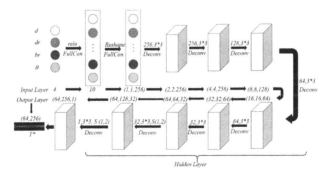

Fig. 7. Specific architecture of Deconv NN

All layers have a similar structure, i.e., batch normalization, the Rectified Linear Unit (ReLU) activation function and dropout (=0.3). There are in total 1,620,115 parameters need to be trained. Batch normalization keeps a normal distribution for the data at every layer to make sure that the distribution is consistent and the original learning features are retained [46]. It also helps to accelerate the training. The choice of the activation is also important to enhance the non-linearity of the neural network. Compared to other activation functions, ReLU is much faster in computing gradients and it is usually acts as the activation function for the hidden layers [47]. Dropout is a method to solve the overfitting and gradient vanishing problems of deep neural networks. Small dataset also performs well in deep learning methods based on dropout [48].

To directly compare the performance of Deconv NN, the quoted error (QE) is defined in Eq. 7. It represents the ratio between the absolute error and the output range.

$$QE = \frac{\frac{1}{m}\sum_i^m |a_i - y_i|}{T^*_{max} - T^*_{min}} \times 100\% = \frac{MAE}{T^*_{max} - T^*_{min}} \times 100\% \qquad (7)$$

where m denotes the number of output neurons, a is model output data and y is origin CFD data, $T^*_{max}(= 1)$ denotes the biggest dimensionless temperature, $T^*_{min}(= 0)$ denotes the minimum dimensionless temperature.

The 729 dataset is randomly spilt into two datasets, where 90% is in the training group, and the rest is in the validation group. Figure 8 shows the comparison of the prediction results by Deconv NN with the CFD data, where frame (a) is the CFD results for a random case in the validation group and frame (b) is the prediction results by Deconv NN for the same case. Figure 8 (c) is the CFD results of a randomly case in the training group and Fig. 8 (d) is the prediction results by Deconv NN for the same case.

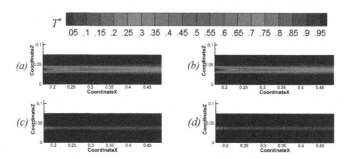

Fig. 8. Comparison for results by Deconv NN and CFD: (a) CFD results of a validation case and (b) prediction results by Deconv NN of the same validation case; (c) CFD results of a training case and (d) prediction results by Deconv NN of the same training case

Actually, the predictions results by Deconv NN are almost the same as the CFD results. Overall, the QE of Deconv NN in validation group is 0.62%. Especially, it is known that the sum of dimensionless temperature and film cooling effectiveness is equal 1. Accordingly, there is no doubt that Deconv NN could predict the film cooling effectiveness fast and accurately.

4   Results and Discussion

4.1   Comparison with Other Methods

To verify which model is the best for film cooling prediction for the 729 dataset, other methods were also adopted to evaluate their performance. The 729 dataset is randomly spilt into two datasets, where 90% is in the training group, and the rest is in the validation group. As Bayesian regression, Kriging method and linear regression method are difficult to achieve high dimensional output, only Deconv NN, MLP, U-net, CGAN are investigated here. Specific architectures of MLP, U-net, CGAN are shown in Figs. 9, 10 and 11, respectively. The number of layer and total parameters for different deep learning methods are given in Table 3. For the MLP, the number of neurons in the output layer is set as $64 \times 256 = 16384$ (see Fig. 9). For the U-net, the temperature field representing dr and the velocity field representing br are loaded into the input A layer [36], and d, θ and angle data are fed into input B layer, as illustrated in Fig. 10. For the CGAN, the generator and discriminator are trained. According to the game theory, in this training process, the generator is trained to generate "fake" images that can be judged by the discriminator as "real" [39]. The generator is just based on Deconv NN and the discriminator is based on CNN.

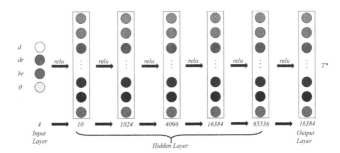

Fig. 9. Architecture of MLP for 2-dimensional prediction

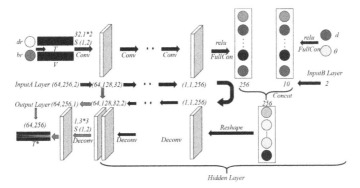

Fig. 10. Architecture of U-net for 2-dimensional prediction

For the MLP, the total number of parameters is quite large. After training with the data set, it is found that its training QE and validating QE are about 95%. In a word, it is nearly impossible to apply MLP to achieve 2-dimensional prediction. On the contrary, the other methods have good performance. Figure 12 shows QE for three methods to compare their performance. It is clearly that Deconv NN has the minimum parameters and the least QE in validation group. It noted that CGAN also shows good performance because its generator is based on Deconv NN.

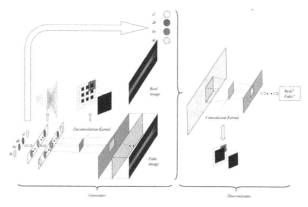

Fig. 11. Architecture of CGAN for 2-dimensional prediction

Table 3. Layers and total parameters for different deep learning methods

Methods	Total layers	Total number of parameters
Deconv NN	11	1,620,115
U-net	19	4,319,071
CGAN	28	1,748,100
MLP for 2D	7	2,219,155,250

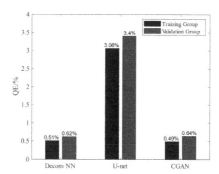

Fig. 12. QE of Deconv NN, U-net and CGAN

4.2   Comparison with Different Data Size

The amount of the data is also important for deep learning performance. Despite the dropout has been employed to prevent the overfit, it is necessary to compare the performance of the methods with different data set size. The Deconv NN was trained using 729 cases and 225 cases. All other settings were kept the same. The QE for these two data sets in validation group is shown in Fig. 13. It is worth nothing that the QE varies slightly with the different dataset size in validation group. The small difference demonstrates that the performance of dropout is good. It also shows that the Deconv NN purposed in this paper is robust for predicting film cooling effectiveness even with small dataset.

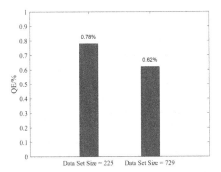

Fig. 13. QE of Deconv NN in validation group with different data size

5   Optimization

Sparrow Search Algorithm (SSA) is a novel swarm intelligence optimization algorithm proposed in 2020. SSA simulates the foraging and anti-predation behaviors of sparrows. There are two different types of sparrows, both the producer and the scrounger. The producers actively search for the food source, while the scroungers obtain food by the producers. Moreover, by biomimetic sparrows searching food process, sparrow that has best fitness is obtained. Furthermore, SSA is able to provide highly competitive results compared with the other state-of-the-art algorithms in terms of searching precision, convergence speed, and stability [49].

In this study, the sparrows' number is set as 50 and the max iteration is 200. The Deconv NN utilized SSA to find the optimum film cooling parameters values for film cooling. The object value γ is the average of outputs, which is defined as:

$$\gamma = \frac{1}{n} \sum_i^n a_i \tag{8}$$

where n is equal 16384(=64 × 256), which denotes the number of outputs and a is the results of Deconv NN. With an increase of iteration steps, the object value γ decreases rapidly until it levels out as shown in Fig. 14. The optimum film cooling parameters found by SSA are given in Table 4.

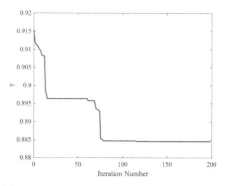

Fig. 14. Object value versus iteration steps during SSA optimization

Table 4. The optimum film cooling parameters

Variables	Deconv NN
d (mm)	14.500
θ (degree)	22.179
dr	1.220
br	0.500

To verify and validate the results in Table 4, Deconv NN and CFD methods were applied to predict the dimensionless temperature distribution on the wall. The CFD results for the optimized case and the reference cases are also compared. The influence of the d, br, and θ are investigated through different reference cases. The parameters values for the optimized case are set as shown in Table 5.

Table 5. The film cooling parameters

Case	d (mm)	θ (°)	dr	br
The optimized case	14.5	22.2	1.2	0.5
The reference case	12.5	35	1.2	1.0
The reference case1	14.5	35	1.2	1.0
The reference case2	12.5	35	1.2	0.5
The reference case3	12.5	22.2	1.2	1.0

Figure 15 (a) shows the CFD results of the optimized case, frame (b) for the prediction results by Deconv NN of the optimized case, frame (c) for the CFD results of the reference case, frame (d) for the CFD results of the reference case1, and frame (e) for the CFD results of the reference case2, frame (f) for the CFD results of the reference case3. As the differences between contour plots are difficult to distinguish, to better evaluate film cooling effectiveness, lateral-averaged results are shown in Fig. 16.

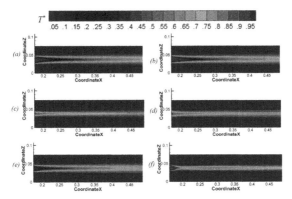

Fig. 15. Wall dimensionless Temperature Contours: (a) CFD results of the optimized case, (b) prediction results by Deconv NN of the optimized case, (c) CFD results of the reference case, (d) CFD results of the reference case1, (e) CFD results of the reference case2, (f) CFD results of the reference case3

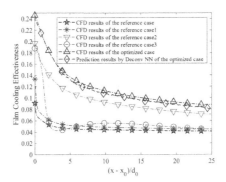

Fig. 16. Lateral-averaged film cooling effectiveness

Figure 17 (a) shows the quoted error of the prediction lateral-averaged results by Deconv NN and CFD results of the optimized case and the quoted error of the CFD lateral-averaged results of different reference cases when compared with the reference case. Frame (b) shows the quoted error of the prediction lateral-averaged results by Deconv NN of the optimized case and the quoted error of the CFD lateral-averaged results of different reference cases when compared with the optimized case.

According to Fig. 17 (a), it can be found that the film cooling effectiveness of the optimized case has been successfully improved with QE 7.35% when compared with the reference case. Moreover, QE of the reference case1 is 0.55%; QE of the reference case2 is 5.05%; QE of the reference case3 is 1.3% compared with the reference case. According to Fig. 17 (b), the QE of the lateral-averaged results of the optimized case

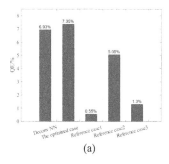 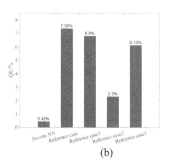

|(a)|(b)|

Fig. 17. QE of other results compared with (a) the reference case, (b) the optimized case

from CFD and Deconv NN is only 0.42%. The film cooling effectiveness of the optimized case has been successfully improved by QE of 6.80% when compared with the reference case1; by QE of 2.30% when compared with the reference case2 and by QE of 6.13% when compared with the reference case3. Obviously, *br* has the highest impact on the film cooling performance, with θ and *d* follow.

6   Conclusion

The current study developed a deep learning approach to predict the film cooling effectiveness on the adiabatic wall downstream of a coolant jet. Parameters that considered are blowing ratio, density ratio, hole inclination angle and hole diameters. Based on the Deconv NN, the non-linear and high-dimensional mapping between the coolant jet parameters and the film cooling effectiveness is developed. Using this model, an efficient optimization framework is proposed. A series of CFD simulations is performed to provide the dataset. With a careful training and validation, it is found that the predicted results are in good agreement with CFD. Additionally, the Deconv NN was compared against different methods and dataset size for model accuracy in predicting film cooling effectiveness. It can be concluded that:

1. The Deconv NN successfully reconstructed the film cooling effectiveness on the wall using only a few film cooling parameters. The quoted error is less than 0.62% in validation group and less than 0.51% in training group.
2. The Deconv NN has the minimum number of parameters and least quoted error in validation group as compared with MLP, U-net and CGAN. The marginal difference of the quoted error from different sizes of datasets demonstrates that the Deconv NN is robust for predicting film cooling effectiveness even for a small dataset.
3. The results of the optimization show that the film cooling effectiveness of the optimized case has been successfully improved by the quoted error of 7.35% when compared with the reference case.

These conclusions were limited to the flat plate cases. As the deconvolution has the potential to collect information from the film cooling parameters, there is potential to consider more film cooling parameters that were not covered in the current study. Moreover, more the experiment datasets could be included in the future to enhance the reliability of the model.

Acknowledgements. This Study was supported in part by the Zhejiang University/University of Illinois at Urbana-Champaign Institute and Natural Science Foundation of Zhejiang Province: LQ19A020003. It was led by Supervisor Jiahuan Cui.

References

1. Wang, W., Cui, J., Qu, S.: Large-eddy simulation of film cooling performance enhancement using vortex generator and semi-sphere. In: ASME Turbo Expo 2020: Turbomachinery Technical Conference and Exposition. American Society of Mechanical Engineers Digital Collection (2020)
2. Goldstein, R.J.: Film cooling. In: Advances in Heat Transfer, vol. 7, pp. 321–379. Elsevier (1971). https://doi.org/10.1016/S0065-2717(08)70020-0
3. Saumweber, C., Schulz, A., Wittig, S.: Free-stream turbulence effects on film cooling with shaped holes. J. Turbomach. **125**(1), 65–73 (2003)
4. Rallabandi, A.P., Grizzle, J., Han, J.-C.: Effect of upstream step on flat plate film-cooling effectiveness using PSP. J. Turbomach. **133**(4), 1–8 (2011). https://doi.org/10.1115/1.400 2422
5. Fric, T.F., Roshko, A.: Vortical structure in the wake of a transverse jet. J. Fluid Mech. **1994**, 1–47 (1994)
6. Kelso, R.M., Lim, T.T., Perry, A.E.: An experimental study of round jets in cross-flow. J. Fluid Mech. **306**, 111–144 (1996)
7. Haven, B.A., Kurosaka, M.: Kidney and anti-kidney vortices in crossflow jets. J. Fluid Mech. **352**, 27–64 (1997)
8. Lee, K.D., Kim, K.Y.: Shape optimization of a fan-shaped hole to enhance film-cooling effectiveness. Int. J. Heat Mass Transf. **53**(15–16), 2996–3005 (2010)
9. Goldstein, R.J., Eckert, E.R.G., Burggraf, F.: Effects of hole geometry and density on three-dimensional film cooling. Int. J. Heat Mass Transf. **17**(5), 595–607 (1974)
10. Gritsch, M., Schulz, A., Wittig, S.: Adiabatic wall effectiveness measurements of film-cooling holes with expanded exits (1998)
11. Yu, Y., Yen, C.H., Shih, T.P., Chyu, M.K., Gogineni, S.: Film cooling effectiveness and heat transfer coefficient distributions around diffusion shaped holes. J. Heat Transfer **124**(5), 820–827 (2002)
12. Kohli, A., Bogard, D.G.: Adiabatic effectiveness, thermal fields, and velocity fields for film cooling with large angle injection. J. Turbomach. **119**(2), 352–358 (1997). https://doi.org/10. 1115/1.2841118
13. Fu, Z., Zhu, H., Liu, C., Wei, J., Zhang, B.: Investigation of the influence of inclination angle and diffusion angle on the film cooling performance of chevron shaped hole. J. Therm. Sci. **27**(6), 580–591 (2018). https://doi.org/10.1007/s11630-018-1070-8
14. Schmidt, D.L., Sen, B., Bogard, D.G.: Film cooling with compound angle holes: adiabatic effectiveness. J. Turbomach. **118**(4), 807–813 (1996). https://doi.org/10.1115/1.2840938
15. Lutum, E., Johnson, B.V.: Influence of the whole length-to-diameter ratio on film cooling with cylindrical holes (1999)
16. Ito, S., Goldstein, R.J., Eckert, E.R.G.: Film cooling of a gas turbine blade. J. Eng. Power **100**(3), 476–481 (1978). https://doi.org/10.1115/1.3446382

17. Pedersen, D.R., Eckert, E.R.G., Goldstein, R.J.: Film cooling with large density differences between the mainstream and the secondary fluid measured by the heat-mass transfer analogy. J. Heat Transf. **99**(4), 620–627 (1977). https://doi.org/10.1115/1.3450752

18. Sinha, A.K., Bogard, D.G., Crawford, M.E.: Film-cooling effectiveness downstream of a single row of holes with variable density ratio. J. Turbomach. **113**(3), 442–449 (1991). https://doi.org/10.1115/1.2927894

19. Pietrzyk, J.R., Bogard, D.G., Crawford, M.E.: Hydrodynamic measurements of jets in cross-flow for gas turbine film cooling applications. J. Turbomach. **111**(2), 139–145 (1989). https://doi.org/10.1115/1.3262248

20. Mayhew, J.E., Baughn, J.W., Byerley, A.R.: The effect of freestream turbulence on film cooling adiabatic effectiveness. Int. J. Heat Fluid Flow **24**(5), 669–679 (2003)

21. New, T.H., Lim, T.T., Luo, S.C.: Effects of jet velocity profiles on a round jet in cross-flow. Exp. Fluids **40**(6), 859–875 (2006)

22. Bhatnagar, S., Afshar, Y., Pan, S., Duraisamy, K., Kaushik, S.: Prediction of aerodynamic flow fields using convolutional neural networks. Comput. Mech. **64**(2), 525–545 (2019). https://doi.org/10.1007/s00466-019-01740-0

23. Jeong, S., Murayama, M., Yamamoto, K.: Efficient optimization design method using kriging model. J. Aircr. **42**(2), 413–420 (2005)

24. Secco, N.R., Mattos, B.S.: Artificial neural networks applied to airplane design. In: 53rd AIAA Aerospace Sciences Meeting, p. 1013 (2015)

25. Chen, L., Qiu, H., Gao, L., Jiang, C., Yang, Z.: Optimization of expensive black-box problems via Gradient-enhanced Kriging. Comput. Methods Appl. Mech. Eng. **362**, 112861 (2020)

26. Baldauf, S., et al.: Correlation of film cooling effectiveness from thermographic measurements at engine like conditions. Turbo Expo. Power. Land. Sea. Air. **36088**, 149–162 (2002)

27. Brunton, S.L., Noack, B.R., Koumoutsakos, P.: Machine learning for fluid mechanics. Annu. Rev. Fluid Mech. **52**, 477–508 (2020)

28. Singh, A.P., Medida, S., Duraisamy, K.: Machine-learning-augmented predictive modeling of turbulent separated flows over airfoils. AIAA J. **55**(7), 2215–2227 (2017)

29. Bai, Z., et al.: Data-driven methods in fluid dynamics: sparse classification from experimental data. In: Pollard, A., Castillo, L., Danaila, L., Glauser, M. (eds.) Whither Turbulence and Big Data in the 21st Century?, pp. 323–342. Springer, Cham (2017). https://doi.org/10.1007/978-3-319-41217-7_17

30. Kutz, J.N.: Deep learning in fluid dynamics. J. Fluid Mech. **814**, 1–4 (2017)

31. Zhang, Z.J., Duraisamy, K.: Machine learning methods for data-driven turbulence modeling. In: 22nd AIAA Computational Fluid Dynamics Conference, p. 2460 (2015)

32. Hassoun, M.H.: Fundamentals of Artificial Neural Networks. MIT Press, Cambridge (1995)

33. Wang, C., Zhang, J., Zhou, J., Alting, S.A.: Prediction of film-cooling effectiveness based on support vector machine. Appl. Therm. Eng. **84**, 82–93 (2015)

34. Milani, P.M., Ling, J., Saez-Mischlich, G., Bodart, J., Eaton, J.K.: A machine learning approach for determining the turbulent diffusivity in film cooling flows. J. Turbomach. **140**(2), 021006 (2018). https://doi.org/10.1115/1.4038275

35. Milani, P.M., Ling, J., Eaton, J.K.: Physical interpretation of machine learning models applied to film cooling flows. J. Turbomach. **141**(1), 011004 (2019). https://doi.org/10.1115/1.4041291

36. Ma, H., Zhang, Y.-X., Haidn, O.J., Thuerey, N., Hu, X.-Y.: Supervised learning mixing characteristics of film cooling in a rocket combustor using convolutional neural networks. Acta Astronautica **175**, 11–18 (2020). https://doi.org/10.1016/j.actaastro.2020.05.021

37. Yang, L., Chen, W., Chyu, M.K.: A convolution modeling method for pore plugging impact on transpiration cooling configurations perforated by straight holes. Int. J. Heat Mass Transf. **126**, 1057–1066 (2018)

38. Yang, L., Rao, Y.: Predicting the adiabatic effectiveness of effusion cooling by the convolution modeling method. In: Turbo Expo: Power for Land, Sea, and Air, Vol. 58646, p. V05AT12A004. American Society of Mechanical Engineers, June 2019

39. Yang, L., Dai, W., Rao, Y., Chyu, M.K.: Optimization of the whole distribution of an effusively cooled surface facing non-uniform incoming temperature using deep learning approaches. Int. J. Heat. Mass. Transf. **145**, 118749 (2019)

40. LeCun, Y., Bottou, L., Bengio, Y., Haffner, P.: Gradient-based learning applied to document recognition. Proc. IEEE **86**(11), 2278–2324 (1998)

41. Farimani, A.B., Gomes, J., Pande, V.S.: Deep learning the physics of transport phenomena (2017). arXiv preprint arXiv:1709.02432

42. Guo, X., Li, W., Iorio, F.: Convolutional neural networks for steady flow approximation. In: Proceedings of the 22nd ACM SIGKDD International Conference on Knowledge Discovery and Data Mining, pp. 481–490, August 2016

43. Sekar, V., Jiang, Q., Shu, C., Khoo, B.C.: Fast flow field prediction over airfoils using deep learning approach. Phys. Fluids. **31**(5), 057103 (2019)

44. Zeiler, M.D., Krishnan, D., Taylor, G.W., Fergus, R.: Deconvolutional networks. In: 2010 IEEE Computer Society Conference on Computer Vision and Pattern Recognition, pp. 2528–2535. IEEE (2010)

45. Zhang, X., Xie, F., Ji, T., Zhu, Z., Zheng, Y.: Multi-fidelity deep neural network surrogate model for aerodynamic shape optimization. Comput. Methods Appl. Mech. Eng. **373**, 113485 (2021)

46. Santurkar, S., Tsipras, D., Ilyas, A., Madry, A.: How does batch normalization help optimization? In: Advances In Neural Information Processing Systems, pp. 2483–2493 (2018)

47. Agarap, A.F.: Deep learning using rectified linear units (RELU) (2018). arXiv preprint arXiv:1803.08375

48. Srivastava, N., Hinton, G., Krizhevsky, A., Sutskever, I., Salakhutdinov, R.: Dropout: a simple way to prevent neural networks from overfitting. J. Mach. Learn. Res. **15**(1), 1929–1958 (2014)

49. Xue, J., Shen, B.: A novel swarm intelligence optimization approach: sparrow search algorithm. Syst. Sci. Control Eng. **8**(1), 22–34 (2020)

Turbomachinery Blade Surrogate Modeling Using Deep Learning

Shirui Luo[1(✉)], Jiahuan Cui[2], Vignesh Sella[1], Jian Liu[2], Seid Koric[1],
and Volodymyr Kindratenko[1]

[1] University of Illinois at Urbana-Champaign, Urbana, IL 61801, USA
{shirui,vsella2,koric,kindrtnk}@illinois.edu
[2] Zhejiang University-University of Illinois at Urbana-Champaign Institute,
Haining, Zhejiang province 314400, China
jiahuancui@intl.zju.edu.cn

Abstract. Recent work has shown that deep learning provides an alternative solution as an efficient function approximation technique for airfoil surrogate modeling. In this paper we present the feasibility of convolutional neural network (CNN) techniques for aerodynamic performance evaluation. CNN approach will enable designer to fully utilize the ability of computers and statistics to interrogate and interpolate the nonlinear relationship between shapes and flow quantities, and rapidly perform a thorough optimization of the wide design space. The principal idea behind the current effort is to uncover the latent constructs and underlying cross-sectional relationships among the shape parameters, categories of flow field features, and quantities of interest in turbo-machinery blade design. The proposed CNN method is proved to automatically detect essential features and effectively estimate the pressure loss and deviation much faster than CFD solver.

Keywords: Turbomachinery blade · Shape parameterization · Deep learning

1 Introduction

Data-driven assisted automated aerodynamic design with affordable computational cost has received substantial attention in the last few decades [1,2]. The idea behind this so-called automated design, or surrogate model, is to first generate high quality data set using full fidelity software, and then an approximate model is constructed to fit the objective function and constraints for further data extrapolation. In turbo-machinery blade design, designers are interested in the surrogate models that capture the relationship between blade geometry parameters with two quantities of interest: 1) the pressure loss coefficient and 2) deviation angle [3]. Pressure loss coefficient is directly related with the reduction of turbine efficiency, while estimation of the deviation angle of flow leaving an annular cascade of blades is also important, since blades must be selected which

© Springer Nature Switzerland AG 2021
H. Jagode et al. (Eds.): ISC High Performance 2021 Workshops, LNCS 12761, pp. 92–104, 2021.
https://doi.org/10.1007/978-3-030-90539-2_6

turn the fluid to the desired direction in order to achieve the desired energy transfer in rotors.

The advantage of such surrogate models is that they are computationally cheap and feasible. The application of computational fluid dynamic (CFD) spans the full design cycle from conceptual to detailed design. Each of design stages require large numbers of steady/unsteady simulations, making the most rudimentary CFD too sophisticated and time consuming, especially at the preliminary design stage when high-resolution solutions are not necessarily required. Figure 1(a) shows the simplified process of aerodynamic design, the design proceeds in several phases and the computational complexity of the analysis codes increases progressively as it advances to the later phases. Typically, at the initial design stage, instead of looking for the finest CFD solution, engineers run sequential simplified simulations (meanline analysis/inviscid simulations) to only achieve a target solution that roughly within the optimal range. Surrogate models can greatly reduce the number of fine CFD simulations and speed up design cycle. Once well trained, surrogate models can efficiently characterize the aerodynamic performance with a speed comparable to empirical models while maintaining the favorable accuracy equivalent to the high-fidelity numerical simulations.

There are a few studies that use machine learning for blade surrogate model. The feasibility of applying artificial neural networks was first investigated by NASA [4,5], with more attention and efforts in the recent years [6–8]. For example, Zhang trained both a Multi-layered perception and CNN model that can learn the lift coefficients of airfoils with a variety of shapes in different Reynolds numbers and angles of attack [7]. The airfoils are from UIUC Airfoil Data Site and the aerodynamic coefficients are obtained from XFOIL simulation. Bhatnagar used Reynolds number, angle of attach, and the shape of airfoil as the inputs to predict the velocity and pressure fields in a shared-encoding and decoding CNN. The fact that only three airfoil shapes in the training dataset is a limit factor in generalization of the model predictability.8 Wu proposed a model that leverage both generative adversarial network and CNN to model the flow field profile using the parameterized airfoil profiles as input [9]. Thuerey adopted a U-net architecture to achieve a model at a mean relative pressure and velocity error of less than 3% compared to Reynolds Averaged Navier Stokes (RANS) solutions [10].

In this paper we explored the feasibility of applying convolutional neural network (CNN) techniques to assist turbomachinery blade design. The principal idea behind the current effort is to build a turbine-specific surrogate model to substitute the computationally intensive RANS simulation with dataset obtained from inviscid simulation. The CNN is introduced as the surrogate model to uncover underlying cross-sectional relationships among the shape parameters, categories of flow field features, and quantities of interest in turbomachinery blade design. The trained CNN model, which maps the blade shape and low-fidelity simulation data with flow quantities from high-fidelity simulations, can be used as a non-linear interpolation in the feature space or in a space of reduced features.

2   Proposed Framework

As previously mentioned, the design of turbomachinery is typically sequential with gradual increment of increasing fidelity, from preliminary design to identify velocity triangles with a 1D meanline model, to detailed design optimization iterations with a 3D CFD solver (Fig. 1a). We propose a surrogate model that utilize the neural networks to combine two simulations with different fidelity. This "multi-fidelity" learning allows training a surrogate model from multiple fidelity of data sources with different accuracy to reduce overall computing costs. The two simulations are RANS and inviscid Euler with different mesh resolutions. Our automated design strategy is summarized as follows (Fig. 1b): 1) Generate a blade shape library with varying parameters to represent the parameter spaces; 2) Mesh and then run both RANS and inviscid Euler CFD solutions for each blade; 3) Data pre-preprocessing and then CNN model training, the input data for training CNN include four channels: blade shape represented in distance function, x-direction velocity, y-direction velocity, and pressure from inviscid simulation, the response for training are the pressure loss and deviation angle obtained from RANS simulations.

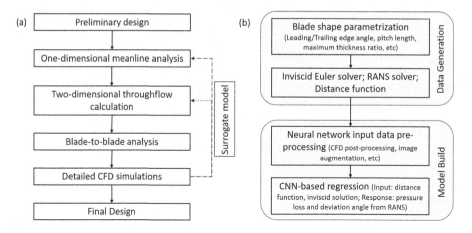

Fig. 1. (a) Simplified schematic diagram of the design process of turbo-machinery blade; (b) Schematic diagram of the proposed CNN assisted surrogate model.

3   Data Generation

One of the key issues in developing effective approaches for design is the ability to model arbitrary flow geometries that can be easily modified in an automated fashion. There have been several blade design models using parametric approach for blade geometry construction, like the classical parameterization technique B-splines [11], freeform deformation technique [12], Bezier polynomial method [13], and the class function/shape function transformation method [14], that are widely used geometry representation methods employed to generate airfoil coordinates. In this paper an open-source package, T-Blade3, was used to generate the blade shape library [15]. T-Blade3 is a general parametric blade geometry builder that can create a variety of blade geometries based on few geometric and aerodynamic parameters. This package uses control points for the definition of splines to modify the blade shapes quickly and smoothly to obtain the desired blade model. The second derivative of the mean-line is controlled using B-splines, a smooth thickness distribution is then added to the airfoil. The geometry of a turbine blade in shown in (Fig. 2-left), where the blades are characterized by a mean camber line halfway between the suction and the pressure surfaces. The blade chord is the straight line connecting the leading and the trailing edges. The blade thickness is the distance between the pressure and suction surfaces, measured perpendicular to the camber line. The axial-tangential view of a turbine stage is shown in (Fig. 2-right). The blade pitch is the circumferential separation between two contiguous blades. The projection of the chord onto the axial direction is known as the axial chord b. The cascade spacing s_c is the axial separation between one blade cascade and the next one. The symbol α is used to denote the absolute flow angle, β is used for the relative flow angle, θ is used for tangential flow angle. For simplicity, only stator blades are considered in the current study. In the parametric representation of blade geometries, the β_{in} ranges (20:3:41), β_{out} ranges (50:3:71), thickness ratio ranges (0.08:0.01:0.15). The pitch has four different length (0.110, 0.135, 0.145, and 0.155), the inflow angle has three values (15,20,25). Therefore, we have $3\times4\times392= 4704$ simulations in total within the data set. For each simulation, the inlet velocity in x-direction is fixed to achieve the Reynolds number $= 8 \times 10^5$ and Mach number $= 0.2$.

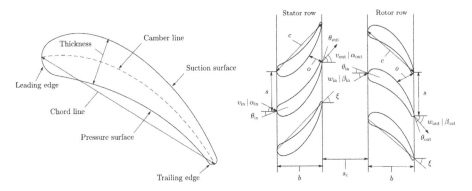

Fig. 2. (Left) Geometry of a blade section; (Right) Axial-tangential view of a cascade.

These generated blades have two uses: 1) The RANS/inviscid simulation will be run for each blade to generate flow data. 2) the blade shape will be the input after signed distance function. The distance function (DF) is used as the geometry representation of the pixelated blade shape [16]. DF returns the shortest distance between the point and surface when passed the coordinates of a point. The DF both defines a boundary and includes spatial information of distances from that boundary. The sign of the return value indicates whether the point is inside that surface or outside. The mathematical definition of the DF of a set of points X measures the shortest distance of a points to a predefined boundary.

The Ansys CFX Computational Fluid Dynamics (CFD) package is used in the current study to run cases. CFX is a mature CFD code based on the finite volume method with focus on the turbomachinery applications. Figure 3 shows the computational domain and the boundary condition for one representative blade profile. All the calculations are performed on the single blade passage with periodic boundary condition applied on the pitchwise direction as shown in the figure. The inflow boundary condition is imposed at 40% chord upstream of the leading edge, whereas the outlet is located at 1.5 chord downstream of the trailing edge. The no-slip wall boundary condition is enforced on the blade surface. As we have too many different blade profile, manually meshing all these geometries is infeasible. Here, only one geometry is manually meshed with Gripro, which is a mesh generation software, and the rest is obtained by the mesh morphing techniques. This automated discretization of the computational domain without human interference is another key for accurate and computationally efficient flow simulations.

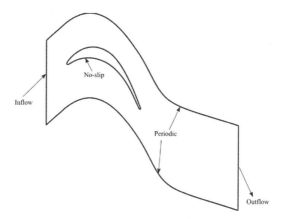

Fig. 3. Boundary conditions for RANS calculations

The RANS is too slow for routine design work at preliminary stage, as it requires a full boundary layer resolution. Practically designers use a much faster viscous-inviscid zonal approach that only solves the Euler equations coupled to some boundary-layer formulation using the displacement thickness concept. This inviscid flow approach typically has a boundary layer analysis so that viscous effects near the boundary can be modeled. In regions not close to solid surfaces, viscous forces are negligibly small compared to inertial or pressure forces. As such, neglecting the viscous terms in such inviscid flow regions greatly simplifies the analysis without much loss in accuracy. A Euler solver has been used to produce aerodynamic results for all blade simulations undertaken during this work. It is shown (Fig. 4) that both the Euler and the RANS methods can predict the global characteristics of the flow. However, the Euler method fails to predict the separation induced by the adverse pressure gradient on the upper side of the blade. This is expected to be more severe at a high angle of attack. As shown in Fig. 4, both viscous and inviscid calculations are performed to generate the dataset. The wake downstream of the blade trailing edge is clearly identified in the viscous calculation, whereas it is not present in the inviscid as expected. As the Reynold number in all the cases is relatively low, boundary layer transition is expected on the suction surface of the blade. Therefore, the transition model $\gamma - Re_\theta$ coupled with SST turbulence model is adopted in all the simulations.

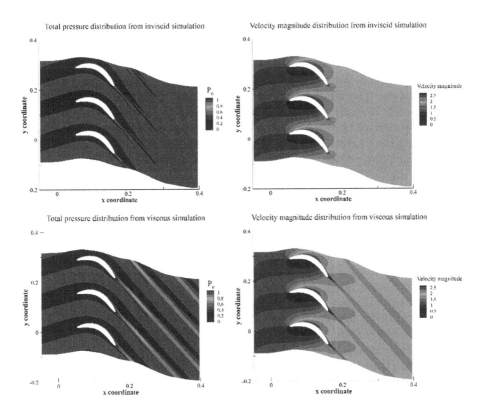

Fig. 4. Inviscid simulation (top) vs RANS simulation (bottom) when pitch $= 0.11$

4   Results and Discussion

In this section we discuss the training and prediction results of two different network architectures with different scenarios. The prediction results are shown in comparison to RANS results, the performance of different architectures is compared to show the capability range of CNN model's predictability for flow over blade dataset. A total set of 4704 RANS and Euler simulations were performed. The whole dataset was randomly split 80% as training and 20% as testing. Figure 5(a) shows the scatter plot of feature spaces for network dataset when the pitch length and inflow angle are fixed. The blue and red are training and testing dataset randomly split. For each sample point in Fig. 5(a), four image-like matrices are created to feed into the CNN as four channels. Figure 5(b-d) are pixelated pressure, x-direction velocity, and y-direction velocity from inviscid simulation to feed as the input for CNN. The true field from CFD simulation has dense and unstructured mesh, here we use linear interpolation to transform the field data into pixelated images with a resolution of 201×201.

The nonlinear models have been studied using response surfaces, generic algorithm, and recently the deep learning to detect patterns and features in the shape parameters [17,18]. The CNN has widely been used for challenging machine-learning tasks like image recognition since the introduction of the LeNet-5 architecture. The CNN can capture the invariance from complex and noisy real-world data in a scalable manner, due to a unique sub-structure of local receptive fields with weight-sharing and subsequent mapping through subsampling layers. The input image and intermediate images are convolved with learned kernels in many successive layers, allowing the network to learn highly nonlinear features. VGG is one CNN model proposed by K. Simonyan and A. Zisserman from the University of Oxford [19]. Based on the VGG model, the aerodynamic modeling requires some modifications on top of this structure. Figure 6 illustrates the modified layout of the VGG for blade dataset regression. First, the last layer of softmax is removed since the learning task is about regression instead of classification, the network outputs are two continuous regressions representing pressure loss and deviation angle instead of a discrete classification. The four channels of CNN input are DFs, pressure distribution, velocity in x-direction, and velocity in y-direction, respectively. These data are standardized, and power transformed in the preprocessing before they are fed to the network. The rectified linear unit (ReLU) is used as the activation function. The batch normalization, which rescale feature maps between layers to improve the scaling of gradients during training, are added. The dropout with rate equal to 0.5 was adapted, in which feature maps are randomly removed from the network during training, reducing the problem of overfitting large networks. All architectures have been implemented in the Python environment using a modern, open-source library for deep learning: Tensorflow. An ensemble of networks was trained, each with randomly initialized weights. Network training was deemed complete when the model error on a held-out validation set of data stopped decreasing. The hyper-parameters were determined through a grid-search process.

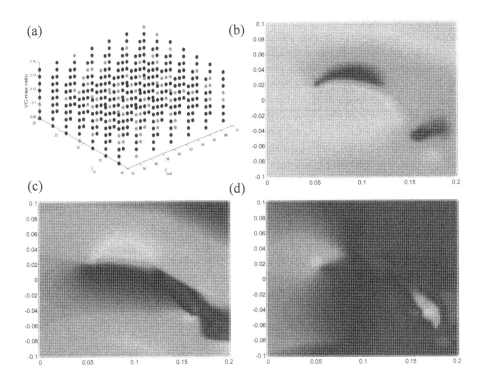

Fig. 5. Scatter plot of feature spaces for network dataset when the pitch length and inflow angle are fixed. (a) The blue and red are training and testing dataset randomly split; (b-d) Pixelated pressure, x velocity, and y velocity from inviscid simulation to feed as the input for CNN (Color figure online)

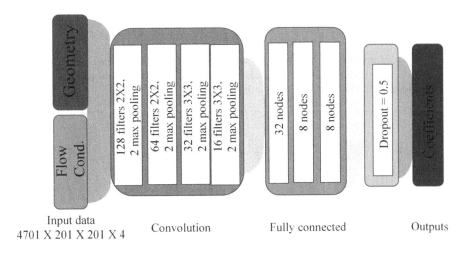

Fig. 6. VGG-based CNN architecture for predicting blade pressure loss and deviation angle

The predictions for pressure loss and deviation angle using the whole dataset are not satisfactory. With the whole dateset, we were not able to train a single model that can both predict the pressure loss and deviation angle very vell. A potential reason is that the data distribution of pressure loss is very skewed (see Fig. 7) even after power transformation. The pressure loss ΔP and deviation angle $\Delta\theta$ vary far more drastically than the variation in blade geometric parameters. New network architectures which have accurate predictions with small and non-normal data sets need to be further explored.

To feed more information into the network and with the hope to gain a better performance, we calculate the blade Zweifel load coefficient and feed this variable in the first fully connected layer after the convolution layers (See Fig. 8). The load coefficient is defined as:

$$Z_w = 2\frac{P}{C}cos^2\alpha_2(tan\alpha_2 + tan\alpha_1) \tag{1}$$

where α_1 and α_2 are the leading and tailing edge angles, P is the pitch, and C is the axial chord, the C is calculated as the maximum in x-coordinate minus

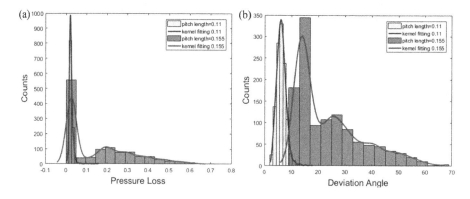

Fig. 7. Histogram plots of the pressure loss and deviation angle when pitch length = 0.11, 0.155. The pressure loss is very skewed towards left side, making prediction on pressure loss more challenging than deviation angle.

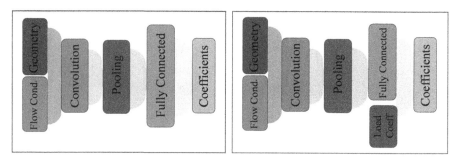

Fig. 8. Two CNN architectures. The right has an additional Load coefficient in the fully connected layer.

the minim, the $U_{x,1}$ and $U_{x,2}$ are equal in our cases. The addition of the fed load coefficient at the first fully connected layer has a profound impact to the prediction, as this value shows up at the very end of the CNN structure.

Beside of the load coefficient, we split the whole dataset into subsets by fixing the pitch length and inflow angle and training a separate model for each individual subset. The reason of this splitting is that it is found the pitch length can affect the flow behavior a lot, while the β_{in}, β_{out}, and $t/C - max$ ratio are less influential. It is expected that the CNN has better prediction as the target will not change drastically by fixing the pitch length and inflow angle. However, a potential drawback is that the dataset becomes smaller after splitting, the smaller dataset (only 1176) may sacrifice CNN's prediction accuracy. Figure 9 shows the prediction performance when the pitch length is fixed at 0.135. The prediction is improved after the load coefficient is included.

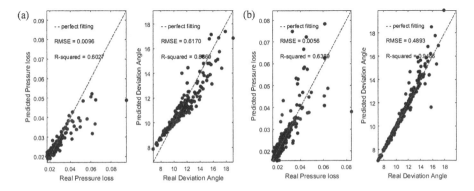

Fig. 9. (a) The real pressure loss vs CNN predicted without load coefficient when pitch length = 0.135; (b) Plot of the real pressure loss vs CNN predicted with load coefficient when pitch length = 0.135

We postulated that the prediction deviation at high pressure loss and deviation angle is due to the intrinsic nature of inviscid simulation. The inviscid simulation needs to perform a boundary layer calculation iteratively to account for the boundary layer effects, this calculation works only when the boundary layer has no separation. When the boundary layer thickness increases and separation occurs, the wake region loss becomes significant, the inviscid solution is more complicated and more different from RANS simulation, thus neural network can no longer map the relationship between two fidelity solutions. As a result, the model performance of cases that have large pressure loss and deviation angle is much worse, as shown in Fig. 9.

To delve into the interpretability of the model and verify that the CNN was indeed learning spatial characteristics that seem appropriate for this problem, we used the Gradient-weighted Class Activation Mapping (Grad-CAM) method to produce saliency maps, or heatmaps, of the features the CNN views as most discriminative [20]. Grad-CAM uses gradient information from the last convolutional layer of a CNN and derives 'importance values' for a particular class. The gradients of the last layer are computed with respect to a particular feature, and then are global-average-pooled over the width and height dimensions. These neuron importance values are used as weights for the forward activation values, and then processed through a ReLU to obtain the heatmap. From Fig. 10, the CNN model can discriminate important features near the blade wall. This information provides some reassurance that the network is taking into account the geometry of each airfoil input.

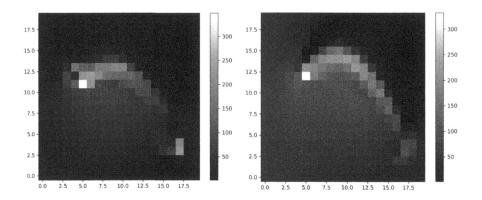

Fig. 10. The salient map with respect to pressure loss and deviation angle.

5   Conclusion

We present a data-driven technique to predict the flow around a blade. To accelerate the process, we propose a CNN framework which predicts the pressure loss and deviation angle of blade given the blade shape, velocity, and pressure distribution from inviscid simulation as input. The synthesis between geometric DFs and flow conditions from inviscid simulation into an image-like array has been successfully used in training the CNN. In summary, as a proof of concept, the proposed CNN architectures demonstrate reasonable performance in learning from the given examples and in predicting pressure loss and deviation angle for unseen blade shapes. This result gives a useful perspective to harness well-developed deep learning techniques in image recognition tasks for automated blade design task.

Acknowledgments. This work utilizes resources supported by the National Science Foundation's Major Research Instrumentation program, grant #1725729, as well as the University of Illinois at Urbana-Champaign.

References

1. Anderson, G.: R and Aftosmis. Adaptive shape parameterization for aerodynamic design. Nat. Aeronaut, Michael J (2015)
2. Ando, K., Takamura, A., Saito, I.: Automotive aerodynamic design exploration employing new optimization methodology based on CFD. SAE Int. J. Passenger Cars-Mech. Syst. **3**, 398–406 (2010)
3. Cho, S.-Y., Yoon, E.-S., Choi, B.-S.: A Study on an axial-type 2-D turbine blade shape for reducing the blade profile loss. KSME Int. J. **16**(8), 1154–1164 (2002)
4. Rai, M.M., Madavan, N.K.: Aerodynamic design using neural networks. AIAA J. **38**(1), 173–182 (2000)
5. Rai, M.M., Madavan, N.K.: Application of artificial neural networks to the design of turbomachinery airfoils. J. Propul. Power **17**(1), 176–183 (2001)
6. Papila, N., Shyy, W., Griffin, L., Dorney, D: Shape optimization of supersonic turbines using response surface and neural network methods. In: 39th Aerospace Sciences Meeting and Exhibit 1065 (2016)
7. Zhang, Y., Sung, W.J., Mavris, D.N.: Application of convolutional neural network to predict airfoil lift coefficient. In: 2018 AIAA/ASCE/AHS/ASC Structures, Structural Dynamics, and Materials Conference 1903 (2018)
8. Bhatnagar, S., Afshar, Y., Pan, S., Duraisamy, K., Kaushik, S.: Prediction of aerodynamic flow fields using convolutional neural networks. Comput. Mech. **64**(2), 525–545 (2019)
9. Wu, H., Liu, X., An, W., Chen, S., Lyu, H.: A deep learning approach for efficiently and accurately evaluating the flow field of supercritical airfoils. Comput. Fluidsr. **198**(2), 104393 (2020)
10. Thuerey, N., Weißenow, K., Prantl, L., Hu, X.: Deep learning methods for Reynolds-averaged Navier-Stokes simulations of airfoil flows. AIAA J. **58**(1), 25–36 (2020)
11. Wang, C., Gao, Z., Huang, J., Zhao, K., Li, J.: Smoothing methods based on coordinate transformation in a linear space and application in airfoil aerodynamic design optimization. Sci. China Technol. Sci. **58**(2), 297–306 (2015)
12. Lassila, T., Rozza, G.: Parametric free-form shape design with PDE models and reduced basis method. Comput. Methods Appl. Mech. Eng. **199**(23–24), 1583–1592 (2010)
13. Antunes, A.P., Azevedo, J.L.F.: Studies in aerodynamic optimization based on genetic algorithm. J. Aircraft. **51**(3), 1002–1012 (2014)
14. Ariyarit, A., Kanazaki, M.: Multi-fidelity multi-objective efficient global optimization applied to airfoil design problems. Appl. Sci. **712**, 1318 (2017)
15. Siddappaji, K.: Parametric 3d blade geometry modeling tool for turbomachinery systemss. University of Cincinnati (2012)
16. Guo, X., Li, W., Iorio, F.: Convolutional neural networks for steady flow approximations. In: Proceedings of the 22nd ACM SIGKDD International Conference on Knowledge Discovery and Data Mining, pp. 481–490 (2016)
17. Liu, X., Zhu, Q., Lu, H.: Modeling multiresponse surfaces for airfoil design with multiple-output-Gaussian-process regression. J. Aircraft. **513**, 740–747 (2014)
18. Hollom, J., Qin, N.: Robustness of natural laminar flow airfoil drag optimization to transition amplification factor. In: 18th AIAA/ISSMO Multidisciplinary Analysis and Optimization Conference, p. 3144 (2017)

19. Simonyan, K., Zisserman, A.: Very deep convolutional networks for large-scale image recognition. J. Aircraft (2014). arXiv preprint: arXiv:1409.1556
20. Selvaraju, R.R., Cogswell, M., Das, A., Vedantam, R., Parikh, D., Batra, D.: Grad-cam: visual explanations from deep networks via gradient-based localization. In: Proceedings of the IEEE International Conference on Computer Vision, pp. 618–626 (2017)

A Data-Driven Wall-Shear Stress Model for LES Using Gradient Boosted Decision Trees

Sarath Radhakrishnan$^{(\boxtimes)}$, Lawrence Adu Gyamfi , Arnau Miró ,
Bernat Font , Joan Calafell , and Oriol Lehmkuhl

Barcelona Supercomputing Center, Barcelona, Spain
`sarath.radhakrishnan@bsc.es`

Abstract. With the recent advances in machine learning, data-driven strategies could augment wall modeling in large eddy simulation (LES). In this work, a wall model based on gradient boosted decision trees is presented. The model is trained to learn the boundary layer of a turbulent channel flow so that it can be used to make predictions for significantly different flows where the equilibrium assumptions are valid. The methodology of building the model is presented in detail. The experiment conducted to choose the data for training is described. The trained model is tested a posteriori on a turbulent channel flow and the flow over a wall-mounted hump. The results from the tests are compared with that of an algebraic equilibrium wall model, and the performance is evaluated. The results show that the model has succeeded in learning the boundary layer, proving the effectiveness of our methodology of data-driven model development, which is extendable to complex flows.

Keywords: Machine learning · XGBoost · Turbulence · Wall models

1 Introduction

As a consequence of the recent developments in high-performance computing (HPC), large eddy simulation (LES) is getting increased attention as a predictive tool in turbulence research. LES essentially resolves the dynamically significant, flow-dependent, energy-containing larger scales and models the smaller ones. For LES to give accurate results, these integral scales of motion need to be completely resolved. Resolving these scales becomes prohibitively expensive at high Reynolds numbers (Re). LES may become computationally unfeasible even at moderate Reynolds numbers when it comes to wall-bounded flows, given the complex flow structure at the boundary layer. The estimated cost of calculation is of the order of $Re^{\frac{13}{7}}$ for wall-resolved LES (WRLES) [1], and it can be even more expensive when the temporal integration cost is considered [2]. Interestingly, over 50% of the computational resources are used to resolve only 10% of the flow [3] even at moderate Re. Therefore, the only economical way to perform LES of wall-bounded high Re flows is by resolving the outer layer alone. Since the grid

© Springer Nature Switzerland AG 2021
H. Jagode et al. (Eds.): ISC High Performance 2021 Workshops, LNCS 12761, pp. 105–121, 2021.
https://doi.org/10.1007/978-3-030-90539-2_7

sizes to resolve the outer layer are too coarse to resolve the viscous sub-layer, the momentum transport by the inner scales needs to be modeled by providing an approximate boundary condition. In this sense, wall-modeled LES (WMLES) lowers the computational cost, and the cost depends loosely on the Re and the model type. Wall models can be classified into two categories: zonal models and equilibrium law-based models. A different set of equations is solved in the zonal approach closer to the wall to determine the boundary condition. Equilibrium law-based models assume that the inner layer dynamics are universal; hence they can be represented by general law, at least in an average sense. A detailed review of different wall modeling strategies is presented in [3–6].

Conventional wall modeling strategies perform reasonably well in both low and high-speed flows [7–11]. However, their industrial utility is still limited because of their poor performance on flows involving separation and heat transfer [12]. With the advances in machine learning, strategies based on data could be used to augment wall modeling in LES. Data-based approaches have already been used in computational fluid dynamics (CFD) for turbulence modeling [13–25] and for the simulation of multi-phase flows [26,27]. These approaches are reviewed in detail by [28] and [29]. However, wall modeling using data-based approaches has just started getting attention from the CFD community. The previous works [30,31] have used neural networks for modeling. In this study, a wall model with XGBoost [32] is presented as a first step towards developing data-based models for complex flows. First, we train models on two different channel flows to select the best a priori model. In addition to testing the model a priori on synthetic data, the model's performance is evaluated a posteriori on two cases, one of which is significantly different from the trained data. The results are compared with that of an algebraic equilibrium wall model (EQWM [33]).

The paper is organised as follows: Sect. 2 provides the background information. In Sect. 3 results are presented. Concluding remarks are found in Sect. 4.

2   Methodology

XGBoost is a non-parametric method built using several "base learners" based on the statistical principle of boosting [34]. The base learners used by XGBoost are decision trees. Methods using decision trees have already been used in the context of turbulence modeling [19,20]. Being a non-parametric model, XGBoost does not assume anything about the data and the data distribution. The number of parameters for such a model is not limited. This also increases the chance of over-fitting the model to the trained data. However, XGBoost also provides hyper-parameters to tune such that over-fitting can be effectively controlled. The complete methodology followed for generating the model is discussed below:

2.1   Datasets

The datasets for the model development are generated from WRLES of turbulent channel flows. A turbulent channel flow is a case where the law of the wall(LoW)

$$u^+ = \begin{cases} y^+ & \text{for } y^+ < 5 \\ \frac{1}{\kappa}\log(y^+) + B & \text{for } y^+ > 30 \end{cases} \tag{1}$$

$$where, \quad u^+ = \frac{u}{u_\tau} \quad and \quad y^+ = \frac{yu_\tau}{\nu}$$

given by Eq. (1) holds. u in Eq. (1) is the local mean velocity parallel to the wall, and y is the normal distance from the wall. $\kappa \approx 0.4$ is the Von Kármán constant, and ν is the dynamic viscosity of the fluid. B is a constant that has a value approximately equal to 5. u_τ is the characteristic velocity of the flow called friction velocity. Most of the turbulent flows exhibit this velocity distribution inside the thin wall layer, so it is considered universal [35]. We intend to train the model to learn the boundary layer (BL) of the channel flow and use the model for turbulent flows significantly different from the channel flow.

WRLES is performed using the in-house multi-physics code Alya [36]. Alya is a low-dissipation finite-element code which solves the incompressible Navier-Stokes equation. Two simulations were run using Alya to generate the datasets, viz. $Re_\tau = 1000$ and $Re_\tau = 180$. Re_τ is the friction Reynolds number given by,

$$Re_\tau = \frac{u_\tau \delta}{\nu}$$

where δ is the half-channel height. Given below are the details of the simulation:

$\boldsymbol{Re_\tau = 180}$: The computational domain for this case is $4\pi\delta \times 2\delta \times \frac{4}{3}\pi\delta$ in the stream-wise, wall-normal and span-wise directions respectively. A mesh of 64^3 elements is used to discretize the domain. The mesh is uniform in the stream-wise and span-wise directions, corresponding to $\Delta x^+ \approx 35$ and $\Delta z^+ \approx 12$ in wall-units respectively. The mesh is stretched in the wall normal direction using a hyperbolic tangent function given by

$$y(i) = \frac{\tanh(\gamma(\frac{2(i-1)}{N_y} - 1))}{\tanh(\gamma)}, \tag{2}$$

where N_y is the number of elements in the wall normal direction, with i ranging from 1 to N_y. γ is the factor which controls the stretching. The value of γ is chosen such that the $\Delta y^+ = 1$. Periodic boundary conditions are applied on the stream-wise and span-wise directions, while a no-slip boundary condition is imposed on the wall boundaries. Flow is driven by a stream-wise constant pressure gradient and the Vreman [37] sub-grid scale(SGS) model is used for turbulence closure.

$\boldsymbol{Re_\tau = 1000}$: The computational domain for this case is $6\pi\delta \times 2\delta \times 3\pi\delta$ in the stream-wise, wall-normal and span-wise directions respectively. A mesh of 128^3 elements is used here. Just as before, The mesh is uniform in the stream-wise and span-wise directions, corresponding to $\Delta x^+ \approx 140$ and $\Delta z^+ \approx 70$ in wall units, respectively. The hyperbolic tangent function of Eq. (2) is used to stretch the mesh in the wall-normal direction. The $\Delta y^+ = 1$ in this simulation as well.

Identical boundary conditions are applied with periodic stream-wise and span-wise boundaries and a no-slip boundary on the walls. A stream-wise constant pressure gradient drives the flow and the integral length-scale approximation (ILSA) [38] SGS model is used as the turbulence closure.

Table 1. Distribution of data for training, validation and testing of the model

	Training data		Validation data		Testing data	
	Sample size	Simulation	Sample size	Simulation	Sample size	Simulation
Case study 1	70%	$Re_\tau = 180$	30%	$Re_\tau = 180$	90%	$Re_\tau = 1000$
			10%	$Re_\tau = 1000$		
Case study 2	70%	$Re_\tau = 1000$	30%	$Re_\tau = 1000$	90%	$Re_\tau = 180$
			10%	$Re_\tau = 180$		

Data from these two simulations are distributed for training, validation, and testing as given in Table 1. Details of the case studies mentioned in the table are explained later in Sect. 2.3. The addition of validation data from another distribution than the training data helps prevent over-fitting and also serves as an early-stop criterion during training.

It is made sure that the data chosen for training are statistically not correlated in time. In addition to these data-sets, a third set of data is synthetically generated from the above data-sets by varying the viscosity (ν) of the flow and the half-height of the channel (δ) and correspondingly scaling the velocity (u) and friction velocities (u_τ). This data-set is an augmentation to the Testing data to assess how well the model can generalize to new flow cases not included in the training. Below are the relations used for the scaling viscosity and the channel heights. The scaling ratios are computed such that the bulk and the friction Reynolds numbers of the flow are unaltered. Four sets of synthetic data are generated, two of which, by modifying ν and the other two by modifying δ. For viscosity modification from ν_{old} to ν_{new}, instantaneous velocity (u_{new}) and frictional velocity ($u_{\tau_{new}}$) are calculated as:

$$u_{new} = u_{old} \frac{\nu_{new}}{\nu_{old}}$$

$$u_{\tau_{new}} = u_{\tau_{old}} \frac{\nu_{new}}{\nu_{old}}$$

For the channel height modification from δ_{old} to δ_{new}, scaled instantaneous velocities (u_{new}) and friction velocity ($u_{\tau_{new}}$) are calculated as:

$$u_{new} = u_{old} \frac{\delta_{old}}{\delta_{new}}$$

$$u_{\tau_{new}} = u_{\tau_{old}} \frac{\delta_{old}}{\delta_{new}}$$

The synthetic data is with $\nu = \{10^{-5}, 10\}$ and $\delta = \{2, 10\}$.

2.2   Model Inputs and Output

The output from the model is u^+, i.e., u/u_τ, from which τ_ω can be easily computed. τ_ω is the output from a typical EQWM, which acts as a boundary condition in WMLES [33]. However, choosing an input is not straightforward. The choice of inputs should be such that the model generated based on these inputs should be extrapolatable to higher Re flows. So the best set of inputs for the model is derived from a series of trial and error experiments. The inputs initially considered were dimensionless velocity and dimensionless wall distance. However, we have found that a single non-dimensional, reference frame invariant quantity here-after called the 'local Reynolds Number (Re^*),' given by Eq. (3) is the best input that preserves the generality.

$$Re^* = \frac{uL}{\nu} \tag{3}$$

L is the wall distance, and u is the instantaneous velocity at each grid point.

2.3   Model Training and Testing

We use the XGBoost package from scikit-learn [39] for generating the model. Six cases with different data-sets are studied. Case studies 1 and 2 decides which is the better data out of the two for training the models. Case studies 3 to 6 are done to evaluate the performance of the model on synthesized general flows. This decides the choice of the inputs for the model. The distribution of the data for training validation and testing are as detailed in the Table 1 in Sect. 2.1. The following sections describe the results from above-mentioned case studies. The size of each 'tree' is controlled by the 'max_depth' parameter. This is set to 3 such that each tree will have 2^3 leaves. The rate at which the learning takes place is controlled by the 'learning_rate' parameter. This is set to 0.01. The rest of the parameters are set as default.

Table 2. Case studies done for each of the model.

Case study	1	2	3–6
Training data	$Re_\tau = 180$	$Re_\tau = 1000$	—
Testing data	$Re_\tau = 1000$	$Re_\tau = 180$	Synthesized data from $Re_\tau = 1000$

Case study 1: Training data from $Re_\tau = 180$, Testing data from $Re_\tau = 1000$. The model is trained on the data from the WRLES of $Re_\tau = 180$ and their performance tested on the data from WRLES of $Re_\tau = 1000$.

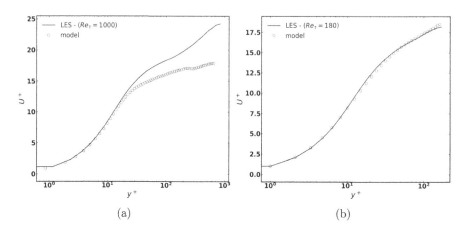

Fig. 1. Model performance: (a) Training data from $Re_\tau = 180$ and Testing data from $Re_\tau = 1000$. (b) Training data from $Re_\tau = 1000$ and Testing data from $Re_\tau = 180$.

Figure 1a shows the mean of the u^+ predicted by the model compared with the results of the WRLES simulations. The velocity profiles are underestimated from the inner region (close to the wall) to the outer region of the boundary layer. This shows the inadequacy of the training data. This is confirmed in the subsequent case study.

Case study 2: Training data from $Re_\tau = 1000$, Testing data from $Re_\tau = 180$. For this test case, the model is trained on the data from the flow case of $Re_\tau = 1000$ and their performance is evaluated data from $Re_\tau = 180$. The results of the test are shown in Figs. 1b. It is observed that the mean u^+ from the predictions by the model follows quite well the results of the LES simulation throughout the boundary layer.

Case Studies 3 to 6: Tests on Synthetic Data. The performance of the model from case study 2 is evaluated on four sets of synthetic data. Figure 2 shows the mean u^+ generated by the predictions by the model when tested on the modified and scaled data sets. The results are compared to the mean velocity profiles of the corresponding data sets. When the height of the channel is increased (assuming the Reynolds number of the flow remains unchanged), the model captures the mean velocity profile as shown in Figs. 2a and 2b. Similar observations (Figs. 2c and 2d) are made when the viscosity is modified and the data set scaled accordingly. The capability of the model to extrapolate to a higher Re_τ flow will be comprehensively done in the a posteriori tests in Sect. 3.

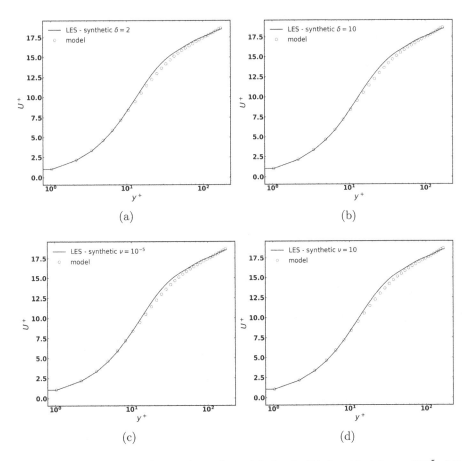

Fig. 2. Test of model on the synthetic data. (a) $\delta = 2$ (b) $\delta = 10$ (c) $\nu = 10^{-5}$ (d) $\nu = 10$

2.4   Model Integration

The trained model is integrated on Alya using a wrapper that communicates between Alya and XGBoost. At each time step, instantaneous velocity from the boundary layer is communicated to the model through the wrapper. The model in exchange gives u^+ corresponding to each of the instantaneous velocities, from which the wall-stresses(τ_ω) are computed; the wall-stresses act as the boundary condition for LES. A schematic of this data exchange is shown in Fig. 3.

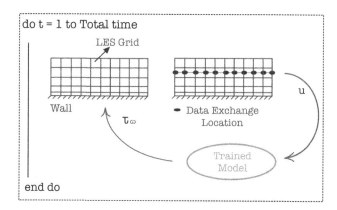

Fig. 3. Schematic showing the data exchange from CFD framework and the machine-learning based wall model

3   Results and Discussion

The performance of the ML-based wall model(MLWM) is evaluated a posteriori on two cases: a) Turbulent channel flow of $Re_\tau = 2005$ and b) Flow over a wall-mounted hump. It is observed that good results a priori need not always guarantee good results a-posteriori [40–42]. The first case is to guarantee that the model works a posteriori. The second case will test the model's performance on complex geometries and strong non-equilibrium conditions. Details of the cases are discussed below:

3.1   Turbulent Channel Flow

The computational domain for the case is $6\pi\delta \times 2\delta \times \times 2\pi\delta$ in the stream-wise, wall-normal and span-wise directions respectively. Three different meshes were used to produce converged results. All the meshes are uniform in the stream-wise, wall-normal, and span-wise directions. Details of the meshes are given in Table 3. Periodic boundary conditions are applied in the stream-wise and span-wise directions, while a no-penetration condition is imposed on the walls as the no-slip condition is no longer valid because of the larger grid size close to the

Table 3. Details of the meshes used for the simulation of the Turbulent channel flow, $Re_\tau = 2005$. N_x, N_y and N_z represent the number of elements in the stream-wise, wall-normal and span-wise directions respectively.

	size($N_x \times N_y \times N_z$)	Δx^+	Δy^+	Δz^+
M1	$64 \times 64 \times 64$	≈ 591	≈ 63	≈ 196
M2	$128 \times 96 \times 96$	≈ 295	≈ 42	≈ 131
M3	$256 \times 128 \times 128$	≈ 147	≈ 31	≈ 98

wall. A stream-wise constant pressure gradient drives flow, and the Vreman [37] SGS model is used for turbulence closure. LES velocity from the third-grid point and the corresponding wall-distance is used to compute Re^*. This is consistent with the direction of LES inputs for wall models as explained in [43]. The results are averaged for 20 flow-through times, where one flow-through time is the time taken by the center-line stream-wise velocity to cover the domain length. Subsequently, spatial averaging is also done and normalized with the friction velocity of the flow.

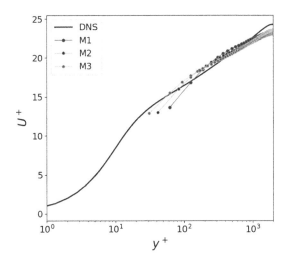

Fig. 4. Mean stream-wise velocity profiles for M1, M2 and M3 compare with DNS.

Numerical Results. Figure 4 shows the mean-stream velocity for M1, M2, and M3 compared with the results from Direct Numeric Simulation(DNS) [44]. The mean-stream velocity profile tends to approach the DNS as the mesh density increases. For all the simulations, the error in u_τ predicted by the model is less than 0.5%. This ability of the model to extrapolate to higher Re_τ channel-flows shows that the model has learned the LoW without explicitly giving any information about LoW as input features. Now the performance of the model is compared with that of the algebraic wall model, EQWM. The mesh used for the simulations is M3. The results are shown in Fig. 5. The mean-stream velocity profiles and the mean fluctuations for both models are very close to each other. This indicates that our non-parametric model trained with the data works well a posteriori and performs as acceptable as a typical EQWM.

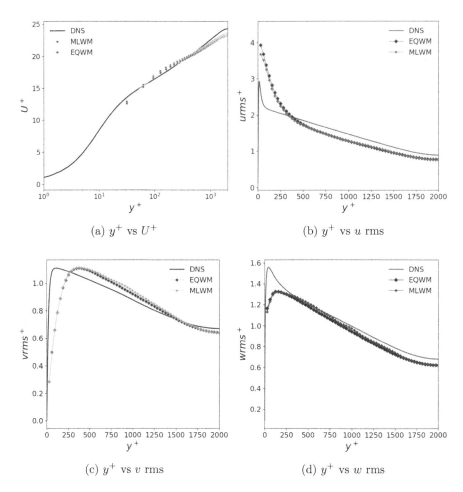

(a) y^+ vs U^+ (b) y^+ vs u rms

(c) y^+ vs v rms   (d) y^+ vs w rms

Fig. 5. Comparison of the model with an algebraic equilibrium law based wall model: (a) shows the Mean stream-wise velocity and (b), (c), (d) show the mean fluctuations.

3.2   Wall-Mounted Hump

In this test, the model is used in the simulation of the flow over a wall-mounted hump. This case is considered a benchmark case to test turbulence models as it involves separation, reattachment, and recovery of the boundary layer, which are the hallmarks of many industrial flows. The geometry is defined following the guidelines of the NASA CFDVAL2004 workshop [45], and the inflow config-uration is based on the work done by Park [46]. The results are compared with the experimental data of Greenblatt et.al. [47]. The performance of the model is also evaluated by comparing the results with that of the EQWM [33].

The computational domain is $4.64c$, $0.909c$ and $0.3c$ in the stream-wise, normal and span-wise directions respectively, where c is the chord-length of the hump. The hump leading edge is set at $x/c = 0$ so that inlet and outlet planes are at $x/c = -2.14$ and $x/c = 2.5$ respectively. In order to account for the effects of the end-plates used in the experiment, the top wall of the domain has a contour from $x/c = -0.5$ to $x/c = 1.5$ as shown in Fig. 6.

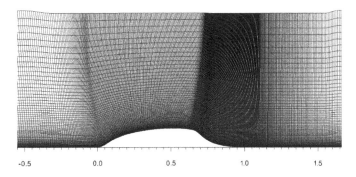

Fig. 6. Computational mesh around the hump. The contour between x/c = −0.5 and x/c = 1.5 is visible

The simulations were conducted on two different grids. The coarse mesh (G1) consists of approximately 3.1 million linear elements, with $742 \times 70 \times 60$ elements in the stream-wise, normal and span-wise directions, respectively. The fine mesh (G2) consists of approximately 8 million linear elements with $900 \times 110 \times 80$ elements in the stream-wise, wall-normal, and span-wise directions, respectively. Figure 7 shows the grid spacing in wall units between $x/c = -0.5$ $x/c = 2.0$. G2 has more refinement in the tangential directions compared to G1. In the normal direction, the mesh growth rate is changed from 1.06 in G1 to 1.03. However, the Δy^+ is maintained the same. The Reynolds number of the flow is $Re = 936000$, based on the hump chord length, c, and the free stream velocity, U_∞ at the inlet. Periodic boundary conditions are imposed on the span-wise direction, while a slip boundary condition is applied at the top boundary. At the bottom wall where the wall stress is predicted, a no-penetration condition is imposed. Vreman [37] SGS model is used for turbulence closure, and synthetic turbulence as described in [48] generated as inflow data such that realistic turbulence evolves before the flow reaches the hump. The MLWM is fed using instantaneous LES data at 12.5% of the boundary layer thickness.

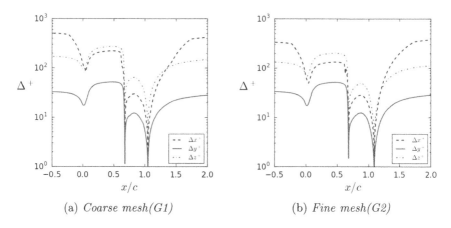

(a) *Coarse mesh(G1)*   (b) *Fine mesh(G2)*

Fig. 7. Grid spacing in wall units for (a) G1 and (b) G2 between x/c = −0.5 and x/c = 2.0.

Numerical Results. Figure 8 shows the Skin friction(C_f) and Pressure coefficients (C_p) for the meshes G1 and G2. The results from both simulations are close to each other except at the re-circulation region. The effect of mesh refinement is reflected in the prediction of C_p. Both simulations fail to capture the primary suction peak before the re-circulation bubble and the secondary suction peak within the bubble, although G2 is qualitatively better.

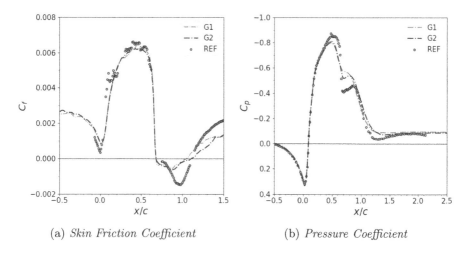

(a) *Skin Friction Coefficient*   (b) *Pressure Coefficient*

Fig. 8. Skin friction and Pressure Coefficients for G1 and G2 compared with experimental results.

Figures 9a and 9b show the comparison of the Skin friction and Pressure coefficients obtained from the mesh G2(MLWM) with that of an EQWM. There are only minor differences in the prediction of C_f by both the models. Both models fail at the re-circulation region. Further, the mean-stream velocity profiles and the Reynolds stresses at the re-circulation region predicted by the two models are also compared in Fig. 10. The profiles compared are obtained from the mesh G1, although similar behavior is observed for G2. The momentum recovery predicted by both models is very close to the experimental data. The percentage error in the re-attachment location is within 5% (cf. Table 4), and it comes down to less than 1% for the fine mesh. The models also agree with each other on the prediction of the Reynolds stresses showing the model's effectiveness on complex flow problems.

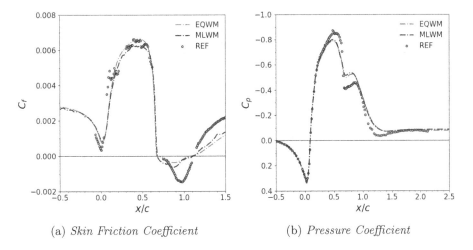

(a) Skin Friction Coefficient   (b) Pressure Coefficient

Fig. 9. Skin friction and pressure coefficients using the machine learning wall model (MLWM) and algebraic wall model (EQWM) compared with experimental results.

Table 4. Details of the re-circulation bubble for MLWM and EQWM on G1. $x/c|_{sep}$ is the location of separtion and $x/c|_{reatt}$ is the location of reattachment. $error|x_{reatt}$ is the percentage error in the location of reattachment.

	Mesh	$/x/c|_{sep}$	$x/c|_{reatt}$	Bubble length	$Error|x_{reatt}$
Experiment [47]	-	∼ 0.665	∼ 1.1	∼ 0.435	-
EQWM	G1	0.67	1.05	0.38	4.5%
MLWM	G1	0.68	1.05	0.37	4.5%

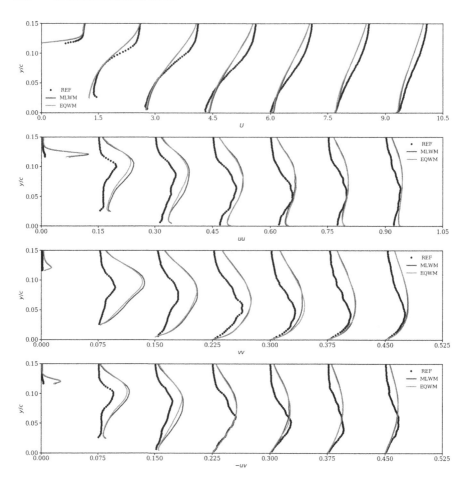

Fig. 10. Mean stream-wise velocity and Reynolds Stress at stream-wise positions: x/c = {0.65, 0.8, 0.9, 1.0, 1.1, 1.2, 1.3}. The profiles are respectively shifted by $\Delta = 1.5$, $\Delta = 0.15$, $\Delta = 0.075$ and $\Delta = 0.075$ units.

4   Conclusions

In this study, a non-parametric machine learning method(XGBoost) based wall model is presented. The model is trained to learn the boundary layer from a channel flow. For training, the data from a wall-resolved LES of channel flow $Re_\tau = 1000$ is used. The performance of the model is evaluated by testing the model a posteriori on the turbulent channel flow $Re_\tau = 2005$ and on the flow over a wall-mounted hump. Promising results were obtained compared with an algebraic equilibrium wall model, thus proving our methodology of data-based model development. The next step is to apply this proven methodology to improve the ML model to perform better in non-equilibrium flows, thus enabling the model's applicability in actual industrial flows.

Acknowledgment. SR acknowledges the financial support by the Ministerio de Ciencia y Innovación y Universidades, for the grant, Ayudas para contratos predoctorales para la formación de doctores(Ref: BES-2017-081982). OL has been partially supported by a Ramon y Cajal postdoctoral contract (Ref: RYC2018-025949-I). We also acknowledge the Barcelona Supercomputing Center for awarding us access to the MareNostrum IV machine based in Barcelona, Spain.

References

1. Choi, H., Moin, P.: Grid-point requirements for large eddy simulation: Chapman's estimates revisited. Phys. Fluids **24**(1), 011702 (2012)
2. Calafell, J., Trias, F.X., Lehmkuhl, O., Oliva, A.: A time-average filtering technique to improve the efficiency of two-layer wall models for large eddy simulation in complex geometries. Comput. Fluids **188**, 44–59 (2019)
3. Piomelli, U.: Wall-layer models for large-eddy simulations. Progr. Aerospace Sci. **44**(6), 437–446 (2008). https://doi.org/10.1016/j.paerosci.2008.06.001. www.sciencedirect.com/science/article/pii/S037604210800047X. Large Eddy Simulation-Current Capabilities and Areas of Needed Research
4. Piomelli, U., Balaras, E.: Wall-layer models for large-eddy simulations. Annual review of fluid mechanics **34**(1), 349–374 (2002)
5. Larsson, J., Kawai, S., Bodart, J., Bermejo-Moreno, I.: Large eddy simulation with modeled wall-stress: recent progress and future directions. Mech. Eng. Rev. **3**(1), 15–00418 (2016). https://doi.org/10.1299/mer.15-00418
6. Bose, S.T., Park, G.I.: Wall-modeled large-eddy simulation for complex turbulent flows. Ann. Rev. Fluid Mech. **50**(1), 535–561 (2018). https://doi.org/10.1146/annurev-fluid-122316-045241
7. Cheng, W., Pullin, D.I., Samtaney, R., Zhang, W., Gao, W.: Large-eddy simulation of flow over a cylinder with re_D from 3.9×10^3 to 8.5×10^5?: a skin-friction perspective. J. Fluid Mech. **820**, 121–158 (2017)
8. Larsson, J., Laurence, S., Bermejo-Moreno, I., Bodart, J., Karl, S., Vicquelin, R.: Incipient thermal choking and stable shock-train formation in the heat-release region of a scramjet combustor. Part II Combust. Flame **162**, 907–920 (2015). Large eddy simulations
9. Iyer, P.S., Park, G.I., Malik, M.R.: Application of wall-modeled LES to turbulent separated flows. In: APS Division of Fluid Dynamics Meeting Abstracts, APS Meeting Abstracts, p. G33.004, November 2016
10. Yang, X.I.A., Urzay, J., Bose, S., Moin, P.: Aerodynamic heating in wall-modeled large-eddy simulation of high-speed flows. AIAA J. **56**(2), 731–742 (2018)
11. Yang, X.I.A., Urzay, J., Moin, P.: Heat-transfer rates in equilibrium-wall-modeled les of supersonic turbulent flows. In: Annual Research Briefs, Center for Turbulence Research, pp. 3–15. Stanford University (2016)
12. Slotnick, J., et al.: CFD vision 2030 study: a path to revolutionary computational aerosciences (2014)
13. Milano, M., Koumoutsakos, P.: Neural network modeling for near wall turbulent flow. J. Comput. Phys. **182**(1), 1–26 (2002)
14. Tracey, B., Duraisamy, K., Alonso, J.: Application of supervised learning to quantify uncertainties in turbulence and combustion modeling. https://arc.aiaa.org/doi/abs/10.2514/6.2013-259

15. Tracey, B.D., Duraisamy, K., Alonso, J.J.: A machine learning strategy to assist turbulence model development. In: 53rd AIAA Aerospace Sciences Meeting, p. 1287 (2015)
16. Duraisamy, K., Zhang, Z.J., Singh, A.P.: New approaches in turbulence and transition modeling using data-driven techniques. In: 53rd AIAA Aerospace Sciences Meeting, p. 1284, (2015)
17. Ling, J., Kurzawski, A., Templeton, J.: Reynolds averaged turbulence modelling using deep neural networks with embedded invariance. J. Fluid Mech. **807**, 155–166 (2016). https://doi.org/10.1017/jfm.2016.615
18. Jin-Long, W., Wang, J.-X., Xiao, H.: A Bayesian calibration-prediction method for reducing model-form uncertainties with application in rans simulations. Flow Turbul. Combust. **97**(3), 761–786 (2016)
19. Wang, J.-X., Jin-Long, W., Xiao, H.: Physics-informed machine learning approach for reconstructing Reynolds stress modeling discrepancies based on DNS data. Phys. Rev. Fluids **2**(3), 034603 (2017)
20. Jin-Long, W., Xiao, H., Paterson, E.: Physics-informed machine learning approach for augmenting turbulence models: a comprehensive framework. Phys. Rev. Fluids **3**(7), 074602 (2018)
21. King, R.N., Hamlington, P.E., Dahm, W.J.A.: Autonomic closure for turbulence simulations. Phys. Rev. E **93**(3), 031301 (2016)
22. Gamahara, M., Hattori, Y.: Searching for turbulence models by artificial neural network. Phys. Rev. Fluids **2**(5), 054604 (2017)
23. Maulik, R., San, O.: A neural network approach for the blind deconvolution of turbulent flows (2017). arXiv preprint: arXiv:1706.00912
24. Vollant, A., Balarac, G., Corre, C.: Subgrid-scale scalar flux modelling based on optimal estimation theory and machine-learning procedures. J. Turbul. **18**(9), 854–878 (2017)
25. Zhang, Z.J., Duraisamy, K.: Machine learning methods for data-driven turbulence modeling. In: 22nd AIAA Computational Fluid Dynamics Conference, p. 2460 (2015)
26. Ma, M., Jiacai, L., Tryggvason, G.: Using statistical learning to close two-fluid multiphase flow equations for a simple bubbly system. Phys. Fluids **27**(9), 092101 (2015)
27. Ma, M., Jiacai, L., Tryggvason, G.: Using statistical learning to close two-fluid multiphase flow equations for bubbly flows in vertical channels. Int. J. Multiphase Flow **85**, 336–347 (2016)
28. Duraisamy, K., Iaccarino, G., Xiao, H.: Turbulence modeling in the age of data. Ann. Rev. Fluid Mech. **51**, 357–377 (2019)
29. Brunton, S.L., Noack, B.R., Koumoutsakos, P.: Machine learning for fluid mechanics. Ann. Rev. Fluid Mech. **52**(1), 477–508 (2020)
30. Yang, X.I.A., Zafar, S., Wang, J.-X., Xiao, H.: Predictive large-eddy-simulation wall modeling via physics-informed neural networks. Phys. Rev. Fluids **4**, 034602 (2019)
31. Lozano-Durán, A., Bae, H.J.: Self-critical machine-learning wall-modeled les for external aerodynamics (2020). arXiv preprint arXiv:2012.10005
32. Chen, T., Guestrin, C.: Xgboost. In: Proceedings of the 22nd ACM SIGKDD International Conference on Knowledge Discovery and Data Mining, August 2016. https://doi.org/10.1145/2939672.2939785
33. Owen, H., et al.: Wall-modeled large-eddy simulation in a finite element framework. Int. J. Numer. Methods Fluids. **92**, 20–37 (2019). https://doi.org/10.1002/fld.4770

34. Friedman, J.H.: Stochastic gradient boosting. Comput. Statist. Data Anal. **38**(4), 367–378 (2002)
35. Marusic, I., Monty, J.P., Hultmark, M., Smits, A.J.: On the logarithmic region in wall turbulence. J. Fluid Mech. **716**, R3 (2013). https://doi.org/10.1017/jfm.2012. 511
36. Vazquez, M., et al.: Alya: multiphysics engineering simulation towards exascale. J. Comput. Sci. **14**, 15–27 (2016). https://doi.org/10.1016/j.jocs.2015.12.007. ISSN 1877-7503. www.sciencedirect.com/science/article/pii/S1877750315300521. The Route to Exascale: Novel Mathematical Methods, Scalable Algorithms and Computational Science Skills
37. Vreman, A.W.: An eddy-viscosity subgrid-scale model for turbulent shear flow: algebraic theory and applications. Phys. Fluids **16**(10), 3670–3681 (2004)
38. Lehmkuhl, O., Piomelli, U., Houzeaux, G.: On the extension of the integral length-scale approximation model to complex geometries. Int. J. Heat Fluid Flow **78**, 108422 (2019)
39. Pedregosa, F., et al.: Scikit-learn: machine learning in Python. J. Mach. Learn. Res. **12**, 2825–2830 (2011)
40. Poroseva, S.V., Colmenares, J.D.F., Murman, S.M.: On the accuracy of RANs simulations with DNS data. Phys. Fluids **28**(11), 115102 (2016)
41. Thompson, R.L., Sampaio, L.E.B., de Bragança Alves, F.A.V., Thais, L., Mompean, G.: A methodology to evaluate statistical errors in DNS data of plane channel flows. Comput. Fluids **130**, 1–7 (2016)
42. Jinlong, W., Xiao, H., Sun, R., Wang, Q.: Reynolds-averaged Navier-stokes equations with explicit data-driven Reynolds stress closure can be ill-conditioned. J. Fluid Mech. **869**, 553–586 (2019)
43. Kawai, S., Larsson, J.: Wall-modeling in large eddy simulation: length scales, grid resolution, and accuracy. Phys. Fluids **24**(1), 015105 (2012)
44. Hoyas, S., Jiménez, J.: Scaling of the velocity fluctuations in turbulent channels up to re τ= 2003. Phys. fluids **18**(1), 011702 (2006)
45. Rumsey, C.L., Gatski, T.B., Sellers, W.L., Vasta, V.N., Viken, S.A.: Summary of the 2004 computational fluid dynamics validation workshop on synthetic jets. AIAA J. **44**(2), 194–207 (2006)
46. Park, G.I.: Wall-modeled large-eddy simulation of a separated flow over the NASA wall-mounted hump by (2015)
47. Naughton, J.W., Viken, S., Greenblatt, D.: Skin friction measurements on the NASA hump model. AIAA J. **44**(6), 1255–1265 (2006)
48. Kempf, A., Klein, M., Janicka, J.: Efficient generation of initial-and inflow-conditions for transient turbulent flows in arbitrary geometries. Flow Turbul. Combust. **74**(1), 67–84 (2005)

Nonlinear Mode Decomposition and Reduced-Order Modeling for Three-Dimensional Cylinder Flow by Distributed Learning on Fugaku

Kazuto Ando[1]([✉]) [iD], Keiji Onishi[1] [iD], Rahul Bale[1] [iD], Makoto Tsubokura[1,2], Akiyoshi Kuroda[1] [iD], and Kazuo Minami[1]

[1] RIKEN Center for Computational Science (R-CCS), Kobe, Japan
kazuto.ando@riken.jp
[2] Kobe University, Kobe, Japan

Abstract. Nonlinear modes of the three-dimensional flow field around a cylinder were extracted by distributed learning on Fugaku. Mode decomposition is an approach used to decompose flow fields into physically important flow structures known as modes. In this study, convolutional neural network-based mode decomposition was applied to the three-dimensional flow field. However, because this process is costly in terms of calculation and memory usage for even a small flow field problem, the enormous computational and memory resources of the supercomputer Fugaku were employed. A hybrid parallelism method combining the distribution of network structure (model parallelism) and the input data (data parallelism) using up to 10,500 nodes on Fugaku was employed for learning. Further, we constructed a reduced-order model to predict the time evolution of latent vector, using the long short-term memory networks. Finally, we compared the reproduced flow field of the model with that of the original full-order model. In addition, we evaluated the execution performance of the learning process. Using a single core memory group, the whole learning process indicates a value of 129.50 GFLOPS being achieved, 7.57% of the single-precision floating-point arithmetic peak performance. Notably, the convolution calculation for backward-propagation achieved 1103.09 GFLOPS, which is 65.39% of the peak. Furthermore, with the weak scaling test, the whole learning process indicates 72.9% with 25,250 nodes (1,212,000 cores) relative to 750 nodes, the sustained performance is 7.8 PFLOPS. In particular, the convolution calculation for backward-propagation indicates a result of 113 PFLOPS (66.2% of the peak performance).

Keywords: Distributed learning · Supercomputer Fugaku · Mode decomposition · Three-dimensional flow field · Reduced-order model · Long short-term memory networks (LSTMs) · Computational fluid dynamics (CFD)

© Springer Nature Switzerland AG 2021
H. Jagode et al. (Eds.): ISC High Performance 2021 Workshops, LNCS 12761, pp. 122–137, 2021.
https://doi.org/10.1007/978-3-030-90539-2_8

1 Introduction

1.1 Mode Decomposition Method

Due to the current advancements in the power of the computational environment, the output data of computational fluid dynamics (CFD) simulations is increasing. Data handling is more laborious in terms of data analysis, moving, and storage. As the method of extracting significant structures representing the physical system, various mode decomposition methods are proposed, such as proper orthogonal decomposition (POD), dynamic mode decomposition (DMD), Koopman analysis, global linear stability analysis, and Resolvent analysis [1]. POD, in particular, is the most popular method owing to its conceptual simplicity [1–7]. The POD mode (which is represented as a basis in linear space) can be obtained as the eigenvector of a covariance matrix constructed by the product of data vectors. Using the mode extracted by POD, we can project the governing equation into subspace spanned by the POD basis (called Galerkin Projection) and construct a reduced-order model (ROM) [4, 8]. In this case, the ROM is represented as the system of ordinary differential equations (ODEs) that describe the time evolution of the variables in the reduced-order space (called the latent vector) [8–10]. For instance, the two-dimensional (2D) flow field around a circular cylinder can be represented with just a few modes, which means that the original flow field can be reconstructed almost perfectly using the ROM of Navier–Stokes equations, which is comprised of a few ODEs. However, this type of ROM, which represents a linear subspace solution, has insufficient prediction accuracy for advection-dominated flows with high Reynolds numbers [11].

1.2 Mode Decomposition with Convolutional Neural Networks (CNNs)

Murata et al. [12] conducted nonlinear mode decomposition for the 2D flow field around a circular cylinder using convolutional neural networks (CNNs). They found that in situations where two modes are used, the reconstruction accuracy is comparable to the six modes extracted by the traditional POD method. This superiority of the neural network is due to its nonlinearity, that is, the conversion between the flow field and the latent vector is represented as a nonlinear function due to containing the nonlinear activation function (e.g., tanh). Meanwhile, Hasegawa et al. [13] demonstrated a ROM utilizing long short-term memory (LSTM) networks [14] which predicts the time evolution of the latent vector for the 2D flow around various shapes of the bluff body using the modes extracted with CNNs. It is naturally conceivable to extend these methods to a three-dimensional (3D) flow field. However, this approach poses two significant challenges. First, CNNs impose huge computational costs when converging the loss value in the learning process. Second, massive memory is required because the network inputs and outputs are 3D grid data points themselves. Therefore, when we apply the mode decomposition to 3D flow field data with CNNs, the distributed learning on the massively parallel distributed system is a realistic option.

Studies have been conducted previously on distributed learning using massively parallel distributed systems. For example, Patton et al. investigated deep learning for electron microscopy using almost the full resources of the Summit supercomputer [15], where they achieved 152 PFLOPS and almost perfect weak scaling up to 4,200 nodes

[16]. Kurth et al. (Gordon Bell winner in SC18) achieved more than 1 ExaFLOPS of AI computing on the same supercomputer system, with a fairly well-established weak scaling value (90.7% in 27,360 GPUs) [17]. Yang et al. reported the performance of a physics-informed generative adversarial network (GAN) on Summit in which their calculations scaled up to 4,584 nodes (27,500 GPUs) with 93.1% weak scaling and 1.2 ExaFLOPS with half-precision [18]. Jia et al. were honored with the Gordon Bell prize in SC20 with the ab initio molecular dynamics simulation enhanced with machine learning [19]. They achieved 91 PFLOPS in double-precision and 162/275 PFLOPS in mixed-single/half-precision on Summit.

Note that all these studies were executed on the GPU-based system. However, to the best of our knowledge, this is the first study that examines the performance and accuracy of the distributed learning for a practical problem executed on a massively parallel CPU(Arm)-based system.

1.3 Supercomputer Fugaku

The supercomputer Fugaku was developed by the RIKEN Center for Computational Science in Kobe, Japan [20, 21]. At the time of writing, this system is the fastest supercomputer in the world, that is, this system came first place in the TOP500 list, published in SC20 [22]. Fugaku has been ranked number one in four benchmarks, including TOP500 for the two consecutive terms, in June and November 2020 [23].

Fugaku is equipped with a single Arm-based central processing unit (CPU) named A64FX™, developed by Fujitsu. The A64FX™ CPU supports an instruction set architecture named Armv8.2-A SVE. SVE refers to Stream Vector Extension and is an extension of the instruction set to execute 512-bit vector instructions.

The A64FX™ is equipped with four core memory groups (CMGs), equivalent to non-uniform memory access (NUMA) nodes, and each CMG has 12 computational cores. Each computational core runs at 2.0 GHz in normal mode and 2.2 GHz in boost mode. The peak arithmetic performance of the CPU when operating in normal mode is 3.072 TFLOPS for double-precision, 6.144 TFLOPS for single-precision, and 12.288 TFLOPS for half-precision. In boost mode, these increase to 3.3792 TFLOPS, 6.7584 TFLOPS, and 13.5168 TFLOPS, respectively.

The A64FX™ also has a 64 KiB 4-way L1 cache in each core and an 8 MiB, 16-way L2 cache shared between CMGs. Each CMG has 8 GiB of HBM2 memory and a total node throughput of 1024 GB/s. Double-precision matrix-matrix multiplication (DGEMM) operations achieve over 90%. efficiency. The Stream Triad performance is 830 + GB/s [24]. The Fugaku nodes are connected with TofuD interconnects. The bandwidth is 6.8 GB/sec per link, and there are six links. As a result, the injection bandwidth is 40.8 GB/sec per node. The system has 158,976 nodes and 7,630,848 cores. The theoretical full system peak performance is 488 PFLOPS in normal mode and 537 PFLOPS in boost mode [25].

To use the abundant computational resources of Fugaku for AI calculations, RIKEN and Fujitsu are currently working to enable high-performance machine learning calculations. It is necessary to optimize the libraries, called from each AI framework, to accelerate the machine learning calculations. The OneAPI Deep Neural Network Library (oneDNN) [26] is currently being optimized for the A64FX™ CPU [27] and will incorporate a high-performance dedicated linear arithmetic library (BLAS). In this study, the PyTorch [28] was used that is ported to Fugaku.

2 Methods

2.1 Flow Field Simulation

We used a complex unified simulation framework 'CUBE' [29] to produce the flow field snapshots used as training data. CUBE is designed to solve industrial flow problems, such as vehicle aerodynamics, based on the hierarchical Cartesian mesh. It was developed by the Complex Phenomena Unified Simulation Research Team in RIKEN R-CCS. CUBE has been executed on various parallel systems such as Intel Xeon, Xeon Phi clusters, and K computer [30]. CUBE can simulate the flow fields around complex geometries, such as car bodies, effectively using the building cube method (BCM) and the immersed boundary method (IBM) [31–34]. In this study, the incompressible fluid solver of CUBE was used. The governing equations are as follows:

$$\rho\left(\frac{\partial u}{\partial t} + (u \cdot \nabla)u\right) = -\nabla p + \mu \nabla^2 u, \tag{1}$$

$$\rho \nabla \cdot u = 0 \tag{2}$$

where $u, p, \rho,$ and μ are the flow velocity, pressure, density, and viscosity, respectively. The simulation settings for generating the flow field snapshots are described in Table 1. This simulation took four days using 60 Intel Xeon Gold 6148 CPUs (1,200 cores at 2.4 GHz)[1]. Although the flow field simulation is conducted using double-precision floating-point calculations, the output data is converted to single-precision in advance to facilitate its use as input to the neural network[2].

2.2 Mode Decomposition

In the following subsections, the details of the mode decomposition method and how to apply a neural network to this problem are described.

Proper Orthogonal Decomposition (POD). The idea behind POD is that n-dimensional data is represented in r-dimensional space ($R \ll n$) such that the basis can adequately represent (i.e., maximize the variance of) the data, as shown in Fig. 1.

POD can be solved as follows [7]. First, represent n-dimensional data $x(t)$ in r-dimensional space using r bases $\{\varphi_k\}_{k=1}^{r}$ and put it back to n-dimensional space.

$$\widetilde{P} x = \sum_{k=1}^{r} \widetilde{\varphi}_k \widetilde{\varphi}_k^T x \tag{3}$$

---

[1] At the time of this calculation, Fugaku was not yet in operation.

[2] Single-precision is sufficient for precise learning and can increase FLOPS by utilizing the SIMD register.

Table 1. Simulation settings.

Parameter	Value
Computational domain	40D[a] × 20D × 2.5D
Cell size	0.026D
Number of cells	1,536 × 768 × 24
Reynolds number	1,000
Time step size	5.0×10^{-3} s
Number of time steps	630,000
Output frequency	Every 50 step (0.25 s.)

D (=1) is the circular cylinder diameter.

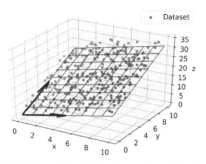

Fig. 1. The idea behind POD. The original 3D data points (blue dots) can be approximately represented on the 2D plane spanned by the two basis vectors (black arrows).

Next, the bases $\{\varphi_k\}_{k=1}^{r}$ are obtained by solving the optimization problem to minimize the time integration of the L_2 norm of the error between original and reconstructed data.

$$\{\varphi_k\}_{k=1}^{r} = \operatorname{argmin} \int_{t_{min}}^{t_{max}} \left\| x(t) - \widetilde{P} \, x(t) \right\|^2 dt \tag{4}$$

In practice, solve the equivalent eigenvalue problem for the covariance matrix R, instead.

$$R = \int_{t_{min}}^{t_{max}} x(t)x^{T}(t)dt \in \mathbb{R}^{n \times n} \tag{5}$$

$$R\varphi_k = \lambda\varphi_k \tag{6}$$

Nonlinear Mode Decomposition with CNN. Murata et al. [12] constructed the neural network, named the mode decomposing convolutional neural network autoencoder (MD-CNN-AE), shown in Fig. 2. This network is based on the structure of the autoencoder [35]. they solved the previously described optimization problem (Eq. (4)) using a neural network. MD-CNN-AE has the same structure as pod; however, with the use of a nonlinear activation function introduces nonlinearity (sigmoid, tanh, ReLU, and softsign).

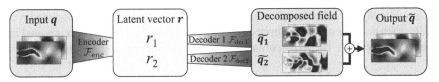

Fig. 2. Schematic of MD-CNN-AE (adapted from [12]).

In this study, the MD-CNN-AE was extended to handle 3D flow field data. Table 2 shows the network structure used in this study. The network consists of two parts, an encoder, and a decoder.

Table 2. Network structure of the 3D extension of the MD-CNN-AE.

Encoder layer	Data size of encoder (X, Y, Z, channel)	Decoder layer	Data size of decoder (X, Y, Z, channel)
Input	(384, 192, 24, 3)	1st Value	(1, 1, 1, 1)
1st 3D convolution	(384, 192, 24, 16)	Fully connected	(6, 3, 3, 4)
1st 3D maxpooling	(192, 96, 12, 16)	1st 3D upsampling	(12, 6, 3, 4)
2nd 3D convolution	(192, 96, 12, 8)	1st 3D convolution	(12, 6, 3, 4)
2nd 3D maxpooling	(96, 48, 6, 8)	2nd 3D upsampling	(24, 12, 3, 4)
3rd 3D convolution	(96, 48, 6, 8)	2nd 3D convolution	(24, 12, 3, 8)
3rd 3D maxpooling	(48, 24, 3, 8)	3rd 3D upsampling	(48, 24, 3, 8)
4th 3D convolution	(48, 24, 3, 8)	3rd 3D convolution	(48, 24, 3, 8)
4th 3D maxpooling	(24, 12, 3, 8)	4th 3D upsampling	(96, 48, 6, 8)
5th 3D convolution	(24, 12, 3, 4)	4th 3D convolution	(96, 48, 6, 8)
5th 3D maxpooling	(12, 6, 3, 4)	5th 3D upsampling	(192, 96, 12, 8)
6th 3D convolution	(12, 6, 3, 4)	5th 3D convolution	(192, 96, 12, 16)
6th 3D maxpooling	(6, 3, 3, 4)	6th 3D upsampling	(384, 192, 24, 16)
Fully connected	(2^{a}, 1, 1, 1)	6th 3D convolution	(384, 192, 24, 3)

a. Equal to the number of modes

In the encoder, the network first inputs the flow field snapshots. The 3D convolutional layer increases the number of channels and then decreases it to cut the computational cost and memory usage growth. The filter size is $3 \times 3 \times 3$ and the output size does not change as the padding size is 1. The tanh function was used as an activation function in this layer (and the fully connected layer described later). In contrast, the max-pooling layers halve the grid size of the flow field. Then, the grid size was decreased to $6 \times 3 \times 3$, and the number of channels decreases to four, after which they are fed into the fully connected layer. Finally, the data size decreased to the number of modes (e.g., 2). There are as many decoder networks as there are modes. One of the values contained in the output vector of the encoder is input to each decoder network. In contrast to the max-pooling layers in the encoder, the size increases twofold in the upsampling layers. Finally, each decoder network outputs the same sized flow field grid as was inputted into the encoder network. The hyperparameters for the learning process are shown in Table 3.

Table 3. Hyperparameters of the learning process for the mode decomposition.

Parameter	Value	Parameter	Value
Filter size	$3 \times 3 \times 3$	Batch size	100
Pooling size	$2 \times 2 \times 2$	Number of epochs	1,000
Weight initializer	Xavier uniform	Number of training data	10,000
Optimizer	Adam	Ratio of validation data	30%
Learning rate	0.001	Number of test data	2,000

Hybrid Parallelization for Distributed Learning. We implemented the distributed learning scheme for the mode decomposition with a hybrid parallelization method, which combines the distribution of the network structure (model parallelism) and the input data (data parallelism). For model parallelization, the encoder and each decoder part of the network were distributed to each MPI process. In addition, for data parallelization, the input data were distributed to each mpi process group in charge of model parallelization (Fig. 3).

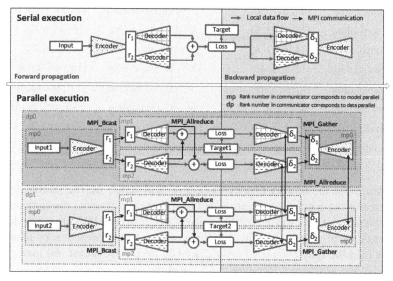

Fig. 3. Schematic of hybrid parallelization for distributed learning. (Example when using two modes)

2.3 Reduced-Order Model with LSTM

We implemented a network that predicts the time variation of the latent vector using long short-term memory networks (LSTMs) [14]. LSTMs are a kind of recursive neural network (RNNs). LSTM recursively inputs its own output, as in a normal RNN, and carefully handles long-term dependencies of the information flow [36]. In this study, the internal procedure of LSTM is formulated as

$$i_t = \sigma\left(W_{ai}a_t + b_{ii} + W_{\tilde{a}i}\tilde{a}_t + b_{hi}\right), \tag{7}$$

$$f_t = \sigma\left(W_{af}a_t + b_{if} + W_{\tilde{a}f}\tilde{a}_t + b_{hf}\right), \tag{8}$$

$$\tilde{c}_t = \tanh\left(W_{a\tilde{c}}a_t + b_{ig} + W_{\tilde{a}\tilde{c}}\tilde{a}_t + b_{hg}\right), \tag{9}$$

$$o_t = \sigma\left(W_{io}a_t + b_{io} + W_{\tilde{a}o}\tilde{a}_t + b_{ho}\right), \tag{10}$$

$$c_t = f_t \odot c_{t-1} + i_t \odot \tilde{c}_t, \tag{11}$$

$$\tilde{a}_{t+1} = o_t \odot \tanh(c_t), \tag{12}$$

where a_t, W, b, i_t, f_t, $\tilde{c}_t$, o_t, c_t, and $\tilde{a}_{t+1}$ represent a latent vector of current time-step, weight, bias, input gate, forget gate, candidate of the new cell state, output gate, new cell state, predicted latent vector of the next time-step, respectively. The network inputs the latent vector for the past 20 steps and outputs that for the past 19 steps and the following one step (Fig. 4). The entire network consists of the parallel arrangement of LSTMs with a different number of features in the hidden state, with reference to Nakamura et al. [37].

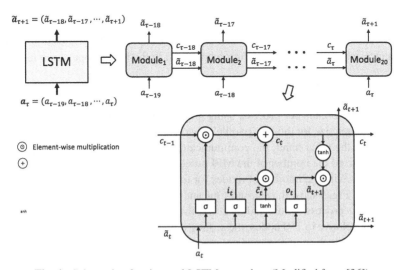

Fig. 4. Schematic of an internal LSTM procedure (Modified from [36]).

3   Results

3.1   Computational Performance

The computational performance of the distributed learning for the mode decomposition of the 3D flow field on Fugaku is described in the following subsections.

Single CMG Performance. In this subsection, the computational performance of the learning process using a single CMG of the A64FX™ of Fugaku is discussed. The sustained performance of the entire learning process was 129.50 GFLOPS in the single-precision calculation, which corresponds to 7.67% relative to the single-precision peak performance of a single CMG. The sustained performance of the entire learning process for one epoch is summarized in Table 4.

Table 4. Computational performance of the single SMG for the learning process.

	Learning process	Convolution
FP performance	129.50 GFLOPS (7.67%[a])	1103.09 GFLOPS (65.39% [a])
Memory bandwidth	10.92 GB/s (4.26% [a])	38.16 GB/s (14.91%[a])
L1D cache miss ratio	2.39% (72.40% [b])	0.34% (7.49% [b])
L2 cache miss ratio	0.67% (17.12% [b])	0.25% (2.92% [b])

a. Ratio of peak performance
b. Demand rate.

The entire learning process can be roughly broken down into forward-propagation, backward-propagation, and weight update; each operation contains some collective communications such as MPI_Bcast, MPI_Gather, and MPI_Allreduce, as shown in Fig. 3. In particular, the convolution operation, the main calculation in the forward- and back-propagation, indicates high calculation performance due to the highly optimized kernel by RIKEN and Fujitsu, as mentioned above. As an example, we show the computational performance achieved by the convolution operation in the back-propagation in Table 4.

Parallel Performance. Next, the weak scaling test results for the learning process using 750–25,250 Fugaku nodes are shown. The measurement job launches four MPI processes and 12 OpenMP threads per process, using 48 computational cores per node. We fixed the communicator size for the data parallelism to 1000, which handles 10,000 snapshots in parallel. On the other hand, the communicator size of the model parallelism can be extended. We fixed the number of the MPI processes for the encoder calculation to one then enlarged it with the number of modes for the decoder calculation.

Table 5 and Fig. 5 show the elapsed-time and FLOPS-based weak scaling test results for the learning process. These indicate that the training cost increased by 19.6% for 25,250 nodes, relative to 750 nodes; the scaling is 72.9%. Although the learning process includes much reduction in communications, the performance degradation is moderate due to the communicator splitting into data parallelism and model parallelism, and the optimized collective communication being tailored for the TofuD interconnect.

Table 6 and Fig. 6 show the weak scaling test results for the convolution operations in the backward-propagation. They demonstrate perfect scaling. The computational
performance is 113 PFLOPS using 25,250 nodes (Fig. 5).

Table 5. Weak scaling test results for the entire learning process.

Number of modes	Number of nodes	Execution time	FLOPS	Scaling
2	750	6.15 s	0.31 PFLOPS	100.0%
20	5,250	6.70 s	1.81 PFLOPS	81.5%
40	10,250	6.83 s	3.43 PFLOPS	79.0%
80	20,250	7.33 s	6.28 PFLOPS	73.3%
100	25,250	7.36 s	7.80 PFLOPS	72.9%

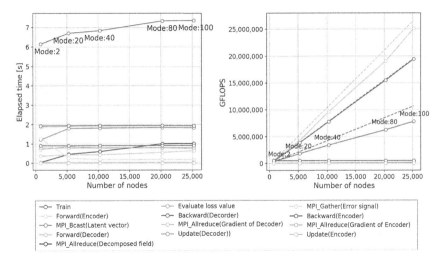

Fig. 5. Weak scaling test results (elapsed-time on the left and FLOPS on the right). The horizontal
axis denotes the number of nodes, and the vertical axes on the left and right denote the elapsed
time and GFLOPS, respectively. The blue, orange, and red lines indicate measured values for
the entire learning process, forward-propagation calculation in the decoder, and back-propagation
calculation in the decoder, respectively.

Table 6. Weak scaling test results for convolution in the back-propagation.

Number of modes	Number of nodes	FLOPS	Scaling
2	750	3.35 PFLOPS	100.0%
20	5,250	23.62 PFLOPS	100.7%
40	10,250	46.14 PFLOPS	100.7%
80	20,250	91.14 PFLOPS	100.7%
100	25,250	113.75 PFLOPS	100.8%

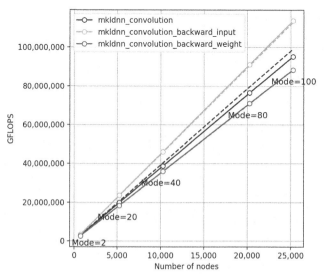

Fig. 6. Weak scaling test results (FLOPS-base). The horizontal axis denotes the number of nodes and the vertical axis the GFLOPS. The blue, right blue, and orange lines indicate measured values for the convolution calculation for the forward-propagation, back-propagation calculating error signal, and back-propagation calculating weight update, respectively (Color figure online).

3.2 Results of ROM Simulation

In this subsection, we show the results of the 3D ROM simulation, conducted using extracted modes with CNN and predicted time series of the latent vector with LSTM.

Flow Field Snapshot. Figure 7 represents the snapshot of the flow field u on the x–y plane at 500 s after starting the simulation. The complicated flow structure of the full-order model (FOM) using CUBE cannot be reproduced with the ROM (when using two or 20 modes).

Full-Order Model   **Reduced-Order Model (2 modes)**   **Reduced-Order Model (20 modes)**

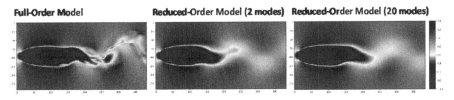

Fig. 7. Snapshot of the flow field u on the x–y plane.

Spatial Distribution of Time-Mean Squared Error. Figure 8 shows the spatial distribution of the time-mean squared error (between the FOM and ROM) of the flow field u on the X-Y plane. The result of rom using two modes has a significant error in the cylinder wake. There is no significant difference between the models based on two and 20 modes. The spatial mean of the time-mean squared error is 1.95×10^{-2} for the two mode model and 1.75×10^{-2} for the 20 mode model.

Reduced-Order Model (2 modes)   **Reduced-Order Model (20 modes)**

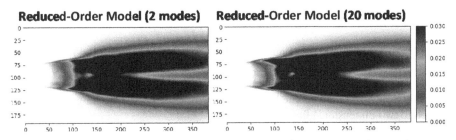

Fig. 8. Spatial distribution of time-mean squared error of flow field u on the x–y plane.

Strouhal Number of Karman Vortex Street. Table 7 shows the strouhal number and period of the Karman vortex street evaluated with the flow field v on the X-Y Plane. The value of the ROM with two modes is closer than that of the 20 modes. we suggest that this result is due to the simple flow field constructed with the two modes having a higher ability to capture two-dimensional oscillation[3].

Table 7. Frequency and Strouhal number of Karman vortex street.

Model	Period	Strouhal number
Full-order model	5.176 s	0.193
Reduced-order model (2 modes)	5.223 s	0.191
Reduced-order model (20 modes)	5.372 s	0.186

---

[3] The first two modes, learned by two and 20 mode models, are not the same because if the number of modes when learning is different, the optimal set of modes to reconstruct the energy of the original field are different.

Visualization of Vortex Structure. Figure 9 Depicts a snapshot of the ISO-surface of the q-criterion (second invariant of the velocity-gradient tensor) at 50 s after starting the simulation. Compared to the FOM, the ROM cannot reproduce a complicated vortex structure in the cylinder wake (in the case of both the two mode and 20 mode models). There is no significant difference between them. This result may indicate that the number of modes chosen, i.e., two or 20, is insufficient to reproduce the FOM's complicated vortex structure.

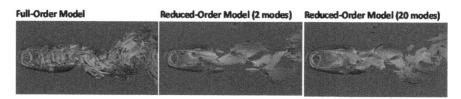

Fig. 9. Iso-surface of the Q-criterion (colored by the velocity magnitude).

Time Average of Flow Field. Figure 10 shows the time-mean of the flow field u at the centerline of the X-Y plane. The reduced-order model using two modes only has a minor deviation from the results of the FOM, the model using 20 modes features greater variation. This result may be due to the ROM with two modes having a greater ability to capture two-dimensional flow field structure.

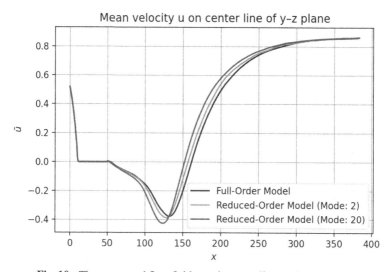

Fig. 10. Time averaged flow field u at the centerline on the y–z plane.

Energy Distribution of Mode. The left side of Fig. 11 represents the energy distribution of each mode obtained by decomposing the flow field of the FOM and ROM with

POD. There is no significant decrease in the energy of the FOM with 40 POD modes. However, there is a significant decrease in the ROM with two modes at a few POD modes. It can be seen that there is a gradual decrease in the ROM with 20 modes.

The right side of Fig. 11 represents the accumulated value of each mode's contribution ratio to the total energy. The FOM reproduces only 60% of the total energy at the number of 40 POD modes. However, the ROM, using two or 20 modes, represents around 90% of the total energy at 3 POD modes. This result indicates that the ROM, using two or 20 modes, cannot sufficiently extract the complicated flow field structure produced with the FOM. Note that 516 POD modes are required to represent 90% of the total energy for the FOM (see inset of the right side of Fig. 11).

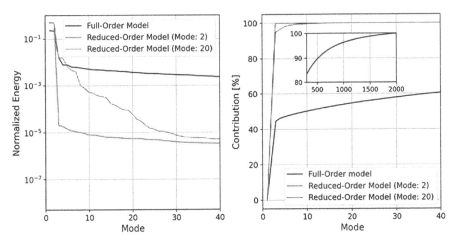

Fig. 11. Energy distribution (on the left) and contribution to the total energy (on the right) of each POD mode.

4 Conclusions

This study implemented a distributed learning scheme for 3D flow field mode decomposition on Fugaku and constructed a reduced-order model with LSTMs. The single CMG performance indicates 129.50 GFLOPS, 7.57% of the single-precision floating-point arithmetic peak performance for the entire learning process, and 1103.09 GFLOPS, which is 65.39% of the peak for the convolution calculation. The weak scaling test indicates 72.9% with 25,250 nodes (1,212,000 cores), and sustained performance is 7.8 PFLOPS for the entire learning process. Notably, the convolution calculation for backward-propagation indicates 113PFLOPS (66.2% of the peak performance). Furthermore, we showed the ROM simulation results and compared them to the FOM. Although the reconstruction accuracy was inadequate, due to the insufficient number of the modes, we will address this issue in future work using a more extensive number of modes, enhancing the large number of nodes on Fugaku and sophisticating the network used for learning.

Acknowledgment. We sincerely appreciate the advice and support of Prof. Koji Fukagata, Mr. Kai Fukami, and Mr. Takaaki Murata of Keio University. This work used computational resources of the supercomputer Fugaku provided by RIKEN.

References

1. Taira, K., et al.: Modal analysis of fluid flows: an overview. AIAA J. **55**(12), 4013–4041 (2017)
2. Jolliffe, I.T.: Principal Component Analysis, Springer Series in Statistics, 2nd edn. Springer, Heidelberg (2002)
3. Lumley, J.L.: The structure of inhomogeneous turbulent flows. In: Yaglom, A.M., Tatarski, V.I. (Eds.) Atmospheric Turbulence and Wave Propagation, pp. 166–178. Nauka (1967)
4. Holmes, P., Lumley, J.L., Berkooz, G., Rowley, C.W.: Turbulence, Coherent Structures, Dynamical Systems and Symmetry, 2nd edn. Cambridge University Press, Cambridge (2012)
5. Chatterjee, A.: An introduction to the proper orthogonal decomposition. Curr. Sci. **78**(7), 808–817 (2000)
6. Berkooz, G., Holmes, P., Lumley, J.L.: The proper orthogonal decomposition in the analysis of turbulent flows. Annu. Rev. Fluid Mech. **25**, 539–575 (1993)
7. Taira, K.: Proper orthogonal decomposition in fluid flow analysis: 1 introduction. Nagare **30**, 115–124 (2011). (in Japanese)
8. Aubry, N., Holmes, P., Lumley, J.L., Stone, E.: The dynamics of coherent structures in the wall region of a turbulent boundary layer. J. Fluid Mech. **192**, 115–173 (1988)
9. Noack, B.R., Morzynski, M., Tadmor, G.: Reduced-Order Modelling for Flow Control. Springer, Heidelberg (2011)
10. Taira, K., et al.: Modal analysis of fluid flows: applications and outlook. AIAA J. **58**(3), 998–1022 (2020)
11. Kim, Y., Choi, Y., Widemann, D., Zohdi, T.: Efficient nonlinear manifold reduced order model (2020). https://arxiv.org/pdf/2011.07727.pdf
12. Murata, T., Fukami, K., Fukagata, K.: Nonlinear mode decomposition with convolutional neural networks for fluid dynamics. J. Fluid Mech. **882**, A13 (2020). https://doi.org/10.1017/jfm.2019.822
13. Hasegawa, K., Fukami, K., Murata, T., Fukagata, K.: Machine-learning-based reduced-order modeling for unsteady flows around bluff bodies of various shapes. Theor. Comput. Fluid Dyn. **34**(4), 367–383 (2020)
14. Hochreiter, S., Schmidhuber, J.: Long short-term memory. Neural Comput. **9**, 1735–1780 (1997)
15. OLCF: Summit system overview (2018). https://www.olcf.ornl.gov/for-users/system-user-guides/summit/system-overview/
16. Patton, R.M., et al.: 167-PFlops deep learning for electron microscopy: from learning physics to atomic manipulation. In: SC18: International Conference for High Performance Computing, Networking, Storage and Analysis, Dallas, TX, USA, pp. 638–648 (2018). https://doi.org/10.1109/SC.2018.00053
17. Kurth, T., et al.: Exascale deep learning for climate analytics. In: Proceedings of the International Conference for High Performance Computing, Networking, Storage, and Analysis, SC 2018, p. 51. IEEE Press, NJ, USA (2018)
18. Yang, L., et al.: Highly-scalable, Physics-Informed GANs for Learning Solutions of Stochastic PDEs. In: 2019 IEEE/ACM Third Workshop on Deep Learning on Supercomputers (DLS), pp. 1–11, November 2019

19. Jia, W., et al.: Pushing the limit of molecular dynamics with ab initio accuracy to 100 million atoms with machine learning. In: 2020 SC20: International Conference for High Performance Computing, Networking, Storage and Analysis (SC), Atlanta, GA, US, pp. 1–14 (2020). https://doi.org/10.1109/SC41405.2020.00009

20. Yoshida, T.: Fujitsu high performance CPU for the post-K computer. Hot Chips **30**, 1–22 (2018)

21. RIKEN Center for Computational Science, Specifications Post-K (Fugaku) Information. https://postk-web.r-ccs.riken.jp/spec.html

22. TOP500.org.: TOP500 Supercomputer Sites (2020)

23. RIKEN Center for Computational Science, Post-K (Fugaku) Information. https://postk-web.r-ccs.riken.jp/perf.html

24. RIKEN: Japan's Fugaku retains title as the world's fastest supercomputer. https://www.riken.jp/en/news_pubs/news/2020/20201117_2/index.html

25. RIKEN Center for Computational Science, Outline of the Development of the Supercomputer Fugaku. https://www.r-ccs.riken.jp/en/fugaku/project/outline

26. OneAPI Deep Neural Network Library (oneDNN). https://01.org/oneDNN

27. Deep Neural Network Library for AArch64. https://github.com/fujitsu/dnnl_aarch64

28. Paszke, A., et al.: Automatic differentiation in PyTorch. In: NIPS-W (2017)

29. Jansson, N., Bale, R., Onishi, K., Tsubokura, M.: CUBE: A scalable framework for large-scale industrial simulations. Int. J. High. Perform. Comput. App. **33**(4), 678–698 (2019). https://doi.org/10.1177/1094342018816377

30. Onishi, K., Tsubokura, M.: Topology-free immersed boundary method for incompressible turbulence flows: an aerodynamic simulation for "dirty" CAD geometry. Comput. Method Appl. Mech. Eng. (2021). https://doi.org/10.1016/j.cma.2021.113734

31. Nakahashi, K.: Building-cube method for flow problems with broadband characteristic length. In: Armfield, S., Morgan, P., Srinivas, K. (Eds) Computational Fluid Dynamics, 77–81. Springer, Berlin Heidelberg (2003). https://doi.org/10.1007/978-3-642-59334-5_7

32. Onishi, K., Obayashi, S., Nakahashi, K., Tsubokura, M.: Use of the immersed boundary method within the building cube method and its application to real vehicle CAD Data. In: 21st AIAA Computational Fluid 1029 Dynamics Conference. American Institute of Aeronautics and Astronautics, San Diego, CA (2013). https://doi.org/10.2514/6.2013-2713

33. Peskin, C.S.: The immersed boundary method. Acta. Numerica. **11**(1032), 479–517 (2002). https://doi.org/10.1017/S0962492902000077

34. Bhalla, A.P.S., Bale, R., Griffith, B.E., Patankar, N.A.: A unified mathematical framework and an adaptive numerical method for fluid-structure interaction with rigid, deforming, and elastic bodies. J. Comput. Phys. **250**(1), 446–476 (2013). https://doi.org/10.1016/j.jcp.2013.04.033

35. Hinton, G.E., Salakhutdinov, R.R.: Reducing the dimensionality of data with neural networks. Science **313**(5786), 504–507 (2006)

36. Olah, C.: Understanding LSTM Networks. http://colah.github.io/posts/2015-08-Understanding-LSTMs/. Accessed 04 Apr 2021

37. Nakamura, T., Fukami, K., Hasegawa, K., Nabae, Y., Fukagata, K.: Convolutional neural network and long short-term memory based reduced order surrogate for minimal turbulent channel flow. Phys. Fluids **33**, 025116 (2021). https://doi.org/10.1017/jfm.2019.238

Using Physics-Informed Enhanced Super-Resolution Generative Adversarial Networks to Reconstruct Mixture Fraction Statistics of Turbulent Jet Flows

Michael Gauding[1]([⊠]) and Mathis Bode[2]

[1] University of Rouen, Rouen, France
michael@gauding.de
[2] Institute for Combustion Technology, RWTH Aachen University, Aachen, Germany
m.bode@itv.rwth-aachen.de

Abstract. This work presents the full reconstruction of coarse-grained turbulence fields in a planar turbulent jet flow by a deep learning framework for large-eddy simulations (LES). Turbulent jet flows are characterized by complex phenomena such as intermittency and external interfaces. These phenomena are strictly non-universal and conventional LES models have shown only limited success in modeling turbulent mixing in such configurations. Therefore, a deep learning approach based on physics-informed enhanced super-resolution generative adversarial networks (Bode et al., Proceedings of the Combustion Institute, 2021) is utilized to reconstruct turbulence and mixture fraction fields from coarse-grained data. The usability of the deep learning model is validated by applying it to data obtained from direct numerical simulations (DNS) with more than 78 Billion degrees of freedom. It is shown that statistics of the mixture fraction field can be recovered from coarse-grained data with good accuracy.

1 Introduction

The motion of turbulent free shear flows is a complex, non-linear, multi-scale phenomenon, posing some of the most fundamental problems in classical physics. A precise prediction of the statistical properties of turbulence based on the governing equations would be of tremendous practical importance for a wide field of applications ranging from geophysics to combustion science. In these disciplines, the turbulent transport and turbulent mixing of a passive scalar species is of special interest. A passive scalar is governed by an advection-diffusion equation but has itself a negligible effect on the flow. The scalar species can be a concentration field, a pollutant, or it can be interpreted as a temperature field in the case that buoyancy forces are small compared to inertial forces. The motion of the scalar field exhibits complex behavior due to the non-linear coupling with the velocity field. An important feature of the scalar field the is the occurrence of very large but relatively rare events that are confined into thin sheet-like structures

© Springer Nature Switzerland AG 2021
H. Jagode et al. (Eds.): ISC High Performance 2021 Workshops, LNCS 12761, pp. 138–153, 2021.
https://doi.org/10.1007/978-3-030-90539-2_9

[18,41,42,48]. This phenomenon is called intermittency and occurs in jet flows at different scales [15,36]. Internal intermittency occurs at the smallest scales and is created by the vortex stretching mechanism. At the larger scales, external intermittency manifests itself at the edge of the flow, where a sharp layer, known as the turbulent/non-turbulent interface (TNTI), separates the turbulent core of the flow from the irrotational surrounding fluid [2,7,49]. Over the thickness of the TNTI, the scalar field varies drastically. The relevance of the TNTI originates from the significant transfer of mass, momentum, and scalars (i.e., heat or species) that takes place across its thickness [51]. Figure 1 illustrates the enstrophy [39] and the TNTI of a turbulent jet flow. Despite decades of research, the statistical modeling of internal and especially external intermittency is still unresolved [21,43,48].

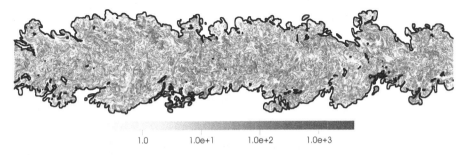

Fig. 1. Visualization of the enstrophy field in a turbulent jet flow. The black contour line represent the turbulent/non-turbulent interface.

Large-eddy simulation (LES) is a well established tool for the modeling of turbulence and turbulent mixing. LES solves for the larger, flow-dependent scales of the flow and models all scales below a particular filter width [22,32]. By assuming that the smaller, unresolved scales (sub-filter scales) reveal certain universal features and decouple from the larger non-universal scales, models for LES can be built from relatively simple, semi-empirical algebraic relations. However, Gauding et al. [21] demonstrated that external intermittency increases the non-universality of small-scale turbulence, which renders the applicability of classical scaling theories in flows with external intermittency questionable. As a consequence, LES has shown only limited success in the modeling of turbulent mixing in jet flows [16]. In this work, we therefore pursue a different approach and reconstruct sub-filter scale features of the scalar field by a data-driven methodology. The method provides highly resolved turbulence data and does not rely on any *ad hoc* scaling relation.

Deep learning (DL) is one of the most emerging research technologies in the age of big data. Examples include image processing [10,24,46,47] and speech recognition [25]. Recently, Bhati et al. [1] used deep learning to accelerate the drug development in the context of the COVID-19 pandemic. The growth of deep learning was made possible by the continued growth of computational power

and the availability of exceptionally large labeled datasets. Data-driven methods and DL have also become more popular over the past years in the field
of fluid mechanics including turbulence research [3,4,6,30,33]. However, simple
networks or small and artificial datasets have often limited these studies. In
this work, we apply the physic-informed enhanced super-resolution generative
adversarial network (PIESRGAN), developed by Bode et al. [6], to model turbulent mixing of a turbulent jet flow subject to strong internal and external
intermittency. The PIESRGAN is derived from the enhanced super-resolution
GAN (ESRGAN) architecture [10], which was extended to three-dimensional
turbulence data and utilizes tailor-made physics-informed loss functions specific
to turbulence. The PIESRGAN was successfully applied by Bode et al. [6] to
decaying turbulence and spray flames. Specifically, it was demonstrated that the
PIESRGAN is able to accurately predict the energy spectra of homogeneous
isotropic decaying turbulence from filtered data over the entire range of scales.
In other words, the PIESRGAN is able to reconstruct small-scale turbulence
from coarse grained data. Consequently, Bode et al. [6] showed that LES clo-
sures based on the PIESRGAN approach are able to correctly predicted the
decay of homogeneous isotropic turbulence and turbulent reactive sprays. It was
also demonstrated how a two-step learning approach can be used to reach good
results for a wide range of Reynolds numbers, making PIESRGAN a flexible
tool.

The remainder of this article is organized as follows. Section 2 describes the
datasets of a turbulent jet flow that is used for the training and validation of the
PIESRGAN. In Sect. 3, details of the data-driven reconstruction methodology
are given. The scalar mixing model is applied to the data in Sect. 4. The paper
finishes with conclusions.

2   Problem Definition and Data-Set Description

The analysis is based on data of a highly-resolved direct numerical simulation
(DNS) of a temporally evolving planar jet flow. The DNS solves the incompressible Navier-Stokes equations together with an advection-diffusion equation for a
mixture fraction variable ϕ, given by

$$\frac{\partial U_k}{\partial x_k} = 0\,,$$

$$\frac{\partial U_j}{\partial t} + U_k \frac{\partial U_j}{\partial x_k} = -\frac{\partial P}{\partial x_j} + \frac{1}{Re_0} \frac{\partial^2 U_j}{\partial x_k \partial x_k}, \quad j = 1,2,3 \tag{1}$$

and

$$\frac{\partial \phi}{\partial t} + U_k \frac{\partial \phi}{\partial x_k} = \frac{1}{Re_0 Sc} \frac{\partial^2 \phi}{\partial x_k \partial x_k}\,, \tag{2}$$

where U denotes the velocity vector with components $(U_1, U_2, U_3)^\intercal$ in stream-
wise, spanwise and crosswise directions, respectively, and P is the pressure. The
dependent variables are functions of space $x = (x_1, x_2, x_3)^\intercal$ and time t. Further,

Einstein's summation convention is used, which implies summation over indices appearing twice. All quantities are non-dimensionalized by the initial centerplane mean velocity U_0 and the initial jet thickness H_0. Without loss of generality, H_0 and U_0 are set to unity. The initial Reynolds number equals 10 000 and is defined as

$$Re_0 = \frac{U_0 H_0}{\nu} \tag{3}$$

with ν being the kinematic viscosity. The Schmidt number Sc is set to unity.

The DNS was carried out on the supercomputer JUQUEEN [44] with the in-house solver psOpen [19, 20, 26]. In order to obtain a high accuracy, spatial derivatives are computed by a sixth-order Pade scheme with spectral-like accuracy [31]. Temporal integration is performed by a low storage, stability-preserving fourth-order Runge-Kutta scheme. The Poisson equation is efficiently solved in spectral space by employing a Helmholtz equation [34, 35]. To reduce aliasing errors, the non-linear terms are formulated in skew-symmetric form [14], and additionally, a sixth-order compact filter is applied. The rectangular computational domain has periodic boundary conditions in streamwise and spanwise directions (denoted by x_1 and x_2), and free-slip boundary conditions in crosswise direction (denoted by x_3). The governing equations are discretized on a mesh with $5376 \times 5376 \times 2688$ grid points to appropriately resolve the smallest scales of the flow. This results in a system of equations with up to 78 billion degrees of freedom which must be solved for each of the approximately 16 000 time steps. For the simulation, all 56 racks (458 752 cores) of the supercomputer JUQUEEN at research center Juelich (Germany) were used for a period of six days, totaling more than 66 Million core-hours. The extremely high resolution of the DNS provides novel insight about the structure of the TNTI and is ideally suited for the training and testing of DL models. A single time step of the DNS has a size of 2.315 TB which provides a tremendous amount of information for a data-driven modeling approach.

Characteristic properties of the DNS at different times (D1 up to D5) are summarized in Table 1. At these times, the jet flow has reached a fully developed turbulent state where the Reynolds number built with the Taylor micro-scale is close to 105.

Figure 2 displays a visualization of the jet flow and the TNTI. The TNTI is defined by a threshold procedure based on the enstrophy field, see da Silva et al. [7] for details on the interface detection. It can be seen that the morphology of the TNTI is highly irregular and exhibits multi-scale structures that are a footprint of the turbulent cascade. This complexity poses a major challenge for models based on deep learning.

3 Modeling

3.1 Turbulent Mixing Models

The key quantity for the modeling of turbulent mixing and turbulent combustion is the mixture fraction ϕ [17, 37, 38]. As the mixture fraction in a turbulent jet

Table 1. Characteristic properties of the jet flow ($Re_0 = 10\,000$) at the centerplane at five different times (denoted by D1–D5). Here, $h_{1/2}$ denotes jet half-width of the jet and Re_λ is the Reynolds number based on the Taylor micro-scale. Further, U_c, $\langle k \rangle$, and $\langle \varepsilon \rangle$ denote the ensemble-averaged mean velocity, turbulent kinetic energy, and dissipation rate at the centerplane.

Case	t	$h_{1/2}$	U_c	Re_λ	$\langle k \rangle \times 10^2$	$\langle \varepsilon \rangle \times 10^3$
D1	13.2	0.86	0.57	105.2	2.87	4.98
D2	15.5	0.93	0.52	105.8	2.39	3.40
D3	18.0	1.00	0.48	105.6	2.02	2.43
D4	20.6	1.06	0.45	107.1	1.76	1.80
D5	23.3	1.16	0.42	107.4	1.57	1.39

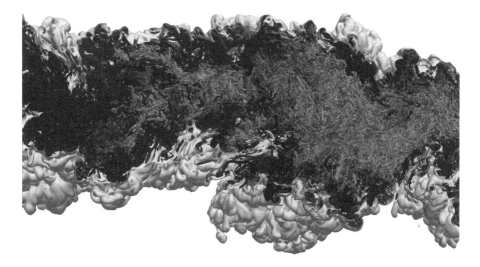

Fig. 2. Illustration of the turbulent jet flow by the Q-criterion [11] (note that only 25% of the computational domain are shown for clarity). The turbulent core is enveloped by the TNTI (grey iso-surface), which reveals a complex, highly convoluted shape.

flow is subject to strong spatio-temporal fluctuations, the accurate prediction of its probability density function (PDF) $P(\phi)$ is of fundamental importance. When this PDF is known, ensemble-averages can be obtained by

$$\langle Y \rangle = \int_0^1 Y(\phi) P(\phi) \mathrm{d}\phi, \tag{4}$$

where Y is a species concentration or temperature, which is known as a function of the mixture fraction from combustion models [37]. Tremendous efforts have been made to model and predict the mixture fraction PDF $P(\phi)$, see Denker et al. [8,9] and references therein. In binary mixtures, $P(\phi)$ is oftentimes modeled by the beta function $P_\beta(\phi)$. The beta function depends only on two parameters,

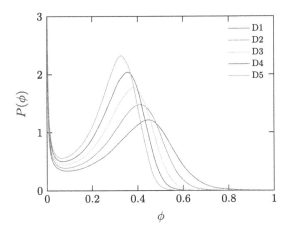

Fig. 3. Temporal evolution of the PDF $P(\phi)$ of the mixture fraction at the times defined in Table 1.

namely the mean $\langle\phi\rangle$ and the variance $\langle\phi'^2\rangle$, with $\phi' = \phi - \langle\phi\rangle$. However, there is substantial evidence that in flows with strong external intermittency, the beta function is not an adequate model for $P(\phi)$ [16]. Figure 3 displays $P(\phi)$ at different times during the decay of the temporally evolving jet flow studied in this work. $P(\phi)$ exhibits a bimodal shape with a singularity at $\phi = 0$ in conjunction with an intermediate local minimum. This minimum is a characteristic footprint of the TNTI [13,50]. The decrease of the local maximum and its shift towards smaller mixture fraction values represent the temporal evolution of turbulent mixing.

Effelsberg and Peters [12] analyzed the effect of external intermittency on $P(\phi)$ and derived a composite PDF model for $P(\phi)$ taking three different regimes into account, i.e., the fully turbulent core region, the irrotational outer flow, as well as a third transitional regime that represents the TNTI. Gampert et al. [16] reported an excellent performance of the composite model in jet flows. However, the practical application of the composite model is still limited. This is because all moments of ϕ up to the fourth order are required for the accurate prediction of the PDF. In turbulent flows, higher-order moments account for the strong, non-universal events and are therefore difficult to obtain in the context of LES models.

Therefore, in this work we pursue a novel route and model $P(\phi)$ by a data-driven deep learning approach. This approach is detailed in what follows.

3.2 Data-Driven Approach

The objective of this work is the reconstruction of the mixture fraction field ϕ by a data-driven approach based on the PIESRGAN [4,6] and the subsequent modeling of the PDF $P(\phi)$. The key feature of the PIESRGAN is the ability to predict instantaneous, fully-resolved three-dimensional flow realizations including scalar fields by knowing solely the coarse-grained data fields. The PIESRGAN generalizes deconvolution techniques as no explicit knowledge of the filter kernel is required. Different from conventional turbulence models, this approach does not only provide statistical quantities but fully-resolved three-dimensional fields.

The PIESRGAN used in this work is predominantly motivated by the previous advancements in the development of single image super-resolution (SISR) networks. A pioneer work for SISR was the super-resolution convolutional neural network (SRCNN) designed by Dong et al. [10]. Great efforts towards SISR had been made through the community since SRCNN first emerged. Yet most of these SISR networks showed the deficiency of producing over-smoothed results, owing to focusing on the peak-signal-to-noise-ratio (PSNR) as the primary metrics. Resultantly, the high frequency details occurring in the ground truth could not be adequately reconstructed. This makes such networks especially fatal for turbulence applications, as the small-scale structures at high wave numbers are exactly what is intended to be restored. Amelioration regarding the PSNR-based SISR networks was elucidated by Johnson et al. [27], who presented the concept "perceptual loss", i.e. a criterion to optimize the performance in the VGG-features space.

The other fundamental framework named generative adversarial network (GAN) was presented by Goodfellow et al. [23]. A GAN is composed of two competing models, a generator that captures the data distribution and generates new data, and a discriminator that learns to distinguish whether a sample stems from the original data distribution (genuine) or the generator (fake). During training, the generator learns to produce samples that are indistinguishable for the discriminator, while the discriminator learns to more accurately judge the genuineness.

In Bode et al. [4,6], we developed the PIESRGAN, which enhances the state-of-art ESRGAN to three-dimensional (3-D) turbulence data and problem-specific, physically-based loss functions. The PIESRGAN is able to recuperate the fully-resolved DNS results from coarse turbulence data, such as LES data. In what follows, we summarize the main features of the PIESRGAN.

The perceptual loss proposed for the ESRGAN based on VGG-feature space is apparently not as suitable for the turbulence data as the geometrical features from VGG19 are not representative for turbulent flows. Hence, a new formulation for the cost function was developed that enforces physical flow constraints.

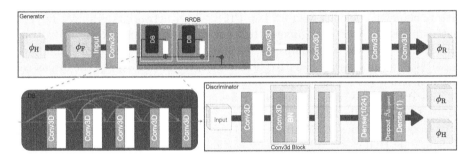

Fig. 4. PIESRGAN network structure. Image from Bode et al. [6].

Before training the PIESRGAN as a combined model, the generator is pre-trained with root-mean-square error (RMSE) due to the complexity of the RRDB. For the combined model, the loss function for reconstructing velocity fields is proposed as

$$l = \beta_1 l_{\mathrm{RADG}} + \beta_2 l_{\mathrm{pixel}} + \beta_3 l_{\mathrm{gradient}} + \beta_4 l_{\mathrm{continuity}} \tag{5}$$

with $\beta_1, \beta_2, \beta_3$, and β_4 being coefficients weighting the different loss term contributions. l_{RADG} is the "relativistic average" discriminator/generator loss, which is the accuracy feedback between discriminator and generator as given by Wang et al. [47]. For a scalar ϕ, the pixel loss l_{pixel} is defined as

$$l_{\mathrm{pixel}} = \mathrm{MSE}(\phi^{\mathrm{predicted}}, \phi^{\mathrm{DNS}}). \tag{6}$$

The mean-scare error (MSE) operator is given by

$$\mathrm{MSE}(\{\cdot\}_1, \{\cdot\}_2) = \frac{1}{N_{\mathrm{samples}}} \sum_{i=1}^{N_{\mathrm{samples}}} (\{\cdot\}_1^i - \{\cdot\}_2^i)^2 \tag{7}$$

with N_{samples} as number of all samples, i. e. the total number of grid points of the reconstructed field. If the MSE operator is applied on tensors including vectors, it is applied to all elements separately. Afterwards the resulting tensor is mapped into a scalar using the 1-norm. The gradient loss l_{gradient} is defined as

$$l_{\mathrm{gradient}} = \mathrm{MSE}(\nabla \phi^{\mathrm{predicted}}, \nabla \phi^{\mathrm{DNS}}) \tag{8}$$

with ∇ being the del operator. The gradient loss l_{gradient} is essential for the prediction of small-scale turbulence and hence for the closure of the LES equations. From a physical perspective, the gradient loss ensures the accuracy of the scalar dissipation rate, defined as

$$\chi = 2D \left(\nabla \phi\right)^2, \tag{9}$$

where D is the molecular diffusivity. $l_{\mathrm{continuity}}$ is the continuity loss, which enforces the continuity equation in the reconstructed field and reads

$$l_{\mathrm{continuity}} = \mathrm{MSE}(\nabla \cdot \boldsymbol{u}^{\mathrm{predicted}}, \boldsymbol{0}) \tag{10}$$

with $\boldsymbol{u}$ being the velocity vector. The PIESRGAN network is graphically presented in Fig. 4. Note that differently from the state-of-art SR networks, the PIESRGAN does not involve up-/ or downsampling layers. The high-/ and low-resolution turbulence data refer to the energy spectral property of the discussed turbulence, not the trivial image resolution.

The PIESRGAN was implemented by using Keras API with TensorFlow backend [5,6], and the training was performed on the JURECA GPU nodes due to the large size of the DNS dataset [4,20]. Input/output operations are handled efficiently by HDF5 [45]. The results for reconstructed velocity and scalar fields are shown in Figs. 5 and 6 for homogeneous isotropic turbulence data to visualize the quality of the deep learning closure. A remarkable agreement between the original DNS data and the reconstructed fields can be observed. The data of homogeneous isotropic turbulence is used later to reconstruct the smaller scales of jet flows, see Sect. 4.

4   Application to Turbulent Jet Flows

In this section, we apply the deep learning approach presented in Sect. 3 to turbulent jet flows. The challenge of reconstructing turbulent jet flows lies firstly in the tremendous range of scales present in the flows and secondly in the complex dynamics that manifest itself at the small scales by internal intermittency and at the large scales by the presence of the TNTI and its connection to external intermittency. In order to account for this flow structure, we extend the training strategy of the PIESRGAN according to Fig. 7. More specifically, we exploit the extrapolation capabilities of the PIESRGAN [6] and the fact that small-scale turbulence is to some degree universal or self-similar [40,43,48]. Universality was first hypothesized by Kolmogorov [28,29] and implies that at sufficiently large Reynolds numbers, the smallest scales of the flow decouple from the larger scales. By this decoupling, the smallest scales are assumed to be independent from the initial or boundary conditions. It is important to note that universality (or self-similarity) of turbulence, and particularly of turbulent jet flows, is restricted to low-order statistics [20,21].

With these considerations, the training strategy for jet flows is defined as follows. The input data ϕ_H of the generator consists of fully resolved three-dimensional fields of homogeneous isotropic turbulence with a Reynolds number similar to that of the jet flow. Additionally, coarse-grained jet flow data is fed into the generator. By this methodology, the generator has information about both small and large scales. The interaction with the discriminator challenges the generator to combine this information with the final goal to reconstruct a realistic, fully resolved jet flow. A comparison between DNS data, coarse-grained data and reconstructed data is given in Fig. 9.

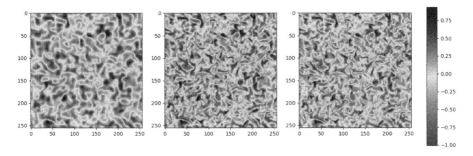

Fig. 5. Velocity reconstruction (from left to right: filtered data, PIESRGAN, DNS). Note that the turbulent field was centered and scaled to unity variance for training and reconstruction.

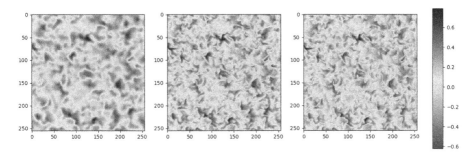

Fig. 6. Passive scalar reconstruction (from left to right: filtered data, PIESRGAN, DNS). Note that the scalar field was centered and scaled to unity variance for training and reconstruction.

Once the reconstructed fields are known, the subgrid stresses $\tau_{ij} = \overline{u_i u_j} - \overline{u}_i \overline{u}_j$ and $\gamma_i = \overline{u_i \phi} - \overline{u}_i \overline{\phi}$ that appear in the filtered governing equations as unclosed terms can be computed. Here, filtered quantities are denoted by an overbar. The PIESRGAN is fully integrated into the simulation code and reconstructs at any time step both velocity field u_i and scalar field ϕ from the coarse-grained fields $\overline{u}_i$ and $\overline{\phi}$.

The performance of the PIESRGAN based turbulence and mixing model is further quantitatively assessed by the mixture fraction PDF $P(\phi)$. Figure 10 displays $P(\phi)$ at two different times. It can be seen that the PIESRGAN based simulation matches very well with the results from DNS. For comparison, $P(\phi)$ is shown for coarse-grained data. The good agreement between the DNS data and the PIESRGAN indicates that the PIESRGAN is able to reconstruct the important characteristics of the TNTI.

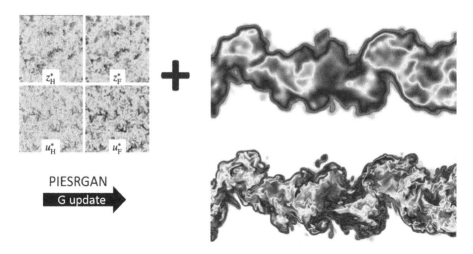

Fig. 7. Illustration of the training strategy of the PIESRGAN to reconstruct turbulent jet flows. The generator is trained with fields of fully resolved homogeneous isotropic turbulence and the large-scale information of the jet flow. The latter is obtained by applying a box filter. With this training strategy, the generator is able to create realistic, scale-resolved data.

Fig. 8. Comparison of the TNTI obtained from DNS data (green line), reconstructed data (red line), and coarse-grained data (black) obtained by filtering with a box filter. (Color figure online)

This assertion is further studied by comparing the TNTI of the reconstructed data with the TNTI of the DNS data in Fig. 8. Additionally, the TNTI of the coarse-grained data is shown. It can be ob observed that the TNTI of the coarse-grained data clearly lacks the fine-scale structure that is present in the DNS data. The PIESRGAN successfully reconstructs this fine scale structure.

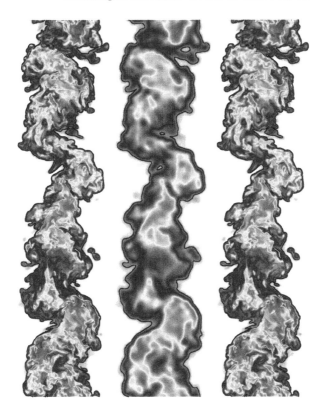

Fig. 9. Comparison of the mixture fraction field: DNS, coarse-grained data, and reconstructed data (from left to right). The TNTI is visualized by a green solid line. (Color figure online)

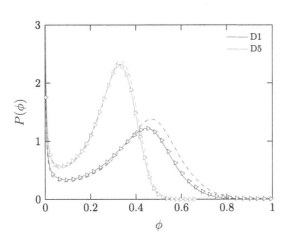

Fig. 10. Modeling of the mixture fraction PDF $P(\phi)$ at two different times D1 and D5. Comparison between DNS (solid lines), reconstructed PDF with the PIESRGAN model (triangles), and under-resolved simulation with no model (dashed lines).

5   Conclusion

The turbulent mixing of a temporally evolving planar jet flow was modeled by a deep learning framework. The deep learning approach utilized the PIESRGAN, which is based on an enhanced super-resolution GAN (ESRGAN) architecture. In order to reconstruct turbulent fields, the ESRGAN architecture was extended to three-dimensional fields and equipped with tailor-made physics-informed loss functions specific to turbulence. In this paper, we demonstrated that the PIES-RGAN is able to successfully reconstruct turbulent mixing fields from coarse-grained data. Specifically, we showed that the characteristics of the TNTI and external intermittency are correctly reproduced by the PIESRGAN. That means that the PIESRGAN accurately accounts for non-trivial and very strong events that do not obey a Gaussian distribution. Consequently, the PIESRGAN can be used to predict mixing statistics with high accuracy. Further work will be devoted to the prediction of statistics of the mixture fraction gradients by the PIESRGAN. Moreover, it will be examined how the quality of the reconstructed data depends on the filter-width and whether a cut-off wave-number exists below which the reconstruction fails.

Acknowledgments. The authors gratefully acknowledge the computing time granted for the projects JHPC55, and TURBULENCESL by the JARA-HPC Vergabegremium and provided on the JARA-HPC Partition part of the supercomputers JUQUEEN, JURECA, and JUWELS at Forschungszentrum Jülich.

References

1. Bhati, A.P., et al.: Pandemic drugs at pandemic speed: Accelerating COVID-19 drug discovery with hybrid machine learning-and physics-based simulations on high performance computers. arXiv preprint arXiv:2103.02843 (2021)
2. Bisset, D.K., Hunt, J.C., Rogers, M.M.: The turbulent/non-turbulent interface bounding a far wake. J. Fluid Mech. **451**, 383–410 (2002)
3. Bode, M., Gauding, M., Göbbert, J.H., Liao, B., Jitsev, J., Pitsch, H.: Towards prediction of turbulent flows at high reynolds numbers using high performance computing data and deep learning. In: Yokota, R., Weiland, M., Shalf, J., Alam, S. (eds.) ISC High Performance 2018. LNCS, vol. 11203, pp. 614–623. Springer, Cham (2018). https://doi.org/10.1007/978-3-030-02465-9_44
4. Bode, M., Gauding, M., Kleinheinz, K., Pitsch, H.: Deep learning at scale for subgrid modeling in turbulent flows: regression and reconstruction. In: Weiland, M., Juckeland, G., Alam, S., Jagode, H. (eds.) ISC High Performance 2019. LNCS, vol. 11887, pp. 541–560. Springer, Cham (2019). https://doi.org/10.1007/978-3-030-34356-9_41
5. Bode, M., Denker, D., Jitsev, J., Pitsch, H.: Sub-grid scale modelling at scale with deep learning and up to 60 billion degrees of freedom. In: NIC Symposium 2020, volume 50 of Publication Series of the John von Neumann Institute for Computing (NIC) NIC Series, pp. 379–388, Jülich, Feb 2020, NIC Symposium 2020, Jülich, Germany, 27 Feb 2020–28 Feb 2020, Forschungszentrum Jülich GmbH Zentralbibliothek, Verlag (2020). https://juser.fz-juelich.de/record/874553

6. Bode, M., et al.: Using physics-informed enhanced super-resolution generative adversarial networks for subfilter modeling in turbulent reactive flows. Proc. Combust. Inst. **38**, 2617–2625 (2021)
7. da Silva, C.B., Hunt, J.C., Eames, I., Westerweel, J.: Interfacial layers between regions of different turbulence intensity. Ann. Rev. Fluid Mech. **46**, 567–590 (2014)
8. Denker, D., et al.: Dissipation element analysis of non-premixed jet flames. J. Fluid Mech. **905** (2020)
9. Denker, D., Attili, A., Gauding, M., Niemietz, K., Bode, M., Pitsch, H.: A new modeling approach for mixture fraction statistics based on dissipation elements. Proc. Combust. Inst. **38**, 2681–2689 (2020)
10. Dong, C., Loy, C.C., He, K., Tang, X.: Learning a deep convolutional network for image super-resolution. In: Fleet, D., Pajdla, T., Schiele, B., Tuytelaars, T. (eds.) ECCV 2014. LNCS, vol. 8692, pp. 184–199. Springer, Cham (2014). https://doi.org/10.1007/978-3-319-10593-2_13
11. Dubief, Y., Delcayre, F.: On coherent-vortex identification in turbulence. J. Turbul. **1**(1), 011 (2000)
12. Effelsberg, E., Peters, N.: A composite model for the conserved scalar pdf. Combust. Flame **50**, 351–360 (1983)
13. Elsinga, G., da Silva, C.: How the turbulent/non-turbulent interface is different from internal turbulence. J. Fluid Mech. **866**, 216–238 (2019)
14. Erlebacher, G., Hussaini, M., Kreiss, H., Sarkar, S.: The analysis and simulation of compressible turbulence. Theoret. Comput. Fluid Dyn. **2**(2), 73–95 (1990)
15. Frisch, U.: Turbulence - The Legacy of A.N. Kolmogorov. Cambridge University Press, Cambridge (1995)
16. Gampert, M., Kleinheinz, K., Peters, N., Pitsch, H.: Experimental and numerical study of the scalar turbulent/non-turbulent interface layer in a jet flow. Flow Turbul. Combust. **92**(1–2), 429–449 (2014)
17. Gauding, M., Wick, A., Pitsch, H., Peters, N.: Generalised scale-by-scale energy-budget equations and large-eddy simulations of anisotropic scalar turbulence at various schmidt numbers. J. Turbul. **15**(12), 857–882 (2014)
18. Gauding, M., Goebbert, J.H., Hasse, C., Peters, N.: Line segments in homogeneous scalar turbulence. Phys. Fluids **27**(9), 095102 (2015)
19. Gauding, M., Wang, L., Goebbert, J.H., Bode, M., Danaila, L., Varea, E.: On the self-similarity of line segments in decaying homogeneous isotropic turbulence. Comput. Fluids **180**, 206–217 (2019)
20. Gauding, M., Bode, M., Brahami, Y., Danaila, L., Varea, E.: Self-similarity of turbulent jet flows with internal and external intermittency. J. Fluid Mech. (2021, submitted)
21. Gauding, M., Bode, M., Denker, D., Brahami, Y., Danaila, L., Varea, E.: On the combined effect of internal and external intermittency in turbulent non-premixed jet flames. Proc. Combust. Inst. **38**, 2767–2774 (2021)
22. Germano, M., Piomelli, U., Moin, P., Cabot, W.H.: A dynamic subgrid-scale eddy viscosity model. Phys. Fluids A: Fluid Dyn. **3**(7), 1760–1765 (1991)
23. Goodfellow, I., et al.:. Generative adversarial nets. In: Advances in Neural Information Processing Systems, pp. 2672–2680 (2014)
24. Greenspan, H., Van Ginneken, B., Summers, R.M.: Guest editorial deep learning in medical imaging: overview and future promise of an exciting new technique. IEEE Trans. Med. Imaging **35**(5), 1153–1159 (2016)
25. Hinton, G., et al.: Deep neural networks for acoustic modeling in speech recognition. IEEE Signal Process. Mag. **29**, 82–97 (2012)

26. Hunger, F., Gauding, M., Hasse, C.: On the impact of the turbulent/non-turbulent interface on differential diffusion in a turbulent jet flow. J. Fluid Mech. **802** (2016)
27. Johnson, J., Alahi, A., Fei-Fei, L.: Perceptual losses for real-time style transfer and super-resolution. In: Leibe, B., Matas, J., Sebe, N., Welling, M. (eds.) ECCV 2016, Part II. LNCS, vol. 9906, pp. 694–711. Springer, Cham (2016). https://doi.org/10.1007/978-3-319-46475-6_43
28. Kolmogorov, A.N.: Dissipation of energy in locally isotropic turbulence. In: Dokl. Akad. Nauk SSSR, vol. 32, pp. 16–18 (1941)
29. Kolmogorov, A.N.: The local structure of turbulence in incompressible viscous fluid for very large Reynolds numbers. In: Dokl. Akad. Nauk SSSR, vol. 30, pp. 299–303 (1941)
30. Kutz, J.N.: Deep learning in fluid dynamics. J. Fluid Mech. **814**, 1–4 (2017)
31. Lele, S.K.: Compact finite difference schemes with spectral-like resolution. J. Comput. Phys. **103**(1), 16–42 (1992)
32. Leonard, A.: Energy cascade in large-eddy simulations of turbulent fluid flows. In: Advances in Geophysics, vol. 18, pp. 237–248. Elsevier (1975)
33. Maulik, R., San, O.: A neural network approach for the blind deconvolution of turbulent flows. J. Fluid Mech. **831**, 151–181 (2017)
34. Mellado, J.P., Ansorge, C.: Factorization of the fourier transform of the pressure-poisson equation using finite differences in colocated grids. ZAMM-J. Appl. Math. Mech./Zeitschrift für Angewandte Mathematik und Mechanik **92**(5), 380–392 (2012)
35. Mellado, J.P., Stevens, B., Schmidt, H., Peters, N.: Two-fluid formulation of the cloud-top mixing layer for direct numerical simulation. Theoret. Comput. Fluid Dyn. **24**(6), 511–536 (2010)
36. Nelkin, M.: Universality and scaling in fully developed turbulence. Adv. Phys. **43**(2), 143–181 (1994)
37. Peters, N.: Turbulent Combustion. Cambridge University Press, Cambridge (2000)
38. Peters, N.: Multiscale combustion and turbulence. Proc. Combust. Inst. **32**(1), 1–25 (2009)
39. Pope, S.B.: Turbulent Flows. Cambridge University Press, Cambridge (2000)
40. Schumacher, J., Scheel, J.D., Krasnov, D., Donzis, D.A., Yakhot, V., Sreenivasan, K.R.: Small-scale universality in fluid turbulence. Proc. Nat. Acad. Sci. **111**(30), 10961–10965 (2014)
41. She, Z.-S., Jackson, E., Orszag, S.A.: Intermittent vortex structures in homogeneous isotropic turbulence. Nature **344**(6263), 226–228 (1990)
42. Shraiman, B.I., Siggia, E.D.: Scalar turbulence. Nature **405**(6787), 639–646 (2000)
43. Sreenivasan, K.R., Antonia, R.: The phenomenology of small-scale turbulence. Ann. Rev. Fluid Mech. **29**(1), 435–472 (1997)
44. Stephan, M., Docter, J.: JUQUEEN: IBM Blue Gene/Q® supercomputer system at the Jülich supercomputing centre. J. Large-Scale Res. Facil. JLSRF **1**, 1 (2015)
45. The HDF Group.: Hierarchical data format version 5, 2000–2010. http://www.hdfgroup.org/HDF5
46. Wang, N., Yeung, D.-Y.: Learning a deep compact image representation for visual tracking. In: Advances in Neural Information Processing Systems, pp. 809–817 (2013)
47. Wang, X., et al.: ESRGAN: enhanced super-resolution generative adversarial networks. In: Leal-Taixé, L., Roth, S. (eds.) ECCV 2018. LNCS, vol. 11133, pp. 63–79. Springer, Cham (2019). https://doi.org/10.1007/978-3-030-11021-5_5
48. Warhaft, Z.: Passive scalars in turbulent flows. Ann. Rev. Fluid Mech. **32**(1), 203–240 (2000)

49. Westerweel, J., Hofmann, T., Fukushima, C., Hunt, J.: The turbulent/non-turbulent interface at the outer boundary of a self-similar turbulent jet. Exp. Fluids **33**(6), 873–878 (2002)
50. Westerweel, J., Fukushima, C., Pedersen, J.M., Hunt, J.: Momentum and scalar transport at the turbulent/non-turbulent interface of a jet. J. Fluid Mech. **631**, 199–230 (2009)
51. Zhou, Y., Vassilicos, J.: Energy cascade at the turbulent/nonturbulent interface. Phys. Rev. Fluids **5**(6), 064604 (2020)

HPC I/O in the Data Center

HPC I/O in the Data Center Workshop (HPC-IODC)

Julian M. Kunkel, Jay Lofstead, and Jean-Thomas Acquaviva

[1] Georg-August-Universität Göttingen, Göttingen, Germany
`julian.kunkel@gwdg.de`
[2] Center for Computing Research, Sandia National Laboratories,
Albuquerque, USA
`gflofst@sandia.gov`
[3] Data Direct Networks, France
`jtacquaviva@ddn.com`

1 Introduction

Many public and privately funded data centers host supercomputers for running large scale simulations and analyzing experimental and observational data. These super-computers run usually tightly coupled parallel applications that require hardware components that deliver the best performance. In contrast, commercial data centers, such as Facebook and Google, execute loosely coupled workloads with a broad assumption of regular failures. The dimension of the data centers is enormous. A 2013 article summarizes commercial data centers' dimensions [4]. It estimates, for example, that Facebook hosts around 100 PB of storage, and Google and Microsoft manage around 1 million servers each – although the hardware is split among several physical data centers – a modus operandi not suitable for HPC centers. With the increasing importance of using machine learning to reveal underlying patterns in data, the data storage rates are accelerating to feed these additional use cases. Combining traditional modeling and simulation with ML workloads yields both a write and read-intensive workload for a single workflow.

Management of the huge amount of data is vital for the effective use of the con-tained information. However, with limited budgets, it is a daunting task for data center operators, especially as the design and storage system required hardware depends heavily on the executed workloads. A co-factor of the increasing difficulty is the increase in complexity of the storage hierarchy with the adoption of SSD and memory class storage technology. The US Department of Energy recognizes the importance of data management, listing it among the top 10 research challenges for Exascale [3].

There are several initiatives, consortia and special tracks in conferences that target RD&E audiences. Examples are the Storage Networking Industry Association (SNIA) for enterprises, the Big Data and Extreme-Scale Computing (BDEC) initiative[1], the Parallel Data Systems Workshop (PDSW) and the HEC FSIO workshop [1].

---

[1] http://www.exascale.org/bdec/.

There are many I/O workloads studies and performance analysis reports for parallel I/O available. Additionally, many surveys of enterprise technology usage include predictions of analysis for future storage technology and the storage market [2]. However, the analysis conducted for HPC typically focuses on applications and not on the data center perspective. Information about data center operational aspects is usually described in file system-specific user groups and meetings or described partially in research papers as part of the evaluation environment.

In the HPC IODC workshop, we bring together I/O experts from data centers and application workflows to share current practices for scientific workflows, issues, and obstacles for both hardware and the software stack, and RD&E to overcome these issues.

Due to the COVID-19 crisis, the ISC HPC conference changed to a digital edition. We preserved the nature of the workshop and organized it as a virtual full-day meeting on the regular workshop day with minimal changes to the agenda. The morning session was served in BigBlueButton while the afternoon session was part of the official ISC HPC conference program and served with Zoom.

2 Organization of the Workshop

The workshop was organized by

- Julian Kunkel (*Georg-August-* Universität Göttingen, *Germany*)
- Jay Lofstead (*Sandia National Labs, USA*)
- Jean-Thomas Acquaviva (*DDN*)

The workshop is supported by the Centre of Excellence in Simulation of Weather and Climate in Europe (ESiWACE), the Virtual Institute for I/O (VI4IO)[2] and the Journal of High-Performance Storage (JHPS)[3].

The workshop covered the following tracks:

- **Research paper presentations** – authors needed to submit a paper regarding relevant state-of-the-practice or research for I/O in the datacenter.
- **Talks from I/O experts** – authors needed to submit a rough outline for the talk related to the operational aspects of the data center.
- **Student Mentoring Session** – students need to submit an abstract for their PhD topic.
- Moderated **discussion** for hot topics to identify key issues and potential solutions in the community

This year, we broadened our scope by including the student mentoring session. To foster the next generation of data-related practitioners and researchers, students are encouraged to submit an abstract aligned with the workshop topics. At the workshop, the students give a lightning talk about what they are working on followed by feedback

---

[2] http://vi4io.org.

[3] https://jhps.vi4io.org/.

of the community about how to further the work, what the impact could be, alternative research directions, and other topics to help the students progress in their studies.

The CFP has been issued at the beginning of January. Important deadlines were:

- Submission deadline: 2021-03-24 AoE
- Author notification: 2021-04-24
- Workshop: 2021-07-02

2.1 Programm Committee

Thomas Boenisch	High-Performance Computing Center Stuttgart
Suren Byna	Lawrence Berkeley National Laboratory
Matthew Curry	Sandia National Laboratories
Philippe Deniel	CEA
Sandro Fiore	University of Trento
Wolfgang Frings	Juelich Supercomputing Centre
Javier Garcia	Blas Carlos III University
Stefano Gorini	Swiss National Supercomputing Centre
Adrian Jackson	The University of Edinburgh
Ivo Jimenez	University of California, Santa Cruz
Anthony Kougkas	Illinois Institute of Technology
Glenn Lockwood	Lawrence Berkeley National Laboratory
Carlos Maltzahn	University of California, Santa Cruz
George S. Markomanolis	Oak Ridge National Laboratory
Sandra Mendez	Barcelona Supercomputing Center
Robert Ross	Argonne National Laboratory
Feiyi Wang	Oak Ridge National Laboratory
Xue Wei	Tsinghua University
Bing Xie	Oak Ridge National Lab

3 Workshop Summary

Over the full-day program, about 35 attendees were constantly connected to the virtual session. In spite of the workshop being held online squarely on European Time zone making attending from North America more difficult. This is in line with the in-person attendance at previous instances and included many North American attendees, including some from the American west coast.

We had a good mix of talks from I/O experts, data center relevant research, and two discussion sessions. A short summary of the presentations is given in the following. The slides and video recordings of the presentations are available on the workshop's webpage: https://hps.vi4io.org/events/2021/iodc.

The morning session covered the three accepted research papers and the four expert talks. For the latter, systems and challenges were discussed for the institutions in CERN, EPCC, CSC and LuxProvide. These research papers and expert talks addressed a wide scope of storage and data issue. For instance new data format such as CERN's RNTuple or the difficulties related to performance evaluation. LuxProvide with its newly established Meluxina system received numerous questions about its architecture, hinting that this system, the greenest in Europe, is triggering a lot of interest.

In the afternoon session, a panel about "The impact of HPC and Cloud convergence on storage" involved five speakers from Amazon, MetOffice, National University of Singapore, Linksfoundation and ECMWF. The panel was structured around individual presentations followed by live discussion based on audience's questions. The panelists acknowledged the on-going convergence between HPC and Cloud, but nevertheless underscored some key differences. Among these differences the workloads diversity in Cloud which brings additional value for heterogeneity in large Cloud Data Center. The notion of Cloud and HPC reflect as well the self-perception of data center: interestingly MetOffice starts a new partnership with a major cloud provider, in order to focus on its core task, weather prediction, without being diverted by the need to host a service. Whereas ECMWF see self hosting as a key part of their success.

The session was followed by the new student mentoring session. In this session, four students presented their PhD works. We believe the feedback from attendees were constructive and received positive feedback from the students and attendees about the session. Therefore, we will include it in the next year's workshop again.

The major distinguishing feature for this workshop compared to other venues is the discussion rounds. The opportunity for themed, open discussions about issues both pressing and relevant to the data center community facilitates sharing experiences, solutions, and problems.

Albeit the workshop was virtual, the discussion covered aspects around use-cases and reasons for doing I/O, standardization of APIs as alternatives for POSIX, i.e., would S3 be sufficient or an object storage API with KV. We also continued the discussion around HPC and cloud convergence.

References

1. Bancroft, M., et al.: Hec fsio 2008 workshop report. In: High End Computing Interagency Working Group (HECIWG), Sponsored File Systems and I/OWorkshop HEC FSIO (2009)
2. IDC: Enterprise storage services survey. http://www.idc.com/getdoc.jsp?contain erId=254468
3. Lucas, R.: Committee Members: Top Ten Exascale Research Challenges. Online http://science.energy.gov/ ~ /media/ascr/ascac/pdf/meetings/20140210/ Top10reportFEB14.pdf (Feb 2014)
4. StorageServers Blog: Facts and stats of world's largest data centers. Online https:// storageservers.wordpress.com/2013/07/17/facts-and-stats-of-worlds-largest-data-centers/ (July 2013)

Toward a Workflow for Identifying Jobs with Similar I/O Behavior Utilizing Time Series Analysis

Julian Kunkel[1(✉)] and Eugen Betke[2]

[1] Georg-August-Universität Göttingen/GWDG, Göttingen, Germany
`julian.kunkel@gwdg.de`
[2] ECMWF, Reading, UK
`eugen.betke@ecmwf.int`

Abstract. One goal of support staff at a data center is to identify inefficient jobs and to improve their efficiency. Therefore, a data center deploys
monitoring systems that capture the behavior of the executed jobs. While
it is easy to utilize statistics to rank jobs based on the utilization of computing, storage, and network, it is tricky to find patterns in 100,000 jobs,
i.e., is there a class of jobs that aren't performing well. Similarly, when
support staff investigates a specific job in detail, e.g., because it is inefficient or highly efficient, it is relevant to identify related jobs to such
a blueprint. This allows staff to understand the usage of the exhibited
behavior better and to assess the optimization potential.

In this article, our goal is to identify jobs similar to an arbitrary reference job. In particular, we sketch a methodology that utilizes temporal
I/O similarity to identify jobs related to the reference job. Practically,
we apply several previously developed time series algorithms. A study is
conducted to explore the effectiveness of the approach by investigating
related jobs for a reference job. The data stem from DKRZ's supercomputer Mistral and include more than 500,000 jobs that have been
executed for more than 6 months of operation. Our analysis shows that
the strategy and algorithms bear the potential to identify similar jobs,
but more testing is necessary.

1 Introduction

Supercomputers execute 1000 s of jobs every day. Support staff at a data center have two goals. Firstly, they provide a service to users to enable them the
convenient execution of their applications. Secondly, they aim to improve the
efficiency of all workflows – represented as batch jobs – in order to allow the
data center to serve more workloads.

In order to optimize a single job, its behavior and resource utilization must
be monitored and then assessed. Rarely, users will liaise with staff and request a
performance analysis and optimization explicitly. Therefore, data centers deploy

© Springer Nature Switzerland AG 2021
H. Jagode et al. (Eds.): ISC High Performance 2021 Workshops, LNCS 12761, pp. 161–173, 2021.
https://doi.org/10.1007/978-3-030-90539-2_10

monitoring systems and staff must pro-actively identify candidates for optimization. Monitoring and analysis tools such as TACC Stats [7], Grafana [4], and XDMod [16] provide various statistics and time-series data for job execution.

The support staff should focus on workloads for which optimization is beneficial, for instance, the analysis of a job that is executed once on 20 nodes may not be a good return of investment. By ranking jobs based on their utilization, it is easy to find a job that exhibits extensive usage of computing, network, and I/O resources. However, would it be beneficial to investigate this workload in detail and potentially optimize it? For instance, a pattern that is observed in many jobs bears potential as the blueprint for optimizing one job may be applied to other jobs as well. This is particularly true when running one application with similar inputs, but also different applications may lead to similar behavior. Knowing details about a problematic or interesting job may be transferred to similar jobs. Therefore, it is useful for support staff (or a user) that investigates a resource-hungry job to identify similar jobs that are executed on the supercomputer.

It is non-trivial to identify jobs with similar behavior from the pool of executed jobs. Re-executing the same job will lead to slightly different behavior, a program may be executed with different inputs or using a different configuration (e.g., number of nodes). Job names are defined by users; while a similar name may hint to be a similar workload, finding other applications with the same I/O behavior would not be possible.

In the paper [2], we developed several distance measures and algorithms for the clustering of jobs based on the time series and their I/O behavior. These distance measures can be applied to jobs with different runtimes and the number of nodes utilized, but differ in the way they define similarity. They showed that the metrics can be used to cluster jobs, however, it remained unclear if the method can be used by data center staff to explore similar jobs effectively. In this paper, we refine these algorithms slightly, include another algorithm, and apply them to rank jobs based on their temporal similarity to a reference job.

We start by introducing related work in Sect. 2. In Sect. 3, we describe briefly the data reduction and the algorithms for similarity analysis. Then, we perform our study by applying the methodology to a reference job, therewith, providing an indicator for the effectiveness of the approach to identify similar jobs. In Sect. 5, the reference job is introduced and quantitative analysis of the job pool is made based on job similarity. In Sect. 6, the 100 most similar jobs are investigated in more detail, and selected timelines are presented. The paper is concluded in Sect. 7.

2   Related Work

Related work can be classified into distance measures, analysis of HPC application performance, inter-comparison of jobs in HPC, and I/O-specific tools.

The ranking of similar jobs performed in this article is related to clustering strategies. Levenshtein (Edit) distance is a widely used distance metric indicating the number of edits needed to convert one string to another [14]. The comparison of the time series using various metrics has been extensively investigated. In [9], an empirical comparison of distance measures for the clustering of multivariate time series is performed. 14 similarity measures are applied to 23 data sets. It shows that no similarity measure produces statistically significant better results than another. However, the Swale scoring model [13] produced the most disjoint clusters.

The performance of applications can be analyzed using one of many tracing tools such as Vampir [18] that record the behavior of an application explicitly or implicitly by collecting information about the resource usage with a monitoring system. Monitoring systems that record statistics about hardware usage are widely deployed in data centers to record system utilization by applications. There are various tools for analyzing the I/O behavior of an application [10].

For Vampir, a popular tool for trace file analysis, in [18] the Comparison View is introduced that allows them to manually compare traces of application runs, e.g., to compare optimized with original code. Vampir generally supports the clustering of process timelines of a single job, allowing to focus on relevant code sections and processes when investigating many processes.

In [8], 11 performance metrics including CPU and network are utilized for agglomerative clustering of jobs, showing the general effectiveness of the approach. In [15], a characterization of the NERSC workload is performed based on job scheduler information (profiles). Profiles that include the MPI activities have shown effective to identify the code that is executed [5]. Many approaches for clustering applications operate on profiles for compute, network, and I/O [1,6,11]. For example, Evalix [6] monitors system statistics (from proc) in 1-minute intervals but for the analysis, they are converted to a profile removing the time dimension, i.e., compute the average CPU, memory, and I/O over the job runtime.

PAS2P [12] extracts the I/O patterns from application traces and then allows users to manually compare them. In [19], a heuristic classifier is developed that analyzes the I/O read/write throughput time series to extract the periodicity of the jobs – similar to Fourier analysis. The LASSi tool [17] periodically monitors Lustre I/O statistics and computes a "risk" factor to identify I/O patterns that stress the file system. In contrast to existing work, our approach allows a user to identify similar activities based on the temporal I/O behavior recorded by a data center-wide deployed monitoring system.

3   Methodology

The purpose of the methodology is to allow users and support staff to explore all executed jobs on a supercomputer in order of their similarity to the reference job. Therefore, we first need to define how a job's data is represented, then describe the algorithms used to compute the similarity, and, the methodology to investigate jobs.

3.1   Job Data

On the Mistral supercomputer at DKRZ, the monitoring system [3] gathers in ten seconds intervals on all nodes nine I/O metrics for the two Lustre file systems together with general job metadata from the SLURM workload manager. The results are 4D data (time, nodes, metrics, file system) per job. The distance measures should handle jobs of different lengths and node count. In the open-access article [2], we discussed a variety of options from 1D job-profiles to data reductions to compare time series data and the general workflow and pre-processing in detail. We will be using this representation. In a nutshell, for each job executed on Mistral, they partitioned it into 10 min segments[1] and compute the arithmetic mean of each metric, categorize the value into NonIO (0), HighIO (1), and CriticalIO (4) for values below 99-percentile, up to 99.9-percentile, and above, respectively. The values are chosen to be 0, 1, and 4 because we arithmetically derive metrics: naturally, the value of 0 will indicate that no I/O issue appears; we weight critical I/O to be 4x as important as high I/O. This strategy ensures that the same approach can be applied to other HPC systems regardless of the actual distribution of these statistics on that data center. After the mean value across nodes is computed for a segment, the resulting numeric value is encoded either using binary (I/O activity on the segment: yes/no) or hexadecimal representation (quantizing the numerical performance value into 0–15) which is then ready for similarity analysis. By pre-filtering jobs with no I/O activity – their sum across all dimensions and time series is equal to zero – the dataset is reduced from 1 million jobs to about 580k jobs.

3.2   Algorithms for Computing Similarity

We reuse the B and Q algorithms developed in [2]: B-all, B-aggz(eros), Q-native, Q-lev, and Q-phases. They differ in the way data similarity is defined; either the time series is encoded in binary or hexadecimal quantization, the distance measure is the Euclidean distance or the Levenshtein distance. B-all determines the similarity between binary codings by means of Levenshtein distance. B-aggz is similar to B-all, but computes similarity on binary codings where subsequent segments of zero activities are replaced by just one zero. Q-lev determines the similarity between quantized codings by using Levenshtein distance. Q-native uses a performance-aware similarity function, i.e., the distance between two jobs for a metric is $\frac{|m_{job1}-m_{job2}|}{16}$. One of our basic considerations is that a short job may run longer, e.g., when restarted with a larger input file (it can stretch the length of the I/O and compute phases) or when run with more simulating steps. There are more alternatives how a longer job is related to a shorter job but we do not consider them for now. In this article, we consider these different behavioral patterns and attempt to identify situations where the I/O pattern of a long job is contained in a shorter job. Therefore, for jobs with different lengths, a sliding-windows approach is applied which finds the location for the shorter job in the

---

[1] We found in preliminary experiments that 10 min reduces compute time and noise, i.e., the variation of the statistics when re-running the same job.

long job with the highest similarity. Q-phases extracts phase information and performs a phase-aware and performance-aware similarity computation. The Q-phases algorithm extracts I/O phases from our 10-min segments and computes the similarity between the most similar I/O phases of both jobs.

3.3   Methodology

Our strategy for localizing similar jobs works as follows:

- A user[2] provides a reference job ID and selects a similarity algorithm.
- The system iterates over all jobs of the job pool, computing the similarity to the reference job using the specified algorithm.
- It sorts the jobs based on the similarity to the reference job.
- It visualizes the cumulative job similarity allowing the user to understand how job similarity is distributed.
- The user starts the inspection by looking at the most similar jobs first.

The user can decide about the criterion when to stop inspecting jobs; based on the similarity, the number of investigated jobs, or the distribution of the job similarity. For the latter, it is interesting to investigate clusters of similar jobs, e.g., if there are many jobs between 80–90% similarity but few between 70–80%.

For the inspection of the jobs, a user may explore the job metadata, search for similarities, and explore the time series of a job's I/O metrics.

4   Reference Job

For this study, we chose the reference job called Job-M: a typical MPI parallel 8-hour compute job on 128 nodes that write time series data after some spin up. The segmented timelines of the job are visualized in Fig. 1 – remember that the mean value is computed across all nodes on which the job ran. This coding is also used for the Q algorithms, thus this representation is what the algorithms will analyze; B algorithms merge all timelines together as described in [2]. The figures show the values of active metrics ($\neq 0$); if few are active, then they are shown in one timeline, otherwise, they are rendered individually to provide a better overview. For example, we can see that several metrics increase in Segment 12. We can also see an interesting result of our categorized coding, the write_bytes are bigger than 0 while write_calls are 0[3].

---

[2] This can be support staff or a data center user that was executing the job.

[3] The reason is that a few write calls transfer many bytes; less than our 90%-quantile, therefore, write calls will be set to 0.

5   Evaluation

In the following, we assume the reference job (Job-M) is given, and we aim to identify similar jobs. For the reference job and each algorithm, we created CSV files with the computed similarity to all other jobs from our job pool (worth 203 days of production of Mistral). During this process, the runtime of the algorithm is recorded. Then we inspect the correlation between the similarity and number of found jobs. Finally, the quantitative behavior of the 100 most similar jobs is investigated.

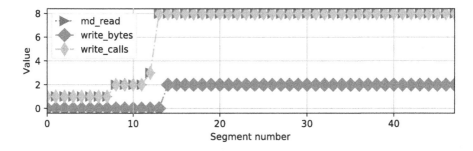

Fig. 1. Segmented timelines of Job-M (runtime = 28,828 s, segments = 48)

5.1   Performance

To measure the performance for computing the similarity to the reference job, the algorithms are executed 10 times on a compute node at DKRZ which is equipped with two Intel Xeon E5-2680v3 @2.50 GHz and 64GB DDR4 RAM. A boxplot for the runtimes is shown in Fig. 2a. The runtime is normalized for 100k jobs, i.e., for B-all it takes about 41 s to process 100k jobs out of the 500k total jobs that this algorithm will process. Generally, the B algorithms are the fastest, while the Q algorithms often take 4-5x as long. Q_phases and Levenshtein-based algorithms are significantly slower. Note that the current algorithms are sequential and executed on just one core. They could easily be parallelized, which would then allow an online analysis.

5.2   Quantitative Analysis

In the quantitative analysis, we explore the different algorithms how the similarity of our pool of jobs behaves to our reference job. The support team in a data center may have time to investigate the most similar jobs. Time for the analysis is typically bound, for instance, the team may analyze the 100 most similar jobs and rank them; we refer to them as the Top 100 jobs, and *Rank i* refers to the job that has the i-th highest similarity to the reference job – sometimes these

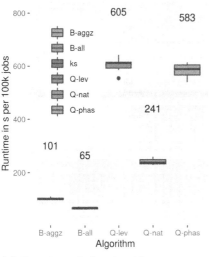

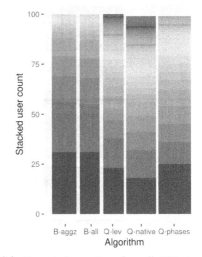

(a) Runtime of the algorithms to compute the similarity to our reference job

(b) User information for all 100 top-ranked jobs. Each color represents a specific user for the given data.

Fig. 2. Algorithm runtime and user distribution (Color figure online)

values can be rather close together as we see in the histogram in Fig. 3 for the actual number of jobs with a given similarity. As we focus on a feasible number of jobs, we crop it at 100 jobs (the total number of jobs is still given). It turns out that both B algorithms produce nearly identical histograms, and we omit one of them. In the figures, we can see again a different behavior of the algorithms depending on the reference job. We can see a cluster with jobs of higher similarity (for B-all and Q-native at a similarity of 75%). Generally, the growth in the relevant section is more steady. Practically, the support team would start with Rank 1 (most similar job, e.g., the reference job) and walk down until the jobs look different, or until a cluster of jobs with close similarity is analyzed.

Inclusivity and Specificity. When analyzing the overall population of jobs executed on a system, we expect that some workloads are executed several times (with different inputs but with the same configuration) or are executed with slightly different configurations (e.g., node counts, timesteps). Thus, potentially our similarity analysis of the job population may just identify the re-execution of the same workload. Typically, the support staff would identify the re-execution of jobs by inspecting job names, which are user-defined generic strings.

To understand if the analysis is inclusive and identifies different applications, we use two approaches with our Top 100 jobs: We explore the distribution of users (and groups), runtime, and node count across jobs. The algorithms should include different users, node counts, and across runtime. To confirm the hypothe-

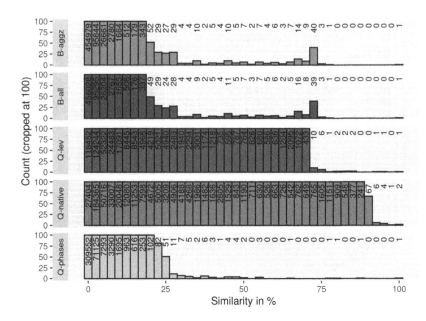

Fig. 3. Histogram for the number of jobs (bin width: 2.5%, numbers are the actual job counts). B-aggz is nearly identical to B-all and therefore omitted.

ses presented, we analyzed the job metadata comparing job names which validate our quantitative results discussed in the following.

User distribution. To understand how the Top 100 are distributed across users, the data is grouped by user ID and counted. Figure 2b shows the stacked user information, where the lowest stack is the user with the most jobs and the topmost user in the stack has the smallest number of jobs. Jobs from 13 users are included; about 25% of jobs stem from the same user; Q-lev and Q-native include more users (29, 33, and 37, respectively) than the other three algorithms. We didn't include the group analysis in the figure as user count and group ID are proportional, at most the number of users is 2x the number of groups. Thus, a user is likely from the same group and the number of groups is similar to the number of unique users.

Node distribution. Fig. 4a shows a boxplot for the node counts in the Top 100 – the red line marks the reference job. All algorithms reduce over the node dimensions, therefore, we naturally expect a big inclusion across the node range as long as the average I/O behavior of the jobs is similar. We can observe that the range of nodes for similar jobs is between 1 and 128.

Runtime distribution. The job runtime of the Top 100 jobs is shown using box-plots in Fig. 4b. While all algorithms can compute the similarity between jobs of different lengths, the B algorithms and Q-native penalize jobs of different lengths, preferring jobs of very similar lengths. Q-phases is able to identify much shorter or longer jobs.

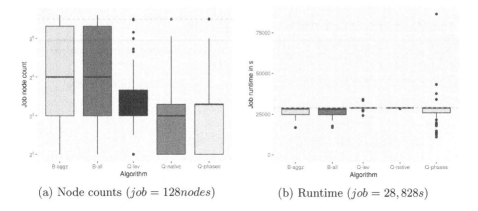

(a) Node counts $(job = 128 nodes)$ (b) Runtime $(job = 28,828s)$

Fig. 4. Distribution for all 100 top-ranked jobs

6 Assessing Timelines for Similar Jobs

To verify the suitability of the similarity metrics, for each algorithm, we carefully investigated the timelines of each of the jobs in the Top 100. We subjectively found that the approach works very well and identifies suitable similar jobs. To demonstrate this, we include a selection of job timelines and selected interesting job profiles. Inspecting the Top 100 is highlighting the differences between the algorithms. All algorithms identify a diverse range of job names for this reference job in the Top 100. The number of unique names is 19, 38, 49, and 51 for B-aggzero, Q-phases, Q-native, and Q-lev, respectively.

When inspecting their timelines, the jobs that are similar according to the B algorithms (see Fig. 5) subjectively appear to us to be different. The reason lies in the definition of the B-* similarity, which aggregates all I/O statistics into one timeline. The other algorithms like Q-lev (Fig. 6) and Q-native (Fig. 7) seem to work as intended: While jobs exhibit short bursts of other active metrics even for low similarity, we can eyeball a relevant similarity particularly for Rank 2 and Rank 3 which have the high similarity of 90+%. For Rank 15 to Rank 100, with around 70% similarity, a partial match of the metrics is still given.

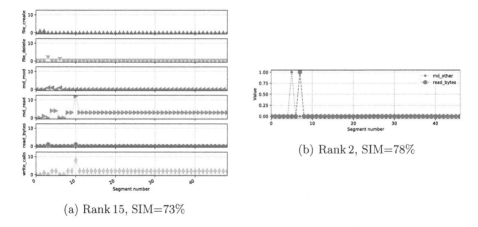

(a) Rank 15, SIM=73%

(b) Rank 2, SIM=78%

Fig. 5. Job-M with Bin-Aggzero, selection of similar jobs

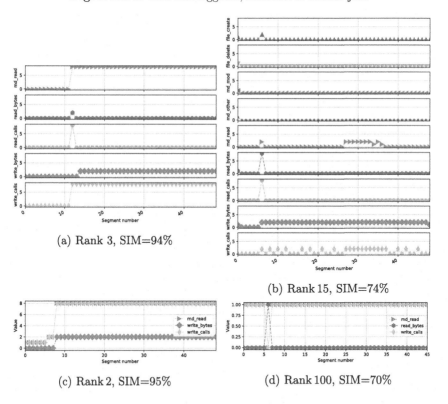

(a) Rank 3, SIM=94%

(b) Rank 15, SIM=74%

(c) Rank 2, SIM=95%

(d) Rank 100, SIM=70%

Fig. 6. Job-M with Q-lev, selection of similar jobs

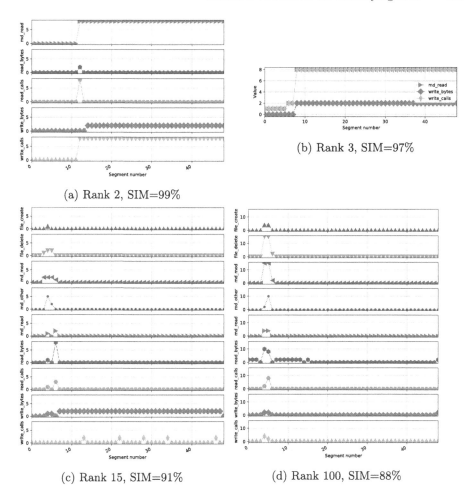

(a) Rank 2, SIM=99%

(b) Rank 3, SIM=97%

(c) Rank 15, SIM=91%

(d) Rank 100, SIM=88%

Fig. 7. Job-M with Q-native, selection of similar jobs

7   Conclusion

We introduced a methodology to identify similar jobs based on timelines of nine
I/O statistics. The quantitative analysis shows that a diverse set of results can
be found and that only a tiny subset of the 500k jobs is very similar to our
reference job representing a typical HPC activity. The Q-lev and Q-native work
best according to our subjective qualitative analysis. Related jobs stem from the
same user/group and may have a related job name, but the approach was able
to find other jobs as well. This was the first exploration of this methodology. In
the future, we will expand the study by comparing more jobs in order to identify
the suitability of the methodology.

References

1. Bang, J., et al.: HPC workload characterization using feature selection and clustering. In: Proceedings of the 3rd International Workshop on Systems and Network Telemetry and Analytics, pp. 33–40 (2020)
2. Betke, E., Kunkel, J.: Classifying temporal characteristics of job I/O using machine learning techniques. J. High Perform. Comput. (1), January 2021. https://doi.org/10.5281/zenodo.4478960
3. Betke, E., Kunkel, J.: The importance of temporal behavior when classifying job IO patterns using machine learning techniques. In: Jagode, H., Anzt, H., Juckeland, G., Ltaief, H. (eds.) ISC High Performance 2020. LNCS, vol. 12321, pp. 191–205. Springer, Cham (2020). https://doi.org/10.1007/978-3-030-59851-8_12
4. Chan, N.: A resource utilization analytics platform using grafana and telegraf for the savio supercluster. In: Proceedings of the Practice and Experience in Advanced Research Computing on Rise of the Machines (learning), pp. 1–6 (2019)
5. DeMasi, O., Samak, T., Bailey, D.H.: Identifying HPC codes via performance logs and machine learning. In: Proceedings of the First Workshop on Changing Landscapes in HPC Security, pp. 23–30 (2013)
6. Emeras, J., Varrette, S., Guzek, M., Bouvry, P.: EVALIX: classification and prediction of job resource consumption on HPC platforms. In: Desai, N., Cirne, W. (eds.) JSSPP 2015-2016. LNCS, vol. 10353, pp. 102–122. Springer, Cham (2017). https://doi.org/10.1007/978-3-319-61756-5_6
7. Evans, T.: Comprehensive resource use monitoring for HPC systems with TACC stats. In: 2014 First International Workshop on HPC User Support Tools, pp. 13–21. IEEE (2014)
8. Halawa, M.S., Díaz Redondo, R.P., Fernández Vilas, A.: Unsupervised KPIs-based clustering of jobs in HPC data centers. Sensors 20(15), 4111 (2020)
9. Khotanlou, H., Salarpour, A.: An empirical comparison of distance measures for multivariate time series clustering. Int. J. Eng. 31(2), 250–262 (2018)
10. Kunkel, J.M., et al.: Tools for analyzing parallel I/O. In: Yokota, R., Weiland, M., Shalf, J., Alam, S. (eds.) ISC High Performance 2018. LNCS, vol. 11203, pp. 49–70. Springer, Cham (2018). https://doi.org/10.1007/978-3-030-02465-9_4
11. Liu, Z., et al.: Characterization and identification of HPC applications at leadership computing facility. In: Proceedings of the 34th ACM International Conference on Supercomputing, pp. 1–12 (2020)
12. Mendez, S., et al.: A new approach for analyzing I/O in parallel scientific applications. Comput. Sci. Technol. Ser. 18, 67–78 (2012)
13. Morse, M.D., Patel, J.M.: An efficient and accurate method for evaluating time series similarity. In: Proceedings of the 2007 ACM SIGMOD International Conference on Management of Data (2007)
14. Navarro, G.: A guided tour to approximate string matching. ACM Comput. Surv. (CSUR) 33(1), 31–88 (2001)
15. Rodrigo, G.P., et al.: Towards understanding HPC users and systems: a NERSC case study. J. Parallel Distrib. Comput. 111, 206–221 (2018)
16. Simakov, N.A., et al.: A workload analysis of NSF's innovative HPC resources using XDMoD. In: arXiv preprint arXiv:1801.04306 (2018)
17. Turner, A., et al.: Analysis of parallel I/O use on the UK national supercomputing service, ARCHER using Cray's LASSi and EPCC SAFE, October 2019

18. Weber, M., Brendel, R., Wagner, M., Dietrich, R., Tschüter, R., Brunst, H.: Visual Comparison of trace files in vampir. In: Bhatele, A., Boehme, D., Levine, J.A., Malony, A.D., Schulz, M. (eds.) ESPT/VPA 2017-2018. LNCS, vol. 11027, pp. 105–121. Springer, Cham (2019). https://doi.org/10.1007/978-3-030-17872-7_7
19. White, J.P., et al.: Automatic characterization of HPC job parallel filesystem I/O patterns. In: Proceedings of the Practice and Experience on Advanced Research Computing, pp. 1–8 (2018)

H3: An Application-Level, Low-Overhead Object Store

Antony Chazapis[1]([✉]), Efstratios Politis[1], Giorgos Kalaentzis[1,2],
Christos Kozanitis[1], and Angelos Bilas[1,2]

[1] Institute of Computer Science,Foundation for Research and Technology - Hellas
(FORTH), Heraklion, Greece
{chazapis,epolitis,gkalaent,kozanitis,bilas}@ics.forth.gr
[2] Computer Science Department, University of Crete, Heraklion, Greece

Abstract. H3 is an embedded object store, backed by a high-performance key-value store. H3 provides a user-friendly object API, similar to Amazon's S3, but is especially tailored for use in "converged" Cloud-HPC environments, where HPC applications expect from the underlying storage services to meet strict latency requirements—even for high-level object operations. By embedding the object store in the application, thus avoiding the REST layer, we show that data operations gain significant performance benefits, especially for smaller sized objects. Additionally, H3's pluggable back-end architecture allows adapting the object store's scale and performance to a variety of deployment requirements. H3 supports several key-value stores, ranging from in-memory services to distributed, RDMA-based implementations. The core of H3 is H3lib, a C library with Python and Java bindings. The H3 ecosystem also includes numerous utilities and compatibility layers: The H3 FUSE filesystem allows object access using file semantics, the CSI H3 implementation uses H3 FUSE for attaching H3-backed persistent volumes in Docker and Kubernetes, while an S3proxy plug-in offers an S3 protocol-compatible endpoint for legacy applications.

1 Introduction

Object storage is a storage architecture in which data and associated metadata are organized in distinct, self-contained units, called *objects*. Object storage provides a filesystem-like abstraction to data management, hiding lower-level operations from the user, such as device administration and block allocations. However, in contrast to "traditional" filesystems, objects are not arranged in a hierarchical structure, but rather placed in a flat address space, called a storage pool, or *bucket*. By simplifying the organizational scheme, object store implementations are able to support Internet-scale storage.

Cloud-based object storage services currently support the majority of Internet-based services and applications, with Amazon's S3 (Simple Storage Service) [1] being by far the most popular. Competitive services include Microsoft's

© Springer Nature Switzerland AG 2021
H. Jagode et al. (Eds.): ISC High Performance 2021 Workshops, LNCS 12761, pp. 174–188, 2021.
https://doi.org/10.1007/978-3-030-90539-2_11

Azure Blob Storage [15] and Google Cloud Storage [9]. Cloud-based object storage completely removes the burden of managing the hardware and software storage infrastructure from application programmers, as simply putting data in some S3 bucket ensures availability without capacity constraints. The term "S3" is often used both in referring to the Amazon service, as well as the underlying communications protocol. Many other service providers strive to provide S3 compatibility (like DigitalOcean Spaces [7] or Wasabi [22]), as the amount of applications already using the protocol through respective libraries is vast. MinIO [16] is an open-source project that provides an S3-compatible server for use on local premises. Also, S3proxy [20] implements an S3 API over a selection of other storage services or a local filesystem.

In local setups, the HTTP-based RESTful web service API, used by S3 and most object store services, greatly inhibits performance and especially latency of storage operations. This can be an important issue, especially in "converged" Cloud-HPC environments: HPC clusters running a combination of typical HPC workloads and cloud-type microservices, or HPC-like cluster setups running on Cloud infrastructure. As an example, consider a "hybrid" HPC application that may use MPI to exchange data at runtime, but store intermediate results or snapshots in an object store. Or a workflow execution framework that passes data between steps through an object store, but runs on a Kubernetes [14] deployment on an HPC cluster. For such cases, it would be preferable that the object store's technology aligns with the available hardware and can exploit its high-performance communication features.

In this paper, we present H3: a *High speed*, *High volume*, and *High availability* storage library, which offers object storage semantics over a high-performance key-value store. H3 provides a cloud-friendly interface, which is similar to S3. It aims to offer both the benefits of Cloud Computing (ease-of-use) and HPC (performance) in converged setups, where volatile or persistent high-speed storage is close to—or even integrated in—the nodes running the application. H3 supports different programming languages through language bindings, and offers additional layers for compatibility, such as a FUSE [8] implementation and an S3proxy extension. H3 also integrates seamlessly with container-based environments, such as Kubernetes.

H3 was built as part of a platform supporting High Performance Data Analytics (HPDA) workflows running on HPC infrastructure. Users of the platform run operational Big Data workflows, originally targeting the Cloud. Workflows are expressed as complex Directed Acyclic Graphs (DAGs), where individual stages are realized by diverse software frameworks or languages. To support the heterogeneity and offer portability and reproducibility of execution, we map each graph node to a container and run the whole graph on Kubernetes. In this environment, each stage may deal with storage in a completely different manner—one using files, one using an object store, another custom libraries, etc. H3 bridges the gaps between stages, by providing a backwards-compatible storage service for existing code, and minimizing overheads when using node-local NVMe devices and memory.

In the following Section we present an overview of the various H3 components, before going into a detailed description of the design and implementation of H3's core, *H3lib*. In Sect. 4, we elaborate on the whole H3 ecosystem and how H3 can be embedded into new code. In Sect. 5 we present evaluation results and then explore related work and suggest future directions before concluding.

2   Overview

The H3 software stack is shown in Fig. 1. At its core is the H3 C library, *H3lib*, which uses key-value store plug-ins at the back end, and API bindings at the front end to offer compatibility with the Python and Java programming languages. We consider any component using the H3 API, an H3 "application". This includes H3 utilities, like *h3cli*, custom user codes linked with H3lib, as well as "legacy" applications, that either need file semantics, so must utilize H3 through the FUSE layer, or rely on an S3-compatible API endpoint, so must reach H3 through S3proxy.

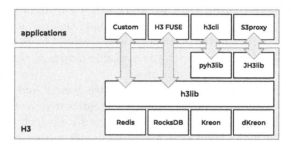

Fig. 1. H3 software stack

H3lib implements a translation layer between the object namespace and a key-value store, similar to how a filesystem provides a hierarchical namespace of files on top of a block device. A key-value store is a high-performance, non-relational database (NoSQL) commonly deployed in HPC and Big Data environments. Keys and values can range from simple strings to complex compound binary large objects (blobs), requiring no upfront data modelling or schema definition. The lack of overall structure makes key-value stores highly partitionable, thus scalable on multiple underlying storage segments or even across a distributed setup of nodes.

In H3 we use a plug-in architecture in the back end to support different key-value implementations, like Redis [17], RocksDB [18], and Kreon [28], each with different characteristics: Redis stores data in memory, RocksDB in disk, while Kreon is optimized for flash-based storage, where CPU overhead and I/O amplification are more significant bottlenecks compared to I/O randomness. H3 plug-ins exploit any optimizations done in the key-value layer. In addition, because H3 is stateless, it requires no synchronization among peer applications that operate on the same back end. Thus, if the key-value store is distributed, H3 can easily scale out across nodes.

3   Design and Implementation

3.1   Data and Metadata Separation

H3lib separates data from metadata at the back end. Each user, bucket, object, and multipart object in H3 has a unique identifier corresponding to a key in the underlying key-value store, where its metadata is stored. "Multipart" objects are objects that are created by uploading different data chunks in separate operations, while specifying their ordering in the object. The multipart object can then be finalized using a *complete* operation or canceled with an *abort*. This allows parallel uploading of large files. Object and multipart object data may consist of a single or multiple parts of variable size, which are stored under different keys. As key-value back ends usually have a size limit on values, we select a part size in H3 and automatically break oversized values into an appropriate number of smaller parts. Table 1 summarizes the keys used by H3, which are discussed in detail in the following paragraphs.

Table 1. Keys used by H3lib

	Field	Key
Metadata	user_id	'@' + <user name>
	bucket_id	<bucket name>
	object_id	<bucket name> + '/' + <object name> (for non-multipart objects)
		<bucket name> + '$' + <object name> (for multipart objects)
	multipart_id	'%' + <UUID>
Data	object_part_id	'_' + <UUID> + '#' + <part number> + ['.' + <subpart number>]

3.2   Metadata Organization

Each user has access only to specific buckets, therefore, to ensure access control, it is required to keep a record of the correlation between users and buckets. We store as user metadata the list of respective bucket names. As bucket metadata we store the time the bucket was created and the user that created it.

User keys are formulated by concatenating the character @ and the user name, for example @user. Bucket keys are mapped directly as the bucket names.

Object keys are produced by concatenating the bucket name, a forward slash and the full object name, for example `mybucket/a.txt`. Multipart objects exist in the namespace that results from concatenating the bucket name with marker `$` and the object name, thus multipart object `a` created in bucket `mybucket`, is stored as key `mybucket$a`, which avoids including incomplete multipart objects in "normal" object listings. There are no limitations on the characters that can be used for object names. Bucket names cannot include forward slashes and must be DNS (Domain Name System) compliant.

As object and multipart object metadata, we store the number and list of parts that comprise the object, as well as statistics about when the object was last read, modified and the last time the metadata were modified. Metadata also includes the size, and the offset of each part inside the object. To avoid resizing values for object metadata very often, we allocate metadata in duplicates of a batch size, where each batch may hold information for several data parts. The same applies to user metadata for storing bucket names.

For multipart objects we also create an additional key at the back end to store the multipart identifier used for operations on the object. Metadata stored in the multipart transaction identifier consist of the user that created it and its object name, in order to ensure that only the user that initiated the multipart is able to complete or abort the operation. Once the multipart is complete, the multipart identifier key is deleted and the multipart object metadata is renamed to use the forward slash marker, effectively placing the object with the given name in the visible object namespace.

By storing object names as keys, we are able to use the key-value store's scan operation to implement object listings. We expect the back end to provide an option to disallow overwriting keys if they already exist, to avoid race conditions when creating resources. If the back end has a limited key size, a respective limitation applies to name identifier lengths. Since most object stores implement the rename operation by copying and then deleting the original object, we assume renaming of an object to be optimally handled by the back end.

3.3   Data Organization

We store the data parts of each object under a Universally Unique Identifier (UUID), generated when the object is created. The UUID is a 128-bit random value, making part identifiers independent of their parent object, thus enabling fast rename operations, considering that a rename operation must be performed only on the key that holds the object's metadata, instead of each data part. The object's data parts are encoded as keys following the format `_<UUID>#i` where `i` signifies that it is the i-th part of the object. For multipart objects, as parts provided by the user can exceed the maximum value size, they may be broken internally into subparts. Thus it is possible to have a second level of data segmentation, encoded in keys as `_<UUID>#i.j`.

3.4   Example

Figure 2 demonstrates how each component of H3lib is mapped to the back-end key space. In this example, an application of user *user*, creates an object named *a.txt* of size 3 MB and stores it under the bucket *mybucket*. Initially the user performs a create bucket operation, that creates key `mybucket` in the back end containing the bucket's metadata, which includes the creation time of the bucket and the user's name. Since the user doesn't already exist in the key-value store, the user name is mapped as key `@user` which holds the user's metadata, in this case a list that contains only the bucket that was created. After the operation is complete, the user performs a create object operation. A new key `mybucket/a.txt` is created, with the object's metadata. The initial metadata consist of the number of parts that comprise the object, the total size, the user's name, and a UUID that is generated during the operation, in this case `d9e24d7ac88e4f5b`. Once the object metadata are written, the value of the object is split into three parts, assuming that parts are limited to 1 MB per value[1]. For each part `i` written, a key `d9e24d7ac88e4f5b#i` is created, holding the corresponding segment of the object's data. After all parts are written, we update the object metadata with a list of the part keys created and the timestamp of the object's creation.

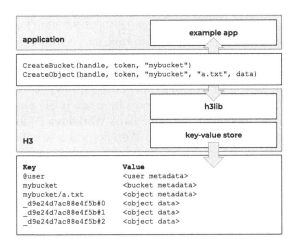

Fig. 2. Example of H3 object to key mapping

The complete H3lib API currently includes 32 calls. In addition to common *create*, *read*, *write*, *list*, and *delete* methods for buckets, objects, and multipart objects, we provide functions to perform data operations directly in the back end: create an object from part of another object, write in an object offset with partial data from another, copy and move objects, and truncate an object to a

---

[1] The 1 MB limit is used here as an example. The maximum part size is configurable.

specific size. H3lib also supports sparse objects and provides functions to read objects directly to local files and vice versa.

4   The H3 Ecosystem

H3lib is written in C, so we implement wrapper functions in Java and Python, for embedding H3lib to a larger set of applications. Java wrapper functions access the store natively, with the use of Java Native Access (JNA) [13]. The Python wrapper functions are implemented as a Python extension module. Furthermore, we provide client libraries on top of the wrapper functions for each programming language, as the wrappers expose internal details that are not required to the end user.

On top of H3lib, we implement H3 FUSE, a FUSE-based filesystem. To support H3 FUSE, we include in H3lib necessary filesystem attributes as part of the object's metadata, such as access permissions and ownership. Directories are created as empty objects ending with a forward slash character. Moreover, through a jclouds plug-in [2] (the library used by S3proxy to perform data operations), we provide a custom version of S3proxy that acts as a bridge between the S3 protocol and a key-value store through H3. Both the filesystem and S3-compatibility layers aim to provide applications with the ability to utilize H3lib, without the need to alter their application code. Considering that the FUSE framework imposes overheads that greatly affect performance [29] and S3 adds back protocol and serialization delays, the user is required to take into consideration the trade-off between compatibility and performance. The primary purpose of these layers is to support legacy applications that are no longer maintained and, consequently, cannot be altered, as well as to enable integrating H3 to existing systems.

We use H3 FUSE in a Container Storage Interface (CSI) plug-in to integrate H3lib in Kubernetes. Also, an H3-specific Argo Workflows [5] fork adds support for H3 as an "artifact repository". Argo Workflows is a workflow management engine for Kubernetes, which allows defining complex execution pipelines as container-based DAGs. Data exchanged between workflow steps are called "artifacts". A workflow may use an artifact repository plug-in to copy in data from an external storage system before a step starts executing, and to copy out data when it ends. We have added a new plug-in for H3 that uses h3cli to interface with H3lib. This also enables downloading such data artifacts from the Argo GUI after each step.

Additionally, we provide utility applications for H3lib. We implement a command line interface, named *h3cli*, and a performance testing tool, named *h3-benchmark*. The benchmark is based on Wasabi Technologies' s3-benchmark [19] and is used to measure *put* and *get* bandwidth. Since h3-benchmark is written in the Go programming language, it can also be used as a sample on how to use H3lib through C wrapper functions in Go code.

All the above software (H3lib and the other components of the H3 ecosystem) are open source and available online [6,10,11]. We also provide respective Docker container images for integration with other software.

5   Evaluation

To evaluate the performance characteristics of H3, we compare it with MinIO, a production grade object store. The two storage systems differ significantly in design, however they do provide a similar end-user feature set. We use two types of servers: type A, equipped with dual Intel Xeon E5-2620v2 CPUs, 128 GB of RAM, and a Samsung 960 EVO 250 GB NVMe, and type B, equipped with dual Intel Xeon E5-2630v3 CPUs, and 256 GB of RAM. All servers run CentOS Linux version 7.3 and communicate over 56 Gbps RDMA-capable Ethernet. The NVMe disks are mounted with the xfs filesystem and have been measured with fio to peak at about 2.8 GB/s of read and 0.5 GB/s of write throughput, 600K read and 80K write IOPS. Load is generated by Wasabi Technologies' s3-benchmark for MinIO, and h3-benchmark for H3, which is an altered version of s3-benchmark that embeds *H3lib*. The benchmarking tools perform *put* and then *get* operations, for a specified duration.

5.1   Single-Node Setup

Figure 3 shows the results reported after 1-minute runs for *put* and *get* operations in a type A server. For *get*s, we have modified the benchmarks to randomly read half the objects that have been inserted, in order to avoid rereading cached values. We focus our single-node evaluation on small object sizes, where the effect of the software stack is more pronounced, and run the benchmarks with 1 or 16 threads. For larger objects and multiple threads, the disk write throughput becomes the primary bottleneck.

For *put* operations, the performance speedup between the MinIO baseline and H3 is larger at the lowest object size of 1K. H3 with the RocksDB back end is about 60× faster for single-thread runs and about 45× in the multi-threaded case. At 1K, Kreon is about 125× faster than MinIO with one thread and about the same as RocksDB with multiple threads. H3/Kreon writes over 1.5 million 1K objects during the 1-minute run, while H3/RocksDB about 750K, and MinIO about 12K. As expected, the exclusion of any networking calls in H3 enables it to perform much better at all object sizes presented. MinIO closes the gap with multiple threads and large objects sizes, where most of the time is spent doing actual I/O at the device and the protocol overheads are hidden.

Note that with RocksDB, the average bandwidth of *put* operations reaches a maximum. Moreover, we have experienced that the larger the run, this average drops, as the more the objects written, the more compactions need to happen at the Log-Structured Merge-Tree (LSM-Tree) [27] structure used. LSM-Trees introduce increasing I/O amplification as their size grows, which decreases overall performance. On the other hand, Kreon stores key-value pairs in a sequential value log and keeps an index with their corresponding locations. The performance benefits of this design are evident when looking at the actual disk I/O during the measurements: RocksDB performs a mix of read and write calls and constantly reorganizes data on the disk, while Kreon writes sequentially with a sustained throughput of about 300 MB/s. Instead, RocksDB consumes less resources when

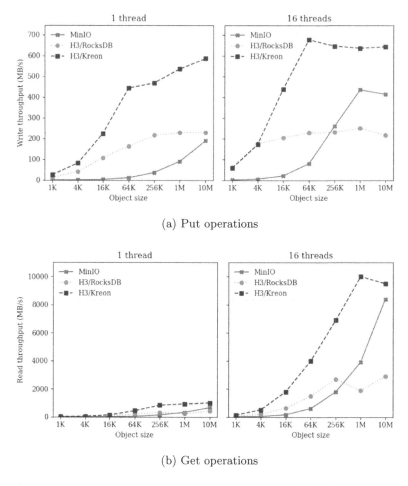

(a) Put operations

(b) Get operations

Fig. 3. Evaluation inside a single server with an NVMe device

running, as it manages the low-level read and write operations directly, using its own internal buffers. Both MinIO and Kreon rely heavily on system caches, which is reflected in both *put* and *get* results.

In a single node, when using H3 with the back-end plug-ins for RocksDB and Kreon, the storage service runs embedded inside the application. MinIO (and any REST-based object store) is deployed as an external service, and the application running in the same machine requires a roundtrip to localhost to reach it. H3/Redis functions similarly to MinIO, however as Redis stores key-values in memory, we configure the MinIO baseline to run over a RAM disk. We run the benchmark again for 1-minute *put*s, and *get* for half the objects, but only in single-threaded mode, as the Redis server is designed to use one CPU only. The results are shown in Fig. 4. H3 is 6–8× faster than MinIO for values up to 16K for both *put*s and *get*s. H3/Redis with a single thread can ingest objects of

256K and larger at a rate of about 300 MB/s. This number grows to about 850 MB/s for multithreaded runs, but can not scale further with one Redis server.

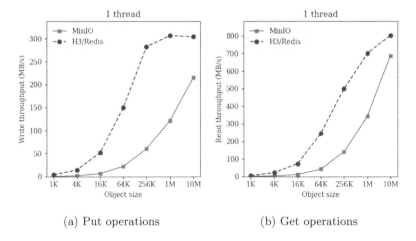

(a) Put operations   (b) Get operations

Fig. 4. Evaluation inside a single server with a RAM disk

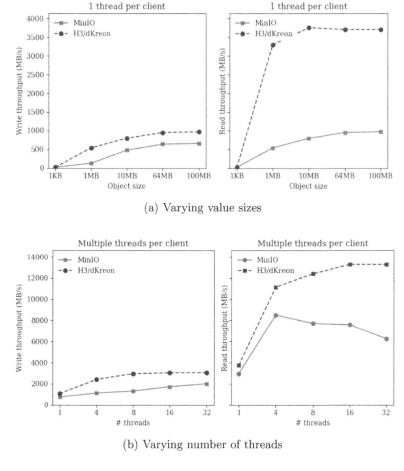

(a) Varying value sizes

(b) Varying number of threads

Fig. 5. Evaluation in a distributed environment

5.2 Distributed Setup

We now extend the testbed to include 4 type A servers running the storage service—either MinIO, or a distributed version of Kreon, *dKreon*—and 4 type B servers for running the benchmark. In the case of dKreon, the 4 servers partition the overall key-value space, and the H3 back-end plug-in at the client side uses RDMA (via the dKreon client library) to reach the appropriate server depending on the key's region. We setup dKreon to keep 2 replicas of each key-value, to match MinIO as closely as possible, which automatically creates redundant data between nodes.

For each measurement, we start an instance of the benchmark on each type B node in parallel, where each *put* and *get* stage runs for 1 min. In Fig. 5a we show runs with a single thread per client, to focus on the behavior of the systems for increasing object sizes. Note that in these runs we use larger objects than in the single-node case. H3 achieves from 1.47× to 4× higher throughput for *put* operations and from 1.27× to 8.2× higher throughput for *get* operations. Furthermore, in the case of H3, we observe an upper limit for *gets*. The current implementation of the dKreon plug-in does not favor large values, because we distribute values to servers based on their key's ASCII representation, thus all data parts for each object are stored at the same endpoint. Another distribution scheme may help increase the paralellization of key-value operations among available dKreon nodes.

Figure 5b shows the performance of the systems when the load increases. We use 100 MB objects and increase the clients' threads. H3's throughput is from 1.54× to 2.29× higher for *put* operations and from 1.27× to 2.13× higher for *get* operations. During the runs, we observe that *put* operations in both cases are constrained by the data replication scheme. MinIO uses erasure coding for data protection, meaning that each *put* requires coordination among all servers.

6   Related Work

The HPC community has been discussing the need of a high performance storage library for converged HPC-Big Data analytics workflows. Systems like DAOS [26], HEPnOS [12], and SAROJA [24], provide applications with such solutions. Although through different interfaces (ranging from key-values to objects), all designs stress the need to bypass the kernel for lower latency and increased throughput. SAROJA is based on libsaroja, a programming library that provides abstract groups of operations, which in turn are implemented with a plug-in architecture similar to H3: metadata operations are converted to a key-value API and served by a noSQL database, data are saved as objects or files, and control functions use some back end service that does synchronization and consensus, like ZooKeeper [4]. SAROJA remains a prototype that has never been released to the public. The ambitions of H3 seem very close, and although we may also separate operation groups at the back end at some point, we envision H3's application-facing API to remain focused on object management.

Ceph [30] is a distributed storage system that implements multiple access interfaces. At its core, Ceph is based on RADOS, a distributed object substrate, which can be utilized directly by applications through librados, or through other services: RBD exposes a block device API, CephFS a filesystem, and RADOS Gateway an S3-compatible object API. Thus, Ceph can be used as a local S3 server, similar to MinIO. In comparison to H3, Ceph provides a richer set of interfaces (i.e., the block API) and features. For example, fault-tolerance is provided by RADOS, which automatically manages data replication and recovery; H3 delegates such functions to the key-value store. A head-to-head comparison with librados is planned, however we believe that the simpler architecture of H3, as well as the fact that some key-value back ends may be designed to avoid kernel-space overheads, will favor our design – in particular when object sizes are small. For the same reasons, related work [25] explores the path of directly using Ceph's BlueStore [23] back end as an object store for HPC applications.

7 Future Extensions

Additional back-end plug-ins in H3lib would enable H3 to cover a wider range of deployment requirements. For example, to exploit multiple processing cores with Redis, requires setting up as many Redis instances. A respective plug-in could function by selecting the appropriate partition for each key. Other plug-in implementations could take advantage of the separation of metadata and data operations at the back end, which would allow to serve each from different stores. A plug-in could, for instance, store metadata in an SQL database, to provide the option of performing elaborate out-of-band metadata queries.

At the core of H3lib, we plan to add extended attributes to objects and utilize them from external controllers, in order to enable supplementary object features, like auto-deletion or conversion to read-only after a specified time period. We are also exploring the idea of integrating multiple storage tiers at the core of H3, allowing objects to move between tiers depending on user-defined attributes that reflect availability or persistence requirements.

We also intend to extend the H3 ecosystem with plug-ins for various programming frameworks, like a Spark [3] connector which would integrate directly to Spark primitives, offering greater performance to Spark applications. Furthermore, we are evaluating the applicability of a TensorFlow [21] plug-in, for machine learning applications.

8 Conclusion

Object storage is a core service of the contemporary Cloud. Cloud-based applications, designed for Internet-scale, typically use the object abstraction for data management and connect to some provider's RESTful web service that performs the actual storage operations. However, when these applications run in private infrastructure and high-speed storage devices are available, it is beneficial to minimize—or completely remove—as many communication layers as possible, since they may introduce significant overheads in the effort to exploit the full hardware's performance. Also, Cloud providers are now offering "exotic" equipment options that may include arrays of NVMe drives or low-latency interconnects, previously only available in HPC clusters. The ongoing convergence of Cloud and HPC environments, introduces novel service requirements, which can only be met by software architectures that bridge respective technologies.

In this paper, we present H3lib, a programming library designed to provide Cloud-like object management over a key-value storage engine. Key-value stores are widely adopted for their scalability and performance. H3lib is extensible, with multiple back-end plug-ins already available and more to follow. Moreover, H3lib sits at the heart of large, growing collection of utilities that allow H3-based objects to be accessed by a diverse set of interfaces, including an S3-compatible service, a filesystem that can easily be mounted in Kubernetes-managed containers, and a workflow execution environment for Kubernetes. Our evaluation confirms that applications modified to use H3 experience much higher write and read performance, especially when using objects of smaller sizes.

Acknowledgements. We thankfully acknowledge the support of the European Commission under the Horizon 2020 Framework Programme for Research and Innovation through the project EVOLVE (Grant Agreement No. 825061).

References

1. Amazon S3. https://aws.amazon.com/s3/
2. Apache jclouds. http://jclouds.apache.org
3. Apache Spark. https://spark.apache.org/
4. Apache Zookeeper. https://zookeeper.apache.org
5. Argo Workflows. https://argoproj.github.io/projects/argo
6. CSI H3: CSI driver for H3. https://github.com/CARV-ICS-FORTH/csi-h3
7. DigitalOcean Spaces. https://www.digitalocean.com/products/spaces/
8. FUSE (Filesystem in USErspace). https://www.kernel.org/doc/html/latest/filesystems/fuse.html
9. Google Cloud Storage. https://cloud.google.com/storage
10. H3: An embedded object store. https://github.com/CARV-ICS-FORTH/H3
11. H3 Benchmark: Performance test for H3. https://github.com/CARV-ICS-FORTH/h3-benchmark
12. Hepnos. https://xgitlab.cels.anl.gov/sds/hep/HEPnOS
13. Java Native Access. https://github.com/java-native-access/jna
14. Kubernetes: Production-Grade Container Orchestration. https://kubernetes.io
15. Microsoft Azure Blob Storage. https://azure.microsoft.com/en-us/services/storage/blobs/
16. MinIO. https://min.io/
17. Redis. https://redis.io/
18. RocksDB. https://rocksdb.org/
19. s3-benchmark. https://github.com/wasabi-tech/s3-benchmark
20. S3Proxy. https://github.com/gaul/s3proxy
21. TensorFlow. https://www.tensorflow.org/
22. Wasabi. https://wasabi.com
23. Aghayev, A., Weil, S., Kuchnik, M., Nelson, M., Ganger, G.R., Amvrosiadis, G.: File systems unfit as distributed storage backends: lessons from 10 years of ceph evolution. In: Proceedings of the 27th ACM Symposium on Operating Systems Principles, SOSP '19, pp. 353–369. Association for Computing Machinery, New York (2019). https://doi.org/10.1145/3341301.3359656
24. Chandrasekar, R.R., Evans, L., Wespetal, R.: An exploration into object storage for exascale supercomputers. In: Proceedings of the 2017 Cray User Group. CUG2017 (2017)
25. Duwe, K., Kuhn, M.: Using ceph's bluestore as object storage in HPC storage framework. In: Proceedings of the Workshop on Challenges and Opportunities of Efficient and Performant Storage Systems, CHEOPS '21. Association for Computing Machinery, New York (2021). https://doi.org/10.1145/3439839.3458734
26. Lofstead, J., Jimenez, I., Maltzahn, C., Koziol, Q., Bent, J., Barton, E.: Daos and friends: a proposal for an exascale storage system. In: SC '16: Proceedings of the International Conference for High Performance Computing, Networking, Storage and Analysis, pp. 585–596 (2016). https://doi.org/10.1109/SC.2016.49
27. O'Neil, P., Cheng, E., Gawlick, D., O'Neil, E.: The log-structured merge-tree (LSM-tree). Acta Inf. **33**(4), 351–385 (1996). https://doi.org/10.1007/s002360050048

28. Papagiannis, A., Saloustros, G., González-Férez, P., Bilas, A.: An efficient memory-mapped key-value store for flash storage. In: Proceedings of the ACM Symposium on Cloud Computing, SoCC '18, pp. 490–502. Association for Computing Machinery, New York (2018). https://doi.org/10.1145/3267809.3267824
29. Vangoor, B.K.R., Tarasov, V., Zadok, E.: To fuse or not to fuse: performance of user-space file systems. In: Proceedings of the 15th Usenix Conference on File and Storage Technologies, FAST'17. pp. 59–72. USENIX Association, USA (2017)
30. Weil, S.A., Brandt, S.A., Miller, E.L., Long, D.D.E., Maltzahn, C.: Ceph: A scalable, high-performance distributed file system. In: Proceedings of the 7th Symposium on Operating Systems Design and Implementation, OSDI '06, pp. 307–320. USENIX Association, USA (2006)

Compiler-assisted Correctness Checking and Performance Optimization for HPC

Automatic Partitioning of MPI Operations in MPI+OpenMP Applications

Tim Jammer[1,2(✉)] and Christian Bischof[2]

[1] Hessian Competence Center for High Performance Computing (HKHLR),
Darmstadt, Germany
[2] Scientific Computing Group, Department of Computer Science,
Technical University Darmstadt, 64283 Darmstadt, Germany
{tim.jammer,christian.bischof}@tu-darmstadt.de

Abstract. The new MPI 4.0 standard includes a new chapter about partitioned point-to-point communication operations. These partitioned operations allow multiple actors of one MPI process (e.g. multiple threads) to contribute data to one communication operation. These operations are designed to mitigate current problems in multithreaded MPI programs, with some work suggesting a substantial performance benefit (up to 26%) when using these operations compared to their existing non-blocking counterparts.

In this work, we explore the possibility for the compiler to automatically partition sending operations across multiple OpenMP threads. For this purpose, we developed an LLVM compiler pass that partitions MPI sending operations across the different iterations of OpenMP for loops. We demonstrate the feasibility of this approach by applying it to 2D stencil codes, observing very little overhead while the correctness of the codes is sustained. Therefore, this approach facilitates the usage of these new additions to the MPI standard for existing codes.

Our code is available on github: https://github.com/tudasc/CommPart.

Keywords: MPI 4.0 · Static analysis · MPI partitioned communication

1 Introduction

The new version 4.0 of the MPI standard includes many changes. In particular, "the largest changes are the addition of persistent collectives, application info assertions, and improvements to the definitions of error handling" [9]. Additionally, the new version includes a whole new chapter on Partitioned Point-to-Point Communication (Chap. 4). Partitioned operations allow "for multiple contributions of data to be made, potentially, from multiple actors (e.g., threads or tasks) in an MPI process to a single communication operation" citempi40. Therefore,

© Springer Nature Switzerland AG 2021
H. Jagode et al. (Eds.): ISC High Performance 2021 Workshops, LNCS 12761, pp. 191–198, 2021.
https://doi.org/10.1007/978-3-030-90539-2_12

```
1  MPI_Psend_init(msg, partitions, count, type, /*...*/
       ↪ &req);
2  MPI_Start(&req);
3  for(i = 0; i < partitions; ++i){ // may be executed in
       ↪ parallel
4      /* compute and fill partition #i, then mark ready: */
5      MPI_Pready(i, &req); }
6  MPI_Wait(&req);
```

Listing 1.1. Illustration of the usage of partitioned communication

the partitioned operations are specifically designed for efficient multi-threaded usage, an area where the usage of traditional non-blocking operations currently lacks performance [11].

The usage of partitioned operations is quite similar to the usage of persistent operations, as shown in Listing 1.1: First, a request object has to be initialized by using the MPI_Psend_Init or MPI_Precv_init functions (line 1). This initializes the request object, but does not start the communication. Starting the communication is done with the MPI_Start routine (line 2). In contrast to a persistent operation, the communication does not start once the MPI_Start operation is used. Rather, each partition separately has to be marked ready with MPI_Pready at which point the message transfer might start (line 5).[1] Similar to persistent and non-blocking operations, a partitioned operation has to be completed by using MPI_Wait or equivalent (line 6).

Partitioned operations were also known as "finepoints" before their adoption to the MPI standard [5], and their use resulted in up to 26% improvement in communication time in the case of a 2D-stencil mini-App [4,5].

Currently, adoption of the already existing persistent operations, on which the partitioned operations are based, is quite low [8]. This strongly suggests that the incorporation of the even more complex partitioned operations into existing codebases will present a challenge. We see a sort of "chicken and egg problem": If no one uses partitioned operations, there is no incentive for implementors to highly optimize these operations in order to harness the full potential of the performance benefits. On the other hand, if there is no real performance gain, programmers will have no incentive to use the partitioned operations.

Therefore, we explore the capabilities of the compiler to help with the adoption and usage of partitioned operations.

Related work on the topic of using the compiler to optimize MPI usage covers the automatic replacement of blocking operations with their non-blocking counterparts [1–3,6,10], as well as the compiler-based detection of the application info assertions [7], which are also included, in the new version of the standard. Some of this work [1] also explored the compiler's capability to replace these operations with persistent operations instead.

---

[1] Meaning that the modification of *this partition* the sending operation is forbidden until the sending operation has completed locally.

In this paper, we extend the existing approaches of replacing blocking operations with their non-blocking counterparts by replacing them with partitioned operations instead. Our replacement tries to partition those operations among different OpenMP threads in OpenMP for loop constructs.

First, we discuss our approach and the resulting tool in Sect. 2. We then demonstrate the feasibility in Sect. 3 and conclude in Sect. 4.

```
1  // allocate/init msg buffer
2  for(int n = 0; n < num_iter; n++){
3       # pragma omp parallel for
4       for(i = 0; i < size; ++i){
5            /* compute and fill buffer[i] */
6       }
7       MPI_Send(buf,/*...*/);
8  }
```

Listing 1.2. Example code before the partitioning.

```
1  MPI_Request req;
2  // allocate/init msg buffer
3  // Instructions to calculate the Loop Access Pattern
4  Init_Partitioned_operation(/*Send Parameters, Loop
       ↪ access pattern*/,&req);
5  for(int n = 0; n < num_iter; n++){
6       MPI_Start(&req);
7       # pragma omp parallel for
8       for(i = 0; i < size; ++i){
9            /* compute and fill buffer[i] */
10           ready_partitions_after_loop_iter(i,&req);}
11      MPI_Wait(&req);
12  }
13  MPI_Request_free(&req);
```

Listing 1.3. Example code after the partitioning.[4]

2 Analysis Approach

We implemented an LLVM compiler pass that replaces blocking MPI_Send operations with a partitioned equivalent if possible. The current version of the pass works on a function level, meaning that it currently is only able to partition sending operations issued in the same function where the parallel region is.

The compiler pass first tries to extend the non-blocking communication window similar to the approaches presented in [1,10]. If our pass finds that the message buffer is modified within an OpenMP for construct, it tries to partition the operation. This happens in 4 steps: First, we use the LLVM scalar evolution

---

[2] Note that this only illustrates the transformation, as the transformation happen on the LLVM IR, no source code is being output.

analysis to calculate the memory access pattern if possible. We do this by analyzing the memory addresses of all store operations inside the OpenMP loop and check if their evolution throughout the different loop iterations is computable and follows a linear pattern. Note that it is sufficient if a linear pattern (based on the loop index) can be computed symbolically, as not all values (e.g. the loop boundaries), might be known at compile time. If no linear pattern (linear in the loop index) can be derived, a partitioning does not seem useful, as the semantics of the MPI partitioned operations require that each partition has the same size, meaning that only a linear partitioning of the message is possible.

If a (symbolic) memory access pattern was computed, our pass transforms the blocking operation into a partitioned one. An example is given in Listings 1.2 and 1.3, which illustrates the transformation done by our pass.

First, our transformation inserts the allocation of a new MPI_Request-alike object (line 1) alongside with the corresponding call to MPI_Request_free (line 13) into the function that contains the parallel region. With the information on the memory access pattern and the loop bounds, the pass will insert the initialization of the partitioned operation (line 4). Instead of directly inserting a call to MPI_Psend_init, we call a self written library function, that also takes the memory access pattern and loop chunk size as arguments. This function then calculates a viable partition size at runtime and calls MPI_Psend_init accordingly. This means that the operations to actually compute the symbolic memory access pattern at runtime will also be inserted into the code.

Once the operation is partitioned, a call to MPI_Start is inserted before the parallel region (line 6) and the original send operation is replaced with the corresponding MPI_Wait call (line 11). Lastly, we need to insert calls to MPI_Pready (line 10). These calls are also wrapped by a library function that is called after every chunk of the loop and determines the partitions that can be marked ready based on the current loop chunk. Listing 1.3 does not illustrate the fact that the library function is called after every chunk of loop iterations instead of after every iteration of the loop, with the chunksize given by OpenMP.

We note that overlapping access patterns are possible. Therefore, our MPI_Request alike object also keeps track of the number of threads that have finished working on a particular partition of the message, with the call to MPI_Pready only being issued once all threads finished working on a particular message partition. The amount of overlap is computed at the initialization of the partitioned operation, as the memory access pattern is already known at this time, keeping the overhead for each loop chunk as low as possible.

One limitation of the current implementation is that the operation has to be partitioned alongside the boundaries of the MPI datatype used. For example, an operation that sends n datamembers of type MPI_DOUBLE can be partitioned, while an operation sending *one* contiguous type[3] containing n doubles cannot be partitioned. In the future, it might be desirable to also allow for the partition of such types.

---

[3] For example a type created by MPI_Type_contiguous.

Currently, the chunksize used to calculate the partition-sizes is the chunksize used by the OpenMP for loop. This means that if the user did not specify a chunksize in the OpenMP for pragma directive, 1 is used as the default (for the used LLVM implementation), which likely will cause a huge overhead if MPI_Pready has to be called after every iteration. We plan to investigate this tradeoff in the future and adjust our tool to also take it into account.

At this point, we only tested the implementation with a static loop schedule, but it can easily be extended to also cover dynamic ones.

For simplicity, we referred to the MPI functions as named in the standard throughout this section, but we implemented a wrapper that is used for correctness checking (e.g. MPIX_Start instead of MPI_Start), meaning that the pass will insert a call to those functions.

3   Demonstration of Feasibility

To demonstrate the feasibility of our approach we consider performance and correctness. We use a 2-dimensional heat dispersion code, based on a 5 point stencil and with block-wise domain decomposition, as an example to demonstrate our approach, as this sort of code was shown to benefit from the usage of partitioned operations [5].

In order to explore if the partitioning done by our tool is correct, we developed a correctness checking wrapper utilizing valgrinds Memcheck tool [12]. Our wrapper functions wrap around the existent persistent communication operations, providing the API defined by the MPI standard for partitioned operations.

The communication itself will only start once the wait call is issued[4], and all partitions are marked ready. This means that our correctness checking wrapper behaves like a blocking communication operation and no performance benefit can be expected. When a Pready call is issued, no data transfer takes place. Instead, our wrapper marks the corresponding part of the message buffer as inaccessible using VALGRIND_MAKE_MEM_NOACCESS. This ensures that every access to this particular part of the message buffer will trigger an error in valgrinds analysis, as modification of the message part that is marked as ready is forbidden by the MPI standard. This might, however, lead to some false positive error reports from valgrind, as reading the data is allowed[5]. Therefore, we developed a script that filters out all false positives from valgrinds output[6]. We do this filtering by specifying a valgrind block handle for each send and receive operation, which gives us the ability to distinguish the send and receive operations to filter out the false positives. This also allows us to distinguish the errors introduced by the message partitioning from other errors that may be present in an application.

---

[4] This is a valid implementation according to the MPI standard.

[5] For a receive operation, reading and writing is forbidden, though.

[6] False positives in the MPI implementation or the application itself are not filtered.

We tested our tool with a handful of different versions of our examplary 2D stencil code, which are semantically the same but use a different set of MPI operations to achieve the halo exchange. The used stencil code is also included in our github repository. In all tested cases, no error was introduced by our message partitioning tool.

In terms of compile performance, we note that our tool uses a reasonable amount of the compilation time: 4.5% of the total 1.3 s for 175 lines of code on optimization Level O2, as reported by clangs -ftimereport option.

For the application performance, we first note that our correctness checking wrapper described above will result in some overhead in and of itself. Nonetheless, we see that even this naive implementation results in very low overhead of 0.8% when executing it with 16 processes using 24 threads each on a cluster[7], when not running under valgrinds supervision.

Some part of the overhead measured results from our library functions that determine the partitions to ready after each chunk of the loop and calculate appropriate partition sizes, while another part likely results from our clearly not optimal implementation of the communication. The distinction which part is actually caused by the "administrative" part rather than the inefficient wrapper is difficult. In the current version of the partitioning, each request is partitioned independently. In future versions, we aim to further lower the required "administrative" part by considering groups of requests together, avoiding unnecessary recalculation of, for example, the loop memory access pattern. Nevertheless, if an optimized implementation is able to achieve close to the suggested 26% performance benefit [5], being able to harness a net gain of 25% will still present a benefit, especially when considering that our approach avoids the need for a human intervention to make use of the partitioned operations.

4   Conclusion

In this work, we demonstrated the compiler's capability to automatically partition MPI operations in some MPI+OpenMP applications by presenting an LLVM compiler pass that is able to partition MPI_Send operations. As our approach results in very low overhead, this allows to harness much of the expected performance benefit without the need for a developer to manually adapt the code. We plan to extend our tool to explore when partitioning makes sense and when the necessary overhead becomes too large. We also plan to refine our implementation with the analysis of different OpenMP loop scheduling and the partition of messages with a contiguous datatype.

In the future, the further evaluation of the performance potential of partitioned operations for other communication patterns besides stencil codes is important. Nonetheless, the presented approach may evolve to be a valuable

---

[7] On the Lichtenberg cluster equipped with Intel Xeon Platinum 9242 CPUs, the execution of unaltered version compiled with clang 11.1 took 614 s on average, while the execution of the automatically partitioned version took 619 s.

additional optimization step in a domain specific stencil compiler as well as provide incentive for highly optimized implementations of these operations.

Our code is available on github: https://github.com/tudasc/CommPart.

Acknowlegements. We especially want to thank Dr. Christian Iwainsky (TU Darmstadt) for fruitful discussion. This work was supported by the Hessian Ministry for Higher Education, Research and the Arts through the Hessian Competence Center for High-Performance Computing. Measurements for this work were conducted on the Lichtenberg high performance computer of the TU Darmstadt. Some of the code analyzing the OpenMP parallel regions originated from CATO [13] (https://github.com/JSquar/cato).

References

1. Ahmed, H., Skjellumh, A., Bangalore, P., Pirkelbauer, P.: Transforming blocking MPI collectives to non-blocking and persistent operations. In: Proceedings of the 24th European MPI Users' Group Meeting, pp. 1–11 (2017)
2. Danalis, A., Pollock, L., Swany, M.: Automatic MPI application transformation with ASPhALT. In: 2007 IEEE International Parallel and Distributed Processing Symposium, pp. 1–8. IEEE (2007)
3. Danalis, A., Pollock, L., Swany, M., Cavazos, J.: MPI-aware compiler optimizations for improving communication-computation overlap. In: Proceedings of the 23rd International Conference on Supercomputing, pp. 316–325 (2009)
4. Grant, R., Skjellum, A., Bangalore, P.V.: Lightweight threading with MPI using Persistent Communications Semantics. Technical report, Sandia National Lab. (SNL-NM), Albuquerque, NM (United States) (2015)
5. Grant, R.E., Dosanjh, M.G.F., Levenhagen, M.J., Brightwell, R., Skjellum, A.: Finepoints: partitioned multithreaded MPI communication. In: Weiland, M., Juckeland, G., Trinitis, C., Sadayappan, P. (eds.) ISC High Performance 2019. LNCS, vol. 11501, pp. 330–350. Springer, Cham (2019). https://doi.org/10.1007/978-3-030-20656-7_17
6. Guo, J., Yi, Q., Meng, J., Zhang, J., Balaji, P.: Compiler-assisted overlapping of communication and computation in MPI applications. In: 2016 IEEE International Conference on Cluster Computing (CLUSTER), pp. 60–69. IEEE (2016)
7. Jammer, T., Iwainsky, C., Bischof, C.: Automatic detection of MPI assertions. In: Jagode, H., Anzt, H., Juckeland, G., Ltaief, H. (eds.) ISC High Performance 2020. LNCS, vol. 12321, pp. 34–42. Springer, Cham (2020). https://doi.org/10.1007/978-3-030-59851-8_3
8. Laguna, I., Marshall, R., Mohror, K., Ruefenacht, M., Skjellum, A., Sultana, N.: A large-scale study of MPI usage in open-source HPC applications. In: Proceedings of the International Conference for High Performance Computing, Networking, Storage and Analysis, SC '19. ACM (2019). https://doi.org/10.1145/3295500.3356176
9. Message Passing Interface Forum: MPI: A Message-Passing Interface Standard Version 4.0 (2021). https://www.mpi-forum.org/docs/mpi-4.0/mpi40-report.pdf
10. Nguyen, V.M., Saillard, E., Jaeger, J., Barthou, D., Carribault, P.: Automatic code motion to extend MPI nonblocking overlap window. In: Jagode, H., Anzt, H., Juckeland, G., Ltaief, H. (eds.) ISC High Performance 2020. LNCS, vol. 12321, pp. 43–54. Springer, Cham (2020). https://doi.org/10.1007/978-3-030-59851-8_4

11. Schonbein, W., Dosanjh, M.G.F., Grant, R.E., Bridges, P.G.: Measuring multi-threaded message matching misery. In: Aldinucci, M., Padovani, L., Torquati, M. (eds.) Euro-Par 2018. LNCS, vol. 11014, pp. 480–491. Springer, Cham (2018). https://doi.org/10.1007/978-3-319-96983-1_34
12. Seward, J., et al.: Memcheck: a memory error detector (2020). https://valgrind.org/docs/manual/mc-manual.html
13. Squar, J., Jammer, T., Blesel, M., Kuhn, M., Ludwig, T.: Compiler assisted source transformation of openmp kernels. In: 2020 19th International Symposium on Parallel and Distributed Computing (ISPDC), pp. 44–51 (2020). https://doi.org/10.1109/ISPDC51135.2020.00016

heimdallr: Improving Compile Time Correctness Checking for Message Passing with Rust

Michael Blesel[1]([☒]) [iD], Michael Kuhn[1] [iD], and Jannek Squar[2] [iD]

[1] Otto von Guericke University Magdeburg, Magdeburg, Germany
{michael.blesel,michael.kuhn}@ovgu.de
[2] Universität Hamburg, Hamburg, Germany
squar@informatik.uni-hamburg.de

Abstract. Message passing is the foremost parallelization method used in high-performance computing (HPC). Parallel programming in general and especially message passing strongly increase the complexity and susceptibility to errors of programs. The de-facto standard technologies used to realize message passing applications in HPC are MPI with C/C++ or Fortran code. These technologies offer high performance but do not come with many compile-time correctness guarantees and are quite error-prone. This paper presents our work on a message passing library implemented in Rust that focuses on compile-time correctness checks. In our design, we apply Rust's memory and concurrency safety features to a message passing context and show how common error classes from MPI applications can be avoided with this approach.

Problems with the type safety of transmitted messages can be mitigated through the use of generic programming concepts at compile time and completely detected during runtime using data serialization methods. Our library is able to use Rust's memory safety features to achieve data buffer safety for non-blocking message passing operations at compile time.

A performance comparison between our proof of concept implementation and MPI is included to evaluate the practicality of our approach. While the performance of MPI could not be beaten, the results still are promising. Moreover, we are able to achieve clear improvements in the aspects of correctness and usability.

Keywords: Message passing · Compile-time checks · Rust · MPI

1 Introduction

Parallelization has become an essential programming technique over the last decades for applications to utilize the full resources of a computing system. In HPC, parallelization is an absolute requirement to run applications on distributed memory systems. The standard technologies used in this context today

© Springer Nature Switzerland AG 2021
H. Jagode et al. (Eds.): ISC High Performance 2021 Workshops, LNCS 12761, pp. 199–211, 2021.
https://doi.org/10.1007/978-3-030-90539-2_13

are message passing via MPI for inter-node parallelization in conjunction with frameworks like OpenMP or manual multi-threading for shared memory intra-node parallelization. Most of these tools are based on C/C++ and Fortran since these languages have traditionally yielded the best performance results for HPC applications and therefore make up the majority of existing HPC codebases.

Parallelization provides significant performance increases and more importantly scalability to applications but it does not come without drawbacks. The code complexity often increases heavily when parallelization is introduced into a program [11]. Additionally new classes of errors such as data races, deadlocks and non-determinism emerge from parallel code [3]. In general, modern compilers have become very good at detecting errors and providing helpful error and warning messages to the user but in respect to parallelization errors they are often still lacking. For MPI applications, not many parallelization errors are caught at compile time. Some static analysis tools such as MPI-Checker [5] exist but often manual debugging by the programmer is required. Better compile time correctness checks for message passing applications are therefore desirable.

Many of these problems can be traced back to the programming languages that are used in HPC applications. Both, C/C++ and Fortran have not been designed with parallel programming in mind. Intrinsic support for parallel programming features and the existing solutions today were either added over time to their specifications or are provided by external libraries.

Rust is a modern system programming language that focuses on memory and concurrency safety with strong compile time correctness checks [12]. One of Rust's unique features is its memory ownership concept which ensures that all data has exactly one owner at all times during a program's runtime and thereby allows the compiler to guarantee the absence of errors like data-races at compile time. This paper explores how Rust's safety mechanisms can be applied to the design of a message passing library that provides stronger compile time correctness checks than existing solutions like MPI.

2   Motivation

The purpose of the work presented in this paper is to show how a message passing library that strongly focuses on compile time correctness checks and usability can be designed in Rust. This section argues why these attributes are desirable and might even be more important than raw performance to users.

The authors of [1] have conducted a study about programming languages for data-intensive HPC applications. They combined an analysis of over one hundred papers from the HPC domain and a survey of HPC experts and concluded that the most desired and important features of programming languages in HPC are usability, performance and portability.

As it can be seen in Fig. 1, usability seems to be the most desired feature for many users. This makes sense when taking into account that a large percentage of the userbase of HPC systems are not necessarily parallel programming experts but rather scientist from other domains. This user group needs to develop scalable parallel applications for supercomputers to facilitate their domain specific

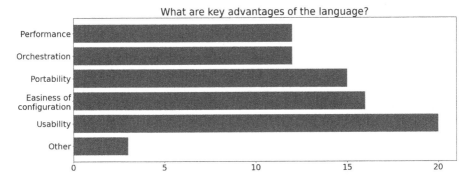

Fig. 1. The most important features of HPC programming languages (based on [1])

research. It is therefore important to provide software solutions that make this process as easy as possible.

Providing better compile time correctness checks for parallel applications can greatly improve the usability of a message passing library by reducing the need for manual debugging, which can be tedious for the users. As the next section will show, MPI and C/C++ have some significant problems in this regard.

Even though Rust is not yet as commonly used in HPC as MPI with C/C++ or Fortran, we chose it due to its fundamental safety and correctness concepts that it was designed with. The following sections will show that they fit very well to the context of message passing. Furthermore, we believe it is important to look into newer technologies that might play a part in the future of HPC. Rust seems like a good candidate since it has seen more wide spread use as a more convenient and safer alternative to C/C++ in the software industry over the last years with support from large companies such as Google, Amazon and Intel [8]. Also when looking at the next generation of HPC developers many will not be as familiar with older languages like C anymore and be more accustomed to modern languages with their design concepts and comfort features.

3   Correctness Problems with MPI

This section highlights some common erroneous coding patterns that can occur in MPI applications and which are currently not caught at compile time without the use of external static analysis tools.

Many common errors in MPI code can be traced back to the use of raw, untyped memory buffers via C's void pointers. This C-style way of working with raw memory addresses yields good performance and gives great control to the programmer, but it also harbors a lot of dangers and hinders the compiler in detecting data type related errors as the following example shows.

3.1   Type Safety Errors in MPI

MPI functions require the programmer to manually specify the data type of
the passed data buffer. This not only introduces a source of errors but can also
be very inconvenient for the user. Listing 1.1 presents an incorrect MPI code
segment where the true type of the sent data buffer does not match the given
MPI_Datatype argument of the send and receive functions. The true type of the
data buffer is double but the MPI functions are given the MPI_FLOAT data type
argument. This is clearly an error by the programmer but it is not detected by
the compiler. What makes this example even more problematic is that the given
code will run without a runtime crash and cause unexpected program results.
This makes it a hard bug to find in a real application with a large codebase.

```
1   double *buf = malloc(sizeof(double) * BUF_SIZE);
2   [...]
3   if (rank == 0) {
4       for (int i = 0; i < BUF_SIZE; ++i)
5           buf[i] = 42.0;
6       MPI_Send(buf, BUF_SIZE, MPI_FLOAT, 1, 0,
                ↪ MPI_COMM_WORLD);
7   }
8   else if (rank == 1) {
9       MPI_Recv(buf, BUF_SIZE, MPI_FLOAT, 0, 0,
                ↪ MPI_COMM_WORLD,
10                  MPI_STATUS_IGNORE);
11  }
```

Listing 1.1. Faulty MPI code that states the wrong MPI_Datatype argument

Errors like this can easily happen when the data type of a buffer variable
has to be changed at some point during development without the programmer
remembering that this also implies modifying all MPI function calls that use
this buffer. This example highlights another problematic aspect of programming
with MPI. Due to the quite low abstraction level of MPI operations it is very
inflexible regarding changes in the code. Even a simple change like switching the
type of a variable can require changes to large parts of the whole program.

3.2   Memory Safety Concerns with Non-blocking Communication

Listing 1.2 shows an example use case of MPI's non-blocking communication
operations. When using non-blocking operations like MPI_Isend from the example
the function immediately returns to the caller and the message passing operation
is processed in the background. This leaves the data buffer that is being sent in
an unsafe state where no other part of the application should access it before
making sure that it is safe to be used again. In the given example the process
with rank 0 does not adhere to this and immediately after calling MPI_Isend it

```
1  if(rank == 0) {
2      MPI_Isend(buf, BUF_SIZE, MPI_DOUBLE, 1, 0,
3                MPI_COMM_WORLD, &req);
4      for(int i = 0; i < BUF_SIZE; ++i)
5          buf[i] = 42.0;
6  }
7  else if(rank == 1) {
8      MPI_Recv(buf, BUF_SIZE, MPI_DOUBLE, 0, 0,
9                MPI_COMM_WORLD, &status);
10 }
```

Listing 1.2. Faulty non-blocking MPI code that writes to an unsafe buffer

starts to modify the buffer. This makes the outcome of the shown code non-deterministic. This error is even harder to detect compared to the last example because the produced results may differ from run to run and the application might even yield the expected results sometimes.

The given code does not conform to the MPI specification, which states that the safety of a buffer, which has been used with non-blocking communication, needs to be verified by calling MPI_Wait or MPI_Test before accessing it again. However, MPI has no way of enforcing this rule in actual code. There will be no compile time warnings or errors if the sequence is not correct, which makes bugs caused by incorrect usage of non-blocking communication hard to track down in more complicated applications.

4   heimdallr: A Proof of Concept Message Passing Library Implementation in Rust

In this section we present our work on a proof of concept message passing library implementation in Rust called heimdallr[1]. The design of the library is focused on strong compile time correctness checks and good usability with clear semantics for all message passing operations. We explain how Rust's safety and correctness mechanics were applied to the design and implementation of basic message passing operations to achieve these goals.

4.1   Type Safety Through Generics and Message Serialization

As discussed in Sect. 3.1, MPI requires the user to manually specify the data type of given data buffers, which can lead to errors. This problem can be solved quite easily in more modern languages that provide stronger support for generic programming than C. Listing 1.3 presents the signatures of heimdallr's blocking,

---

[1] https://github.com/parcio/heimdallr.

```
1  pub fn send<T>(&self, data: &T, dest: u32, id: u32)
2       -> std::io::Result<()>
3
4  pub fn receive<T>(&self, source: u32, id: u32)
5       -> std::io::Result<T>
```

Listing 1.3. Function signatures of heimdallr's blocking, synchronous send and receive operations

synchronous send and receive functions. They work with Rust's generic types for their data buffer arguments, which already removes the burden of having to state the correct data type from the user and leaves it to the compiler. This may seem like a small and obvious change but it eliminates a lot of potential errors, makes the message passing code more flexible regarding data type changes and makes the function signatures more concise.

Leaving the local data buffer type deduction up to the compiler however only solves half of the problem of type safety for message passing. The other aspect is to make sure that all processes that are participating in a message exchange agree about the type of the message's data. For reasons that are discussed in Sect. 6.3, this problem is hard to solve at compile time. Therefore, in its current state, heimdallr is only able to detect errors of this kind at runtime. To make sure that the data type of a received message is interpreted correctly, heimdallr uses serialization. This adds some computational overhead to the message passing procedure when compared to working on raw byte streams, but it can ensure that the message data type cannot be misinterpreted on the receiving side. heimdallr makes use of the established Rust serialization crate Serde [9] and uses the bincode [7] serialization protocol. This also allows users to easily send custom made types if they implement Serde's *Serialize* and *Deserialize* traits. These traits can be automatically generated by Rust if the user simply adds a `#[derive(Serialize, Deserialize)]` statement to the declaration of a custom type. This feature is a nice step up in usability compared to the steps that are needed in MPI to send user defined types.

4.2 Ensuring Buffer Safety for Non-blocking Communication

One of Rust's unique selling points are its compile time guarantees for memory safety without needing a garbage collector. The central feature that allows the compiler to achieve this is called *Ownership*. All data that is allocated in a Rust program has to have exactly one owner. If the owner variable goes out of scope the memory is automatically deallocated. This concept can be applied very well to the previously described problems with unsafe data buffers for MPI's non-blocking operations. Listing 1.4 presents the signatures of heimdallr's non-blocking send and receive functions. They are very similar to the blocking versions from the last section but contain two significant changes. Instead of a reference to the data buffer the non-blocking send function takes ownership of the buffer from the function caller. This means that after the function call has returned the caller no longer has access to the buffer. Modifying it like in the MPI example from Listing 1.2 would lead to a compilation error due to accessing data whose ownership has been moved into the send function. This protects the buffer while the message passing operation is processed in the background. For retrieving ownership of the data buffer the non-blocking send function returns a data handle type, which provides member functions comparable to `MPI_Wait`.

```
1  pub fn send_nb<T>(&self, data: T, dest: u32, id: u32)
2      -> std::io::Result<NbDataHandle<std::io::Result<T>>>
3
4  pub fn receive_nb<T>(&self, source: u32, id: u32)
5      -> std::io::Result<NbDataHandle<std::io::Result<T>>>
```

Listing 1.4. Function signatures of heimdallr's non-blocking send and receive operations

As we can see, the workflow of using non-blocking communication in heimdallr is more or less the same as in MPI but Rust's ownership concept allows the library to actually enforce the rules of having to verify the safety status of data buffers before being able to access them again. This approach works very well from the perspective of safety but it does have some drawbacks. Data ownership can only be moved for entire objects. Many HPC applications contain a core data structure such as a matrix of which only certain parts need to be communicated via message passing. Using heimdallr's non-blocking operations in such a scenario would mean that the whole data structure becomes inaccessible until the ownership has been retrieved. This is not acceptable for algorithms that need to work on other parts of the data while the non-blocking message passing takes place in the background. Therefore, using heimdallr might require some restructuring of distributed data structures where the parts of the data that are used in message passing are isolated as separate objects. This might impact the performance negatively for reasons such as worsened cache-locality.

```
1  match client.id {
2    0 => nb = client.send_nb(buf, 1, 0).unwrap(),
3    1 => buf = client.receive(0,0).unwrap(),
4  }
5  match client.id {
6    0 => {
7      buf = nb.data().unwrap();
8      println!("{:?}", buf);
9    },
10   1 =>  println!("{:?}", buf), // THIS DOES NOT COMPILE!
11 }
```

Listing 1.5. Simplified example of a use pattern of heimdallr's non-blocking communication that produces compilation errors

Listing 1.5 showcases a second problem with the usage of heimdallr's non-blocking operations. In the first match statement of the example in line 2 the process 0 uses a non-blocking send operation to transmit a buffer to process 1. In the second match statement in line 7 the ownership of the buffer is requested back from process 0 and both processes try to access it by printing the buffer's contents. Getting the ownership of the data back works well for process 0 but this example does not compile because of process 1's access on the buffer variable in line 10. Rust's borrow-checking algorithm is not able to correctly analyse the control flow of this example program and instead detects that process 1 might not have ownership of the buffer variable because it was moved in the previous match statement by process 0.

This is problematic because the code pattern given in Listing 1.5, where a non-blocking operation that is only executed conditionally based on the process ID and then later concluded in a similar conditional block, appears frequently in message passing applications. Up until this point we could not find a generalizable solution for this problem. Depending on the context most often the code can be restructured in a way that the compiler will accept it in the end, but doing so will add more complexity to the code and and make it less readable. We hope that future improvements on the Rust borrow checker algorithm like those presented in [6] will fix this problem but currently workarounds in the code need to be used to implement these kind of message passing code patterns.

5   Related Work

When looking at the traditional approach of using MPI with C/C++ or Fortran, static analysis methods are the most promising for detecting errors in the code or communication scheme of parallel applications. The MPI-Checker [5] project is a static analysis tool built upon LLVM's C/C++ compiler frontend Clang. It is able to detect some process local errors such as type mismatches between the true data type of a buffer and the stated `MPI_Datatype` and incorrect buffer referencing where the passed void pointer does not point to valid data. Furthermore, it is able to detect some common errors in the communication scheme of applications. This encompasses deadlock detection and missing communication partners for point-to-point message passing. Additionally it can analyze and detect some errors with MPI's non-blocking communication such as missing `MPI_Wait` calls. As this paper has shown, many of these error classes are already caught automatically at compile time by our Rust implementation.

One reason why MPI applications are so error-prone is that end users have to use the low-level MPI operations to parallelize their applications. From a usability standpoint, a higher abstraction level as well as easy-to-use parallel data structures and algorithms would be preferable. The desire for such solutions is apparent when looking at the popularity of OpenMP, which provides such features for a multi-threading context. The Chapel [4] project is one example for such a solution. Chapel is a special purpose language that is designed for scientific computing in an HPC context. It provides automatically distributed data structures and algorithms to the user with a syntax that is comparable to writing sequential code. Most of the parallelization logic is hidden from the user, which avoids possible parallelization errors. This approach has great usability advantages but being its own special purpose programming language, the barrier of entry is higher compared to using general purpose languages like C or Rust.

MPI bindings for Rust exist in the form of *rsmpi* [10], which supports a subset of MPI's operations containing all two-sided communication functions and most collective operations. The syntax of the message passing operations is in a more Rust-like style that looks quite different from traditional MPI code. Improvements like automatic data type deduction for buffers and some guarantees for better handling of `MPI_Requests` for non-blocking communication are present, where the latter is handled quite different than in our implementation. For users who are not familiar with MPI code, the rsmpi syntax might prove a bit challenging.

For our work, we decided against an approach that is reliant on an existing MPI implementation. Building our Rust message passing library from scratch allowed for a more concise interface and clearer semantics of message passing functions. Furthermore, we were able to experiment with some ideas that do not exist in MPI, such as shared distributed data structures and a central daemon process that can participate in the message passing at runtime.

6   Evaluation

In this section we perform an evaluation on our work with heimdallr. In Sects. 6.1 and 6.2 the performance of heimdallr is compared to equivalent MPI applications. All measurements for the benchmarks in this sections where done on identical computing nodes with the following specs:

- 4x AMD Opteron Processor 6344 (48 cores total)
- 128 GB RAM
- 40 GBit/s InfiniBand network (using TCP over InfiniBand)

For a fair comparison, MPI and heimdallr both used TCP over InfiniBand, because heimdallr currently only works with TCP. All results presented in this section are averaged over three separate benchmark runs.

6.1   Performance Comparison on a Realistic Application

This benchmark uses a realistic scientific application called partdiff that was developed for teaching purposes at the University of Hamburg's Scientific Computing group. It solves a partial differential equation by continuously iterating over a distributed matrix with a stencil operator. This type of application can be categorized as a *structured grid* approach and belongs to the so-called *seven dwarfs of HPC* [2], which makes it a good benchmark candidate to compare both message passing implementations. The original partdiff is written in C and

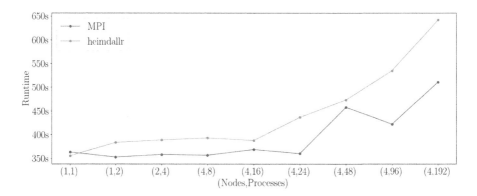

Fig. 2. Weak scaling benchmark for MPI and heimdallr versions of the partdiff application with increasing (#Nodes,#Total processes)

parallelized with MPI. We implemented an equivalent Rust version that uses our heimdallr library for the message passing aspects.

Figure 2 presents a runtime comparison of the two partdiff versions for different configurations of computing nodes and process counts. The weak scaling behaviour of both applications was examined. The results show that from a performance standpoint heimdallr is beaten by MPI. However, this was expected since the performance of MPI implementations has been optimized for decades and for our proof of concept implementation pure performance was not the main focus. The runtime differences can mainly be attributed to two factors. Firstly, the serialization of message data will always produce more overhead than MPI's approach of sending raw byte streams that are written directly into memory at the receiver's end. Secondly, since we only had four computing nodes available the later data points spawn a lot of processes on the same nodes. This leads to a lot of intra-node communication, for which MPI features optimizations that are not yet implemented in heimdallr.

Overall, for most data points heimdallr does not perform significantly worse than MPI and we believe that the provided benefits from better compile time correctness checking and its usability advantages make up for the performance differences.

6.2   Micro Benchmarks for Message Passing Operations

While the previous benchmark shows heimdallr's comparable performance in the context of a realistic application, it does not expose the direct performance difference between the individual message passing operations. Table 1 refers to a micro benchmark that only measures message passing performance without any other unrelated computations. It exchanges 1,000 messages in total between two processes on different computing nodes. Multiple measurements with increasing message sizes were done for the blocking send and receive operations of MPI and heimdallr. The results show that heimdallr's message passing operations have a

Table 1. Performance comparison of heimdallr and MPI for 1000 sent messages between two computing nodes with increasing data size

	$1000 \times 100\,\mathrm{KB}$	$1000 \times 1\,\mathrm{KB}$	$1000 \times 10\,\mathrm{KB}$	$1000 \times 100\,\mathrm{KB}$	$1000 \times 1\,\mathrm{MB}$
MPI	0.0257 s	0.0284 s	0.0456 s	0.2116 s	1.2426 s
heimdallr	0.1661 s	0.1822 s	0.3650 s	2.1253 s	19.303 s
Serialization time	0.0012 s	0.0119 s	0.1192 s	1.1795 s	12.056 s
Serialization time share	0.7%	6.5%	32.7%	55.5%	62.5%

significant computational overhead compared to their MPI equivalents. A significant part of this is due to the serialization of the message data that is performed by heimdallr. In the second table row the serialization and deserialization time of the data buffers has been isolated. It turns out that the time spent in the serialization procedure is above average compared to the message size. This is a trade-off in heimdallr between safety/usability and performance. Serialization allows for transmitting nearly any user defined type and also gives runtime error checks for type correctness of message passing operations but will always require additional computations for the transformation of the transmitted data.

6.3 Limitations of Compile Time Correctness Checks for Message Passing Applications

All compile time correctness checks of heimdallr have in common that they only consider errors that are local to one process of the parallel heimdallr application. Parallelization errors such as deadlocks caused by blocking operations or missing communication partners for send/receive operations are not caught by the compiler. This is due to the fact that the compiler does not know about the broader context of the message passing code. Without knowledge of the actual parallel execution configuration in which heimdallr library calls will be communicating with each other, there is no way to detect these types of errors at compile time.

At this point, there are two possible solutions to include such correctness checks. Firstly, an external static analysis tool like MPI-Checker [5] could be developed for heimdallr. Secondly, direct modifications to the Rust compiler could be made to make it aware of the logic and semantics of message passing applications. The first solutions seems more feasible at the current time. With a static analysis approach that is aware of the parallel context of SPMD applications and the semantics of the used message passing library more thorough correctness checks for process interactions could be deployed.

7 Conclusion and Future Work

This paper shows that the Rust programming language is very applicable for message passing applications. Our heimdallr implementation is able to provide a much safer environment for parallel programming by leveraging Rust's compile time correctness guarantees. Compared to MPI, the performance of heimdallr is lacking behind, but not by unacceptable margins. In addition, our implementation is not production ready yet but a proof of concept to demonstrate the benefits of concepts such as *Ownership* for message passing.

Even though improvements in memory and type safety were made, compile time correctness checks for the validity of an application's communication scheme are still missing and would require the help of external static analysis tools or improved compiler support. We plan to integrate static analysis checks as mentioned in Sect. 6.3 into the build process of heimdallr applications.

This work shows that improvements in correctness checking of parallel message passing applications can be achieved without the need for direct compiler modifications but a more complete solution would require awareness by the compiler about the context of message passing. Rust's correctness checks for multi-threaded code are able to detect errors such as data-races because the compiler is aware of the semantics of such concurrent programs. Integrating comparable correctness checking procedures for SPMD parallelization schemes directly into the Rust compiler might yield even stronger correctness guarantees for message passing applications and presents itself to be promising follow-up research on this topic.

Since most of the existing HPC infrastructure today is built upon MPI and C/C++ it would be interesting to further explore whether Rust's safety concepts such as ownership could be applied there retroactively via the use of static analysis and source-to-source translation methods.

It also seems feasible that at least some of the correctness features of heimdallr could be implemented in modern C++ bindings for MPI by using templates for the type safety aspects and smart pointer types such as `unique_ptr` for data buffer protection in the context of non-blocking communication.

References

1. Amaral, V., et al.: Programming languages for data-intensive HPC applications: a systematic mapping study. Parallel Comput. **91**, 102584 (2020). https://doi.org/10.1016/j.parco.2019.102584
2. Asanović, K., et al.: The landscape of parallel computing research: a view from Berkeley. Technical report UCB/EECS-2006-183, EECS Department, University of California, Berkeley (2006). http://www2.eecs.berkeley.edu/Pubs/TechRpts/2006/EECS-2006-183.html
3. Ba, T.N., Arora, R.: Towards developing a repository of logical errors observed in parallel code for teaching code correctness. In: EduHPC@SC, pp. 69–77. IEEE (2018)
4. Chamberlain, B.L., Callahan, D., Zima, H.P.: Parallel programmability and the chapel language. Int. J. High Perform. Comput. Appl. **21**(3), 291–312 (2007)
5. Droste, A., Kuhn, M., Ludwig, T.: MPI-checker: static analysis for MPI. In: LLVM@SC, pp. 3:1–3:10. ACM (2015)

6. Matsakis, N.D.: An alias-based formulation of the borrow checker. http:// smallcultfollowing.com/babysteps/blog/2018/04/27/an-alias-based-formulation- of-the-borrow-checker/ (2018). Accessed on Mar 2021
7. bincode org: Bincode. https://github.com/bincode-org/bincode (2021). Accessed on Mar 2021
8. R, B.: "Rust is the future of systems programming, C is the new assembly": intel principal engineer, Josh Triplett. https://hub.packtpub.com/rust-is-the- future-of-systems-programming-c-is-the-new-assembly-intel-principal-engineer- josh-triplett/ (2019). Accessed on Mar 2021
9. serde rs: Serde. https://serde.rs/ (2021). Accessed on Mar 2021
10. rsmpi: rsmpi. https://github.com/rsmpi/rsmpi (2021). Accessed on Mar 2021
11. Vanderwiel, S.P., Nathanson, D., Lilja, D.J.: Complexity and performance in par- allel programming languages. In: HIPS, p. 3. IEEE Computer Society (1997)
12. Yu, Z., Song, L., Zhang, Y.: Fearless Concurrency? Understanding Concurrent Programming Safety in Real-World Rust Software. ArXiv: CoRR abs/1902.01906 (2019)

Potential of Interpreter Specialization
for Data Analysis

Wei He$^{(\boxtimes)}$ and Michelle Mills Strout

University of Arizona, Tucson, AZ 85721, USA
{hewei,mstrout}@email.arizona.edu

Abstract. Scientists frequently implement data analyses in high-level programming languages such as Python, Perl, Lu, and R. Many of these languages are inefficient due to the overhead of being dynamically typed and interpreted. In this paper, we report the potential performance improvement of domain-specific interpreter specialization for data analysis workloads and evaluate how the characteristics of data analysis workloads affect the specialization, both positively and negatively. Assisted by compilers, we specialize the Lu and CPython interpreters at source-level using the script being interpreted and the data types during the interpretation as invariants for five common tasks from real data analysis workloads. Through experiments, we measure 9.0–39.6% performance improvement for Lu and 11.0–17.2% performance improvement for CPython for benchmarks that perform data loading, histogram computation, data filtering, data transformation, and dataset shuffle. This specialization does not include misspeculation checks of data types at possible type conversion code that may be necessary for other workloads. We report the details of our evaluation and present a semi-automatic method for specializing the interpreters.

Keywords: Interpreter specialization · Profile-based optimization · Compiler-assisted specialization

1 Introduction

In recent years, interpreted languages such as Python, Perl, and R have come to dominate data analysis software development in many areas of science: for example, a 2017 study [14] of software used in PubMed publications showed that over 67% of them were implemented in languages that are typically interpreted: R (31.9%), Python (12.1%), Matlab (11.8%), Perl (8.9%), and JavaScript (2.7%). Such languages have been referred to as productivity languages [4]. The high-level abstractions supported by such languages enable rapid prototyping which, together with the re-use of contributed code from the scientific community, has led to productivity gains in the development of data analysis programs/scripts.

Unfortunately, some of the features that make these languages productive, e.g., dynamic typing, dynamic error checking, and being interpreted, incur significant runtime overheads. This can lead to scientists waiting hours, days, weeks,

© Springer Nature Switzerland AG 2021
H. Jagode et al. (Eds.): ISC High Performance 2021 Workshops, LNCS 12761, pp. 212–225, 2021.
https://doi.org/10.1007/978-3-030-90539-2_14

or months to test their under-development data analysis scripts on realistic datasets. Alternatives for dealing with this performance problem include (1) reducing the accuracy of their analysis results by sampling larger datasets in some application-specific way; (2) using language-specific, but general, compilers or JIT compilers such as TraceMonkey [11], PyPy [3], or McVM [7]; (3) using performance-optimized libraries such as NumPy in Python [24] or the Image Processing Toolbox in Matlab [23]; and (4) porting data analysis development to more performant programming languages such as Julia [2], Chapel [5], or C/C++ and OpenMP.

The application-specific modification of algorithms is not a general solution. JIT compilers need to be generally applicable and thus typically have a small scope of optimization that is possible that must be balanced with runtime overhead. Using performance-optimized libraries only works well if all of the expensive computations map to these interfaces. Porting code requires extra development time, limiting scientists' ability to rapidly prototype solutions.

Another long-standing approach to optimizing an interpreter is to specialize the interpreter for a particular input script, also known as the first Futamura projection [10]. A profile-directed approach for interpreter specialization based on an input script called Invariant-induced Pattern based Loop Specialization (IPLS) was presented by Oh et al. [17,18] and can be used with interpreters that can be compiled into LLVM [13]. However, this approach aims to be generally applicable to all possible input scripts.

It has not been studied how much performance improvement the interpreter specialization can bring for scientific workloads, specifically data analysis scripts. In particular, since input datasets of data analysis are often in tabular formats where a column of data is usually of the same type, we hypothesize that the runtime data types rarely change, thus enabling specializations to reduce runtime type examinations.

In addition, for specializations on script invariants and data types, runtime misspeculation happens when a specialized interpretation encounters an unseen bytecode instruction or different data type values from the profile, thus requiring extra runtime checks on the specialized values and fallback to unspecialized code if a check fails. Both of these, if frequent, diminish the performance of the specialization. Therefore, we also hypothesize that full script coverage can be achieved during profiling to eliminate misspeculation on script invariants for non-self-modifying languages.

In this paper, we evaluate the characteristics of data analysis workloads and our hypotheses, and analyze how they affect the specialization opportunities and misspeculation handling for the Python and Lu language interpreters. We measure the performance improvement of the specialization with manually identified script invariants and data types, and a semi-automatic source-level specialization method assisted by compiler optimizations. We find that (1) data types are mostly stable throughout the script interpretations, thus enabling specialization on those types, and (2) achieving full script coverage is not generally feasible due to the wide use of libraries, hence we can only reduce the chance of misspeculation in the user's script. With only 2283 SLOC changes for the CPython interpreter and 1509 SLOC changes for the Lu interpreter, it was possible to achieve 9% to 39.6% performance improvement to five common data analysis tasks from Kaggle [1].

This result is based on specialization using stable data types from a profile. Further protection by runtime misspeculation checks of data types at possible dynamic type conversions may be necessary for other workloads.

In this paper, we make the following contributions:

– We identify characteristics of data analysis workloads and report their impacts on the performance of interpreter specialization.
– We present a compiler-assisted semi-automatic method for interpreter specialization through a source-level specialization that only requires developers to create a bee template for each distinct bytecode operator with newly declared scalar variables replacing the original invariant variables, and to instantiate the templates in order according to the input script.
– We evaluate the performance improvement of the Lu and CPython interpreter specialization with five common data analysis tasks from Kaggle and report 9.0–39.6% and 11.0–17.2% overall performance improvement for Lu and CPython respectively.

2   Motivating Example

In Fig. 1, we illustrate the interpretation overhead that can be specialized out through an unrolled interpretation according to an example script. Potential benefits come from the elimination of the interpretation loop overhead, opcode dispatch, and runtime checks on data types. We specialize the highlighted interpreter operations by adding assignments that trigger traditional compiler optimizations such as constant propagation and dead-code elimination. Thus, the instruction fetches and the data type checks will be automatically removed based on the runtime invariant values.

Domain-Specific Runtime Invariants. Since the interpreted bytecode program does not change during an interpretation, Lines 3–4 in Fig. 1(a) can be determined beforehand. Also, because the data types in this example do not change, we specialize on the data type values at Lines 8–9 and 21. We obtain the values of these invariants by instrumenting the interpreter to print out runtime values.

To eliminate the interpretation overhead, we unroll the interpretation for-loop according to the input bytecode program, i.e., copy the loop body that corresponds to each bytecode instruction one by one and place them in order. We then replace the invariants with scalar variables of their values to enable compiler-assisted constant propagation and dead-code elimination. The resulting specialization is given in Fig. 1(d)–(e).

```
1   for (;;) {
2     Instruction i; ...
3     fetch_next_instruction(i);
4     dispatch (GET_OPCODE(i)) {
5       case OP_ADD: {
6         Value *op1 = get_operand_1(i);
7         Value *op2 = get_operand_2(i);
8         if (op1->type == TYPE_INT
9              && op2->type == TYPE_INT) { ...
10        } else if (tonumber(op1, &num1)
11                 && tonumber(op2, &num2)) { ...
12        } else { ... }
13        break;
14      }
15      case OP_SUB: ...
16      ...
17    }
18  }
19  ...
20  int tonumber(Value *obj, Number *num) {
21    if (obj->type == TYPE_INT) ...
22    ...
23  }                    Original interpretation loop
```

(a)

```
local a = <input from file>
local b = <input from file>
if a < b then
  a = a + b
  b = a + b
end
                          Interpreted script
```

(b)

```
LOAD_FAST 0 ...
LOAD_FAST 1 ...
LT 0 1
JMP 7   //jump to RETURN
ADD 0 0 1
ADD 1 0 1
RETURN

                          Interpreted bytecode
                                  program
```

(c)

```
1   #define spec_ADD(i_val,
2                     op1_type_val,
3                     op2_type_val) {
4     assert(i == i_val);
5     i = i_val;
6     Value *op1 = get_operand_1(i);
7     Value *op2 = get_operand_2(i);
8     assert(op1->type == op1_type_val);
9     assert(op2->type == op2_type_val);
10    int op1_type = op1_type_val;
11    int op2_type = op2_type_val;
12    if (op1_type == TYPE_INT
13        && op2_type == TYPE_INT) { ...
14    } else if (spec_tonumber(op1, &num1, op1_type)
15             && spec_tonumber(op2, &num2, op2_type)) {
16      ...
17    } else { ... }
18  }
19  ...
20  inline int spec_tonumber(Value *obj, Number *num,
21                     enum Type obj_type) {
22    if (obj_type == TYPE_INT) ...
23    ...
24  }                    Specialization template
```

(d)

```
void spec_interpretation(...) {
  ...
  fetch_next_instruction(i);
  spec_LOAD_FAST(...);

  fetch_next_instruction(i);
  spec_LOAD_FAST(...);

  fetch_next_instruction(i);
  spec_LT(...);

  fetch_next_instruction(i);
  spec_JMP(..., jump_target);

  fetch_next_instruction(i);
  spec_ADD(16397, TYPE_INT, TYPE_INT);

  fetch_next_instruction(i);
  spec_ADD(12615757, TYPE_INT, TYPE_INT);

jump_target:
  fetch_next_instruction(i);
  spec_RETURN();              Specialized
}                              interpretation
```

(e)

Fig. 1. Original and specialized interpretation loop

Impact of Misspeculations. Since the specialization uses values from profiles, misspeculation happens during an execution if these values become different from the ones observed in profiles. Misspeculation is expensive because once it happens, the execution has to return to the unspecialized code or even terminate. Runtime checks on invariant values to detect such situations also have to be placed in the specialized code, thus may add extra overhead. So reducing the chances of misspeculation is desired.

Unstable input data types can cause misspeculation. For example, the types of a and b in Fig. 1(b) are determined by values in the input files that may become unexpected and cause misspeculation in an execution. If the input dataset of a workload is of the typical tabular format and all values in the same column have the same type, we say this workload has *stable input data types*.

Misspeculation could also happen if there are unexpected data type changes at runtime. For example, if the output `a` of the first `ADD` instruction could have different types depending on runtime values, it causes misspeculation on the operand type of `a` at the second `ADD` instruction (which is not the case in our example). If an operand data type at a bytecode instruction always keeps the same given stable input data types, we say this operand data type at this instruction is *stable*.

Another source of misspeculation is an execution may encounter a bytecode instruction not observed in the profile due to insufficient script coverage during profiling. We say an interpreter profile has *full script coverage* if all execution paths in the script are taken at least once in the profile. We aim to eliminate chances of script invariant misspeculation via full script coverage during profiling.

3   Characteristics of Data Analysis Workloads

In this section, we evaluate two hypotheses that, if true, enable specializations on data types and provides a way to eliminate misspeculation on script invariants.

1. Runtime checks on data types comprise substantial performance overhead, but the examined data types are mostly stable in data analysis script executions.
2. Misspeculations could cause substantial overhead, but full script coverage during profiling can eliminate misspeculation on script invariants.

If the first hypothesis is true, we can expect substantial performance gain by specializing on data type values. With the second hypothesis being true, the chance of misspeculation can be reduced and runtime checks against script invariant misspeculation can be removed.

Through experiments, we found that runtime data types are mostly stable and could lead to 3.8–7.2% potential savings from the specialization in estimation. Our experiment result in Sect. 5 shows 1.4–10.1% improvement in reality. Also, profiling with full script coverage can help avoid misspeculation that potentially affects the specialization improvement, but the use of external libraries in data analysis scripts makes it difficult to achieve full script coverage.

3.1   Methodology

We examine scripts for typical data analysis tasks with the Lu-5.3.5 and CPython-3.6.2 interpreters. Specifically, we collect the twelve top-voted real scripts for five top-voted datasets on Kaggle, namely, (i) COVID-19 Open Research Dataset Challenge, (ii) Credit Card Fraud Detection, (iii) Novel Corona Virus 2019 Dataset, (iv) Heart Disease UCI, and (v) Netflix Movies and TV Shows. We then extract the five most common tasks from these scripts, including (1) data loading from CSV files, (2) histogram computation, (3) column scan and filtering (such as counting NULL values in a column), (4) column transformation into a new column, and (5) dataset shuffle and split (in descending order of their commonality).

These tasks are typically performed by calling external libraries in the real scripts. To exclude the influence of external libraries from the initial study of the workload characteristics, we re-implement these tasks from scratch without external library calls. We analyze the impact of using external libraries on the specialization in Sect. 3.4. Additionally, since the Python Standard Library implements the data loading from CSV files through efficient C code, we do not examine the first task for CPython.

3.2   Hypothesis of Stable Data Types

In this section, we examine the input data type stability. We also estimate the percentage of assembly instructions spent on data type checks and report the percentage of bytecode instructions that do not observe operand types changing throughout the examined interpretations.

Stability of Input Data Types. Among the five examined datasets that consist of 8–31 columns each, we found that three of them have stable data types columnwise, i.e., all values except NULLs in a column are of the same type. The other two datasets each contain one column that mixes integers and floating-point numbers together, which can be easily unified before the script interpretations through preprocessing. So we claim it is reasonable to assume stable input data types for tabular datasets of data analysis workloads.

Runtime Overhead of Data Type Examinations and Stability of Data Types. To estimate the percentage of assembly instructions on type checks, we obtain the total amount of assembly instruction using Callgrind [9] and count the number of data type examinations by instrumenting the interpreters. We then assume each check consists of three or four assembly instructions, for loading the data type descriptor, optionally loading a constant data type (in CPython), a comparison, and a conditional jump. We estimate the percentage of bytecode instruction operands of stable types by instrumenting the interpreter to print out the examined type values.

Approximately 5.8–7.8% of assembly instructions of the script interpretations are spent on runtime data type checks in the Lu interpreter, and 4.4–6.0% in CPython. Meanwhile, the type stability is 100% for all examined scripts in CPython and is over 92% for four scripts in the Lu interpreter. Overall, 87–100% of the examined data types do not change throughout the interpretation, leading to 3.8–7.2% overhead possibly avoidable through specialization on the type values in arithmetic.

Note that the reported numbers are based on scripts that have been preprocessed to separate the code running over multiple columns of different data types by creating a copy of the code for each individual data type. This separation ideally should be handled inside the specialized interpreter code. For our initial study, however, we separate the code in the script and profile the interpretations again. This simplification should bring equivalent performance to that of handling the code reuse in the specialized interpreter.

3.3   Hypothesis About Full Script Coverage

Since conditional branches in scripts can cause insufficient coverage in profiles, we estimate the chances of misspeculation on script invariants with the percentage of dynamic conditional-jump bytecode instructions in the interpretations. We found that in the Lu interpreter, 11.8–21.8% bytecode instructions were conditional jumps for if-statements in the scripts of data-loading, histogram-computation, and scan-and-filtering, while 8.0–21.8% bytecode instructions were spent on conditional jumps for loop termination checks in all scripts except the data-loading one. In the CPython interpreter, 7.7–10.3% bytecode instructions were conditional jumps for if-statements in the scan-and-filtering and dataset-shuffle scripts, while 4.4–10.3% bytecode instructions were conditional jumps at loop termination checks in all examined scripts. The amount of conditional jumps in the interpretations of data analysis tasks is notable which allows potential misspeculation when the execution of the specialized code takes an uncovered branch in the profile.

We then examine the cost of misspeculation checks. For both the Lu and CPython interpreters, we found that the conditional-jump bytecode operators are implemented with if-statements that can be the de facto misspeculation checks and thus introduce no additional cost. In general, every introduced misspeculation check takes at least three assembly instructions (for loading the current bytecode instruction, performing a comparison, and jumping based on the result) and executes as many times as the conditional-jump bytecode instruction.

Finally, we examine whether full script coverage is achievable during profiling to reduce the chances of misspeculation on script invariants. We ran the examined scripts with their full input datasets and measured the script coverage with Coverage.py [8] for Python and LuCov [15] for Lu. We found that all examined scripts achieved full script coverage during the interpretations. This result suggests aiming for full coverage of user scripts during profiling is reasonable.

3.4   Impact of the Use of Libraries

There are two potential impacts on interpreter specialization from the use of libraries in the interpreted script:

1. Library calls that are not interpreted cannot be specialized.
2. Full script coverage of the library code is hard to guarantee during profiling.

We found that all of the twelve examined data analysis scripts use at least one library. Besides the Python Standard Library, the top commonly-used external libraries in descending order of their frequencies are pandas [16], NumPy [19], Matplotlib [12], scikit-learn [20], seaborn [22], plotly [21], and SciPy [25]. To the best of our knowledge, NumPy [24] and SciPy [25] are known to execute through lower-level code such as C code, thus cannot be specialized through the interpreter specialization.

To understand how the second impact affects specialization, we looked into the interpretation of a histogram computation using the plotly library as an example. We found that with the full data inputs, 4919 scripts in the plotly library are interpreted and the coverage reported by Coverage.py of the library scripts is only 70% on average. This is because each library script usually contains code for many interface functions whereas a single user's script cannot use them all. So this script-level coverage number is too coarse-grained to indicate whether the profile has a full coverage of the interpreted code. As the result, specialization of the library functions requires a function-level coverage analysis for the interpreted functions only.

4   Semi-Automatic Source-Level Specialization via Compiler Optimizations

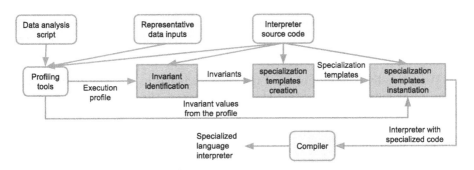

Fig. 2. Workflow of the specialization. Manual steps are highlighted in blue. (Color figure online)

To understand how much performance improvement can be achieved through interpreter specialization for data analysis workloads, experimental evaluation is necessary. Developing a fully automatic technique to identify invariants and perform the specializations is complicated as language interpreters are typically written in low-level languages such as C/C++ where intensive uses of pointers can obfuscate program analysis. However, semi-automatically applied microspecialization has been shown to be effective in the context of interpretation in database management systems [26–28], thus we borrow ideas from that approach.

Therefore, we apply a source-level specialization on interpreters with profiles of full script coverage and manually-identified invariants using domain knowledge about the data type stability. Since the specialization requires unrolling the interpretation loop and making code transformation throughout, which can take a good amount of effort and is error-prone, we developed a semi-automatic, compiler-assisted approach to specialize the interpreter at source-level by using traditional compiler optimizations. It requires developers to write a specialization prototype template for each distinct bytecode operator used in the interpretation with new scalar variables replacing the invariant variables, and instantiate the templates in order according to the interpreted bytecode program. A compiler then compiles this code and performs constant propagation and dead-code elimination to remove the interpretation overhead. The workflow of the specialization process is illustrated in Fig. 2 where blue boxes represent the manual steps. This section presents details of this semi-automatic specialization method.

4.1 Identify the Interpretation Loop and Invariants

We locate the interpretation loop as the hot loop in the hottest function in a Callgrind profile of the interpreter. We then identify two kinds of invariants:

1. Data-type "invariants": values of data type descriptors or expressions involving data types and constants in the interpreter code that are observed to keep the same in the profile. These values are likely to be invariants based on domain knowledge of data analysis workloads.
2. Script invariants: values representing the interpreted script or expressions involving these values and constants in the interpreter code, such as the interpreted bytecode instructions.

We manually identify potential invariant variables in the interpreter source code by looking for data structures that represent the bytecode instructions and type descriptors, attributes that represent the usage of particular language features in data structures of interpretation context states, and expressions that consist of invariants and constants (such as expressions with pointer-based invariants in CPython). A value at a bytecode instruction is an invariant only if it stays the same at this instruction throughout the profile. We obtain a source-level trace of the values of variables that are possibly invariant by instrumenting the original interpreter with print-statements and running the script with a small representative data input.

4.2 Specialization via Code Templates

Instead of manually optimizing the interpreter code where invariant values are known, we employ traditional compilers to automate most of the code transformations. The overall idea of the source-level specialization is to unroll the interpretation loop and specialize every iteration according to the interpreted bytecode instruction to eliminate the overhead of the interpreter dispatch loop. At every iteration, we replace accesses to each invariant variable through pointers in the interpreter source code with accesses to a newly added local scalar variable of the literal invariant values. After these changes, we compile this modified interpreter source code with $-O3$ compiler optimizations. The replacement of variables makes the data flow easy to understand for a traditional compiler to propagate constant values and perform dead-code elimination, thus realizing the code transformations we expect.

To ease the code modification for many bytecode instructions, we create a macro template as the specialization prototype for the interpreter code block of each bytecode operator, and make the runtime invariant values as arguments to the templates. An example is given in Fig. 1(d). Developers need to provide the invariant values extracted from the profile to instantiate the templates in order according to the bytecode program of the interpreted script. This template instantiation step can potentially be automated in the future.

We follow the steps below to specialize the interpretation loop for a script:

1. Recognize interpreter functions called in the interpretation loop through a function-level profile with calling information such as Callgrind. Also, recognize macros used in the interpretation loop by comparing the interpreter source code before and after a C-preprocessor expansion.
2. Create a specialization prototype template for each bytecode operator by replacing each invariant accessed through pointers with a new local scalar variable as mentioned before. Do the same to functions and macros used in this template and declare specialized functions as inline functions. References to invariants in macros can be easily identified after C-preprocessing. The example in Fig. 1(d) highlights the introduced scalar variables in red.
3. In a new function, instantiate the macro templates with invariant values from the profile and place them in order according to the interpreter bytecode program. An example is given in Fig. 1(e).
4. Find a signal in the original interpreter code that indicates the start of the interpretation of the script and redirect the execution to the function of the specialized interpretation. Possible signals include interpretation context state that keeps the current interpreted function name, or the value of the first bytecode instruction in the script.
5. Optionally, to verify the invariant values, place assertions of these values before the specialization on them in the macro templates and run the specialized code with the full input dataset. This allows the unexpected runtime values to be caught. (Notice that the assertions are for verification purposes only, not for protection against misspeculation.) We highlight such assertations in blue in the example in Fig. 1(d).

4.3   Protect Against Misspeculation on Data Types

A naive method for protecting against runtime misspeculation on data types is to check for a data type value wherever it is specialized and catch the mismatch between the values at runtime and in the profile. However, this approach is too expensive as the overhead of runtime checks will offset the performance gain from the specialization. Therefore, we analyze where data types could change at runtime and place misspeculation checks only at the type specializations being affected.

Since we assume stable input data types, misspeculation on data types could only come from unexpected type changes at runtime. One example is the conversion of integer size in CPython when the integer value increases. Such type changes at runtime could cause misspeculation if the type is specialized where it is used later. An instance is mentioned in Sect. 2 where the output of a bytecode instruction could have different types depending on runtime values while another bytecode instruction takes it as an operand and has its type specialized.

In our experiments, we identified bytecode instructions that produced intermediate result data objects of unstable data types, and found their data types were not specialized. We identified these intermediate result data objects by instrumenting the interpreter to print out the data types of manually identified outputs at every bytecode operator and running the instrumented interpreter with the examined scripts and full inputs. We then looked for bytecode instructions that used these outputs by analyzing the data flow of the bytecode program. We found that our specialization had already avoided specializing on these unstable data types. This is because our specialization was based on a profile of a small representative data input that already captured these data type changes. So we did not add misspeculation checks of data types to the specialized interpreter. However, a full specialization technique for other workloads needs to protect against misspeculation of data types in the interpreter.

5   Evaluation of Potential Performance Improvement

With the source-level specialization, we measure the performance improvement the specialization can achieve and analyze how characteristics of data analysis workloads affect interpreter specialization.

We use scripts for the same five common data analysis tasks from Kaggle as those in Sect. 3. But we adjust the scripts to repeat the tasks many times to make the execution time measurement more accurate. We specialize the interpreters of Lu-5.3.5 and CPython-3.6.2, and compile the specialized code using GCC-4.8.4 with the -O3 optimization option. The experiments are conducted on a machine of 2.50 GHz Intel i5-4200M CPU and 4 GB memory. Both Level-1 instruction (L1i) cache and data (L1d) cache are 32 KB in size. There are also 256 KB Level-2 (L2) and 3072 KB Level-3 (L3) caches.

We specialized the interpreters with script invariants and data type values for the examined workloads. The overall execution time improvement is reported in the second and fourth columns of Table 1. To understand where the performance improvement came from, we also measured the performance improvement of the specialization only on script invariants, as given in the third and fifth columns of the same table. The specialization on script invariants brings 6.1–29.7% improvement while specialization on data types brings 1.4–10.1% improvement (i.e., the difference between the overall improvement and the improvement from script invariants only), so both types of invariants are necessary for interpreter specializations.

Table 1. Execution time improvement of Lu and CPython interpreter specializations

Task	Lu time	Lu time (script only)	CPython time	CPython time (script only)
Loading data from file	12.8%	9.0%	N/A	N/A
Computing histograms	35.8%	25.7%	17.2%	14.5%
Scan and filtering	12.1%	9.6%	14.6%	13.2%
Transforming columns	9.0%	6.6%	16.4%	10.3%
Shuffling and splitting dataset	39.6%	29.7%	11.0%	6.1%
Average	21.9%	16.1%	14.8%	11.0%

For all examined scripts in total, we specialized 25 bytecode operators in the Lu interpreter with 11 script invariants and 32 data-type invariants, and 26 bytecode operators in the CPython interpreter with 18 script invariants and 60 data-type invariants. We modified about 230 SLOC of both interpreters for specialization templates, and 520–800 SLOC for instantiating and calling the specialized code. In total, we made 1509 SLOC and 2283 SLOC changes in the Lu and CPython interpreters respectively, which amounts to 9.1% of the Lu interpreter and 0.2% of the CPython interpreter codebases.

For all the examined scripts, we ensured the profiles had the full script coverage, therefore no misspeculation on script invariants happens. During the executions of the specialized code, we observed no runtime misspeculation of invariant values, which indicates that the specialization is reliable. Since the performance improvement of interpreter specialization is significant, we believe interpreter specialization is a good approach to speed up data analysis workloads.

6   Conclusion and Future Work

This paper presents an initial study to examine how the characteristics of data analysis workloads affect the profile-based interpreter specialization and report the potential performance improvement from it. We found that runtime data types tend to be stable for data analysis workloads and full script coverage during profiling helps reduce the chances of misspeculation, but the use of libraries makes full script coverage hard to achieve. An experimental performance evaluation reports 9.0–39.6% performance improvement for Lu and 11.0–17.2% performance improvement for CPython for five common basic data analysis tasks.

This study demonstrates that domain knowledge about the interpreted workloads, e.g., data type stability, can help reveal specialization opportunities after simple preprocessing that brings substantial performance improvement. Also, specialization through constant propagation and dead-code elimination can be effectively semi-automated via traditional compilers to reduce the manual efforts for a source-level specialization. Interpreter specialization for other dynamically typed and non-self-modifying languages should gain similar, if not more, performance improvement since we do not specialize on language-specific features.

For determining where to place misspeculation checks, *type freezing* for reducing misspeculation checks for type specialization in the context of JIT compilation [6] can be taken. We also notice that interpreters may maintain secondary data type information, such as the size of integer data objects, that could change depending on runtime values even if the primary type remains the same. We do not specialize on the integer size in our current work, but since the integer size is checked at every integer comparison, bitwise shift, logical, and arithmetic operations, we think it would be interesting to explore its specialization in the future. Other interesting problems include (1) the possibility to specialize the reference counting and expression stack accesses in interpreters and (2) performance comparison between the presented specialization and other performance improvement approaches such as JIT and performance-optimized libraries.

References

1. Kaggle. https://www.kaggle.com/. Accessed on Apr 2021
2. Bezanson, J., Edelman, A., Karpinski, S., Shah, V.B.: Julia: A fresh approach to numerical computing. Technical report arXiv:1411.1607v4, MIT and Julia Computing (2015)
3. Bolz, C.F., Cuni, A., Fijalkowski, M., Rigo, A.: Tracing the meta-level: pypy's tracing JIT compiler. In: Proceedings of the 4th Workshop on the Implementation, Compilation, Optimization of Object-Oriented Languages and Programming Systems, pp. 18–25 (2009)
4. Catanzaro, B., et al.: SEJITS: getting productivity and performance with selective embedded JIT specialization. Technical report. UCB/EECS-2010-23, EECS Department, University of California, Berkeley (2010)
5. Chamberlain, B.L., et al.: Chapel comes of age: making scalable programming productive. In: Cray User Group Conference (2018)
6. Cheng, L., Ilbeyi, B., Bolz-Tereick, C.F., Batten, C.: Type freezing: exploiting attribute type monomorphism in tracing JIT compilers. In: Proceedings of the 18th ACM/IEEE International Symposium on Code Generation and Optimization, pp. 16–29 (2020)
7. Chevalier-Boisvert, M., Hendren, L., Verbrugge, C.: Optimizing MATLAB through Just-In-Time specialization. In: Gupta, R. (ed.) CC 2010. LNCS, vol. 6011, pp. 46–65. Springer, Heidelberg (2010). https://doi.org/10.1007/978-3-642-11970-5_4
8. Coverage.py Developers: Coverage.py 5.5 documentation (2021). https://coverage.readthedocs.io/en/coverage-5.5/. Accessed on Apr 2021
9. Valgrind Developers: Callgrind: a call-graph generating cache and branch prediction profiler. Valgrind (2021). http://valgrind.org/docs/manual/cl-manual.html. Accessed on Apr 2021
10. Futamura, Y.: Partial evaluation of computation process-an approach to a compiler-compiler. Higher-Order Symbolic Comput. **12**(4), 381–391 (1999)
11. Gal, A., Eich, B., Shaver, M., Anderson, D., Mandelin, D., Haghighat, M.R., Kaplan, B., Hoare, G., Zbarsky, B., Orendorff, J., et al.: Trace-based Just-In-Time type specialization for dynamic languages. ACM Sigplan Not. **44**(6), 465–478 (2009)
12. Hunter, J.D.: Matplotlib: A 2D Graphics Environment. IEEE Ann. Hist. Comput. **9**(03), 90–95 (2007)

13. Lattner, C., Adve, V.: LLVM: a compilation framework for lifelong program analysis & transformation. In: International Symposium on Code Generation and Optimization, 2004. CGO 2004, pp. 75–86. IEEE (2004)
14. Lindenbaum, P.: Programming language use distribution from recent programs/articles (2017). https://www.biostars.org/p/251002/
15. LuCov Developers: LuCov - Coverage analysis for Lu scripts (2021). https://keplerproject.github.io/luacov/. Accessed on Apr 2021
16. McKinney, W., et al.: pandas: a foundational python library for data analysis and statistics. Python High Perform. Sci. Comput. **14**(9), 1–9 (2011)
17. Oh, T., Beard, S.R., Johnson, N.P., Popovych, S., August, D.I.: A generalized framework for automatic scripting language parallelization. In: In the Proceedings of the 26th International Conference on Parallel Architectures and Compilation Techniques (PACT) (2017)
18. Oh, T., Kim, H., Johnson, N.P., Lee, J.W., August, D.I.: Practical automatic loop specialization. In: Proceedings of the Eighteenth International Conference on Architectural Support for Programming Languages and Operating Systems, pp. 419–430. ASPLOS 2013, ACM, New York, NY, USA (2013)
19. Oliphant, T.E.: Guide to NumPy, vol. 1. Trelgol Publishing USA (2006)
20. Pedregosa, F., et al.: Scikit-learn: Machine Learning in Python. J. Mach. Learn. Res. **12**, 2825–2830 (2011)
21. Plotly Developers: Plotly Python Open Source Graphing Library (2021). https://plotly.com/python/. Accessed on Apr 2021
22. Seaborn Developers: seaborn: statistical data visualization (2021). https://seaborn.pydata.org/. Accessed on Apr 2021
23. Shoelson, B., Tannenbaum, B.: New features for high-performance image processing in MATLAB (2012). https://www.mathworks.com/company/newsletters/articles/new-features-for-high-performance-image-processing-in-matlab.html
24. van der Walt, S., Colbert, S.C., Varoquaux, G.: The NumPy array: a structure for efficient numerical computation. Comput. Sci. Eng. **13**(2), 22–30 (2011)
25. Virtanen, P., et al.: SciPy 1.0: fundamental algorithms for scientific computing in Python. Nat. Methods **17**(3), 261–272 (2020)
26. Zhang, R., Debray, S., Snodgrass, R.T.: Micro-specialization: dynamic code specialization of database management systems. In: Proceedings of the Tenth International Symposium on Code Generation and Optimization, pp. 63–73 (2012)
27. Zhang, R., Snodgrass, R.T., Debray, S.: Application of micro-specialization to query evaluation operators. In: 2012 IEEE 28th International Conference on Data Engineering Workshops, pp. 315–321. IEEE (2012)
28. Zhang, R., Snodgrass, R.T., Debray, S.: Micro-specialization in DBMSes. In: 2012 IEEE 28th International Conference on Data Engineering, pp. 690–701. IEEE (2012)

Refactoring for Performance with Semantic Patching: Case Study with Recipes

Michele Martone[1(✉)] [ID] and Julia Lawall[2]

[1] Leibniz Supercomputing Centre, Garching bei Muenchen, Germany
Michele.Martone@lrz.de
[2] Inria-Paris, Paris, France
Julia.Lawall@inria.fr

Abstract. Development of an HPC *simulation code* may take years
of a domain scientists' work. Over that timespan, the computing landscape evolves, efficient programming best practices change, APIs of *performance libraries* change, etc. A moment then comes when the entire
codebase requires a thorough performance lift. In the luckiest case, the
required intervention is limited to a few *hot loops*. In practice, much more
is needed. This paper describes an activity of *programmatic* refactoring
of ≈200k lines of C code by means of source-to-source translation. The
context is that of a so-called *high level support* provided to the domain
scientist community by a HPC service center. The motivation of this
short paper is the immediate reuse potential of these techniques.

1 Introduction

GADGET3 (from now on, GADGET) is a code simulating *large-scale structure (galaxies and clusters) formation.* Not counting forks, it has a codebase of
around 200 kLOC (thousands of Lines of Code) in C. It is being developed by
a geographically sparse community of domain scientists (astrophysicists). Code
revisions progress using a revision control system.

GADGET revolves around the concept of *particle.* A particle and its associated quantities are modeled using a few C `struct`s, e.g.: `struct P {float
x,y,z;} *p;`. Here three quantities are shown; GADGET has around a hun-
dred of them, enabled/disabled via several `#ifdef`s. Memory use is dominated
by a few dynamically allocated global arrays of similar `struct`s. The *number
crunching* defining most of the code accesses these arrays using expressions similar to `p[e].x` (`e` being an indexing *expression*). This data layout goes by the
name of *Arrays of Structures* (AoS). The GADGET community finds this layout very handy: the AoS definitions reside in one single header maintained by
the project lead. Collaborators maintain separate source files with functionality
(in jargon, *physics modules*) de-/activated by `#ifdef`s.

While appreciated by the community, AoS performs suboptimally on the
frequently occurring *streaming access* loops. On current architectures, the *complementary* layout – *Structures of Arrays* (SoA) – performs better here, for

© Springer Nature Switzerland AG 2021
H. Jagode et al. (Eds.): ISC High Performance 2021 Workshops, LNCS 12761, pp. 226–232, 2021.
https://doi.org/10.1007/978-3-030-90539-2_15

it favours *compiler autovectorization* [5]. The SoA equivalent of the previously sketched AoS is: `struct P {float *x,*y,*z;} p;`, with dynamically allocated arrays `p.x`, `p.y`, and `p.z`. Besides redefinition of *particle* `struct`s and introducing a few new variables, porting AoS to SoA requires rewriting the bulk of the code. Namely, translating all the non-trivial expressions containing combinations of AoS accesses like `p[e].x` into using the `p.x[e]`-like syntax. Still, operations that move particles are more practical with AoS, than on structures scattered across a few hundred arrays. Thus, one may want to retain the AoS definitions, and use *scatter/gather* operations to occasionally convert *to/from* SoA, like in sorting or *load balancing* across distributed processes over MPI.

GADGET is a major astrophysical code and improving its performance is highly desirable. Baruffa et al. [2] estimated a performance improvement with SoA as exceeding 2×, but their study was limited to an excerpt of circa 1kLOC. The present article tackles the problem of *backporting SoA* to the entire ≈200 kLOC code, respecting its many build-time `#ifdef` variants.

The present work has been carried within a longer-term (so-called *high level support*) activity at LRZ, and has targeted both a legacy version (P-GADGET3) and a development one (codenamed OPENGADGET3, from non-public source repositories) forks, both from the Max-Planck Institute for Astrophysics in Garching, Germany. These [6,7] are derivatives of GADGET2 [8]

This article applies to both and addresses either by the namesake GADGET. Although we are aware of C++-based techniques to use a SoA semantics with AoS syntax, we had to rule those out: keeping the code in C has been a project requirement.

2   Prospective Factorization Steps and Tool Choice

Essential to any AoS to SoA translation are: 1. Identifying AoS members to be made into SoA arrays; 2. Declaring new SoA types and variables in a global scope; 3. For each new SoA array, adding de-/allocation and AoS ↔ SoA gather/scatter primitives; 4. Accessing each new SoA array by mutating corresponding AoS *expressions*. Such changes are constrained by interrelated factors:

- *timeliness*: How to quickly change so many lines of code?
- *correctness*: How to avoid introducing mistakes? Note the aggravation of having numerous build-time *code paths* implied by the `#ifdef`s.
- *flexibility*: Can we enact only a *partial* SoA translation, possibly on demand?
- *continuity*: Can we develop in AoS, transforming only before *build and run*?
- *acceptance*: How to have the community *accept* the proposed solution?

Timeliness requires an automated tool. *Correctness* calls for a tool having a model of a C program. A programmable, or at least parametric solution in choosing AoS quantities would be best: we do not know which *subset* of a complete SoA transition is most performant under which configuration (moreover, several code forks exist). *Continuity* by preserving the current AoS development culture would maximize *acceptance*.

Existing Integrated Development Environments (IDEs) are too primitive for these changes. *Regular expressions* are tempting but brittle: C *expressions* may span multiple lines, and do not generally fit regular expressions. ROSE is a compiler-based infrastructure for developing program analyses and transformations. It requires working at the AST level and regenerates the affected code. Manipulating ASTs can be awkward for the developer, who is more familiar with the code base in its source code representation. The regenerated code does not follow the whitespace usage of the original code, which can lead to many superfluous diffs between the old and new versions. This is especially problematic in the case of a legacy code base, where users are mostly concerned with stability and any changes have to be checked carefully.

These factors suggested the use of the COCCINELLE rule-based language for transforming C code [3,4]. COCCINELLE is a *metalanguage* routinely used by the **Linux kernel** developer community for large-scale updating of API usages and data structure layouts. The use of COCCINELLE on driver code results in mostly short **diffs**, which is not the case here. Its use in HPC is in its inception.

3   Thinking Out COCCINELLE Transformation Rules

COCCINELLE's rule syntax is a variant of the familiar **patch** syntax, thus also serving as documentation of the performed changes. A rule may *match* code at a function, definition, or declaration level, etc. Matching is independent of code layout, sensitive to control-flow, and takes into account type information. The modification specification is intermingled in the rule: that motivates terming this technology *semantic patching*. Rules can be chained; they involve notions of existential and universal quantifiers, as often found in *logic programming languages*.

Section 2 has enumerated well-defined factorization steps. Below, we describe their counterpart as real-life semantic patches.

3.1   Identify AoS Variables for Reuse in SoA

GADGET AoS variables involve variables of type **particle_data** and **sph_parti-cle_data**, and their members. The variables are found by the COCCINELLE rule prtcl_str , at right. Such a rule has two parts. Lines 1-7 describe a set of metavariables, which match any term of the indicated kind: id (line 2) matches any identifier, limited to a set of possible names (**particle_data** and **sph_particle_data**), while I matches any identifier without

```
1  @prtcl_str@
2  identifier id = {
       particle_data,
       sph_particle_data};
3  field list fs;
4  identifier I;
5  declaration d;
6  type ST;
7  @@
8  (
9    struct id { fs } *I;
10 &
11   ST         { fs } *I;
12 &
13   d
14 )
```

restriction. Lines 8–14 provide a *pattern* that matches a structure declaration. This pattern matches the declaration in three ways, connected as a *conjunction* by the enclosing (and) (lines 8 and 14), and by the occurrences of & on lines 10 and 12. The first pattern (line 9) exposes the details of the declaration, matching id to the name of the structure type, fs to the list of members (referred to by COCCINELLE as a field list) and I to the name of the declared variable. The second pattern (line 11) matches ST to the entire type. The third pattern (line 13) matches d to the complete declaration. A match against a declaration in the C code only succeeds if all three patterns match the declaration.

Identifying members within the types of the variables matched by the previous rule is done by the following rule. This rule matches members of a previously selected structure (referenced by the redeclaration of id on line 2), such that the members are restricted to have one of a specified list of type s (line 5). Ellipses (...) (line 7) match the context around each matching member. This rule is applied once for each struct name for which a variable was found by the previous rule. There may furthermore be many matching members. This rule (and those dependent on it) is applied on each possible match.

```
1 @prtcl_str_mmbrs@
2 identifier prtcl_str.id;
3 identifier M, P;
4 typedef MyDouble, MyFloat, MyLongDouble, MyDoublePos, MyBigFloat;
5 type MT={double,float,MyDouble,MyFloat,MyLongDouble,MyDoublePos,MyBigFloat
        };
6 @@
7 struct id { ... MT M; ... } *P;
```

3.2   Clone Structures and Make Them SoA

Firstly, we want to derive SoA type identifiers id1 from previously matched AoS identifiers id . For this, we exploit the PYTHON scripting functionality. Likewise, we create SoA variable identifiers.

```
1 @script:python                    1 @script:python new_prtcl_str_var_id@
    new_prtcl_str_id@                2 I << prtcl_str.I;
2 id << prtcl_str.id;               3 J;// same as fresh identifier J=I ## "_soa
3 id1;                                 ";
4 @@                                4 @@
5 coccinelle.id1="%s_soa_t"%(id)    5 coccinelle.J="%s_soa"%(I)
```

Once the SoA identifiers are ready, we can add the new type definitions in the main header, extern variable declarations in most sources, and the variables themselves in one specific point. The choice of the *attach points* is crucial here.

```
1 @insert_new_prtcl_str depends on   1 @insert_new_prtcl_str_var_extr@
    prtcl_str@                       2 identifier new_prtcl_str_id.id1;
2 identifier new_prtcl_str_id.id1;   3 identifier prtcl_str.I;
3 field list prtcl_str.fs;           4 fresh identifier J = I ## "_soa";
4 type T;                            5 @@
5 @@                                 6 struct id1 { ... };
6 extern int maxThreads;             7 ++extern struct id1 J;
7 ++struct id1 { fs };
```

```
1 @insert_new_prtcl_str_var@
2 identifier new_prtcl_str_id.id1, prtcl_str.I, new_prtcl_str_var_id.J;
3 @@
4 struct global_data_all_processes All;
5 ++struct id1 J;
```

A few adjustments are still needed in SoA: we want to exclude union s. So we first match them, then erase them from the recently created definitions.

```
1 @match_anon_union@
2 identifier id;
3 identifier J;
4 field list[n] fs;
5 identifier new_prtcl_str_id.id1;
6 @@
7 struct id1 { fs
8   union { ... } J;
9   ... };
```

```
1 @rm_union_from_struct
2   depends on match_anon_union@
3 field list[match_anon_union.n] fs
    ;
4 identifier new_prtcl_str_id.id1;
5 field fld;
6 @@
7 struct id1 { fs
8 - fld
9   ... };
```

One can *shortlist* member types to be made into allocatable C arrays. The remaining members, which are not transformed into pointers, can be deleted.

```
1 @make_ptr@
2 identifier new_prtcl_str_id.id1, M;
3 typedef MyDouble, MyFloat, MyLongDouble,
      MyDoublePos, MyBigFloat;
4 type MT={double,float,MyDouble,MyFloat,
      MyLongDouble,MyDoublePos,MyBigFloat};
5 @@
6 struct id1 { ...
7 - MT   M;
8 + MT *M;
9   ... };
```

```
1 @del_non_ptr@
2 identifier new_prtcl_str_id.id1, J;
3 type T;
4 type P != {T*};
5 @@
6 struct id1 { ...
7 - P J;
8   ... };
```

Only pointer fields now remain – these will serve as the allocatable SoA arrays. Now a little trick is needed, to overcome COCCINELLE's limited preprocessor support. We insert a special __define symbol just before each member (to be later replaced with #define via a script). At compile time that symbol will only be defined if the member had no deactivating #ifdef context.

```
1 @define_per_field_syms@
2 identifier new_prtcl_str_id.id1, M; type MT;
3 typedef __define; fresh identifier si = "HAVE__"##id1##"__"##M;
4 @@
5 struct id1 { ...
6 + __define si;
7   MT *M; ... };
```

3.3   Helper Functions for SoA Array Memory Management

Each of the new SoA structs's arrays needs memory management statements. We cluster those in specific new functions.

```
1 @insert_per_type_soa_functions@
2 identifier new_prtcl_str_id.id1;
3 fresh identifier soa_init_fid="soa_init__"##id1;
4 fresh identifier soa_alloc_fid="soa_alloc__"##id1;
5 fresh identifier soa_free_fid="soa_free__"##id1;
6 @@
7 void allocate_memory(...) { ... }
8 ++ void soa_init_fid(struct id1*P) { }
9 ++ void soa_alloc_fid(struct id1*P, size_t N) { }
10 ++ void soa_free_fid(struct id1*P) { }
```

Populating them with `malloc`/etc. statements proceeds by referring to members `P.M` of `id1` . In order to support multiple build-time configurations, each `P.M` allocation statement needs a surrouning `#ifdef`/`#endif` unique to that `id1` , `M` pair (recall `define_per_field_syms.si`). Given the overlap with previous rules, we omit these rules. We proceed similarly for deallocation and *gather/scatter* to/from AoS (e.g. in I/O and network communication).

3.4   Transform Expressions from AoS to SoA, Globally

Rules in this section can be independently applied to the bulk of source files. As in Sec. 3.1, matching begins on the original AoS particle structures.

```
1  @ostr@
2  identifier id = {particle_data,sph_particle_data};
3  identifier P;
4  type ST;
5  @@
6  (
7    struct id { ... } *P;
8  &
9    ST { ... } *P;
10 )
```

Create an SoA `struct` type `id1` based on AoS `id` , and match it in `nt` .

```
1  @script:python pps@
2  id << ostr.id;
3  id1;
4  @@
5  coccinelle.id1="%s_soa_t"%(id)
```

```
1  @nt@
2  identifier pps.id1, I;
3  type T;
4  @@
5  struct id1 { ...  T I; ... };
```

Create SoA identifiers `S` based on AoS `P` and substitute in all expressions.

```
1  @script:python pid@
2  id1 << pps.id1;
3  P << ostr.P;
4  S;
5  @@
6  coccinelle.S="%s_soa"%(P)
```

```
1  @soa_access@
2  identifier ostr.P, pid.S, nt.I;
3  expression E;
4  @@
5  - P[E].I
6  + S.I[E]
```

Here we exploit the fact that the variables referred to by *metavariables* `P` and `S` are declared globally. Their members `I` instead are bound to the given `struct`. `E` matches arbitrarily complicated index expressions.

At the cost of flexibility, one may have as well written SoA `struct`s by hand and applied only this section's rules: they account for the near totality of the code changed.

4   Current Status and Conclusions

This paper describes a technique to obtain an SoA port of GADGET. A copy of the original set of semantic patches has been added to Coccinelle's test suite (filenames prefixed by `gadget`). Preprocessor-related complications required a few small by-hand code changes. Besides that, as long as the matching points in the code remain stable, these *semantic patches* will stay valid and applicable. This preserves the original AoS-based development model; the *semantic patches* plus helper scripts are ready for use in the GADGET repository. Worthwhile to note, the SoA conversion adds or removes $12k$ lines. A few last steps are still pending before an SoA-GADGET can be fully usable, and the expected $> 2\times$ speedup verified: I/O and MPI related functions need more intervention, postponed to a future collaboration with the GADGET lead developers. The quality of the changes has been ensured by using the internal test suite and a few self-developed custom check scripts. The semantic patches have been developed on extracts of the code, which allowed quick and terse visual inspection of the changes. COCCINELLE preserves existing coding style (e.g. spacing, indentation) very well, which leads to a minimal `diff`.

Generally, HPC is witnessing a divergence in APIs and programming models. This may be a problem for small, geographically sparse domain scientist teams working on large codebases, risking 1) premature code obsolescence, 2) wasted, repeated effort, and 3) operation of hardware at below-optimal performance. This paper illustrated a novel use of a source-to-source translator in such a context. Adapting these recipes to introduce SoA in another codebase may be straightforward. However, the cleaner a codebase is, the easier it is to develop *semantic patches*. Adopting *coding guidelines* and following emerging *research software engineering* practices [1] will help, no matter how small the team.

References

1. Anzt, H., et al.: An environment for sustainable research software in Germany and beyond: current state, open challenges, and call for action. F1000Research **9**, 295 (2020). https://doi.org/10.12688/f1000research.23224.1
2. Baruffa, F., Iapichino, L., Hammer, N.J., Karakasis, V.: Performance optimisation of smoothed particle hydrodynamics algorithms for multi/many-core architectures. CoRR ArXiv:abs/1612.06090 (2016). http://arxiv.org/abs/1612.06090
3. Coccinelle: https://archive.softwareheritage.org/browse/snapshot/207d182d085fcff 85a70deb765336ffe63db5c2a/directory/?origin_url=https://github.com/coccinelle /coccinelle
4. Lawall, J., Muller, G.: Coccinelle: 10 years of automated evolution in the Linux kernel. In: 2018 USENIX Annual Technical Conference, USENIX ATC, pp. 601–614 (2018)
5. Pennycook, S.J., Hughes, C.J., Smelyanskiy, M.: Optimizing gather/scatter patterns. In: Reinders, J., Jeffers, J. (eds.) High Performance Parallelism Pearls, pp. 143–157. Morgan Kaufmann, Boston (2015). https://doi.org/10.1016/B978-0-12-802118-7.00008-X
6. Ragagnin, A., et al.: Gadget-3 on GPUs with OpenACC. In: Parallel Computing: Technology Trends, Proceedings of the International Conference on Parallel Computing (ParCo). Advances in Parallel Computing, vol. 36, pp. 209–218. IOS Press (2019). https://doi.org/10.3233/APC200043
7. Ragagnin, A., Tchipev, N., Bader, M., Dolag, K., Hammer, N.: Exploiting the space filling curve ordering of particles in the neighbour search of Gadget-3. In: Parallel Computing: On the Road to Exascale, Proceedings of the International Conference on Parallel Computing (ParCo). Advances in Parallel Computing, vol. 27, pp. 411–420. IOS Press (2015). https://doi.org/10.3233/978-1-61499-621-7-411
8. Springel, V.: The cosmological simulation code GADGET-2. MNRAS **364**, 1105–1134 (2005). https://doi.org/10.1111/j.1365-2966.2005.09655.x

Negative Perceptions About the Applicability of Source-to-Source Compilers in HPC: A Literature Review

Reed Milewicz[1(✉)], Peter Pirkelbauer[2], Prema Soundararajan[3], Hadia Ahmed[4], and Tony Skjellum[5]

[1] Sandia National Laboratories, Albuquerque, USA
rmilewi@sandia.gov
[2] Lawrence Livermore National Laboratory, Livermore, USA
pirkelbauer2@llnl.gov
[3] University of Alabama at Birmingham, Birmingham, USA
prema@uab.edu
[4] bodo.ai, San Francisco, USA
[5] University of Tennessee at Chattanooga, Chattanooga, USA
Tony-Skjellum@utc.edu

Abstract. A source-to-source compiler is a type of translator that accepts the source code of a program written in a programming language as its input and produces an equivalent source code in the same or different programming language. S2S techniques are commonly used to enable fluent translation between high-level programming languages, to perform large-scale refactoring operations, and to facilitate instrumentation for dynamic analysis. Negative perceptions about S2S's applicability in High Performance Computing (HPC) are studied and evaluated here. This is a first study that brings to light reasons why scientists do not use source-to-source techniques for HPC. The primary audience for this paper are those considering S2S technology in their HPC application work.

1 Introduction

Source-to-source compilation (also known as S2S compilation, transcompilation or transpilation), refers to tools that accept the source code of a program written in a programming language as its input and produce an equivalent source code in the same or different programming language [3]. S2S compilers are distinct from conventional compilers (source-to-binary), decompilers (binary-to-source), and recompilers (binary-to-binary); this definition also excludes low-level IR frameworks like LLVM [28] and MLIR [29] which are typically used to generate binary end products. In the world of conventional software, S2S techniques are commonly used to enable fluent translation between high-level programming languages, to perform large-scale refactoring operations, and to facilitate instrumentation for dynamic analysis. Over the past three decades, numerous S2S compiler frameworks targeting HPC platforms and applications have emerged, including ROSE [46], Mercurium [5], Cetus [12], Clang [28], and Insieme [23].

© Springer Nature Switzerland AG 2021
H. Jagode et al. (Eds.): ISC High Performance 2021 Workshops, LNCS 12761, pp. 233–246, 2021.
https://doi.org/10.1007/978-3-030-90539-2_16

S2S technologies enjoy a diverse range of uses in HPC, including automatic differentiation [38], designing domain-specific languages for scientific computing [33], performance tuning [18], data layout optimizations [34], loop optimizations [51], automatic parallelization [44], porting applications to new platforms [26], code rejuvenation [2], fault tolerant computing [31], instrumentation for checkpointing [11], error checking [40], and converting between parallelization constructs and libraries [25].

S2S solutions are attractive in that they introduce transparency, flexibility, and extensibility into a domain of technology that is often viewed as an inscrutable black box. The key benefits of S2S tools are rooted in the fact that they output source code, which can be inspected by humans for validation, further processed by any other tool that is capable of handling the output language, and compiled by compilers on different target systems. However, in a review of the literature, we have found that a significant number of HPC practitioners who have encountered limitations in S2S tools that prevented them from realizing these benefits; this points towards a need for more engagement with the community and more investment in S2S frameworks to address gaps in capabilities.

The contributions of this paper are: (1) a first study that brings to light reasons why practitioners choose not to adopt source-to-source techniques; (2) demonstrate capabilities of S2S tools; (3) present list of limitations to S2S on where there tool falls short.

The rest of the paper is outlined as follows: Sect. 2 describes the methodology we used to identify the relevant corpus; Section 3 discusses the reasons stated in the literature in detail; Section 4 and Sect. 5 discuss our findings and threats to the validity of our study; Section 6 lists related work; and Sect. 7 presents our conclusion.

2   Methodology

The results presented in this paper are an offshoot of a broader systematic literature review on the use of source-to-source compilers in HPC. While conducting our review, we found a significant number of papers where authors avoided the use of source-to-source technologies in favor of another approach and gave reasons for doing so. Seeing an opportunity to better understand those concerns and to help framework developers address them, we arrived at our research question:

Research Question: In what contexts and for what reasons do HPC practitioners and researchers choose *not* to use source-to-source compiler frameworks?

2.1   Search Process

As a foundational, cross-cutting technology, source-to-source compilers are employed in many different contexts within HPC, and source-to-source compilers can show up in publications across different journals, conferences, and domains of study. As a result, it can be challenging to measure the extent of use and popularity of these tools. For that reason we opted to use Google Scholar to mine the literature rather than targeting specific academic databases or venues.

To conduct our search, we used Harzing's Publish or Perish (version 7.22) to anonymously fetch results from Google Scholar. We defined two queries to bound our search (plus an additional, supplemental query), which are described in Table 1.

Table 1. Search strings used in this paper

Query	Search string
Source-to-source terminology	("source-to-source compiler" OR "s2s"
	OR "transcompiler" OR "transpiler")
	AND ("high performance computing" OR "HPC")
Popular source-to-source frameworks	("compiler" AND
	("ROSE" OR "Mercurium" OR "Insieme"
	OR "Clang" OR "OpenARC" OR "Xevolver"
	OR "Omni" OR "Pluto" OR "Clava"))
	AND ("high performance computing" OR "HPC")
Supplementary search	("source-to-source" OR "s2s" OR "transcompiler" OR "transpiler")
	AND ("weakness" OR "drawback" OR "limitation" OR "shortcoming")
	AND ("high performance computing" OR "HPC")

The first two queries were executed in October 2020, and the third executed in March 2021. We limited the search results to articles that were published between January 1st, 2014 and December 31st, 2019 to focus on recent literature. Google Scholar returned the top 1000 search results for each query, and we merged these results to form our initial corpus of literature with 1766 unique entries.

2.2 Inclusion and Exclusion Criteria

A diagram of our literature review process can be found in Fig. 1. We eliminated papers that did not meet the following criteria:

– Papers that were not focused on high-performance computing (e.g., source-to-source in finance, medical imaging, or web development).
– Papers that did not mention or use source-to-source tools or frameworks (e.g., binary instrumentation or LLVM-IR-based approaches that do not generate source code).
– Documents that were not peer-reviewed (e.g., patents, white papers). Note that we opted to include PhD dissertations, which are internally reviewed and often contain a more complete treatment of exploratory and prototyping work than most conference papers.
– Introductory papers for special issues, books, and workshops.
– Duplicate reports of the same study in different sources.
– Papers not written in English.

Each paper was initially reviewed by one researcher. Where there was doubt or uncertainty about how to categorize a paper, we set the paper aside and held a best of three vote to include or exclude that paper; this happened in 186 cases.

After initial review and voting, we labeled 480 papers that involved the design or use of source-to-source technologies in an HPC context. Of the 1286 papers that did not meet that criterion, we downselected 17 papers that had considered using a source-to-source approach, but explicitly chose not to. We also added 12 papers from our supplementary search results, giving us a total of 29 papers.

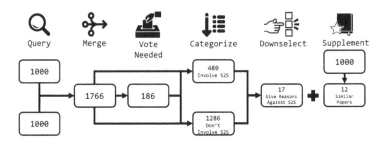

Fig. 1. A diagram illustrating the review process for the literature presented in this study.

2.3   Qualitative Analysis

Next, the authors of this study worked together to assess the rationales of papers that avoided the use of source-to-source approaches. We divided up the papers among us and extracted lines of text that gave arguments against source-to-source. As an example, in a paper on domain-specific language design for HPC, McCormick et al. [36] makes the following claim:

> ✎ *"We posit that [a source-to-source approach] is valuable for exploration but in the long term is likely to result in a lack of adoption. Specifically, we claim that to maximize overall developer productivity the abstractions provided by a DSL must persist throughout the toolchain, particularly for optimization and debugging. Furthermore, and most importantly, the loss of domain-specific knowledge is inherent in source-to-source compilation techniques that (by design) split the toolchain into disjoint infrastructures"* [36].

After compiling our list of references and extracting relevant quotations, each author independently labeled the excerpts using an open coding approach (e.g., "S2S is too complicated"), then we met to converge on an agreed upon set of qualitative categories for those excerpts. Based on our categorization, we summarize the trends and themes in arguments against the use of source-to-source technologies.

3   Results

(R1) S2S Transformations Interfere with or are Oblivious to Downstream Compiler Optimizations: A strength of S2S tools is the ability to work with source code as-is while remaining decoupled from and agnostic to the compiler. A side effect of transforming the source code is that the generated program may exhibit subtle behavioral changes, for example in terms of runtime. Thus, the source code modifications could render the output less useful when the S2S transformation is applied for the purpose of dynamic analysis. In this case, the instrumented code may prevent compiler optimizations [48].

Denis et al., in looking to build a tool to assess floating point accuracy in scientific codes, found that S2S instrumentation could prevent floating-point compiler optimizations taking place, making problematic floating point optimizations invisible to analysis [14]. Huck et al., examining the task of performance profiling, make a similar statement, arguing that "source instrumentation can also prevent compiler and/or runtime optimizations" [22].

For using shared libraries in the context of a reversible computing framework, Cingolani et al. considered the use of binary and S2S translation, and found neither approach ideal. They state "While static binary instrumentation and source-to-source transformation could be directly used on these shared libraries to make them reversible, their applicability might fall either due to the lack of source code (in the case of closed-source libraries) or due to the fact that instrumenting shared objects could produce system-wide effects to other programs not related to optimistic simulation" [10]. Kruse et al. note that while S2S-based polyhedral optimizers can produce effective results, modern compiler mid-ends are increasingly using tactics like static single assignment that may undo or limit the effectiveness of source-level transformations [27].

Meanwhile, some use case scenarios prefer the use of low-level program representations. Adamski et al., for instance, found that they preferred using low-level LLVM solution to an S2S solution because LLVM's support for the single static assignment rule would greatly expose data dependencies and program flow [1]. Chen, meanwhile, argued that S2S techniques provide no control of generated native instructions and allocated registers, something which was indispensable to their use case [9]. McCormick et al. arrive at a similar conclusion in attempting to design the Scout DSL, arguing that incorporating S2S approaches into compiler toolchains leads to disjoint infrastructures that can't effectively communicate information between different components [36].

(R2) S2S Tools are Difficult to Extend to Support New Programming Models: S2S frameworks make it easy to introduce or convert library calls, directives, and macros to port applications between different parallel programming models. However, many such tools are simply source-level pattern-matchers that do not understand the semantics of the transformations they perform, meaning that adapting a tool for a new use case requires significant effort on a case-by-case basis.

Ortega et al. argue that S2S solutions have to be tailored to a specific translation scheme (e.g., sequential C to CUDA) and can't easily be extended to support new models and can't intelligently mix and match different parallel models [43]. Weber and Goesele, in developing an auto-tuner for CUDA applications, claim that using an S2S approach, while feasible, would imply a future maintainability burden because of the need to continually evolve the tool to stay current with the latest version of CUDA [52]. This was the same pitfall encountered by Medina, who found that "available source-to-source translators handle only a subset of CUDA or its assembly language (PTX)" [37]. Meanwhile, Luley and Qiu, examining state-of-the-art optimization S2S tools for GPU resource utilization, argue that S2S tools are fine-tuned to work for specific use cases, and this inherently "[limits] the generality of the solution for future applications and hardware" [32]; the same concern about adapting to future architectures was raised by Yilmaz [53]. Ayres et al. makes a similar claim, stating that dependence on S2S translators, which may not be up-to-date on the latest programming models, presented a potential development risk [4]. Huck et al. note that certain features, like untied tasks in OpenMP, are intrinsically difficult to manage through a solely S2S approach [22]. Meanwhile, Meyer et al. noted that many automatic differentiation tools rely on S2S techniques, but a significant drawback is that none of the tools could handle parallel programming models in an intelligent, fully automated way [39].

(R3) S2S Approaches Lead to Complex and Fragile Workflows: Several authors found that S2S toolchains were difficult to design and equally difficult to maintain and extend.

Degomme et al., reporting on their work to develop a MPI application simulator, noted that early versions of their tool relied on automatic S2S transformation, but that this proved to be too fragile for real-world use [13]. Khammassi claims that S2S-based DSLs are at a major disadvantage because they "require long development time to reach the maturity and performance of traditional compilers" [24]. Novillo, on the subject of instrumentation-based profiling, notes that source instrumentation is often tied to the control structures of programs, meaning that even small changes to the source code can make past profiling runs unusable [42]. Weber and Goesele implemented the MATOG programming interface for array layout optimization for CUDA programs using a code generator. They avoided the use of an S2S translator because "to support platform independence and easy maintainability, we decided to use code generation instead of an own source-to-source compiler, so no changes to the compile chain have to be applied" [52]. Finally, we found several authors of non-S2S tools who believed that their solution was preferable because they did not require S2S support and therefore their solution had fewer moving parts [30,47].

(R4) Parsing Source Code is Inherently Difficult: Parsing is the first and most important step in any S2S solution, and having strong language support is a selling point for major S2S frameworks – perhaps even a point of pride for framework developers.

However, many HPC practitioners believe that parsing is far from a solved problem, and that this is a compelling reason to avoid S2S altogether. Castro et al. claims that approaching code through low-level IRs is simpler than at the source code level, which requires complex input languages [8]. Likewise, Besnard et al. caution against S2S approaches, noting the "the inherent complexity associated with the parsing of language constructs (particularly in C++)" [6]. Huck et al. echo these concerns, noting that "automated source instrumentation can be problematic if the source code includes complex preprocessor macros or language features that are not well supported by the parser in the instrumentation framework" [22]. Along similar lines, several authors noted that the unavailability of source code can be a barrier to using S2S techniques [7,22]; instrumentation, for instance, is limited to the visible and accessible parts of a codebase.

(R5) S2S is a Response to Missing Features Elsewhere: Multiple sources we considered reported that S2S techniques were used to fill gaps in languages and libraries. That is, where pre-existing capabilities could serve the same function as S2S tools, it is better to avoid using those tools. Moreover, as new capabilities emerge, they can diminish the need for S2S solutions.

In several cases, authors considered the use of S2S compilers to implement solutions, but found that they could meet their needs using language features like template meta-programming. Masnada argues that, compared to S2S solutions, a "meta-programming approach goes further by giving more flexibility to the programmer as it provides a higher level of abstraction. It consists in using high level languages to describe the computation and the optimizations. This allows the programmer to propose optimizations that the compiler would not be allowed to do." [35]; other authors make similar arguments for meta-programming strategies [16,21,45]. Similarly, Sulyok et al. found that their DSL for GPU cache optimization, unlike other similar DSLs which required S2S compiler support, could be implemented entirely using macros, obviating the need for an S2S approach [49].

Meanwhile, several authors in our corpus found that advances in languages and libraries eventually eliminated the need for S2S solutions. Holland found that previous works addressing OpenCL support for FGPAs required S2S transformations to map kernel functions to accelerators generated by HLS, but since that time Xilinx Vivado HLS added native support for OpenCL C, meaning that an S2S solution was no longer necessary [20]. Milic et al. reported a similar outcome, commenting that past work on data placement for NVIDIA GPUs required an S2S approach, but that the rollout of NVIDIA's Unified Virtual Addressing and NVLink had removed the need for S2S transformations [41]. Diener et al., studying the performance capabilities of Adaptive MPI (AMPI), found that AMPI could achieve the same quality of results as changing the source code, reducing the need for source code modification (whether manual or automated) [15].

4   Discussion

We have reviewed numerous papers that rejected the application of S2S transformations to solving their problems. We believe that all authors have carefully weighed advantages and disadvantages of the alternatives they considered. Common issues raised include interference with compiler optimizations, the difficulty of extending S2S tools to new programming models, the fragility and complexity of S2S toolchains, challenges with parsing source code, and the tendency

Table 2. Summary of findings of our study.

Label	Perception about S2S	Sources	Potential Solutions
R1	S2S transformations interfere with or are oblivious to down-stream compiler optimizations.	[1,9,10, 14,22, 27,36]	Promote co-design across the compiler toolchain to allow S2S compilers and backend compilers to communicate information about optimizations more transparently.
R2	S2S tools are difficult to extend to support new programming models.	[4,22, 32,37, 39,43, 52,53]	Develop metamodels for parallel programming constructs that enable tool developers to express transformations at an appropriate level of abstraction.
R3	S2S approaches lead to complex and fragile workflows.	[13,24, 30,42, 47,52]	Provide lowering transformations that normalize the code structure, reducing complexity and improving maintainability.
R4	Parsing source code is inherently difficult.	[6–8,22]	Shorten the learning curve of S2S tools by providing online learning tools.
R5	S2S is a response to missing features elsewhere.	[15,16, 20,21, 35,41, 45,49]	Add more user-friendly support for commonplace use cases outside of research prototyping (e.g., refactoring).

of S2S to be used as a stop-gap measure for missing features in languages and libraries rather than as a durable, long-term solution. Our intent is not to change someone's opinion about whether to use or not use S2S for solving their domain problems.

However, we do believe that S2S has strong advantages when it comes to portability, maintainability, and human validation of transformations. By studying these publications that argue against S2S, we and the S2S community can learn lessons and seek new opportunities. A summary of our findings and recommended solutions can be found in Table 2.

One crucial lesson is that for many application domains, the support and availability of easy to use standard transformations is important. Several articles prefer the normalized form often found in low-level code representation. Examples include code represented in static single assignment (SSA) form [50], or the uniform representation of loop structures. In that vein, S2S frameworks could provide lowering transformations that normalize the code structure. Programmers could write analysis passes for the normalized representation. If retaining the original source code is important, the S2S system would also need to offer support to map the analysis results back to the original source code. The lowering to a normalized representation would also benefit S2S users that view transformations as pattern matching, where each syntactic feature needs to be expressed as separate pattern.

With respect to barriers to S2S tool extensibility (R2), we find that S2S tool developer find themselves writing highly granular and concrete transformations to accomplish complex tasks like converting between parallel programming models. Given that developers will likely want to adapt that tool to address new use cases as they emerge, there is a need for S2S frameworks to provide features to facilitate that work. One potential solution would be to build in support for parallel programming metamodels that would enable tool developers to express transformations at an appropriate level of abstraction.

Another lesson specifically from users that implement DSLs is that in this domain the S2S translation systems need better support for debugging that allows to map the output back to the code in the DSL in order to facilitate source-level debugging. Another need from the DSL community is support to simplify the implementations of optimizing transformations before the source code level and before the backend compiler is invoked. Otherwise, high-level specific properties get lost and opportunities for optimizations are not realized. More generally, this points towards an opportunity for co-design across the compiler toolchain to allow S2S compilers and backend compilers to communicate information about optimizations more transparently.

Next, we noted potential users who rejected the use of S2S due to the complexity of parsing. It is precisely this point where S2S shines, as it relieves users from many tedious tasks of constructing a full compiler frontend (lexer, parser, intermediate representation, backend). However, it is up to the S2S community to reach out to potential users and articulate the benefits more clearly. One way to make this clear and shorten the learning curve of S2S tools is by providing online learning tools (*e.g.,* [17]).

Finally, there were several authors who found that S2S techniques which were previously used to solve a problem were no longer needed thanks advances elsewhere (*e.g.,* in libraries, languages, compilers, or hardware). This is to be expected: a primary use case for S2S frameworks in HPC is to prototype research concepts that may eventually be achieved without S2S. However, insofar as S2S frameworks are seen as a temporary means to an end, this can have the unintended side effect of disincentivizing S2S users from investing energy into learning how to use those frameworks or building more robust, reusable S2S tools. To fully realize the impact of S2S technologies in HPC, it is important that the S2S community builds a critical mass of knowledgeable users. Fortunately, there are also range of perennial use cases for S2S technologies; this includes instrumentation for performance measurement, refactoring, static analysis, and DSL development. We argue that the more familiar developers are with S2S for regular use cases, the more comfortable they will be with using S2S techniques to solve complex, one-off problems. For this reason, S2S framework developers should focus their attention on developing more user-friendly, built-in support for those perennial use cases.

5   Threats to Validity

In deriving categories for the papers we analyzed, we used no measure of inter-rater reliability to compare similarity of participants' categorizations of the texts. However, we opted to focus on a small number of papers that clearly articulated perspectives on the use of S2S compilers, and there were no significant disagreements in how we chose to organize the results. Another limiting factor in our work is relying on self-reported perspectives and experiences about S2S technologies. It is possible – indeed likely – that many more people chose not to use S2S technologies in their works but opted not to mention that in their papers, and therefore there may be more unstated objections than we captured in our study. Follow-up work using surveys or interviews targeting the HPC community could reveal a more comprehensive picture.

6   Related Work

While S2S compilers have made significant impacts inside and outside the HPC community, there have been very few meta-analyses or secondary studies on the use of S2S compilers. To be clear, there is some ambiguity in how the term "source-to-source" is operationalized; in a formal languages sense, S2S transformations run the gamut of the Chomsky hierarchy, some of which can be accomplished with modest implements (e.g., regular expressions) and others entailing deep, context-sensitive operations. S2S compilers sit on the far end of that spectrum: tools capable of fluently parsing, interrogating, and manipulating source code written in a general-purpose programming language. Within an HPC context, the closest work we can find is by Harel et al., a comparative study of the strengths and weaknesses of different source-to-source compilers for auto-parallelization tasks [19]. We also did not find any studies that compared S2S compilers to alternative solutions. To the best of our knowledge, ours is the first work to systematically investigate reported limitations of S2S compilers in HPC.

7   Conclusion

In this study, we have analyzed a large corpus of publications related to source-to-source translation for high-performance computer system. We identified a subset of papers where authors opted not to use S2S technologies but instead favored an alternative approach. A summary of these alternatives is in itself interesting. In addition, we found several works that relied on alternative approaches although S2S would have provided benefits. Bringing these reasons to light will hopefully help the S2S community to improve the support for potential users.

Acknowledgements. Sandia National Laboratories is a multimission laboratory managed and operated by National Technology and Engineering Solutions of Sandia, LLC, a wholly owned subsidiary of Honeywell International, Inc., for the U.S.

Department of Energy's National Nuclear Security Administration under contract DE-NA-0003525. Images used by permission. SAND2021-9377 C.

This work was performed under the auspices of the U.S. Department of Energy by Lawrence Livermore National Laboratory under Contract DE-AC52-07NA27344. LLNL-CONF-821299.

References

1. Adamski, D., Szydłowski, M., Jabłoński, G., Lasoń, J.: Dynamic tiling optimization for polly compiler. Int. J. Microelectron. Comput. Sci. **8**(4) (2017)
2. Ahmed, H., Skjellum, A., Bangalore, P., Pirkelbauer, P.: Transforming blocking MPI collectives to non-blocking and persistent operations. In: Proceedings of the 24th European MPI Users' Group Meeting. EuroMPI 2017. Association for Computing Machinery, New York (2017). https://doi.org/10.1145/3127024.3127033
3. Appel, A.W.: Modern Compiler Implementation in C. Cambridge University Press, Cambridge (2004)
4. Ayres, D.L., Cummings, M.P.: Heterogeneous hardware support in BEAGLE, a high-performance computing library for statistical phylogenetics. In: 2017 46th International Conference on Parallel Processing Workshops (ICPPW), pp. 23–32. IEEE (2017)
5. Balart, J., Duran, A., Gonzàlez, M., Martorell, X., Ayguadé, E., Labarta, J.: Nanos Mercurium: a research compiler for OpenMP. In: Proceedings of the European Workshop on OpenMP, vol. 8, p. 56 (2004)
6. Besnard, J.B., et al.: Introducing task-containers as an alternative to runtime-stacking. In: Proceedings of the 23rd European MPI Users' Group Meeting, pp. 51–63 (2016)
7. Capodieci, N., Cavicchioli, R., Bertogna, M., Paramakuru, A.: Deadline-based scheduling for GPU with preemption support. In: 2018 IEEE Real-Time Systems Symposium (RTSS), pp. 119–130. IEEE (2018)
8. Castro, P.D.O., Akel, C., Petit, E., Popov, M., Jalby, W.: Cere: LLVM-based codelet extractor and replayer for piecewise benchmarking and optimization. ACM Trans. Arch. Code Optim. (TACO) **12**(1), 1–24 (2015)
9. Chen, Y.: Software simultaneous multithreading through compilation. Ph.D. thesis, University of Delaware (2018)
10. Cingolani, D., Pellegrini, A., Schordan, M., Quaglia, F., Jefferson, D.R.: Dealing with reversibility of shared libraries in PDES. In: Proceedings of the 2017 ACM SIGSIM Conference on Principles of Advanced Discrete Simulation. SIGSIM-PADS 2017, pp. 41–52. Association for Computing Machinery, New York (2017). https://doi.org/10.1145/3064911.3064927
11. Cores, I., Rodríguez, G., González, P., Martín, M.J.: Failure avoidance in MPI applications using an application-level approach. Comput. J. **57**(1), 100–114 (2014)
12. Dave, C., Bae, H., Min, S.J., Lee, S., Eigenmann, R., Midkiff, S.: Cetus: a source-to-source compiler infrastructure for multicores. Computer **42**(12), 36–42 (2009)
13. Degomme, A., Legrand, A., Markomanolis, G.S., Quinson, M., Stillwell, M., Suter, F.: Simulating MPI applications: the SMPI approach. IEEE Trans. Parallel Distrib. Syst. **28**(8), 2387–2400 (2017)
14. Denis, C., Castro, P.D.O., Petit, E.: Verificarlo: checking floating point accuracy through Monte Carlo arithmetic. In: 2016 IEEE 23nd Symposium on Computer Arithmetic (ARITH), pp. 55–62. IEEE (2016)

15. Diener, M., White, S., Kale, L.V., Campbell, M., Bodony, D.J., Freund, J.B.: Improving the memory access locality of hybrid MPI applications. In: Proceedings of the 24th European MPI Users' Group Meeting. EuroMPI 2017. Association for Computing Machinery, New York (2017). https://doi.org/10.1145/3127024.3127038

16. Fukuda, K., Matsuda, M., Maruyama, N., Yokota, R., Taura, K., Matsuoka, S.: Tapas: an implicitly parallel programming framework for hierarchical n-body algorithms. In: 2016 IEEE 22nd International Conference on Parallel and Distributed Systems (ICPADS), pp. 1100–1109. IEEE (2016)

17. Gosselin, J., Wang, A., Pirkelbauer, P., Liao, C., Yan, Y., Dechev, D.: Extending freecompilercamp.org as an onlineself-learning platform for compiler development. In: Workshop on Education for High Performance Computing (EduHPC-20), November 2020

18. Gschwandtner, P., Durillo, J.J., Fahringer, T.: Multi-objective auto-tuning with Insieme: optimization and trade-off analysis for time, energy and resource usage. In: Silva, F., Dutra, I., Santos Costa, V. (eds.) Euro-Par 2014. LNCS, vol. 8632, pp. 87–98. Springer, Cham (2014). https://doi.org/10.1007/978-3-319-09873-9_8

19. Harel, R., Mosseri, I., Levin, H., Alon, L.O., Rusanovsky, M., Oren, G.: Source-to-source parallelization compilers for scientific shared-memory multi-core and accelerated multiprocessing: analysis, pitfalls, enhancement and potential. Int. J. Parallel Program. **48**(1), 1–31 (2020)

20. Holland, G.: Abstracting OpenCL for multi-application workloads on CPU-FPGA clusters. Ph.D. thesis, Applied Sciences: School of Engineering Science (2019)

21. Hollman, D.S., Bennett, J.C., Kolla, H., Lifflander, J., Slattengren, N., Wilke, J.: Metaprogramming-enabled parallel execution of apparently sequential C++ code. In: 2016 Second International Workshop on Extreme Scale Programming Models and Middlewar (ESPM2), pp. 24–31 (2016)

22. Huck, K.A., Malony, A.D., Shende, S., Jacobsen, D.W.: Integrated measurement for cross-platform OpenMP performance analysis. In: DeRose, L., de Supinski, B.R., Olivier, S.L., Chapman, B.M., Müller, M.S. (eds.) IWOMP 2014. LNCS, vol. 8766, pp. 146–160. Springer, Cham (2014). https://doi.org/10.1007/978-3-319-11454-5_11

23. Jordan, H.: Insieme-a compiler infrastructure for parallel programs. Ph.D. thesis, Ph. D. dissertation, University of Innsbruck (2014)

24. Khammassi, N.: High-level structured programming models for explicit and automatic parallelization on multicore architectures. Ph.D. thesis, Université de Bretagne Sud (2014)

25. Kim, J., Lee, Y.J., Park, J., Lee, J.: Translating OpenMP device constructs to OpenCL using unnecessary data transfer elimination. In: SC 2016: Proceedings of the International Conference for High Performance Computing, Networking, Storage and Analysis, pp. 597–608. IEEE (2016)

26. Komatsu, K., Egawa, R., Hirasawa, S., Takizawa, H., Itakura, K., Kobayashi, H.: Migration of an atmospheric simulation code to an OpenACC platform using the xevolver framework. In: 2015 Third International Symposium on Computing and Networking (CANDAR), pp. 515–520. IEEE (2015)

27. Kruse, M., Grosser, T.: DeLICM: scalar dependence removal at zero memory cost. In: Proceedings of the 2018 International Symposium on Code Generation and Optimization, pp. 241–253 (2018)

28. Lattner, C.: LLVM and clang: next generation compiler technology. In: The BSD Conference, vol. 5 (2008)

29. Lattner, C., et al.: MLIR: a compiler infrastructure for the end of Moore's law. arXiv e-prints, pp. arXiv-2002 (2020)
30. Li, J., Guo, B., Shen, Y., Li, D., Huang, Y.: Kernel scheduling approach for reducing GPU energy consumption. J. Comput. Sci. **28**, 360–368 (2018)
31. Lidman, J., Quinlan, D.J., Liao, C., McKee, S.A.: Rose::fttransform - a source-to-source translation framework for exascale fault-tolerance research. In: IEEE/IFIP International Conference on Dependable Systems and Networks Workshops (DSN 2012), pp. 1–6 (2012)
32. Luley, R.S., Qiu, Q.: Effective utilization of CUDA Hyper-Q for improved power and performance efficiency. In: 2016 IEEE International Parallel and Distributed Processing Symposium Workshops (IPDPSW), pp. 1160–1169. IEEE (2016)
33. Macià, S., Martínez-Ferrer, P.J., Mateo, S., Beltran, V., Ayguadé, E.: Assembling a high-productivity DSL for computational fluid dynamics. In: Proceedings of the Platform for Advanced Scientific Computing Conference, pp. 1–11 (2019)
34. Majeti, D., Meel, K.S., Barik, R., Sarkar, V.: Automatic data layout generation and kernel mapping for CPU+GPU architectures. In: Proceedings of the 25th International Conference on Compiler Construction, pp. 240–250 (2016)
35. Masnada, S.: Semi-automatic performance optimization of HPC kernels. Ph.D. thesis, Université Grenoble Alpes (2016)
36. McCormick, P., et al.: Exploring the construction of a domain-aware toolchain for high-performance computing. In: 2014 Fourth International Workshop on Domain-Specific Languages and High-Level Frameworks for High Performance Computing, pp. 1–10. IEEE (2014)
37. Medina, D.: Okl: a unified language for parallel architectures. Technical report, TR15-04, Rice University, June 2015
38. Menon, H., et al.: Adapt: algorithmic differentiation applied to floating-point precision tuning. In: SC18: International Conference for High Performance Computing, Networking, Storage and Analysis, pp. 614–626. IEEE (2018)
39. Meyer, X., Chopard, B., Salamin, N.: Scheduling finite difference approximations for DAG-modeled large scale applications. In: Proceedings of the Platform for Advanced Scientific Computing Conference. PASC 2017. Association for Computing Machinery, New York (2017). https://doi.org/10.1145/3093172.3093231
40. Milewicz, R., Vanka, R., Tuck, J., Quinlan, D., Pirkelbauer, P.: Runtime checking C programs. In: Proceedings of the 30th Annual ACM Symposium on Applied Computing. SAC 2015, pp. 2107–2114. Association for Computing Machinery, New York (2015). https://doi.org/10.1145/2695664.2695906
41. Milic, U., et al.: Beyond the socket: NUMA-aware GPUs. In: Proceedings of the 50th Annual IEEE/ACM International Symposium on Microarchitecture, pp. 123–135 (2017)
42. Novillo, D.: SamplePGO - the power of profile guided optimizations without the usability burden. In: 2014 LLVM Compiler Infrastructure in HPC, pp. 22–28 (2014)
43. Ortega-Arranz, H., Torres, Y., Gonzalez-Escribano, A., Llanos, D.R.: TuCCompi: a multi-layer model for distributed heterogeneous computing with tuning capabilities. Int. J. Parallel Prog. **43**(5), 939–960 (2015)
44. Palkowski, M., Bielecki, W.: TRACO: source-to-source parallelizing compiler. Comput. Inform. **35**(6), 1277–1306 (2016)
45. Penuchot, J., Falcou, J., Khabou, A.: Modern generative programming for optimizing small matrix-vector multiplication. In: 2018 International Conference on High Performance Computing and Simulation (HPCS), pp. 508–514. IEEE (2018)

46. Quinlan, D., Liao, C.: The ROSE source-to-source compiler infrastructure. In: Cetus Users and Compiler Infrastructure Workshop, in Conjunction with PACT, vol. 2011, p. 1. Citeseer (2011)
47. Sangaiah, K., et al.: Synchrotrace: synchronization-aware architecture-agnostic traces for lightweight multicore simulation of CMP and HPC workloads. ACM Trans. Arch. Code Optim. (TACO) 15(1), 1–26 (2018)
48. Shen, D., Song, S.L., Li, A., Liu, X.: CudaAdvisor: LLVM-based runtime profiling for modern GPUs. In: Proceedings of the 2018 International Symposium on Code Generation and Optimization. CGO 2018, pp. 214–227. ACM, New York (2018). https://doi.org/10.1145/3168831
49. Sulyok, A.A., Balogh, G.D., Reguly, I.Z., Mudalige, G.R.: Improving locality of unstructured mesh algorithms on GPUs. arXiv preprint arXiv:1802.03749 (2018)
50. Torczon, L., Cooper, K.: Engineering A Compiler, 2nd edn. Morgan Kaufmann Publishers Inc., San Francisco (2007)
51. Wahib, M., Maruyama, N.: Scalable kernel fusion for memory-bound GPU applications. In: SC 2014: Proceedings of the International Conference for High Performance Computing, Networking, Storage and Analysis, pp. 191–202. IEEE (2014)
52. Weber, N., Goesele, M.: MATOG: array layout auto-tuning for CUDA. ACM Trans. Archit. Code Optim. 14(3) (2017). https://doi.org/10.1145/3106341
53. Yilmaz, B.: Runtime specialization and autotuning of sparse matrix-vector multiplication. Ph.D. thesis, Ph. D. dissertation, Ozyegin University (2015)

Machine Learning on HPC Systems

Automatic Tuning of Tensorflow's CPU Backend Using Gradient-Free Optimization Algorithms

Derssie Mebratu[1], Niranjan Hasabnis[2(✉)], Pietro Mercati[2], Gaurit Sharma[1], and Shamima Najnin[1]

[1] Intel Corporation, Hillsboro, OR, USA
{derssie.d.mebratu,gaurit.sharma,shamima.najnin}@intel.com
[2] Intel Labs, Santa Clara, CA, USA
{niranjan.hasabnis,pietro.mercati}@intel.com

Abstract. Modern deep learning (DL) applications are built using DL libraries and frameworks such as TensorFlow and PyTorch. These frameworks have complex parameters and tuning them to obtain good training and inference performance is challenging for typical users, such as DL developers and data scientists. Manual tuning requires deep knowledge of the user-controllable parameters of DL frameworks as well as the underlying hardware. It is a slow and tedious process, and it typically delivers sub-optimal solutions. In this paper, we treat the problem of tuning parameters of DL frameworks to improve training and inference performance as a black-box optimization problem. We then investigate applicability and effectiveness of Bayesian optimization, genetic algorithm, and Nelder-Mead simplex to tune the parameters of TensorFlow's CPU backend. While prior work has already investigated the use of Nelder-Mead simplex for a similar problem, it does not provide insights into the applicability of other more popular algorithms. Towards that end, we provide a systematic comparative analysis of all three algorithms in tuning TensorFlow's CPU backend on a variety of DL models. Our findings reveal that Bayesian optimization performs the best on the majority of models. There are, however, cases where it does not deliver the best results.

Keywords: Deep learning · Gradient-free optimizations · Gaussian process · Auto-tuning

1 Introduction

In recent years, deep learning has gained significant momentum in academic research as well as in production to solve real-world problems. For example, deep learning applications in the areas of speech recognition (e.g., Amazon Alexa, Apple Siri, Google Assistant, etc.), language translation (e.g., Google Translate), and recommendation systems (e.g., Netflix movie recommendations, Amazon product recommendations, etc.) are already part of everyday life. Interest in

---

D. Mebratu and N. Hasabnis—Equal contribution.

© Springer Nature Switzerland AG 2021
H. Jagode et al. (Eds.): ISC High Performance 2021 Workshops, LNCS 12761, pp. 249–266, 2021.
https://doi.org/10.1007/978-3-030-90539-2_17

deep learning is fueled by the vast availability of both open-source and proprietary data as well as by the continuous development of heterogeneous computing platforms (e.g., CPU, GPU, TPU, etc.) and cloud resources (e.g., Amazon AWS, Google Cloud, Microsoft Azure, etc.) to process that data.

The availability of open-source deep learning software frameworks, such as PyTorch [11] and TensorFlow [1], along with the suites of neural network models [15] enables fast deployment of deep learning models. Although deep learning frameworks are relatively new software systems, they essentially employ software designs that are similar to other existing software systems, particularly compilers. Deep learning frameworks accept models written in high-level languages such as Python. Similar to the compilers for high-level languages, these models are either interpreted directly (as for Python itself) or converted ("lowered", in compilers parlance, such as for C and C++ languages) into a low-level data-flow graph that is later executed. Before the models are executed, the framework runtime schedules the computations from their data-flow graphs onto the backends for the hardware devices [1]. Consequently, the training or inference performance of a deep learning model partly depends upon runtime's scheduling decisions.

TensorFlow's default CPU backend is implemented using an open-source library named Eigen [3]. TensorFlow's Eigen CPU backend enables efficient execution on multicore CPUs by offering a configurable threading model to exploit the concurrency that is typically present in TensorFlow's data-flow graphs. Specifically, vertices in TensorFlow's data-flow graphs represent computations, and they can have data dependencies (i.e., input edges from other vertices) and control dependencies (i.e., a scheduling constraint specified by the user or TensorFlow framework). The Eigen CPU backend relies on PThreads library for multi-threading, and its threading model offers two configurable parameters: *(i)* `inter_op_parallelism_threads`: the maximum number of independent computations to execute in parallel, and *(ii)* `intra_op_parallelism_threads`: the maximum number of threads to use for executing a single computation. Unfortunately, the Eigen CPU backend has shown sub-optimal performance on several Intel Xeon CPU platforms [5,10]. Consequently, Intel contributes with its own CPU backend to TensorFlow [17] that delivers orders of magnitude of performance improvement over the Eigen CPU backend. Intel's CPU backend uses the OpenMP [9] library for multi-threading and adds another configurable parameter to TensorFlow's threading model: *(iii)* `OMP_NUM_THREADS`: the number of OpenMP threads to use for executing a single computation with Intel's backend.

TensorFlow's configurable CPU threading model enables end-users to improve performance of their models by tuning TensorFlow to the target hardware. As mentioned in TensorFlow's "Binary Configuration" section [14], a savvy user can tune the model by finding values of `inter_op_parallelism_threads` and `intra_op_parallelism_threads` by "finding the right configuration for their specific workload and environment". The guide, however, does not discuss how to find the right configuration in practice. Unfortunately, it is unrealistic to expect that a deep learning application developer or a data scientist would know the optimal parameter configurations as these configurations are intimately related to detailed knowledge of the framework and the underlying hardware. Considering this limitation, Intel provides specific configurations [19] for popular deep learning models, such as ResNet50, on commonly-used Intel Xeon platforms, such as the latest generation Intel Xeon CPUs (codenamed IceLake). However, any deviation from this standard setup, for example with a new model or a new hardware platform, could mean that the provided settings may not deliver the optimal performance. The alternative of relying on the default values of the parameters can be acceptable in some situations such as early prototyping. However, they usually deliver sub-optimal performance [5].

A common approach to search for the optimal configuration is manual search. Manual search, however, is a tedious activity, leading to sampling only a few configurations, and it also relies on the expertise of the user. A naive approach of exhaustive search is feasible for small search spaces, but becomes unfeasible as the search time grows exponentially in the number of parameters. For instance, in our experiments, the exhaustive search run for the optimal configuration of TensorFlow's threading model for ResNet50 inference took close to a month of CPU time on a multi-core Intel Xeon platform. The search space consisted of roughly 50000 points. While this could be acceptable in research and development settings, it would not be acceptable in production environments.

Hasabnis [5] offers an excellent description of the problem and an auto-tuning solution, called TensorTuner, to configure TensorFlow's threading model for CPU backend. Specifically, TensorTuner uses a black-box optimization algorithm named Nelder-Mead simplex. This solution addresses both the issues described earlier: obtaining the best performance and systematically configuring the parameters of the threading model. Nelder-Mead simplex, however, is a local optimization algorithm. And popular global optimization algorithms, such as Bayesian optimization and genetic algorithm, have been demonstrated to perform successfully in system tuning tasks [8]. Hasabnis does not consider these alternatives and leaves the open question of the best algorithm for this problem.

In this paper, we analyze the effectiveness of Bayesian optimization, genetic algorithm, and Nelder-Mead simplex to tune TensorFlow's threading model for various deep learning models. Unlike TensorTuner that focuses solely on deep learning models from image recognition domain, we consider models belonging to a variety of domains. Furthermore, we also consider a larger set of performance-sensitive parameters by considering `batch_size` and `KMP_BLOCKTIME`, which are not considered by TensorTuner. Finally, we perform detailed comparative analysis of the performance of all three algorithms and discuss our findings.

1.1 Contributions

In this paper we make following contributions:

1. We evaluate and compare the effectiveness of Bayesian optimization, genetic algorithm, and Nelder-Mead simplex to automatically tune performance-critical parameters of TensorFlow's Intel-CPU backend.

2. We consider several deep learning models, written for a variety of use cases such as image recognition, language translation, etc. Prior work for this problem has focused on the models used in image recognition only.
3. We analyze performance of each optimization algorithm. The analysis provides us insights on the performance behavior of the algorithms and the classes of problems for which they could be more successful.

This paper is organized as follows. Section 2 provides the necessary background information about TensorFlow and black-box optimization algorithms. Section 3 and Sect. 4 present our evaluation methodology and results, respectively. Section 5 presents the related work, while Sect. 6 concludes the paper.

2   Background

This section provides a brief introduction to TensorFlow, Bayesian optimization, genetic algorithm, and Nelder-Mead simplex algorithm. The description is not meant to be exhaustive, but sufficient to understand the results presented in the experimental section.

2.1   TensorFlow

TensorFlow [1], initially released in 2015, is an open-source library for machine learning and deep learning that is developed by the Google brain team. It is a multi-system library that supports Linux, MacOS and Windows and is implemented primarily in Python, C++, and CUDA.

TensorFlow supports machine learning and deep Learning models implemented in languages such as Python and Javascript. It also offers high-level Keras APIs to enable quick model development and prototyping. It supports execution on various hardware devices such as CPUs, GPUs, TPUs, etc., and provides a variety of tools (e.g., TensorFlow eXtended, TensorFlow Lite, TensorFlow.js, etc.) that enable easy deployment of trained models on those devices.

Execution Modes. TensorFlow's current version (version 2) supports two modes of execution: eager mode and graph mode. The eager mode is similar to Python's interpreter mode in that Keras/Python APIs invoked by programmers are interpreted immediately. The graph mode, on the other hand, leverages the concept of *lazy evaluation* and builds an intermediate data-flow graph representation before executing it. Although the eager mode enables faster prototyping and model development, its performance is typically lower than the graph mode. This is because the graph mode can perform global optimizations over the data-flow graphs that are not possible in the eager mode.

```
import tensorflow as tf
from tf.keras import Input, Model
from tf.keras.layers import Dense
from tf.nn import relu

in = Input(shape=(3,),
              batch_size=2)
out = Dense(4,
              use_bias=True,
              activation=relu)(in)
model = Model(in, out)
```

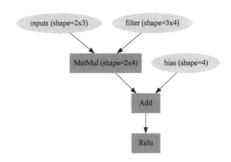

(a) Python implementation of the model for $y = W.x + b$

(b) Data-flow graph for the model (yellow boxes show computations, while gray boxes show variables/tensors)

Fig. 1. TensorFlow model for $y = W.x + b$ (left) and its data-flow graph (right) (Color figure online)

Tensors and Data-Flow Graph. TensorFlow's data-flow graph represents high-level machine learning models by representing computations as vertices and inputs/outputs of the computations as incoming and outgoing edges. In Tensor-Flow, inputs and outputs of the computations are called *tensors*. This name, borrowed from algebra, indicates objects that can be represented as N-dimensional matrices. Edges in the data-flow graph carry tensors between the computations, and thus the name "data-flow" graph. Figure 1 shows a Python implementation of the model for $(y = W.x + b)$, a basic operation of a neural network, written using TensorFlow's Keras APIs. The figure also shows its corresponding data-flow graph. The arrows in the figure represent tensors, and the directions of the arrows correspond to the directions of the data flow.

Scheduling and Execution. Edges in TensorFlow's data-flow graph can represent two different types of dependencies: *data dependencies* and *control dependencies*. An edge that feeds an output of an operation X to an operation Y constitutes a data dependency of the operation Y on the operation X. It means that the operation Y cannot be executed or scheduled for execution until the operation X has finished its execution. Control dependencies, on the other hand, represent scheduling constraints between the operations and can be inserted (by the user or automatically) to enforce a particular scheduling order. As an example, solid arrows in Fig. 1 only show data dependencies. There are no control dependencies in the figure.

CPU Threading Model. Data and control dependencies in TensorFlow's data-flow graph help in enforcing a particular execution order of the operations. However, the execution order can still be partial. In particular, operations in the data-flow graph that do not have any direct or indirect dependencies can be executed in any order. With reference to Fig. 1, variables `inputs` and `filter` of `MatMul` can be accessed either concurrently or serially (`inputs` after `filter` or vice versa.) Ten-sorFlow's threading model for multi-core CPU devices allows users to exploit this *concurrency* in the data-flow graphs by setting two parameters of the threading model: `inter_op_parallelism_threads` and `intra_op_parallelism_threads`. `inter_op_parallelism_threads` specifies the maximum number of operations that can be executed concurrently, while `intra_op_parallelism_threads` spec-ifies the maximum number of threads that can be used by a single operation. Both parameters together restrict the total number of threads that will be used to execute a data-flow graph. Therefore, they are used to control over-subscription of a device. The default values of these parameters are decided by TensorFlow's runtime depending on the underlying platform. The default values, however, are not adapted further to the input machine learning model, thus missing an opportunity for performance improvement.

2.2 Black-Box Optimization Algorithms

Tuning the parameters of a software system to improve performance metrics, such as execution time or memory consumption, can be formulated as a black-box optimization problem. "Black-box" here refers to any system for which analytical description or gradients is not available, and instead it is only possible to query a configuration of the inputs and measure the corresponding output. Therefore, the problem cannot be solved with gradient-based techniques, but requires gradient-free optimization algorithms of non-linear systems. The algorithms investigated in this work belong to the class of gradient-free optimization algorithms, and all can solve this problem. However, they have fundamentally different behaviors as explained in the following sections.

Formally, a black-box has input $x \in X$, where X is the solution space. Note that X has, in general, d dimensions, so $x = x_0, x_1, ..., x_{d-1}$. The system can be described by an objective function f, which is unknown but measurable. A measurement or evaluation corresponding to input x would be $y = f(x)$. The optimization problem can be formulated as:

$$\min_{x \in X} f(x)$$

The solution to this problem would be an input configuration $x^* = argmin f(x)$, also called minimizer, and the only information that can be leveraged to find this solution is the history of past n measurements $D = \{(x_i, y_i)\}_{i=0}^{n-1}$.

Different classes of algorithms have been developed to address black-box systems, most notably model-based, evolutionary and heuristic, and all of them are iterative in nature.

Bayesian optimization (BO) is a model-based algorithm, meaning that it uses system evaluations to construct a surrogate model of the optimization objective, and leverages the knowledge of the model to guide the selection of the next configuration to evaluate. It is called Bayesian, because the model employed is probabilistic, often a Gaussian Process, which is fundamental to trade global exploration in the regions of large uncertainty with local exploitation around the best solutions observed. This is different from more traditional models such as linear regression or neural network regression that only return a predicted value for each input. Instead, a probabilistic model returns both a prediction and an estimate of uncertainty for that prediction. This information is leveraged by BO at each iteration to guide the selection of candidate solutions. For this, predictions and uncertainties are used to evaluate an acquisition function, which takes large values in the vicinity of promising past measurements or in the regions with large uncertainty. After the initial model is ready, usually trained with a few random evaluations, BO starts a loop of iterations. First, it computes and maximizes the acquisition function. The solution maximizing the acquisition function is selected as the next configuration to evaluate. Second, this configuration is applied to the system and evaluated. Finally, the measurement provides a new data point, which is used to update the surrogate model.

In this work we use Gaussian Processes (GPs) as the surrogate models. The GP is highly "data-efficient", thus it achieves good accuracy with a relatively small number of training points, and can be customized to model different classes of functions by changing its "kernel" function. Finally, GPs have convenient analytical properties that allow to train them with a closed-form approach. For the acquisition function we adopt "SMSego", because it is fast to compute and delivers state-of-the-art performance. For each point in the solution space, this function accepts the prediction and the uncertainty from the surrogate model and estimates how likely they can extend the best evaluation observed so far. SMSego has been shown to have performance comparable to other best acquisition functions, which are harder to implement and require approximations.

Genetic algorithm (GA) belongs to the family of evolutionary algorithms, which draw inspiration from biological phenomena such as reproduction. Instead of building an internal model, at each iterations, GA relies upon a fitness function to select two "best parent configurations" from the history of the evaluated configurations. Then, the parent configurations are manipulated via crossover and mutation operations to generate a "child" configuration. GA reflects the process of natural evolution, in which genes determining a better adaptation are mixed together with occasional mutations, which leads to stronger and healthier generations. More formally, the GA would take the history as an input and reorder the input-output pairs based on a certain fitness function $g(x_i, y_i)$. Then, it would pick the inputs of the two fittest pairs, called "parents", and generate a new input by copying part of the components from the first parent and the other from the second parent. This operation is called crossover. Then, it might also change one or more component to purely random values. This is referred to as mutation. Evolutionary algorithms are broadly used for their ease of implementation and configuration.

Finally, Nelder-Mead simplex (NMS) is a direct search heuristic method that uses evaluations to build a simplex object in the space of objective function. The next configuration to evaluate is selected by manipulating the simplex via reflection, expansion and contraction operations. While simple to implement and intuitive, NMS has a tendency to get stuck in local optima.

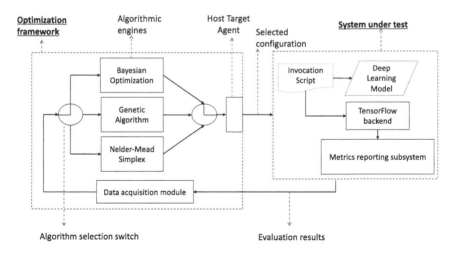

Fig. 2. Optimization framework and methodology

3   Optimization Framework and Methodology

In this section, we describe our automated optimization methodology for black-box optimization of TensorFlow's CPU backend.

Figure 2 shows the block diagram of the optimization setup. The optimization framework (on the left) has different components, and it runs on the host system. The algorithmic engines implement the black-box optimization algorithms described in the previous section: Bayesian optimization, genetic algorithm and Nelder-Mead simplex. The algorithm selection switch is configured to exercise one engine at a time. This ensures that all engines can use the same interface to TensorFlow for converting and applying the chosen parameters and the same data acquisition module to retrieve evaluation results and update the evaluation history. On the right, the system under test is the target system, and generically, it is any computing system that can execute TensorFlow models. The only requirement on the system is that it allows applying the parameters and measuring the corresponding output via some metric reporting subsystem (e.g. a log file in the simplest case). A clear separation of components ensures that the workload performance is not affected by interference from the optimization algorithm. It also enables us to run optimization algorithm on a relatively less-powerful machine than the target machine.

The mapping of the optimization problem is realized as following. At each iteration, an algorithmic engine selects a configuration x of TensorFlow's threading model parameters. Through the TensorFlow interface, the configuration x is converted into a command to set the values of parameters on the target system. Then, the optimization framework runs an evaluation on the target system and evaluates the objective function $f(x)$ of the metric of interest, such as images processed per second in the case of ResNet50. The evaluation provides a new data point, which is added to the global history of evaluations. In case of Bayesian optimization, this is then used to retrain the Gaussian process model, recompute the acquisition function and maximize to select the next configuration.

4   Evaluation

In this section, we discuss our evaluation of genetic algorithm, Bayesian optimization, and Nelder-Mead simplex algorithm to tune the inference throughput of the selected deep learning models. In other words, the objective function was to maximize the throughput of performing inference over every model.

4.1   Experimental Setup

Before we present our results, we describe the evaluation setup.

Hardware Configurations: We used a dual-socket, 22-core Intel Xeon E5-2699 v4 processor (codenamed Broadwell) as the host system and a dual-socket, 24-core 2nd-generation Intel Xeon Scalable Gold 6252 processor (codenamed Cascade Lake) as the target system. The processor for the host system was configured to run at 3.6 GHz with 384 GB of physical memory, while the processor for the target system was configured to run at 3.9 GHz with hyper-threading turned on and with 512 GB of physical memory. Both the servers were running Ubuntu-18.04 operating system.

Software Configurations: We installed Intel-optimized TensorFlow v1.15 [17] on the target system to run the deep learning models. This TensorFlow version uses version v0.20.6 of Intel's Math Kernel Library for Deep Neural Networks (oneDNN). oneDNN is an open-source, cross-platform high-performance library of basic building blocks for deep learning applications [7]. We used Python 3.7.7 to run the TensorFlow benchmarks.

TensorFlow Models: Intel Model Zoo [6] provides a suite of popular deep learning models that are optimized for various versions of Intel-optimized TensorFlow. We used SSD Mobilenet, ResNet50, Transformer-LT, BERT, and NCF models from the Intel provided suite. We selected the models such that they cover a variety of application domains, such as image recognition, language translation.

Configuration of the Parameter Search Space: We considered five parameters of TensorFlow's threading model for our experiments. We described `inter_op_parallelism_threads` and `intra_op_parallelism_threads` parameters in the Background section (Sect. 2). We provide a brief background of the other three parameters below. In addition, we describe rationale for selecting particular ranges of values to tune these parameters. The range is defined with an upper bound, a lower bound, and a step size value as shown in Table 1.

inter_op_parallelism_threads: Since this parameter controls the maximum number of concurrent operations from the data-flow graph, we set this parameter's range from 1 to 4 at step size of 1. These values were obtained from Intel's recommendation of setting this parameter based on the number of sockets.

Table 1. Tuning parameters and their ranges (min, max, step size)

Parameters		Range
inter_op_parallelism_threads		[1, 4, 1]
intra_op_parallelism_threads		[1, 56, 1]
batch_size	NCF	[64, 256, 64]
	SSD-MobileNet	
	ResNet50	[64, 1024, 64]
	Transformer-LT	
	BERT	[32, 64, 32]
KMP_BLOCKTIME		[0, 200, 10]
OMP_NUM_THREADS		[1, 56, 1]

intra_op_parallelism_threads: Since this parameter controls the maximum number of threads to be used for operations from the data-flow graphs, we set its range from 1 to 56 at the step size of 1. This decision was based on Intel's recommendation of setting intra_op_parallelism_threads based on the number of cores in the system. Intel Xeon CPUs have per-socket core count of up to 56.

batch_size: This parameter controls the number of examples provided to the deep-learning models as input. Setting the value to 1 allows us to obtain latency of inference, while higher values allow us to obtain throughput. We note that the batch size is a performance-sensitive parameter—a multi-core system could be under-utilized for lower batch size values. Higher batch sizes thus allow us to explore the saturation points of a system. Furthermore, some models are computationally-less intensive than others. To ensure that the target system is satured for all the models, we used different batch sizes for different models.

KMP_BLOCKTIME: This and the next parameter are tunable parameters of OpenMP runtime library, and they are applicable to Intel-optimized Tensor-Flow, since its CPU backend relies on oneDNN library that uses OpenMP library. KMP_BLOCKTIME sets the time that a thread should wait before sleeping after completing the execution of a *parallel region*. Most deep-learning primitives in oneDNN are implemented using parallel-programming primitives such as `parallel for`. The block of code following this primitive is called "parallel region" in OpenMP. OpenMP tuning guide [9] recommends to set this parameter to 200, but our prior experiments demonstrated that value of 0 is also sometimes effective. Consequently, we set the range for this parameter from 0 to 200 with the step size of 10.

OMP_NUM_THREADS: This parameter is used to set the maximum number of threads to use in OpenMP parallel regions. Setting this parameter to a value higher than 1 enables parallel regions to use multiple cores of multi-core CPUs concurrently. Intel's guide [19] recommends setting this parameter to the number of cores in the system. So we set the range of this parameter to be same as intra_op_parallelism_threads.

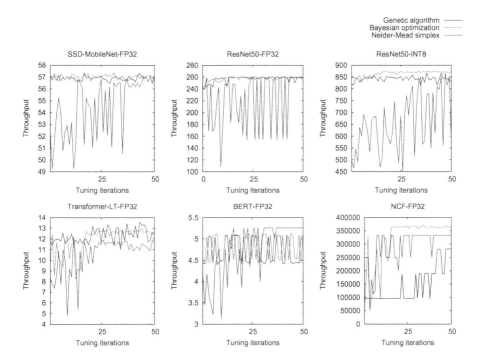

Fig. 3. Results of auto-tuning TensorFlow's threading model using Bayesian optimization, genetic algorithm, and Nelder-Mead simplex

4.2   Results

We now discuss the results of our tuning experiments. In our experiments, the models were configured to use 32-bit floating point (FP32) data type. Additionally, for ResNet50 model, we evaluated it with 8-bit integer (INT8) data type, which produces a compact model and also reduces its memory footprint.

Figure 3 shows the results of tuning the selected deep learning models using different optimization algorithms. The X axis in the figure represents tuning iterations (capped at 50), and the Y axis represents the throughput value (examples/second)—a higher throughput value represents better performance. Also, in the figure, green, blue and orange plots represent the performance of Nelder-Mead simplex, genetic algorithm, and Bayesian optimization, respectively.

Out of the 6 plots, the top 3 plots for SSD-MobileNet-FP32, ResNet50-FP32, and ResNet50-INT8 show similar characteristics. Specifically, Bayesian optimization and genetic algorithm perform similarly and deliver close to peak throughput, while Nelder-Mead simplex struggles with a considerable variation in the throughput. For the bottom 3 plots, namely Transformer-LT-FP32, BERT-FP32, and NCF-FP32, the optimization algorithms perform differently. Specifically, except for BERT-FP32, plots for Bayesian optimization and genetic algorithm for other two models look different. Additionally, while Bayesian optimization

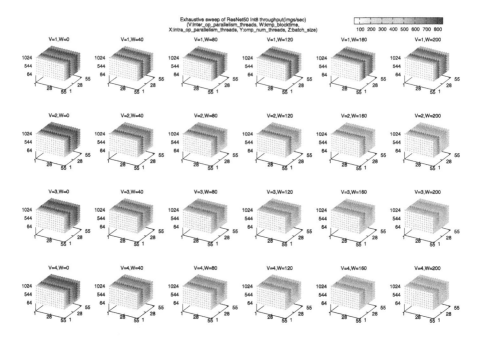

Fig. 4. Exhaustive sweep of ResNet50-INT8 throughput across all five parameters. Labels for different axes are in the legend. Colors indicate different throughput values (dark blue being the highest, and yellow being the lowest.) (Color figure online)

delivers the best performance on tuning NCF-FP32 throughput, it struggles on BERT-FP32, for which Nelder-Mead simplex delivers the best throughput. For Transformer-LT model, genetic algorithm performs better than Nelder-Mead simplex and Bayesian optimization.

Overall, the results show that no single optimization algorithm consistently outperforms others in tuning the selected deep learning models. Nevertheless, Bayesian optimization demonstrates to be the most competitive overall for the selection of the models.

4.3   Comparison of the Optimization Algorithms

Exhaustive Sweep. In order to understand the effect of different parameters on the performance of the deep learning models, we performed exhaustive sweep of ResNet50's performance for INT8 precision across all the five parameters. Figure 4 shows the throughput of ResNet50 for different parameter values.

We report some salient observations from Fig. 4:

– KMP_BLOCKTIME of 0 delivers better performance than others, for a given value of inter_op_parallelism_threads. 3D plots become lighter in color as KMP_BLOCKTIME value increases (from left to right).

- All 3D plots have a common pattern: as the value of `OMP_NUM_THREADS` increases (along the Y-axis) the throughput also increases, suggesting that this parameter has considerable impact on the performance.
- Performance does not vary considerably (and noticeably) for different values of `intra_op_parallelism_threads` (along the X-axis), suggesting that ResNet50's INT8 model does not utilize deep learning operators that leverage Eigen threadpool (which relies on the value of this parameter). It also suggests that we can possibly drop this parameter from the list of tunable parameters to prune the search space.
- Batch size (along the Z-axis) has relatively less impact on the throughput than other parameters, suggesting that it could be dropped from the list of tunable parameters as well.

Exploration-Exploitation Balance. After obtaining the shape of the performance function for the ResNet50-INT8 model, we compared the effectiveness of all three algorithms in obtaining optimal configurations. The objective is to understand the tradeoff between exploitation and exploration delivered by all three algorithms. For this purpose, we plotted the ResNet50-INT8 throughput as a function of the sampled parameter values. Since we have 5 different parameters for tuning, we transformed the 5-dimensional plot into multiple pairplots that represent throughput as a function of the pairs of the sampled parameter values. Figure 5a shows the ResNet50-INT8 pairplot for Nelder-Mead simplex. For instance, the plot on the lower left corner between X and W in Fig. 5a represents the ResNet50-INT8 throughput values in terms of sampled values of X and W parameters. Darker values represent higher throughput values; lighter values represent lower throughput values. Figure 5c shows the pairplot for Bayesian optimization, and Fig. 5b shows the pairplot for genetic algorithm.

There are a few interesting observations that emerge from these pairplots:

- Bayesian optimization samples min and max ranges of all the parameters (squares in pairplots). Moreover, it also samples all the parameters fairly uniformly, displaying a fair balance between exploitation and exploration.
- Nelder-Mead simplex algorithm samples clusters of points, indicating that the algorithm has a higher chance of getting stuck in a local optimum. In other words, Nelder-Mead simplex devotes more time to exploitation, i.e. local search in the vicinity of the promising solutions. Note also that Nelder-Mead simplex presents another limitation in that it does not sample points along min and max ranges of some of the parameters (e.g., Y and Z),
- Genetic algorithm, on the other hand, has neither clusters of points nor samples along min and max ranges (e.g. parameter V, more white spaces in pairplots), indicating a poor exploration/exploitation balance.
- Bayesian optimization also has more darker points than Nelder-Mead simplex and genetic algorithm, suggesting that Bayesian optimization delivers the best balance between exploitation and exploration. This is unsurprising as this is one of the commonly known advantages of Bayesian optimization.

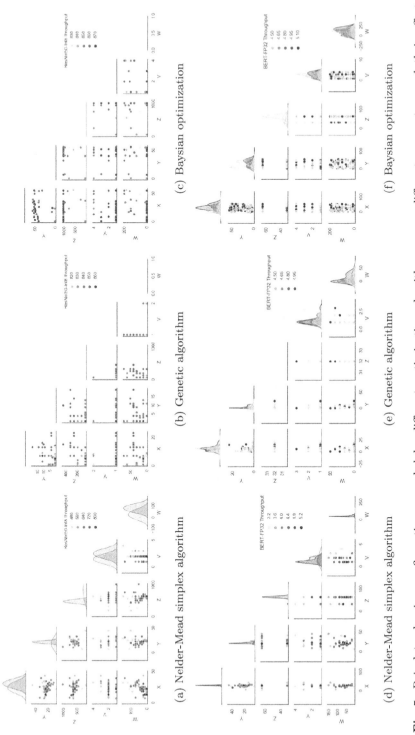

Fig. 5. Pairplots showing configurations sampled by different optimization algorithms across different parameters and their effect on throughput for ResNet50-INT8 (top row) and BERT-FP32 (bottom row) models. Parameters: X = intra_op_parallelism_ threads, Y = OMP_NUM_THREADS, Z = batch_size, V = inter_op_parallelism_threads, W = KMP_BLOCKTIME

Table 2. Min/max ranges for different parameters sampled by Bayesian optimization (BO), genetic algorithm (GA), and Nelder-Mead simplex (NMS) vs. tunable ranges. Percentages are obtained by dividing the ranges of the sampled values by the tunable ranges. Parameters: X = intra_op_parallelism_threads, Y = omp_num_threads, Z = batch_size, V = inter_op_parallelism_threads, W = kmp_blocktime

Description	ResNet50-INT8					BERT-FP32				
	X	Y	Z	V	W	X	Y	Z	V	W
Tunable range	[1, 56]	[1, 56]	[64, 1024]	[1, 4]	[0, 200]	[1, 56]	[1, 56]	[32, 64]	[1, 4]	[0, 200]
NMS (min, max)	[7, 43]	[8, 45]	[192, 1024]	[1, 4]	[0, 150]	[7, 44]	[6, 45]	[32, 64]	[1, 4]	[10, 150]
GA (min, max)	[1, 23]	[1, 19]	[64, 448]	[1, 2]	[0, 70]	[1, 22]	[1, 23]	[32, 32]	[1, 3]	[0, 50]
BO (min, max)	[1, 56]	[1, 56]	[64, 1024]	[1, 4]	[0, 200]	[1, 56]	[1, 56]	[32, 64]	[1, 4]	[0, 200]
NMS sampled range (%)	65	67	86	100	75	67	70	100	100	70
GA sampled range (%)	40	32	40	33	35	38	40	50	66	25
BO sampled range (%)	100	100	100	100	100	100	100	100	100	100

To further understand the exploration-exploitation behavior of all three algorithms, we obtained their pairplots for the BERT-FP32 model. Figures 5d, 5f, 5e shows the pairplots for Nelder-Mead simplex algorithm, Bayesian optimization, and genetic algorithm, respectively. Observations similar to those of ResNet50-INT8 can be made in BERT's case also. Specifically, genetic algorithm neither has clusters of points nor samples min/max ranges, suggesting poor exploration-exploitation strategy. Nelder-Mead simplex algorithm has clusters of points, similar to that for ResNet50-INT8 model, suggesting that Nelder-Mead simplex algorithm exploits more than exploring the space (visible from not sampling min/max values of parameter V). However, it still samples better than genetic algorithm in a sense that there is much less white space in Nelder-Mead simplex's pairplots than in genetics algorithm's pairplots. Bayesian optimization, on the other hand, has a cluster of points as well as samples near min/max values, suggesting better balance between exploration and exploitation.

Overall, these experiments suggest that Bayesian optimization maintains a fair balance between exploration and exploitation and can sample solutions in different regions of the search space. Nelder-Mead simplex algorithm and genetic algorithm, instead, struggle to maintain this balance, although Nelder-Mead simplex algorithm in these cases ends up exploring more than genetic algorithm. This can also been seen from the data in Table 2, which shows the sampled ranges, shown as (min,max), for different parameters against their tunable ranges for different optimization algorithms. As can be seen, Bayesian optimization explores min and max values of all the parameters, both in case of ResNet50-INT8 and BERT-FP32. It explores 100% of the tunable ranges for all the parameters for both the models. Genetic algorithm, on the other hand, explores less than 50% of the ranges for most of the parameters for both the models, suggesting that it exploits more than explores.

In summary, we found that no single optimization algorithm can be used to find the optimal throughput for the selected deep learning workloads. Nevertheless, Bayesian optimization demonstrates a more robust and reliable behavior and delivers quality solutions with a limited number of iterations. Besides, each algorithm took different time to search the maximum throughput. For instance, Nelder-Mead simplex algorithm took a relatively short amount of time for searching the maximum throughput in BERT-FP32 compared with the others. Similarly, genetic algorithm took less time to search for the maximum throughput than Bayesian optimization in SSD-MobileNet-FP32. Moreover, we run our experiments multiple times, and we observed that the throughput values with both genetic algorithm and Bayesian optimization are very close in SSD-MobileNet-FP32, ResNet50-FP32 and BERT-FP32 model.

5   Related Work

In the machine learning domain, auto-tuning is routinely applied to the problem of hyper-parameter tuning. Although, there exists a number of commercial and open-source hyper-parameter tuning systems such as HyperOpt [2], MOE [20], Spearmint [13], AutoWeka [16], SigOpt [12], Google's Vizier [4], etc., we are not aware of existing work that systematically analyzes tuning of performance-sensitive parameters of TensorFlow framework on multi-core CPU platforms used in data centers. The closest to our work is TensorTuner [5], which uses Nelder-Mead simplex algorithm to tune TensorFlow's CPU backend. This work, however, neither considers other optimization algorithms nor provides insights into the applicability of Nelder-Mead simplex algorithm to the problem. Nelder-Mead simplex is known to be a local optimization algorithm, and global optimization algorithms such as Bayesian optimization and genetic algorithm exist already. We seek to provide this comparative evaluation and analysis among different optimization algorithms on several TensorFlow models, written for a variety of usecases such as image recognition, language translation, and recommendation system. TensorTuner, on the other hand, focuses on models used in image recognition problem. We also consider a larger set of performance-sensitive tunable parameters, thus expanding the search space of the configurations. Our work, in this sense, can be considered as an extension of TensorTuner.

Alternative to the auto-tuning based approach considered in this work, Wang et al. [18] develops a formula to set `inter_op_parallelism_threads` and `intra_op_parallelism_threads` by analyzing the data-flow graphs of the deep learning models. They develop this formula by analyzing data-flow graphs of various models and their relationship with the optimal values of these parameters.

Their approach, however, treats TensorFlow's CPU backend as a white-box and requires intrusive changes to the TensorFlow framework. Furthermore, operating as a part of TensorFlow framework, this approach cannot set other performance-sensitive parameters such as `batch_size`. Nevertheless, it is a promising approach in a sense that it can directly set the values of the parameters by analyzing data-flow graph of a model and thus eliminate the need of multiple rounds of online or offline tuning.

6   Conclusion

Overall, our evaluation across a variety of deep learning models for Tensor-Flow demonstrates that Bayesian optimization generally maintains good balance between exploration and exploitation (explores 100% of the tunable ranges for all the parameters for ResNet50-INT8 and BERT-FP32 models) and explores most of the search spaces, if not all. Genetic algorithm, on the other hand, explores less than 50% of the ranges for several models and struggles to maintain the balance between exploration and exploitation. Nelder-Mead simplex falls in between Bayesian optimization and genetic algorithm in terms of the exploration-exploitation balance. Nonetheless, we also found out that no particular optimization algorithm performs the best across all the models—Nelder-Mead simplex performs the best on BERT-FP32, while it lags behind Bayesian optimization and genetic algorithm on the others.

Acknowledgements. We would like to thank Michael Kishinevsky and Boris Serafimov from Intel for providing access to the implementation of the optimization algorithms that we used in our experiments.

References

1. Abadi, M., et al.: TensorFlow: a system for large-scale machine learning. In: 12th USENIX Symposium on Operating Systems Design and Implementation (OSDI 2016) (2016). https://www.usenix.org/system/files/conference/osdi16/osdi16-abadi.pdf
2. Bergstra, J., Yamins, D., Cox, D.D., et al.: Hyperopt: a python library for optimizing the hyperparameters of machine learning algorithms. In: Proceedings of the 12th Python in Science Conference (2013)
3. Eigen: Eigen C++ Template Library. https://eigen.tuxfamily.org
4. Golovin, D., Solnik, B., Moitra, S., Kochanski, G., Karro, J., Sculley, D.: Google vizier: a service for black-box optimization. In: Proceedings of the 23rd ACM SIGKDD International Conference on Knowledge Discovery and Data Mining. KDD 2017 (2017). https://doi.org/10.1145/3097983.3098043
5. Hasabnis, N.: Auto-tuning TensorFlow threading model for CPU backend. In: 2018 IEEE/ACM Machine Learning in HPC Environments (MLHPC) (2018). https://doi.org/10.1109/MLHPC.2018.8638636
6. Intel Corporation: Model Zoo for Intel Architecture (2021). https://github.com/IntelAI/models

7. Intel Corporation: oneAPI Deep Neural Network Library (oneDNN) (2021). https://github.com/oneapi-src/oneDNN
8. Li, Q., et al.: RAMBO: resource allocation for microservices using Bayesian optimization. IEEE Comput. Archit. Lett. (2021). https://doi.org/10.1109/LCA.2021.3066142
9. OpenMP: The OpenMP API Specification for Parallel Programming (2021). https://www.openmp.org/
10. Ould-Ahmed-Vall, E., et al.: Accelerating TensorFlow on modern intel architectures. In: First International Workshop on Architectures for Intelligent Machines (2017). http://aim2017.cse.psu.edu/
11. Paszke, A., et al.: PyTorch: an imperative style, high-performance deep learning library. In: Advances in Neural Information Processing Systems (2019)
12. SigOpt: SigOpt (2021). https://sigopt.com/
13. Snoek, J., Larochelle, H., Adams, R.P.: Practical Bayesian optimization of machine learning algorithms. In: Proceedings of the 25th International Conference on Neural Information Processing Systems - NIPS 2012, vol. 2 (2012)
14. TensorFlow: Performance Guide (2021). https://www.tensorflow.org/tfx/serving/performance
15. The TensorFlow Authors: TensorFlow Model Garden (2021). https://github.com/tensorflow/models
16. Thornton, C., Hutter, F., Hoos, H.H., Leyton-Brown, K.: Auto-WEKA: combined selection and hyperparameter optimization of classification algorithms. In: Proceedings of the 19th ACM SIGKDD International Conference on Knowledge Discovery and Data Mining. KDD 2013 (2013). https://doi.org/10.1145/2487575.2487629
17. Venkatesh, P., Xu, J.: Intel Optimization for TensorFlow Installation Guide (2020). https://software.intel.com/content/www/us/en/develop/articles/intel-optimization-for-tensorflow-installation-guide.html
18. Wang, Y.E., Wu, C.J., Wang, X., Hazelwood, K., Brooks, D.: Exploiting parallelism opportunities with deep learning frameworks. ACM Trans. Archit. Code Optim. (2021). https://doi.org/10.1145/3431388
19. Xu, J., Venkatesh, P., Tsai, H.J.: Maximize TensorFlow* Performance on CPU: Considerations and Recommendations for Inference Workloads (2021). https://software.intel.com/content/www/us/en/develop/articles/maximize-tensorflow-performance-on-cpu-considerations-and-recommendations-for-inference.html
20. Yelp Inc.: A Global, Black-Box Optimization Engine for Real World Metric Optimization (2014). https://github.com/Yelp/MOE

MSM: Multi-stage Multicuts for Scalable Image Clustering

Kalun Ho[1,3(✉)], Avraam Chatzimichailidis[1], Margret Keuper[3], and Janis Keuper[2]

[1] CC-HPC, Fraunhofer ITWM, Fraunhofer-Platz 1, 67663 Kaiserslautern, Germany
kalun.ho@itwm.fhg.de
[2] Institute for Machine Learning and Analytics, Offenburg University, Offenburg, Germany
[3] Data and Web Science Group, University of Mannheim, Mannheim, Germany

Abstract. Correlation Clustering, also called the minimum cost Multicut problem, is the process of grouping data by pairwise similarities. It has proven to be effective on clustering problems, where the number of classes is unknown. However, not only is the Multicut problem NP-hard, an undirected graph G with n vertices representing single images has at most $\frac{n(n-1)}{2}$ edges, thus making it challenging to implement correlation clustering for large datasets. In this work, we propose Multi-Stage Multicuts (MSM) as a scalable approach for image clustering. Specifically, we solve minimum cost Multicut problems across multiple distributed compute units. Our approach not only allows to solve problem instances which are too large to fit into the shared memory of a single compute node, but it also achieves significant speedups while preserving the clustering accuracy at the same time. We evaluate our proposed method on the CIFAR10 and CelebA image datasets. Furthermore, we also provide the proof for the theoretical speedup.

1 Introduction

Clustering data based on some feature measure has been a major interest in machine learning. Specifically, when pairwise similarities between data points in a set are given, one can partition (e.g. cluster) the data without determining the number of clusters a priori. This is important as data specific knowledge remains unknown for real world problems. Correlational Clustering, also called the minimum cost Multicut problem, solves such clustering tasks globally and in a deterministic way. Data points (e.g. nodes) form a graph G with a cost on the edges between each other, where these costs are often computed using some features based on deep learning models (details in Sect. 3.1). The graph is partitioned based on this cost. Although G can be either a complete graph or a graph with arbitrary number of edges, solving the minimum cost Multicut problem is know to be NP-hard. With the increase in data size (e.g. nodes in G), solving such a task remains a challenge.

K. Ho and A. Chatzimichailidis—Equal contribution.

Electronic supplementary material The online version of this chapter (https://doi.org/10.1007/978-3-030-90539-2_18) contains supplementary material, which is available to authorized users.

H. Jagode et al. (Eds.): ISC High Performance 2021 Workshops, LNCS 12761, pp. 267–284, 2021.
https://doi.org/10.1007/978-3-030-90539-2_18

Contributions. In this work, we propose MSM (Multi-Stage Multicuts) to solve the minimum cost Multicut problem on large graphs. Specifically, MSM utilizes data parallelism to achieve significant speedup while preserving the performance on image clustering tasks. This straightforward method divides a single, large clustering problem into small disjoint sets across different CPU threads on a shared memory system. This has two main advantages: (1) the clustering tasks become smaller on each thread and (2) the optimization on each set is done concurrently. Our key contributions of this paper are summarized as follows:

- We provide MSM: Multi-Stage Mulicuts approach based on minimum cost Multicuts that is capable of solving large graphs using features from deep neural networks. MSM runs concurrently on multiple CPU threads, allowing to solve large image clustering problems.
- We provide a theoretical proof of speedup for our proposed method
- The performance of MSM is evaluated on multiple scenarios based on image clustering tasks on CelebA, CIFAR10 and CIFAR100 dataset.

2 Related Work

Image Clustering. The goal of image clustering is to assign class labels to a given set of data based on their semantic features. These semantic features for clustering are often obtained via convolutional neural networks (CNN) [5,21], where dimensions are successively reduced via non-linear mapping functions on each layer. A joint optimization approach is proposed in [2,3], where these features are learned and clustered via assigned pseudo-labels. However, [31] shows that this method leads to unstable training and propose a decomposing feature clustering approach to tackle this issue. [11] propose a Graph-Convolutional Network approach with LSTM for a density-aware face clustering. [23] seeks fairness in clustering by hiding sensitive features that are based on min-max game strategy. Other methods, such as autoencoders [10,30], generative models [9,25] or transformer [4] have also been proposed to solve image clustering tasks.

Minimum Cost Multicuts. Minimum Cost Multicuts, also called Correlational clustering [6,8] is a graph-based clustering technique, where data points are represented in a graph and pairwise similarities between the nodes are utilized to optimize (e.g. cluster) the overall problem. This technique has shown success in various computer vision applications, such as multiple object tracking [17], motion and image segmentation [15,29], pose estimation [27] and image clustering [13]. The minimum cost Multicut problem is known to be NP-hard [8]. However, the use of heuristic solvers [1,16] yield reasonable results in practice.

Parallel Computing. Parallel computing describes the process of partitioning a problem into smaller ones and solving these sub problems simultaneously. Recently data parallelism [7,19] and model parallelism [12,14] have been explored in the context of deep learning. In [26], a parallel Multicuts approach for binary graphs is proposed. In order to scale to bigger datasets, our proposed MSM makes use of the data parallel approach, where each worker holds a copy of the full model locally, as well as a fraction of the whole dataset.

3   Notation and Methods

In this section, we explain our proposed algorithm: Multi-Stage Multicuts (MSM), which allows parallelization across multiple CPU threads (worker) with shared memory in order to solve a large image clustering problem. Through this work, we will use the term *worker*. Given a set of available workers $|S_k|$ at stage k, each individual CPU thread is represented as $s_{i,k} \in S_k$ with $\forall i \in \mathbb{N} : 1 \le i \le w$. At stage S_1, the number of workers is set to $|S_1| = w$. Furthermore, a defined number of stage $L = k$ is given, where the number of workers are reduced successively:

$$|S_k| < |S_{k-1}| \tag{1}$$

A dataset X with a total size of $|X|$ is randomly divided into disjoint sets across the workers $|S_1|$. At stage one, each worker $s_{i,1} \in S_1$ holds $n = \frac{|X|}{|S_1|}$ samples of X. Since MSM is based on pairwise comparison of data, the permutation of the splits as well as the distribution of the classes within a batch will not affect the clustering performance in noticeable way (we show this in our experiments).

In order to obtain the cluster labels $y_{i,k}$, each individual worker solves an instance of minimum cost Multicut problem with respect to the graph G, which is explained in Subsect. 3.1. Each cluster label $y_{i,k}$ is then forwarded during the next stage to S_{k+1} to compute the joint solution (red arrow). Details are explained in Sect. 3.3. This process is repeated until the final stage L is reached. The results of S_{L-1} are forwarded to one single worker $|S_L| = 1$. Cluster labels are then sent back to all other workers via backpropagation (green arrow).

The following section is divided into four parts. First, we define the notation and explain the minimum cost Multicut problem. Section 3.2 describes the image clustering task using Multicuts. Our algorithm is introduced in Sect. 3.3.

3.1   Minimum Cost Mulitcut Problem

We consider an undirected graph $G = (V, E)$, where nodes $v \in V$ represent data points x_i of the given dataset X and edges $e \in E$ with real valued costs $c : E \to \mathbb{R}$ on all edges. The cost affects whether nodes are being separated or joined together, which are represented as edge labels $y : E \to \{0, 1\}$. For image clustering problems, we want to infer the *edge* labels, which define the cuts and joins in a way, that every cluster or partition belongs to corresponding class label. This can be achieved by solving instances of the minimum cost Multicut problem with respect to the graph G and costs c, which is defined as follows (Fig. 1):

$$\min_{y \in \{0,1\}^E} \sum_{e \in E} c_e y_e \tag{2}$$

$$s.t. \quad \forall C \in cycles(G) \quad \forall e \in C : y_e \le \sum_{e' \in C \setminus \{e\}} y_{e'} \tag{3}$$

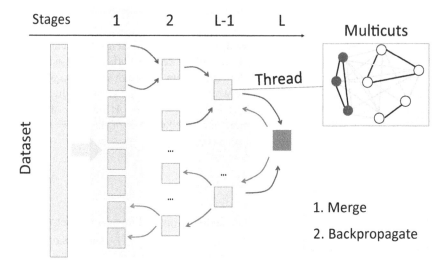

Fig. 1. Our Multi-Stage Multicuts (MSM) procedure: at stage 1, we evenly divide a given dataset into small, disjoint sets and distribute this to individual computing units to solve the minimum cost multicut problem concurrently. The results are forwarded to the next units in the following stage, where the intermediate results are being merged (red arrow). This process is repeated until the final stage L is reached. The merge result is sent back to all previous computing units via backpropagation (green arrow). (Color figure online)

The partitioning of graph G is achieved by cutting edges with negative costs c_e. Equation (3) ensures that for each cycle in G, a cut is only allowed if there is at least another edge being cut as well. This was shown in [6] to be sufficient to enforce on all *chordless* cycles, i.e. all cycles. In practice, a cut probability between two nodes are converted into such edge cost via the *logit* function $\text{logit}(p) = \log \frac{p}{1-p}$, thus resulting in a positive and negative real value.

3.2   Image Clustering with Multicuts

The advantage of Multicuts clustering is the fact that pairwise comparisons are performed. In contrast, centroid-based clustering methods such as *K-Means* assumes data of same clusters to be distributed evenly around its center or have the same density. However, such assumptions do not perform well on real-world face clustering [11]. We assume that each pair of nodes of the undirected graph G has at most one edge with a cost c. Consequently, a complete graph with n nodes has in total $|E| = \frac{n(n-1)}{2}$ edges.

Sparsity. In context of image clustering using Multicuts, it is desired to have as many edges as possible during the graph creation (e.g. complete) as more pairs of images are being compared with. Figure 2 a) depicts the final cluster accuracy (in blue) on the CIFAR10 [20] Test dataset as well as the file size (in red) against the sparsity of the graph: 1.0 represents a complete graph while 0.5 means that half of the edges are being utilized. This experiment uses a single worker for solving the Minimum Cost Multicut Problem. We observe the clustering accuracy converges to a value at roughly 80%. Since this is the case, it is safe to assume that at sparsity = 1.0 (e.g. complete graph), the highest clustering accuracy is reached. When using very few edges only (sparsity at around 0.01), performance drops significantly. The red box depicts an area with higher standard deviation. At the same time, the size of the graph file is increasing. Figure 2 b) illustrates the runtime and file size of a complete graph (e.g. sparsity = 1.0) for different dataset size. One can observe that the larger the dataset size, the longer is the runtime for solving the problem and more memory it consumes.

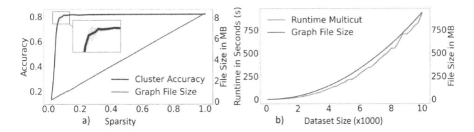

Fig. 2. Minimum Cost Multicuts for image clustering task on a single worker. In a), a subset of CIFAR10 (1000 images) is used to evaluate the clustering performance as well as the graph size for different sparsity setups. A sparty of 0.5 means that half of the edges are removed during the construction of G. In b), a complete graph (e.g. sparsity = 1.0) is being evaluated for different dataset size. Graph file is stored uncompressed as an edge list.

3.3   MSM: Multi-stage Multicuts

Our approach is based on the idea to use multiple CPU threads (worker) on a shared memory system to solve the image clustering problem. The dataset X is decomposed into disjoint sets with equal size, reducing the size of graph G in order to solve the minimum cost Multicut problem in a reasonable amount of time. Figure 2 b) shows the relation between runtime and number of data (e.g. nodes in G).

At the initial stage $k = 1$, each worker of $s_{i,1} \in |S_1|$ with $|S_1| = w$ carries $n = \frac{|X|}{w}$ samples of $|X|$, which represents the number of nodes in G. The higher the available resource (number of workers w), the faster MSM processes at S_1 since n gets smaller. The output class labels $y_{i,k} \in Y_k$ for each sample are forwarded to stage S_{k+1} and the joint solution is computed by worker $s_{i,k+1} \in S_{k+1}$.

Merge Process. An illustration is shown in Fig. 3 a): the results of two disjoint sets are merged together. At stage S_2, the goal is to find the same cluster in workers from the previous stage $s_{i,1} \in S_1$ and $s_{i+1,1} \in S_1$. Figure 3 b) depicts the merge process: the centroid of the individual clusters using their class labels is computed. The centroids are used as new nodes, allowing the next stage to form a graph of centroids for the minimum cost Multicut problem. The size of the graph (thus the runtime) of the next stage mainly depends on the number of output clusters y_i from previous stage as well as the number of incoming disjoint sets (e.g. number of workers), that are being merged. The number of samples for $s_{i,k} \in S_k$ with $k > 1$ is defined as follows:

$$n_{i,k} = \sum_{j \in I_{i,k}} unique(y_{j,k-1}) \tag{4}$$

where $I_{i,k}$ represents the set of all workers in the prior stage that are joint together to worker $s_{i,k}$. The full MSM algorithm is described in Algorithm 1: MSM runs parallel after the dataset is distributed to different workers (line 3). We precompute the embedding z_n for data sample x_n offline, using a deep neural network. Since $|S_{k+1}|$ output its own class label, we need to reassign them to the workers in $|S_k|$ (line 14). The number of workers w as well as the number of stages L are considered as hyperparameters of MSM.

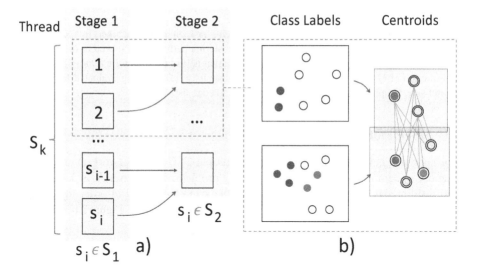

Fig. 3. Combining results of disjoint sets from two different workers: a) two sets are being merged for the next stage. In b), the centroids of different clusters from previous stage are being used to form a new minimum cost Multicut problem.

Algorithm 1. MSM: Multi-Stage Multicuts

1: **Input:** data X, number of workers w, Stages L
2: Set $k = 1$
3: Split data X to worker $s_i \in S_1$
4: Extract embedding z_n via deep neural network
5: Obtain clusters y_n based on z_n using Multicuts
6: **while** Final Stage L not reached **do**
7:    S_k sends y_n and z_n to S_{k+1}
8:    S_{k+1} compute centroids: $\tilde{z}_n$
9:    Obtain new clusters y_n based on $\tilde{z}_n$ using Multicuts
10:    $k = k + 1$
11: **end while**
12: **for** All stages **do**
13:    Backpropagate cluster labels y_n
14:    y_n = Translate y_n
15: **end for**
16: **Output:** y_n

3.4 Theoretical Proof

Here, we formally show the theoretical speed up of MSM. Given a set of n nodes V, we split V into k disjoint subsets $V_1, V_2, ..., V_k$. ($V_i \cap V_j = \varnothing$ for $i \neq j$ and $\bigcup\limits_{i=1}^{k} V_i = V$)

We denote the resulting graph that is built from set V_i as $G_i(V_i, E_i)$.

$$\min_y G_i^{(k)}(V_i^{(k)}, E_i^{(k)}) \tag{5}$$

$$z_i^{(k+1)} = f(V_i^{(k)}, y_i^{(k)}) \tag{6}$$

$$V_l^{(k+1)} = \bigcup_{i \in I_l^{(k+1)}} z_i^{(k+1)} \tag{7}$$

The function f computes the centroids of the nodes in $V_i^{(k)}$. $I_l^{(k+1)}$ is the set of indices of workers in stage k whose results are combined for worker l in stage $k + 1$.

The function $h^{(k+1)}(C_l^{(k)}) = y_l^{(k+1)}$ relates the indices found by the Multicuts with index in $I_l^{(k+1)}$ to the indices found by the Multicut of worker l in the next stage. The set of indices that are combined for worker l in the stage $k+1$ is $C_l^{(k)} = \{y_i^{(k)} | i \in I_l^{(k+1)}\}$. This is done in order to backpropagate the indices found in the last stage to the input data with $h^{-1}(y_l^{(k+1)})$. In our case the function h is a lookup table that keeps track of all the indices at a given stage.

For a fully connected Multicut with number of nodes $|V| = n$ the algorithm scales in $\mathcal{O}(\frac{n^2(n-1)}{2})$ [28]. For L stages with S_k workers at stage k one obtains the following complexity

$$\sum_{k=1}^{L} \underbrace{\sum_{i=1}^{S_k} \frac{n_{k,i}^2(n_{k,i} - 1)}{2}}_{R_k} \tag{8}$$

where $n_{k,i}$ is the number of nodes for worker i in stage k.

Let $g_k = \sum_{k=1}^{L} n_{k,i}$ be the number of nodes of all workers in stage k. Note that $g_1 = n$, the size of the original dataset.

Assumption 1. In order to find an upper bound we assume a balanced data allocation for each worker in each stage, therefore

$$n_{k,i} = \frac{g_k}{S_k} \tag{9}$$

The total number of nodes in stage k, g_k, does not grow in size in the next round, $g_{k+1} \leq g_k$.

The following relationship holds

$$g_k = p_{k-1} g_{k-1} \tag{10}$$

with $0 < p_k \leq 1$.

Assumption 2. The series of $(p_k)_{1 \leq k}$ is monotonically increasing and satisfies the following inequality

$$p_k \geq p_{k-1}^{\frac{k-1}{k}} \tag{11}$$

This is in line with what is being observed in the case of continually decreasing workers. The workers in the first stage are able to cluster most of the dataset, resulting in a much smaller p than what is achieved in later stages.

Assumption 3. The number of workers S_k is decreasing with each stage k, $S_{k+1} < S_k$.

In stage k one has a complexity of

$$R_k \overset{(9)}{=} \sum_{i=1}^{S_k} \frac{(\frac{g_k}{S_k})^2(\frac{g_k}{S_k} - 1)}{2}$$

$$= S_k \frac{(\frac{g_k}{S_k})^2(\frac{g_k}{S_k} - 1)}{2} \tag{12}$$

Since $1 \leq S_k$ we have

$$S_k \frac{(\frac{g_k}{S_k})^2(\frac{g_k}{S_k} - 1)}{2} \leq \frac{1}{S_k^2} \frac{g_k^2(g_k - 1)}{2} \tag{13}$$

Given $g_1 = n$ one can observe that

$$g_k = n \prod_{i=1}^{k-1} p_i \leq n p_{k-1}^{k-1} \tag{14}$$

With this relationship we can simplify expression (13)

$$\frac{1}{S_k^2} \frac{g_k^2(g_k - 1)}{2} \leq \frac{1}{S_k^2} \frac{(n p_{k-1}^{k-1})^2(n p_{k-1}^{k-1} - 1)}{2} \tag{15}$$

since $p_i \leq 1$ we obtain for stage k the following expression

$$R_k \leq \frac{1}{S_k^2} \frac{(n p_{k-1}^{k-1})^2(n p_{k-1}^{k-1} - 1)}{2} \leq \frac{p_{k-1}^{3(k-1)}}{S_k^2} \frac{n^2(n - 1)}{2} \tag{16}$$

If we set this back into expression (8), we obtain for an L-stage Multicut

$$\sum_{k=1}^{L} R_k \leq \frac{n^2(n - 1)}{2} \sum_{k=1}^{L} \frac{p_{k-1}^{3(k-1)}}{S_k^2} \tag{17}$$

Note that we have $S_L = 1$ and $\frac{1}{S_k} \leq 1$. Since $S_{k+1} < S_k$ we can write

$$\frac{n^2(n - 1)}{2} \sum_{k=1}^{L} \frac{p_{k-1}^{3(k-1)}}{S_k^2} \leq \frac{n^2(n - 1)}{2} \sum_{k=1}^{L} \frac{p_{k-1}^{3(k-1)}}{(L + 1 - k)^2} \tag{18}$$

Since we have $p_0 = 1$, the first term is split off the sum

$$\frac{n^2(n - 1)}{2} \sum_{k=1}^{L} \frac{p_{k-1}^{3(k-1)}}{S_k^2} = \frac{n^2(n - 1)}{2} \left(\underbrace{\sum_{k=2}^{L} \frac{p_{k-1}^{3(k-1)}}{(L + 1 - k)^2}}_{(I)} + \frac{1}{L^2} \right) \tag{19}$$

Now focus on term (I) from Eq. (19):

$$\sum_{k=2}^{L} \frac{p_{k-1}^{3(k-1)}}{(L + 1 - k)^2} = \sum_{k=1}^{L-1} \frac{p_k^{3k}}{(L - k)^2} \tag{20}$$

Denote $l_k = p_k^{3k}$. Since p_k is monotonically increasing, with p_k satisfying (11), we also have l_k monotonically increasing. Therefore we have that the maximum of $(l_k)_{1 \leq k \leq L-1}$ is $l_{L-1} = \max(\{l_k : k = 1, ..., L-1\})$. Thus we have

$$\sum_{k=1}^{L-1} \frac{l_k}{(L-k)^2} < l_{L-1} \sum_{k=1}^{L-1} \frac{1}{(L-k)^2} \tag{21}$$

One can rearrange the term in the sum so that one obtains

$$l_{L-1} \sum_{k=1}^{L-1} \frac{1}{(L-k)^2} = p_{L-1}^{3(L-1)} \sum_{k=1}^{L-1} \frac{1}{k^2} \tag{22}$$

We have that

$$\sum_{k=1}^{L-1} \frac{1}{k^2} = \frac{\pi^2}{6} - \psi^{(1)}(L) \tag{23}$$

Here $\psi^{(1)}(x)$ represents the first derivative of the digamma function.

$$\psi^{(1)}(x) = \sum_{k=0}^{\infty} \frac{1}{(k+x)^2} > \frac{1}{x^2} \tag{24}$$

Using the inequality in (24) this allows us to put an upper bound on expression (23)

$$\sum_{k=1}^{L-1} \frac{1}{k^2} = \frac{\pi^2}{6} - \psi^{(1)}(L) < \frac{\pi^2}{6} - \frac{1}{L^2} \tag{25}$$

Putting this result back into Eq. (22)

$$p_{L-1}^{3(L-1)} \underbrace{\sum_{k=1}^{L-1} \frac{1}{k^2}}_{(I)} < p_{L-1}^{3(L-1)} \left(\frac{\pi^2}{6} - \frac{1}{L^2} \right) \tag{26}$$

Putting (26) into (19) and (19) into (17) we obtain the following upper bound for the complexity for an L-stage Multicut under Assumptions 1–3:

$$\sum_{k=1}^{L} \sum_{i=1}^{S_k} \frac{n_{k,i}^2(n_{k,i}-1)}{2} < \frac{n^2(n-1)}{2} \underbrace{\left(p_{L-1}^{3(L-1)} \left(\frac{\pi^2}{6} - \frac{1}{L^2} \right) + \frac{1}{L^2} \right)}_{h(p_{L-1},L)} \tag{27}$$

Inequality (27) gives an upper bound to the complexity of our algorithm. It also relates the complexity of the L-stage Multicut to the regular approach that has complexity of $\frac{n^2(n-1)}{2}$. Whether the L-stage Multicut has lower computational complexity depends on the function $h(p_{L-1}, L)$. If $h(p_{L-1}, L) \leq 1$ the L-stage Multicut has lower complexity than a single Multicut on the entire dataset. The function $h(p_{L-1}, L)$ can be seen in Fig. 4 for different numbers of stages L.

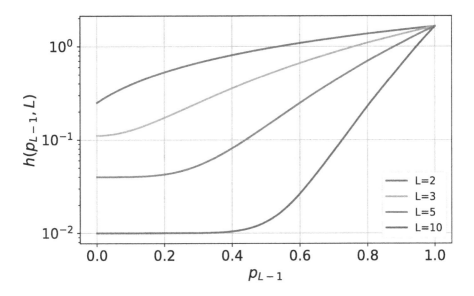

Fig. 4. Visualization of the function $h(p_{L-1}, L)$ for different stages L.

The memory complexity of the naive Multicut approach on a dataset of size n scales with a complexity of $\frac{n^2(n-1)}{2}$.

On the other hand, in the MSM approach, the memory scales at most like
$$\frac{n^2(n-1)}{2} \max_{k \in [1,L]} \frac{\left(\prod_{i=1}^{k-1} p_k\right)^3}{S_k^2}.$$

This allows a reduction in the very first stage by $\frac{1}{S_1^2}$. In later stages p is much smaller than one, thus the memory requirement on different workers are still much smaller than the naive approach. This allows to train much bigger datasets than what has previously been possible.

Table 1. Datasets used for image clustering tasks.

Dataset	Train size	Test size	# Classes
CELEBA	12.293	101.642	5
CIFAR10	50.000	10.000	10
CIFAR100	50.000	10.000	100

4   Experiments

In this section, we evaluate MSM algorithm on various datasets (Table 1) for image clustering tasks. We measure the runtime in seconds as well as the cluster accuracy, finding the best matches between the predicted cluster and true label as in [22]. All experiments are run on the same hardware and setup with multiple runs. If not specified, we report the mean number over five runs as well as its standard deviation.

The features are extracted from models based on supervised learning. We specify this in the according subsection of each experiment. The aim is to show, that, for a given problem, MSM can speedup clustering using Multicuts clustering method without any noticeable performance drop. The rest of this section explains the experiments on the datasets.

4.1   Two-Stage Approach on CIFAR10 Dataset

In this experiment, we evaluate our MSM on CIFAR10 based on a two-stage approach ($L = 2$), meaning that we split the dataset across S_1 workers during the first stage as shown in Fig. 3. In the second stage, we forward all intermediate results to one worker ($S_2 = 1$) to compute the final results.

Embeddings. We follow the approach of [13] to train a deep neural network with modified triplet loss for Multicuts. The threshold for cuts and joins are derived from the training parameters, which are provided in the supplementary materials. We also compute all the embeddings offline. This way, the GPUs are not required to extract the embeddings during the clustering task.

Results. We are comparing this method in terms of runtime as well as clustering accuracy on the full test dataset. As shown previously in Fig. 2, one single worker takes on average 930.64 ± 8.44 s to solve the problem. Increasing the number of workers by 2 using MSM ($S_1 = 2$) reduces the runtime of the problem by more than half (361.29 ± 16.4587 s). While the runtime is decreasing, the cluster accuracy remains the same, which is $80.54\% \pm 0.36\%$, as shown in Fig. 5.

4.2   Sparsity is Influencing the Runtime on Merge

In this experiment, we evaluate MSM on CelebA dataset [24]. We use the attribute *haircolors* for the image clustering task, which consists of five following classes: *bald*, *gray_hair*, *blond_hair*, *black_hair* and *brown_hair*.

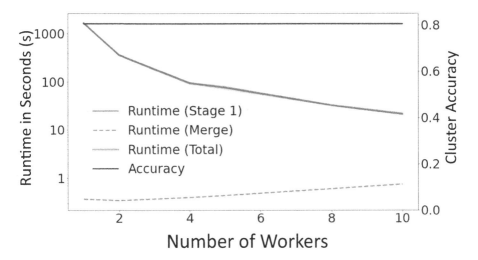

Fig. 5. Runtime and Cluster Accuracy on CIFAR10 test dataset using different number of workers in first stage (S_1). The Multicut runtime is reduced significantly when more workers are utilized. The runtime for merge (e.g. second stage) remains very low and the cluster accuracy is consistently around 80%.

Embeddings. We trained a deep neural network as in the previous experiment, using a modified Triplet Loss [13]. Here we swapped the train and test (see Table 1). We show the performance of MSM on a larger image clustering problem. The top row of Fig. 6 shows the performance of MSM on CelebA dataset for a two stage clustering $L = 2$ (as in Sect. 4.1). However, in this particular experiment, we enforce sparsity, where the number of total edges are reduced. Having less edges will speed up the algorithm but tends to produce more clusters thus decreasing the total cluster accuracy (as shown previously in Fig. 2). We also use up to $S_1 = 40$ workers for this image clustering task. The grey line depicts the runtime of each individual, concurrent worker for the clustering task via Multicuts while the dashed line shows the runtime for merging the results (e.g. the last stage $|S_L|$). The sum of both (total runtime) is represented as red line.

Results. The runtime decreases when adding more workers to MSM. Moreover, only a small drop in clustering performance is observed (blue line). However, Fig. 6 top left shows, that at roughly $S_1 = 25$ workers, the runtime of merge process (dashed line) of MSM begins to overtake the runtime of each individual Multicut process (gray line).

This effect is amplified by further removing more edges from the initial graph (sparsity = 0.01) at S_1. This is illustrated in Fig. 6 top right. Not only does the performance of the clustering task drop, but also the total runtime increases when using more workers. When increasing the sparsity of the graph (=overcluster), the merge process in $S_2 = 1$ becomes the bottleneck and no performance gain is achieved but rather the opposite instead.

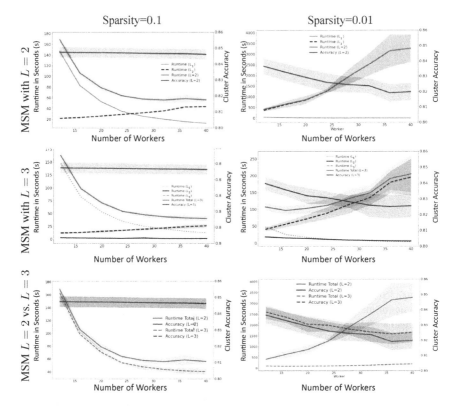

Fig. 6. Evaluation of MSM on CelebA Dataset: $L = 2$ vs. $L = 3$ using different (sparse) input graphs on CelebA Dataset. We compare the performance in terms of runtime (in seconds) and cluster accuracy. First row: MSM with two stages ($L = 2$). Second row: MSM with three stages ($L = 3$). Third row: comparison of $L = 2$ and $L = 3$. The columns represent different sparse graph for the initial stage. When using a two stage approach ($L = 2$) with graphs as depicted on first row, second column, adding more workers will increase the runtime significantly since we merge all results to one single worker in the last stage. We can avoid such *bottleneck* by adding an additional stage ($L = 3$), which is shown in the second row, second column (be aware of the scaling). (Color figure online)

4.3   MSM with 3-Stages on CelebA

When the output of S_k becomes too large, sending all the intermediate solutions to one single worker (e.g. $S_{k+1} = 1$) for processing the final result is not beneficial for MSM as it creates a bottleneck. We therefore investigate the effects of MSM with $L = 3$ stages on image clustering tasks. Specifically, we ran the same experiments as previously. On each intermediate stage, we reduce the number of workers by half. For instance if we set $S_1 = 40$, then $S_2 = 20$ and $S_3 = 1$, respectively. This way, we successively reduce the number of data on each layer.

Results. Figure 6 second row illustrates the performance of MSM with $L = 3$ stages. The total runtime slightly improves compared to MSM with $L = 2$ stages. However, on second row right, we see a significant performance increase for $L = 3$. Similarly, we also observe a drop in cluster accuracy when increasing the number of workers. The last row shows the direct comparison between $L = 2$ vs. $L = 3$ stages MSM.

4.4 MSM with 4-Stages on CIFAR100

CIFAR100 Test dataset has in total 10.000 samples with 100 unique, balanced clusters. These 100 unique clusters are further grouped into 20 super clusters, for instance the class *trees* consists of $tree = \{maple, oak, palm, pine, willow\}$ Fig. 7 shows the cluster accuracy as well as the total runtime in seconds. We use the embedding from [18] and evaluated MSM for $L = 3$ and $L = 4$.

Results. While the clustering accuracy remains very stable (average of $75.7\% \pm 0.4\%$), we observe different runtimes for $L3$ and $L4$. The fastest clustering solution (115.83 s ± 1.75 s) in this experiment is obtained with $L = 4$ and 12 workers for the initial stage ($S_1 = 12$), which is circled in back on Fig. 7. Increasing the number of workers slows down MSM. The best clustering accuracy is 75.7% with 578 unique clusters in total.

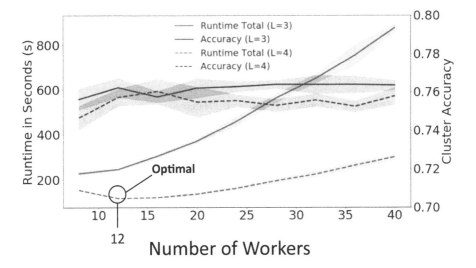

Fig. 7. Evaluation of MSM on CIFAR100 dataset: $L = 3$ vs. $L = 4$. We compare the performance in terms of runtime (in seconds) and cluster accuracy. The optimal runtime for $L = 4$ is achieved with $S_1 = 12$ workers.

5   Conclusion and Future Work

In this paper, we presented MSM, a Multi-Stage parallel Multicut algorithm for clustering data based on a given graph of pair-wise distances between entities. We showed that MSM provides good scalability on shared memory systems, while preserving the accuracy of the originally sequential Multicut clustering and provided a theoretical proof.

The advantage of Multicut clustering is the fact, that it is possible to perform pairwise comparisons of data. This allow us to overcome certain assumptions of data distributions, such as a priors known numbers of clusters or priors on cluster density and shape as in popular methods like K-Means and DB-Scan. However, optimizing such a data requires significant amount of resources such as memory and computation time. We observe that for image clustering task, MSM provides significant speedup using without any noticeable drop in cluster accuracy. We reported the runtime in seconds on different datasets with different number of classes, for example MSM is clusters a dataset of 100.000 images in one minute. Our aim is to provide a Multicuts clustering approach that is capable of solving a large graph within a reasonable amount of time. We believe that Multicuts clustering approaches enable new possibilities for research towards unsupervised learning.

Future Work. MSM introduces different hyperparameters such as sparsity of the input graphs, number of available resources and number of stages. We plan to investigate a heuristic for automatically finding the optimal setup for a given problem and dataset. Furthermore, we also plan to scale up the problem on a distributed setup.

References

1. Beier, T., Kroeger, T., Kappes, J.H., Kothe, U., Hamprecht, F.A.: Cut, glue & cut: a fast, approximate solver for multicut partitioning. In: Proceedings of the IEEE Conference on Computer Vision and Pattern Recognition, pp. 73–80 (2014)
2. Caron, M., Bojanowski, P., Joulin, A., Douze, M.: Deep clustering for unsupervised learning of visual features. In: Proceedings of the European Conference on Computer Vision (ECCV), pp. 132–149 (2018)
3. Caron, M., Bojanowski, P., Mairal, J., Joulin, A.: Unsupervised pre-training of image features on non-curated data. In: Proceedings of the IEEE/CVF International Conference on Computer Vision, pp. 2959–2968 (2019)
4. Caron, M., et al.: Emerging properties in self-supervised vision transformers. arXiv preprint arXiv:2104.14294 (2021)
5. Chen, T., Kornblith, S., Norouzi, M., Hinton, G.: A simple framework for contrastive learning of visual representations. In: International Conference on Machine Learning, pp. 1597–1607. PMLR (2020)
6. Chopra, S., Rao, M.R.: The partition problem. Math. Program. **59**(1–3), 87–115 (1993). https://doi.org/10.1007/BF01581239
7. Dean, J., et al.: Large scale distributed deep networks. In: Pereira, F., Burges, C.J.C., Bottou, L., Weinberger, K.Q. (eds.) Advances in Neural Information Processing Systems, vol. 25, pp. 1223–1231. Curran Associates Inc. (2012)

8. Demaine, E.D., Emanuel, D., Fiat, A., Immorlica, N.: Correlation clustering in general weighted graphs. Theor. Comput. Sci. **361**(2–3), 172–187 (2006)
9. Ghasedi, K., Wang, X., Deng, C., Huang, H.: Balanced self-paced learning for generative adversarial clustering network. In: Proceedings of the IEEE/CVF Conference on Computer Vision and Pattern Recognition, pp. 4391–4400 (2019)
10. Ghasedi Dizaji, K., Herandi, A., Deng, C., Cai, W., Huang, H.: Deep clustering via joint convolutional autoencoder embedding and relative entropy minimization. In: Proceedings of the IEEE International Conference on Computer Vision, pp. 5736–5745 (2017)
11. Guo, S., Xu, J., Chen, D., Zhang, C., Wang, X., Zhao, R.: Density-aware feature embedding for face clustering. In: Proceedings of the IEEE/CVF Conference on Computer Vision and Pattern Recognition, pp. 6698–6706 (2020)
12. Harlap, A., et al.: PipeDream: fast and efficient pipeline parallel DNN training. CoRR arXiv:1806.03377 (2018)
13. Ho, K., Keuper, J., Pfreundt, F., Keuper, M.: Learning embeddings for image clustering: an empirical study of triplet loss approaches. arXiv preprint arXiv:2007.03123 (2020)
14. Huang, Y., et al.: GPipe: efficient training of giant neural networks using pipeline parallelism. CoRR arXiv:1811.06965 (2018)
15. Kardoost, A., Ho, K., Ochs, P., Keuper, M.: Self-supervised sparse to dense motion segmentation. In: Proceedings of the Asian Conference on Computer Vision (2020)
16. Kernighan, B.W., Lin, S.: An efficient heuristic procedure for partitioning graphs. Bell Syst. Tech. J. **49**(2), 291–307 (1970)
17. Keuper, M., Tang, S., Andres, B., Brox, T., Schiele, B.: Motion segmentation & multiple object tracking by correlation co-clustering. IEEE Trans. Pattern Anal. Mach. Intell. **42**(1), 140–153 (2018)
18. Kolesnikov, A., et al.: Big transfer (bit): general visual representation learning, vol. 6, no. 2, p. 8. arXiv preprint arXiv:1912.11370 (2019)
19. Krizhevsky, A.: One weird trick for parallelizing convolutional neural networks. CoRR arXiv:1404.5997 (2014)
20. Krizhevsky, A., Hinton, G., et al.: Learning multiple layers of features from tiny images. Technical report, Citeseer (2009)
21. Krizhevsky, A., Sutskever, I., Hinton, G.E.: ImageNet classification with deep convolutional neural networks. In: Advances in Neural Information Processing Systems, vol. 25, pp. 1097–1105 (2012)
22. Kuhn, H.W.: The Hungarian method for the assignment problem. Naval Res. Logist. (NRL) **52**(1), 7–21 (2005)
23. Li, P., Zhao, H., Liu, H.: Deep fair clustering for visual learning. In: Proceedings of the IEEE/CVF Conference on Computer Vision and Pattern Recognition, pp. 9070–9079 (2020)
24. Liu, Z., Luo, P., Wang, X., Tang, X.: Deep learning face attributes in the wild. In: Proceedings of International Conference on Computer Vision (ICCV), December 2015
25. Mukherjee, S., Asnani, H., Lin, E., Kannan, S.: ClusterGAN: latent space clustering in generative adversarial networks. In: Proceedings of the AAAI Conference on Artificial Intelligence, vol. 33, pp. 4610–4617 (2019)
26. Pan, X., Papailiopoulos, D., Oymak, S., Recht, B., Ramchandran, K., Jordan, M.I.: Parallel correlation clustering on big graphs. arXiv preprint arXiv:1507.05086 (2015)
27. Pishchulin, L., et al.: DeepCut: joint subset partition and labeling for multi person pose estimation. In: Proceedings of the IEEE Conference on Computer Vision and Pattern Recognition, pp. 4929–4937 (2016)
28. Tang, S., Andres, B., Andriluka, M., Schiele, B.: Multi-person tracking by multicut and deep matching. CoRR arXiv:1608.05404 (2016)
29. Wolf, S., et al.: The mutex watershed and its objective: efficient, parameter-free graph partitioning. IEEE Trans. Pattern Anal. Mach. Intell. **43**(10), 3724–3738 (2020)

30. Xie, J., Girshick, R., Farhadi, A.: Unsupervised deep embedding for clustering analysis. In: International Conference on Machine Learning, pp. 478–487. PMLR (2016)
31. Zhan, X., Xie, J., Liu, Z., Ong, Y., Loy, C.C.: Online deep clustering for unsupervised representation learning. In: Proceedings of the IEEE/CVF Conference on Computer Vision and Pattern Recognition, pp. 6688–6697 (2020)

OmniOpt – A Tool for Hyperparameter Optimization on HPC

Peter Winkler[1]([✉]), Norman Koch[1], Andreas Hornig[2], and Johannes Gerritzen[2]

[1] Center for Information Services and High Performance Computing (ZIH),
Technische Universität Dresden, 01187 Dresden, Germany
peter.winkler1@tu-dresden.de
[2] Institute of Lightweight Engineering and Polymer Technology (ILK),
Technische Universität Dresden, 01307 Dresden, Germany
https://tu-dresden.de/zih/

Abstract. Hyperparameter optimization is a crucial task in numerous applications of numerical modelling techniques. Methods as diverse as classical simulations and the great variety of machine learning techniques used nowadays, require an appropriate choice of their hyperparameters (HPs). While for classical simulations, calibration to measured data by numerical optimization techniques has a long tradition, the HPs of neural networks are often chosen by a mixture of grid search, random search and manual tuning.

In the present study the expert tool "OmniOpt" is introduced, which allows to optimize the HPs of a wide range of problems, ranging from classical simulations to different kinds of neural networks. Thereby, the emphasis is on versatility and flexibility for the user in terms of the applications and the choice of its HPs to be optimized. Moreover, the optimization procedure – which is usually a very time-consuming task – should be performed in a highly parallel way on the HPC system Taurus at TU Dresden. To this end, a Bayesian stochastic optimization algorithm (TPE) has been implemented on the Taurus system and connected to a user-friendly graphical user interface (GUI). In addition to the automatic optimization service, there is a variety of tools for analyzing and graphically displaying the results of the optimization.

The application of OmniOpt to a practical problem from material science is presented as an example.

Keywords: Hyperparameter optimization · High performance computing · Neural networks

1 Introduction

Most machine learning (ML) algorithms have a set of configuration parameters determining the architecture of the system, details of the training procedure and

This work was supported by the German Federal Ministry of Education and Research (BMBF, 01/S18026A-F) by funding the competence center for Big Data and AI "ScaDS.AI Dresden/Leipzig".

© Springer Nature Switzerland AG 2021
H. Jagode et al. (Eds.): ISC High Performance 2021 Workshops, LNCS 12761, pp. 285–296, 2021.
https://doi.org/10.1007/978-3-030-90539-2_19

data flow. This statement holds not only for ML systems like neural networks or decision trees, but also for classical numerical simulations. These control parameters, which are set by the user, are called hyperparameters (HPs). In the case of neural networks (NNs), which have become increasingly popular over the last decade, HPs determine the network's architecture, activation functions, regularization, optimization, etc.

In general, the choice of HPs has a profound effect on the performance, efficiency and transferability of the algorithm used. Therefore, an appropriate choice of HPs is a crucial task for both, ML applications and numerical simulations. Naturally, HPs tuned for a specific case usually outperform the default settings provided by common ML libraries. Thereby, an automated HP optimization has several advantages over manual parameter tuning: it helps to reduce the often tedious procedure of repeatedly running the application to be optimized with different HP sets and tuning them manually. In case of a complex or high-dimensional parameter space it is very likely to overlook the areas of highest information gain of the HP space by manual search. Moreover, an automated approach is reproducible and allows unbiased comparisons between different methods [1].

Often, automated HP optimization is a challenging problem, because in many cases the parameter space is complex and high-dimensional. The choice of the HPs to be optimized as well as the choice of their boundaries is not clear a priori. Moreover, huge computational effort can be expected due to the multitude of training (or simulation) runs that have to be performed with different HP sets. Therefore, use of high performance computing (HPC) resources may be necessary in order to facilitate HP optimization.

Generally, optimization methods which do not require the gradient of the objective function with respect to the HPs can be used for HP optimization. The simplest approach is grid search, where the objective function is evaluated for all points on a regular grid spanned across the parameter space. This is, however, known to be numerically inefficient as the computational effort grows exponentially with the number of dimensions of the HP space. A simple alternative to grid search is random search [2]. Here, the points are chosen at random from the HP space. In many cases this approach is more efficient and yields more satisfying results than grid search. Moreover, it can easily be parallelized on an HPC system. Random search is often useful to provide an overview over the HP space and to choose reasonable parameter boundaries for more sophisticated optimization methods.

One of the most common approaches for global optimization on complex and high-dimensional parameter spaces is Bayesian optimization [3]. The present work makes use of the Hyperopt package [4] which is a highly parallel implementation of Bayesian optimization. The basics of this method will be outlined in Sect. 2. There are several HP optimization packages available, mainly focused on the optimization of ML applications. Two recent examples are: the Python library AutoSKlearn, which aims at freeing a ML user from algorithm selection and HP tuning [5] and makes use of Bayesian optimization algorithms. Another useful Python-based tool is Tune [6] which belongs to the Ray library [7]. Tune supports most popular ML frameworks and integrates a variety of optimization libraries including Hyperopt [4] and Nevergrad [8]. For efficient parallelization on multiple GPUs there is an integration of Tune into Horovod which is a distributed deep learning training framework for TensorFlow, Keras, PyTorch, and Apache MXNet [9]. For a more comprehensive overview of HP optimization approaches we refer to the excellent review article by Feurer et al. [1] and the references therein.

1.1 Outline

The present work describes the HP optimization tool OmniOpt which is focused on user-friendliness, versatility regarding the applications to be optimised (ML applications as well as classical simulations – practically every application returning an objective function), versatility regarding the programming languages of the user's code (practically all languages running on Linux systems can be used) and flexibility in the setup of the optimization process (choice of HP and their borders, free choice of the ML method or simulation technique). It is a tailor-made solution for the HPC system Taurus [10] at TU Dresden which is open to the scientific community worldwide. OmniOpt uses a Bayesian optimization algorithm, the tree-structured Parzen optimizer (TPE) [11] implemented by the Hyperopt project. Parallelisation is done automatically by the system and there is a graphical user interface (GUI) for preparing the user's input as well as tools for automatic evaluation and plotting of the results.

In the results section an application of OmniOpt to a practically relevant problem from material science is presented.

2 Methods and Tools

OmniOpt is versatile and user-friendly HP optimization tool which is automatically parallelized on the HPC system Taurus which is operated by the Centre for Information Services and High Performance Computing (ZIH) of Technische Universität (TU) Dresden.

2.1 The HPC System

The HPC cluster Taurus [10] has more than 60000 CPU cores, 720 GPUs of which 272 are Nvidia A100, 192 are Nvidia V100 and 256 are Nvidia K80 units. Moreover, there is a flexible storage hierarchy with a total capacity of 16 PB. The operating system is Bullx [12], a Linux system specially designed for supercomputers. Jobs are scheduled by the open-source workload management system Slurm [13]. A variety of pre-installed software is available to all users. Free access to Taurus is possible for the whole scientific community i.e. universities and other research institutes as well as non-profit organizations. To gain access, a short project application is required.

2.2   Features of OmniOpt

OmniOpt is designed as black box optimization tool. The application provided by the user has to fulfil the following conditions:

- It can be written in any programming language running on Linux systems. The most popular examples supported by the HPC system Taurus are Python, C++, R, Java, Perl and Fortran. The common deep learning frameworks for Python, like TensorFlow, PyTorch or Keras are also supported. Special software packages that are not pre-installed on Taurus may be installed by the user within a container or a virtual environment. Generally, any numerical simulation, the HPs of which are to be optimised, can be handled. In principle also binary files are possible. However, this is not recommended as minor changes on the code might be helpful for an efficient processing.
- The user's application has to read the HPs to be optimized from the command line as arguments. This enables the algorithm to update the HPs during the optimization process.
- The application has to write the value of the objective function to the standard output (stdout). Here, the user has to choose an objective function appropriate for the problem to be optimized. In the case of NNs, the validation loss will be a good choice in many cases, where the choice of the loss function – again – depends on the demands of the user. Multi-criterial optimization, i.e. optimizing with respect to more than one objective function, is not supported by OmniOpt at this stage of the work.

The OmniOpt GUI allows the user to start an optimization without directly interacting with the batch system of the HPC system. By using this GUI the user can control the optimization process, the parameter space and the computational resources. It requires the following input parameters:

- Use of GPUs or CPUs. In both cases hardware with different specifications can be chosen.
- Number of workers. In case of CPUs several thousands are possible whereas more than 50 GPUs may be requested. Note, that the choice of a very large number of GPUs may cause the application to be scheduled with lower priority.
- Memory (RAM) per worker.
- Maximal computing time (wall clock time).
- Maximum number of HP sets to be evaluated.
- Type of optimization algorithm: random search or TPE (a Bayesian method outlined below).
- Name and location of the objective program (the user's application).
- Number of HPs to be optimized.
- Type of each HP (discrete or continuous).
- Boundaries of each HP.
- Choose linear or logarithmic scale for each HP.

The OmniOpt repository includes automatic tools to analyze and visualize of the results of the optimization process. Some of the options are:

- Writing a complete table of the HP sets evaluated during the optimization to a text file. This includes the values of the HPs, the corresponding value of the objective function, runtimes of the specific evaluation, a time stamp, and the ID of the worker used.
- Creating graphs which show all HP sets evaluated in the HP space. Due to the usually high dimension of the HP space, a graphical representation in a single graph is hardly possible. Therefore individual graphs for each possible pair of HPs are displayed. The quality of the results (i.e. the value of the objective function) is indicated by a color code. A threshold may be given in order to show only HP sets that are above a certain quality level defined by the user. Examples will be shown in the Results section.
- Creating graphs showing the GPU usage over time.
- An automatic analysis of jobs which may have failed (based on logfiles).
- Control over running jobs, e.g. a live view of the standard output and the possibility to shut down individual jobs while the whole optimization process is still running.

2.3   Architecture of OmniOpt

OmniOpt offers two different optimization algorithms: random search and the TPE [11] which is a state-of-the-art Bayesian optimization method. In short, Bayesian methods are iterative algorithms using the following basic concept: they start by calculating the objective function for a set of random configurations in the HP space. In each further step a probability distribution (called surrogate model) is determined by fitting to the results calculated so far (i.e. the values of the objective function as a function of the HPs). In a more qualitative picture, the surrogate model describes, where 'good' HP configurations are likely to be found in the HP space. Then, an acquisition function chooses a new set of HPs for the next iteration. Thereby, a trade-off between the predictions of the surrogate model and exploration of the full HP space is made. So, on the one hand the whole HP space is considered and on the other hand the promising regions therein are preferred by the algorithm. This concept enables global optimization with a moderate number of function evaluations. This feature is highly relevant as the evaluation of the objective function is usually the computationally most expensive part of the optimization process. More details as well as the mathematical background can be found in [3].

In this work, the Hyperopt project [4], a Python library containing implementations of both, random search and TPE, has been applied. The communication between the optimization routines from Hyperopt and the HPC system Taurus is governed by a data base, specifically a MongoDB [14]. At the beginning of the optimization process, a MongoDB server is started on one node which is accessible from all other nodes. The results of all evaluations of the objective function are stored in this data base. This enables the algorithm to create the surrogate model and choose a new set of HPs for the next iteration. To this end a Hyperopt-script called `fmin.py` periodically checks the data base, determines the next HP sets to be tried and writes them back into the data base. Another script created by the authors governs the communication to the Slurm batch system of Taurus: first, after some sanity checks of the input data, it starts the number of workers requested by the user. Subsequently the evaluations of the objective function are started, each as an individual job on one worker. Whenever there is a new set of HPs in the MongoDB, this script will automatically start a new job. This means that the whole process is embarrassingly parallel: *one* function evaluation for *one* set of HPs is evaluated on *one* worker (CPU or GPU). The number of workers, and hence the number of parallel processes, is determined by the user. This has the advantage, that the user does not have to care about the parallelization of the application. As for both, TPE and random search, a high number of independent function evaluations are necessary, this is an efficient approach avoiding more complex parallelization approaches. Thereby, the intrinsic parallelization on GPUs offered by most popular ML frameworks remains intact. The optimization process ends when either the maximum number of evaluations or the maximal computation time is reached (both chosen by the user in the GUI).

2.4   Application to a Problem from Material Science

OmniOpt has been tested for several practical applications. One example from material science – the prediction of material parameters from strain-stress curves – is described in the following.

The material behaviour of fibre reinforced plastics, represented by the stress-strain relation, is of highly non-linear nature. Therefore models accurately describing such behaviour are complex and depend on a multitude of parameters [15–17]. This poses a high initial hurdle to employ new models. Oftentimes the models have to be understood to get into the position to precisely determine the material parameters. The aim of the presented approach is therefore to transfer the task of parameter identification – and with that the required understanding – to a NN and subsequently facilitate the usage of non-linear material models.

For this work, a minimalistic yet highly non-linear material model has been chosen. It depends on the two material parameters G_0, which corresponds to the initial response of the material to an external load and a, which describes how soon into the loading process and how strongly the material's response diverges from the initial one.

Since the amount of data required for training cannot be obtained experimentally, synthetic training data were created based on the non-linear material model, using 50 variations per parameter and full factorial assembling. To account for experimental variation, the strain has been uniformly varied in a range of 0.15 to 0.25, the stress has been superimposed with a random noise of maximum amplitude 1 MPa (maximum stresses in a range of 15 to 450 MPa) and the number of data points per case has been varied between 150 and 250. To fit the constant input size of 200, each series has either been filled up with zeros and an additional flag was added, clarifying these were only padding values, or random points were dropped. This results in a data set with a total of 12500 stress-strain curves containing 200 points with 3 values (strain, stress, flag) each. Due to the material parameters being of different orders of magnitude, they were normalized to a range of 0 to 1.

In order to predict the material parameters based on the respective stress-strain curve, a NN was built up using TensorFlow [18]. The model contains two 1d convolutional layers, each followed by a max pooling layer. The output of the second pooling layer is flattened and piped through a dense layer, with the last one giving the predictions for the normalized parameters.

25% of the available data is used for validation. As loss function the sum of the mean squared errors (MSE) of the material parameters G_0 and a is chosen. The same quantity, evaluated for the validation data, is used as objective function for the HP optimization.

3   Results

Here we show the results of the HP optimization of the above-mentioned application.

3.1   Initial Tests

Manual tests have shown that the most important HPs are the number of epochs, the learning rate and the number of filters in the two convolutional layers, whereas the batch size – as expected – has significant effects on the computation time. Changing other HPs like the number of convolutional layers and the type of optimizer for the training had only minor effects on the quality of the results. Whereas, the superiority of a 1d-convolutional network over a dense network was so clear that the network type has not been included in the set of HPs to be optimized. This lead us to the following five HPs for optimization by OmniOpt: the number of epochs, the learning rate, the batch size and the number of filters in the first and second convolutional layer, respectively.

The above-mentioned manual tests suggested the HP boundaries summarized in Table 1. For all five HPs a uniform distribution within the interval has been chosen.

Table 1. Boundaries and best values found for the HPs to be optimized.

HP	Minimum	Maximum	Type	Best value found
Number of epochs	20	1000	Discrete	922
Learning rate	10^{-5}	10^{-3}	Continuous	$5.3 \cdot 10^{-4}$
Batch size	10	200	Discrete	17
Number of filters in layer a	20	70	Discrete	30
Number of filters in layer b	20	70	Discrete	41

The computational resources used for the optimization run are summarized in Table 2. The use of GPUs and CPUs has been tested beforehand. Performing the training on a GPU lead to a rather low GPU usage of around 30%. This is due to a moderate amount of training data (59 MB) in combination with low batch sizes appropriate for this problem. On the other hand, the training of the application on a single CPU was computationally rather inexpensive (depending on the number of epochs maximally one hour). Therefore, the use of GPUs is not advisable in this case. However, for most applications with more expensive training procedures (larger networks and large amounts of training data) GPUs should be the first choice. As there is a large number of CPUs available at Taurus (60000 in total, 500 used here) the use of CPUs lead to a moderate wall clock time of 4 h and 22 min for the whole HP optimization process using the specifications in Table 2.

Table 2. Computational resources and other parameters.

Number of CPUs	500
Number of GPUs	0
CPU type	amd64
Memory per CPU	2540 MB
Number of HP sets evaluated	3000
Optimization method	TPE
Wall clock time	4 h 22 min

3.2   Optimization Results

The best HPs found in a TPE optimization run with 3000 evaluations are shown in the last column of Table 1. This set of HPs leads to the mean squared errors $6.05 \cdot 10^{-4}$ for G_0 and $1.756 \cdot 10^{-3}$ for a. Consequently, the minimal value of the objective function is $\text{MSE}(G_0) + \text{MSE}(a) = 2.361 \cdot 10^{-3}$. These values indicate a satisfying accuracy for the prediction of the material parameters under consideration. This is illustrated in Fig. 1 where the strain-stress-curves for ten different materials are shown. Each pair of lines with the same color belongs to one specimen. The full lines are data from the validation set of the synthetic data, whereas the dashed lines are calculated by the material model using the predicted values of G_0 and a. The agreement is highly satisfying from an engineer's point of view.

3.3   Visualization in the HP Space

To gain more insight in the optimization process, the OmniOpt repository contains a tool for automatic visualization of the HP sets evaluated. To this end, scatterplots for each possible pair of HPs are created. In case of five HPs this amounts to a number of ten graphs. Each of them represents a two-dimensional

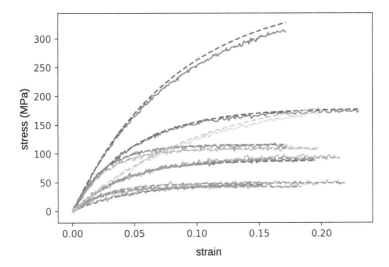

Fig. 1. Strain-stress-curves for ten different materials. Validation data (full lines) are compared to the predicted curves (dashed lines).

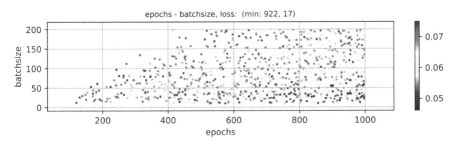

Fig. 2. HP sets evaluated: batch size versus number of epochs. (Color figure online)

subspace of the five-dimensional HP space. Three examples will be discussed in the following.

In Figs. 2, 3 and 4 the color of the dots indicates the quality of the results measured by the square-root of the objective function. As indicated in the legend, the best results are in dark blue corresponding to low values of the objective function. Note, that only 1334 of the 3000 HP sets evaluated are represented in the plots. This is due to a threshold of 0.075 for the square-root of the objective function which excludes higher values. This threshold can be chosen individually by the user. It will lead to more concise and understandable plots if carefully chosen.

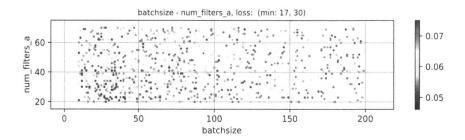

Fig. 3. HP sets evaluated: number of filters in convolutional layer 'a' versus batch size. (Color figure online)

In Fig. 2 the batch size is plotted versus the number of epochs. Clearly, there is a tendency to very small batch sizes, the minimum being at 17. On the other hand, the optimal number of epochs (922) is quite close to the upper boundary of its interval [10, 1000]. This indicates that another optimization run allowing for even higher numbers of epochs might be useful. However, the very satisfying accuracy and rather low computation time of the results presented here, do not necessitate a further increase of the interval. Generally, this rather surprising result (a very low batch size and a high number of epochs) is a strong argument for automated HP optimization: tuning the HPs manually, such a configuration will be found only through lengthy experiments.

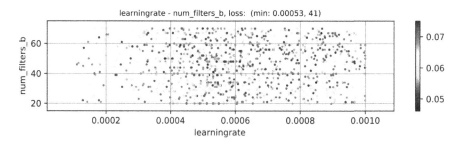

Fig. 4. HP sets evaluated: number of filters in convolutional layer 'b' versus learning rate. (Color figure online)

Figure 3 shows the plot for the number of filters in convolutional layer 'a' versus the batch size. Here, the picture is less clear than in the previous plot. Still, there is a tendency towards a low number of filters, the minimum being at 30.

In Fig. 4 the number of filters in convolutional layer 'b' is plotted versus the learning rate. It can be observed that both HPs tend to intermediate values. The learning rate is a very sensitive parameter with the best results in the small interval $[5 \cdot 10^{-4}, 6.2 \cdot 10^{-4}]$.

All three figures show, that the TPE algorithm chooses the HP configurations in an intelligent way: In the 'interesting' regions of the HP space, the points are much more densely scattered than elsewhere.

It should be mentioned that for an in-depth analysis of a multi-dimensional HP space different visualization techniques are available. A simple yet powerful approach is the use of parallel coordinates [19].

4   Conclusions

OmniOpt is an expert tool for hyperparameter optimization on the HPC cluster Taurus of the TU Dresden. It is a free tool which is open to the scientific community. Its focus is on versatility and flexibility for the user: in contrast to other HP optimization frameworks it is not restricted to neural networks. Also other ML applications, e.g. random forests as well as classical simulations may be optimised. All common programming languages and ML frameworks running on Linux systems are supported. The user is free in the choice of the HPs to be optimized.

A user-friendly GUI helps to control the optimization process in a convenient way. The parallelization on the HPC system is performed automatically according to the resources requested. However, OmniOpt is not a fully automatic framework. The user is expected to handle the tool in an intelligent way: the network (or simulation) architecture as well as the objective function has to be supplied by the user as black box. HP boundaries have to be chosen carefully by performing initial manual tests. In many cases an initial optimization run may suggest to adjust the choice of the HPs or their boundaries and then performing another optimization.

For problems with inexpensive evaluation of the objective function, e.g. NNs with a small number of training data, the use of CPUs will be the first choice. For larger compute-intensive problems and problems with large amounts of data several hundred state-of-the-art GPUs are available.

Application of OmniOpt to a convolutional neural network for determination of material parameters from strain-stress-curves has been successfully performed. In future, application to problems of different size and complexity from different disciplines is desired.

Acknowledgments. The authors would like to thank Taras Lazariv for his feedback and support which helped to improve this work.

References

1. Feurer, M., Hutter, F.: Hyperparameter optimization. In: Hutter, F., Kotthoff, L., Vanschoren, J. (eds.) Automated Machine Learning. TSSCML, pp. 3–33. Springer, Cham (2019). https://doi.org/10.1007/978-3-030-05318-5_1
2. Bergstra, J., Bengio, Y.: Random search for hyper-parameter optimization. J. Mach. Learn. Res. **13**, 281–305 (2012)

3. Shahriari, B., Swersky, K., Wang, Z., Adams, R., de Freitas, N.: Taking the human out of the loop: a review of Bayesian optimization. Proc. IEEE **104**(1), 148–175 (2016)
4. Bergstra, J., et al.: Hyperopt: a Python library for model selection and hyperparameter optimization. Comput. Sci. Discov. **8**, 014008 (2015). https://doi.org/10.1088/1749-4699/8/1/014008
5. Feurer, M., Klein, A., Eggensperger, K., Springenberg, J., Blum, M., Hutter, F.: Efficient and robust automated machine learning. In: Cortes, C., Lawrence, N.D., Lee, D.D., Sugiyama, M., Garnett, R. (eds.) Advances in Neural Information Processing Systems, vol. 28, pp. 2962–2970. Curran Associates, Inc. (2015)
6. Liaw, R., Liang, E., Nishihara, R., Moritz, P., Gonzalez, J.E., Stoica, I.: Tune: a research platform for distributed model selection and training. arXiv:1807.05118 (2018)
7. Moritz, P., et al.: Ray: a distributed framework for emerging AI applications. arXiv:1712.05889 (2017)
8. Rapin, J., Teytaud O.: Nevergrad – a gradient-free optimization platform, GitHub repository (2018). https://GitHub.com/FacebookResearch/Nevergrad
9. Sergeev A., Del Balso, M.: Horovod: fast and easy distributed deep learning in TensorFlow. arXiv:1802.05799 (2018)
10. ZIH homepage. https://tu-dresden.de/zih/hochleistungsrechnen/hpc
11. Bergstra, J., Bardenet, R., Bengio, Y., Kégl, B.: Algorithms for hyperparameter optimization. In: Advances in Neural Information Processing Systems, vol. 24 (2011). https://papers.nips.cc/paper/2011/file/86e8f7ab32cfd12577bc2619bc635690-Paper.pdf
12. Bullx documentation. https://www.dkrz.de/pdfs/docs/docu-mistral/bullx_scs_4_r4_de_2014-01.pdf
13. Yoo, A.B., Jette, M.A., Grondona, M.: SLURM: simple linux utility for resource management. https://doi.org/10.1007/10968987
14. MongoDB homepage. https://www.mongodb.com/
15. Zscheyge, M., Böhm, R., Hornig, A., Gerritzen, J., Gude, M.: Rate dependent non-linear mechanical behaviour of continuous fibre-reinforced thermoplastic composites – experimental characterisation and viscoelastic-plastic damage modelling. Mater. Des. **193**, 108827 (2020)
16. Böhm, R., Gude, M., Hufenbach, W.: A phenomenologically based damage model for textile composites with crimped reinforcement. Comput. Sci. Technol. **70**, 81–87 (2010)
17. Gude, M., Hufenbach, W., Ebert, C.: The strain-rate-dependent material and failure behaviour of 2D and 3D non-crimp glass-fibre-reinforced composites. Mech. Compos. Mater. **45**, 467 (2009). https://doi.org/10.1007/s11029-009-9108-3
18. Abadi, M., et al.: TensorFlow: large-scale machine learning on heterogeneous systems (2015). https://www.tensorflow.org/
19. Heinrich, J., Weiskopf, D.: State of the art of parallel coordinates. In: Sbert, M., Szirmay-Kalos, L. (eds.) Eurographics 2013 - State of the Art Reports, pp. 95–116 (2013). https://doi.org/10.2312/conf/EG2013/stars/095-116

Parallel/Distributed Intelligent Hyperparameters Search for Generative Artificial Neural Networks

Mathias Esteban[1] , Jamal Toutouh[2,3(✉)] , and Sergio Nesmachnow[1]

[1] Universidad de la República, Montevideo, Uruguay
{mathias.esteban,sergion}@fing.edu.uy
[2] University of Malaga, Malaga, Spain
[3] Massachusetts Institute of Technology, Cambridge, MA, USA
toutouh@mit.edu

Abstract. This article presents a parallel/distributed methodology for the intelligent search of the hyperparameters configuration for generative artificial neural networks (GANs). Finding the configuration that best fits a GAN for a specific problem is challenging because GANs simultaneously train two deep neural networks. Thus, in general, GANs have more configuration parameters than other deep learning methods. The proposed system applies the iterated racing approach taking advantage of parallel/distributed computing for the efficient use of resources for configuration. The main results of the experimental evaluation performed on the MNIST dataset showed that the parallel system is able to efficiently use the GPU, achieving a high level of parallelism and reducing the computational wall clock time by 78%, while providing competitive comparable results to the sequential hyperparameters search.

Keywords: Hyperparameters search · Artificial neural networks · Generative adversarial networks · Iterated race

1 Introduction

Generative Adversarial Networks (GANs) are emerging powerful methods to train deep generative models. GANs have demonstrated being a successful tool for many applications, especially those concerning multimedia information (e.g., images, sound, and video), science, healthcare, and other areas [9,18,23].

To construct a generative model, GAN training considers two artificial neural networks (ANN), a generator and a discriminator, that apply adversarial learning to optimize their parameters by defining a minmax optimization problem. The mark of a successful GAN is a generator that produces accurate synthetic samples. However, during GAN training, the adversarial dynamics may give rise to different convergence pathologies, e.g., gradient vanishing and mode collapse [10]. Co-evolutionary training methods have shown to be resilient to the degenerate behavior of GAN training by evolving two populations of ANN (one of generators against one of discriminators) towards convergence.

© Springer Nature Switzerland AG 2021
H. Jagode et al. (Eds.): ISC High Performance 2021 Workshops, LNCS 12761, pp. 297–313, 2021.
https://doi.org/10.1007/978-3-030-90539-2_20

This work focuses on Lipizzaner [20], a GAN library that applies a spatially distributed co-evolutionary training method to addresses the minmax optimization problems by fostering arms races between the populations. The appropriate selection of hyperparameters strongly determines the success of deep learning methods. When dealing with GANs, that simultaneously train two ANN, picking the correct configuration for the hyperparameters is even more critical.

In this line of work, this article proposes a parallel/distributed system for the automatic configuration of relevant GAN parameters, implemented over a high performance computing infrastructure. The proposed system applies a two-level parallel approach, combining distributed memory and shared memory GPU-based training, to efficiently execute the hyperparameters search proposed by *iterated racing* (IRACE), a well-known configuration tool for tuning optimization algorithms [13].

IRACE implements an iterated racing algorithm to search through the parameter space, looking for a configuration that minimizes the experiment target function. A race is a competition between a set of candidate configurations where individual parameters are drawn from independent normal distributions. During a race, configurations that perform statistically worse than the rest are discarded as soon as possible. Candidate configurations are compared with non-parametric Friedman's two-way analysis of variance by ranks. Races are performed until the specified computation budget is exhausted. Surviving configurations proceed to the next race and bias sampling distributions towards themselves.

In the proposed system, the iterated race approach is distributed to efficiently search the parameter space of GANs, to provide a useful high-level configuration algorithm capable of taking advantage of the computing power of large supercomputing facilities. The main training parameters in Lipizzaner are studied: the *initial learning rate* (the step size of the change of the weights), the *number of steps the discriminator skips learning*, to avoid early convergence and subpar results due to vanishing gradient issues, the *mutation probability*, and the *standard deviation* of the normal distribution used in the Gaussian mutation.

Configuration experiments are performed for a standard image processing problem: the generation of handwritten digits. Training data are 60,000 grayscale images of handwritten digits from the MNIST dataset. Experiments are performed on the infrastructure provided by National Supercomputing Center Uruguay [17]. The accuracy of the obtained generative model is measured in terms of Frechet inception distance score, a black box, discriminator-independent metric, that computes image similarity of the synthesized samples to the samples in the training dataset. In any case, the proposed methodology can be applied to study the configuration of GANs for other relevant applications, such as the parallel/distributed GAN for data augmentation of COVID-19 training images [24].

The contributions of the research are the implementation and validation of an automatic procedure to efficiently search the Lipizzaner parametric space. The proposed methodology will allow computing the most effective parameter values, significantly reducing the execution time demanded by brute force approaches.

The article is organized as follows. Section 2 introduces the subject of automatic hyperparameter configuration in GANs, it presents the main software components devised and used in our research, and it briefly presents a review of related works. Section 3 describes the proposed parallel/distributed approach to automatically tune GANs. The experimental evaluation and results are reported and discussed in Sect. 4. Finally, the conclusions and the main lines for future work are presented in Sect. 5.

2   Automatic Parameter Configuration of GANs

This section describes the approach for automatic parameter configuration of GANs and the software libraries used in the proposed system. It also presents a review of related works.

2.1   Parameter Configutation of GANs

In the machine learning domain, the selection of the appropriate hyperparameter configuration has been a subject of study over the years [15,22,28]. Hyperparameter optimization methods can be grouped into two main groups: manual exploration-based approaches, which usually are led by expert knowledge; and automatic search-based methods, such as, random, grid, and racing search [3]. The number of parameters to configure machine learning algorithms and the alternatives for each parameter are extremely large. Therefore, the hyperparameter optimization problem deals with high-dimensional search spaces. Besides, most methods are based on trial-and-error, which means that they need to run the algorithm and evaluate numerically its accuracy to assess the tentative solution (hyperparameter configuration), which in general is very time consuming. The search huge search space and the time consuming evaluation process severely affects the application of the search of hyperparameters.

This research focuses on the use of racing hyperparameter search methods. Racing search methods allow the rapid search of *good* hyperparameter configurations [5]. These search algorithms define a race among different tentative hyperparameter configurations and keep in the race the most promising configurations, while discarding the least competitive ones. The racing method allows an efficient use of computational resources by guiding the search through the search space area that defines the most promising hyperparameters configurations.

This article aims at solving the problem of automatically tuning the hyperparameters that command the algorithm of GAN training. In order to obtain a generative model, GANs train two deep neural networks: the generative model (*generator*) and a discriminative model (*discriminator*), which apply an adversarial learning to learn from each other [9]. As most of deep learning approaches, the network weights of both the generator and the discriminator are updated/optimized by using a variation of stochastic gradient decent approach. Therefore, the complexity of finding the hyperparameter configuration that best fit algorithm is rather more difficult than in other deep learning methods, because GANs consider the simultaneous training of two different deep neural networks.

GANs are notoriously hard to train, frequently showing degenerative behaviors or pathologies, such as mode collapse or vanishing gradients [2,29]. In order to mitigate these problems, different approaches inspired on co-evolutionary algorithms have been proposed, e.g., Lipizzaner [21] or Mustangs [25]. Thus, this article proposes using an automatic hyperparameter configuration method for Lipizzaner algorithm.

2.2 Software Libraries Used in the Proposed System

This subsection describes the software components integrated in the proposed parallel system.

Lipizzaner. In our study, Lipizzaner GAN training framework is used to train the generative models [21]. Lipizzaner implements a co-evolutionary distributed GAN training method, in which two set of generations (i.e., populations) are trained against each other, one for generators and one for discriminators. The networks (i.e., individuals in each population) are located in a two-dimensional spatial grid. The concept of neighborhood is applied to define those individuals that participate in the training phase for both generators and discriminators. Lipizzaner has shown to be effective overcoming the main pathologies in GAN training (e.g., mode collapse and non-convergence). In turn, cellular training allows implementing a data-parallel approach where each cell is trained using reduced subsets of training dataset, allowing to improve the computational efficiency of the training process because less training data batches are needed, while providing comparable quality results [26].

IRACE. The IRACE software package is an automatic hyperparameter configurator based on a racing procedure [13]. It was initially devised to tune metaheuristic optimization algorithms, which the quality of their solutions are highly dependent on their configurations. In IRACE, a race consists of three steps: i) sampling new parametric configurations, ii) testing configurations on the target algorithm, iii) discard configurations that are outperformed as soon as possible. At the end of the race, the sampling distribution is biased towards the best parameters and the process is repeated.

Linking IRACE and Lipizzaner. The search logic implemented by IRACE is abstracted from the specific domain problem. A middleware component named *target runner* is required to allow communication between IRACE and the algorithm to be optimized. This component is responsible for testing parametric configurations sent by IRACE on Lipizzaner, and returning the results back. It is also the target runner responsibility to verify that the minimum required resources to run Lipizzaner are available before execution.

2.3   Related Work

The hyperparameter optimization manually carried out by human experts requires bounded computational resources. Humans can easily and quickly appreciate poor hyperparameter configurations by examining the stochastic gradient descent results after a few steps. This is helpful to rapidly terminate training of algorithms that are performing bad due to the hyperparameter selection. However, the use of human experts have some disadvantages: it is time intense of human effort, few design alternatives and hyperparameter settings are explored, and the configurations are typically evaluated only on limited set of instances.

Automatic hyperparameter configuration search algorithms have been proposed to overcome the drawbacks of manual search [31]. The most intuitive approach is the grid or Cartesian hyperparameter search [4]. This method makes an exhaustive search of the best configuration by evaluating each combination of possible values of hyperparameters. The evaluation is carried out according to a predefined performance metric and using cross validation. This method can theoretically find the best (global optimum) hyperparameter configuration. However, the number of parameters and their range of values make the use of grid search computationally cost prohibitive.

Random search algorithms have been proposed to sample the hyperparameters search space. Basically, it tires random combinations of a range of values. His search is less expensive (in terms of computational cost) than grid search [4]. Thus, it is more efficient in high-dimensional hyperparameters spaces. However, it has been shown that random search is unreliable for finding hyperparameters for some complex models [4].

Finding the hyperparameter configuration that best fit an algorithm to solve a given problem can be defined as an optimization problem where the objective function is a black-box function. However, classic optimization approaches such as the ones based on the gradient descent or Newton methods are impractical to address the hyperparameter configuration problem. Thus, some authors have proposed different optimization techniques to tune hyperparameters in machine learning, such as metaheuristics [1] or Bayesian optimization [28] methods.

A number of studies have focused on using metaheuristics to configure hyperparameters in deep neural networks [1]. For example, a convolutional neural network classifier for tumor-specific microRNA signatures was configured by using an evolutionary algorithm (EA) [16]. In this approach, the authors tuned 10 hyperparameters and the quality of the configuration was evaluated on a 10-fold validation process. The same type of neural network, a CNN, was tuned by using another EA [11]. In this case the authors considered nine hyperparameters and they evaluated their approach over different image datasets such as, MNIST and CIFAR. Besides, metaheuristics have been applied to address the same problem with other deep neural networks, such as, recurrent neural networks (RNN). For example, evolutionary strategies (ES) were used to find the best configuration of RNNs taking into account the hyperparameters that define the network architecture and the look back for addressing synthetic [6] and car park occupancy [7] forecasting problems.

Bayesian optimization has shown being an effective method to solve hyperparameter optimization [30]. Bayesian optimization was used to configure CNNs to address the classification on CIFAR image dataset [28]. In this case, the authors optimized four hyperparameters of the CNN learning algorithm (including the DNN depth). This type of hyperparameter optimization method was applied to configure an RNN applied to estimate the disaggregation household power consumption forecasting (i.e., predict the power load signal per appliance) [12].

Racing hyperparameter configuration methods emerged as automatic tuning methods that find good configurations through statistically guided experimental evaluations [5]. The main idea is that the method defines a race of sequentially generated candidate configurations, evaluates them via several independent runs, and discards the less competitive ones as soon as there is a statistical evidence that is performing worst than the other configurations. Removing from the race the least promising solutions improves the search, allows evaluating promising configurations on more instances, and obtaining reliable estimates of their behavior. An example of racing algorithm is the F-race, which is based on racing and Friedman's non-parametric two-way analysis of variance by ranks [5].

An improvement over F-race is the iterative F-race (I/F-race), which is the method implemented by IRACE and it is applied in our study. In this case, the set of initial tentative configurations are created by sampling the parameter space and, when there is a statistical evidence that a configuration is performing worse than the best ones, this worst configuration is discarded, and a new configuration is generated by randomly modifying the best ones [13]. This method allows to speed up the search providing comparative results, while critically reducing the computational costs. At the time of writing this article, racing methods (such as the one implemented in IRACE) have not been applied to deal with deep learning methods, but to machine learning (mainly to tune metaheuristics) [14,19,27].

This article proposes applying an automatic approach to tune GANs. The main differences of our approach regarding the current state of the art are that (a) an automatic tool is applied to configure the hyperparameters of GAN training algorithm and (b) IRACE is used to explore the tentative configurations of such special type of machine learning/deep learning approach.

3   The Proposed Parallel/Distributed Approach for Hyperparameters Search

This section describes the proposed approach for parallel/distributed search of hyperparameters values of GANs.

3.1   Overall Description

The proposed system integrates IRACE, Lipizzaner, and parallel programming in distributed memory platforms. The building block for the proposed system is the traditional sequential search for hyperparameters implemented in IRACE, as described in Fig. 1.

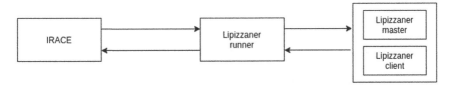

Fig. 1. Sequential hyperparameters search.

During a race, the sequential approach of IRACE executes one parametric configuration at a time. The race algorithm implemented by IRACE evaluates surviving parametric configurations on a fixed number of instances before performing the applied statistical comparison. As a consequence, the evaluation of several instances is suitable for parallelism, by applying the domain decomposition approach. Furthermore, as the executions are independent, no data or control communications are required between processes.

Three parallel schemes are supported by IRACE to perform fixed executions. The *parallel processes* scheme is based on creating multiple spawn processes using the parallel R package. The *MPI* scheme applies a distributed memory approach, where parallel processes are controlled using the Message Passing Interface protocol. Both previous schemes are mainly conceived for interactive processing. Finally, the *batch jobs cluster* parallel scheme allows off-line process execution by using submission scripts of standard workload management systems (Torque, SLURM, etc.) to submit multiple executions of the target algorithm as independent jobs. The off-line execution is supported by submissions to a batch queue and waiting for processes to finish. In any case, the number of parallel call is configurable.

The proposed parallel approach for hyperparameters search of GANs is based on the parallel process scheme of IRACE. The basic schema proposed for execution on a single computer/server is extended for proper execution on a larger, non-dedicated infrastructure, such as the one available in modern supercomputing centers. This type of facilities has a very important impact on e-Science by promoting a collaborative approach where financial resources is scarce, such as in Latin America [8].

For execution on a large, shared computing infrastructure, parallel processes that share limited resources (e.g., GPU, RAM memory, and ports for communication) must be properly controlled. In consequence, a new component is incorporated in the solution architecture, the *Execution Manager*. The main job of the Execution Manager is monitoring the execution environment and taking proper decisions to allow or stop IRACE from launching new Lipizzaner instances, based on the available computing resources. Two specific resources are monitored and evaluated: i) the number of available GPU and the free GPU memory on each one, and ii) the availability of network ports for communication between master and slave processes in Lipizzaner.

Thus, the proposed parallel search requires two new parameters as input:

1. The GPU memory required to run a single instance of Lipizzaner, and
2. The range of port numbers where Lippizaner instances are allowed to attach.

In the developed implementation of the parallel approach, the Execution Manager is a Python class pickled in the filesystem. The responsibility for changing and saving the Execution Manager state is delegated to runners. This design decision guarantee that every runner is able to read the Execution Manager in a safe way by locking the pickle file. Thus, specific modifications are required in the parallel version of the Lipizzaner runner algorithm.

The developed parallel version of the Lipizzaner runner is detailed in Algorithm 1.

Algorithm 1. Lipizzaner runner algorithm in the parallel search approach

---

Require: learning rate, α, μ, skip steps
1: finish = **False**
2: **while** finish **is not True do**
3:     resources = executionManager.allocateResources()
4:     **if** resources **is not None then**
5:         config = prepareLipizzaner(lr, α, μ, skip_steps)
6:         score = runLipizzaner(config)
7:         executionManager.freeResources()
8:         finish = **True**
9:     **else**
10:         sleep()
11:     **end if**
12: **end while**
13: **return** *score*

Algorithm 1 requires four parameters to set up the Lipizzaner configuration file. These parameters are sent by IRACE to test a specific parametric configuration on Lipizzaner and are explained in Subsect. 4. The main body of the runner algorithm is the loop in lines 2–12. The iteration is performed until Lipizzaner results are retrieved (line 6) and the resources have been released (line 7). If there are no available resources to allocate (line 9), the runner process sleeps between 15 and 30 s before a new try (line 10). Finally, the score is returned.

Figure 2 shows a diagram of the parallel architecture. The main software components are identified and data flows between processes are represented by directed arrows.

4   Experimental Evaluation

This section describes the experimental evaluation of the proposed parallel approach for the intelligent search of Lipizzaner hyperparameters.

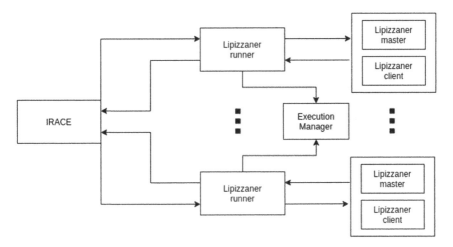

Fig. 2. The implemented parallel hyperparameters search.

4.1 Evaluation Methodology

Methodology. The experimental evaluation is focused on analyzing the execution time improvement of the parallel approach and the quality of the generated images during the search. The specific domain task is the MNIST handwritten digit generation, described in the next paragraph. The grid used for Lipizzaner has dimension 1×1, which essentially trains a single pair of generator/discriminator networks with learning rate mutation. In order to evaluate parallelism, the computational efficiency results are studied, considering a sequential IRACE search as reference baseline. The speedup and scalability of the proposed system is evaluated by increasing the number of parallel executions of Lipizzaner to 2, 4, 6, and 8. The Execution Manager was constrained to allow up to 4 instances of Lipizzaner running on each GPU.

Generation Task. The goal of the proposed GANs is to generate diverse and good quality images from the MNIST dataset. MNIST database is composed of 28×28 pixel images of handwritten digits. Digits are centered and size-normalized. The training dataset contains 60000 images and test dataset 10000.

Metrics. The Fréchet Inception Distance (FID) metric is used to assess the quality and diversity of generated images. The FID score is based on a hidden layer of the inception_v3 model, a deep convolutional neural network trained to classify images into 1000 classes. The FID is calculated in three steps: i) feed real and generated images through the inception network; ii) gather activations from the last hidden layer; and iii) compute the Fréchet distance between activations distributions. A lower FID indicates better-quality and more-diverse images. The computational efficiency is evaluated in terms of execution time and GPU usage. The execution time is retrieved from the job accounting log file of the workload management system. GPU usage is gathered from the output of the *nvidia-smi* command, available in CUDA environments.

IRACE Search. The Lipizzaner parameters to be explored in the search are: i) the initial learning rate (l_0) for the Adam optimization algorithm, ii) the Gaussian mutation probability (mu), i.e., the probability of mutating the current value of the Adam learning rate after each epoch; iii) the mutation regularization factor ($alpha$), which adjust the mean of the Gaussian mutation distribution; and iv) the number of updates to the generator network for each update of the discriminatory network (*skip_steps*). This parameter is used to avoid diminished gradient problems, as generator network is trained *skip_steps* times before updating discriminator weights.

IRACE Parameters. In order to perform a statistically robust search, IRACE constrains the minimum number of the target runnner executions (*minBudget*). The *minBudget* value is computed based on the number of parameters to be explored (*n_params*) as defined in Eq. 1, where *minSurvival* is the number of configurations needed to continue the execution of each race, *n_iter* is the number of races according to Eq. 2, *m* is a parameter used to define the number of configurations sampled and evaluated at each iteration, *eachTest* is the number of instances evaluated between elimination tests, and T_{new} is the number of new instances added to the execution list. The default values for the studied parameters are *minSurvival* = 4, *m* = 5, *eachTest* = 1, and T_{new} = 1.

$$
\begin{aligned}
minBudget = &(minSurvival + 1) \times n\_iter \times \\
&(m + eachTest + (n\_iter - 1) \times \max(eachTest, T_{new}))
\end{aligned} \tag{1}
$$

$$
n\_iter = 2 + log_2(n\_params) \tag{2}
$$

The default parameter values of IRACE were used to explore four parameters of Lipizzaner, thus the minBudget value defined by Eq. 1 is 180. The maximum number of Lipizzaner executions for a whole search was set to 200.

Development and Execution Platform. The proposed system was implemented in Python 3.6 and R 4.1.0. Libraries used are Lipizzaner 1.0 and IRACE 3.4.1.9. The experimental analysis was performed on high-end servers with two Xeon Gold 6138 processors (40 cores each), two Nvidia Tesla P100 GPUs (12 GB memory), 128 GB RAM memory, and 10 GbE from National Supercomputing Center (Cluster-UY), Uruguay

4.2   Numerical Results

This subsection reports the numerical results of the proposed parallel approach to explore the parameter space of Lipizzaner with IRACE.

Execution Time. Table 1 reports the execution time of the proposed search for the five parallelization levels studied. The sequential approach required a considerable long time to complete the run (about 60 h). Considering that a space of just four parameters is explored, this execution time can be prohibitive to complete accurate parameter configurations in reasonable execution times. Then, as the number of parallel Lipizzaner calls performed by IRACE increased, the execution time decreased. The best (minimum) value was 16.81 h for the execution using 8 parallel calls. These execution time values demosntrate that the proposed system is able to reduce the wall time for configuration in a factor of 3.56×.

Table 1. Execution time results.

Experiment	Execution time
Sequential	59.8 h
2 parallel calls	41.5 h
4 parallel calls	23.21 h
6 parallel calls	20.05 h
8 parallel calls	16.81 h

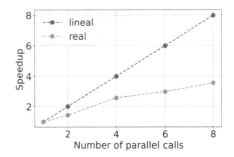

Fig. 3. Speedup analysis.

The speedup analysis is reported in Fig. 3, showing that the execution time reduction is sub-linear with respect to the number of parallel calls. This behavior is mainly due to the non-determinism in the parallel execution, which generate idle times for processes and resources. In addition, the actual number of parallel processes is limited to the number of surviving configurations; in the final stages of a race, few parametric configurations are evaluated, thus searches with 4, 6, and 8 parallel calls achieve the same degree of parallelization. Finally, there is a relatively low overhead for communication with the Execution Manager.

Figure 4 reports the number of completed Lipizzaner executions over time for each search. Results demonstrate the usefulness of the proposed approach, which is able to complete a significantly larger number of executions within a given time. For example, considering a time limit of 1000 min, the search using 8 parallel calls is able to complete 194 executions of Lipizzaner, whereas the sequential search is only able to complete 58. These results imply a significant better throughput of the parallel executions, improving 3.35× over the sequential.

GPU Memory Utilization. Video cards are powerful and expensive hardware components that speed up the training process of deep learning algorithms. Then, optimizing the GPU utilization is desired to improve performance and reduce costs. Table 2 reports the workload of the two available GPUs (gpu0 and gpu1) during the experimental evaluation as the percentage of the total memory in use. Load values were gathered every 60 s using the NVIDIA System Management Interface.

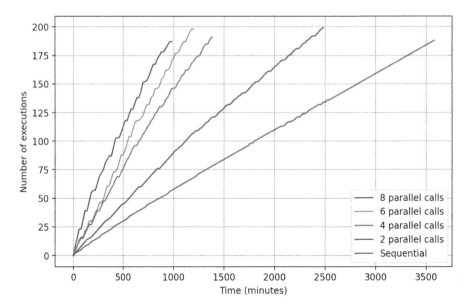

Fig. 4. Number of Lipizzaner executions over time.

Load results do not follow a normal distribution, thus values of the median, interquantile range (IQR), and maximum are reported as relevant estimators in Table 2.

Table 2. GPU utilization percentage results.

Experiment	GPU	Median	IQR	Maximum
Sequential	gpu 0	10	6	26
	gpu 1	0	0	3
2 parallel calls	gpu 0	13	17	52
	gpu 1	0	0	3
4 parallel calls	gpu 0	26	36	87
	gpu 1	0	0	4
6 parallel calls	gpu 0	27	37	66
	gpu 1	0	19	51
8 parallel calls	gpu 0	34	35	71
	gpu 1	7	22	80

Results in Table 2 show that in experiments that executed less than four instances of Lipizzaner at a time, the second GPU (gpu1) remained idle, as the required video memory at every moment is bellow 12 GB. In contrast, in searches with 6 and 8 parallel calls, a single GPU cannot handle all processes and a proportion of the load is delegated to gpu1. As the number of parallel calls increases, load measures also increase, thus the system is able to make a better use of the available resources. The median of usage percentage distribution on gpu0 was 3.4 times greater on the 8 parallel calls search compared to the sequential search. On gpu 1, the 8 parallel calls had a load median of 7% and the maximum load reached 80%, whereas the sequential search never used a second GPU.

Lipizzaner Results. The search tasks performed by the different experiments evaluated here are the same. However, the non-determinism of some of the operations carried out by IRACE influences on how the search evolves, and therefore, on the results computed by Lipizzaner. Thus, each experiment explored different hyperparameters and provided different FID scores. Here, we evaluate the whole distribution of the FID results returned by Lipizzaner during the search. Thus, Fig. 5 shows these results by showing the results in a histogram. The first group of the histogram (group 1) illustrates the frequency of the Lipizzaner configurations that returned FID scores between 0 and 99; the second, the frequency of FID scores between 100 and 199, and so on (i.e., the group i in the histogram represents the frequency of the Lipizzaner runs that provided FID$\in [(i-1) \times 100, (i \times 100) - 1]$).

According to the histograms in Fig. 5, there is not a significance difference among the distributions of the results of the five experiments. All histograms show that most of Lipizzaner configurations computed during the search provide FID scores in the first decile, i.e., between 0 and 99. Thus, this confirms that, even the stochastic nature of IRACE search, all the experiments carried out a similar hyperparameters search.

Finally, Fig. 6 presents images generated during different iterations of the IRACE by using 8 parallel calls search. This figure allows the reader to observe the quality and diversity of the samples according to the FID score. It can be seen that with FID score 1061, the generator produces only noise; when the FID decreases to 380, the quality of the samples improves but the diversity is still limited; and with FID score 55, the generator synthesizes better quality and diversity digits (images).

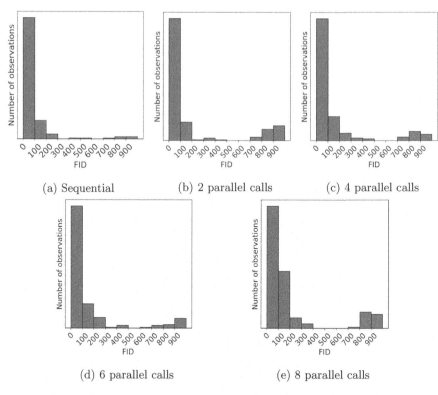

(a) Sequential   (b) 2 parallel calls   (c) 4 parallel calls

(d) 6 parallel calls   (e) 8 parallel calls

Fig. 5. FID histograms of Lipizzaner executions.

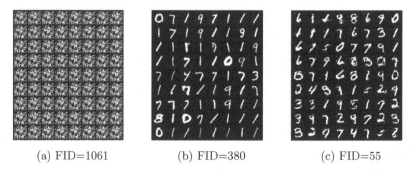

(a) FID=1061   (b) FID=380   (c) FID=55

Fig. 6. Generated images (digits) during the 8 parallel calls search.

5   Conclusions and Future Work

This article presented a proposal for a parallel intelligent hyperparameters search for generative artificial neural networks. The proposed implementation is an automatic procedure to efficiently search through the hyperparameter space of Lipizzaner by the means of racing. The main goal of the parallel approach is to reduce the execution time required to perform a parameters search using IRACE and maximize the use of available resources. This goal was achieved by parallelizing independent executions of Lipizzaner in a controlled way, using middleware components that manage Lipizzaner processes and monitor the GPU memory utilization.

Experimental evaluation results showed that the parallel system was able to significantly reduce execution time of a sequential IRACE search. Execution time decreased 72% when 8 parallel calls were allowed. The implementation monitored available resources and avoided overloading hardware components. Experiments showed that the degree of parallelism is constrained not only by the number of parallel processes and GPU memory, but also the number of surviving configurations in a race. This indicates that the implementation is suitable for IRACE searches were a high number of configurations is desired to be sampled in each race. In all experiments good quality images were generated during the search process.

The main lines for future work include implementing a new version of the Execution Manager using more advanced inter process communication techniques to reduce idle time of Lipizzaner processes and GPU resources. Other interesting line is studying the search capabilities of IRACE with an extended computational budget and a larger number of configuration candidates per race. The proposed solution should also be applied to more complex problems using a bigger population of generator and discriminator networks in Lipizzaner.

Acknowledgements. This research was partially funded by European Union's Horizon 2020 research and innovation program under the Marie Skodowska-Curie grant agreement No 799078 and by the European Union H2020-ICT-2019-3.

References

1. Akay, B., Karaboga, D., Akay, R.: A comprehensive survey on optimizing deep learning models by metaheuristics. Artificial Intelligence Review, pp. 1–66 (2021)
2. Al-Dujaili, A., Schmiedlechner, T., Hemberg, E., O'Reilly, U.M.: Towards distributed coevolutionary GANs. In: AAAI Symposium (2018)
3. Bergstra, J., Bardenet, R., Bengio, Y., Kégl, B.: Algorithms for hyper-parameter optimization. Advances in Neural Information Processing Systems, vol. 24 (2011)
4. Bergstra, J., Bengio, Y.: Random search for hyper-parameter optimization. Journal of Machine Learning Research, vol. 13, no. 2 (2012)
5. Birattari, M., Stützle, T., Paquete, L., Varrentrapp, K., et al.: A racing algorithm for configuring metaheuristics. In: Gecco, vol. 2 (2002)
6. Camero, A., Toutouh, J., Alba, E.: Random error sampling-based recurrent neural network architecture optimization. Eng. Appl. Artif. Intell. **96**, 103946 (2020)
7. Camero, A., Toutouh, J., Stolfi, D.H., Alba, E.: Evolutionary deep learning for car park occupancy prediction in smart cities. In: Battiti, R., Brunato, M., Kotsireas, I., Pardalos, P.M. (eds.) LION 12 2018. LNCS, vol. 11353, pp. 386–401. Springer, Cham (2019). https://doi.org/10.1007/978-3-030-05348-2_32
8. Gitler, I., Gomes, A.T.A., Nesmachnow, S.: The latin american supercomputing ecosystem for science. Commun. ACM **63**(11), 66–71 (2020)

9. Goodfellow, I., et al.: Generative adversarial nets. In: Advances in Neural Information Processing Systems, pp. 2672–2680 (2014)

10. Hemberg, E., Toutouh, J., Al-Dujaili, A., Schmiedlechner, T., O'Reilly U-M.: Spatial coevolution for generative adversarial network training. ACM Trans. Evol. Learn. Optim. **2**(1) (2021). Article 6, 28 p. https://doi.org/10.1145/3458845

11. Hinz, T., Navarro-Guerrero, N., Magg, S., Wermter, S.: Speeding up the hyperparameter optimization of deep convolutional neural networks. Int. J. Comput. Intell. Appl. **17**(02), 1850008 (2018)

12. Kaselimi, M., Doulamis, N., Doulamis, A., Voulodimos, A., Protopapadakis, E.: Bayesian-optimized bidirectional lstm regression model for non-intrusive load monitoring. In: ICASSP 2019–2019 IEEE International Conference on Acoustics, Speech and Signal Processing (ICASSP), pp. 2747–2751 (2019). https://doi.org/10.1109/ICASSP.2019.8683110

13. López-Ibáñez, M., Dubois-Lacoste, J., Cáceres, L.P., Birattari, M., Stützle, T.: The IRACE package: iterated racing for automatic algorithm configuration. Oper. Res. Perspect. **3**, 43–58 (2016)

14. Lopez-Ibanez, M., Stutzle, T.: The automatic design of multiobjective ant colony optimization algorithms. IEEE Trans. Evol. Comput. **16**(6), 861–875 (2012)

15. López-Ibáñez, M., Stützle, T.: Automatically improving the anytime behaviour of optimisation algorithms. Eur. J. Oper. Res. **235**(3), 569–582 (2014)

16. Lopez-Rincon, A., Tonda, A., Elati, M., Schwander, O., Piwowarski, B., Gallinari, P.: Evolutionary optimization of convolutional neural networks for cancer mirna biomarkers classification. Appl. Soft Comput. **65**, 91–100 (2018)

17. Nesmachnow, S., Iturriaga, S.: Cluster-UY: collaborative scientific high performance computing in uruguay. In: Torres, M., Klapp, J. (eds.) ISUM 2019. CCIS, vol. 1151, pp. 188–202. Springer, Cham (2019). https://doi.org/10.1007/978-3-030-38043-4_16

18. Pan, Z., Yu, W., Yi, X., Khan, A., Yuan, F., Zheng, Y.: Recent progress on generative adversarial networks (GANs): a survey. IEEE Access **7**, 36322–36333 (2019)

19. Prestes, L., Delgado, M.R., Lüders, R., Gonçalves, R., Almeida, C.P.: Boosting the performance of moea/d-dra with a multi-objective hyper-heuristic based on irace and ucb method for heuristic selection. In: 2018 IEEE Congress on Evolutionary Computation (CEC), pp. 1–8. IEEE (2018)

20. Schmiedlechner, T., Yong, I., Al-Dujaili, A., Hemberg, E., O'Reilly, U.: Lipizzaner: a system that scales robust generative adversarial network training. In: 32nd Conference on Neural Information Processing Systems (2018)

21. Schmiedlechner, T., Yong, I.N.Z., Al-Dujaili, A., Hemberg, E., O'Reilly, U.M.: Lipizzaner: a system that scales robust generative adversarial network training. In: the 32nd Conference on Neural Information Processing Systems (NeurIPS 2018) Workshop on Systems for ML and Open Source Software (2018)

22. Thornton, C., Hutter, F., Hoos, H.H., Leyton-Brown, K.: Auto-weka: combined selection and hyperparameter optimization of classification algorithms. In: Proceedings of the 19th ACM SIGKDD International Conference on Knowledge Discovery and Data Mining, pp. 847–855 (2013)

23. Toutouh, J., Esteban, M., Nesmachnow., S.: Parallel/distributed generative adversarial neural networks for data augmentation of covid-19 training images. In: Latin America High Performance Computing Conference (CARLA 2020), p. 10 (2020)

24. Toutouh, J., Esteban, M., Nesmachnow, S.: Parallel/distributed generative adversarial neural networks for data augmentation of COVID-19 training images. In: Nesmachnow, S., Castro, H., Tchernykh, A. (eds.) CARLA 2020. CCIS, vol. 1327, pp. 162–177. Springer, Cham (2021). https://doi.org/10.1007/978-3-030-68035-0_12
25. Toutouh, J., Hemberg, E., O'Reilly, U.M.: Spatial evolutionary generative adversarial networks. In: Proceedings of the Genetic and Evolutionary Computation Conference, pp. 472–480. GECCO '19, Association for Computing Machinery, New York, NY, USA (2019)
26. Toutouh, J., Hemberg, E., O'Reilly, U.-M.: Data dieting in GAN training. In: Iba, H., Noman, N. (eds.) Deep Neural Evolution. NCS, pp. 379–400. Springer, Singapore (2020). https://doi.org/10.1007/978-981-15-3685-4_14
27. Ugolotti, R., Nashed, Y.S., Mesejo, P., Cagnoni, S.: Algorithm configuration using gpu-based metaheuristics. In: Proceedings of the 15th Annual Conference Companion on Genetic and Evolutionary Computation, pp. 221–222 (2013)
28. Victoria, A.H., Maragatham, G.: Automatic tuning of hyperparameters using bayesian optimization. Evolving Syst. **12**, 217–223 (2021)
29. Wang, C., Xu, C., Yao, X., Tao, D.: Evolutionary generative adversarial networks. IEEE Trans. Evol. Comput. **23**(6), 921–934 (2019)
30. Wu, J., Chen, X.Y., Zhang, H., Xiong, L.D., Lei, H., Deng, S.H.: Hyperparameter optimization for machine learning models based on bayesian optimization. J. Electron. Sci. Technol. **17**(1), 26–40 (2019)
31. Yang, L., Shami, A.: On hyperparameter optimization of machine learning algorithms: theory and practice. Neurocomputing **415**, 295–316 (2020)

Machine Learning for Generic Energy Models of High Performance Computing Resources

Jonathan Muraña[1]([⊠]) [iD], Carmen Navarrete[2] [iD], and Sergio Nesmachnow[1] [iD]

[1] Universidad de la República, Montevideo, Uruguay
{jmurana,sergion}@fing.edu.uy
[2] Leibniz Supercomputing Center, Munich, Germany
carmen.navarrete@lrz.de

Abstract. This article presents an study of the generalization capabilities of forecasting techniques of empirical energy consumption models of high performance computing resources. This is a relevant subject, considering the large energy utilization of modern supercomputing facilities. Different energy models are built, considering several forecasting techniques and using information from the execution of a benchmark over different hardware. A cross-evaluation is performed and the training information of each model is gradually extended with information about other hardware. Each model is analyzed to evaluate how new information impacts on the prediction capabilities. The main results indicate that neural network approaches achieve the highest quality results when the training data of the models is expanded with minimal information from new scenarios.

Keywords: Power consumption models · Artifical neural networks · High performance computing

1 Introduction

Reducing energy consumption is crucial in nowadays high performance computing facilities, as it represents a large fraction of the operation costs and because of its environmental consequences due to its carbon footprint [8]. In addition, the load limitations of the power grid introduce additional constraints on the available and required power. This has led most supercomputing facilities to enforce energy aware policies.

Energy aware policies are mainly focused on optimizing the use of hardware and cooling system, and also the utilization of renewable energy [11,13]. The optimization is carried out through intelligent job distribution, and/or planning on/off air-conditioning, among other strategies. In any case, gather specific knowledge about the power profile, e.g. by forecasting the energy consumption of computing resources, is a key input for any energy aware strategy. A common approach for forecasting consists in using energy models, oriented to capturing the relationship between the energy consumption, hardware features, and specific characteristics of the executed software.

© Springer Nature Switzerland AG 2021
H. Jagode et al. (Eds.): ISC High Performance 2021 Workshops, LNCS 12761, pp. 314–330, 2021.
https://doi.org/10.1007/978-3-030-90539-2_21

Energy models are applied for estimating the energy consumption entailed by a given workload on a specific computing resource. Energy models can be classified as hardware-centric, based in hardware component specification such chip-set and physical memory, or software-centric, where workload computing and memory requirements are considered to determine the energy consumption. In the construction process of software-centric energy models, three main phases are identified: i) benchmarks are executed over different hardware and the information about resources utilization and energy consumption is recorded; ii) the recorded information is processed and used to adjust the parameters of the models, i.e. the *training stage*; iii) the resulting models are tested to evaluate the prediction quality. Several mathematical and computational techniques are used to predict the energy consumption from recorded data [5].

Related works have shown that accurate energy predictions can be computed by considering characteristics if both workload and resources [2,15]. However, models built for specific workload on specific hardware usually are inaccurate for estimating power consumption for applications and resources that differ from the training scenario [9]. Inaccurate predictions for unseen scenarios might lead to implementing inefficient energy-aware policies, entailing financial losses and energy waste. Larger error values can also force the models to be periodically re-trained to better capture the features of new workloads and/or computing resources. Reducing the gap between real and estimated energy for unseen scenarios is very useful in heterogeneous computing facilities where the type of software executed and the hardware characteristics change frequently. Overall, the observed lack of generality of existing energy models can have a major impact on their applicability, thus affecting the efficacy of energy-aware planning strategies.

In this line of work, this article proposes a study of the generalization capabilities of forecasting techniques of empirical energy models. Two main goals led the research. The first goal was performing a comparative analysis of different estimation techniques for building energy models, in order to identify the technique(s) that achieve the best accuracy in unseen scenarios. For the reasons mentioned in the previous paragraph, the techniques that show generalization capabilities, being able to transfer knowledge learned in training from one scenario to another, are more appropriate than those techniques that generate specific models. The second goal was determining how much training effort each technique requires to achieve a quality of prediction over a given threshold. Both, the achieved prediction quality and the effort required for each technique are compared.

The proposed methodology consists in build different energy models with well-know forecasting techniques, using information from the execution of a benchmark over different high performance computing (HPC) hardware. A model is built for each technique and each hardware considered. Then, a cross-evaluation is performed and the training information of each model is gradually extended by including information about the execution on other hardware. Each model is analyzed to evaluate how new information impacts on the prediction quality.

The main results of the analysis indicate that although models based on neural networks do not show the best generalization capabilities when they do not use information about other scenarios, they are able to achieve the highest quality results when the training data of the models is expanded with minimal information from new scenarios.

The article is organized as follows. Section 2 introduces the problem of generalization of energy models in HPC hardware and reviews related works. The proposed techniques, data structure, hardware details, and research methodology are presented in Sect. 3. The experimental results are reported and discussed in Sect. 4. Finally, the conclusions and the main lines for future work are formulated in Sect. 5.

2   Generalization of HPC Energy Models

This section presents an overview of the problems of power consumption prediction and the generalization of energy models in HPC hardware and reviews related work.

2.1   Energy Consumption Models

Modeling the energy consumption of HPC hardware is a main concern in modern supercomputing facilities, since it allows applying intelligent energy management, saving money, and reducing the carbon footprint. On the downside, building accurate energy models demands high effort specially in those facilities with heterogeneous characteristics. One source of heterogeneity is due providing services to a wide variety of users, which execute different type of software. Another common source of heterogeneity usually emerges in incremental platforms, built by the periodic acquisition and aggregation of commodity hardware, in which the main characteristics of the platform change rather frequently.

A different alternative is to develop models capable of transferring, to some extent, knowledge about energy consumption acquired on the training stage on a certain software-hardware to another. This alternative allows building an agnostic software-hardware model, thus reducing the maintenance cost of energy management [12]. In turn, having pre-trained models to speed up the training stage of models for new hardware and software leads to an improved energy management of HPC facilities. The proposed study aims at answering the following questions:

1. How does energy models built using forecasting techniques adapt to situations where the evaluated data is different from the training data, i.e. different hardware and software?
2. In what extent does information about additional software and hardware incorporated to the training data allow improving the estimation of each technique?
3. How much information, i.e., training effort, is needed to achieve a certain quality threshold on the energy consumption prediction?

The addressed problem of forecasting the power consumption of HPC hardware can be described as a mathematical extrapolation problem of finding a function $f(x_1, x_2, \ldots, x_n) = y_j$, where x_i are the independent variables (features) and y_j is a value such that $|Y - \hat{Y}| < \epsilon$, with $Y = (y_1, y_2, \ldots, y_m)$, $\hat{Y} = \hat{y}_1, \hat{y}_2, \ldots, \hat{y}_m$ the real measurements, and ϵ is the value to minimize for the forecasting technique.

The proposal developed in this article aims at finding a function f that minimize the error for the data set $x_1, x_2, \ldots, x_n, \hat{Y}$, but at the same time presents low error values for other unseen datasets $x'_1, x'_2, \ldots, x'_n, \hat{Y}'$, corresponding to different HPC hardware.

The proposed methodology consist in build energy models applying well-know forecasting techniques such as a linear regression, a fully connected neural network and a convolutional neural network. The techniques were selected to cover diverse machine learning methods with different complexity and specialized in modeling linear and nonlinear problems.

2.2   Related Work

Power consumption models for HPC hardware has been an important concern in the last years. A review of relevant related work is presented next.

Auweter et al. [2] proposed a linear energy model to predict the energy consumption of a workload based in its CPU cycles and memory requirements. The model was built assuming a linear relationship between CPU frequency and power consumption, that allow extrapolating the energy consumption from one reference frequency to another. The proposed model was trained considering a single reference frequency, and then used as input of a workload manager to estimate the energy on any frequency. To take advantaged of the model characteristics, the workload manager was able to adjust the frequency of the HPC hardware dynamically, by applying the Dynamic Voltage and Frequency Scaling (DVFS) technology. Several scientific workload were studied in the experimental evaluation, executed over one HPC hardware. The validation of the energy models, specific for each workload and hardware, yielded estimation errors from 1% to 7%.

The work of Auweter et al. was applied in the context of the recent project DEEP–Extreme Scale Technologies [1], considering modern HPC hardware, new synthetic benchmarks, and real applications for building a power consumption model. Also, additional software characteristic were considered as input, such as cache misses and the number of scalar and vector operations. The importance of these characteristics for power consumption estimation was evaluated applying Principal Component Analysis (PCA). The data of synthetic benchmarks recorded in the DEEP project was used in our work for the construction of the models.

Imes et al. [7] presented machine learning classifier to find energy efficient runtime settings of HPC hardware, including CPU frequency, number of socket allocation, and the use of hyperthreading. The classifier was trained using information about memory usage and CPU utilization benchmarks, collected from performance counters in benchmarks executions. The classifier was integrated to a scheduler and it reduced by 20% (on average), when compared with a strategy based on executing as fast as possible. However, the scheduler was not able to outperform an Oracle scheduler based in DVFS that achieved 28.1% on average of energy savings.

Sayadi et al. [14] presented a machine leaning predictor to estimate the energy efficiency in a composite cores architecture. Several multi-threading benchmarks were executed using different parameters (core type, voltage/frequency level, and number of threads) to collect training data from twelve performance counters. The authors applied PCA for reducing the number of independent variables and determined four performance counters as the most important to estimate the energy consumption: L1 D-cache access, L2 cache access, L2 cache misses, and brand miss prediction. Then, three forecasting techniques were compared: a linear regression, a neural network and a decision tree. The best result were achieved by the decision tree (94.5% of accuracy) and the second best result, close to the first one, was achieved by the neural network (93%).

Barreda et al. [3] presented a convolutional neural networks to estimate the performance and energy consumption of a memory-bound application to calculate the sparse matrix-vector product. The number of L2/L3 cache misses was proposed as a relevant metric for evaluation, since it is directly related to the energy consumption due to the sparse structure of the considered matrices. Two independent networks were built for estimating performance and energy consumption using an architecture including two dimensional convolution layers with a custom activation function followed by a max-pooling layer, and fully connected layers followed by dropout layers. The experimental results showed relative prediction errors between 0.5% and 14%.

Our previous articles [9,10] developed energy consumption models based in application type (CPU-bound, memory bound, or disk-bound) and hardware utilization level. The input of the models was the percentage of each application type on the HPC hardware, and the output was the power consumption. To model construction, energy consumption of several benchmarks executions over two HPC hardware were recorded using both external power meter and internal CPU counters. Different polynomial regressions were used as forecasting techniques. This article extends this line of research by considering different forecasting techniques, low-level model inputs, and the evaluation of generalization capabilities of models.

The analysis of related works allowed concluding that, although there is an extensive literature on the use of machine learning to estimate energy models, no articles has explicitly studied the generalization capabilities of learning techniques for HPC energy models. Thus, there is room to contribute in this line of research, in line with the main contributions of this article.

3   Generalization Capabilities of HPC Power Consumption Models Models

This section describes the main concepts about the proposal for studying the generalization capabilities of HPC power consumption models

3.1   Overview

The research proposed evaluating the generalization capabilities of power consumption models built using machines learning methods.

The rationale behind the proposed approach relies on the assumption that both the energy consumption and the performance behavior of scientific applications can be characterized by a small set of application-specific and architecture independent performance factors [6]. Three forecasting techniques are compared: a linear regression (LRG), a fully connected neural network (FCN), and a convolutional neural network (CNN). These techniques are described in the following subsection. The data used to build the models correspond to the execution of a computing benchmark over three high performance hardware. The details about the considered data are presented in Subsect. 3.3.

3.2   Description of the Evaluated Techniques

Regarding the forecasting approach, the evaluated techniques are:

- LRG follows the traditional approach of approximating an objective function with a linear combination of the independent variables, and evaluating the error of the approximation using a least square approach. This approach has been widely used for energy consumption models, assuming a linear relationship between resource utilization and the energy consumption [1,2,9,11]. In the proposed implementation, no interceptor is considered.
- FCN is a type of artificial neural network in which all neurons of a layer are connected with all networks of the next layer. FCN methods have been applied for predicting the energy consumption from software and hardware characteristics, obtaining accurate results [7,14]. In the proposed implementation implementation a sequential network is used; it has two layers, the first one with 256 neurons and the second one with one neuron. Linear activation is used in all layers. The input dimension of the network is six, corresponding to the number of features.
- CNN is a type of deep neural network that contains a convolution layer, this, a layer where filter are applied to the original input. CNNs extend the FCN model by including a specific mechanism to prevent overfitting, taking advantage of assembling hierarchical patterns detected in data, allowing computing improved results for energy consumption forecasting problems [3]. In the proposed implementation a sequential network is used; it contains four layers: a convolution layer with 64 filters and three kernels, a fully connected layer with 64 neurons and ReLu activation, a fully connected layer with 128 neurons and linear activation, and the output layer with one neuron and linear activation.

3.3   Training Data for Building the Models

The training data used for the proposed energy consumption models consist on information from the execution of specific benchmarks over different HPC hardware. The test suite of executed applications extended the Apex-MAP benchmark [16]. Applications were conceived such that the combination of memory accesses and computational intensity is the dominant factor on performance; thus, several typical memory access patterns are included.

The Performance Application Programming Interface [17] was used to collect performance counter values, which are directly related to the energy consumption [6]. Recorded data contains values for six performance counters: the number of CPU instructions, the number of L2 cache misses, the number of L3 cache misses, the number of double precision float operations, the ratio of vectorization per cycle of double precision floating point operations (using 128-bit, 256-bit and 512-bit vectorization per CPU cycle), and the number of CPU cycles. These counters were identified as the most relevant for characterizing energy consumption in the PCA analysis performed in the DEEP project.

The information collected during each execution is called a *trace*. A trace is obtained by recording the values of each of the studied performance counter during the executions of the Apex-MAP benchmark, considering different parameters combination, over one HPC resource (there are one trace per HPC resource). Values of six parameters are combined resulting in 6000 different executions of the benchmark, this is, 6000 points per trace.

Three HPC resources are considered in the experiments:

- CN node: 2 Intel Xeon Golden 6146, Skylake microarchitecture, 12 cores (24 threads) 3.2 GHz. 192 GB RAM.
- ESB node: 1 Intel Xeon Silver 4215, Cascade Lake microarchitecture, 8 cores 2.50 GHz. 48 GB RAM.
- DAM node: 2 Intel Xeon Platinum 8260M, Cascade Lake microarchitecture, 24 cores 2.4 GHz. 384 GB RAM.

4   Experimental Evaluation

This section describes the experimental evaluation of the proposed energy consumption models, reporting and commenting the methodology and the obtained results for each case studied.

4.1   Design of Experiments

An incremental approach was applied for the design of experiments, in order to analyze the prediction capabilities of each model in different scenarios. A three-stage methodology was proposed for single and cross-validation.

In the first stage, the accuracy of each technique (and the resulting model) is evaluated over the same trace used for training. Given traces t_i with $i = 1, 2, 3$ and models m_k with $k = 1, 2, 3$, the first stage consists in training model m_k using trace t_i, and then evaluating the accuracy of model m_k over the same trace t_i. The standard partitioning approach is used, splitting the whole dataset into two disjoint training (containing 80% of the recorded information) and testing (containing 20% of the recorded information) subsets. Accuracy results obtained in the first stage allows directly comparing prediction techniques and resulting energy consumption models for specific hardware. They also provide baseline accuracy values to be considered in experiments performed in the next stages.

In the second stage, the accuracy of each technique is evaluated over other traces, different to the ones used for training. Following the previous nomenclature, m_k is trained using t_i trace and then its accuracy is tested using t_j. Thus, the generalization capabilities of the studied techniques are analyzed to determine how the knowledge acquired in the training phase is transferred by each technique from one trace to another. As in the previous stage, training datasets correspond to 80% of each training trace and testing datasets correspond to 20% of each testing trace. Data was selected using the `train_test_split` method from the `sklearn` machine learning library for Python [4].

In the third stage, the models are trained in a given trace adding additional information about other traces, and tested in all traces. This is, each model m_k is trained using t_i plus a percentage of each trace t_j, and then m_k is tested in t_j. This third stage analyzes the cost (in terms of amount of new information needed) of retraining each model for fine-tuning, to achieve a given accuracy considering all traces. Figure 1 summarizes the proposed experimental design.

first stage	second stage	third stage
train(t_i) → test(t_i)	train(t_i) → test(t_j)	train($t_i + \%t_j$) → test(t_j)

Fig. 1. Three-stage approach for the experimental design

In all training stages, 50 epochs were considering for the FCN method, and five epochs were considering for CNN (since a larger number caused overfitting). Both neural network techniques used the Adam optimizer and the Mean Absolute Error as loss function for training.

4.2 Metrics Considered in the Evaluation

The prediction quality of the proposed models is evaluated using the normalized root mean square error (NRSME) and the ad-hoc d_0 metrics.

The NRSME metric allows comparing the estimations of models with different scales, since error values are normalized considering the absolute value of the y coordinate (i.e., the energy values). Thus, NRSME allows comparing the prediction quality of models for different hardware. Equation 1 shows the NRSME formulation, where $\hat{y}_i$ is the real energy consumption and y_i is the estimation of the evaluated model. The maximum value of the real energy consumption in all samples $(max(\hat{y}_i))$ is considered for normalization.

In turn, given $NRSME(m_k, t_i, t_j)$ of the evaluation of trace t_j, using model m_k trained on t_i, Eq. 2 define the d_0 metric.

$$\text{NRSME} = \frac{\sqrt{\sum_{i=1}^{n}(\hat{y}_i - y_i)^2/n}}{max(\hat{y}_i)} \times 100 \quad (1) \qquad d_0 = \sqrt{\sum_{j=1}^{L} \text{NRSME}(m_k, t_i, t_j)^2} \tag{2}$$

Metric d_0 is the Euclidean distance of the vector of the NRSME of a model trained in a given trace, to the vector 0^L (where L is the total number of traces). This metric allows comparing models considering its evaluation results globally.

4.3   Results

This subsection report the numerical results for each stage in the evaluation.

First Stage: Testing in Same Trace of the Training Phase. Table 1 reports the NRMSE for models evaluated in the same trace of the training phase. Rows correspond to the studied techniques and columns correspond to the traces used for training and testing. Also, the average error considering all traces is reported. Results indicate that the convolution approach achieves the best prediction error for all scenarios.

Table 1. NRSME of each technique in the same trace of the training

Technique	Trace			Average
	CN	ESB	DAM	
LRG	5.80	7.57	7.22	6.86
FCN	6.00	5.40	5.30	5.57
CNN	**4.80**	**4.68**	**3.37**	**4.28**

Results in Table 1 indicate that the FCN approach outperformed the linear regression, achieving a difference of 1.29. on average in the NRSME. In turn, CNN outperformed the linear regression by a difference of 2.58 on average.

Second Stage: Testing in Different Traces to the Training Phase.
Table 2 reports the NRMSE and d_0 metrics for the second stage, where models were evaluated in different traces than the ones used for training. Rows correspond to techniques and columns correspond to traces used for testing, grouped by training traces. This way, the first three columns are the results of each techniques training using CN traces and testing using CN, ESB, and DAM respectively, and the second three columns are the results of each technique training using ESB trace and testing using CN, ESB, and DAM respectively, and so on.

Table 2. Evaluation of the NRSME of each technique in other traces

	Training in CN				Training in ESB				Training in DAM			
	CN	ESB	DAM	d_0	CN	ESB	DAM	d_0	CN	ESB	DAM	d_0
LRG	5.80	**10.14**	9.70	15.18	7.56	7.57	10.67	15.11	**8.27**	**22.86**	7.22	**25.36**
FCN	6.00	10.75	**8.35**	**14.88**	14.95	5.40	15.78	22.40	11.48	82.97	5.30	83.93
CNN	**4.80**	46.90	18.86	50.78	**7.17**	**4.68**	**8.81**	**12.29**	14.37	111.39	**3.37**	112.36

Results in Table 2 show that the CNN approach achieved the best prediction error in six evaluations, LRG in three evaluations, and FCN in just one evaluation. However, different results are obtained when using different training data. When training in CN, no conclusive results are obtained, as the three studied methods get the best result in one instance. When training in ESB, the CNN approach consistently achieves the best results on the three studied instances. Finally, when training in DAM, the LRG method computed the best results in two evaluations, and CNN in the other one.

Results clearly show that the training data significantly influences in the prediction accuracy. Regarding the generalization capabilities, no clear superiority of more complex models (using neural networks) is observed, as demonstrated when considering only those evaluations on different datasets than the ones using for training (in fact, the LRG method computed better results in three evaluations and CNN in just two evaluations). This result suggests that there is room to improve the proposed learning approaches to get better knowledge transfer by including additional information in the training phase, as evaluated in the next subsection.

Third Stage: Adding information of Other Traces to the Training Phase. Tables 3–11 report the values of the NRMSE and d_0 metrics for experiments in the third stage, where information about other hardware, different to the training one, is gradually added to the training process of the models presented in the second stage. The added percentage of the each new trace is in the interval [0%,30%]. CN^+, ESB^+, and DAM^+ denote the augmented training sets, where 80% of the training data correspond to the base dataset and the rest is the corresponding data from the other traces.

Table 3. NRSME/d_0, LRG trained in CN^+

ESB	NRSME	DAM 0%	5%	10%	15%	20%	25%	30%
0%	CN	5.8	5.83	5.91	5.99	6.08	6.16	6.25
	ESB	10.14	10.57	11.53	12.24	12.96	13.49	14
	DAM	9.7	9.28	8.88	8.63	8.42	8.27	8.15
	d_0	15.18	15.23	15.71	16.13	16.61	16.98	17.36
5%	CN	5.79	5.82	5.89	5.97	6.06	6.13	6.22
	ESB	9.45	10.01	10.76	11.35	11.96	12.44	12.9
	DAM	9.75	9.32	8.93	8.67	8.46	8.31	8.19
	d_0	14.76	14.86	15.17	15.48	15.85	16.17	16.5
10%	CN	5.79	5.81	5.88	5.96	6.04	6.12	6.2
	ESB	9.18	9.58	10.16	10.64	11.15	11.57	11.98
	DAM	9.79	9.37	8.97	8.71	8.5	8.35	8.22
	d_0	14.62	14.61	14.77	14.99	15.27	15.53	15.8
15%	CN	5.8	5.81	5.88	5.95	6.03	6.11	6.18
	ESB	8.99	9.26	9.7	10.09	10.5	10.86	11.22
	DAM	9.82	9.4	9.01	8.75	8.53	8.38	8.25
	d_0	14.52	14.42	14.49	14.62	14.81	15.02	15.24
20%	CN	5.8	5.81	5.88	5.95	6.03	6.1	6.18
	ESB	8.91	9.13	9.5	9.82	10.18	10.49	10.81
	DAM	9.83	9.42	9.03	8.77	8.55	8.4	8.27
	d_0	14.48	14.35	14.37	14.45	14.6	14.76	14.95
25%	CN	5.8	5.82	5.88	5.95	6.03	6.1	6.18
	ESB	8.86	9.03	9.35	9.63	9.94	10.22	10.51
	DAM	9.84	9.43	9.04	8.78	8.57	8.42	8.29
	d_0	14.46	14.29	14.27	14.33	14.44	14.58	14.74
30%	CN	5.8	5.82	5.88	5.95	6.03	6.1	6.18
	ESB	8.81	8.95	9.22	9.46	9.73	9.99	10.25
	DAM	9.84	9.44	9.05	8.8	8.58	8.43	8.3
	d_0	14.43	14.25	14.19	14.22	14.31	14.42	14.57

Table 4. NRSME/d_0, LRG trained in ESB^+

CN	NRSME	DAM 0%	5%	10%	15%	20%	25%	30%
0%	CN	7.56	6.76	7.18	7.37	7.53	7.61	7.67
	ESB	7.57	8.26	8.74	9.02	9.19	9.31	9.46
	DAM	10.67	8.24	7.85	7.72	7.65	7.61	7.58
	d_0	15.11	13.48	13.77	13.97	14.13	14.23	14.34
5%	CN	6.1	6.36	6.8	7.04	7.23	7.33	7.42
	ESB	7.87	8.28	8.63	8.88	9.04	9.17	9.33
	DAM	9.87	8.44	7.98	7.82	7.72	7.67	7.62
	d_0	14.02	13.43	13.58	13.77	13.91	14.02	14.15
10%	CN	5.93	6.19	6.58	6.81	7	7.12	7.22
	ESB	8.1	8.3	8.56	8.76	8.91	9.04	9.2
	DAM	9.75	8.64	8.14	7.94	7.81	7.74	7.68
	d_0	13.99	13.49	13.52	13.64	13.76	13.87	13.99
15%	CN	5.91	6.11	6.43	6.65	6.84	6.97	7.08
	ESB	8.13	8.28	8.5	8.69	8.83	8.97	9.13
	DAM	9.74	8.78	8.26	8.04	7.89	7.8	7.74
	d_0	14	13.53	13.48	13.58	13.68	13.78	13.91
20%	CN	5.88	6.04	6.32	6.52	6.7	6.83	6.94
	ESB	8.21	8.31	8.5	8.67	8.8	8.93	9.09
	DAM	9.75	8.9	8.38	8.14	7.97	7.87	7.8
	d_0	14.04	13.59	13.51	13.56	13.63	13.72	13.84
25%	CN	5.86	5.98	6.22	6.4	6.57	6.7	6.81
	ESB	8.26	8.32	8.48	8.63	8.75	8.88	9.04
	DAM	9.82	9.03	8.5	8.24	8.06	7.95	7.86
	d_0	14.11	13.66	13.52	13.54	13.59	13.67	13.78
30%	CN	5.84	5.94	6.14	6.31	6.48	6.6	6.71
	ESB	8.34	8.38	8.52	8.65	8.77	8.9	9.05
	DAM	9.83	9.11	8.59	8.33	8.13	8.01	7.92
	d_0	14.15	13.73	13.57	13.57	13.6	13.67	13.77

Results indicate that the accuracy of neural network approaches improved when additional information is added to the training phase. The best method was CNN, which in average improved 46.59 in the d_0 metric over results obtained in the second stage when training with additional data. In turn, including additional training data also helped to significantly reduce the worst observed prediction errors from the second stage, e.g., for CNN, the value of metric d_0 reduced from 112.36 to 13.66 in the training set DAM^+ when including 10% of training data from CN and 25% of training data from ESB. Thus, significant improvements are obtained over the results reported for experiments of the second stage, and neural network models showed improved generalization capabilities.

Table 5. NRSME/d_0, LRG trained in DAM$^+$

CN	NRSME	ESB						
		0%	5%	10%	15%	20%	25%	30%
0%	CN	8.27	8.13	8.06	8.02	8.00	7.98	7.97
	ESB	22.86	18.50	16.17	14.45	13.56	12.93	12.41
	DAM	7.22	7.23	7.26	7.29	7.31	7.33	7.35
	d_0	25.36	21.46	19.47	18.06	17.361	16.87	16.48
5%	CN	8.08	7.96	7.89	7.86	7.84	7.83	7.82
	ESB	21.25	18.19	16.01	14.36	13.50	12.88	12.36
	DAM	7.23	7.25	7.28	7.31	7.33	7.35	7.37
	d_0	23.86	21.14	19.28	17.93	17.25	16.77	16.38
10%	CN	7.91	7.81	7.75	7.72	7.71	7.70	7.69
	ESB	20.37	17.66	15.68	14.15	13.34	12.74	12.25
	DAM	7.25	7.27	7.30	7.33	7.35	7.37	7.39
	d_0	23.02	20.63	18.95	17.71	17.07	16.61	16.24
15%	CN	7.78	7.69	7.64	7.62	7.60	7.59	7.58
	ESB	19.87	17.41	15.55	14.09	13.31	12.73	12.24
	DAM	7.27	7.29	7.32	7.35	7.37	7.38	7.40
	d_0	22.54	20.38	18.81	17.62	17.01	16.56	16.19
20%	CN	7.65	7.58	7.53	7.51	7.50	7.49	7.48
	ESB	19.28	17.06	15.35	13.98	13.23	12.67	12.19
	DAM	7.30	7.32	7.34	7.37	7.39	7.41	7.42
	d_0	21.99	20.05	18.61	17.50	16.91	16.48	16.11
25%	CN	7.53	7.47	7.42	7.40	7.39	7.38	7.38
	ESB	18.83	16.78	15.18	13.87	13.14	12.60	12.14
	DAM	7.32	7.35	7.37	7.40	7.42	7.43	7.45
	d_0	21.56	19.78	18.43	17.38	16.80	16.38	16.04
30%	CN	7.45	7.38	7.34	7.32	7.31	7.30	7.30
	ESB	18.59	16.68	15.15	13.88	13.18	12.64	12.18
	DAM	7.35	7.37	7.39	7.42	7.44	7.45	7.47
	d_0	21.33	19.67	18.39	17.36	16.81	16.39	16.05

Table 6. NRSME/d_0, FCN trained in CN$^+$

DAM	NRSME	ESB						
		0%	5%	10%	15%	20%	25%	30%
0%	CN	6.00	5.97	5.97	5.88	5.99	5.91	6.04
	ESB	10.75	9.19	8.76	7.7	7.88	7.37	7.51
	DAM	8.35	8.5	8.65	8.9	8.74	8.95	8.78
	d_0	14.88	13.87	13.68	13.16	13.2	13.01	13.04
5%	CN	5.99	5.94	6.15	6.08	6.07	5.94	6.03
	ESB	11.22	9.71	8.2	7.79	7.19	7.61	7.29
	DAM	8.31	8.54	8.19	8.36	8.47	8.72	8.67
	d_0	15.19	14.23	13.12	12.94	12.66	13.01	12.83
10%	CN	6.11	6.07	6.1	6.1	6.09	6.08	6.1
	ESB	12.11	9.58	8.7	8.25	7.65	7.5	7.72
	DAM	7.86	8.25	8.28	8.23	8.41	8.49	8.32
	d_0	15.68	14.02	13.47	13.15	12.9	12.86	12.89
15%	CN	6.14	6.13	6.06	6.12	6.09	6.24	6.12
	ESB	16.11	10.86	9.53	7.57	7.75	7.4	7.38
	DAM	7.59	7.95	8.13	8.28	8.37	8.4	8.36
	d_0	18.84	14.79	13.92	12.78	12.93	12.82	12.72
20%	CN	6.21	6.25	6.26	6.12	6.17	6.22	6.09
	ESB	14.56	11.78	9.63	8.38	8.15	7.67	7.84
	DAM	7.58	7.66	7.94	8.2	8.07	8.11	8.28
	d_0	17.55	15.38	13.96	13.23	13.02	12.78	12.93
25%	CN	6.19	6.16	6.15	6.2	6.29	6.23	6.31
	ESB	15.47	12.27	9.18	10.46	8.76	8.18	7.23
	DAM	7.6	7.78	8	7.9	7.93	8	8.09
	d_0	18.31	15.78	13.64	14.5	13.39	13.03	12.55
30%	CN	6.04	6.11	6.05	6.18	6.26	6.3	6.32
	ESB	7.51	7.2	7.32	7.17	7.6	7.28	8.27
	DAM	8.78	8.47	8.44	8.29	8.07	8.07	7.91
	d_0	13.04	12.69	12.71	12.58	12.73	12.56	13.07

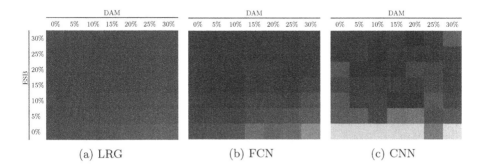

(a) LRG   (b) FCN   (c) CNN

Fig. 2. Progression of the d_0 metric of models trained in CN$^+$ (Color figure online)

The heatmaps in Figs. 2–4 graphically summarizes the results of the d_0 metric for each training set. Best accuracy values correspond to darker green, and worse prediction errors correspond to light green.

Table 7. NRSME/d_0, FCN trained in ESB$^+$

DAM	NRSME CN	0%	5%	10%	15%	20%	25%	30%
0%	CN	14.95	8.82	7.24	6.66	6.42	6.42	6.54
	ESB	5.40	6.07	6.39	6.61	6.74	6.78	6.72
	DAM	15.78	9.04	8.26	8.26	8.37	8.37	8.26
	d_0	22.40	14.01	12.71	12.5	12.52	12.54	12.5
5%	CN	9.01	7.13	6.71	7.33	6.62	6.61	6.36
	ESB	6.14	6.48	6.59	6.42	6.64	6.7	6.81
	DAM	9.1	8.11	8.2	8.32	8.2	8.08	8.28
	d_0	14.2	12.59	12.48	12.81	12.46	12.4	12.47
10%	CN	8.12	7.43	6.97	6.91	6.89	6.37	6.39
	ESB	6.3	6.49	6.51	6.58	6.55	6.82	6.78
	DAM	8.42	8.08	8.14	8.01	8.12	8.19	8.37
	d_0	13.29	12.75	12.54	12.46	12.5	12.42	12.52
15%	CN	8.06	6.84	7.49	6.62	6.72	6.57	6.47
	ESB	6.41	6.6	6.43	6.69	6.66	6.74	6.86
	DAM	8.19	8.1	8.08	8.02	8.13	8.08	8.09
	d_0	13.16	12.49	12.76	12.37	12.47	12.4	12.42
20%	CN	7.4	7.31	7.09	6.78	6.93	6.63	6.66
	ESB	6.59	6.51	6.58	6.69	6.63	6.8	6.69
	DAM	7.94	8	7.92	7.92	7.93	7.94	8.19
	d_0	12.7	12.64	12.5	12.39	12.44	12.38	12.5
25%	CN	7.14	7.18	6.98	7.18	6.63	6.64	6.5
	ESB	6.67	6.75	6.76	6.6	6.91	6.72	6.77
	DAM	7.89	7.81	7.82	7.94	7.92	8.02	8.08
	d_0	12.56	12.57	12.47	12.58	12.43	12.39	12.38
30%	CN	7.53	7.14	7.2	6.81	7.02	6.69	6.69
	ESB	6.59	6.73	6.71	6.67	6.7	6.64	6.73
	DAM	7.89	7.79	7.79	7.93	7.84	8.03	7.95
	d_0	12.74	12.53	12.55	12.4	12.48	12.38	12.38

Table 8. NRSME/d_0, FCN trained in DAM$^+$

ESB	NRSME CN	0%	5%	10%	15%	20%	25%	30%
0%	CN	11.48	11	10.65	10.19	9.5	9.1	8.23
	ESB	82.97	76.82	74.43	67.81	62.44	59.66	49.87
	DAM	5.30	5.35	5.37	5.41	5.51	5.65	5.85
	d_0	83.93	77.79	75.38	68.78	63.4	60.61	50.88
5%	CN	9.88	9.33	8.63	8.41	7.94	8.01	7.69
	ESB	63.52	59.38	50.55	44.96	39.54	40.8	35.65
	DAM	5.52	5.61	5.75	5.85	6.02	6.01	6.22
	d_0	64.52	60.37	51.6	46.11	40.78	42.01	37
10%	CN	8.56	7.88	7.67	7.65	7.31	7.21	7.21
	ESB	42.68	32.35	30.91	28.04	28.86	24.46	24.32
	DAM	5.93	6.21	6.25	6.43	6.38	6.57	6.61
	d_0	43.93	33.87	32.45	29.77	30.45	26.33	26.21
15%	CN	7.67	7.61	7.46	7.48	7.09	7.21	7.08
	ESB	16.78	15.8	16.66	17.91	15	15.35	16.06
	DAM	6.81	6.86	6.86	6.79	6.99	6.97	6.96
	d_0	19.67	18.83	19.5	20.56	18	18.34	18.88
20%	CN	7.76	7.66	7.53	7.35	7.23	6.98	6.75
	ESB	11.16	11.08	11.6	12.41	11.48	12.45	11.65
	DAM	7.12	7.12	7.1	7.05	7.17	7.15	7.27
	d_0	15.34	15.24	15.55	16.05	15.35	15.96	15.3
25%	CN	8.03	7.53	7.71	7.2	7.16	7.15	6.92
	ESB	10.53	9.63	9.97	9.71	11.6	9.54	10.37
	DAM	7.19	7.23	7.21	7.31	7.16	7.31	7.29
	d_0	15.07	14.2	14.52	14.13	15.4	13.98	14.44
30%	CN	7.77	7.53	7.36	7.35	7.06	7.16	6.92
	ESB	9.63	9.63	8.65	10.15	10.33	9.53	10.24
	DAM	7.24	7.23	7.34	7.22	7.25	7.31	7.31
	d_0	14.34	14.2	13.52	14.46	14.46	13.98	14.36

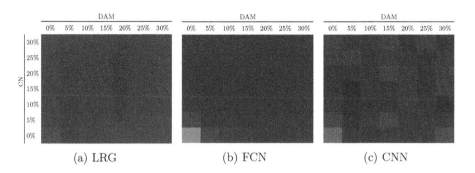

(a) LRG   (b) FCN   (c) CNN

Fig. 3. Progression of the d_0 metric of models trained in ESB$^+$ (Color figure online)

Heatmaps clearly show that both CNN and FCN obtained more accurate predictions than LRG, as long as the additional information from training in different hardware increases, in all evaluated traces.

Table 9. NRSME/d_0, CNN trained in CN$^+$

DAM	NRSME	ESB						
		0%	5%	10%	15%	20%	25%	30%
0%	CN	4.80	5.68	5.52	5.77	5.31	5.4	5.95
	ESB	46.90	10.06	10.39	6.07	6.35	5.57	5.67
	DAM	18.86	12.26	11.43	11.46	13.43	10.2	10.13
	d_0	50.78	16.85	16.4	14.19	15.78	12.82	13.04
5%	CN	3.89	5.63	5.99	6.23	5.7	6.21	5.88
	ESB	39.79	14.12	8.19	6.18	5.79	6.47	5.77
	DAM	13.57	9.11	10.17	9.07	9.71	9.5	9.68
	d_0	42.22	17.72	14.37	12.62	12.66	13.06	12.71
10%	CN	5.36	5.82	6.05	5.75	6.5	6.23	6.51
	ESB	40.21	8.5	7.23	7.38	5.69	6.02	7.13
	DAM	9.3	9.67	8.77	9.08	8.51	8.58	8.63
	d_0	41.62	14.13	12.88	13.04	12.13	12.19	12.95
15%	CN	6.31	5.13	6.19	6.61	5.8	6.26	5.92
	ESB	31.3	17.07	6.79	6.15	8.15	7.28	6.08
	DAM	7.89	6.81	8.77	8.18	9.94	8.49	9.76
	d_0	32.89	19.08	12.7	12.18	14.1	12.82	12.93
20%	CN	6.02	6.19	5.08	6.79	6.23	6.23	4.9
	ESB	31.57	17.23	8.8	7.67	5.83	7.76	7.22
	DAM	7.45	7.71	7.54	8.79	8.34	8.06	8
	d_0	32.99	19.87	12.65	13.5	11.93	12.81	11.84
25%	CN	7.32	6.22	5.8	5.84	5.01	5.91	4.99
	ESB	17.16	10.94	13.31	9.58	10.31	7.16	9.43
	DAM	7.64	8.24	6.98	9.05	8.4	9.08	7.4
	d_0	20.16	15.04	16.11	14.41	14.21	12.99	12.98
30%	CN	6.26	6.73	6.35	6.27	6.07	6.45	5.85
	ESB	34.26	11.95	9.51	7.82	8.2	8.57	8.59
	DAM	7.07	7.7	7.71	8.66	8.47	7.61	8.21
	d_0	35.54	15.73	13.79	13.25	13.26	13.15	13.24

Table 10. NRSME/d_0, CNN trained in ESB$^+$

DAM	NRSME	CN						
		0%	5%	10%	15%	20%	25%	30%
0%	CN	7.17	6.27	5.99	6.41	6.48	6.1	5.81
	ESB	4.68	5.1	5.18	5.63	5.01	6.07	5.25
	DAM	8.81	11.28	9.89	9.42	9.13	10.01	11.03
	d_0	12.29	13.88	12.67	12.71	12.27	13.2	13.53
5%	CN	7.54	8.19	6.59	6.92	6.1	6.27	5.92
	ESB	5.06	5.31	4.31	6.75	4.81	5.89	5.51
	DAM	8.21	8.87	8.52	9.39	8.73	10.19	9.96
	d_0	12.24	13.19	11.6	13.48	11.69	13.34	12.83
10%	CN	7.99	7.75	7.59	7.49	6.18	6.28	6.04
	ESB	4.45	6.17	6.21	5.35	4.52	5.34	5.69
	DAM	7.44	7.58	8.5	8.28	8.18	8.62	7.45
	d_0	11.79	12.47	12.98	12.38	11.2	11.93	11.15
15%	CN	7.51	7.86	6.74	7.5	6.99	6.49	5.91
	ESB	4.67	6.64	5.22	5.78	6.38	5.74	7.8
	DAM	8.26	8.62	8.06	8.05	8.2	8.54	8.01
	d_0	12.1	13.42	11.73	12.43	12.52	12.17	12.65
20%	CN	7.58	7.82	7.89	7.57	7.45	7.29	6.99
	ESB	5.26	5.19	5.48	5.58	6.11	5.44	6.14
	DAM	7.73	7.76	8.14	8.33	6.89	7.89	8.83
	d_0	12.04	12.18	12.59	12.56	11.85	12.04	12.83
25%	CN	7.91	7.86	7.66	7.33	7.18	6.39	6.67
	ESB	5.58	5.52	5.41	5.35	5.59	5.54	4.67
	DAM	7.45	7.57	7.63	7.77	7.8	8.34	7.7
	d_0	12.22	12.23	12.09	11.95	11.99	11.88	11.21
30%	CN	8.68	7.16	7.77	8.33	8.42	6.43	7.22
	ESB	6.48	5.59	5.44	5.29	5.3	6.18	6.18
	DAM	9.01	7.88	5.83	8.26	8.18	8.34	7.82
	d_0	14.09	12.03	11.13	12.87	12.88	12.21	12.31

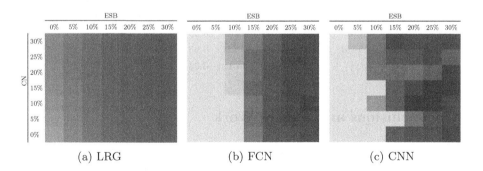

(a) LRG   (b) FCN   (c) CNN

Fig. 4. Progression of the d_0 metric of models trained in DAM$^+$ (Color figure online)

Table 11. NRSME/d_0, CNN trained in DAM$^+$

ESB	NRSME	CN						
		0%	5%	10%	15%	20%	25%	30%
0%	CN	14.37	11.21	10.75	10.09	9.76	9.68	8.37
	ESB	111.39	93.47	79.54	67.52	65.25	61.48	56.22
	DAM	3.37	5.09	5.04	5.14	5.27	5.33	5.43
	d_0	112.36	94.28	80.42	68.46	66.19	62.47	57.1
5%	CN	10.57	9.01	8.51	7.95	8.75	8.13	8.42
	ESB	27.56	52.58	51.87	42	41.47	43.69	42.89
	DAM	4.77	5.29	5.68	6.42	5.68	5.93	6.15
	d_0	29.9	53.61	52.87	43.23	42.76	44.83	44.14
10%	CN	9.34	8.72	8.18	8.35	8.08	7.82	7.91
	ESB	31.86	47.24	22.37	30.39	9.83	15.5	16.87
	DAM	6.84	5.65	6.58	6.45	4.78	6.77	6.81
	d_0	33.9	48.37	24.71	32.17	13.59	18.63	19.84
15%	CN	8.87	7.71	8.6	8.14	7.46	7.46	8.17
	ESB	11.77	29.28	12.22	10.85	16.24	12.17	15.03
	DAM	6.88	6.52	6.81	7.59	6.84	6.78	7.07
	d_0	16.26	30.97	16.42	15.54	19.14	15.8	18.51
20%	CN	9.66	7.71	8.04	8.98	8.43	7.24	6.7
	ESB	9.21	16.71	7.19	8.77	15.81	11.84	9.8
	DAM	6.89	6.86	7.14	6.86	6.71	7.46	7.28
	d_0	15.02	19.64	12.94	14.3	19.13	15.76	13.93
25%	CN	9.36	9.16	8.04	7.72	8.07	7.38	8.18
	ESB	8.92	10.3	8.42	7.72	13.38	9.87	10.46
	DAM	6.92	6.9	5.08	6.6	6.94	7.35	4.93
	d_0	14.67	15.41	12.7	12.76	17.1	14.35	14.16
30%	CN	9.23	8.94	7.54	8.35	8.03	6.91	7.3
	ESB	8.69	8.1	9.47	8.69	8.01	13.44	9.18
	DAM	4.91	7.04	7.27	4.95	7.42	7.36	7.01
	d_0	13.59	13.97	14.12	13.03	13.55	16.81	13.66

5   Conclusions and Future Work

This article presented an study of the generalization capabilities of forecasting techniques of empirical energy consumption models of high performance computing resources.

Improving energy efficiency of supercomputing facilities has become a relevant subject to reduce operational cost and environmental impacts. Furthermore, shifting from fossil fuels to renewable energy sources requires intelligent energy management for predicting and adapting to events both processing demand and energy availability. Accurate forecasting of the energy consumption of HPC resources plays a fundamental role in the energy management, and to have energy consumption models capable of quality prediction in heterogeneous scenarios allows implementing efficient energy policies.

In this article, different energy models were built, considering three forecasting techniques: a linear regression, a fully connected neural network, and a convolutional neural network. Models were built using information from the execution of a benchmark over three different HPC hardware.

The design of the experiments included tree stages. In the first stage each model was trained with information of only one HPC hardware and the prediction error was evaluated for the same hardware. In the second stage, the prediction error of the built models was evaluated for other HPC hardware. In the third stage, training information of each model was gradually extended with information about other hardware, and then each model was analyzed to evaluate how new information impacts on the prediction and generalization capabilities.

Results of the first stage indicated that CNN was the best technique, outperforming both the linear regression and the FCN method. CNN improved the prediction accuracy (evaluated by the NRMSE metric) in 2.58 over LRG and 1.29 over FCN. In the second stage, results showed that the training data significantly influences in the prediction accuracy. No clear superiority of neural networks over LRG was observed.

In turn, results of the third stage showed that network approaches were able to significantly improve the prediction accuracy when the training data is expanded by including information from other training instances. The generalization capabilities improved too, allowing to overcome some pathological results observed in the cross-validation performed in the second stage.

The reported results are very relevant for advancing towards building general models for energy consumption in HPC infrastructures. The empirical analysis showed that models based on neural network are able to improve their learning capabilities and properly generalize to unseen scenarios, when including few additional data in the training phase. This behavior is promising for cases where hardware and software with different features are operated and used.

The main lines for future work are related to extend the analysis of the proposed models by considering different learning strategies and including training data from the execution of both specific software and generic benchmarks on representative hardware architectures of modern supercomputing facilities.

References

1. DEEP-Extreme Scale Technologies project. https://www.deep-projects.eu/. Accessed 08 Jul 2021
2. Auweter, A., et al.: A case study of energy aware scheduling on SuperMUC. In: Supercomputing, pp. 394–409 (2014)
3. Barreda, M., Dolz, M., Castaño, M.: Convolutional neural nets for estimating the run time and energy consumption of the sparse matrix-vector product. Int. J. High Perform. Comput. Appl. **35**(3), 268–281 (2021)
4. Buitinck, L., et al.: API design for machine learning software: experiences from the scikit-learn project. In: Workshop: Languages for Data Mining and Machine Learning, pp. 108–122 (2013)

5. Dayarathna, M., Wen, Y., Fan, R.: Data center energy consumption modeling: a survey. IEEE Commun. Surv. Tutorials **18**(1), 732–794 (2016)
6. Hähnel, M., Döbel, B., Völp, M., Härtig, H.: Measuring energy consumption for short code paths using RAPL. ACM SIGMETRICS Perform. Eval. Rev. **40**(3), 13–17 (2012)
7. Imes, C., Hofmeyr, S., Hoffmann, H.: Energy-efficient application resource scheduling using machine learning classifiers. In: 47th International Conference on Parallel Processing (2018)
8. Malmodin, J., Lundén, D.: The energy and carbon footprint of the global ICT and E&M sectors 2010–2015. Sustainability **10**(9), 3027 (2018)
9. Muraña, J., Nesmachnow, S., Armenta, F., Tchernykh, A.: Characterization, modeling and scheduling of power consumption of scientific computing applications in multicores. Cluster Comput. **22**(3), 839–859 (2019). https://doi.org/10.1007/s10586-018-2882-8
10. Nesmachnow, S., et al.: Demand response and ancillary services for supercomputing and datacenters. In: Torres, M., Klapp, J. (eds.) ISUM 2019. CCIS, vol. 1151, pp. 203–217. Springer, Cham (2019). https://doi.org/10.1007/978-3-030-38043-4_17
11. Nesmachnow, S., Perfumo, C., Goiri, Í.: Holistic multiobjective planning of datacenters powered by renewable energy. Cluster Comput. **18**(4), 1379–1397 (2015). https://doi.org/10.1007/s10586-015-0485-1
12. Pan, S.J., Yang, Q.: A survey on transfer learning. IEEE Trans. Knowl. Data Eng. **22**(10), 1345–1359 (2010)
13. Rong, H., Zhang, H., Xiao, S., Li, C., Hu, C.: Optimizing energy consumption for data centers. Renew. Sustain. Energy Rev. **58**, 674–691 (2016)
14. Sayadi, H., Patel, N., Sasan, A., Homayoun, H.: Machine learning-based approaches for energy-efficiency prediction and scheduling in composite cores architectures. In: International Conference on Computer Design, pp. 129–136 (2017)
15. Schöne, R., et al.: Automatic application tuning for HPC architectures. Sci. Program. **22**, 1–11 (2014)
16. Strohmaier, E., Shan, H.: Apex-Map: a global data access benchmark to analyze hpc systems and parallel programming paradigms. In: 2005 ACM/IEEE Conference on Supercomputing, pp. 49–49 (2005)
17. Terpstra, D., Jagode, H., You, H., Dongarra, J.: Collecting performance data with PAPI-C. In: Tools for High Performance Computing, pp. 157–173 (2010)

Fourth International Workshop on Interoperability of Supercomputing and Cloud Technologies

Automation for Data-Driven Research with the NERSC Superfacility API

Deborah J. Bard, Mark R. Day, Bjoern Enders,
Rebecca J. Hartman–Baker, John Riney III, Cory Snavely(✉),
and Gabor Torok

National Energy Research Scientific Computing Center (NERSC),
Lawrence Berkeley National Laboratory, Berkeley, CA, USA
{djbard,mrday,benders,rjhartmanbaker,riney,csnavely,gtorok}@lbl.gov
https://www.nersc.gov

Abstract. The Superfacility API brings automation to the use of High Performance Computing (HPC) systems. Our aim is to enable scientists to reliably automate their interactions with computational resources at the National Energy Research Scientific Computing Center (NERSC), removing human intervention from the process of transferring, analyzing, and managing data. In this paper, we describe the science use cases that drive the API design, our schema of API endpoints, and implementation details and considerations, including authentication and authorization. We also discuss future plans, working toward our vision of supporting entirely automated experiment-network-HPC workflows.

Keywords: HPC · Supercomputing · RESTful API · Workflows

1 Introduction and Motivation

Large-scale analysis of experimental data is an increasingly important type of workload at supercomputing facilities. The National Energy Scientific Computing Center (NERSC), the mission HPC and data center for the United States Department of Energy (DOE), has supported such experimental computing workloads since its inception as a general-purpose supercomputing facility.

Until recently, the data volumes produced at instrument facilities such as light sources, telescopes, and other specialized detectors and the corresponding computational demands for processing and analyzing those data have generally been met by on-site HPC clusters. However, Moore's Law applies differently to detectors than computers, and today, as the projects using these detectors have begun to exceed the capability of local resources, supercomputing facilities like NERSC become a more attractive resource for data processing and analysis. Re-engineering workflow pipelines to handle data collection and analysis at large

This research was supported by the National Energy Research Scientific Computing Center (NERSC), a U.S. Department of Energy Office of Science User Facility operated under Contract No. DE-AC02-05CH11231.

H. Jagode et al. (Eds.): ISC High Performance 2021 Workshops, LNCS 12761, pp. 333–345, 2021.
https://doi.org/10.1007/978-3-030-90539-2_22

scale across a distributed architecture—spanning separate instrument and super-computing facilities, management structures, authentication and authorizations systems, and other technical and organizational disparities—requires reliable, easily programmable interfaces to HPC resources that are based on common, industry-standard tools and reusable by multiple science communities. The API described in this paper was designed and built to meet this emergent need.

We view the Superfacility API as a key enabling technology for projects that use modern instrument facilities, allowing them to continue their natural upward scaling by leveraging off-site supercomputing resources as easily as they have leveraged on-site HPC clusters in the past. With these resources at their disposal, researchers will be able to benefit from higher detector resolutions, faster sampling rates, on-demand computation for scheduled data collection windows, and other exciting capabilities of modern scientific instrument facilities.

The development of the API is one facet of the Superfacility project [6] at Lawrence Berkeley National Laboratory, which aims to create a unified, seam-less environment combining hardware solutions, application software, and data management tools to deliver breakthrough science. Automation is a key part of the Superfacility concept, which envisions science teams at experimental facili-ties orchestrating automated data analysis pipelines which move data from the instrument to the computing site, perform analysis, and disseminate results—all without human intervention. An API must therefore have the capability to access and manage data and compute at the HPC center and to interface with the batch scheduler to control and monitor job submission. In this paper we describe how we have developed an API to meet these needs at NERSC. We discuss the motivating use cases, describe the basic functions and software architecture, and explain implementation considerations made in integrating with backend sys-tems. We also describe the authentication model, which was designed to both meet modern security standards and support the long-running, non-interactive workflows that research demands.

2   Related and Prior Work

2.1   Similar HPC APIs

The development of the Superfacility API was inspired by work at various HPC centers to offer RESTful API [8] interfaces to resources:

- At NERSC, the NEWT (*NE*RSC *W*eb development *T*oolkit) project [3] was created to provide API access to web science gateways, presenting computa-tional and data resources through simple transactions against URIs.
- The Tapis/Agave project [5] at the Texas Advanced Computing Center (TACC) was developed around the same time as a "Science-as-a-Service" plat-form with even broader functionality, allowing users to query system health, control compute jobs, manage user groups, and perform other necessary func-tions.

– At the Swiss National Supercomputing Centre (CSCS), an API interface called FirecREST [4] has been developed that allows users to execute simple and complex tasks alike on the CSCS compute and storage infrastructure, such as managing compute jobs and moving data between file systems.

Our work aims to introduce functional compatibility with these projects and additionally to push their collective boundaries by envisioning API endpoints for every part of an HPC center, with the ultimate goal of totally automated use of NERSC, integrating everything from compute to storage.

2.2   Comparison to the Superfacility API

Our aim in developing a successor to NEWT (NERSC's first API) is to develop an API based on modern standards and security practices and to included features to support automated workflows (rather than only web applications). So, while the Superfacility API implements some functionality similar to NEWT, its predecessor, there are fundamental differences that make it more similar to Tapis and FirecREST in usage and/or function.

The syntax of the API hierarchically groups related functions into URL sub-paths (e.g., /account, /status, etc.) for increased ease of use ("ergonomics") for developers using similar APIs elsewhere. Such groupings are in line with conventions for modern REST APIs. In particular, we chose to align the syntax with that of FirecREST due to its similar stage of development and strong functional similarities. We also looked at Tapis for inspiration, especially its authentication model; though as a more mature API, it incorporates a number of more specialized features than the Superfacility API.

Unlike NEWT, which uses HTTP Basic Authentication (usernames and passwords), the Superfacility API uses OAuth2 access tokens to authenticate the caller. These tokens are less vulnerable to theft because they are short-lived—expiring after just 10 min—and their creation is secured by a private/public key pair, which makes them cryptographically verifiable. The process of creating access tokens is documented as part of the OAuth2 standard and supported by freely available Python libraries, simplifying the adoption of this authentication framework. Similar libraries are available for other programming environments. The FirecREST API also uses access tokens for authentication.

Since NEWT uses usernames and passwords for authentication, integrating it with a web application is convenient. In contrast, the Superfacility API is meant to be used from long-running workflow-type applications in environments where storing a password is undesirable. Eventually, we also plan to support calls to the new API from web applications.

3   Summary of API Functions

Table 1 below is a current list of the high-level categories of endpoints and their intended uses. Additional details, including the precise call syntax and parameters, are available at the online Swagger documentation[1] for the API.

Table 1. Summary of high-level endpoint categories and their intended uses.

Category	Usage
/account	Get accounting data about the user's projects, roles, groups and compute and storage allocations
/compute	Run batch jobs and query job and queue statuses on NERSC compute resources
/status	Query the status of NERSC component systems
/storage	Transfer files between Globus endpoints
/utilities	Traverse the file system, upload and download small files, and execute commands
/tasks	Query the status and results of asynchronous operations (See below; most endpoints are asynchronous, and will run in the background until complete.)
/reservations	Make and amend requests for NERSC compute resources ahead of time (Currently under implementation)

API calls are either synchronous (blocking reads) or asynchronous. All endpoints using the HTTP GET method will block until they retrieve data. Endpoints using POST and PUT calls schedule their work on a message queue and return immediately with a *task_id* that can be looked up via the /tasks endpoints.

As mentioned, the various API endpoints were chosen to match the call syntax of the FirecREST API. It should be noted that the endpoint names and their groupings were intentionally oriented to functions or tasks that would intuitively make sense to existing NERSC users, not specific underlying NERSC systems (except where particularly relevant). Our guiding philosophy here was to model the basic procedural building blocks that scientists currently use to conduct their research, in order to provide a meaningful abstraction over NERSC resources that will remain consistent over time, as the API matures and underlying systems change. As new usage patterns develop, we can adapt and augment the API in a backwards-compatible fashion to provide more nuanced endpoints that correspond to new features and capabilities.

---

[1] Superfacility API documentation generated using the Swagger toolset, available at https://api.nersc.gov/api/v1.2/.

4   General Use-Case Drivers for API Functionality

Experiments often require HPC-scale computing at short notice because detector output, the driver of compute demand, often varies cyclically. Some experiments may even arrange for multiple compute sites to be available to handle workloads on demand. To build a truly automated and resilient workflow, scientists need to be able to query the health and status of a facility and make real-time decisions based on the response; for example, if a file system is unavailable, the workflow pipeline must not send data to it. Providing the center status via a standardized API interface is therefore a key requirement.

Science teams often comprise tens or hundreds of members at different organizations worldwide, with differing needs for data access. These collaborations need a way for PIs to automate the management of their team members' accounts at the HPC facility—for example, to set access permissions. They also need to manage petabyte-scale data sets across multiple file systems, and move data into and out of the HPC facility as needed. Including these functions within the scope of an API allows automation of these tasks.

Over the years, NERSC staff has observed that many research workflow operations naturally form patterns of recurring actions that are carried out when analyzing data. Traditionally, the interfaces to these tasks are made for humans parsing the information and reacting accordingly. This suffices as long as each workload on an HPC is paired with a human, but the approach becomes untenable at large scale or fast rates, or when interfacing with an external user group (or machine) that runs patterns of tasks rapidly. Table 2 describes many of these common workflow tasks.

Let's illustrate these abstract actions with a concrete example. A growing community of NERSC users from experimental facilities such as the Advanced Light Source, National Center for Electron Microscopy or the Linac Coherent Light Source (LCLS) produce so much data with their advanced cameras that the data rate can outrun the local compute capacity [1,7]. The most basic workflow for these facility partners is to iterate the following steps for each data set produced by an experiment:

1. *Move* the data to a HPC facility with a transfer tool,
2. *Submit* a job for analysis, and
3. *Move* the result back for interpretation and/or archive the data.

We find these essential workflow components in Table 2. Looking at the API spec in Table 1, such a workflow could be implemented using the `/compute` and `/storage` endpoints. However, more elements are needed in order to build truly resilient workflows where data acquisition occurs around the clock (nearly) every day, and where the analysis step is a crucial feedback component that drives the experiment. The larger goal, therefore, is to create a fully closed-loop operation, with HPC *embedded into the experiment.*

Before any work can even begin, the scientist must determine whether the HPC facility is up and available to handle the workload, which prompts them to *check the status* of required subsystems and employ a mitigation strategy if not.

Table 2. Common workflow tasks.

Action	Before SuperFacility API	After SuperFacility API
Check status	SSH in or ping specific services	Query the /status API endpoint.
Submit job	SSH in and submit jobs with the sbatch command.	Manage jobs using calls to the /compute endpoint.
Monitor job	SSH in (again) and perform ad-hoc queries with complex commands using squeue | grep | sort | ...	Develop a web gateway that calls the /compute endpoint and presents a custom view of workflow progress.
Plan ahead	Read the NERSC MOTD to see if any down time is planned.	Query the /status API endpoint for planned outages.
Move data	SSH in and run file transfer tools to move data.	Call the /storage API endpoint.
Automate	Chain jobs, maintain job state, check state to coordinate a workflow.	*Future capability:* Register callbacks at the /tasks API that fire when steps complete.
Reserve	File a ticket to create a reservation, discuss plans with NERSC staff, and negotiate for workable timing.	*Future capability:* Call the /reservations API endpoint.
Manage	As PI, go to https://iris.nersc.gov/ to manually sort your users into groups and check quotas.	Add users to groups via the /account/groups API endpoint, check compute quotas via /account/projects

(This could entail switching to an alternate compute resource or deferring the task to a later date.) NERSC provides a human-parsable interface for this: a web page[2] with a listing of system status. Likewise, the API provides the /status endpoint to return the status of NERSC resources.

Keeping with the example above, a workflow engine would first query the status of /status/dtns and /status/community_filesystem in order to find out the health of NERSC's data transfer nodes and the Community File System, respectively. A JSON-formatted return looks like this:

```
{"name": "dtns",
 "full_name": "Data Transfer Nodes",
 "description": "System is active",
 "system_type": "filesystem",
 "notes": [],
 "status": "active",
 "updated_at": "2021-05-21T07:55:00"}
```

A status of "active" indicates that the resources are operational and the data transfer can start.

---

[2] NERSC live status page https://www.nersc.gov/live-status/motd/.

While short unexpected interruptions can always occur, the scientist also needs to *plan ahead* and determine whether all required resources will be available during the experiment's time window, or if NERSC has any conflicting scheduled outages (e.g., using `/status/outages/planned`).

An experimental user facility like a light source will continuously run many experiments in parallel, each producing data set after data set, and for each it will direct the analysis to HPC on behalf of their users. Manually interacting with the remote compute backend for large-scale experiments is impractical for local support staff. Hence the "scientist" in the previous sections must be replaced with a "workflow engine" doing the same task. Having reliable, machine-readable APIs for these operations is crucial for the transition to automation.

4.1 Example: Integrating the Superfacility API into an LCLS-II Pipeline

An early adopter of the Superfacility API is the AutoSFX project at the LCLS [2]. Here, the LCLS data management system integrated the API into its automation engine (ARP) to provision NERSC computing resources as an endpoint for data analysis. Data management events (such as the beginning or the end of an experiment), file transfers, or other operations automatically trigger analysis jobs on NERSC's Cori supercomputer, or other everyday tasks such as shell commands, which are then initiated, monitored and managed with queries to `/compute/jobs/cori` and `/utilities`, respectively. Updates from the running code as well as job status update (also obtained via `/compute/jobs/cori`) are collected, curated, and then pushed to the browser to form a visual representation of the progress in a web interface.

The entire AutoSFX workflow is modeled as multiple analysis steps which are expressed as a Directed Acyclic Graph (DAG) in Apache Airflow.[3] Each node in the DAG is executed by ARP as mentioned above, and summary results are copied back to the experiment folders using `/utilities/download` and displayed in the web UI. As ARP frequently calls asynchronous endpoints (e.g., `/compute/jobs` or `/utilities`) where each POST call generates a task, so it also queries `/tasks` to check their status and advance their state in the DAG.

5 API Design and Architecture

5.1 Deployment Details and Integration with Underlying Systems

The Superfacility API endpoint layer is built as a set of Docker[4] containers and runs in Spin [10], NERSC's Containers-as-a-Service platform. A Docker-based implementation allows for fast deployment, high availability, and simple scaling, among other benefits.

---

[3] https://airflow.apache.org/.
[4] https://www.docker.com/.

The code for the API endpoint layer consists of about 4500 lines of Python code and took about six months to complete with a team of two engineers. It uses Flask and the **flask_restx** (formerly **flask_RESTPlus**)[5] library to model and annotate the API code. The library translates JSON to and from a set of model objects, as well as providing automatic Swagger documentation.

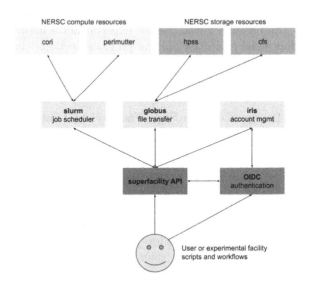

Fig. 1. API architecture and underlying NERSC systems.

The main role of the API endpoint layer is to orchestrate connections to backend systems and databases, consolidate authentication and authorization across these disparate backend systems, asynchronously manage long-running tasks, and provide self-hosted documentation. Thus, as a system whose primary goal is to simplify a unified access mechanism into the NERSC environment, the API overlays and relies on the functionality provided by numerous NERSC internal systems, as depicted in Fig. 1. Several of these systems are not designed for direct access by NERSC users, making the API endpoint layer a critical component to securely expose those capabilities for programmatic control. Accordingly, most of the API code is simply a normalized shell that either secures and abstracts the details of interaction with underlying NERSC systems or services them internally, such as the /tasks endpoint, which calls an internal database.

– Accounting data served by the /account endpoints comes from NERSC's Iris [11] allocation banking and identity access management system, which has its own API. Iris provides access to compute allocation and storage usage accounting information and settings, and allows for manipulation of user groups.

---

[5] https://flask-restx.readthedocs.io/en/latest/.

- The `/compute` endpoint integrates with the Slurm[6] workload manager and enables submission and other manipulation of compute jobs. Notably, integration with Slurm for `/compute` (and `/reservations`, below) is handled via SSH internally, but will eventually use a Slurm API currently being developed by SchedMD. This thin abstraction over the native Slurm command-line interface or native API, which is designed for administrator use, allows for more precise access control and selective exposure of the functionality that is meant to be end-user-facing.
- The `/utility` endpoints help users accomplish miscellaneous tasks, such as uploading or downloading small files, listing directories, or running shell commands.
- Calls to the `/storage` endpoint wrap the Globus API and are used to manage data transfers. This allows efficient large file transfer in and out of NERSC or between various NERSC storage tiers. While it is possible for users to call the Globus API directly, this abstraction layer allows for less coding as well as allowing other file transfer tools to be added in the future, and transfer functionality to be further abstracted, if needed.
- The `/status` endpoint uses the same backend data source that reports planned and unplanned outages to the NERSC web site and login messages, but in an easily parsable format.
- The `/tasks` endpoint queries the state of asynchronous background tasks. As the execution and monitoring of tasks is managed within the API service itself, their state is being continuously updated in an internal database.
- The `/reservations` endpoint—which allows users to reserve future compute time—is one of the more complex integrations. When called, the API will validate the request against business rules, including checking for planned maintenance (as with the `/status` endpoint). If policies require human intervention to review the request, it will then be queued in Iris. At two weeks before the start time, an approved request will be automatically "guaranteed" with an independent call to the Slurm backend.

5.2 Authentication and Authorization Model

The Superfacility API uses OAuth2 bearer tokens for authentication and authorization. OAuth2 has a number of features that make it attractive for our purposes:

- It is an Internet Engineering Task Force (IETF) standards track protocol that is well understood by developers.
- It provides authorization grant types appropriate for both individual users (client credentials grant) as well as for workflow managers working on behalf of many users and across allocations (authorization code grant).
- Its short-lived access tokens allow for quick access revocation, satisfying the strict security requirements of our center.

---

[6] https://slurm.schedmd.com/.

To use the API, users must complete a one-time process of creating an OAuth2 "client" in Iris, the NERSC user dashboard, which consists of an identifier and symmetric (private/public) key pair. The client can be customized with security controls, such as source IP restrictions, which allow it to have a longer lifetime; this is important for long-running, non-interactive workflows. Once the client is obtained, the user uses their client ID and private key to create a signed client assertion in the form of a JSON web token (JWT) and exchanges it for an access token against our OAuth2 server. This exchange can be accomplished with standard programming libraries or command-line tools. The access token can then be passed in the `Authorization:` header of the API request. The API endpoint layer validates the token and maps it to the appropriate user and allocation for authorization.

While SSH remains a popular tool for interactive access and can also be leveraged for non-interactive access, we believe that using an API via access tokens is a better path forward. With SSH, users have unobstructed access to the entire system which, while convenient for users, presents challenges for NERSC both in enforcing granular security policy and understanding how NERSC users are interacting with computational resources. In contrast, using the OAuth2 model enhances security because individual clients can be restricted in capabilities and access lifetime. Having end users access the center via an API also allows NERSC to gather more granular and more meaningful statistics on usage patterns and, in the future, to build specific API endpoints to better serve the needs of the science community. Lastly, using OAuth2 in conjunction with an API is a natural integration for coders, complete with supporting software libraries, and allows for easier coding of multifaceted workflows where NERSC is just one component. We therefore expect that while SSH will remain a prominent means of HPC access for some time, it will be used for a narrower set of purposes.

5.3   API Internal Message Queue and Call Handling Sequence

Because the API interacts with various backend systems for both synchronous and asynchronous tasks, it needs a reliable internal mechanism to dispatch requests, track outstanding backend responses as necessary, and deliver payloads back to the caller. Synchronous blocking operations interact directly with backend systems, but an internal message queue was built into the system to handle asynchronous tasks.

Figure 2 illustrates how the API handles an example call sequence from initial authentication, followed by an asynchronous task, and finally a synchronous task.

As described above, to prepare for using the API, the researcher manually obtains an OAuth2 client credential from Iris, the NERSC user dashboard. When the credential is securely stored and accessible to the workflow orchestration software, automation can continue non-interactively.

– First, authentication libraries in the workflow software supply the OAuth 2 client ID and key to Connect2Id, the API authentication server, which will respond with a short-lived access token that is used for subsequent API calls.

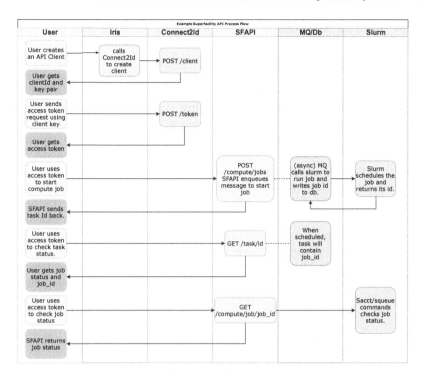

Fig. 2. Example API call sequence.

- Next, the software makes a call to enqueue a job. Job submission is treated asynchronously because a response may not always be immediate. The API creates a new message on the queue and assigns it a task ID, and the message persists.
- To monitor progress, the workflow software can repeatedly query the task ID to check the status of the job submission.
- In the background, when the job submission has completed, the Slurm job ID is populated into the message and is then included in the responses to task status.
- Finally, when the task status indicates the job has been scheduled and contains a job ID, the software can query detailed job status using the job ID. As this is a direct call to the Slurm backend, it is handled synchronously, and does not rely on the message queue.

6   Remarks on Portability

The Superfacility API provides an abstraction layer that obscures the complexity of the NERSC environment and idiosyncrasies of individual component systems, exposing high-level operations as easy-to-understand functions that are common across supercomputing facilities. This notion of exposing HPC as a callable software construct, and orienting its usage by function rather than system, introduces a paradigm change in accessibility, with the potential to transform how users interact with HPC resources and automate the processes that use them.

It is our hope that other compute facilities will build similar capabilities, and moreover, that they will choose to align their API implementations similarly, or engage in discussions to extend functionality through a collaborative process. By keeping the call syntax, functional groupings, and data payloads compatible, we enable users of HPC APIs to organize their workflow logic to a common set of actions and write code to a common convention, with the ultimate goal of making workflow engine code agnostic to any particular compute facility!

Seamless integration with commercial cloud providers is also of interest to many researchers. While these systems differ considerably from HPC in their architecture and modes of use, there are common elements that can help to simplify development. For example, the use of standards-based OAuth2 authentication, described in more detail in the next section, prevents developers from having to integrate multiple authentication libraries in workflow software that needs to operate against both the Superfacility API and a commercial cloud provider.

7 Future Capabilities Envisioned

The first released version of the Superfacility API works well for most basic use cases that NERSC users or experimental facilities need. However, we are also designing features for near- and long-term future API releases.

Additional features planned or under consideration includes the following:

- Extend the authentication procedure to allow SAML assertions to be exchanged for an access token, thereby allowing single-page web apps to use the API as well. This would allow us to deprecate NEWT.
- Enhance the reservation feature by incorporating more business rules for more autonomous operation, e.g., automating the approval procedure and allowing users to upload an entire task set to execute during the reservation. Automating approvals will require codifying policy and will likely involve the development of predictive metrics to ensure that accepting reservations does not adversely impact system utilization.
- Add the ability for users to register event handlers in the API using the /tasks endpoint. These event handlers could send notifications, call a URL, start another job, etc., upon task completion.
- Integrate with ESNet's SENSE project [9], which aims to deliver smart, on-demand networking configuration at the WAN level. Work in this area would also make use of NERSC SDN capabilities to complete SENSE's "last mile."

While much of the Superfacility API implementation is specific to NERSC, and would therefore be of minimal utility to the general open source community, we believe that there is value in open-sourcing a general interface framework that the API implements, and will consider making this available with a future release. Such a framework could define a basic set of endpoints with well-documented inputs and outputs, and serve as a standard for future HPC centers creating similar APIs. The interface API standard could be managed by a team of individuals representing participating institutions and could form the basis for a registry of implementations.

References

1. Blair, J., et al.: High performance data management and analysis for tomography. In: Stock, S.R. (ed.) Developments in X-Ray Tomography IX, vol. 9212, pp. 374–382. International Society for Optics and Photonics, SPIE (2014). https://doi.org/10.1117/12.2069862
2. Blaschke, J.P., et al.: Real-time XFEL data analysis at SLAC and NERSC: a trial run of nascent exascale experimental data analysis (2021)
3. Cholia, S., Skinner, D., Boverhof, J.: NEWT: A RESTful service for building high performance computing web applications. In: 2010 Gateway Computing Environments Workshop (GCE), pp. 1–11 (2010). https://doi.org/10.1109/GCE.2010.5676125
4. Cruz, F.A., et al.: FirecREST: a RESTful API to HPC systems. In: 2020 IEEE/ACM International Workshop on Interoperability of Supercomputing and Cloud Technologies (SuperCompCloud), pp. 21–26 (2020). https://doi.org/10.1109/SuperCompCloud51944.2020.00009
5. Dooley, R., Brandt, S.R., Fonner, J.: The Agave platform: An open, science-as-a-service platform for digital science. In: Proceedings of the Practice and Experience on Advanced Research Computing. PEARC '18, Association for Computing Machinery, New York, NY, USA (2018). https://doi.org/10.1145/3219104.3219129
6. Enders, B., et al.: Cross-facility science with the superfacility project at LBNL. In: 2020 IEEE/ACM 2nd Annual Workshop on Extreme-scale Experiment-in-the-Loop Computing (XLOOP), pp. 1–7 (2020). https://doi.org/10.1109/XLOOP51963.2020.00006
7. Enders, B., et al.: Dataflow at the cosmic beamline - stream processing and supercomputing. Microscopy Microanal. **24**(S2), 56–57 (2018). https://doi.org/10.1017/S1431927618012710
8. Fielding, R.T.: Architectural Styles and the Design of Network-based Software Architectures. Ph.D. thesis, Irvine, California, USA (2000)
9. Monga, I., et al.: SDN for End-to-end Networked Science at the Exascale (SENSE). In: 2018 IEEE/ACM Innovating the Network for Data-Intensive Science (INDIS), pp. 33–44. IEEE Computer Society, Los Alamitos, CA, USA (2018). https://doi.org/10.1109/INDIS.2018.00007
10. Snavely, C., Alvarez, G., Hendrix, V., Cholia, S., Lasiewski, S.: Spin: a docker-based platform for deploying science gateways at NERSC. In: Gateways 2018: The 13th Gateway Computing Environments Conference. figshare, October 2018. https://doi.org/10.6084/m9.figshare.7071770.v3
11. Torok, G., Day, M.R., Hartman-Baker, R.J., Snavely, C.: Iris: allocation banking and identity and access management for the exascale era. In: SC20: International Conference for High Performance Computing, Networking, Storage and Analysis, pp. 1–11 (2020). https://doi.org/10.1109/SC41405.2020.00046

A Middleware Supporting Data Movement in Complex and Software-Defined Storage and Memory Architectures

Christopher Haine[1], Utz-Uwe Haus[1], Maxime Martinasso[2], Dirk Pleiter[3,4]([⊠]),
François Tessier[6], Domokos Sarmany[5], Simon Smart[5], Tiago Quintino[5],
and Adrian Tate[7]

[1] HPE HPC/AI Research Lab, Basel, Switzerland
[2] CSCS, Swiss National Supercomputing Centre, 6900 Lugano, Switzerland
[3] Forschungszentrum Jülich, 52425 Jülich, Germany
[4] KTH, 100 44 Stockholm, Sweden
pleiter@kth.se
[5] European Centre for Medium-Range Weather Forecasts (ECMWF),
Reading RG2 9AX, UK
[6] Inria Rennes Bretagne-Atlantique, 35042 Rennes, France
[7] NAG, Oxford, UK

Abstract. Among the broad variety of challenges that arise from workloads in a converged HPC and Cloud infrastructure, data movement is of paramount importance, especially oncoming exascale systems featuring multiple tiers of memory and storage. While the focus has, for years, been primarily on optimizing computations, the importance of improving data handling on such architectures is now well understood. As optimization techniques can be applied at different stages (operating system, run-time system, programming environment, and so on), a middleware providing a uniform and consistent data awareness becomes necessary. In this paper, we introduce a novel memory- and data-aware middleware called Maestro, designed for data orchestration.

Keywords: HPC and cloud infrastructures · Software-defined infrastructures · Workflows

1 Introduction

The multiplicity of emerging memory and storage technologies as well as the evolution towards converged HPC and Cloud architectures requires that we rethink the way data is managed. We have seen for years the development of new types of memory and storage layers on large-scale systems to overcome the data movement bottleneck. Node-local storage, burst buffer nodes [10] or storage-class memory [8], to name a few, are now becoming widely available. Those new tiers

© Springer Nature Switzerland AG 2021
H. Jagode et al. (Eds.): ISC High Performance 2021 Workshops, LNCS 12761, pp. 346–357, 2021.
https://doi.org/10.1007/978-3-030-90539-2_23

come with their own characteristics, whether it is in terms of performance (capacity, bandwidth, latency) or in terms of access (byte or block addressable) [18].

On the other hand, applications and workflows are becoming dominated by data movement [14]. The ever-increasing resolution from scientific simulations as well as the diversity of workloads (such as Big Data analytics or AI for instance) tend to generate a growing amount of data that has to be properly handled to minimize its impact on performance. For example, the operational weather forecasting workflow at the European Centre for Medium-Range Weather Forecasts (ECMWF) currently generates around 30 TiB per time-critical one-hour forecast four times per day and estimates that this volume of data produced will continue increasing by 40% per year [19]. Data-locality requirements are expected to be a major driver for creating converged infrastructures based on HPC and Cloud technologies, which have to be highly flexible to support different workflows with a variety of requirements, in particular with respect to data handling, on top of a complex hardware architecture (see, e.g., the case of numerical weather prediction [6]).

Therefore, it is useful to develop data movement optimization techniques that can base their decisions on both the way data is accessed (pattern, I/O method) and the underlying hardware (memory and storage hierarchy). The variety in the former poses problems for systems software, and results in an inability to make use of the semantics of data-movement across the entire software stack. This constraint could be addressed with a unified data model. On the hardware side, while it is clear that user-software should not be concerned with non-portable hardware details, higher-level software making data movement decisions cannot do so without some form of locality information being available. An approach is to keep the locality information visible from the user through an abstracted, hierarchical model providing hardware information to any level of the software stack consistently.

In order to address the aforementioned challenges, we introduce Maestro, a memory- and data-aware middleware for data movement orchestration within workflows. Its central element is a pool of resources that each workflow component contributes to. The data, encapsulated in objects along with metadata, is submitted or requested to/from the pool while the data movements are handled and optimized by Maestro. In this document in particular, we present the core data model providing common and consistent access to multiple software layers regardless of the current location in the memory system.

The key contributions of our work are as follows:

- The design of a memory- and data-aware middleware
- A light-weight annotation- and object-based data model for manipulating user data
- An API for easily handling objects within and across applications and workflows

The outline of this paper is the following. In Sect. 6, we introduce the state of the art memory- and data-aware abstractions for optimized data movement. Then, we introduce in Sect. 2 the architecture of the Maestro middleware while we detail both our data abstraction and our data management API in Sect. 3. Section 4 is dedicated to an evaluation of our model based on our implementation of the Maestro middleware. Section 5 puts Maestro in a workflow perspective. We present early results obtained with a component of a major weather forecasting workflow. Finally, we conclude this paper while putting the emphasis on the limitations of our approach and our future work to resolve them.

2   Architecture

The Maestro middleware is built around the idea that applications should be empowered to delegate the access and movement of the data they provide and/or require to a smart middleware. This middleware should then reason about the system characteristics, data-movement cost, and workflow-level scheduling of data placement. At the same time, data should not be required to be allocated in Maestro-defined data structures. Instead, low-overhead annotation of existing data should be sufficient to inform the middleware and permit it to handle such application-defined and -managed data.

The Maestro middleware can be understood to provide its features at three different levels:

- As a data management layer for all memory tiers of a system inside a single process, e.g. across multiple threads, to use the abstraction of *core data objects* (CDOs, detailed in Sect. 3) to better structure data exchanges between program parts, across devices (e.g., GPUs), and to use convenient data transformations provided by the library.
- As a data management layer for all memory tiers of a system across multiple execution domains (compute nodes, processes, workload manager jobs, and/or allocations), including the coupling of applications by their CDO dependencies.
- As an enabler of a workflow-management solution, which enables the workflow manager to observe and influence data availability, demand, locality, and transfer without the applications knowing about the workflow they are embedded within.

To support these features, Maestro is based on an architecture centred around a CDO pool to (from) which CDOs can be offered (requested). CDOs are managed by the pool on basis of a system model that allows assessing the availability of storage resources or the costs of data movement as well as data transformations. The Maestro APIs are defined such that seamless access to various memory layers is supported.

This architecture supports the following usage patterns:

- Data objects (CDOs) are declared using a workflow-level unique name.
- Attributes (Maestro-specific or user-specific) can be added to each CDO (e.g. concerning lifetime).
- Data objects are offered to other participants of a workflow or requested from other participants via a conceptual pool.

– Participants eventually withdraw the object they contributed to the pool
– During the time an object is pooled, and only in this phase, Maestro takes full control over it; it may move, re-layout, redistribute, or copy the data as it sees fit across the entire union of resources available to the workflow, including the resources contributed by participants in the form of CDOs.

Maestro being a middleware, its use will be triggered by different means. The design is catering to these in a consistent way, so that the different usage scenarios will be able to interact seamlessly.

Application-level Usage of Maestro to Simplify Data Management – In this case a user application, typically a scientific application, will directly use `libmaestro` as a library, from C/C++/FORTRAN or a scripting language to take advantage of the memory management facilities and the feature to offer application data to unknown consumers, or request data from unknown sources. Other applications of this use case are compilation tools, compilers implementing advanced data layout or movement transformations, the implementation of tasking frameworks, or programming environments like OpenMP, MPI, or UPC.

Workflow-Controlled Usage of Maestro as a Coupling Tool – In this case a workflow description language is used to coordinate the execution of multiple applications, including resource provisioning. Translation to an execution schedule may occur statically, or dynamically with the workflow-manager or dedicated watcher components observing data-object creation and requests. Using object attributes, it is possible for the workflow manager to steer the behaviour of the Maestro middleware; using telemetry information, it is possible to implement feedback profiling or online re-scheduling or re-resourcing.

This is the usage scenario we believe will be most prevalent for end users: minimal application changes to annotate the core data objects required for coupling applications will be combined with a powerful workflow description, and execution strategies will be controlled and tuned at the workflow manager level, with the middleware in the position to minimize data transfer cost transparently.

On the core middleware side, automatic multi-application rendezvous is implemented with the help of a dedicated pool manager component using `libfabric`[1], and using a `protobuf`-based protocol[2], avoiding user selection of network interfaces, or administrative permissions/daemons.

The pool client component, which is implemented as an in-process Maestro core instance, is the interface between the application and the pool manager, which handles API calls that translate into pool protocol, that includes the CDO management API, and the subsequent network communication towards the pool manager. A four-step protocol, detailed in Sect. 3, specifies the way that an application and Maestro share ownership of data objects. Broadly speaking, "Give-Take" semantics describe applications giving data objects to Maestro pool and taking data objects back from Maestro pool. In case of "Take" on a CDO,

---

[1] http://libfabric.org/.
[2] https://developers.google.com/protocol-buffers.

be it in a multithreaded context or not, the first check the Maestro middleware performs is to look-up the presence of the "Taken" CDO in the local pool – the set of resources tied to the process. If it is indeed present, the "Take" can be satisfied promptly without wasting pool manager time. This also allows for a single application Maestro usage, without the need to launch a dedicated pool manager application.

CDO transport is decoupled from the pool operations, which means CDO "Take" resolution and layout metadata transfer are decoupled from the actual CDO content transfer. It makes the pool operations fast, and independent of CDO storage resource handling, transport methods, and layout transformations.

3   Core Middleware API

A core data object (CDO) combines all available information from both the hardware/storage side and the software/semantic side. As the most complete understanding that the middleware can obtain about a particular data object, the CDO is how applications communicate intentions with Maestro. The CDO typically represents real data and their physical location (if known).

CDOs possess two binary states that dictate how Maestro can interact with the CDO

1. ACCESSIBLE defines whether the contents of a CDO can be accessed via Maestro accessor functions (e.g. elemental/tile set/get).
2. POOLED defines whether a CDO has been given to the Maestro management pool or not.

These states are used to indicate whether it is the application or Maestro that is in control of the object. When a CDO is POOLED, Maestro may move, copy or transform the CDO. When a CDO is ACCESSIBLE, then its content and structure can be queried by an application, and a set of accessor methods allows setting and retrieval of the data. If an application creates a POOLED CDO, the application is relinquishing control of the CDO to the middleware.

CDOs encapsulate additional CDO information or metadata – otherwise referred to as attributes in Maestro core language. We will refer to the attributes proposed by default by Maestro core as *core attributes*, as opposed to *user-defined attributes*, which Maestro core supports via schemata, and typically correspond to domain-specific key-value metadata.

A CDO contains optional metadata related to its usage context, such as access relations and relations to other CDOs. Layout attributes are part of the core attributes as well, and allow users to add data semantics to Maestro – either manually or via a static-analysis tool that can infer these attributes and automatically inject them into the code – in order to take advantage of its automatic transformations.

An extra API is needed to allow users to add their specific metadata. In order to incorporate user-defined attributes within CDOs, Maestro core expects the user to provide a YAML schema that user-defined attribute operations will have to be compliant with, essentially consisting of a key-value list of possibly optional keys.

A four-step protocol specifies the way that an application and Maestro share ownership of data objects. Broadly speaking, "Give-Take" semantics describe applications giving data objects to Maestro pool and taking data objects back from Maestro pool. To accommodate the necessary differentiation between data producer and data consumer use cases, "give" and "take" have bilateral counterparts. The overall give-take API is composed of DECLARE, OFFER/REQUIRE, WITHDRAW/DEMAND/RETRACT, and DISPOSE. They represent four distinct steps in the lifetime of a CDO as detailed below, namely:

1. CDO declaration,
2. CDO pool injection,
3. CDO pool retraction,
4. CDO disposal.

In all of the operations, CDOs are referred to on the application side by an application-defined name at DECLARE time, and then referenced by a *handle* that corresponds to a (Maestro-internal) object identifier (UUID). Declaration is done through DECLARE and allows an application to describe a CDO to Maestro. The application then obtains a handle that will be needed for any future communication about this object. Maestro can, depending on the object attributes used in the declaration, allocate resources, prepare and plan for necessary transfers, schedule other workflow components, etc.

Pool injection is done through OFFER as a producer and REQUIRE as a consumer, the two GIVE variants that take CDO definitions from Maestro to the CDO Management Pool. After this operation the CDO content may not be accessed by the application. It is entirely up to Maestro where the CDO content resides or even whether its content is consistent with any previous or future state. Maestro can, depending on the object attributes used in the declaration, allocate resources, prepare and plan for necessary transfers, schedule other workflow components, etc. It can even use the CDO's storage allocation for other purposes.

Pool retraction is conveyed by WITHDRAW on the producer side, and DEMAND/ RETRACT on the consumer side. "Take" is the moment at which CDO ownership is transferred (back) to the application. This operation is blocking: Maestro may choose to delay all operations until this point (permitting lazy CDO handling semantics).

CDO disposal is done through DISPOSE, which is the inverse of the DECLARE operation. It indicates the end of the CDO's lifetime. If resources were provided by Maestro for the CDO they may be deallocated.

As part of Maestro's metadata support, it is also possible for a client to inspect the state and properties of a CDO, such as its attributes or whether it has been DECLAREDed or OFFERed to the pool. It also allows for user applications to retrieve CDOs based on their attributes.

4   Performance Evaluation

One of many applications that may greatly benefit from the Maestro middleware is numerical weather forecasting. The transfer between the data producers of a time-critical forecast run and the post-processing consumers is the bottleneck in many global numerical weather forecasting workloads, including the one run by ECMWF. Its global numerical model, the Integrated Forecast System (IFS), outputs its forecast data via a domain-specific I/O library, called `multio` [2], which is responsible for routing the data to multiple datasinks, such as the domain-specific object store FDB [19].

We have created a backend to the `multio` library that supports data output to the Maestro core middleware. To simulate the output process without having to run the actual forecast model, we have also built a tool, called `multio-hammer` on top of the `multio` library. It takes sample data as input and permutes it through the range of metadata required for a forecast run, thus outputting dummy data with various sets of metadata. This data is output through the full I/O stack used in normal operations. In this way it simulates the forecast model from the I/O perspective.

We aim to evaluate the metadata performance of the Maestro management API for producer-consumer applications and its support for domain-specific attributes. For this purpose, we have set up a test experiment that communicates all necessary metadata without initiating any data transfer. The experiment consists of: *a)* a user-defined YAML schema of weather-forecasting-specific attributes; *b)* a pool manager running on one node; *c)* a single consumer application running on another node, polling for OFFERed CDOs; and *d)* various numbers of `multio-hammer` instances, each running on a separate node and executing three forecast steps.

Each forecast step creates 22236 CDOs with unique metadata. We measure, for each step, the time it takes to create and inject the 22236 CDOs and the time it takes for the consumer application to inspect all CDOs for possible retrieval.

We have run these tests on a 60-node Atos Linux cluster with Infiniband interconnects and Slurm submission system. The machine is the prototype and test machine for the next set of HPC systems that will be used at ECMWF for both operations and research.

This setup primarily aims to verify part of the Maestro management API that interfaces with the data producers, although it also uses Maestro's metadata introspection to verify that communication between the producer and consumer based on metadata can be established via the pool manager. It measures the overhead of metadata operations and the interaction with the Maestro middleware API. For every CDO, a producer makes a CDO declaration, sets the core attributes, sets all the user-defined attributes, seals the CDO declaration, offers the CDO to the management pool and, finally, disposes of the CDO.

Figure 1a shows for a single time step the time in seconds to create all 22236 CDOs. The steps are grouped according to the number of different nodes on which an instance of the producer task `multio-hammer` is running.

In terms of the scaling of metadata operations, the time for the CDO creation per step goes from around 5s on single node to around 5–8 on 20 nodes. In other words, it takes at most 60% longer for the pool manager to process 20 times more data. These numbers roughly corresponds to an overhead of a few percent on top of the generation of mock data, which in turn is much faster than the generation of actual data.

Figure 1b shows the amounts of times it takes to detect (inspect) all CDOs produced (OFFERed) by the different number of producers. The measurements include the acknowledgements sent back to the pool manager that the event has been handled. The plot indicates linear relation in the range of 1–20 nodes, as expected. The results from the 20-node setup translate to creating more than 50000 CDOs per second.

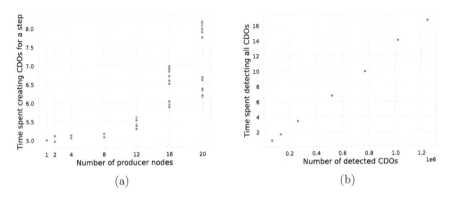

(a)   (b)

Fig. 1. Time in seconds to complete a single time step, creating 22236 CDOs per node (left), and to detect (inspect) all CDOs produced in three time steps (right)

5   Dynamic Provisioning and Workflow Support

To facilitate on-demand availability of storage resources to Maestro-enabled workflows, one tool has been developed for software-defined provisioning of storage resources. The concept of on-demand storage resources enables a workflow to deploy a specific data manager or parallel file system into the targeted infrastructure. To provide higher degree of performance, the selected data manager offers a specific feature , such as caching, that increases I/O throughput of the workflow. Moreover, the data manager is deployed on near-compute storage resources.

In a first proof-of-concept, it has been demonstrated how a parallel file system, e.g. BeeGFS, can be deployed on top of near-compute storage nodes, e.g. HPE/Cray DataWarp nodes, connected on the same network layer as the compute nodes [21]. Later, other data managers have been added to demonstrate the capability of the dynamic provisioning tool. Support of object stores using MinIO and databases using Cassandra have been added. The design of the dynamic provisioning enables an easy integration of other types of data managers by the usage of containers.

In the next proof-of-concept, we integrated the use of Maestro middleware and dynamically provided storage resources for workflows based on Pegasus. The on-demand data manager is deployed as a job by the batch scheduler installed on the infrastructure. As Pegasus is using a batch scheduler to execute workflow tasks, the dynamic provisioning is simply integrated as a new task in a Pegasus workflow. To create such task, a tool has been developed to semi-automatically augment workflow descriptions in Pegasus format with information and tasks that take care of dynamic resource provisioning and start-up of the Maestro middleware.

6   Related Work

Data access relies on two overlapping research topics: data model and API.

New data models have been proposed over the years as architectures have evolved [16,23]. HDF5 [7], for instance, provides namespace-like characteristics to parts of user data, but with an assumption that the data will be stored in a (potentially virtual) filesystem. With a similar idea but focusing on in-memory storage, Conduit [5] provides a hierarchical scheme for relating program data structures to the contents of DRAM, with no means to extend the hierarchy into the fileystem or to split between, for example, flash and DRAM. Another related project is ADIOS [13]. ADIOS is an abstraction layer that allows the user to annotate their I/O operations using an API, but through which a multitude of real I/O libraries, servers and transport layers can be activated. Finally, NetCDF [11] proposes an abstract data type in the form of arrays and an API to manipulate the data-structure. Maestro differs from those approaches in that Maestro is not only focused on I/O but data movement at all levels, I/O in the application, I/O in the workflow and data movement in the memory system.

Another area relevant to data-models is data stagers. One example is the DataStager [4] framework, which comprises a client library which provides the basic methods required for creating data objects and transporting them. At the crossroads of data models and data stagers, we find research works such as LABIOS [12]. LABIOS is a distributed I/O system enabling transparent asynchronous I/O on heterogeneous and elastic storage resources. Data is abstracted in a *label*, a structure made of a pointer to the data, pointers to functions for data transformation and metadata. Very similar concepts are realised in Maestro. However, our approach is more general and not limited to asynchronous data objects in the context of I/O. Another interesting work in that domain, by Tang et al. [20], proposes to encapsulate scientific data in an object-oriented manner.

ADIOS2 [9] and XIOS [15] also share some goals with Maestro. ADIOS2, the Adaptable Input Output System, focuses on asynchronous coupling of applications by user-defined variables, while XIOS is primarily used as an (XML) I/O-server build on top of the existing NetCDF data model for weather and climate simulations. Maestro, by contrast, puts major significance on extensive user-defined attribute handling, programmatic observability of availability of data objects, and awareness and handling of the memory hierarchy. Applications do not need to know how to communicate and transport to other applications in Maestro, and synchronization can be achieved by data objects. This permits easier composition of Maestro-enabled applications and workflows, including dynamically changing numbers of producers and consumers. Implementing an ADIOS2 Engine based on Maestro will be the topic of a future study. Similarly, it is conceptually possible to implement data transport in XIOS using Maestro instead of MPI.

Unity [3] also shares philosophical intentions with Maestro, being an attempt to unify the memory and storage spaces. Its focus is on data-intensive processing and mixed workloads and the close integration of HPC with data analytics. At a lower level, Perarneau et al. [17] and Unat et al. [22] have been working on low-level abstraction of data layout in memory. Work on SharP also brings a low-level abstraction layer for data management [24].

The Maestro design uses similar concepts to some of these projects - it uses HDF5-like namespacing, it abstracts I/O like ADIOS, it provides a unified memory/storage scheme like Unity and it also provides common data models to different components. However, while many of the mentioned projects are an explicit API, Maestro differs from each of the data models in that it is a middleware layer designed to be used in a variety of environments. It provides an API but can be used in other ways and users can avoid using any explicit calls to the Maestro library if preferred. Maestro therefore has the potential to provide better legacy support than most of these libraries, but also serve as a powerful foundation for new software and frameworks.

7   Conclusion

Taking into account the movements of data on current and future architectures is crucial. The increasing amount of data generated by scientific applications and workflows is concomitant with a relative decline in I/O performance on supercomputers. However, the HPC software stack was not designed with this in mind.

In this paper, we present the data model and API at the base of the Maestro middleware whose goal is to orchestrate data movement. In particular, we detail a model based on the encapsulation of data and metadata into objects as well as its data-access semantics. The preliminary results are encouraging and confirm our approach. A test experiment based on the production of weather-forecast data has shown that the Maestro middleware is able to handle the injection of more than 50000 CDOs/s (together with their domain-specific metadata) on a 20-node setup. This represents an overhead of just a few percent on top of the generation of mock data, which we deem on track to meet the future objective of scaling to an operational configuration.

For the metadata communication presented in this paper, libfabric high-speed interconnect has already been used. Work is ongoing to implement a Maestro

I/O (MIO) interface as an abstraction layer to different object store technologies. It initially focuses on Cortx [1], later it will be extended to Ceph using the RADOS [25] service.

References

1. CORTX object store. https://github.com/Seagate/cortx
2. MultIO - a multiplexing I/O library. https://github.com/ecmwf/multio
3. Jones, T., et al.: Unity: Unified memory and file space. In: Ross '17 Proceedings of the 7th International Workshop on Runtime and Operating Systems for Supercomputers Ross 2017, article no. 6 (2017). https://doi.org/10.1145/3095770.3095776
4. Abbasi, H., Wolf, M., Eisenhauer, G., Klasky, S., Schwan, K., Zheng, F.: Datastager: Scalable data staging services for petascale applications. Cluster Comput. **13**, 277–290 (2009). https://doi.org/10.1007/s10586-010-0135-6
5. Aspesi, G., Bai, J., Deese, R., Shin, L.: Havery mudd 2014–2015 computer science conduit clinic final report (2015). https://doi.org/10.2172/1184132. https://www.osti.gov/biblio/1184132-havery-mudd-computer-science-conduit-clinic-final-report
6. Bauer, P., Dueben, P.D., Hoefler, T., Quintino, T., Schulthess, T.C., Wedi, N.P.: The digital revolution of earth-system science. Nat. Comput. Sci. **1**(2), 104–113 (2021)
7. Folk, M., Heber, G., Koziol, Q., Pourmal, E., Robinson, D.: An overview of the hdf5 technology suite and its applications. In: Proceedings of the EDBT/ICDT 2011 Workshop on Array Databases, pp. 36–47. AD '11, Association for Computing Machinery, New York, NY, USA (2011). https://doi.org/10.1145/1966895.1966900
8. Freitas, R.F., Wilcke, W.W.: Storage-class memory: the next storage system technology. IBM J. Res. Dev. **52**(4.5), 439–447 (2008)
9. Godoy, W.F., et al.: Adios 2: The adaptable input output system. A framework for high-performance data management. SoftwareX **12**, 100561 (2020). https://doi.org/10.1016/j.softx.2020.100561, http://www.sciencedirect.com/science/article/pii/S2352711019302560
10. Henseler, D., Landsteiner, B., Petesch, D., Wright, C., Wright, N.J.: Architecture and design of Cray DataWarp. In: Proceedings of 2016 Cray User Group (CUG) Meeting (2016)
11. Jianwei, L., et al.: Parallel netCDF: A high-performance scientific I/O interface. In: SC '03: Proceedings of the 2003 ACM/IEEE Conference on Supercomputing, pp. 39–39 (2003)
12. Kougkas, A., Devarajan, H., Lofstead, J., Sun, X.H.: Labios: A distributed label-based I/O system. In: Proceedings of the 28th International Symposium on High-Performance Parallel and Distributed Computing, pp. 13–24. HPDC '19, Association for Computing Machinery, New York, NY, USA (2019). https://doi.org/10.1145/3307681.3325405
13. Liu, Q., et al.: Hello adios: The challenges and lessons of developing leadership class I/O frameworks. Concurrency Comput. Pract. Experience **26**(7), 1453–1473 (2014)
14. Luu, H., et al.: A multiplatform study of I/O behavior on petascale supercomputers. In: Proceedings of the 24th International Symposium on High-Performance Parallel and Distributed Computing, pp. 33–44. HPDC '15, Association for Computing Machinery, New York, NY, USA (2015). https://doi.org/10.1145/2749246.2749269

15. Meurdesoif, Y.: XIOS current developments and roadmap (2020). https://forge.ipsl.jussieu.fr/ioserver/raw-attachment/wiki/WikiStart/XIOS-ROADMAP-15102020.pdf
16. Otstott, D., Zhao, M., Williams, S., Ionkov, L., Lang, M.: A foundation for automated placement of data. In: 2019 IEEE/ACM Fourth International Parallel Data Systems Workshop (PDSW), pp. 50–59 (2019)
17. Perarnau, S., Videau, B., Denoyelle, N., Monna, F., Iskra, K., Beckman, P.: Explicit data layout management for autotuning exploration on complex memory topologies. In: 2019 IEEE/ACM Workshop on Memory Centric High Performance Computing (MCHPC), pp. 58–63 (2019)
18. Ross, R., et al.: Storage systems and I/O: Organizing, storing, and accessing data for scientific discovery. Report for the DOE ASCR Workshop on Storage Systems and I/O (2018). https://doi.org/10.2172/1491994
19. Smart, S., Quintino, T., Raoult, B.: A high-performance distributed object-store for exascale numerical weather prediction and climate. In: Proceedings of the Platform for Advanced Scientific Computing Conference, pp. 1–11 (2019)
20. Tang, H., et al.: Toward scalable and asynchronous object-centric data management for HPC. In: 2018 18th IEEE/ACM International Symposium on Cluster, Cloud and Grid Computing (CCGRID), pp. 113–122 (2018)
21. Tessier, F., Martinasso, M., Chesi, M., Klein, M., Gila, M.: Dynamic provisioning of storage resources: a case study with burst buffers. In: 2020 IEEE International Parallel and Distributed Processing Symposium Workshops (IPDPSW), pp. 1027–1035 (2020). https://doi.org/10.1109/IPDPSW50202.2020.00173
22. Unat, D., et al.: Tida: high-level programming abstractions for data locality management. In: Kunkel, J.M., Balaji, P., Dongarra, J. (eds.) High Performance Computing, pp. 116–135. Springer International Publishing, Cham (2016). https://doi.org/10.1007/978-3-319-41321-1_7
23. Unat, D., Shalf, J., Hoefler, T., Schulthess, T., (Editors), A.D., Besta, M., et al.: Programming Abstractions for Data Locality. Technical report (2014)
24. Venkata, M.G., Aderholdt, F., Parchman, Z.: Sharp: towards programming extreme-scale systems with hierarchical heterogeneous memory. In: 2017 46th International Conference on Parallel Processing Workshops (ICPPW), pp. 145–154 (2017)
25. Weil, S.A., Leung, A.W., Brandt, S.A., Maltzahn, C.: Rados: a scalable, reliable storage service for petabyte-scale storage clusters. In: Proceedings of the 2nd International Workshop on Petascale Data Storage: Held in Conjunction with Supercomputing'07, pp. 35–44 (2007)

Second International Workshop on Monitoring and Operational Data Analytics

2nd International Workshop on Monitoring and Data Analytics (MODA21)

Florina Ciorba[1], Utz-Uwe Haus[2], Nicolas Lachiche[3], and Daniele Tafani[4]

[1] University of Basel, Switzerland
[2] HPE HPC/AI EMEA Research Lab, Switzerland
[3] University of Strasbourg, France
[4] Nvidia, Germany

1 Introduction

The Exascale computing race poses significant challenges for the collection and analysis of the vast amount of data that current pre- and future Exascale HPC systems will produce, in terms of increasing complexity of the machines, scalability of the adopted monitoring solution, minimizing monitoring intrusiveness and maximizing the effectiveness of inference and interpretability driven by the acquired data.

After a very successful first installment of the International Workshop on Monitoring and Operational Data Analytics in 2021, we were excited to organize the 2nd ISC-HPC International Workshop on Monitoring and Operational Data Analytics (MODA21).

The goal of the MODA workshop series is to provide a venue for sharing insights into current trends in MODA for HPC systems and data centres, identify potential gaps, and offer an outlook into the future of the involved fields of high performance computing, databases, machine learning, and possible solutions for upcoming Exascale systems. To this end, we solicited contributions related to:

- Currently envisioned solutions and practices for monitoring systems at data centers and HPC sites. Of particular focus are operational data collection mechanisms i) covering different system levels, from building infrastructure sensor data to CPU-core performance metrics, and ii) targeting different end-users, from system administrators to application developers and computational scientists, respectively.
- Effective strategies for analyzing and interpreting the collected operational data. Of articular focus are different visualization approaches and machine learning-based techniques, potentially inferring knowledge of the system behavior and allowing for the realization of a proactive control loop.

Topics not targeted by the MODA workshop series include: new solutions proposed in the context of application performance modeling and/or application performance analysis tools; and novel contributions in the area of compiler analysis, debugging, programming models, and/or sustainability of scientific software.

While MODA is becoming common practice at various international HPC sites, each site adopts a different, insular approach, rarely adopted in production environments and mostly limited to the visualization of the system and building infrastructure metrics for health check purposes. In this regard, we observe a gap between the collection of operational data and its meaningful and effective analysis and exploitation, which prevents the closing of the feedback loop between the monitored HPC system, its operation, and its end-users.

Under these premises, the **goals of the MODA21 workshop** can then be summarized as:

1. Gather and share knowledge and establish a common ground within the international community with respect to best practices in monitoring and operational data analytics.
2. Discuss future strategies and alternatives for MODA, potentially improving existing solutions and envisioning a common baseline approach in HPC sites and data centers.
3. Establish a debate on the usefulness and applicability of AI techniques on collected operational data for optimizing the operation of production systems (e.g. for practices such as predictive maintenance, runtime optimization, optimal resource allocation and scheduling).

MODA21 offered a forum for invited presentations, technical contributions, and discussions on:

- State-of-the-practice methods, tools, techniques in monitoring at various HPC sites.
- Solutions for monitoring and analysis of operational data that work very well on large- to extreme-scale systems with a large number of users.
- Solutions that have proven limitations in terms of efficiency of operational data collection in real-time or in terms of the quality of the collected data.
- Opportunities and challenges of using machine learning methods for efficient monitoring and analysis of operational data.
- Integration of monitoring and analysis practices into production system software (energy and resource management) and runtime systems (scheduling and resource allocation).
- Explicit gaps between operational data collection, processing, effective analysis, highly useful exploitation, and propose new approaches to closing these gaps for the benefit of improving HPC and data centres planning, operations, and research.
- Other monitoring and operational data analysis challenges and approaches (data storage, visualisation, integration into system software, adoption).
- Means to identify misuse, intentional or unintentional, of resources, and methods to mitigate the effects of these: taking automatic steps to contain the effects of one application/job/user allocation on others, supporting users to identify causes for the misbehavior of their application, linking to intrusion detection and safe multitenancy.
- Concepts to integrate MODA into the system design at all levels, including dedicated hardware components, middleware features, and tool support that make "monitoring by default" a viable option without sacrificing performance.
- FAIR data practices, including sharing of monitoring workflows and tools across sites while ensuring compliance with GDPR regulations and user access agreements.

2 Workshop Organisation

The workshop organising and program committees consist of academics and researchers at leading HPC sites and in industry. The workshop is unique to the European HPC arena being the among the few to address the topic of monitoring and operational data analytics for improving HPC operations and research.

Organising Committee

Florina Ciorba	University of Basel, Switzerland
Utz-Uwe Haus	HPE HPC/AI EMEA Research Lab, Switzerland
Nicolas Lachiche	University of Strasbourg, France
Daniele Tafani	NVIDIA, Germany

Program Committee

Andrea Bartolini	University of Bologna, Italy
Daniele Cesarini	CINECA, Italy
Ann Gentile	Sandia National Laboratories, USA
Thomas Ilsche	Technische Universität Dresden, Germany
Jacques-Charles Lafoucriere	CEA, France
Erwin Laure	TU Munich & Max Planck Computing and Data Facility, Germany
Filippo Mantovani	BSC, Spain
Diana Moise	Cray/HPE, Switzerland
Alesio Netti	Leibniz Supercomputing Centre, Garching, Germany
Melissa Romanus	NERSC Lawrence Berkeley National Laboratory, USA
Dominik Strassel	Fraunhofer ITWM Kaiserslautern, Germany
Ugo Varetto	Pawsey Supercomputing Centre, Australia
Keiji Yamamoto	RIKEN, Japan
Aleš Zamuda	University of Maribor, Slovenia

Technical Program

The reviewing of the submitted papers was balanced among the program committee members and ensured a high quality of the reviews. Based on the submissions and their reviews, two papers were accepted and presented at MODA20:

- *An Explainable model for Fault Detection in HPC Systems*, by Martin Molan, Andrea Borghesi, Francesco Beneventi, Massimiliano Guarrasi, and Andrea Bartolini
- *An Operational Data Collecting and Monitoring Platform for Fugaku: System Overview and Case Study in the Prelaunch Service Period*, by Masaaki Terai, Keiji Yamamoto, Shin'Ichi Miura, and Fumiyoshi Shoji

MODA21 was held as an online half-day workshop with a balanced mix between technical paper presentations, keynote and invited talks, and a discussion panel. The full live program is available on the MODA21 website[1].

The workshop debuted with the live keynote address by Dr. Ann Gentile and Dr. Jim Brandt (Sandia National Laboratories, USA) with the title *Integrating Systems Operations into CoDesign* followed by a lively questions and answers (Q&A) session.

The workshop continued with live presentations of the two contributed paper (see above), that initiated an interactive real time exchange of questions and answers via the Zoom chat functionality. The last session consisted of three invited talks:

- *The KrakenMare Exascale Monitoring Toolkit*, by Torsten Wilde (HPE)
- *Monitoring and Operational Data Analytics from a User Perspective at First EuroCC HPC Vega Supercomputer and Nation-wide in Slovenia*, by Aleš Zamuda (University of Maribor, Slovenia)
- *Framework for deploying HPC ODA*, by Natalie Bates (Energy Efficiency HPC Working Group)

MODA21 was concluded with a panel discussion on *Monitoring and Operational Data Analysis: past, present, and future* which very early turned in to a free-form discussion with the entire audience.

3 Conclusion

The MODA21 presentations and discussions show the broad scope of topics addressed, and that some aspects warrant significantly more attention:

- training of next generation workforce on monitoring issues
- challenges in incentivizing and opening access to monitoring data
- opportunity in tightening communication between users and system operators (or administrators) to support the transition from hindsight to insight and, finally, to foresight
- data collected with data analytic method in mind
- need for holistic monitoring
- need common data format(s) to enable analytic models and algorithms to be exchangeable, portable, and applicable across systems
- need for data analytic methods that work in general cases
- need for legitimate advances in analytics that go beyond toy examples
- coding challenge for MODA

The *coding challenge for MODA* involves curating data sets and defining concrete challenges to implement analytics thereupon. One goal of such a challenge would be to understand how different data sources or different data formats influence the analytics that can be performed. Additional goals include understanding the best way to prepare the data (how to insert or annotate events) to increase their likelihood of being

---

[1] https://moda21.sciencesconf.org/resource/page/id/4

identified with analytic methods. In defining such a coding challenge for MODA, care must be taken to understand what should be found by the analysis challenge. This requires well-defined questions and appropriate data sets. We believe that realizing such a coding challenge is highly valuable, can propel the community forward, as well as attract and engage young talent.

We hope that these and other aspects will figure prominently in submissions to the next edition(s) of the MODA workshop series.

An Operational Data Collecting and Monitoring Platform for Fugaku: System Overviews and Case Studies in the Prelaunch Service Period

Masaaki Terai$^{(\boxtimes)}$, Keiji Yamamoto, Shin'ichi Miura, and Fumiyoshi Shoji

RIKEN Center for Computational Science, 7–1–26 Minatojima-minami-machi, Chuo-ku, Kobe, Hyogo 650-0047, Japan
{teraim,keiji.yamamoto,shinichi.miura,shoji}@riken.jp

Abstract. After a seven-year long-term development process, the supercomputer Fugaku was officially launched as the successor to the K computer in March 2021. During this development process, we upgraded various system components and the data center infrastructure for official service in Fugaku. It was also necessary to upgrade the K computer operational data collection/monitoring platform for use in Fugaku. As a result, we are now in the process of developing and deploying an operational data collection/monitoring platform based on a three-tier pipeline architecture. In the first stage, the HPC system produces various types of log/metric data that are used to identify and monitor troubleshooting issues. Additionally, several thousand sensors operated by the building management system (BMS) generate metrics for power supply and cooling equipment. In the second stage, we aggregate the data into time-series databases and then visualize the results via a dashboard in the third stage. The dashboard provides an interactive interface for multiple data of the HPC system and data center infrastructure. During the course of this project, we resolved some issues found in the previous K computer platform. By using the redundant cores of the A64FX to allocate agents, it was determined that the new platform takes less than 20 s to collect metrics from over 150k compute nodes and finally write them to persistent storage. This paper introduces the design of the system architecture and reports on the current state of the platform renewal project, and provides overviews of two use cases encountered during the prelaunch service period.

Keywords: Operational data · Monitoring · Log · Metrics · Dashboard · Open-source software · Prometheus · Elasticsearch · ODA · HPC

1 Introduction

A modern exascale supercomputer system depends on various information technology (IT) component types (e.g., servers, storage, and network systems) and

© Springer Nature Switzerland AG 2021
H. Jagode et al. (Eds.): ISC High Performance 2021 Workshops, LNCS 12761, pp. 365–377, 2021.
https://doi.org/10.1007/978-3-030-90539-2_24

facility equipment types (e.g., power supply and cooling systems), and each system component constantly produces a huge number of time-series log/metric data regardless of whether or not it has failure possibilities. While those log/metric data are most often used by operators/vendors to monitor the system behavior and identify issues during troubleshooting, such data have significant potential as sources for insights into supercomputing/data center operations. Accordingly, as far back as the startup of the K computer operations, we focused on the development of an operational data collection and monitoring platform [27] that would allow us to exploit as well as monitor the massive data produced during our operations. As applications of that platform, we launched various projects and have reported their results [15, 18, 19, 25].

Fugaku [8], the successor of the K computer, is an exascale supercomputer system. The basic system architecture concept, except for the microprocessor, is based on enhancements to the K computer design. The number of compute nodes with Arm-based microprocessors has reached 158,976 nodes, and over 500 PFLOPS have been achieved in the TOP500 benchmark [9]. On the other hand, we adopted a retrofit approach for the facility upgrades. While part of the facility equipment (including the electrical transformers, a heat exchanger, and a chiller with a cooling tower) for the power supply and cooling system was upgraded to handle 30 MW-scale power consumption, most of the K computer facility equipment was integrated into the Fugaku operation without major enhancements. Due to the total growth in power consumption, a rapid number of job submissions can cause megawatts level power consumption fluctuations that could result in temporary cooling capacity shortages. Since maintaining stable operations of both the HPC system and the data center infrastructure is imperative, it was necessary to implement a comprehensive monitoring system of the entire center in order to fully understand the energy usage issue.

The replacement process resulted in the need to develop a new operational data collection and monitoring platform that was created almost from scratch. In particular, our aim was to address the following issues that had been identified in the K computer collection and monitoring platform.

- In the K computer operation, we installed `fluentd` as an agent to collect log and metric data. However, `fluentd`, which is written in Ruby, consumes excessive amounts of memory.
- Due to the need to prevent performance interference, we could not install collector tools (agents) in the compute nodes of the K computer.
- `ZABBIX`, which was used in the K computer operation, is limited to 30k metrics per second due to a bottleneck in the relational database management system (RDBMS). There could have been an issue in terms of sampling frequency in the environment of Fugaku, which has more than 150k compute nodes.
- The building management system (BMS) for the facility is a subsystem of the collection system. (Due to the need to avoid expensive developments, we developed the platform separately.) However, the overhead of the loading metrics from the BMS subsystem will need to be considered if we are to achieve a near-real-time system.

The platform development is an ongoing project. Based on the issues above, we have attempted to improve the previous platform implementations and have resolved several technical issues in the process. In this paper, we report the current state of the project along with two use cases involving the platform.

- To reduce memory usage, we use `logstash` and `filebeat` instead of `fluentd` in the Fugaku environment.
- Since Fugaku's microprocessor has redundant cores (assistant cores) in a node, we can assign collector agents to the cores without any interference to compute cores of the node and can monitor precise states than the K computer operations.
- We use `Prometheus` instead of `Zabbix`. `Prometheus` can collect up to 1M metrics per second. Finally, the platform can collect data from over 150k compute nodes and write them to persistent storage within 20 s.

The rest of the paper is organized as follows: Sect. 2 presents related work, while Sect. 3 provides the platform renewal project state, including an overview of data sources from the HPC system and data center infrastructure, and the architecture design of the operational data collection and monitoring platform. Section 4 describes use cases involving a dashboard. In Sect. 5, we present a summary and discuss our future work.

2   Related Works

For large-scale IT systems, a reliable monitoring and reporting system is essential for operating and identifying problems during troubleshooting processes. Historically, such monitoring is performed within the context of surveillance. Today, the monitoring processes cover numerous targets, including servers, network devices, storage, applications, and peripheral infrastructure. Meanwhile, as part of efforts to obtain operation/business insights, some data centers have begun considering analytics based on their collection and monitoring platforms [13,16,22]. Within the context of high-performance computing, some supercomputing centers now use Operational Data Analytics (ODA) [11,12,17] as a formalization process, and most ODA monitoring systems consider not only HPC systems but also peripheral data center infrastructures. Those consolidating platforms often focus on energy efficiency.

In terms of tools, those ODA platforms employ various types of open-source software [1–7]. Along with their pipeline mechanisms, those are roughly classified as collectors, message brokers, time-series databases, dashboards (visualization), and analysis tools. In ODA platforms, the time-series database plays a key role in enabling mass data collection with low overheads. One of the tools, `Prometheus`, is an open-source monitoring/reporting toolkit that is widely used in monitoring processes that can integrate a third-party database depending on the system. Some ODA projects outside the scope of this paper have used or attempted `Apache Cassandra`, `KairosDB`, `influxDB`, and `Victoria Metrics` [21]. Since dashboard systems also provide interactive visualization environments, some supercomputing centers have attempted to adopt dashboards into their sites and have reported their results [10, 23, 24].

3   Operational Data Collection and Monitoring Platform in the Fugaku Environment

The development of the operational data collection and monitoring platform is a relatively new project among all the projects in Fugaku and is an ongoing project. In this section, we mention the overview of data sources and the architecture design in the platform.

3.1   Overview of Data Sources

In the Fugaku environment, there are two types of data sources available. One data group is derived from the HPC system, including compute nodes, boot I/O nodes, peripheral nodes (e.g., login nodes, pre/post nodes, and so on), storage (e.g., a Lustre-based parallel file system), and network devices (e.g., switches, routers, and firewalls). The other group is derived from the data center infrastructure, including the power supply and cooling equipment. The details of these data sources are explained below.

HPC System. Firstly, we begin with a brief overview of the Fugaku HPC system and peripheral IT equipment. Fugaku employs Arm-based A64FX processors [20] enhanced to fit into the current trends of various HPC applications. Each microprocessor has four core memory groups (CMGs), each of which integrates 13 cores, an L2-cache shared by those cores, a memory controller, and a ring bus network on a chip. Of the 13 cores, one works as a redundant (or assistant) core that is used for multi-purpose operating processes. A core memory group (CMG) directly connects a single second-generation High Bandwidth Memory (HBM2) unit. Each CMG can access external HBM2 units belonging to the other CMGs of the processor via the ring bus network. The A64FX processor has a hardware performance monitoring unit (PMU) to measure dynamic program behavior (e.g., number of CPU cycles, number of instructions, floating-point operations, and cache misses) [14]. These metrics are useful not only for performance profiling tools but also for our operations to survey workloads' behaviors.

Fugaku consists of 432 racks with 158,976 compute nodes. By connecting the compute nodes with the high-speed interconnect (Tofu interconnect D), Fugaku can be organized as a single huge system to provide exascale computing resources. In addition, there are various peripheral servers, including login nodes with x86/Arm-based microprocessors, directory service nodes with Lightweight Directory Access Protocol (LDAP), job scheduler nodes, pre/post nodes with a graphics processing unit (GPU)/large-capacity memory, various management servers, and network devices.

In addition, Fugaku uses a Lustre-based parallel file system as with the K computer. During the K computer operations, the global file storage system shared a portion of the compute racks installed in the computer room, which degraded system maintainability. In contrast, the Fugaku storage system has been installed in the data storage room and can be operated separately from the compute system. The storage capacity is up to 150 PB available in total. At the time this paper was written, we divided the storage into six file volumes. In terms of monitoring, the storage system consists of many servers, including management service (MGS), metadata service (MDS), object storage service (OSS) servers, and so on. These are monitoring targets in our operation.

To monitor the system's behavior and keep operators informed, the HPC system produces a huge number of log data and metrics. Most of the log data (e.g., syslog messages, job scheduler logs, parallel file system logs, and audit logs) are recorded by servers. Additionally, some of the network devices generate syslog messages. Generally, these are time-series event data in a text-based semi-/unstructured format. The servers also measure various metrics (e.g., load average, network transfer bytes, memory usage, microprocessors and board temperature, Self-Monitoring, Analysis and Reporting Technology (S.M.A.R.T.), and electric power consumption on power supply units). The PMU metrics are also classified in this metric type. Further, network devices generate Simple Network Management Protocol (SNMP) messages. Generally, these metrics are time-series data provided in a scalar/vector numerical structured format.

Data Center Infrastructure. Our supercomputing center has dedicated facilities for power supply and cooling systems. In the Fugaku development project, while the IT equipment was mostly built from scratch, the concept of power supply and cooling systems resembles the previous design of the K computer and reuse most of the installed equipment without additional major enhancements. In the section below, we introduce the facility overviews.

As well as the K computer, Fugaku uses two-type energy sources—electricity purchased from a public utility company and energy produced by the gas turbine power generators. The new HPC system is designed to consume electricity up to 37 MW, which is approximately three times more than the K computer. Prior to the Fugaku installation, part of the facility components (e.g., transformers, a heat exchanger, chillers and cooling towers, and a thermal storage tank) had been enhanced to address the increased power consumption. Accordingly, we used a retrofit approach and reused many facilities installed for the K computer. For instance, we continue to use the co-generation system (CGS) without additional enhancements in the Fugaku operation.

Like the HPC system, the data center infrastructure produces various types of metrics (e.g., air/water temperature, pump flow rate, generated electric power, and purchased electric power from a public utility company) and miscellaneous log data. Basically, the log data volume is smaller than the metrics. All the metrics in the facility are collected by the building management system (BMS), which works as a subsystem of the operational data collection and monitoring system. When we enhanced the facility, we also added sensors to the facility equipment at the same time. At the time of this writing, the number of sensors had reached five thousand.

3.2   System Architecture

The operational data collection/monitoring platform consists of a three-tier data pipeline, as shown in Fig. 1. The first tier is data sources, including the HPC system and the data center infrastructure, as discussed in Subsect. 3.1. The second tier is a data lake used to store the log/metric data in the databases (e.g., time-series databases, distributed full-text databases, traditional transactional databases, and a Portable Operating System Interface (POSIX) file system). The third tier, which is the end of the pipeline, provides visualization/business intelligence (BI) tools that can be used to exploit insights. The platform began operations during the Fugaku prelaunch service period. In the remainder of this section, the current state of the system architecture is explained.

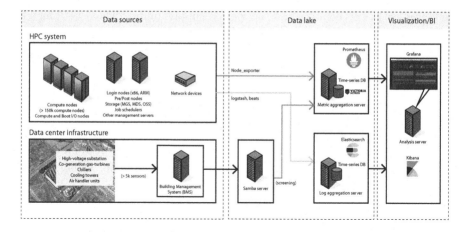

Fig. 1. Overview of the collection and monitoring platform.

Data Collection System. In the data lake tier, the data collection system uses two-type databases depending on the data type. For the metric data, we use a time-series database (TSDB) provided by `Prometheus` [6] as an open-source monitoring/alerting tool. For the log data, we use `Elasticsearch` [1] with `logstash` [4] as a data aggregation tool. To form the pipeline between the data sources and the data lake tier, we installed `Prometheus exporter` to serve as a data collection tool for each compute node and the boot I/O nodes. This tool is a shipper agent that captures metrics and sends them to the `Prometheus` server. Additionally, the exporter has been installed in other servers, including the login nodes, pre/post nodes, and the MGS/MDS/OSS servers. On top of those, we installed `filebeat` in boot I/O nodes and the abovementioned servers. That is also a shipper agent in front of `logstash`.

During K computer operations, we could not deploy any data collection tools in the compute nodes because the microprocessor did not have any redundant cores that could be used to assign collectors. In the context of the HPC, performance is the primary concern. Therefore, we needed the ability to prevent a kind of performance interference (e.g., operating system jitter) that can be caused by the collectors running as a background daemon. In Fugaku, this issue was resolved by using the redundant cores.

Monitoring System. To monitor and visualize the time-series data stored in the databases, we use `Grafana` [2] and `Kibana` [3] as front-end tools for `Prometheus` and `Elasticsearch`, respectively. Both tools have fancy dashboards that allow users to customize their interfaces to meet specific requirements depending on the operators.

`Grafana` provides various graphical interfaces (e.g., line graphs, stacked graphs, heatmaps, tables, and so on). Also, `Kibana` has similar features that can be used to visualize log data. Both are managed via graphical user interfaces.

`Grafana` and `Kibana` focus on providing effective monitoring and reporting environments for troubleshooting. While those backend databases have derived query languages for use when searching data, the query languages impose some initial learning costs. In the K computer operations, we used `redash` [7] in addition to `Grafana` and `Kibana` to visualize metrics and data. `Kibana` is used to search data with the standard SQL language, which seems to be easier to learn than domain-specific languages. However, at the time of this writing, we have only deployed `Grafana` and `Kibana` for visualization, and our `Kibana` environment is not yet mature enough for use in practical operations because it still requires additional dashboard customization. Also, we believe that `Jupyter` [5] may be a more appropriate tool for more general users. Those general analysis tools (e.g. `redash`, `Jupyter`, and so on) in the third tier are outside the scope of this paper.

4   Results

In this section, we report on the implementation of monitoring dashboards with `Grafana` and introduce two use cases.

4.1   Case 1: The Integrated Monitoring Platform for the HPC System and the Data Center Infrastructure

Modern supercomputer systems require a complicated power supply and cooling facility management as with common plant operations. Hence, facility operators are required to monitor the power consumption of the entire center area 24 h a day, seven days a week, and efficiently manage CGS operations to ensure backup electricity available for the IT equipment and to supply steam for the chillers as needed. From the facility operators' perspective, the amount of electricity supplied to the IT equipment is strongly dependent on workload behavior (e.g., memory throughput, flops, and communication frequency among compute nodes). While the job scheduler may play a key role in controlling workloads running simultaneously depending on the available electricity, it does not have a feature that can create supply-and-demand balances between the available electricity and the workloads. Accordingly, at the time of this writing, facility operators used the BMS that was installed at almost the same time the facility began operations to manage the power supply and cooling systems. That BMS was implemented on the intranet with access restrictions for security reasons. However, IT equipment operators also need online information regarding facility operations.

Based on the background, to integrate both the IT equipment information and the facility information, we implemented a combined dashboard. In Fig. 2, we show a portion of the facility metrics extracted from the dashboard, which were measured during the prelaunch service period that finished in early March 2021. The missing values in the middle of November were the result of planned maintenance. The dashboard can show the power consumption for the entire center as well as for Fugaku. Except for early October, the average power consumption was about 17.8 MW because the period of early October had a benchmarking campaign (e.g., HPL). Besides, the dashboard can visualize detailed power consumption (not shown in the figure) for each group of racks installed in the computer room. It can also show electricity supplied from the two CGSs and the public utility company. Although, the amount of purchased electricity was dominant in the total. Also, we confirmed that the switching operations with two CGSs within a certain period of time. That operations seem to extend the lifetime of the equipment and make it easier to maintain. Additionally, power usage effectiveness (PUE) is commonly used as a comparable metric to evaluate energy efficiency operations in data centers. Based on the results shown in the figure, the average PUE is about 1.2. Finally, we confirmed that all the results are consistent with the related study [26].

4.2   Case 2: Monitoring Overloading Jobs on the Lustre-Based Parallel File System

As with the K computer, Fugaku has a Lustre-based parallel distributed file system allocated to the home and working directories used by workloads. Although the Lustre-based file system is designed for use in large-scale parallel computing systems, it has encountered various issues when dealing with specific I/O patterns. For example, when a number of workloads write to a single file, those flooding I/Os often cause blocking responses or do not complete the processing due to the overloading because those transactions are serialized per file. Ideally, issues of this type would be resolved by modifying the user program itself. However, it is currently difficult to prevent the situation, and they are generally considered to be accidental issues. From the operators' perspective, it is

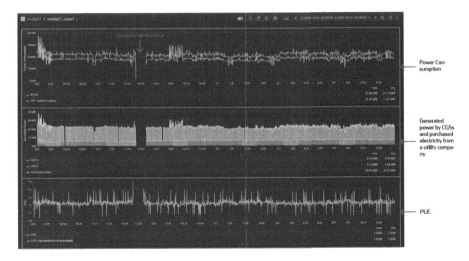

Fig. 2. A screenshot of electricity supply-and-demand and PUE during the prelaunch service period. The topmost graph (upper red box) shows power consumption for R-CCS as a whole and for the HPC system (only Fugaku). The middle graph (middle red box) shows the power generated by two CGSs and the purchased power from a public utility company. The bottommost graph (lower red box) shows the PUE and the exponential moving average of the PUE.

clear that the ability to detect the workload behavior and thus prevent accidental situations where file system overloading can result in system-wide failures is required. As shown in Figs. 3 and 4, we use the dashboard to monitor the Lustre-based file system state. Figure 3 describes OST write I/O performance using dd with parameters: bs=1M, count=768, oflag=direct. dd is issued at between 150 and 300-second intervals, avoiding simultaneous execution to the OSTs to be monitored.

The dashboard can output in CSV format. Tables 1 and 2 show sorted lists converted from a CSV file regarding the write I/O throughput for the OSTs of a volume (vol00004) shown in the Fig. 3. For instance, for a slow and fluctuated OST, it's not necessarily a malfunction, but it is likely to have some sort of problem. In this case, OST16 is appeared in both tables. While we showed that the case focuses on large fluctuations in Table 2, it is assumed that a case with small fluctuations can also be used for identifying issues. In addition, Fig. 4 describes MGS/MDS/OSS nodes performance. These dashboards are useful for finding and isolating the problem in operations.

5   Summary and Future Work

As we move toward bringing Fugaku into official service, we can report that most of the HPC system and a portion of the data center infrastructure have been upgraded to handle an unprecedented power consumption level of 30 MW.

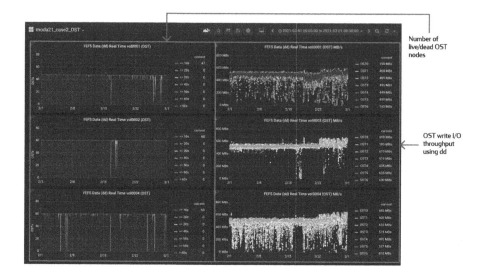

Fig. 3. An example of the Lustre-based file system state (OST write I/O performance). The left graphs describe the number of live/dead OST nodes using dd. If many OSTs have a long response time (60 s is used as a criterion.), the possibility of failure is considered. The right graphs describe the OST write I/O throughput using dd.

Table 1. List of the ten slowest OSTs among the 60 OSTs of vol0004 shown in Fig. 3. The list is arranged in ascending order by average (mean).

OST name	mean [MB/s]	min [MB/s]	max [MB/s]	std [MB/s]
OST16	437.2	2.0	609.5	115.2
OST22	438.8	2.1	604.7	109.0
OST58	440.5	2.3	619.4	111.1
OST55	441.4	1.6	634.7	110.9
OST25	442.0	1.3	619.4	112.2
OST19	442.5	2.1	614.4	108.0
OST46	443.4	2.2	614.4	111.9
OST52	443.6	2.3	640.0	111.2
OST49	444.8	2.2	614.4	108.7
OST7	444.9	2.0	634.7	111.3

Table 2. List of the most fluctuated ten OSTs among the 60 OSTs of vol0004 shown in Fig. 3. The list is arranged in descending order by the standard deviation (std).

OST name	mean [MB/s]	min [MB/s]	max [MB/s]	std [MB/s]
OST47	459.2	2.2	629.5	117.0
OST16	437.2	2.0	609.5	115.2
OST53	462.1	1.4	640.0	114.2
OST32	460.2	2.1	629.5	114.1
OST0	469.7	3.5	645.4	114.0
OST17	459.2	2.0	619.4	113.6
OST20	457.3	2.1	629.5	113.1
OST23	456.5	2.1	614.4	112.8
OST26	455.6	2.1	609.5	112.7
OST2	466.3	3.5	629.5	112.7

Among the other necessary enhancements, we installed a new operational data collection and monitoring platform to operate in the Fugaku environment. In this paper, we reported the current state of this project to renew the platform.

The data collection and monitoring platform that was developed and deployed in this project is based on the three-tier data pipeline architecture. The first stage of the pipeline is data sources, including the HPC system and the data center

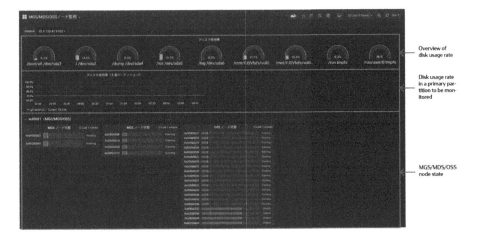

Fig. 4. An example of the Lustre-based file system state (MGS/MDS/OSS nodes performance). The topmost area (upper red box) describes an overview of disk usage rate in an MDS node of the Lustre-based filesystem. The middle graph (middle red box) describes disk usage rate in a primary partition to be monitored. The bottommost area (lower red box) describes updates on the part of the state of an MGS/MDS/OSS node. (Color figure online)

infrastructure. The second stage is a data lake used to store the log/metric data within time-series databases. The third stage, which is the end of the pipeline, provides visualization/BI features to exploit insights. To avoid vendor lock-in, various open-source software components have been adopted for use in this platform. At the time of this writing, the dashboard with Grafana was used to provides an interactive interface for multiple data provided by the HPC system and data center infrastructure. We also introduced two use cases describing the prelaunch service period. The first case showed comprehensive energy usage and the PUE metric of the center. The second case showed how the state for the Lustre-based filesystem was monitored to avoid overloading. In our future work, we will continue our efforts to resolve the ODA issue found in the K computer.

Acknowledgements. We would like to thank colleagues, especially Dr. Toshiyuki Tsukamoto (RIKEN R-CCS), who provided excellent advice and abundant materials regarding facility operations, and Dr. Yuichi Tsujita (RIKEN R-CCS) for valuable comments based on his expertise. We thank Mr. Kensuke Matsumoto (Fujitsu Limited), Mr. Naoki Ikeda (Fujitsu Limited), Mr. Yoshitaka Furutani (Fujitsu Limited), and Mr. Nobuo Ohgushi (Fujitsu Limited) for technical support and comments during the course of this project.

References

1. Elastic. github.com/elastic
2. Grafana. github.com/grafana/grafana

3. Kibana. github.com/elastic/kibana
4. logstash. github.com/elastic/logstash
5. Project Jupyter. github.com/jupyter
6. Prometheus. github.com/prometheus
7. redash. github.com/getredash/redash
8. Top500. www.top500.org/system/179807/
9. Wikipedia. en.wikipedia.org/wiki/Fugaku(supercomputer)
10. Bates, N., Hsu, C., Imam, N., Wilde, T., Sartor, D.: Re-examining HPC energy efficiency dashboard elements. In: 2016 IEEE International Parallel and Distributed Processing Symposium Workshops (IPDPSW), pp. 1106–1109 (2016)
11. Bautista, E., Romanus, M., Davis, T., Whitney, C., Kubaska, T.: Collecting, monitoring, and analyzing facility and systems data at the national energy research scientific computing center. In: Proceedings of the 48th International Conference on Parallel Processing: Workshops. ICPP 2019, Association for Computing Machinery (2019)
12. Bourassa, N., et al.: Operational data analytics: optimizing the national energy research scientific computing center cooling systems. In: Proceedings of the 48th International Conference on Parallel Processing: Workshops. ICPP 2019, Association for Computing Machinery (2019)
13. Chen, J., Tan, R., Xing, G., Wang, X.: Ptec: a system for predictive thermal and energy control in data centers. In: 2014 IEEE Real-Time Systems Symposiumm, pp. 218–227 (2014)
14. Fujitsu: A64fx microarchitecture manual. github.com/fujitsu/A64FX
15. Matsuda, M., Matsuba, H., Nonaka, J., Yamamoto, K., Shibata, H., Tsukamoto, T.: Modeling the existing cooling system to learn its behavior for post-k supercomputer at riken r-ccs. In: Proceedings of the 48th International Conference on Parallel Processing: Workshops. ICPP 2019, Association for Computing Machinery (2019)
16. Minet, P., Renault, E., Khoufi, I., Boumerdassi, S.: Analyzing traces from a Google Data Center. In: 2018 14th International Wireless Communications Mobile Computing Conference (IWCMC), pp. 1167–1172 (2018). https://doi.org/10.1109/IWCMC.2018.8450304
17. Netti, A., et al.: Dcdb wintermute: enabling online and holistic operational data analytics on HPC systems. In: Proceedings of the 29th International Symposium on High-Performance Parallel and Distributed Computing (2020)
18. Nonaka, J., Hanawa, T., Shoji, F.: Analysis of cooling water temperature impact on computing performance and energy consumption. In: 2020 IEEE International Conference on Cluster Computing (CLUSTER), pp. 169–175 (2020)
19. Nonaka, J., Yamamoto, K., Kuroda, A., Tsukamoto, T., Koiso, K., Sakamoto, N.: A view from the facility operations side on the water/air cooling system of the k computer (2019). sc19.supercomputing.org/proceedings/tech/poster/tech/poster/pages/rpost246.html
20. Okazaki, R., et al.: Supercomputer fugaku CPU A64FX realizing high performance, high-density packaging, and low power consumption. Tech. Rep. Fujitsu Tech. Rev. (2020)
21. Ott, M., et al.: Global experiences with HPC operational data measurement, collection and analysis. In: 2020 IEEE International Conference on Cluster Computing (CLUSTER), pp. 499–508 (2020)
22. Santos, D., Mataloto, B., Ferreira, J.C.: Data center environment monitoring system. In: CCIOT 2019: Proceedings of the 2019 4th International Conference on Cloud Computing and Internet of Things, pp. 75–81. CCIOT 2019, Association for Computing Machinery (2019)

23. Sartor, D., Mahdavi, R., Radhakrishnan, B.D., Bates, N., Bailey, A.M., Wescott, R.: General recommendations for high performance computing data center energy management dashboard display. In: 2013 IEEE International Symposium on Parallel Distributed Processing, Workshops and Phd Forum, pp. 892–898 (2013)
24. (SRCC), S.R.C.C.: HPC dashboards. github.com/stanford-rc/hpc-dashboards
25. Terai, M., Shoji, F., Tsukamoto, T., Yamochi, Y.: A study of operational impact on power usage effectiveness using facility metrics and server operation logs in the K computer. In: 2020 IEEE International Conference on Cluster Computing (CLUSTER), pp. 509–513 (2020)
26. Terai, M., Tsukamoto, T., Shoji, F.: Study on the facility enhancement by operational data analysis: a comparison of the operations in the K computer and fugaku. In: ISC 2021 Digital Research Poster (2021)
27. Yamamoto, K.: Operational data processing pipeline. In: SC19 BoF: Operational Data Analytics (2019). eehpcwg.llnl.gov/assets/sc19/bof/operational/data/processing/pipeline.pdf

An Explainable Model for Fault Detection in HPC Systems

Martin Molan[1]([✉]) [ID], Andrea Borghesi[1] [ID], Francesco Beneventi[1],
Massimiliano Guarrasi[2] [ID], and Andrea Bartolini[1] [ID]

[1] University of Bologna, Bologna, Italy
{martin.molan2,andrea.borghesi3,francesco.beneventi,a.bartolini}@unibo.it
[2] CINECA, Reno, Italy
m.guarrasi@cincea.it

Abstract. Large supercomputers are composed of numerous components that risk to break down or behave in unwanted manners. Identifying broken components is a daunting task for system administrators. Hence an automated tool would be a boon for the systems resiliency. The wealth of data available in a supercomputer can be used for this task. In this work we propose an approach to take advantage of holistic data centre monitoring, system administrator node status labeling and an explainable model for fault detection in supercomputing nodes. The proposed model aims at classifying the different states of the computing nodes thanks to the labeled data describing the supercomputer behaviour, data which is typically collected by system administrators but not integrated in holistic monitoring infrastructure for data center automation. In comparison the other method, the one proposed here is robust and provide explainable predictions. The model has been trained and validated on data gathered from a tier-0 supercomputer in production.

Keywords: Machine learning · High performance computing · Fault detection

1 Introduction

High Performance Computing (HPC) systems are large machines composed by hundreds of thousands (up to millions) of smaller components (both software and hardware), all interacting in complex manners. A key challenge to be addressed by researchers in this area is the detection of anomalies and fault conditions that can arise due to the incorrect or sub-optimal behaviour of a wide variety of components. The large scale of the problem motivates the development of an automated procedure for anomaly detection in current supercomputers, and this need will become even more pressing for future Exascale systems [25].

Supported by University of Bologna and CINECA, Italy.

The original version of this chapter was revised: The spelling of the first author's name was corrected. The correction to this chapter is available at
https://doi.org/10.1007/978-3-030-90539-2_36

© Springer Nature Switzerland AG 2021, corrected publication 2021
H. Jagode et al. (Eds.): ISC High Performance 2021 Workshops, LNCS 12761, pp. 378–391, 2021.
https://doi.org/10.1007/978-3-030-90539-2_25

In this situation, a great help comes from the fact that the performance and operative status of HPC systems are continuously monitored by different reporting and monitoring services, that gather data from software and hardware components [15]. Thanks to this data, it is possible to evaluate the health status of the system. These monitoring services are designed for and used by HPC system administrators who monitor the operation of the whole system, and who can manually disable certain parts to prevent serious damage to hardware components, or negative effects to system availability.

Best practice (default operation) of the HPC system or a data center relies on the use of tools for event monitoring, software service and node status reporting [2]. These services/software tools warn system administrators about critical conditions; system administrators can then verify the automatically generated alarms by manually inspecting the system status. Based on the result of the inspection, it is decided if it was a false alarm or if the compute node has to be "drained" from the production. Node downtime is recorded in logs and it is then used for post-mortem analysis. The current trend in data center information is systematic recording of system information data such as data coming from physical sensors' telemetry (temperature, power), micro-architectural events (IPC, cache misses), data coming from the computing resources and infrastructure data from cooling and power equipment (DCIM) [5,6,19]. This data is stored in the form of multivariate time series. However, in current HPC systems servicereporting tools are decoupled from physical monitoring infrastructure. *The first contribution of this paper is combining both the traditional (based on reporting services) and industry 4.0 (based on granular) data sources.* Concretely: we extend the Examon [5,6] framework with Nagios data [3]. Our goal is to detect critical HPC node failures that are recorded by system administrators via Nagios as DOWN+DRAIN events (in the rest of the paper *system failure* and *label* is synonymous with DOWN+DRAIN event).

Using this data we build the second contribution of this work: *an explainable fault detection/classification model based on Machine Learning* (ML). The model will classify HPC node state depending on the monitored data. We call the model *TrueExplain* as it is based on *TrueSkill* model originally developed by Microsoft research [13]. This model benefits the administrators of the HPC system in two ways. First, it automates fault detection; this could shorten the elapsed time between recognition of system failure and reaction by administrators. Secondly, the proposed model provides *insights* into the dynamics of HPC system operation. The *insight generation* capability of the ML model can support the decision process that hinges on the model's predictions. Identified root cause of the suspected fault can be interpreted by a human user. Explainable ML models can also be more reliable as they can be validated by a domain expert. Despite explainable AI not being a novel concept, this is the first time it has been applied to resiliency in HPC systems and trained on real data from HPC production.

As a final contribution, it must be stressed out that the model was trained and validated using labeled data collected on a tier-0 supercomputer hosted by the Italian Supercomputing Center (Cineca) [1]. We dealt with the real anomalies from a production machine unlike most approaches in the literature that deal with "synthetic" or artificially injected anomalies.

2   Related Works

Previous research works have made preliminary exploration towards the creation of model for fault detection in HPC systems. There have been approaches based on large quantity of data with scarce labels. These approaches belong to the *semi-supervised* field. For instance, Borghesi et al. [7–9] propose the usage of a particular type of Deep Neural Network (DNN) called autoencoder to learn the characteristic behaviour of a supercomputer in healthy state. These trained DNNs are then used to classify between normal and anomalous points in incoming data streams.

When the labels are available researchers have employed *supervised* ML-inspired algorithms to perform anomaly detection with high accuracy. Tuncer et al. [24] deal with the problem of diagnosing performance variations in HPC systems, using labeled data collected from a HPC simulator. The authors train different ML algorithms to classify the behaviour of the supercomputer using the gathered data. In a similar fashion, Netti et al. [18] propose a model based on Random Forest to classify different types of faults that can happen in a HPC node.

The previously described methods have been proven to be useful and have good accuracy. The important difference between existing work and the work presented in this paper is the use of data from real HPC production. Existing work such as [18] uses anomaly injection to *artificially* create faults that are then approximated with a machine learning model. As such there can be doubt about the generalization capabilities of such models; ML approach that is capable of recognising the dynamics and characteristics of fault injection might not be able to recognise the dynamic of *actual failures*. The dynamics of failures might be more complex and more difficult to model than the dynamics of injected anomalies. Additionally, from a ML perspective, training on a real dataset brings additional challenges in the form of noise in the data. Instead, in this work, we deal with real, noisy data.

Additionally we aim at a fault detection model whose predictions could be explained. We have thus obtained a tool for data center automation that can be adopted by system administrator and facility owners more willingly, as it is possible to interpret its decision on a human-understandable way. The outputs of explainable models can be cross-referenced and checked by domain experts. Black box models can never truly be validated by domain experts - the very prominent (and in recent years popular with researchers) filed of research that deals with *fairness* and *bias* in artificial intelligence is largely the result of the inherent impossibility to examine the rules learned by complex black-box models [16]. It is shown that just trusting the black box models can lead to models that make ultimately wrong decisions [16].

Explaining ML models has been a rich source of research works. A baseline explainable approaches are feature importance explanation models like [26]. Another possible approach are inherently explainable models [11]. Among explainable models, Bayesian models are very promising. In particular a recent work by Microsoft Research [13] proposes a scalable Bayesian approach called *True Skill*. The basic idea is similar to ELO rating in chess [21] and is based on predicted skill of two opponents and their previous interactions. As opposed to ELO rating, the skill is a Gaussian variable (not a scalar value). The update of this variable depends both on it's mean and it's variance. The skill estimates (model priors) are updated so that the score of the winner is increased and score of the loser is decreased. The score update (increase for the winner and decrease for the looser) depends on the relative skills of the opponents. In general, this process could require a lot of previous data (not available for new players) and to overcome this limitation TrueSkill models player score as a Gaussian random variable instead of as a scalar value; the additional information obtained via the probability distribution – in particular the variance – allows for the more efficient update of players' scores.

The basic idea of TrueSkill can be adopted to other problems where interaction can be modeled as opposition between two agents. For instance, *TrueLearn* was developed by Bulathwela and et al. [10] to model the learning path of students consuming educational materials. The opposing agents are the learner and the material; the estimated parameters are material difficulty and learner's skill. Similarly, Molan et al. generalize TrueSkill [17] to assist blind students. In this case, the model learns student's accessibility preferences and uses those preferences to rank materials in terms of suitability. The idea of two opposing agents in Bayesian learning can also be abstracted for classification settings. This method was explored by Graepel et al. [12] to learn user preference with regards to different types of ads.

In this paper, we will extend the usage of TrueSkill to the context of fault classification in HPC systems, as described in the following section.

3   Methodology

The aim of this work is to construct an explainable ML model, trained on real data that I) is accurate and robust and II) provides justification for its decision. Robust models stay the same (and have the same predictions) when they are trained multiple times on the same dataset. We limit our focus on the binary classification, that is distinguishing the normal state of a HPC node from a faulty one. For this scope, the critical element is the identification of the most relevant attributes and of their relative contributions. To this end, we develop a Bayesian approach based on TrueSkill [13] aimed at estimating the relative importance of the input features. We name this approach *TrueExplain*. TrueExplain is compared to the standard for explainable classification models: decision trees. Decision trees serve as a baseline against which our novel ML apprach will be evaluated.

As a classifier, we opted to implement DTs as a baseline as they are simple to implement and tend to provide good accuracy [24]. Furthermore, in this work we are not only interested in the classification accuracy *per se*, but rather on the explainability of the model – and DTs are notoriously more "transparent" compared to model such as neural networks. Secondarily, we want to obtain a robust model, that is a model capable of making consistent predictions over multiple runs.

TrueExplain is an extension of *TrueSkill* that can be used for classification. It is a form of Bayesian method, that aims to increase the robustness of the overall approach and provide the explainability in the form of feature importance. The feature importance is modeled as a Gaussian variable with its mean and variance; the variance can be interpreted in terms of uncertainty about the model prediction. Additionally, the Bayesian approach True Explain is more robust and has consistent classification performance across different subsets of data – which is not necessarily the case for decision trees.

Our approach TrueExplain exploits the the Bayesian approach introduced by TrueSkill – it is an *opposition-based classifier*. Binary classification can be interpreted as an opposition of two agents as presented in Table 1. Currently, TrueExplain only works for one-hot encoded discrete (nominal) variables; generalization to continuous variables is a topic of ongoing research. Hence, TrueExplain expects data composed by a set of examples (or rows), each one possessing a collection of binary features assuming only values 0 or 1 and a binary label; if the original data set contains non-categorical data, one-hot encoding needs to be applied.

TrueExplain is trained through iterating over rows of the data set – the model is updated after each row (each example in the training set). In order to understand an update after a single row, it is important to understand how to construct two opposing teams from a single line in a data set. The binary classification problem (an example can represent either a normal data point or a fault) is presented as a "game" between two opposing teams (the core scheme of TrueSkll). One team is represented by active (hot) features (features with value 1) and it is described by a Gaussian variable whose parameters have to be learned through the training process. The other team is a dummy one described by a (deformed) variable with zero mean and zero variance. The dummy team is the same size as a feature team. Both teams are presented in Table 1. Information about the label is interpreted as the *outcome* of the opposition; if the label is 1 the feature team won - otherwise the dummy team won.

Table 1. Representation of two opposing teams. G(0,0) designates a deformed Gaussian distribution. G(f) denotes a learned Gaussian for a feature f.

G(f2)	G(f3)	G(f5)	...	G(f(N-1))
		vs.		
G(0,0)	G(0,0)	G(0,0)	...	G(0,0)

The main advantage of using the scalable Bayesian approach as a classifier are interpretability and robustness. A Gaussian variable is associated to each feature and its parameters are learned during training. The mean value represents the relative feature importance and the variance represents the estimated confidence.

4   Case Study: Marconi HPC System

A very important aspect for the anomaly detection approach is the availability of large quantity of data that monitors and describes the state of a supercomputer. To test our approach we take advantage of a supercomputer with an integrated monitoring infrastructure able to handle large amounts of data coming from several different sources. We opted for a supercomputer hosted by Cineca, Italy, named Marconi [14] (peak performance 20PFlops), already endowed with a holistic monitoring infrastructure called Examon [4,6]. We collect three kinds of data: i) physical data measured with sensors; ii) workload information obtained from the job dispatcher; iii) information about the state of the system and its services collected by Nagios [3], a tool to provide alerts for system administrators. In this work we propose to use the information about the system services provided by Nagios to characterize Marconi's nodes. In Nagios the labels have been manually annotated by system administrators by reporting the nodes which experienced a failure in the considered time-frame. Nagios information consists of a set of categorical values for each alert probe set up during the configuration phase; this data type is well-suited for the one-hot encoding required by True-Explain (see Sect. 3). To the best of the authors knowledge this is the first work proposing to use Nagios data integrated with a holistic monitoring infrastructure.

4.1   Dataset

The dataset consists of data collected from Marconi over a period of over 4 months[1]. The size of the collected data is 1GB. The data set is composed by combining high level status reporting information and corresponding system availability information – both recorded by Nagios reporting system. The label (target) consists of two values: 0 describing normal operation and 1 describing fault (DOWN+DRAIN event as recorded by Nagios). The label is provided by system administrators. On average we have recorded 1.5 faults per node (in the time period) with a maximum of 10 and minimum of 0 faults. The data sampling frequency is 15 min, as determined by Nagios monitoring functionalities. 15 min is the maximum possible sampling frequency. The data about a single computing node's availability (manual shutting down of nodes – our label), is referenced to subsystem availability reporting intervals – each 15 min interval is annotated by information about node availability at that time interval.

All the data, discussed in this paper, was collected on the A1 partition of the Marconi system that consists of 1521 nodes with 36 cores and 128GB of

---

[1] April-July 2019.

RAM. All nodes were manufactured by the same supplier. All nodes also report the same data back to the monitoring system. Since all the nodes are part of the same partition and were in full production, they were similarly frequently used. We have specifically chosen the observation period where all nodes were in production. We have no information about the job status on the nodes; this could be a useful additional information but it is the subject of further work.

4.2   Raw Data Pre-processing

The data is stored as system logs, one log for each service monitored by Nagios (including node availability – our label), and divided in multiple files depending on nodes and time stamp. This raw data format (shown in Table 2) is not suitable for training ML models. It has been reshaped by a pre-processing phase which included merging data from different Nagios services (including label data).

Table 2. Raw dataset as recorded in system logs.

Time stamp	Node	Reporting service	State
1256953732	r033c01s04	CPU temp	Warning (1)

To have a suitable training set for TrueExplain, raw data is transformed to an attribute-value description, that is each instance is described by values of selected attributes (and a target variable) [22]. The transformation produces the data in the new format summarized in Table 3.

Table 3. Section of attribute-value representation of data.

Node	Time stamp	CPU temp	...	Downtime/Target
r033c01s04	1256953732	Warning (1)	...	Available (0)

For each time stamp and for each node, information for all reporting services are recorded alongside the log (downtime label) information. The downtime label also serves as a target class (label) while building the fault detection model. The data transformation is performed via parallel jobs executed on another supercomputer hosted at CINECA, namely Galileo HPC system. Galileo is also used for training and testing TrueExplain; Galileo is composed by 1022 nodes equipped with 2 x 18-cores Intel Xeon E5-2697 v4 (Broadwell) at 2.30 GHz. Overall, the data transformation was run on 60 nodes and it took a few minutes less than 3 h.

4.3   Data Description

The data set consists of 31 attributes and a target nominal attribute *Fault*. Attributes correspond to available monitoring services; Fault is a binary attribute describing whether the system is at Fault at a given timestamp. Fault events are identified through the logs annotated by system administrators under normal Marconi usage – *we did not require any additional annotation operation besides those performed for typical system maintenance.* As each node will have its own fault detection model (trained and tested on its own data), the data is grouped accordingly. Two of the 31 attributes are then not informative for TrueExplain – timestamp and node[2] – and are discarded.

The input features/attributes are listed in Table 4. They represent the statuses of various subsystems of the supercomputer nodes. All 29 attributes are categorical attributes with three possible values: 0 denotes normal operational condition, 3 denotes a warning situation and 2 denotes a potentially serious (abnormal) condition[3]. These values come from configuration of Nagios on Marconi.

Table 4. Attributes used in construction of a model. The attributes are in the format - component::service::status or component::status.

alive::ping	backup::local::status	cluster::status::availability
cluster::status::criticality	cluster::status::internal	dev::raid::status
dev::swc::confcheckself	filesys::local::avail	filesys::local::mount
filesys::shared::mount	memory::phys::total	ssh::daemon
sys::ldap_srv::status	batchs::JobsH	filesys::eurofusion::mount
sys::gpfs::status	dev::ipmi::events	dev::swc::bntfru
dev::swc::bnthealth	dev::swc::bnttemp	dev::swc::confcheck
batchs::client::state	batchs::client	net::opa::pciwidth
net::opa	sys::orphaned_cgroups::count	core::total
sys::cpus::freq	batchs::client::serverrespond	

5   Experimental Results

In this work we focus on obtaining a model that is explainable and robust (and not necessarily the most accurate). We have trained and tested different standard supervised classification methods from the literature, namely: Decision Trees (DT), Linear Support Vector Machine (L-SVM), Nearest Neighbors (NN), Radial Basis Function SVM (RBF-SVM), and Random Forest (RF)[4]. All standard ML techniques are implemented in Python 3 (Python 3.6) using Scikit-learn [20]; TrueExplain is implemented in Python 3 as an extension of TrueSkill.

---

[2] Timestampsuniquelyidentifiesrows/examples.

[3] Value 1 is unused.

[4] Hyperparameters: DT max dept equal to none, splitting heuristic Gini impurity, min samples leaf equal to 1; L-SVM loss function squared hinge, regularization *l*2; NN number of neighbours equal to 5, uniform weights, euclidean metric; RBF-SVM has RBF kernel, regularization parameter equal to 1, RF number of estimators equal to 10, base estimator parameters same as DT.

The performance of different classification algorithms is evaluated on the pre-processed data set. All algorithms receive the same data that is processed in the same manner.F-score for the algorithms was calculated on a 20% test set. Each algorithm was trained and tested on 57 different nodes of Marconi. The average accuracy results (measured as F-Score) over all nodes are presented in Table 5.

Table 5. Average accuracy of classification methods across all nodes.

Decision trees (DT)	0.97
Linear SVM	0.51
Nearest neighbors	0.83
RBF SVM	0.66
Random forest (RF)	0.91
TrueLearn	0.77

These experimental results reveal that TrueLearn is not the most accurate method. Its accuracy is on par with other methods, being outperformed only by DT-based classifiers. As mentioned earlier, in this work we do not aim at finding the most accurate ML model for fault detection, but we rather focus on obtaining a model that is explainable and *robust*. In the following section we discuss the robustness results; in particular we compare the robustness of TrueLearn with the robustness of the best explainable method, that is decision tree.

We do not measure the robustness since we are comparing a method that gives the same result in *every* run against the method (decision trees) that gives multiple different results. If we had multiple methods that produce different models between different runs, we could measure robustness of those methods by similarity of the models (e.g. similarity of decision tree graphs). In our case, robustness is the inherent characteristic of the design of the TrueLearn.

5.1   Fault Detection Robustness

Standard implementations of decision tree classifier [23] use random choice for splitting feature if more than one feature carry the same information about target label. This is the reason why decision trees, as well as their accuracy, can *change between different runs on the same dataset*. Results of 100 runs on the same dataset, validated by chronological 80/20 split are presented in a Table 6. This is in stark contrast with TrueLearn which provides the *exact same accuracy level on all runs*; this is a significant boost in terms of model robustness and reliability. As seen in the Table 6 the biggest difference between min, max and average accuracy is on the node $r104c14s02$. This node is the same as other nodes in terms of configuration but it serves as a good example of instability of decision trees. There are three possible induced decision trees on that dataset; the induced decision trees are presented on Figs. 1a, 1b and 1c. All three possible decision tree graphs are equally likely and each one occurs in $\frac{1}{3}$ of the cases.

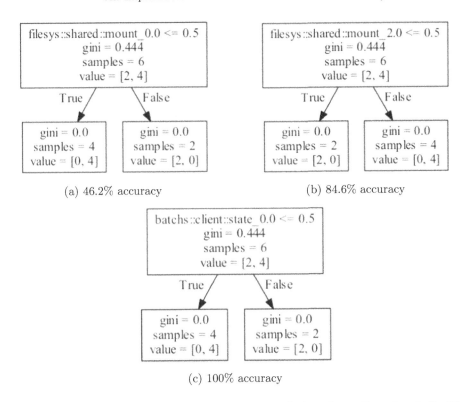

(a) 46.2% accuracy   (b) 84.6% accuracy

(c) 100% accuracy

Fig. 1. Different decision trees on node r104c14s02. Left node predicts class 1 (fault) and right one class 0 (no fault). Reported is the accuracy on the test set.

5.2 Visualization of Learned Parameters for Bayesian Classifier TrueExplain

On the same node - node r104c14s02 - where decision trees experienced most fluctuation in terms of performance, TrueExplain classifier is also trained. Performance of TrueExplain classifier *is the same on all runs*. Distributions can also be visualized and plotted as Gaussians as presented in Fig. 2.

6 Discussion

In general explainable classification models perform well compared to black box models. This is probably mostly the result of very informative features; reporting services (NAGIOS) already transform low level diagnostics data into higher level features. As such this dataset (beyond the frame of this work) could serve as a nice practical dataset for explainable classification models. Comparing the two explainable models (decision trees and Bayesian classifier TrueExplain) we see that decision trees outperform Bayesian approach in both the average and the best case. It is the worst case scenario for Decision trees that is worrying - on

Table 6. Average, min and max accuracy in 100 runs of decision tree algorithm on the same dataset - results on selected nodes with average calculated on all nodes.

Node	Average accuracy	Max accuracy	Min accuracy
r070c13s04	1.00	1.00	1.00
r075c13s02	0.85	1.00	0.53
r078c14s01	0.72	0.72	0.72
r090c14s02	1.00	1.00	0.99
r093c15s03	0.99	0.99	0.98
r094c04s03	1.00	1.00	1.00
r098c05s02	0.86	1.00	0.77
r103c11s02	0.86	0.86	0.86
r104c12s02	0.81	1.00	0.46
r104c14s02	0.83	1.00	0.46
r112c02s02	1.00	1.00	0.99
r145c10s04	0.99	1.00	0.98
r162c15s01	0.87	1.00	0.81
r169c11s04	0.70	0.97	0.65
r170c13s04	0.99	1.00	0.96
Average	0.974	0.992	0.951

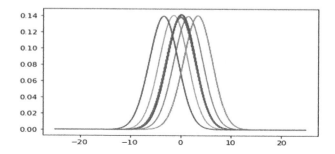

Fig. 2. Plotted weight distributions form TrueExplain, learned from node r104c14s02. The performance of TrueExplain is constant across different runs.

this problem one has no guarantee that decision trees will be able to learn and produce usable predictions.

Exploring the most problematic node for decision trees - node r104c14s02 - illustrates the nature of the problem with decision trees. After training decision tree classifier on train dataset (80% of the data) it is apparent that the algorithm recognizes multiple features as equally informative on the *train set*. Thus the algorithm randomly chooses between three possible models (Figs. 1a, 1b and 1c). Only model Fig, 1c however performs equally well on the test set. Diving into the nature of the underlying problem it can be assumed that different reporting services report errors simultaneously. Only one error is however the real cause of the fault that can be generalized to the test set. Decision trees however have no guarantee of recognizing the real culprit. Described problem is especially characteristic for small dataset (per node models) and can be addressed by accumulating more data.

Bayesian model TrueExplain recognizes and increases the weights of all possible causes of a system failure. This system (on such a small dataset) protects against false negative errors that decision trees can make. The main advantage of the Bayesian approach is that it can recognize multiple factors as equally important in predicting a malfunction. For each attribute, TrueExplain learns two parameters μ (expected value) and σ. μ denotes expected contribution to class 1 (positive μ) or class 0 (negative μ). Additionally Bayesian learner TrueExplain also communicates prediction certainty. Variance (curve width) carries information about parameter certainty – as the certainty increases the width of the curve decreases (the Gaussian curve slowly tends towards a constant).

We are using the one-hot encoding for features; each feature is split into three sub-features according to it's critical state (0, 2, 3). Let us focus on a node where decision trees achieve poor performance: *r104c14s02*. Investigating the outputs of the TrueExplain for node r104c14s02, it can be seen that the model identifies as the most influential features (highest negative expected value - μ) contributing to class 0: *filesys::shared::mount, sys::gpfs::status, batchs::client::state*, all with critical state 0. Interestingly the same three factors, when they have critical state 2 (fault), are the most relevant to class 1. This means that, for this specific node, these three factors really determine if the node is available or not. In other words, these three factors explain the availability of examined node. Identification of pairs of important attributes (similar importance of the same feature with critical state 0 and critical state 2) is also in line with domain expectations for the problem. If a fault of a subsystem means the downtime of the node, than the normal operation of the subsystem should indicate availability of the node.

7 Conclusions

In this paper we tackle the problem of anomaly recognition in HPC systems. We propose a novel approach to characterize the behaviour of a supercomputing node, through the combination of I) measurements from hardware/software sensors and II) labels(system availability) provided by system administrators. Using this labeled data, we created and trained *TrueExplain*, a Bayesian classifier for distinguishing normal and anomalous states in supercomputing nodes. We have empirically shown that TrueExplain is I) robust, II) its decision offers a possibility for interpretation, and III) it works on smaller training set. The last point is very beneficial in terms of implementation on HPC systems, as it means that explainable and efficient models can be constructed for individual or multiple nodes relatively early on in the operational life of a new HPC system. Based on the work presented here, informative models for each individual node can be constructed in just a few months of operation. Another additional benefit of the proposed Bayesian model is that it is inherently an online training algorithm – which means it can be trained in real time.

TrueExplain also can greatly help HPC system administrators as it accurately detects undesired states, thus improving the supercomputer resilience. This result is boosted by empirically proven robustness of the presented approach, as it is capable of consistently providing the same classification results over different nodes and hundreds of runs. Furthermore, the fact that our model is relatively simple to explain means that predictions can greatly help HPC operators in identifying the malfunctioning components and fault root causes.

8   Code Access

Code for a classifier, implemented in this work is accessible at: https://github. com/MolanM/TrueExplain

Acknowledgements. This research was partly supported by the
EU H2020-ICT-11–2018-2019 IoTwins project (g.a. 857191),
the H2020-JTI-EuroHPC-2019–1 Regale project (g.a. 956560)
and Emilia-Romagna POR-FESR 2014–2020 project "SUPER: SuperComputing Unifier Platform - Emilia-Romagna".
We also thank CINECA for the collaboration and access to their machines.

References

1. Cineca inter-university consortium web site. www.cineca.it//en. Accessed 29 Jun 2018
2. Sensu go: Sensu go 5.20, docs.sensu.io/sensu-go/latest/
3. Barth, W.: Nagios: system and network monitoring. No Starch Press (2008)
4. Bartolini, A., Borghesi, A., et al.: The D.A.V.I.D.E. big-data-powered fine-grain power and performance monitoring support. In: Proceedings of the 15th ACM International Conference on Computing Frontiers, Ischia, Italy, 2018 (2018)
5. Bartolini, A., Beneventi, F., Borghesi, A., Cesarini, D., Libri, A., Benini, L., Cavazzoni, C.: Paving the way toward energy-aware and automated datacentre. In: Proceedings of the 48th International Conference on Parallel Processing: Workshops. ICPP 2019, Association for Computing Machinery, New York, NY, USA (2019). https://doi.org/10.1145/3339186.3339215
6. Beneventi, F., Bartolini, A., et al.: Continuous learning of hpc infrastructure models using big data analytics and in-memory processing tools. In: Proceedings of the Conference on Design, Automation and Test in Europe, pp. 1038–1043. European Design and Automation Association (2017)
7. Borghesi, A., Bartolini, A., et al.: Anomaly detection using autoencoders in hpc systems. In: Proceedings of the AAAI Conference on Artificial Intelligence (2019)
8. Borghesi, A., Bartolini, A., et al.: A semisupervised autoencoder-based approach for anomaly detection in high performance computing systems. Eng. Appl. Artif. Intell. **85**, 634–644 (2019)
9. Borghesi, A., Libri, A., et al.: Online anomaly detection in hpc systems. In: 2019 IEEE International Conference on Artificial Intelligence Circuits and Systems (AICAS), pp. 229–233. IEEE (2019)

10. Bulathwela, S., Perez-Ortiz, M., et al.: Truelearn: a family of bayesian algorithms to match lifelong learners to open educational resources. In: Proceedings of the AAAI Conference on Artificial Intelligence (2020)

11. Burkart, N., Huber, M.F.: A survey on the explainability of supervised machine learning. CoRR abs/2011.07876 (2020). arxiv.org/abs/2011.07876

12. Graepel, T., Candela, J., et al.: Web-scale bayesian click-through rate prediction for sponsored search advertising in microsoft's bing search engine. Omnipress (2010)

13. Herbrich, R., Minka, T., Graepel, T.: Trueskill^{TM}: a bayesian skill rating system. In: Advances in neural information processing systems, pp. 569–576 (2007)

14. Iannone, F., Bracco, G., et al.: Marconi-fusion: the new high performance computing facility for european nuclear fusion modelling. Fusion Eng. Design **129**, 354–358 (2018)

15. Massie, M.: Monitoring with Ganglia. O'Reilly Media, Sebastopol, CA (2012)

16. Mehrabi, N., Morstatter, F., Saxena, N., Lerman, K., Galstyan, A.: A survey on bias and fairness in machine learning. arXiv preprint arXiv:1908.09635 (2019)

17. Molan, M., Bulathwela, S., Orlic, D.: Accessibility recommendation system. In: Proceedings of the OER20: Open Education Conference (2020)

18. Netti, A., Kiziltan, Z., et al.: A machine learning approach to online fault classification in hpc systems. Future Gener. Comput. Syst. (2019)

19. Netti, A., Mueller, M., Guillen, C., Ott, M., Tafani, D., Ozer, G., Schulz, M.: Dcdb wintermute: enabling online and holistic operational data analytics on hpc systems (2019)

20. Pedregosa, F., Varoquaux, G., Gramfort, A., et al.: Scikit-learn: machine learning in Python. J. Mach. Learn. Res. **12**, 2825–2830 (2011)

21. Pelánek, R.: Applications of the elo rating system in adaptive educational systems. Comput. Educ. **98**, 169–179 (2016)

22. Sammut, C., Webb, G.I. (eds.): Attribute-value learning. Springer, US (2010)

23. Sharma, H., Kumar, S.: A survey on decision tree algorithms of classification in data mining. Int. J. Sci. Res. (IJSR) 5(4) (2016)

24. Tuncer, O., et al.: Diagnosing performance variations in HPC applications using machine learning. In: Kunkel, J., Yokota, R., Balaji, P., Keyes, D. (eds) High Performance Computing. ISC 2017. Lecture Notes in Computer Science, vol. 10266. Springer, Cham (2017). https://doi.org/10.1007/978-3-319-58667-0_19

25. Yang, X., Wang, Z., Xue, J., Zhou, Y.: The reliability wall for exascale supercomputing. IEEE Trans. Comput. **61**(6), 767–779 (2012)

26. Zamuda, A., Zarges, C., Stiglic, G., Hrovat, G.: Stability selection using a genetic algorithm and logistic linear regression on healthcare records. In: Proceedings of the Genetic and Evolutionary Computation Conference Companion, p. 143–144. GECCO '17, Association for Computing Machinery, New York, NY, USA (2017). https://doi.org/10.1145/3067695.3076077

Sixteenth Workshop on Virtualization in High–Performance Cloud Computing

A Scalable Cloud Deployment Architecture for High-Performance Real-Time Online Applications

Sezar Jarrous-Holtrup[1]([✉]), Folker Schamel[2], Kerstin Hofer[2],
and Sergei Gorlatch[1]

[1] University of Muenster, Muenster, Germany
{s_jarr01,gorlatch}@uni-muenster.de
[2] Spinor GmbH, Munich, Germany
{fms,kerstin.hofer}@spinor.com

Abstract. We study high-performance Real-Time Online Interactive Applications (ROIAs), with use cases like product configurators in the Configure-Price-Quote market, e-learning, multiplayer online gaming, and digital twins of production facilities for the Industry 4.0 market. While core components of ROIAs, e.g., interactive real-time 3D rendering, still widely run on local devices, it is very desirable to run them on cloud resources to benefit from the advantages of cloud computing, e.g., better quality provided by high-performance compute resources and accessibility. In this paper, we design and implement a novel cloud service deployment architecture for ROIAs, which addresses three major challenges: meeting the high Quality of Service (QoS) requirements, autoscalability, and resource usage optimization. Compared to previous work, our deployment approach is based on the concept of session slots that combines a high level of QoS with the economic use of resources like CPU, GPU, and memory. We describe a prototype implementation of a ROIA use case - a car configurator running on a Kubernetes cluster. Experimental evaluation demonstrates that our architecture avoids the traffic and latency bottleneck of a classical cloud load balancer, provides significantly more efficient resource usage, and can autoscale well.

Keywords: Cloud computing · Real-time 3D rendering ·
High-performance computing · Deployment architecture · Autoscaling

1 Introduction

High-performance Real-Time Online Interactive Applications (ROIAs) form a class of technically challenging distributed applications. They include, for example, product configurators in the Configure-Price-Quote market (e.g., for the car industry), e-learning applications like virtual classrooms, online computer games reaching from fast-paced action games to large-scale massively multiplayer online games (MMOG), as well as Industry 4.0 applications, like digital twins of production facilities which use interactive real-time 3D visualization for analyzing

© Springer Nature Switzerland AG 2021
H. Jagode et al. (Eds.): ISC High Performance 2021 Workshops, LNCS 12761, pp. 395–405, 2021.
https://doi.org/10.1007/978-3-030-90539-2_26

production processes. High-performance ROIAs need to be efficient and optimized for frequent transfers of data for a high number of concurrent users [13] with a workload that may typically change quickly within seconds [4].

Today core components of high-performance ROIAs, e.g., interactive real-time 3D rendering of a commercial product or a factory processing line, still widely run on local devices [14]. However, it is often desirable for high-performance ROIA operators to run them on cloud resources. This avoids installation hurdles and achieves shorter loading times (by not having to transfer larger amounts of 3D data before rendering) and more realistic rendering quality (by using high-performance hardware like better GPUs than available on many end-user devices). Optimizing the resource usage and, therefore, minimizing operating costs is especially important for running ROIAs in a cloud environment: high-performance ROIA services, in particular, when using server-side real-time 3D rendering, often require significantly more resources than other cloud applications and use expensive specialized hardware like GPUs [14].

Lift-and-Shift (LaS) [2] is a strategy for moving an existing application or operation from on-premises infrastructure to the cloud without redesigning the application or operations workflow. LaS reduces the on-premises infrastructure costs in the short term. However, applying LaS for legacy applications typically leads to inefficient results [2], especially for 3D ROIAs. Since those applications were originally designed as a single-user application running on a local device, they are only able to handle a single user session. Transferring such high-performance ROIAs to a cloud environment via LaS often results in huge costs, mainly because a full-service instance of the ROIA will be needed for each user session.

In previous work, the problem of using service-oriented architectures for ROIAs is solved by Service-Oriented Interactive Media (SOIM) engines based on service-oriented networking [7] and different deployment algorithms [12], where multiple parallel user sessions are supported per service instance [1]. While for some applications it is acceptable to become slower under heavy load, ROIAs require a very stable delivery quality, e.g., 30 frames per second (fps), and a low response time, e.g., 100 ms: Failing to deliver timely updates leads to a degraded application experience, such that annoyed users may leave the application and close their accounts [6]. Therefore, SOIM engines use the concept of session slots by setting a hard limit on the number of concurrent user sessions running on a service instance without loss of Quality of Service (QoS) [7,16]. For good QoS of ROIAs, service placement should also take latency into account [9,10]. Unfortunately, existing container orchestration systems cannot deal with the concept of session slots.

Addressing these needs of high-performance ROIAs on a cloud infrastructure requires a suitable service deployment architecture [15]. Container orchestration systems, e.g., Kubernetes [8], provide service deployment architectures with integrated load balancing as well as autoscaling services. However, such solutions are not primarily designed to deal with the challenges of ROIAs and are insufficient for ROIAs for the following reasons: 1) they do not support the session slot concept of SOIM engines; and 2) since ROIAs often have a massive data throughput (e.g., media data) and sessions in ROIAs typically have a long duration, the load-balancing service may become overloaded.

In this paper, we propose and implement a novel scalable cloud service deployment architecture for high-performance ROIAs called Scalable Real-time Service Deployment (SRSD), which both meets the strict QoS of high-performance ROIAs and keeps the costs of computing resources on the cloud as low as possible. Our approach is based not on classical metrics, but rather on the session slots concept. It also avoids the load balancer bottleneck and provides reduced latency by providing a direct service endpoint exposure [17], i.e., the user device can directly connect to a service instance without the data having to go through other nodes like a load balancer.

The paper is structured as follows. Our new deployment architecture is described in Sect. 2. Section 3 analyses the performance of this deployment architecture by measurements on a small prototype implementation and by simulating a large-scale system. Section 4 summarizes our findings.

2   Our Scalable Cloud Deployment Architecture for High-Performance ROIAs

Figure 1 shows the core components of our proposed deployment architecture: a scalable Session Slots Database (SSD), a scalable stateless Session Slots Orchestrator (SSO), and a scalable stateless Session Slot Autoscaler (SSA). The SSO and the SSD replace traditional load balancers. They manage the session slots, sessions, as well as direct endpoint exposure of the 3D-service instances, and they also collect session slots usage data. The SSA ensures the availability of a sufficient number of session slots, based on the startup times of new service instances and the history of session slot usage collected by the SSO and stored in the SSD. The SSA component also ensures meeting the strict QoS of ROIAs on the one hand and the avoidance of an overprovisioning of too many service instances on the other hand.

Every service instance registers all its session slots in the SSD at its start and unregisters them at termination. The SSA permanently evaluates the history of session slot usage and launches and terminates nodes and service instances in the cluster accordingly. In particular, it predicts the future session slot requirements by regression analysis of the recent usage patterns, taking into account the deployment and startup time of new service instances.

Figure 1 shows the interaction steps between the users and the application:

1. A client connects to a web server.
2. The website of the application is loaded.
3. The web application requests a session slot from the SSO.
4. The SSO requests a free session slot from the SSD.
5. The SSD sets the status of the determined session slot as "reserved" and sends the slot information to the SSO.

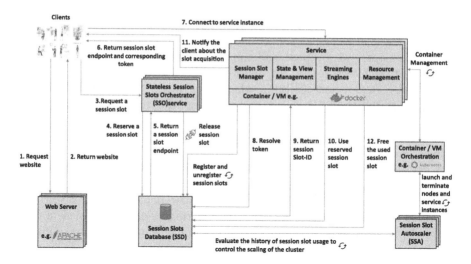

Fig. 1. The overall architecture of SRSD.

6. The SSO returns the session slot endpoint and a generated token to the client. If the user fails to connect the service instance, e.g., due to connectivity problems or malicious intent, the SSO releases the reserved slot as soon as the user is disconnected and the slot is not used yet.

7. The client connects to the service instance using the connection endpoint and the token.

8. The service instance resolves the token from the SSD.

9. The SSD returns the ID of the session slot to the service instance.

10. The SSD sets the corresponding session slot to "used".

11. The service instance notifies the client about the slot acquisition. Only then the client disconnects from the SSO.

12. When the client gets disconnected from the service instance, the SSD sets the status of the session slot to "free".

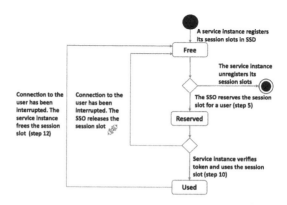

Fig. 2. State diagram of the session slots.

Figure 2 shows the state diagram of the session slots, from creation till termination.

We intentionally design the SSO and SSA components to be stateless in order to make them easily scalable. We also design all SSD database operations to work as SQL statements without transaction based locking over network to ensure the following properties:

- Effective scalability, since atomic SQL statements lock the database for a much shorter time than network locks do: the latter would include one or more network turnaround times.
- Avoiding temporary or total freezing of the whole system when client locks take longer (e.g., because of network problems) or there is a heavy CPU load on the SSA or SSO components, or a crash happens.

3   Use Case and Evaluation

We implement, evaluate, and simulate our proposed service deployment architecture for the use case of product configurator prototype in the car industry.

Fig. 3. Use case of ROIA: an interior and an exterior screenshot of a high-quality interactive real-time 3D product visualization for the car industry.

Figure 3 shows our use case of the car configurator that uses high-performance, high-quality, real-time 3D rendering. In this use case, customers visit the website of a car vendor to configure cars they would like to consider for purchase. The website provides the customers with a web application for 3D real-time visualization, giving the customers the possibility to configure the desired features of the car (e.g., colors, seat type, rim style). The customer is able to zoom in and out, rotate the camera, and change the surrounding area in real-time. In real-world deployments, such a configurator is used by a mass of concurrent users (e.g., multiple thousand).

Our prototype implementation of the interactive car configurator consists of a service that provides server-side GPU-based real-time 3D rendering [1]. The scene of 4.8M polygons uses various lighting techniques implemented by highly parallelized shaders, delivered by a 25 Mbps low-latency 1080p video stream at 30 fps. The service is packaged as a Docker container image [3] and instantiated inside pods on a Kubernetes cluster [8]. We have chosen to use Docker and Kubernetes, since they are the most common containerization and orchestration systems. To avoid setting up a huge infrastructure for the experiments, we use a deployment setup consisting of only two session slots, but perform the measurements for 14 h instead.

Our application experiments run on a computer with an Intel Core i7-9700K CPU 3.6 GHz with 8 cores, 16 GB RAM, a Nvidia GeForce RTX 2070 8 GB, and an Intel Ethernet Connection I219-LM network interface controller. We merge the results of the measurements, consisting of packages of timestamps and amount of bytes, into a one-minute time period. The results represent the traffic of approximately 500 concurrent users of the application.

Using this prototype, we evaluate the benefits of the direct endpoint exposure by comparing the data traffic that passes through the SSO in our SRSD against the traffic that passes through a simulated traditional round-robin load balancer. Each service instance in the application has two main logical communication channels to the web browser running on the user's end devices: a real-time, low-latency custom protocol-based remote method invocation (RMI) channel, and a real-time video stream channel.

In our experiments, we compare three different scenarios, as follows:

1. The first scenario is a traditional load balancer using a single network connection for both communication channels. In practice, applications of this scenario typically use a WebSocket connection for both the RMI channel and the transfer of the video data. That traffic has to go through the load balancer. Instead of implementing an additional deployment for traditional load balancers, we measured the traffic of both channels for our new deployment setup.

2. The second scenario is a traditional load balancer using directly exposed video streaming endpoints. In practice, applications of this scenario often use the WebRTC protocol for video streaming, which provides a direct endpoint exposure. That means that the traffic of video streaming does not have to go through the load balancer. However, WebRTC is typically not used for the RMI channel, because of the instability of that connection caused by reconnects that can happen frequently for WebRTC connections. Instead, these applications typically use a WebSocket for the RMI calls. This means that the RMI traffic still has to go through the load balancer. Also in this scenario, we do not implement an additional deployment but measure the RMI traffic of our deployment setup.

3. The third scenario is using our proposed SRSD, where the load balancer is replaced by the SSO and the SSD. In this scenario, the SSO represents the relevant bottleneck of the application.

Figure 4 shows that our SRSD reduces the bottleneck traffic of the load balancer from more than 10 GB/min in the first scenario and about 10 MB/min in the second scenario to about 1 MB/min in SRSD. The reason for this significant improvement is that both communication channels in SRSD, unlike in other scenarios, run through the direct endpoint exposure between service consumer and service instance.

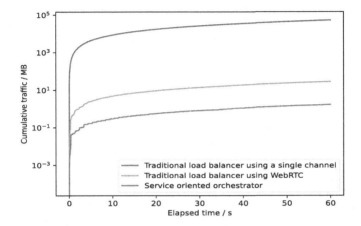

Fig. 4. Evaluating the data traffic for the three scenarios. Due to the high number of concurrent users and because the cumulative traffic is displayed, the variance decreases fast and the graph becomes quite smooth very quickly after a few seconds.

In our second series of experiments, we compare the QoS of Kubernetes service deployment architectures with QoS in our solution, depending on the provided server resources. As a metric for a poor QoS, we use the Denial of Service (DoS) rate P_d, which is the fraction of ROIA session requests that are denied because the load balancer routes the requests to a server that cannot handle an additional ROIA session. For commercial applications, the DoS rate P_d should be below 0.1%. As a metric for server resources, we use an overprovisioning ratio defined as:

$$r_o := \frac{N_d - \nu_0}{\nu_0}, \tag{1}$$

where N_d the number of deployed session slots, and the Average Concurrent Users (ACU) ν_0 is defined as:

$$\nu_0 := \frac{\nu_r T_s}{T_r}, \tag{2}$$

where T_s is the Average Session Duration (ASD), and ν_r is the average number of session requests issued in the time interval T_r.

In our evaluation, we determine the dependency of the DoS rate of our prototype depending on the overprovisioning ratio for the load balancer algorithms Round Robin (RR) [5], Least Connection (LC) [5], and our SRSD. The first two modes are supported by the Linux IPVS load balancer [8] and exposed to

Kubernetes services. For measurements, we implement a session slot allocations simulation in Python running on the same computer as specified above. The simulation is performed for six use cases. Each use case measures the DoS rate for 10k session requests depending on the overprovisioning ratio for one load balancer algorithm and a given number of concurrent users in two variants, either 250 or 1000 ACU. Each user requests a ROIA session at a random time, with equal probability for all users within the total time interval of the simulation execution. As a probability distribution $P(t)$ of the positive duration t of each session, we use the exponential function:

$$P(t) = \frac{1}{T_s} \exp\left(-\frac{t}{T_s}\right), \qquad \text{for } t > 0, \tag{3}$$

This function does not make specific assumptions about the user behavior, but allows any session duration up to infinity.

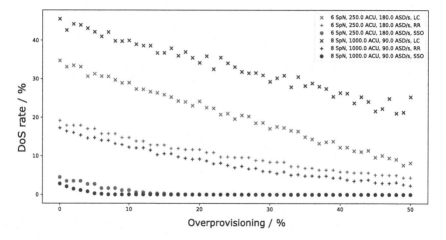

Fig. 5. DoS rate (lower is better) for: Least Connection (LC), Round Robin (RR), and Session Slots Orchestrator (SSO), with different Slots per Node (SpN), Average Concurrent Users (ACU), and Average Session Duration (ASD). The experiments in red present the measurements of 250 ACU, 6 SpN and 180 s ASD. The experiments in blue present the measurements of 1000 ACU, 8 SpN and 90 s ASD. (Color figure online)

Figure 5 shows the results of the simulation. The two upper curves show how the DoS rate depends on the overprovisioning when the Least Connection (LC) approach is used, the next two - for the RR approach, and the two lower curves show the DoS rate for our SSO approach. We observe that when having on average 1000 (or 250) concurrent users, the classical architectures lead to DoS rates of 30% (respectively 10%) for LC and 5% (respectively 3%) for RR even for the high overprovisioning ratio (and thus additional costs) of 50%. The reasons are as follows. TCP's TIME_WAIT [11] often leads to just routing repeatedly to the same server, which does not have a free session slot available. Without TCP's TIME_WAIT, the LC algorithm would be equivalent to our SRSD architecture, but would still not solve the bottleneck issue described above. RR provides better results than LC; however, since the service instance of a 3D ROIA has a hard limit on the number of sessions it can handle in parallel, depending on the underlying hardware of the node, it is a game of chance for a new session request to get routed to a server which can handle another session. Our architecture directly ensures that each ROIA session request is fulfilled as long as at least one of the servers can handle it. Therefore, we can get close to perfect QoS by using a relatively small overprovisioning rate of only 10%.

We conduct a plausibility check of these simulation results, as follows. When assuming that session slots are requested statistically independently and ignoring autocorrelation and correlation of session slot usages of different nodes, the number of currently used or desired session slots at a given time is per definition given by the Poisson distribution P_p. A realistic assumption is that each server node supports 8 session slots. If we have on average 5 concurrent user sessions per server node, this corresponds to a quite high overprovisioning ratio of 60% (but still only about 1.3 times the standard deviation). In this case the DoS is $P_p(\mu = 5, n > 8) = 7\%$, which is quite high. However, when using all available session slots effectively as in our architecture, we can achieve a better avoidance of a DoS by a lower overprovisioning ratio. For example, when having 1000 concurrent users using SRSD on average by an overprovisioning ratio of only 10% (but nevertheless about 3 times the standard deviation), the probability of having a DoS is $P_p(\mu = 1000, n > 1100) = 0.09\%$, which is significantly lower than traditional deployment architectures. This plausibility check mathematically confirms the results of our simulation scenarios.

4 Conclusion and Future Work

In this paper, we propose and implement the novel Scalable Real-time Service Deployment (SRSD) architecture for high-performance Real-Time Online Interactive Applications (ROIAs). While using Kubernetes, our architecture does not rely on classic metrics, but rather uses the session slots concept. The SRSD architecture provides an efficiently auto-scalable cloud environment for high-performance ROIAs which meets the strict QoS requirements of such RIOAs on the one hand and keeps the costs of computing resources on the cloud as low as possible on the other hand. The presented experimental evaluations demonstrates the following two advantages of SRSD: 1) we remove the bottleneck effect of traditional load balancers; 2) we achieve a significant improvement in the usage of the underlying cloud infrastructure resources by achieving a near-zero DoS rate with an overprovisioning ratio of only 10%.

As future work, we plan to further optimize our SSA component by using different prediction algorithms for future session slot requirements. An appropriate prediction algorithm will significantly increase the efficiency of resource usage. We expect this to be especially valuable for high-performance ROIAs since infrastructure costs are a fundamental aspect of ROIAs, which employ high-performance computing components like real-time 3D rendering.

References

1. Aly, M., Franke, M., Kretz, M., Schamel, F., Simoens, P.: Service oriented interactive media (SOIM) engines enabled by optimized resource sharing. In: 2016 IEEE Symposium on Service-Oriented System Engineering (SOSE), pp. 231–237 (2016). https://doi.org/10.1109/SOSE.2016.47
2. Bernstein, C.: TechTarget Homepage. https://whatis.techtarget.com/definition/lift-and-shift. Accessed 14 Mar 2021
3. Docker Homepage. https://www.docker.com. Accessed 20 Mar 2021
4. Ferris, J., Surridge, M., Glinka, F., et al.: Securing real-time on-line interactive applications in edutain@grid. In: César, E. (ed.) Euro-Par 2008. LNCS, vol. 5415, pp. 371–381. Springer, Heidelberg (2009). https://doi.org/10.1007/978-3-642-00955-6_42
5. GitHub Homepage. https://github.com/kubernetes/kubernetes/blob/d1525ec808c2c2ac6987f12cc68acf0b5a776650/pkg/proxy/apis/config/types.go#L189-L194. Accessed 14 Mar 2021
6. Gorlatch, S., Glinka, F., Ploss, A.: Towards a scalable real-time cyberinfrastructure for online computer games. In: 2009 15th International Conference on Parallel and Distributed Systems, pp. 722–727 (2009). https://doi.org/10.1109/ICPADS.2009.94
7. Griffin, D., et al.: Service oriented networking. In: 2014 European Conference on Networks and Communications (EuCNC), pp. 1–5 (2014). https://doi.org/10.1109/EuCNC.2014.6882684
8. Kubernetes Homepage. https://kubernetes.io/docs/concepts/services-networking/service/#proxy-mode-ipvs. Accessed 14 Mar 2021
9. Landa, R., Araújo, J.T., Clegg, R.G., Mykoniati, E., Griffin, D., Rio, M.: The large-scale geography of Internet round trip times. In: 2013 IFIP Networking Conference, pp. 1–9 (2013)
10. Landa, R., Clegg, R.G., Araujo, J.T., Mykoniati, E., Griffin, D., Rio, M.: Measuring the relationships between Internet geography and RTT. In: 2013 22nd International Conference on Computer Communication and Networks (ICCCN), pp. 1–7 (2013). https://doi.org/10.1109/ICCCN.2013.6614151
11. Linux Virtual Server Homepage. http://kb.linuxvirtualserver.org/wiki/Least-Connection_Scheduling. Accessed 14 Mar 2021
12. Maini, E., Phan, T.K., Griffin, D., Rio, M.: Hierarchical service placement for demanding applications. In: 2016 IEEE Globecom Workshops (GC Wkshps), pp. 1–6 (2016). https://doi.org/10.1109/GLOCOMW.2016.7848922
13. Ploss, A., Glinka, F., Gorlatch, S., et al.: A case study on using RTF for developing multi-player online games. In: César, E. (ed.) Euro-Par 2008. LNCS, vol. 5415, pp. 390–400. Springer, Heidelberg (2009). https://doi.org/10.1007/978-3-642-00955-6_44
14. Sawicki, B., Chaber, B.: Efficient visualization of 3D models by web browser. Computing 95, 661–673 (2013). https://doi.org/10.1007/s00607-012-0275-z

15. Unkelos-Shpigel, N., Hadar, I.: A multitude of requirements and yet sole deployment architecture: predictors of successful software deployment. In: 2013 2nd International Workshop on the Twin Peaks of Requirements and Architecture (TwinPeaks), pp. 19–23 (2013). https://doi.org/10.1109/TwinPeaks.2013.6614719
16. Vandeputte, F., et al.: Evaluator services for optimised service placement in distributed heterogeneous cloud infrastructures. In: 2015 European Conference on Networks and Communications (EuCNC), pp. 439–444 (2015). https://doi.org/10.1109/EuCNC.2015.7194114
17. W3C Consortium Homepage. https://www.w3.org/TR/wsdl20/#Endpoint. Accessed 14 Mar 2021

Leveraging HW Approximation for Exploiting Performance-Energy Trade-offs Within the Edge-Cloud Computing Continuum

Argyris Kokkinis$^{(\boxtimes)}$, Aggelos Ferikoglou, Dimitrios Danopoulos, Dimosthenis Masouros, and Kostas Siozios

Aristotle University of Thessaloniki, Thessaloniki, Greece
{akokkino,aferikog,ddanopou,dmasoura,ksiop}@physics.auth.gr

Abstract. Today, the need for real-time analytics and faster decision making mechanisms has led to the adoption of hardware accelerators, such as GPUs and FPGAs, within the edge-cloud computing continuum. Moreover, the need for energy-, yet performance-efficient solutions both in the edge and cloud has led to the rise of approximate computing as a promising paradigm, where "acceptable errors" are introduced to error-tolerant applications, thus, providing significant power-saving gains. In this work, we leverage approximate computing for exploiting performance-energy trade-offs of FPGA accelerated kernels with faster design time though an extended source-to-source HLS compiler based on Xilinx Vitis framework. We introduce a novel programming interface that operates at a high level of abstraction, thus, enabling automatic optimizations to the existing HLS design flow supporting both embedded and cloud devices through a common API. We evaluate our approach over three different application from DSP and machine learning domains and show that a decrease of 27% and 28% in power consumption, 61% and 69% in DSP utilization and 7% in clock period is achieved for Alveo U200 and ZCU104 FPGA platforms, on average.

Keywords: Edge & cloud computing · FPGA · HW approximation · High Level Synthesis · Source-to-source compiler

1 Introduction

Nowadays, the explosive growth and increasing power of IoT devices along with the rise of 5G networks have resulted in unprecedented volumes of data. Emerging use cases around autonomous vehicles, smart-cities, and smart factories require data processing and decision making closer to the point of data generation due to mission-critical, low-latency and near-real time requirements of such deployments. To this end, multi-layered computing architectures are emerging, where computing resources and applications are distributed from the edge of the network, closer to where data are gathered, to the cloud, realizing the edge-cloud computing continuum [15].

© Springer Nature Switzerland AG 2021
H. Jagode et al. (Eds.): ISC High Performance 2021 Workshops, LNCS 12761, pp. 406–415, 2021.
https://doi.org/10.1007/978-3-030-90539-2_27

Even though edge-cloud architectures expand the computing capacity of the traditional cloud paradigm by introducing an additional huge pool of computing resources, the inefficiency of traditional CPUs to provide fast, near real-time executions has also led to the introduction of hardware accelerators, such as GPUs and FPGAs, to the aforementioned hierarchy. Typical examples of accelerators include power-efficient devices at the edge (e.g., NVIDIA Jetson and Xilinx MPSoC), to high-performance, massively-parallel devices at the cloud (e.g., NVIDIA Ampere and Xilinx Alveo). While hardware accelerators provide increased performance gains, these benefits do not come for free, as such devices typically require more power to operate. From the edge point of view, energy efficiency has always been a first class system-design concern, to provide low-power embedded systems design. On the cloud side, the considerable share of electricity expenses over the total cost of ownership (TCO) [2], as well as the shift towards energy-efficient (green) computing at the data-center level, also indicate the need for efficient hardware acceleration.

Towards building more energy proportional computing systems, approximation techniques have been identified as a promising solution to reduce energy consumption and increase performance while retaining the output quality of applications. *Approximate computing* is based on the observation that many applications feature intristic error-resilience properties [3] (i.e. in DSP or machine learning domain). On top of that, automatic compilation flows have been leveraged to apply hardware transformations in FPGA designs in order to achieve faster and more optimal results.

In this paper, we employ approximate computing for exploring performance-energy trade-offs of FPGA accelerated kernels. Specifically, the novel contributions of this paper are as follows:

- We develop an extension for Vitis framework based on word-length optimizations that takes into account resource and accuracy constraints.
- We build an end-to-end compilation flow by creating a novel source-to-source HLS compiler that can achieve significant improvements with resource-power-accuracy trade-offs.
- We provide support for both embedded and cloud FPGAs in the framework by utilizing a standardized software interface that enables seamless interoperability between devices. We evaluate our proposed framework on three popular algorithms from DSP and ML domains for both a cloud (Xilinx Alveo U200) and an embedded (MPSoC ZCU104) FPGA device.

2   Background and Related Work

2.1   HLS and RTL Approaches for FPGA Design

FPGA devices have been proven to perform really well when programmed with optimal configuration [4]. However, hardware can be designed at varying levels of abstraction with the commonly used levels of abstraction being the gate level, register-transfer level (RTL) and algorithmic level. These methodologies differ with one another; RTL or many times described as hardware description language (HDL) (i.e. VHDL, Verilog) is used for circuit-level programming while behavioral approaches such as High Level Synthesis (HLS) are used at the algorithmic level [7,9].

RTL Design Methodology: With HDL like Verilog and VHDL developers can create low-level representations of an AI model or function, from which ultimately actual wiring can be derived. Unlike in software compiler design, RTL takes as input the register transfer level representation and involves constructs such as cells, functions, and multi-bit registers. In order to accelerate an AI algorithm on hardware several Processing Elements (PEs) that perform multiply-accumulate operations are hand-written in Verilog or VHDL code that are designed and optimized based on the constraints of the target platform (i.e. the number of multipliers, etc.). Mapping an AI model's computational operations to matrix-matrix or matrix-vector multiplication modules has been widely applied in prior studies [7,8,13]. Also, usually tiling and ping-pong double buffers techniques are then employed to improve the throughput along with other optimizations on the RTL level.

HLS Design Methodology: Employing High Level Synthesis for FPGA design enables a fast development process and high flexibility. Although using HLS provides a software-like tool flow (i.e. Xilinx Vitis or Intel Quartus Prime), the developer must still learn hardware-centric concepts, such as pipelining and routing, that they may have not been exposed to in writing C-code for traditional processors. Also, studies have shown that HLS can simulate faster the effects of data type precision and other hardware approximations which are often utilized on AI applications [14,16]. HLS automatically generates an RTL testbench which is driven by vectors generated by the original C++ code. Last, previous work has shown that HLS designs can exploit significant parallelism compared with RTL approaches and achieve similar latency improvements [5,11].

2.2 Approximation Techniques

Approximate computing techniques are used widely in error-resilient applications, trading-off algorithmic performance with power consumption and resource utilization. The rising computational complexity of many machine learning (ML) and math tasks makes imperative the use of techniques that mitigate the power and resource expenses while keeping the application's performance in the desired levels. Reducing the operands bit widths and exploiting inexact hardware are two popular techniques that are used in approximate computing in a wide range of different applications.

Precision Scaling: A technique that changes the bit-width of input or intermediate operands to reduce storage and computing requirements. Jong Hwan Ko et al. [10] leverage the benefits of precision scaling in neural networks for audio processing achieving up to 30x processing time speedup while the performance impact degradation is less than 3.14% in the case of classification tasks. Xilinx [1] provides tools and libraries that support a wide range of fixed point precision data types. It has been noted, that FPGA design implementations using fixed point arithmetics are more efficient than their equivalent floating point due to their limited power and resource consumption. According to [6] power savings of up to 50% have been noticed for designs that have been migrated from floating to fixed point.

Approximate Multipliers/Adders: Hardware oriented approximate techniques have been proposed. Approximate adders and multipliers modify the typical addition and multiplication process for error resilient applications. The majority of the approximate integer and floating point multiplication approaches leverage logarithmic properties to minimize the computational overhead for a given error tolerance. Saadat et al. [12] proposed a custom floating-point multiplier that achieves x57 and x28 power and area improvement respectively when used as the multiplication block in AlexNet, with no significant degradation in the accuracy.

3   Proposed Framework Extension

In this section we describe the programming interface for our HLS compiler. The motivation behind this tool is to study how our HW optimizations can benefit from automation. We extend the Vitis HLS compiler with a word-length optimization tool packaged as an extension that can automatically optimize HLS kernels by applying source-to-source transformations and can generalize to different kinds of applications. Also, three use cases were selected for demonstration which are also described in this section.

3.1   Common FPGA Interface

We built our applications on top of Xilinx Runtime library (XRT) which is an open-source software stack that facilitates management and usage of FPGA devices. The interface supports either like C/C++ or Python on host code which enabled us to generalize more the framework using a unified API. XRT was implemented as a combination of userspace and kernel driver components that provided standardized software interface in our source-to-source HLS compiler enabling seamless device interoperability.

3.2   Building a Source-to-Source HLS Compiler

Automatic source-to-source transformation techniques have been applied in software compilation and optimization but are also an ideal solution for HLS transformations. They can greatly benefit the FPGA accelerator design in a high-level synthesis design flow because there are many temporal/spatial resource and optimization directives that HLS tools provide. The goal of our source-to-source compiler was to enable the fully automated FPGA design flows which is especially important for deploying FPGAs seamlessly both in edge and cloud domains. Figure 1 shows the whole development process and the HLS compiler utilizing our extension for word-optimization along with the XRT interface to support edge and cloud devices such as MPSoC or Alveo FPGAs.

High-Level Synthesis Under Accuracy Constraint. HLS vendors have enriched the HLS-C language with integer and fixed-point types of arbitrary size. The constraint function of the optimization problem corresponded to the fixed-point numerical accuracy. The case study in this work on Vitis tool is a transformation that applies to floating-point multiplications and additions on a loop's critical path. The number of bits for each part becomes fixed, I_w is the number of bits for the integer part integrating the sign bit, D_w is the number of bits for the decimal part, while $F_w = I_w + D_w$ is the total number of bits. The quantization mode Q_m which dictates the behavior when greater precision is generated than can be defined by smallest fractional bit in the variable used to store the result was set to round to plus infinity. Last, in the hardware context, we also configured the number scaling from float to fixed point types to tailor the accuracy requirements of the application.

High-Level Synthesis Under Resource Constraint. In the resource optimization scheme, the word-lengths are first optimized and then the architecture is synthesized. The first step gave a fixed-point specification that respects the accuracy constraint. For this constraint, a dedicated resource is used for each operation which can be defined by the HLS compiler. Also, when there are enough resources and high performance is required larger word lengths can be used where the heuristic limits the search space and obtain reasonable optimization time.

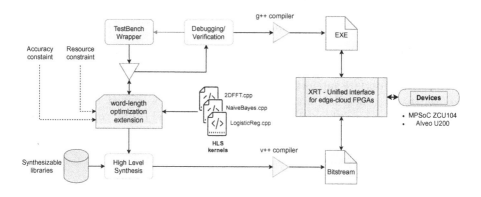

Fig. 1. HLS compiler extension

3.3   Kernels and Algorithms Tested

In this study, we intentionally focused on evaluating the performance of popular algorithms as they are used as backend kernels to many frameworks in machine learning and math tasks. For this reason, we used for evaluation three kernels: Logistic Regression, 2D FFT and Gaussian Naive Bayes. All kernels were initially optimized according to the FPGA principles for high performance using HLS optimizations such as loop unrolling, pipelining and memory partition.

Case Study 1: Two-Dimensional FFT. A fast Fourier transform (FFT) is an algorithm that computes the discrete Fourier transform (DFT) of a sequence. For our case study we selected a slightly different version of the classical algorithm namely 2D-FFT (two-dimensional Fast Fourier Transform) which can be used to analyze the frequency spectrum of 2D signal (matrix) data based on the primitives of 1D-FFT. First it computes the one-dimensional FFT along one dimension (row or column) then it computes the FFT of the output of the first step along the other dimension (column or row).

Case Study 2: Logistic Regression. Logistic regression is one of the most popular methods for building predictive models for many complex pattern-matching and classification problems. It can label a sample with integer from 0 to $L-1$ in which L is class number. For a L class label, it needs $L-1$ vector to calculate $L-1$ margins. Its prediction function's output is linear to samples. The equation can be seen as below:

$$margin_i = \beta_{i,0} + \beta_{i,1}x_1 + \beta_{i,2}x_2 + ... + \beta_{i,n}x_n$$

Then label is decided according to L $-$ 1 margins based on formula below:

$$Label = \begin{cases} 0, & \text{if } \text{maxMargin} \leqslant 0 \\ k, & \text{if } margin_k = \text{maxMargin} > 0 \end{cases}$$

Case Study 3: Gaussian Naive Bayes. In machine learning, naive Bayes classifiers are a family of simple "probabilistic classifiers" based on applying Bayes' theorem with strong (naive) independence assumptions between the features. We chose to implement the extension of Naive Bayes which is the Gaussian Naive Bayes which supports real-valued attributes, most commonly by assuming a Gaussian distribution. The likelihood of the features is as below:

$$P(x_i \mid y) = \frac{1}{\sqrt{2\pi\sigma_y^2}} \exp\left(-\frac{(x_i - \mu_y)^2}{2\sigma_y^2}\right)$$

4   Evaluation

In each of the case studies we evaluate our word-length optimization extension using the proposed compilation flow. The trade offs of the approximation techniques are evident in terms of accuracy, power consumption and resource utilization. The provided results underline the importance of the proposed HLS source-to-source compiler for designing approximate algorithms under a set of constraints in an automated manner.

Device Setup

For the device setup we evaluated our algorithms on a Zynq UltraScale+ MPSoC ZCU104 edge FPGA and an Alveo U200 cloud FPGA. The MPSoC is a System on a Chip (SoC) which has a 16 nm XCZU9EG FPGA with 504K logic cells and 48 mb of total on-chip memory. The SoC also includes a quad-core ARM Cortex-A53 CPU with 4 GB 64-bit DDR4 memory. Regarding the Alveo U200,

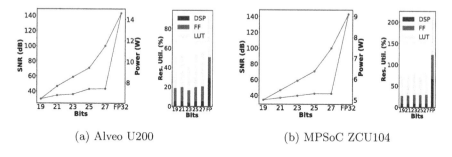

(a) Alveo U200   (b) MPSoC ZCU104

Fig. 2. Signal to noise ratio, power and utilization percentage per resource vs decimal bits for 2D FFT algorithm in U200 (a) and ZCU104 (b) platforms

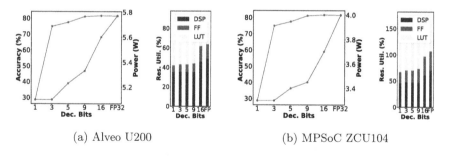

(a) Alveo U200   (b) MPSoC ZCU104

Fig. 3. Accuracy, power and utilization percentage per resource vs decimal bits for logistic regression algorithm in U200 (a) and ZCU104 (b) platforms

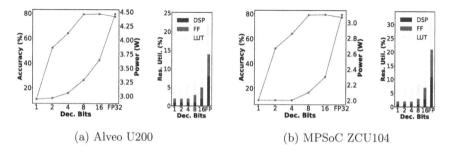

(a) Alveo U200   (b) MPSoC ZCU104

Fig. 4. Accuracy, power and utilization percentage per resource vs decimal bits for gaussian naive bayes algorithm in U200 (a) and ZCU104 (b) platforms

it is a PCIe attachable FPGA card built on 16 nm architecture with 64 GB DDR4 off-chip memory of 77 GB/s bandwidth and 35 MB on-chip memory of 31 TB/s total bandwidth.

4.1 Resource Utilization and Algorithmic Performance

Figures 2, 3 and 4 show the performance, power consumption (on-chip) and resource utilization for different decimal bit approximations for the aforementioned case studies. The implemented kernels were simulated on Alveo U200 and MPSoC ZCU104 platforms with 300 MHz target clock frequency. Power analysis was performed on RTL level for each kernel using Vivado Design Suite.

Figures 2a and 2b show the relation between accuracy, power and resource utilization for different levels of approximation for the 2D FFT kernel. An increase in decimal bits results to a rise in algorithm's accuracy and power consumption for both platforms. From 19 to 27 decimal bits there is a linear increase in Signal-to-Noise Ratio (SNR) reaching 80 dBs, while the power consumption for U200 and ZCU104 does not exceed 8 W and 5.5 W respectively. In the case of U200 for up to 27 bits the resource utilization does not significantly differentiate, with the utilization of digital signal processing (DSP) units, flip flops (FF) and lookup tables (LUT) not exceeding 5.4%, 15.4% and 34.4%. Similar results are observed in the ZCU104 platform with the utilization percentages reaching values up to 9%, 21% and 51%. The utilization per resource type for the same number of decimal bits is higher in the case of ZCU104 due to fewer available resources of the MPSoC FPGAs compared to U200.

Figures 3a and 3b show the effect of precision scaling on logistic regression algorithm. For up to 5 decimal bits there is a disproportionate rise between algorithmic performance and resource utilization with the percentage of utilized DSPs, LUTs and FFs not exceeding 21%, 11% and 17% in the case of U200 platform. At the same time, the algorithm's accuracy increases from 28.7% to 77.5% and reaches a plateau. Specifically, any further increase at the decimal bits causes fluctuations up to 5.3% in accuracy while the rise in power consumption may reach 0.6 W on both platforms.

Finally, Figs. 4a and 4b present the results for gaussian naive bayes algorithm. Regarding the relationship between power consumption, accuracy and decimal bits, the same trend as in Figs. 3a and 3b can be observed. In particular, for 8 decimal bits the achieved accuracy is almost equal to the floating point (79.25%) while the power consumption is 1 W lower for both U200 and ZCU104. Additionally, resource utilization figures depict that for up to 8 decimal bits the utilization of DSPs, FFs and LUTs does not exceed 1%, 2% and 6% for U200 and 1%, 2% and 5% for ZCU104. For the floating point data type, an increase in DSPs (x8 and x11), FFs (x3 and x5) and LUTs (x1.7 and x2.4) is observed compared to 8 decimal bits for both platforms.

4.2 Approximate and Default Algorithm Comparative Analysis

In Fig. 5, the floating point implementation of each case study is compared with the corresponding approximate implementation that satisfies the predefined

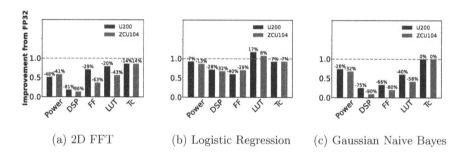

(a) 2D FFT   (b) Logistic Regression   (c) Gaussian Naive Bayes

Fig. 5. Savings in power consumption, resource utilization and maximization of the achievable target clock frequency due to the employment of approximate techniques for 2D FFT, logistic regression and gaussian naive bayes algorithms.

performance criteria (SNR above 95 dBs and accuracy above 95% of the floating point) in terms of power, resource utilization and achieved clock frequency. Figures 5a, 5b and 5c exhibit the advantages of the proposed HLS approximation mechanism for the studied ML and DSP algorithms derived from our source-to-source HLS compiler automatically. Our compiler extension leads to a decrease of 27% and 28% in power consumption and a decrease of 61% and 69% in DSP utilization for U200 and ZCU104 platforms, on average. Meanwhile, the significant reduction in used resources and hence in critical paths, leads to lower Tc (clock period) and as a result higher clock frequency (7% lower clock period for both platforms).

5   Conclusion

In this work we proposed a new programming interface based on the new Xilinx Vitis framework. Our optimizations were implemented as an extension to our source-to-source HLS compiler that operates at a high level of abstraction enabling automatic accuracy and resource optimizations to the existing HLS design flow. Also, we provided a common API to support both embedded and cloud FPGAs using the standardized XRT software interface. The HLS transformations were tested on three applications producing a diverse set of kernel versions which gave a broad range of resource-accuracy-power tradeoffs. From a research point of view, we are focusing on adding further functionality to our framework with additional approximation features. The spectrum of possible design space tradeoffs is vast but this work shed some light to the area with successful results aiming to make FPGAs contribute fundamentally with minimum programming effort into the software-hardware ecosystem.

Acknowledgment. This work has been supported by the E.C. funded program SERRANO under H2020 Grant Agreement No: 101017168.

References

1. Xilinx. https://www.xilinx.com/
2. Barroso, L.A., Hölzle, U.: The case for energy-proportional computing. Computer **40**(12), 33–37 (2007)
3. Chippa, V.K., Chakradhar, S.T., Roy, K., Raghunathan, A.: Analysis and characterization of inherent application resilience for approximate computing. In: 2013 50th ACM/EDAC/IEEE Design Automation Conference (DAC), pp. 1–9 (2013). https://doi.org/10.1145/2463209.2488873
4. Danopoulos, D., Kachris, C., Soudris, D.: A quantitative comparison for image recognition on accelerated heterogeneous cloud infrastructures, pp. 171–189 (September 2019). https://doi.org/10.1201/9780429399602-8
5. Danopoulos, D., Kachris, C., Soudris, D.: Utilizing cloud FPGAs towards the open neural network standard. Sustain. Comput.: Inform. Syst. **30**, 100520 (2021)
6. Finnerty, A., Ratigner, H.: Reduce power and cost by converting from floating point to fixed point. WP491 (v1. 0) (2017)
7. Guan, Y., et al.: FP-DNN: an automated framework for mapping deep neural networks onto FPGAs with RTL-HLS hybrid templates. In: 2017 IEEE 25th Annual International Symposium on Field-Programmable Custom Computing Machines (FCCM), pp. 152–159 (2017). https://doi.org/10.1109/FCCM.2017.25
8. Guo, K., et al.: Angel-eye: a complete design flow for mapping CNN onto customized hardware. In: 2016 IEEE Computer Society Annual Symposium on VLSI (ISVLSI), pp. 24–29 (2016). https://doi.org/10.1109/ISVLSI.2016.129
9. Homsirikamol, E., George, K.G.: Toward a new HLS-based methodology for FPGA benchmarking of candidates in cryptographic competitions: the Caesar contest case study. In: 2017 International Conference on Field Programmable Technology (ICFPT), pp. 120–127 (2017). https://doi.org/10.1109/FPT.2017.8280129
10. Ko, J.H., Fromm, J., Philipose, M., Tashev, I., Zarar, S.: Precision scaling of neural networks for efficient audio processing. arXiv preprint arXiv:1712.01340 (2017)
11. Nane, R., et al.: A survey and evaluation of FPGA high-level synthesis tools. IEEE Trans. Comput.-Aided Des. Integr. Circuits Syst. **35**, 1591–1604 (2015). https://doi.org/10.1109/TCAD.2015.2513673
12. Saadat, H., Bokhari, H., Parameswaran, S.: Minimally biased multipliers for approximate integer and floating-point multiplication. IEEE Trans. Comput.-Aided Des. Integr. Circuits Syst. **37**(11), 2623–2635 (2018)
13. Sharma, H., et al.: Bit fusion: bit-level dynamically composable architecture for accelerating deep neural network. In: 2018 ACM/IEEE 45th Annual International Symposium on Computer Architecture (ISCA), pp. 764–775 (2018)
14. Shawahna, A., Sait, S.M., El-Maleh, A.: FPGA-based accelerators of deep learning networks for learning and classification: a review. IEEE Access **7**, 7823–7859 (2019). https://doi.org/10.1109/ACCESS.2018.2890150
15. Shi, W., Cao, J., Zhang, Q., Li, Y., Xu, L.: Edge computing: vision and challenges. IEEE Internet Things J. **3**(5), 637–646 (2016)
16. Wess, M., Manoj, P.D.S., Jantsch, A.: Neural network based ECG anomaly detection on FPGA and trade-off analysis, pp. 1–4 (May 2017). https://doi.org/10.1109/ISCAS.2017.8050805

Datashim and Its Applications in Bioinformatics

Yiannis Gkoufas[1], David Yu Yuan[2](✉) ⓘ, Christian Pinto[1],
Panagiotis Koutsovasilis[1], and Srikumar Venugopal[1]

[1] IBM Research, Dublin, Ireland
yiannisg@ie.ibm.com
[2] Technology and Science Integration, European Bioinformatics Institute,
European Molecular Biology Laboratory, Cambridge, United Kingdom
davidyuan@ebi.ac.uk
https://www.ibm.com/, https://www.ebi.ac.uk/

Abstract. Bioinformatics pipelines depend on shared POSIX filesystems for its input, output and intermediate data storage. Containerization makes it more difficult for the workloads to access the shared file systems. In our previous study, we were able to run both ML and non-ML pipelines on Kubeflow successfully. However, the storage solutions were complex and less optimal.

In this article, we are introducing a new concept of Dataset and its corresponding resource as a native Kubernetes object. We have implemented the concept with a new framework Datashim which takes care of all the low-level details about data access in Kubernetes pods. Its pluggable architecture is designed for the development of caching, scheduling and governance plugins. Together, they manage the entire lifecycle of the custom resource Dataset.

We use Datashim to serve data from object stores to both ML and non-ML pipelines on Kubeflow. We feed training data into ML models directly with Datashim instead of downloading it to the local disks, which makes the input scalable. We have enhanced the durability of training metadata by storing it into a dataset, which also simplifies the setup of the TensorBoard, independent of the notebook server. For the non-ML pipeline, we have simplified the 1000 Genome Project pipeline with datasets injected into the pipeline dynamically. We have now established a new resource type Dataset to represent the concept of data source on Kubernetes with our novel framework Datashim to manage its lifecycle.

Keywords: Datashim · Kubeflow · Kubernetes · Bioinformatics.

1 Introduction

Bioinformatics pipelines make extensive use of HPC for batch processing. Ever-increasing demands of computational resources by the pipelines make migration to clouds necessary. In our previous studies [1–3], we ported the pipelines from Platform Load Sharing Facility (LSF) to Kubernetes (K8S) [4] and Kubeflow

© Springer Nature Switzerland AG 2021
H. Jagode et al. (Eds.): ISC High Performance 2021 Workshops, LNCS 12761, pp. 416–427, 2021.
https://doi.org/10.1007/978-3-030-90539-2_28

(KF) [5] to make the pipelines more efficient with containerization. This made it harder to access cloud-agnostic global shared file systems similar to ones in HPC clusters due to the limited choices of persistent volumes [6] supporting RWX access mode. We made many attempts, but we were never satisfied with the performance, security and ease of use with the previous solutions.

There are no established resource types to represent the concept of data source on Kubernetes. End users are burdened with configuring and optimising the data access. We are to introduce a new concept Dataset on Kubernetes and to create a novel framework Datashim to manage its lifecycle. Datashim [7] enables users to access remote data sources via a mount-point within their container-ized workloads. It is extensible and can potentially support additional storage mechanisms with the Container Storage Interface (CSI) [8] plugins.

Dataset is a higher level construct implemented as a Custom Resource Defi-nition (CRD). Each Dataset is a pointer to an existing remote data source and is materialized as a Persistent Volume Claim [15]. With the integration of Datashim on Kubeflow, we were able to mount object stores as Persistent Volumes Claims and present them to Bioinformatics pipelines as a POSIX-like file system. The developers of Bioinformatics Pipelines can focus on the methodologies and the results of the experiments and not on installing and tuning CSI Plugins. In addition, Datashim makes use of Kubernetes access control and secrets so that pipelines do not need to be run with escalated privilege or to handle secret keys. This makes the platform more secure. Under the hood, Datashim can accelerate data access by transparently caching Datasets which are frequently accessed.

We have conducted functional analysis on Google Kubernetes Engine (GKE). The conclusions are applicable to existing Kubernetes clusters on all clouds. Through both ML and non-ML Bioinformatics pipelines, we have demonstrated the capabilities of Datashim to access input from GCS, S3 and web server with S3 and H3 protocols securely. We have managed to simplify our pipelines on Kube-flow via all three usage scenarios: creating dataset statically, injecting mount points with ConfigMap and creating dataset dynamically. In addition, we have benchmarked our variant calling pipeline for the 1000 Genomes Project access-ing large number of genome assemblies via Datashim with and without cache. Our result shows that we can access data on Kubeflow easily and securely with Datashim. The new concept Dataset and its implementation Datashim can be a valuable addition to enhance Kubernetes for batch processing.

2   Method

Datashim aims at providing a higher level of abstraction for dynamic provision-ing of storage for the users' applications. It introduces the concept of Dataset to represent available storage or pre-existing data provided by any cloud-based storage solution, like S3 Object Store or NFS. In the following sections we will outline the basic specifications and components of the framework.

2.1   Dataset Custom Resource Definition

Every entity (pod, deployment, job, etc.) in the Kubernetes world can be expressed as a resource accompanied by a specification. As an example, when the user wants to create a new pod, they need to create a pod resource following the related specification in terms of mandatory fields, possible values etc. The default Kubernetes resources are materialized by Kubernetes in a well-defined way. For instance, when the user creates a new pod, the associated containers will be launched in one of the available nodes of the cluster. The mechanisms of Kubernetes enable service providers to define their own Custom Resource Definitions (CRD) to bring the domain-specific logic they desire to their Kubernetes-managed infrastructure. Tapping on those capabilities, the Datashim introduces the Dataset CRD. A Dataset object is a reference to a storage provided by a cloud-based storage solution, potentially populated with pre-existing data. Our framework is completely agnostic to where/how a specific Dataset is stored, as long as the endpoint is accessible by the nodes within the Kubernetes cluster, in which the framework is deployed. Currently, the framework supports any Cloud Object Storage solution which exposes an S3 or NFS compatible endpoint. An example Dataset is displayed in Fig. 1.

```
apiVersion: com.ie.ibm.hpsys/v1alpha1
kind: Dataset
metadata:
  name: example-dataset
spec:
  local:
    type: "COS"
    accessKeyID: "accesskey"
    secretAccessKey: "secret_accesskey"
    endpoint: "http://s3.endpoint.cloud"
    bucket: "my-bucket"

<example-dataset.yaml>
```

Fig. 1. Dataset Spec

The user can specify the type of the remote data storage. For Datasets stored in COS (Cloud Object Store) the mandatory fields are: `endpoint`, `bucket`, `accessKeyID` and `secretAccessKey`. As described above, the only requirement for the endpoint is that it must be a reachable address from the Kubernetes nodes. The bucket entry creates a one-to-one mapping relationship between a Dataset object and a bucket in the Cloud Object Store. The fields `accessKeyID` and `secretAccessKey` are the necessary credentials to allow access to the specific bucket. Finally, in the specific example the user or an administrator who creates this Dataset object defines a name for the Dataset, in this case `example-dataset`. In Kubernetes the various resources are logically grouped under a namespace, and the users who have access granted to a specific namespace can access all the resources created within it. This is valid for the Dataset objects as well, access is restricted to only a specific namespace. To accelerate the development process of Kubernetes-based applications and workloads, it is very likely that a different persona would create a Dataset object (like the administrator or the data provider) and a different persona would use a Dataset within their application.

2.2 Dataset Operator

We have described above the specification of a Dataset object. Creating a Custom Resource Definition is just the first step to add custom logic in the Kubernetes cluster. The next step would be to create a component that has embedded the domain-specific application logic for the CRD. Essentially, a service provider needs to develop and install a component which reacts to the various events which are part of the lifecycle of a CRD (creation, deletion) and implements the desired functionality. This would have required significant amount of boilerplate code and there was no established standard for developing such component a few years ago. Fortunately, the opensource operator-sdk [16] provides the necessary tooling and automation to assist in the development of these components. We have utilized the operator-sdk to create our Dataset Operator. Its main functionality is to react to the creation of a new Dataset and materialize the specific object.

As mentioned above, the way to provide access to a data source within an application running on Kubernetes is via PVCs (Persistent Volume Claim). A PVC is linked to a specific `storage class` corresponding to the underlying storage mechanism. However, the support for storage is not flexible when it comes to provisioning new volume types. Recently Kubernetes has adopted the Container Storage Interface (CSI) [8] that facilitates the introduction of volume plugins without the need of modifying the core of Kubernetes itself. For our work we are maintaining an opensource implementation of CSI-based volumes for S3. When a new dataset of type COS (Cloud Object Store) is created, the operator is the component responsible for 1) creating a new PVC with the corresponding Storage Class and 2) creating the Kubernetes secrets to store the access credentials for the new Dataset. The pair PVC-Secret associated with this Dataset is passed to the CSI-S3 implementation which provides a mount point as a way for any pod to consume the Dataset. An example flow is presented in Fig. 2, where hexagons represent components of the framework and the squares are the Kubernetes resources created as a result of submitting a new Dataset.

2.3 Pods Admission Controller

With the components we have outlined so far, we enable the end user to define a Dataset representing a remote data source and we create the associated PVC. This PVC can be mounted to any pod and provide access to a deployed application. We have taken an extra-step to offer a transparent way for the users to

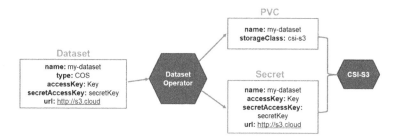

Fig. 2. Dataset operator

access their Datasets within their pods. With our framework the only requirement from the user is to annotate their pods according to our convention and
the Dataset will become available to the pod via a mount point as shown in
Fig. 3.

Fig. 3. Pods Admission Controller functions

The user needs to define the fields `id` and `useas` for every dataset. The `id`
field should correspond to a dataset name (as created above). The `useas` dictates the way that the user wants to access the specific dataset. The user can
access it via a mount directory within their pod, but also it's possible for users
to get the datasets access credentials (e.g., S3 ID and KEY) injected into application pods. Access to data in this latter case will be explicitly handled by the
application code using whatever native interface exposed by the dataset source
(e.g., S3). The extra labels required to operate with datasets are handled by a
dedicated Kubernetes component following the Admission Controller pattern.
Such components can modify objects upon creation and decorate them with
additional fields. In our use case, we monitor the pods with the specific type
of labels and add the necessary information to enable pods mounting the PVC
linked to each Dataset. As a convention, a dataset with id `my-dataset` would be
mounted inside the pod on `/mnt/datasets/my-dataset`. The user is also able
to override the desired mount path as shown in Fig. 4

3   Result

We have been using Kubeflow as an efficient platform for both ML and non-ML
pipelines in Bioinformatics. The pipelines are unable to read from and write

```
apiVersion: v1
kind: Pod
metadata:
  name: nginx
  labels:
    dataset.0.id: "example-dataset"
    dataset.0.useas: "mount"
spec:
  containers:
    - name: nginx
      image: nginx
      volumeMounts:
      - mountPath: "/mount/dataset1"
        name: "example-dataset"
```

Fig. 4. Pod definition with user defined dataset mount point

to object stores or to access HTTP archives directly. They all assume the local access of files on shared file systems. It is often impractical to download or upload large amount of files or to rewrite the pipelines to make use of the cloud-native storages. We use Datashim to bridge the gap.

Datashim enables us to access very different input from different sources via different protocols uniformly. We choose a private Google Cloud Storage (GCS) bucket for cardiomyocyte images for the ML pipeline. We use a public S3 bucket on AWS for DNA alignments from the 1000 Genomes Project for the non-ML pipeline. We also access a public gzip archive at European Bioinformatics Institute (EBI) for human reference genome GRCh37 for the non-ML pipeline. The S3 access is authenticated with the access key and secret. The data is made available to both ML and non-ML pipelines in containers as if local POSIX files mounted onto pods via PVC dynamically.

Datasets can be mapped into Persistent Volume Claims (PVCs) and pod injection. There are three methods to access datasets in the context of Kubeflow:

1. Option 1 - Mount Datasets via Persistent Volume Claims (see Sect. 3.1.)
2. Option 2 - Mount Datasets via pod injection with annotation (see Sect. 3.2.)
3. Option 3 - Mount Datasets dynamically in a pipeline via Kubeflow Pipeline (KFP) Domain Specific Language (DSL) [9] (see Sect. 3.3.)

3.1 ML: Data Volumes for Notebook Servers

In our previous study, we used Keras API to download files to the local file system [10] so that the microscopic images can be used for training and validation later in the notebook. It was very slow to download one file at a time via the OMERO 5.6.0 JSON API [12]. The Keras API get_file() provided a simple-minded caching mechanism of skipping files with the same name. This can speed up the process but was error-prone.

With Datashim, we created our own repository of images from Image Data Repository (IDR) [13] deposited by Nirschl, J.J., et al. [11]. The repository is a storage bucket on GCS set up via the following process.

1. GCS - Copy the images into an empty bucket.
2. K8S - Define a dataset backed by the newly created bucket in the namespace used by notebooks via kubectl
3. KF - Create a notebook server mounting the dataset via its PVC (option 1).

With the one-time setup in the first two steps, the notebooks in the same Kubernetes namespace can access the images directly from the data volume as if they were on a POSIX filesystem. They do not need to download their own copies of images. In addition, the GCS bucket can survive the deletion of the notebook, the notebook server, the Kubeflow instance, and the Kubernetes cluster. The private repository can be used by new notebooks on new Kubeflow instances or by multiple Kubernetes clusters at the same time.

ML pipelines typically process GiBs to TiBs of images in training. For ML in timelapse videos (e.g. embryo development), the data size gets into TiB to PiB range. Downloading images via REST calls can quickly become impractical for time and storage space. The Datasets backed by object storage provide nearly infinite scalability. In addition, ML pipelines prototyped on POSIX file systems can access images in object stores conveniently without modification.

3.2   ML: Pod Labels for TensorBoard

The default notebook server images have included TensorBoard as a notebook extension. It requires four steps to set it up in addition to invoke the TensorBoard callback:

1. Load the extension in the notebook: `%load_ext tensorboard`
2. Start the TensorBoard in the notebook: `%tensorboard --logdir='<log_dir>'`
3. Enable port forward in a command terminal on the local client:
   – `kubectl port-forward -n <namespace> <notebook_pod> 8080:6006`
4. Access the TensorBoard in a web browser: `http://localhost:8080/`

This approach does not involve Datashim and it has the following issues:

1. The process is very manual and inconvenient.
2. The training metadata can not survive the deletion of the notebook or the kubernetes cluster.
3. This approach would not work if a custom image does not have the TensorBoard extension.

We take a fairly new Tensorflow image `tensorflow/tensorflow:2.2.1-py3` and wrap it into a Deployment. The TensorBoard gets exposed via a Service and an Istio CRD VirtualService so that it can be accessed via a custom URI from the same host as the Kubeflow dashboard. More importantly, the Deployment is configured with two labels so that pods can access a Dataset backed by an object store for the TensorBoard (option 2).

A Deployment is labelled with `dataset.0.id` and `dataset.0.uses` to get Datashim to inject the default mount point `/mnt/datasets/<dataset_name>/` into a pod, similar to Fig. 4. The namespace has to be labelled for Datashim to monitor the lifecycle of the datasets in the namespace, for example:

```
kubectl label namespace "$namespace"
monitor-pods-datasets=enabled --overwrite=true
```

The Kubeflow community has noticed the same issue between the notebook and the TensorBoard. They are taking a similar approach to create TensorBoards independent of notebooks in a future release. We have shared this article and advised them to use Datashim or something similar for the training metadata as described here (internal communications).

3.3   Non-ML: Dynamic Dataset with Kubeflow Pipelines APIs

Kubeflow Pipeline can access existing Datasets via PipelineVolumes. This is similar to how Persistent Volumes are accessed statically in Kubernetes. A more convenient approach is to define Datasets dynamically, again similar to how PVCs can be used to create PVs dynamically (option 3).

The overall processes for both static and dynamic approaches are similar. The dynamic approach gives more control to the pipeline users, similar to how PVCs are used statically or dynamically. The code snippet below shows how we have implemented the dynamic approach with the KFP APIs in Fig. 5.

```
def k8s_ds_op(name: str,
              manifest: str,
              action: str = "apply") -> PipelineVolume:
    with open(manifest, 'r') as fp:
        yml = yaml.safe_load(fp)
    k8s_resource = V1beta1CustomResourceDefinition(api_version=yml['apiVersion'],
                                                   kind=yml['kind'],
                                                   metadata=yml['metadata'],
                                                   spec=yml['spec'])
    rop = ResourceOp(name=name,
                     k8s_resource=k8s_resource,
                     action=action)
    return PipelineVolume(pvc=name).after(rop)


<1000g.py>
```

Fig. 5. Datashim dataset created dynamically in KFP

3.4   Pipeline for 1000 Genomes Project Simplified

Before the integration with Datashim, the output of our G1K pipeline was uploaded to an S3 bucket. The input was downloaded from three different sources to PVCs backed by an NFS server for ReadWriteMany (RWX) access:

1. Human reference genome GRCh37 on a public FTP server downloaded via curl.
2. G1K queries, a list of 1046 alignments (i.e. BAM file names) on a private S3 bucket downloaded via AWS CLI in a custom Docker container.
3. G1K genomes, the actual BAM files and their indexes (i.e. BAI files) on a private NFS volume accessed via Onedata.

The total size of alignments are about 230 TiBs. It is impractical to download such a large volume of data and store it on the NFS server. It is estimated to take 14 h to transfer the files and $2,000/day to store them. We use Onedata [14] to access the alignments when they are needed as shown in Fig. 6. As we have discussed in detail in our previous paper [1], we have spent very significant effort (compiling Freebayes from the source and merging images via multi-stage builds) to create a custom Docker image because Onedata does not support Kubernetes. We also have a maintenance issue to keep updating the Onedata client and Freebays whenever these components change, compounded by poor backward compatibility of Onedata. In addition, Onedata client requires root privileges to mount file systems at runtime. This implies significant security risk for these custom pods to run with the escalated privilege.

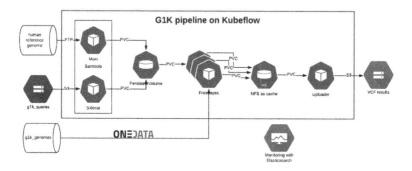

Fig. 6. Complicated pipeline implementation without Datashim

Datashim has enabled us to simplify the pipeline significantly (See Fig. 7). We do not download or upload files from or to storage buckets with S3 protocol. The sidecar and uploader in Fig. 6 are removed. In addition, the process in Freebayes can copy results to the output directly. We no longer need an NFS Persistent Volume in RWX mode to cache the results for the uploader. These processes can use their local ephemeral disk for caching, which has improved IO throughput very significantly. This is because the processes are writing to local disks with completely isolated parallel IOs. They no longer have to fight for the shared Persistent Volume backed by an NFS server. Finally, Onedata client is no longer used. We can simply use the binaries of Freebayes maintained by Anaconda to augment Miniconda image and run pods without escalated privileges.

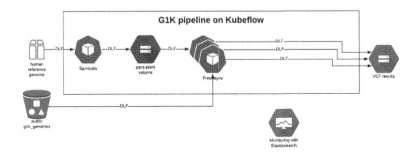

Fig. 7. Simplified pipeline implementation with Datashim

Comparing the two implementations of our G1K pipeline, we can definitively conclude that Datashim has simplified the implementation significantly. In addition, we have improved security by running pods as non-root by removing the dependency on Onedata. The bottleneck of the NFS Persistent Volume and a custom S3 uploader for caching are eliminated.

4   Discussion

The adoption of the Dataset object as a declarative way to provision and use PVCs within Kubernetes pods brings benefits not only to the end users but also on other data-oriented Kubernetes frameworks, especially those providing Caching and Scheduling capabilities. In Datashim we are supporting a pluggable caching mechanism: if there is a caching plugin available in the Kubernetes Cluster, then Datashim will utilize it in a completely transparent way for the end user. We have added experimental support for a custom Ceph-based solution [17], Noobaa [19] and Spectrum Scale [18]. Initial results have been very promising about performance gains, but it's out of the scope of the current paper and detailed evaluation on Bioinformatics applications will be part of a follow-up paper.

We have decided not to compare the performance of the two versions of the variant calling pipeline with Onedata and with Datashim in this study. This is because the architecture of the pipeline has changed significantly. Thus, we are unable to compare these two utilities side-by-side to draw meaningful conclusions. We have some empirical evidence that the simplification of the pipeline has resulted in the improvements of the overall throughput.

For Bioinformatics pipelines for both Machine Learning (ML) and classic algorithms (non-ML), we store input data and output results in object stores for nearly unlimited scalability. It is common knowledge that object stores do not perform well compared with NAS or local storages. Bioinformatics tend to have smaller numbers of larger data files (e.g. thousands of files with the size of MiB or more such as genomic sequences, research literature and images). Datashim can provide a nice POSIX-like facade for Bioinformatics pipelines for sequential reads and writes. The implementation of Datashim is cloud-agnostic, depending on a Kubernetes cluster only. The conclusion drawn from the study is applicable to any cloud with a pre-existing Kubernetes cluster.

This paper only discussed the application of Datashim in Bioinformatics. However, we believe that Datashim would work just as well with other research pipelines by simplifying the integration with cloud-native object stores. If pipelines require shared global POSIX file systems especially for sequential reads and writes, Datashim can be helpful to ease the transition for such applications from HPC to clouds.

5   Conclusion

Datashim provides a high level construct based on CSI. It introduces a concept of dataset to represent available storage or existing data backed by cloud-native storage. In particular, it creates Dataset CRDs on Kubernetes to describe the remote data storage. It uses Dataset Operator to manage the lifecycles of the CRDs. As a result, the corresponding PVCs are created to present the COS to the containers in pods such that application can access the remote data directly. In addition, Pods Admission Controller injects the mount points into pods via custom annotation dynamically.

Bioinformatics pipelines have deep roots in HPC and assume local access to files on shared file systems. Containerised pipelines can now access cloud-native data stores via Datashim from various sources via various protocols (for example GCS, S3 and HTTP archive). Both non-ML pipelines and newer ML pipelines can make use of Datasets created by Datashim statically or dynamically, and have mount points injected via annotations. The use of Dataset simplifies the pipelines, improves security comparing with Onedata.

Datashim addresses the requirement to access files locally by pipelines originated in HPC so that they can access cloud-native data stores on Kubeflow in Kubernetes environment directly. This integration is not only extremely useful in Bioinformatics but also potentially beneficial to all pipelines developed in HPC. It solves one of the major issues for HPC pipelines migrating into the clouds.

Acknowledgements. Datashim has received support as an incubation project by Linux Foundation AI & Data Foundation. In addition, this project has received funding from the European Union's Horizon 2020 research and innovation programme "evolve" under grant agreement No 825061. It is also supported by the internal funding from European Bioinformatics Institute, European Molecular Biology Laboratory. The authors would like to thank funding agencies and organisations for their generous support.

References

1. Yuan, D.Y., Wildish, T.: Bioinformatics application with Kubeflow for batch processing in clouds. In: Jagode, H., Anzt, H., Juckeland, G., Ltaief, H. (eds.) ISC High Performance 2020. LNCS, vol. 12321, pp. 355–367. Springer, Cham (2020). https://doi.org/10.1007/978-3-030-59851-8_24
2. Yuan, D.: RSEConUK 2019, University of Birmingham, 17–19 September 2019, Case Study of Porting a Bioinformatics Pipeline into Clouds (2019). https://sched.co/QSRc
3. Yuan, D.Y., Wildish, T.: Workflow platform for machine learning [version 1]. F1000Research 2020 **9**(ISCB Comm J), 822 (2020). https://doi.org/10.7490/f1000research.1118095.1
4. Kubernetes (2021). https://kubernetes.io/
5. Kubeflow (2021). https://www.kubeflow.org/docs/started/kubeflow-overview/
6. Persistent volume access modes in Kubernetes (2021). https://kubernetes.io/docs/concepts/storage/persistent-volumes/#access-modes
7. Datashim (2021). https://github.com/datashim-io/datashim/
8. Kubernetes Container Storage Interface (CSI) Documentation (2021). https://kubernetes-csi.github.io/docs/
9. Kubeflow Pipelines SDK API reference (2021). https://kubeflow-pipelines.readthedocs.io/en/stable/
10. Notebook download microscopic images from IDR with Keras (2020). https://gitlab.ebi.ac.uk/TSI/kubeflow/-/blob/latest/notebooks/imgcls/gcp/IDR0042.classification.tf2.1.0.v3.timing.ipynb
11. OMERO 5.6.0 JSON API (2021). https://docs.openmicroscopy.org/omero/5.6.0/developers/json-api.html
12. Nirschl, J.J., et al.: A deep-learning classifier identifies patients with clinical heart failure using whole-slide images of H&E tissue (2018). https://www.ncbi.nlm.nih.gov/pmc/articles/PMC5882098/
13. IDR: Image Data Repository (2018). https://idr.openmicroscopy.org/webclient/?show=project-402
14. OneData (2021). https://onedata.org/
15. Persistent Volume Claim (2021). https://kubernetes.io/docs/concepts/storage/persistent-volumes/
16. Operator SDK (2020). https://sdk.operatorframework.io/
17. Ceph Pull Request (2020). https://github.com/ceph/ceph/pull/37212
18. Spectrum Scale (2021). https://www.ibm.com/products/spectrum-scale
19. NooBaa (2021). https://www.noobaa.io/

FaaS and Curious: Performance Implications of Serverless Functions on Edge Computing Platforms

Achilleas Tzenetopoulos[✉], Evangelos Apostolakis, Aphrodite Tzomaka,
Christos Papakostopoulos, Konstantinos Stavrakakis, Manolis Katsaragakis,
Ioannis Oroutzoglou, Dimosthenis Masouros, Sotirios Xydis,
and Dimitrios Soudris

National Technical University of Athens, Athens, Greece
microlab@microlab.ntua.gr

Abstract. Serverless is an emerging paradigm that greatly simplifies
the usage of cloud resources providing unprecedented auto-scaling, simplicity, and cost-efficiency features. Thus, more and more individuals
and organizations adopt it, to increase their productivity and focus
exclusively on the functionality of their application. Additionally, the
cloud is expanding towards the deep edge, forming a continuum in
which the event-driven nature of the serverless paradigm seems to make
a perfect match. The extreme heterogeneity introduced, in terms of
diverse hardware resources and frameworks available, requires systematic approaches for evaluating serverless deployments. In this paper, we
propose a methodology for evaluating serverless frameworks deployed
on hybrid edge-cloud clusters. Our methodology focuses on key performance knobs of the serverless paradigm and applies a systematic
way for evaluating these aspects in hybrid edge-cloud environments.
We apply our methodology on three open-source serverless frameworks,
OpenFaaS, Openwhisk, and Lean Openwhisk respectively, and we provide key insights regarding their performance implications over resource-
constrained edge devices.

Keywords: Serverless-computing · Edge-computing ·
Function-as-a-Service · Cloud · Kubernetes · Openwhisk · OpenFaaS

1 Introduction

Serverless computing represents the next frontier in the evolution of cloud computing being an emerging paradigm that segregates computing infrastructure
from software development and deployment. This results to resource elasticity

This work is partially funded by the EU Horizon 2020 research and innovation programme, under project EVOLVE, grant agreement No 825061 and under project AIat-
EDGE, grant agreement No 101015922.

H. Jagode et al. (Eds.): ISC High Performance 2021 Workshops, LNCS 12761, pp. 428–438, 2021.
https://doi.org/10.1007/978-3-030-90539-2_29

and seamless scalability combined with lower operational costs. In serverless, also known as Function-as-a-Service (Faas), short-lived, stateless, event-driven functions are usually triggered by various sources. Today several public cloud vendors already support serverless, e.g., AWS Lambda (Amazon) [2] and Google Cloud Functions [3], while the global market size of serverless is projected to triplicate by the end of 2025 [8].

While originally designed for the cloud, the benefits of serverless architectures have the potential to be employed in edge computing environments, where computational resources and applications are distributed across the edge-cloud continuum [16]. In fact, serverless shares many common principles with the edge computing paradigm, which allows for low-latency response and Quality-of-Service (QoS) guarantees to event triggers, by collocating computing resources closer to the source of data. Moreover, the development of lightweight containers [20], orchestrators [4,26] and serverless frameworks [12] for edge devices also paves the way towards the consolidation of edge and serverless paradigms.

Nonetheless, the potential benefits of such a combination can be obtained only if efficiently designed, implemented and deployed. Otherwise, the energy- and computation-limited nature of edge computing devices can lead to inconsistent and unreliable systems [10]. While previous research works have put effort on characterizing the performance of serverless infrastructures and identifying potential bottlenecks and limitations, they rely mostly on serverless solutions provided by public cloud vendors [17,25] or custom deployments on high-end computing resources [18,24]. However, the extreme heterogeneity both in terms of hardware resources, as well as serverless solutions available, found in edge/cloud environments requires systematic methodologies for identifying and evaluating the implications of such deployments on the performance of the system.

In this paper, we propose a methodical approach for the evaluation of serverless frameworks on hybrid edge-cloud infrastructures. Our methodology takes into account key performance knobs of serverless frameworks and exposes their implications on resource-constrained edge deployments. We apply our methodology on three open-source serverless frameworks, i.e., Apache Openwhisk [11], Lean Openwhisk [12] and OpenFaaS [6] deployed on top of a hybrid cluster, combining both high-end servers and resource-constrained edge devices.

2   Background and Related Work

Although cloud computing has been significantly improved over the last years, its full-potential has not been released yet. Cloud users continue to bear a burden from resource provisioning operations and the pay-as-you-go promise has not yet been fulfilled by the traditional cloud offerings. *Serverless computing* aims to overcome these limitations by introducing a new layer of abstraction to developers, i.e., remove the burden of server management from the end user (-less), delegating them to the platform.

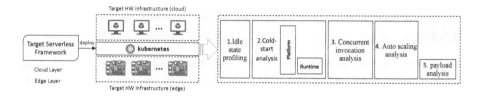

Fig. 1. Proposed methodology for systematic analysis of serverless infrastructures

From the developers' point of view, responsibilities are limited to the source code submission in the serverless platform; they are relieved from pre- and post-development tasks (e.g., infrastructure setup, resource provisioning). In addition, the key economic incentive for clients stems from the cost savings due to fine-grained billing (e.g., 1 ms billing granularity in AWS Lambda). Scaling down to zero, combined with the demand-driven resource elasticity, precludes clients from paying for idle resources. Providers, on the other hand, are given the opportunity to maximize their data-centers' utilization, by performing fine-grained resource multiplexing due to the short run time and stateless nature of functions.

While previous research efforts have examined the performance implications of serverless frameworks [13,17,24,25,27], these works mainly focus on serverless deployments on the cloud, thus, neglecting the potentials of serverless deployment on the edge. *Compared to conventional cloud serverless deployments, serverless on the edge reveals new challenges that need to be undertaken* [10]. Several research works have designed custom, lightweight frameworks, designated for the edge, by either utilizing WebAssembly [14,15] or application level isolation through multi-threading [21]. Authors in [23] optimize existing open-source frameworks and furtherly encourage [22] the serverless on edge paradigm adoption. However, these approaches either refer to single-node deployments or neglect the heterogeneity found in hybrid edge-cloud infrastructures.

3   Systematic Analysis of Serverless Infrastructures

In this section, we describe our proposed methodology for systematically evaluating serveless infrastructures over hybrid edge-cloud deployments. This methodology, illustrated in Fig. 1, includes the evaluation of key features for serverless platforms at the edge.

3.1   Proposed Methodology

Our systematic way of evaluating serverless frameworks relies on key enablers and open challenges that characterize such infrastructures. More specifically, our methodology consists of 5 evaluation steps (Fig. 1), which are described below:

1. Idle state profiling: Due to the inefficient and insufficient resources found at the edge, idle-state resource utilization is a key factor for a platform's evaluation.

As a first step of our approach, we examine the additional overhead introduced by the target platform when deployed on the underlying infrastructure.

2. Cold-start Analysis: In existing serverless platforms, delays incurred during function instantiation can lead to significant execution time overheads, compared to native execution. From the platform's point of view, this additional latency includes a) the time required to start the sandbox and b) the time required for runtime initialization. While there have been different sandboxes proposed in academia [19] and industry[9] for lightweight virtualization, in this study, we focus on performance characteristics of Docker containers, which currently form the most typical way of deploying applications to the cloud. From application's perspective, this latency delay occurs due to the different runtimes of modern programming languages, e.g., Node.js, Python, Go, each of which induces different performance overheads. This variability may get even worse when those functions are deployed on heterogeneous edge devices.

3. Concurrent invocation analysis: Serverless functions hosted on edge devices may be invoked concurrently by multiple clients or triggers. Therefore, bottlenecks on different components of a serverless platform may incur latency on invocations' end to end execution time. Thus, this step evaluates the latency distribution on different levels of invocation concurrency.

4. Auto-scaling analysis: In order to minimize costs, (e.g., energy, billing) serverless platforms need to provide elastic scalability. At the same time they need to address bursts on invocation frequency efficiently. We evaluate the responsiveness of serverless platforms on different invocation per second intensities.

5. Payload analysis: In serverless computing, storage and computation are decoupled. Thus, fine-grained state sharing between application becomes difficult. Most platforms utilize external object storage services, like AWS S3, which induce additional costs and latency overhead on data sharing, especially on edge environments with limited network bandwidth. As a next step of our methodology, we measure the delays provoked by payload transfer between functions through the framework gateway.

3.2   Target Serverless Frameworks

Our methodology can be applied for evaluating open-source serverless frameworks that support deployment over container orchestration frameworks (e.g., Kubernetes) that manage resource-constrained edge devices, as well as conventional x86 machines. For the purposes of this work, we focus on three open-source serverless frameworks, i.e., Apache Openwhisk [11] and OpenFaaS [6], as well as a lightweight version of Openwhisk (Lean Openwhisk [12]) specifically designed for edge computing environments. Since Openwhisk currently supports only x86 machines, we modified and recompiled the necessary components and runtimes to address deployments on `aarch64` architectures. Below, we provide an overview of the operation mechanisms for each one of the aforementioned serverless frameworks.

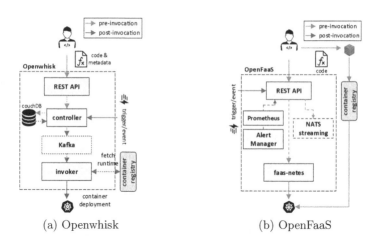

(a) Openwhisk   (b) OpenFaaS

Fig. 2. Architecture overview

Openwhisk Architecture Overview: Apache Openwhisk is an open-source, distributed serverless platform, initially developed by IBM. In Openwhisk, developers register their functions, also referred to as `Actions`, which can be triggered either from associated events, external sources, or HTTP requests. Moreover, `Triggers` provide endpoints that can be triggered by event sources, such as databases, stream processing engines and others. Finally, through `Rules`, developers create loosely coupled associations between them.

From an architectural point of view, Openwhisk relies on four main components for handling and executing function codes (Fig. 2a). First, Openwhisk exposes a public RESTful API which can be reached by developers to register their Actions, Triggers and Rules. After a request passes through the API, it triggers the `controller` component, which acts as the governor of the system. The controller communicates with a database instance (`couchDB`), which maintains and manages the state of the overall system and keeps information regarding credentials, metadata, namespaces as well as the definitions of Actions, Triggers and Rules registered by developers. Once an event triggers a new invocation, the `controller` after authenticating the invocation request, retrieves the function code, and selects the most appropriate node (`Invoker`) to handle the request. Afterwards, it publishes a message containing the code along with invocation-related meta-data, (e.g., resource allocation, input arguments) to Apache Kafka [1]. Finally, the `Invoker` builds the function code, encapsulates it in a predefined runtime container, initializes and executes it.

Lean Openwhisk Architecture Overview: Lean Openwhisk [12] is a customized, downsized distribution of Openwhisk which, however, shares the same design principles. By replacing Kafka with an in-memory queue, and compiling jointly some other parts, Lean Openwhisk is designed to enable the serverless paradigm within resource-constrained edge devices. Yet, to the best of our knowledge Lean Openwhisk only supports single-node setups.

Table 1. VMs and edge nodes specifications

	Server	Agent 1	Agent 2	Rasp. Pi 3b+	Rasp. Pi 4b
Processor model	Intel®Xeon® E5-2658A v3	Intel®Xeon® E5-2658A v3	Intel®Xeon® Silver 4210	Cortex-A53 (ARMv8)	Cortex-A72 (ARMv8)
Cores	4(vCPUs)	4(vCPUs)	8(vCPUs)	4	4
RAM(GB)	8	4	8	1	4

OpenFaaS Architecture Overview: OpenFaaS (Fig. 2b), unlike Openwhisk, utilizes a container orchestrator, e.g., Kubernetes, to manage the lifecycle of the containers through a custom controller. An end-to-end workflow starts with a call to the OpenFaaS API which interacts with Kubernetes objects (Pod, Deployment, Service) leveraging the OpenFaaS controller (`faas-netes`). According to the default settings, functions auto-scale up or down depending on the requests per second, by utilizing Prometheus [7] alert manager and monitoring. In addition, OpenFaaS utilizes a message bus for asynchronous function invocation. Compared to Openwhisk, OpenFaaS does not dynamically pack and execute code at runtime. Instead, developers have to pre-define containers containing their function code and are always up and running on the cluster by default. These containers are augmented by OpenFaaS with an additional process, called `watchdog`. The watchdog is responsible for processing incoming event triggers and also for initializing and monitoring the functional logic of the container.

3.3   Target Cluster Infrastructure

Our experiments have been performed on a distributed cluster, that consists of VMs deployed on top of high-end servers as well as typical, resource-constrained edge devices, the specifications of which are outlined in Table 1. Moreover, we utilize K3s as our container orchestrator, which is a lightweight distribution of conventional Kubernetes, built for IoT and edge computing devices.

4   Evaluation

In this section we apply the profiling and analysis steps of our proposed methodology to assess and evaluate our target serverless frameworks (Sect. 3.2) over our cluster infrastructure (Sect. 3.3). For the purposes of our experiments, we intentionally place all the required components for the frameworks' functionality, (e.g., Apache Kafka, CouchDB, Prometheus), on the Server node, which is dedicated to orchestration rather than workload execution. Therefore, resources of VM agents and edge devices (Raspberry Pis) are exclusively exploited by the scheduled applications. Additionaly, in order to evaluate the performance of Openwhisk on edge devices, we place the Invoker component either externally (Agents) or internally (RPi4), utilizing the *Kubernetes container factory*, which allows the placement of Openwhisk to be managed solely by Kubernetes.

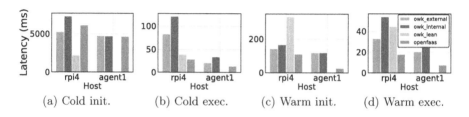

Fig. 3. Per platform Cold and Warm start latency breakdown

Idle-State Profiling: Regarding the resource consumption of our container orchestrator, K3s introduces neglectable utilization. Its resource utilization sums up to 10 millicpu and 200 MB of RAM on average. Openwhisk, due to its complicated components, has considerable resource needs. While the agents need 600 millicpu and 161 MB of RAM when hosting the Invoker, its main components deployed on the Server node contribute 1800 millicpu and 2.4 GB of RAM jointly. The Lean, single-node version of Openwhisk uses 5 millicpu and 218.93 MB of RAM on Rpi4. OpenFaaS, on the other side, being closely integrated with Kubernetes, contributes a modest footprint on the Server node that sums up to 66 millicpu and 83 MB of RAM on the Server node. Agent and edge nodes experience negligible overhead.

Cold-Start Latency Analysis: The resource-constrained edge devices increase the latency of container fetching, creation and initialization.

Platform Dependence: Figure 3 illustrates the cold/warm initialization and execution time of a simple Node.js function on Rpi4 and on Agent1. As initialization latency, we define the time elapsed between function invocation and the runtime execution. In every platform, while we observe higher latency on the edge node, the impact of function initialization remains tremendous. As mentioned before (Fig. 2a), since Openwhisk alleviates more tasks (e.g., source code injection), additional post-invocation overhead is added. However, when the Invoker is hosted externally, Openwhisk post-invocation procedure is accelerated and results in decreased instantiation and execution time. Lean Openwhisk supporting only Node.js-6 runtime presents the less overhead on coldstart function instantiation. Yet, since the operational logic of the framework is embedded to a single edge node, the warm times are increased. On the contrary, on warm invocations, we observe decreased latency on OpenFaaS, which requires more pre-invocation tasks, e.g., function container deployment, (Fig. 2b) from the user.

Runtime Dependence: In the OpenFaaS platform, which offers greater flexibility on multi-arch runtimes, we deploy a `helloworld` function on different language runtimes to Rpi3 and Rpi4 to examine the invocation latency breakdown. We execute each experiment 5 times for consistency, and the average latency is illustrated in Fig. 4. Cold start latency is high for every language runtime. The difference for function initialization between the warm and cold start is 8 s for the Rpi3 and 5 s for the Rpi4, respectively. Therefore, the inefficient and heterogeneous resources at the edge may vary in the latency incurred during

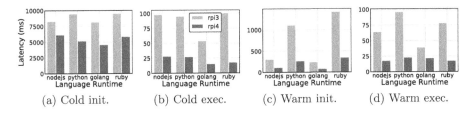

(a) Cold init.   (b) Cold exec.   (c) Warm init.   (d) Warm exec.

Fig. 4. Per language runtime Cold and Warm start latency breakdown

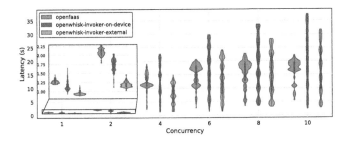

Fig. 5. Applications relative performance in different workload density.

container fetching, creation and initialization. In the warm start cases, latency is decreased up to 4.3x in Rpi4. Comparing the alternative programming languages, Python and Ruby runtimes provoke the greatest latency even in the warm start cases (Fig. 4c, 4d), while Golang seems to offer the modest latency footprint among them. Finally, except for the performance variability in function instantiation between cold/warm start and edge device, similar results are observed in function execution time. Post-initialization (exec.) latency is smaller after a warm compared with a cold start. Possible reasons for this phenomenon may be trained branch predictors, or cache locality.

Concurrent Invocation Analysis: Figure 5 depicts the distribution of 120 warm invocations of an `Optical Character Recognition` (OCR) (164KB *png* image) function in Node.js on Rpi4, when invoked concurrently by multiple sources. Invocations were generated using the `loadtest` [5] tool on the Server. In both platforms, latency increases drastically when 4 or more invocations occur concurrently. The high standard deviation of Openwhisk workload distribution depicts the accumulated congestion occurring in its complicated pipeline after the function invocation. Thus, there is a great performance improvement when the Invoker is offloaded externally (Agent2). While OpenFaaS provides a more robust distribution for higher numbers of concurrent requests (32% lower 90th percentile latency for 10 requests), it is outperformed by Openwhisk for lower numbers of concurrent requests which delivers lower median end-to-end latency.

Auto-scaling: In order to evaluate the auto-scaling, we invoke the OCR application with 1,2 and 3 invocations per second (ips). This time, instead of the default OpenFaaS auto-scaler which utilizes Prometheus monitoring, we employ

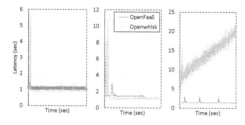 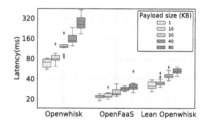

Fig. 6. Auto-Scaling: 1, 2 and 3 ips   **Fig. 7.** Payload transfer

the Horizontal Kubernetes Auto-scaler. We assign 500 millicpus per function and define 75% as the limit that must be exceeded before scaling up. In Fig. 6 is illustrated the latency of Openwhisk (external Invoker) and OpenFaaS overtime on a Rpi4 for different densities. While Openwhisk provides gradual, finer-grained scalability, additional latency is built-up overtime due to its complex components. Moreover, another inefficiency observed is that invocation requests are assigned to function replicas before they are instantiated. OpenFaaS scales the function much less aggressively, but it applies more efficient load balancing.

Payload Transfer: Figure 7 illustrates the payload transfer latency distribution of 10 experiment repetitions for data sizes 1-80 KB on Rpi4. Again, Openwhisk requires increased latency on routing and passing the request to the message queue. However, OpenFaaS and Lean Openwhisk incur modest latency on data transfer; therefore local state passing to avoid data transfers from the serverless edge environments to the Cloud, forms a promising field for further study.

5   Conclusion and Future Work

This paper proposes a systematic methodology for evaluating serverless platforms at hybrid edge-cloud infrastructures. We apply our methodology by deploying a Kubernetes cluster on top of an heterogeneous pool of devices and evaluate three of the most widely used open-source serverless platforms, i.e., OpenFaaS, Openwhisk and Lean Openwhisk. As future steps, we aim to extend our methodology for applying to real-world serverless applications and examine the performance implications of serverless frameworks on function chains and workflows, as well as to investigate function orchestration schemes in the edge/cloud computing continuum.

References

1. Apache kafka. https://kafka.apache.org/
2. AWS lambda. https://aws.amazon.com/lambda/
3. Google cloud functions. https://cloud.google.com/functions
4. Lightweight kubernetes - k3s. https://k3s.io/

5. Loadtest. https://github.com/alexfernandez/loadtest
6. Openfaas. https://www.openfaas.com/
7. Prometheus. https://prometheus.io. Accessed 7 Apr 2021
8. Serverless architecture market. https://www.marketsandmarkets.com/PressReleases/serverless-architecture.asp
9. Agache, A., et al.: Firecracker: Lightweight virtualization for serverless applications. In: 17th USENIX Symposium on Networked Systems Design and Implementation (NSDI 2020), pp. 419–434 (2020)
10. Aslanpour, M.S., et al.: Serverless edge computing: vision and challenges. In: 2021 Australasian Computer Science Week Multiconference, pp. 1–10 (2021)
11. Baldini, I., et al.: Cloud-native, event-based programming for mobile applications. In: Proceedings of the International Conference on Mobile Software Engineering and Systems, pp. 287–288 (2016)
12. Breitgand, D.: Lean openwhisk. https://medium.com/openwhisk/lean-openwhisk-open-source-faas-for-edge-computing-fb823c6bbb9b. Accessed 7 Apr 2021
13. Copik, M., Kwasniewski, G., Besta, M., Podstawski, M., Hoefler, T.: SEBS: a serverless benchmark suite for function-as-a-service computing. arXiv preprint arXiv:2012.14132 (2020)
14. Gadepalli, P.K., Peach, G., Cherkasova, L., Aitken, R., Parmer, G.: Challenges and opportunities for efficient serverless computing at the edge. In: 2019 38th Symposium on Reliable Distributed Systems (SRDS), pp. 261–2615. IEEE (2019)
15. Hall, A., Ramachandran, U.: An execution model for serverless functions at the edge. In: Proceedings of the International Conference on Internet of Things Design and Implementation, pp. 225–236 (2019)
16. Jonas, E., et al.: Cloud programming simplified: a Berkeley view on serverless computing. arXiv preprint arXiv:1902.03383 (2019)
17. Lee, H., Satyam, K., Fox, G.: Evaluation of production serverless computing environments. In: 2018 IEEE 11th International Conference on Cloud Computing (CLOUD), pp. 442–450. IEEE (2018)
18. Li, J., Kulkarni, S.G., Ramakrishnan, K., Li, D.: Understanding open source serverless platforms: Design considerations and performance. In: Proceedings of the 5th International Workshop on Serverless Computing, pp. 37–42 (2019)
19. Nikolos, O.L., Papazafeiropoulos, K., Psomadakis, S., Nanos, A., Koziris, N.: Extending storage support for unikernel containers. In: Proceedings of the 5th International Workshop on Serverless Computing, pp. 31–36 (2019)
20. Park, M., Bhardwaj, K., Gavrilovska, A.: Toward lighter containers for the edge. In: 3rd USENIX Workshop on Hot Topics in Edge Computing (HotEdge 2020) (2020)
21. Pfandzelter, T., Bermbach, D.: TinyFaas: a lightweight FaaS platform for edge environments. In: 2020 IEEE International Conference on Fog Computing (ICFC), pp. 17–24. IEEE (2020)
22. Rausch, T., Hummer, W., Muthusamy, V., Rashed, A., Dustdar, S.: Towards a serverless platform for edge AI. In: 2nd USENIX Workshop on Hot Topics in Edge Computing (HotEdge 2019) (2019)
23. Rausch, T., Rashed, A., Dustdar, S.: Optimized container scheduling for data-intensive serverless edge computing. Future Gener. Comput. Syst. **114**, 259–271 (2021)
24. Shahrad, M., Balkind, J., Wentzlaff, D.: Architectural implications of function-as-a-service computing. In: Proceedings of the 52nd Annual IEEE/ACM International Symposium on Microarchitecture, pp. 1063–1075 (2019)

25. Wang, L., Li, M., Zhang, Y., Ristenpart, T., Swift, M.: Peeking behind the curtains of serverless platforms. In: 2018 USENIX Annual Technical Conference (USENIX ATC 2018), pp. 133–146 (2018)
26. Xiong, Y., Sun, Y., Xing, L., Huang, Y.: Extend cloud to edge with KubeEdge. In: 2018 IEEE/ACM Symposium on Edge Computing (SEC), pp. 373–377. IEEE (2018)
27. Yu, T., et al.: Characterizing serverless platforms with serverlessbench. In: Proceedings of the 11th ACM Symposium on Cloud Computing, pp. 30–44 (2020)

Differentiated Performance in NoSQL Database Access for Hybrid Cloud-HPC Workloads

Remo Andreoli$^{(\boxtimes)}$ and Tommaso Cucinotta

Scuola Superiore Sant'Anna, Pisa, Italy
{r.andreoli,t.cucinotta}@santannapisa.it

Abstract. In recent years, the demand for cloud-based high-performance computing applications and services has grown in order to sustain the computational and statistical challenges of big-data analytics scenarios. In this context, there is a growing need for reliable large-scale NoSQL data stores capable of efficiently serving mixed high-performance and interactive cloud workloads. This paper deals with the problem of designing such NoSQL database service: to this purpose, a set of modifications to the popular MongoDB software are presented. The modified MongoDB lets clients submit individual requests or even carry out whole sessions at different priority levels, so that the higher-priority requests are served with shorter response times that exhibit less variance, with respect to lower-priority requests. Experimental results carried out on two big multi-core servers using synthetic workload scenarios demonstrate the effectiveness of the proposed approach in providing differentiated performance levels, highlighting what trade-offs are available between maximum achievable throughput for the platform, and the response-time reduction for higher-priority requests.

1 Introduction

Cloud Computing has become increasingly popular over the past decade as an affordable solution for all size businesses, thanks to virtualization technologies (and containerization, more recently) that add flexibility in the management of the physical infrastructure. For instance, public cloud providers are able to maximize resource utilization by multiplexing its access across a wide number of tenants that can deploy widely heterogeneous workloads. With the increasingly distributed nature of applications and services, cloud providers have been playing a key role in providing reliable storage solutions, thanks to their ability to replicate data on multiple sites and fault-independent availability zones. Storage services are at the heart of distributed cloud-native and big-data processing applications, where the always increasing need for higher and higher capacity, performance and scalability requirements pushed towards departing from traditional relational data-base architectures to embrace more lightweight, less feature-rich, NoSQL architectures. The selling points of NoSQL data stores is

© Springer Nature Switzerland AG 2021
H. Jagode et al. (Eds.): ISC High Performance 2021 Workshops, LNCS 12761, pp. 439–449, 2021.
https://doi.org/10.1007/978-3-030-90539-2_30

massive scalability and the ability to deal with arbitrary table sizes and numbers of concurrent clients. The historical work in [8] discussed how such data stores can be effectively and productively used in cloud services, without any need for relying on expensive reliable hardware, but achieving reliability by distribution of the workload across various inexpensive nodes. Later, those principles were reused for engineering AWS DynamoDB, the industrial real-time data-base offering in AWS.

In cloud providers, it has become commonplace to find fully managed 24/7 data store services which can be directly and conveniently used by a plethora of clients submitting widely heterogeneous workload patterns. On one hand, the elasticity of the Cloud has brought the traditionally owner-centric High Performance Computing (HPC) community to explore, in a number of cases, cloud-based solutions in order to deal with the emergence of extreme-scale simulations and big-data processing [11,25]. On the other hand, time-sensitive applications are being increasingly hosted in cloud environments, where a great component of the end-to-end latency (and its variability) is due to the time needed to access one or more data stores. Therefore, a cloud provider must be capable of designing evolved NoSQL data store services for virtualized/containerized applications exhibiting highly heterogeneous workloads. These include a mix of high-performance applications and services, that need to process high volumes of data at the maximum average throughput, as well as (soft) real-time ones that need to process relatively smaller amounts of data, but with tight timing constraints for individual requests. A widely adopted mechanism in real-time systems is the use of priorities, so that higher priority workloads may be served earlier than lower-priority ones. In this work, we propose a modification to the popular MongoDB [7] NoSQL data store in order to achieve differentiated per-client and per-request performance using the aforementioned prioritized access principle.

1.1   Contributions

This paper extends our prior work, RT-MongoDB [2], which exploits *UNIX nice level* combining them with two design choices of MongoDB, the per-client threading model and optimistic concurrency control, in order to achieve differentiated performance. The additional modifications we introduced pay special care to avoid penalizing the achievable throughput in presence of mixed-priority workloads, keeping effectiveness in separating performance among different-priority requests. This is crucial when serving both HPC and interactive cloud workloads from the same MongoDB instance. We present for the first time results performed under a heavy-stress for a multi-core MongoDB instance deployed over a pair of 20-cores Xeon-based servers, with a variety of mixed HPC/interactive workload scenarios, showing the effectiveness of the proposed approach.

2 Related Work

In the research literature, a number of proposals can be found dealing with optimizing the performance of databases, including NoSQL data stores for cloud computing, so to support scenarios with mixed workload types and requirements.

For example, the old concept of a real-time database system (RTDBS) [6,15, 24] refers to a data management system with predictable timing of the operations requested by clients. Research efforts in this area complemented research on scheduling of processes on the CPU [3], with investigations on scheduling of on-disk transactions. Cumbersome issues that have been tackled in the last decade include: how to work around the high seek latencies of traditional rotational disk drives, dealt with by switching to memory-only data management systems [12], or recently introducing solid-state drives; the presence of dynamic workload conditions, that pushed towards the adoption of adaptive feedback-based scheduling techniques [1,14]. Thanks to their capability of guaranteeing predictable access times, real-time database systems found applications in traditional hard real-time application domains, like mission control in aerospace, process control in industrial plants, telecommunication systems and stock trading [14]. Unfortunately, the great focus of real-time database research on hard real-time systems, and the necessarily pessimistic analysis accompanying their design, causing poor utilization at run-time, caused these systems to remain of interest only in a restricted domain area.

In contrast, research on distributed and cloud systems has a traditional focus on maximizing average-case performance and overall throughput, neglecting predictability for individual requests. Here, the typical feature-richness and ideal consistency model of relational databases has been progressively dropped, in favour of NoSQL architectures [13,22] with relaxed consistency models that implement essentially reliable/replicated distributed hash tables with the ability to ingest arbitrarily high volumes of data, scaling at will on several nodes.

However, the growing interest in deploying time-sensitive web-based applications and services in cloud infrastructures, led to a return of interest in enriching these lightweight NoSQL databases with predictability features, albeit the focus is not on guaranteeing every single request, but rather to control a sufficiently high percentile of the response-time distributions. For example, the DynamoDB[1] solution from AWS, designed around lessons learnt from the Dynamo project [9], has been among the first solutions with the capability of providing guaranteed levels of read and write operations per second for each table, as required by customers, keeping also a per-request latency (99th percentile) lower than 10ms.

More recently, real-time stream processing [4,17,28] solutions have gained momentum. These process data as soon as it comes from various sources, without necessarily storing data on disk, using arbitrarily complex topologies of processing functions. This way, the results of the computation are made available with a very short latency from when new data arrives. Thanks to cloud technologies, it is possible to let these systems scale to several nodes, so that end-to-end latency

---

[1] See: https://aws.amazon.com/dynamodb/.

can be controlled by applying elastic scaling to individual processing functions. A few works [20, 27] tried to build empirical performance models of these system, so to employ more precise control logics for the end-to-end performance.

ZHT [21] is a key-value data store for extreme-scale system services hosted on clouds and supercomputers, designed as a zero-hop distributed hash table. SILT [23] is a high-performance key-value store that uses new fast and compact indexing data structures to balance the use of memory, storage and computations. Xyza [26] proposes an extension of MongoDB that combines multiple concurrency control techniques to achieve high performance and scalability. Moreover, several studies combine MongoDB and Hadoop to build reliable storage solutions for HPC-Cloud environments [10, 16].

Along with MongoDB, another NoSQL data store that gained significant popularity is Cassandra [18]. This has become also an interesting target for researchers willing to demonstrate applicability of differentiated performance methods. For example, a quality-of-service aware allocator (AQUAS) [29] has been proposed, with the capability of allocating physical resources in a Cassandra deployment to satisfy individual clients' performance requirements.

3   Proposed Approach

This paper extends the modified version of MongoDB we presented in [2], improving the flexibility in replicated scenarios where higher data durability is required. The key to ensure reliability and data consistency in MongoDB is to deploy a *replica set*, a group of multiple database instances residing on different physical machines that share the same data set, and then reply to a user write request only after a number of such instances have locally replicated the operation. In this system configuration, the write operations are all issued to the same database instance, called the *primary* node, which logs them in the *oplog*, a MongoDB capped collection that stores the history of logical writes to the database. Each oplog entry is paired with a timestamp in order to assert the operations order and avoid data corruptions. The other MongoDB instances, namely the *secondary* nodes, rely on the oplog to replicate the state of the data set. For the sake of performance, the replication internals elaborate new oplog entries in batches, carefully crafted by the so-called *OplogBatcher* to be applicable in parallel to the local storage unit. Thus each batch represents a "limbo" state where chronological order is not enforced. While this certainly leads to a mismatch between how history is depicted by each replica node, the underlying storage unit, WiredTiger, stores multiple versions of the data in a tree-based structure [5] and thus is able to return the correct state of the data set to the user, based on the query timestamp.

These observations suggest that it is not possible to properly propagate priorities to the secondary nodes[2] due to the inevitable priority inversion of using batches: this is particularly noticeable when enforcing data durability, because the database does not reply to users until the secondaries finish replicating the

---

[2] As of MongoDB v4.4.

corresponding batch. The checkpoint system conceived in our previous work attempts to minimize this *unbiased replication problem*, by providing a prioritized channel to temporarily revoke the database access based on the user priority: *low-priority*, *normal-priority* or *high-priority*. In practice, the checkpoint system defines an entry and exit point to the processing state of the user session life-cycle through the means of two primitives, *check-in* and *check-out* (Fig. 1). The checkpoint eventually blocks the underlying worker thread in charge of serving a certain user, based on these simple rules: low priority users are blocked whenever normal or high-priority requests are being processed, while normal priority requests are blocked when high-priority ones are being processed. The major drawback of this solution is the impact on overall throughput: the lower-priority requests are completely halted at the checkpoint if there is even just 1 higher priority request under processing. This design choice effectively reduces the parallelism capabilities of the MongoDB architecture, which on HPC workloads with many-core servers is excessively penalizing, considering the underlying hardware. This paper proposes two additions to RT-MongoDB in order to tackle the issue:

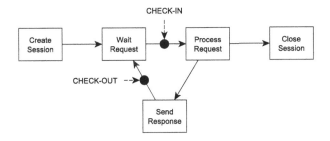

Fig. 1. A simplified view of the user session life-cycle, highlighting the positions of the checkpoint entry and exit point. Each user connection to the database is handled by a distinct worker thread

1. A customizable *checkpoint activation threshold* to specify the maximum number of high-priority requests under processing below which lower-priority requests are still brought forward at the checkpoint. This option allows to fine-tune the drop in parallelism: a high value implies a lower rate of activations, whereas a low value implies a higher rate.
2. A collection of *CPU pools*, user-defined CPU sets that specify the *working space* of the underlying threads based on user priorities, so that it is possible to restrict the number of cores available to those threads serving lower-priority users whenever higher ones are being processed. In this way, high-priority users are serviced with reduced interference, without necessarily halting completely the lower-priority ones.

Regarding the first point, it might be useful to set a high checkpoint activation threshold in scenarios where data durability is not required, since the primary node does not have to wait for the replication process to finish, and thus priority inversion does not occur. Regarding the last point, the current prototype allows for three CPU pools: the *restricted pool*, which is used by lower-priority users whenever higher ones are being processed; the *priority pool*, dedicated to high-priority users for the duration of their session; the *standard pool*, which serves the lower-priority users whenever higher priority sessions are present but not in processing state. The idea is to allocate a sufficient number of cores for high-priority worker threads and a very small restricted working space, so that lower-priority ones are slowed down (but not completely halted). Figure 2 shows a possible allocation of working spaces on a 10-core CPU. Note that this novel mechanism is integrated to the checkpoint system, thus the migration between working spaces follows the workflow already depicted in Fig. 1.

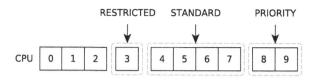

Fig. 2. A possible working space allocation on a 10-core CPU: 1 physical core for the restricted pool, 4 for the standard pool and 2 for the priority pool

In conclusion, the goal is to offer a pair of parameters to database administrators so that they can adjust the trade-off between reduced response times for priority users and total throughput, depending on the scenario. The user API remains mostly unchanged from the previous version of RT-MongoDB, with the only difference being the addition of the `setCpuPools` command to configure the working spaces. A user alters the throughput of its queries by specifying its priority via the `setClientPriority` command. Note that the setting persists for the duration of the session, or until it is changed again. In order to prioritize a single request only, the client should issue the query with `runCommand`, specifying the optional `priority` parameter.

4   Experimental Evaluation

The modifications to MongoDB described in Sect. 3 have been experimentally tested with various (synthetic) stress workloads and the resulting performance has been compared with the original MongoDB. The test environment comprises three distinct multi-core server-class NUMA machines: two 20-core servers (Dell R630 with 2 Intel Xeon E5-2640 CPUs and 64 GB of RAM) to host a 2-member replica set and one 96-core (Arm 64 server with 2 ThunderX 88XX CPUs and 64 GB of RAM) to execute the client processes concurrently. Note that of the 20 cores, 4 will be dedicated to the mandatory MongoDB activities that are not related to the management of a user connection in order to avoid unnecessary CPU contention. Moreover, hyperthreading and turbo-boost are disabled on every machine, and each user process on the 96-core server is pinned to a different physical core in order to simulate an isolated scenario with stable performance.

The stress workload consists of write operations only, since in high concurrency scenarios they put more stress than reads on the database. Every operation waits for the changes to be replicated to the secondary node, in order to simulate a high reliability scenario. Our experimental scenarios are composed of the following steps: each user declares its priority (*high-priority* or *normal-priority*, for simplicity) with `setClientPriority`, waits a randomized amount of time uniformly distributed between 0 and $300\,\mu s$ and then issues 1000 insert operations, sequentially and without delays in-between. The goal of the following experiments is to show how the trade-off between reduced response times and overall throughput can be adjusted.

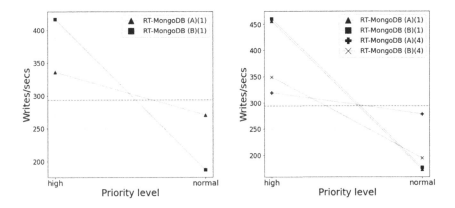

Fig. 3. Writes per second comparison in the 2 cases of: 1 high-priority and 29 normal-priority concurrent users using two different parameter configurations (left); 4 high-priority and 26 normal-priority concurrent users using four different parameter configurations (right). The dashed line corresponds to the average write throughput of the original version of MongoDB

The first two charts, depicted in Fig. 3, show how the average throughput is affected due to priorities in a 30-user scenario. Each line plot corresponds to a different parameter configuration of RT-MongoDB: (A) does not use CPU pools, (B) defines a restricted, standard and priority pool of respectively 2, 10 and 4 physical cores, leaving the remaining 4 for the auxiliary MongoDB activities. The activation threshold is specified in a similar manner: for instance, the configuration (A)(4) corresponds to RT-MongoDB with no CPU pools and checkpoint activation threshold of 4. Figure 3 (left) presents the average throughput of 29 normal-priority users concurring with 1 high-priority one. In both configurations, the checkpoint system activates as soon as a priority request is being processed, thus threshold activation is set to 1 and (A)(1) corresponds to the version of RT-MongoDB proposed in our previous work. The configuration with CPU pools

(B) is able to service the high-priority user at higher rates with respect to (A), achieving 80 more operations per second at the cost of drastic reduction in performance for the remaining users. This is due to the fact that lower-priority users are forced to compete over the 10 cores of the standard pool, while the high-priority user has is own interference-free working space. Note that in this case the restricted pool is never used due to the activation threshold configuration.

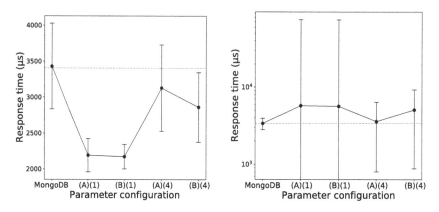

Fig. 4. Average response time and variance for a high-priority user (left) and normal-priority user (right). The scenario comprises 4 high-and 26 normal-priority users. The dashed line and the first data point corresponds to the average response time and variance of the original version of MongoDB

The following paragraph describes a more interesting scenario involving multiple concurrent high-priority users, thus allowing for a greater customization on the activation threshold. Figure 3 (right) presents a 30-user scenario similar to the previous experiment, but with 4 high-priority users. The two configurations with activation threshold (1) achieve similar results, because the checkpoint activates whenever the database receives at least one high-priority request: since this happens with high probability at any given time in the case of 4 concurrent high-priority users, the CPU pool parameter (B) is useless. Consequently, the throughput for high-priority users is very high, because they monopolize the database access. The other configurations show that it is possible to adjust the trade-off between overall throughput and responsiveness for high-priority requests: for example (A)(4) services high-priority requests with a higher rate with respect to the original MongoDB, while still being able to provide a good average throughput for the other users, because they are allowed to be serviced whenever at least one high-priority request is not being processed. It is reasonable to think that the variance for high-priority users is higher using the more "relaxed" configurations, as clearly depicted in Fig. 4, which presents the average response time and variance for high and normal priority users (left and right plots, respectively). The average variance for high-priority users is of 600 microseconds in the worst case scenario, which is equal to the variance experienced by a user using an unmodified version of MongoDB, while still perceiving better response times.

Summarizing the above results, the new version of RT-MongoDB is capable of better adapting to the requirements of HPC-Cloud workloads: one can use a very confined working space (restricted resources) for lower-priority users and 1 as activation threshold to reduce response times of higher-priority requests to a minimum, or fine-tune the available parameters to avoid an excessive degradation in the overall throughput of the system.

5   Conclusions

This paper discussed improvements to our RT-MongoDB variant of the MongoDB database, to enable differentiated per-user/request performance on a priority basis. The focus was to adapt it to the key requirements of hybrid HPC-Cloud workloads, providing the database administrator with a basic set of Quality-of-Service parameters to tune the trade-off between reduced response time for high priority queries and overall system throughput.

A future work is to couple RT-MongoDB with the use of more advanced scheduling techniques, like SCHED_DEADLINE [19], and provide a similar interface to that of DynamoDB, where the users declare the number of read/write requests so as to allow the system to set up a reasonable end-point with performance guarantees.

References

1. Amirijoo, M., Hansson, J., Son, S.H.: Specification and management of QoS in real-time databases supporting imprecise computations. IEEE Trans. Comput. **55**(3), 304–319 (2006)
2. Ferguson, D., Pahl, C., Helfert, M. (eds.): CLOSER 2020. CCIS, vol. 1399. Springer, Cham (2021). https://doi.org/10.1007/978-3-030-72369-9
3. Baruah, S., Bertogna, M., Buttazzo, G.: Multiprocessor Scheduling for Real-Time Systems. ES, Springer, Cham (2015). https://doi.org/10.1007/978-3-319-08696-5
4. Basanta-Val, P., Fernández-García, N., Sánchez-Fernández, L., Arias-Fisteus, J.: Patterns for distributed real-time stream processing. IEEE Trans. Parallel Distrib. Syst. **28**(11), 3243–3257 (2017)
5. Bernstein, P.A., Goodman, N.: Multiversion concurrency control-theory and algorithms. ACM Trans. Database Syst. **8**(4), 465–483 (1983)
6. Bestavros, A., Lin, K.J., Son, S.H.: Real-Time Database Systems: Issues and Applications. Springer, New York (1997). https://doi.org/10.1007/978-1-4615-6161-3
7. Chodorow, K.: MongoDB: The Definitive Guide: Powerful and Scalable Data Storage. O'Reilly Media, Inc., New York (2013)
8. DeCandia, G., et al.: Dynamo: Amazon's highly available key-value store. In: Proceedings of Twenty-First ACM SIGOPS Symposium on Operating Systems Principles, pp. 205–220. SOSP 2007. Association for Computing Machinery, New York, NY, USA (2007)

9. DeCandia, G., et al.: Dynamo: Amazon's highly available key-value store. SIGOPS Oper. Syst. Rev. **41**(6), 205–220 (2007)
10. Dede, E., Govindaraju, M., Gunter, D., Canon, R.S., Ramakrishnan, L.: Performance evaluation of a MongoDB and Hadoop platform for scientific data analysis. In: Proceedings of the 4th ACM Workshop on Scientific Cloud Computing, pp. 13–20. Science Cloud 2013. Association for Computing Machinery, New York, NY, USA (2013)
11. Fox, G., Qiu, J., Jha, S., Ekanayake, S., Kamburugamuve, S.: Big data, simulations and HPC convergence. In: Rabl, T., Nambiar, R., Baru, C., Bhandarkar, M., Poess, M., Pyne, S. (eds.) Big Data Benchmarking, pp. 3–17. Springer, Cham (2016)
12. Garcia-Molina, H., Salem, K.: Main memory database systems: an overview. IEEE Trans. Knowl. Data Eng. **4**(6), 509–516 (1992)
13. Han, J., Haihong, E., Le, G., Du, J.: Survey on NoSQL database. In: 6th International Conference on Pervasive Computing and Applications, pp. 363–366 (2011)
14. Kang, K., Oh, J., Son, S.H.: Chronos: feedback control of a real database system performance. In: 28th IEEE International Real-Time Systems Symposium (RTSS 2007), pp. 267–276 (Dec 2007)
15. Kao, B., Garcia-Molina, H.: An overview of real-time database systems. In: Halang, W.A., Stoyenko, A.D. (eds.) Real Time Computing, pp. 261–282. Springer, Heidelberg (1994)
16. Karim, L., Boulmakoul, A., Lbath, A.: Real time analytics of urban congestion trajectories on Hadoop-MongoDB cloud ecosystem. In: Proceedings of the Second International Conference on Internet of Things, Data and Cloud Computing, ICC 2017. Association for Computing Machinery, New York, NY, USA (2017)
17. Kulkarni, S., et al.: Twitter heron: stream processing at scale. In: Proceedings of the 2015 ACM SIGMOD International Conference on Management of Data, pp. 239–250, SIGMOD 2015. ACM, New York, NY, USA (2015)
18. Lakshman, A., Malik, P.: Cassandra: a decentralized structured storage system. ACM SIGOPS Oper. Syst. Rev. **44**(2), 35–40 (2010)
19. Lelli, J., Scordino, C., Abeni, L., Faggioli, D.: Deadline scheduling in the linux kernel. Softw. Pract. Exper. **46**(6), 821–839 (2016)
20. Li, T., Tang, J., Xu, J.: Performance modeling and predictive scheduling for distributed stream data processing. IEEE Trans. Big Data **2**(4), 353–364 (2016)
21. Li, T., Raicu, I.: Distributed NoSQL storage for extreme-scale system services. IEEE/ACM Supercomputing Ph.D. Showcase (2015)
22. Li, Y., Manoharan, S.: A performance comparison of SQL and NoSQL databases. In: 2013 IEEE Pacific Rim Conference on Communications, Computers and Signal Processing (PACRIM), pp. 15–19, August 2013
23. Lim, H., Fan, B., Andersen, D.G., Kaminsky, M.: Silt: a memory-efficient, high-performance key-value store. In: Proceedings of the Twenty-Third ACM Symposium on Operating Systems Principles, pp. 1–13, SOSP 2011. Association for Computing Machinery, New York, NY, USA (2011)
24. Lindström, J.: Real Time Database Systems, pp. 1–13. American Cancer Society (2008)
25. Netto, M.A.S., Calheiros, R.N., Rodrigues, E.R., Cunha, R.L.F., Buyya, R.: HPC cloud for scientific and business applications: taxonomy, vision, and research challenges. ACM Comput. Surv. **51**(1), 1–29 (2018)

26. Patel, Y., Verma, M., Arpaci-Dusseau, A.C., Arpaci-Dusseau, R.H.: Revisiting concurrency in high-performance nosql databases. In: 10th USENIX Workshop on Hot Topics in Storage and File Systems (HotStorage 2018). USENIX Association, Boston, MA, July 2018. https://www.usenix.org/conference/hotstorage18/presentation/patel

27. Theeten, B., Bedini, I., Cogan, P., Sala, A., Cucinotta, T.: Towards the optimization of a parallel streaming engine for telco applications. Bell Labs Tech. J. **18**(4), 181–197 (2014)

28. Wingerath, W., Gessert, F., Friedrich, S., Ritter, N.: Real-time stream processing for big data. IT - Inf. Technol. **58**(4), 186–194 (2016). https://www.degruyter.com/view/journals/itit/58/4/article-p186.xml

29. Xu, C., Xia, F., Sharaf, M.A., Zhou, M., Zhou, A.: Aquas: a quality-aware scheduler for NoSQL data stores. In: 2014 IEEE 30th International Conference on Data Engineering, pp. 1210–1213 (2014)

Deep Learning on Supercomputers

JUWELS Booster – A Supercomputer for Large-Scale AI Research

Stefan Kesselheim[1](✉), Andreas Herten[1], Kai Krajsek[1], Jan Ebert[1],
Jenia Jitsev[1], Mehdi Cherti[1], Michael Langguth[1], Bing Gong[1],
Scarlet Stadtler[1], Amirpasha Mozaffari[1], Gabriele Cavallaro[1], Rocco Sedona[1,2],
Alexander Schug[1,3], Alexandre Strube[1], Roshni Kamath[1], Martin G. Schultz[1],
Morris Riedel[1,2], and Thomas Lippert[1]

[1] Jülich Supercomputing Centre, Forschungszentrum Jülich GmbH, Jülich, Germany
{s.kesselheim,a.herten,k.krajsek,ja.ebert,j.jitsev,m.cherti,m.langguth,
b.gong,s.stadtler,a.mozaffari,g.cavallaro,r.sedona,a.schug,a.strube,
r.kamath,m.schultz,m.riedel,t.lippert}@fz-juelich.de
[2] School of Engineering and Natural Sciences, University of Iceland,
Reykjavik, Iceland
[3] University of Duisburg-Essen, Duisburg, Germany

Abstract. In this article, we present JUWELS Booster, a recently commissioned high-performance computing system at the Jülich Supercomputing Center. With its system architecture, most importantly its large number of powerful Graphics Processing Units (GPUs) and its fast interconnect via InfiniBand, it is an ideal machine for large-scale Artificial Intelligence (AI) research and applications. We detail its system architecture, parallel, distributed model training, and benchmarks indicating its outstanding performance. We exemplify its potential for research application by presenting large-scale AI research highlights from various scientific fields that require such a facility.

Keywords: Artificial Intelligence · Deep learning · GPU ·
High-performance computing · Machine learning · Jülich
supercomputing centre

1 Introduction

In recent years, deep learning methods brought up radical transformation across various disciplines of technology and science, sparking interest in the previously academic field of Artificial Intelligence (AI), and extending it far beyond academia. Progress is notified and valued in mainstream and business media and widely discussed. Without disparaging many other ingenious contributions, it can be said that a single paper started the boom: in 2012, Alex Krizhevsky, Ilya

S. Kesselheim, A. Herten, K. Krajsek, J. Ebert, J. Jitsev, M. Cherti, M. Langguth, B. Gong, S. Stadtler, A. Mozaffari, G. Cavallaro, R. Sedona, A. Schug—Equal contribution.

H. Jagode et al. (Eds.): ISC High Performance 2021 Workshops, LNCS 12761, pp. 453–468, 2021.
https://doi.org/10.1007/978-3-030-90539-2_31

Sutskever and Geoffrey Hinton had shown that a deep neural network outperforms the state-of-the-art in image classification in the ImageNet competition, by a large margin [34]. Since then, interest has skyrocketed, and the number of publications on AI has grown exponentially [70].

A vital ingredient of this success was the availability of computational resources for AlexNet: two NVIDIA GeForce GTX 580 graphics processing units (GPUs). Since then, not only the cumulated amount of compute has increased tremendously, but also the computational resources needed by AI models. Amodei et. al observed a 300 000-fold increase in six years of the computational effort required for the largest models [6]. This trend extends over all fields of machine learning (ML), ranging from Computer Vision (CV), over Natural Language Processing (NLP) to Reinforcement learning (RL).

A prominent example with a lot of media echo is the GPT-3 model, a transformer-based NLP architecture consisting of 175 billion parameters trained on a corpus of 45 TB of text [11]. The impressive NLP model is capable of performing "in-context learning", i.e. it can pick up novel tasks at inference time without re-training by just providing an input that verbally describes the task or gives the context of the desired outcome.

In the CV field, the BigTransfer (BiT) work follows similar lines. A very large model is pre-trained on an extremely large dataset: up to 300 million images, allowing for fine-tuning the model in an extremely data-efficient way for downstream tasks [33]. This idea is further detailed in Sect. 3.1. Self-supervised approaches make it possible to also use data that has not been manually annotated for pre-training [13]. Such approaches heavily rely on large models and extensive training procedures but have the potential to reach learning from only a few examples. An even greater source of visual data enclosing also the temporal dimension are videos as shown e.g. in Ref. [44].

While the previous examples involve the private sector, also in the academic world, large scale training have been performed. Kurth et al. trained an ML-based large scale climate model on the Piz Daint and Summit supercomputers, reaching 1 EFlop/s peak in FP16 [35]. Other typical situations in science are inverse problems, in which an accurate forward simulation model is available, but the practical task is the inference of parameters. In an example of Laanait et al., electron densities were inferred from diffraction patterns by an ML model, a computation that involved a training data set of 500 TB and up 27 600 GPUs on Summit [36]. A further example is the evolutionary search of network architectures in cancer research [46]. Here, the objective was to find an architecture that could analyze microscopic tissue slides to support cancer diagnosis and that is suitable for usage in a desktop PC application, requiring an extensive search for the optimal model.

Reproducibility is an indispensable factor for AI research [59]. While many academic papers are accompanied with dedicated repositories, reproducing the largest models from the industry sector are especially difficult, for neither of the examples GPT-3, AlphaZero, AlphaFold or DALL-E the full source code or trained models have been released. Initiatives dedicated to reproducing such results can make very important contributions to the field, yet require considerable computational resources[1].

To support these trends, a new supercomputer has been installed at the Jülich Supercomputing Centre (JSC) for Forschungszentrum Jülich. The machine is installed as a booster module for the modular supercomputer JUWELS (Jülich Wizard for European Leadership Science) and referred to as JUWELS Booster. Almost 4000 high-performance GPUs render it both one of the fastest and most energy efficient computers in the world, currently ranked no. 7 in the Top500 list and no. 3 in the Green500 list, as well as the fastest supercomputer in Europe. It is intended as a machine that not only supports AI research, but can act as a substrate for a blooming AI community.

In this paper, we will explain the rationale behind the system design, indicate its technological capabilities, and demonstrate its potential by showing several research highlights from Forschungszentrum Jülich. This paper is structured as follows. After the introduction in Sect. 1, we present JUWELS' ecosystem in Sect. 2. Here, we discuss its architecture, parallel model training techniques and ML benchmark results. In Sect. 3, we present four examples of large scale AI applications. This includes large scale transfer learning, deep-learning driven weather forecast, multispectral remote sensing image classification, and RNA structure analysis. We conclude with a summary and an outlook.

2   JUWELS Booster System

2.1   JSC Supercomputer Ecosystem

The Jülich Supercomputing Centre operates different supercomputers of various sizes. The two largest ones are JURECA and JUWELS. JUWELS is a *Gauss Centre for Supercomputing* Tier 0/1 machine [30], currently consisting of two modules: JUWELS Cluster and JUWELS Booster. While the JUWELS Cluster module provides general-purpose computational resources with more than 2300 compute nodes based on Intel Skylake CPUs, JUWELS Booster is the system's highly scalable module, leveraging GPUs to provide computing performance. Both modules are combined through their network fabric and file system and can be used together, by heterogeneous jobs, through a tight integration via the workload manager.

2.2   JUWELS Booster

Commissioned in 2020, JUWELS Booster features the latest GPU, CPU, and network technology available. 936 compute nodes host four GPUs each, providing access to 3744 GPUs. The installed GPUs are NVIDIA A100 Tensor Core GPUs (40 GB), providing 19.5 TFLOP/s of $FP64_{TC}$ computing performance each. The GPUs are hosted by AMD EPYC 7402 CPUs with 2×24 cores (SMT-2) per node. Each node is equipped with 512 GB of RAM.

---

[1] See e.g. https://github.com/EleutherAI/the-pile.

The network of JUWELS Booster is based on Mellanox HDR200 InfiniBand, with four Mellanox ConnectX 6 devices per node, each providing 200 Gbit/s of bandwidth per direction. The network is designed as a DragonFly+ network; the nodes are aligned in sets of 48 in a local switch group (*cell*). While nodes in a cell are tightly connected as a full fat-tree with two levels of switches, each cell connects to the other cell with 10 links. The resulting total bi-section bandwidth is 400 Tbit/s between the cells. Dedicated network links are available to connect to JUWELS Cluster. These links also provide access to a highly-parallel, flash-based file system with 1400 GB/s peak bandwidth. The storage cluster, JUST, can be reached with a peak of 400 GB/s bandwidth via gateway nodes.

The NVIDIA A100 GPUs installed into JUWELS Booster provide different computing performance depending on the precision used. Within the 400 W TDP, the following peak performance is available: 9.7TFLOP/s (FP64), 19.5TFLOP/s $FP64_{TC}$ and FP32, 78TFLOP/s FP16, 156TFLOP/s $TF32_{TC}$, 312TFLOP/s $FP16_{TC}$, where *TC* denotes the usage of Tensor Cores. With respect to the FP64 Tensor Cores, an excellent peak efficiency of 48,75GFLOP/s can be reached. Indeed, JUWELS Booster ranks highest in the Green500 list of November 2020 as the most energy-efficient supercomputer within the first 100 places of the Top500 with 25GFLOP/s.

The software stack on JUWELS is managed via EasyBuild and accessed via environment modules, enabling finely-tuned, homogeneous software environments across the modules of the system. In addition, containers are supported via Singularity, either by using pre-made containers from registries, or by building containers directly from the system through a dedicated container build service.

2.3   Distributed Model Training on JUWELS Booster

The execution of efficient AI algorithms on JUWELS Booster requires different levels of parallelism: At the level of basic numerical operations, at the level of parallelization of deep learning models, and at the level in the training procedure of the deep learning models.

Modern deep learning models transform n-dimensional tensors by applying element-wise operations, e.g. activation functions, convolution operations, or matrix multiplication in fully connected layers. While element-wise operations are embarrassingly parallelizable, convolution operations and matrix multiplication require special, sophisticated parallelization strategies. The development of parallel matrix operations and convolutions that can themselves be reduced to matrix operations is mature and results in highly optimized libraries such as MKL [1], cuBLAS [2], and cuDNN [15]. JUWELS Booster's GPUs contain Tensor Cores, hardware that specializes in matrix multiplications in the context of AI. In conjunction with cuBLAS, it is possible to apply efficient convolution operations and matrix multiplications in GPUs. Depending on the dimension of the input tensor and its data type, the most efficient algorithm is automatically selected by the cuBLAS library. While it is not necessary to optimize these operations manually, AI applications can be tuned by choosing optimal input dimensions and data types, i.e. Tensor Cores work most efficiently when the data dimension is divisible by a certain number depending on the data type. Reducing the precision of the data type, for example from FP32 to FP16, can also lead to a significant speed-up. The deep learning frameworks installed on JUWELS Booster (Tensor-Flow [4] and PyTorch [45]) provide modules (e.g. `torch.cuda.amp` in PyTorch) to automatically reduce precision for operations where precision is a minor concern. While operator-level parallelization is performed on a single GPU, model-level parallelization enables usage of all 3744 GPUs of the JUWELS Booster system. A common method for parallelizing the training of neural networks is data parallelism. This involves replicating the model on several GPUs, each of which is trained with a different batch of the training data. Apart from batch normalization [29], all operations in modern deep learning models can be performed independently on the different computing devices. After calculating the gradient of the model parameters, the gradients are averaged over the different replicants, which effectively gives the same result as training a model on a large batch – the combination of all distributed data batches. The averaging of the gradients as well as the batch normalization operation require collective communication across different GPUs, and can become a bottleneck when scaling the training process. To overcome these problems, one usually changes the training procedure in a distributed environment. For example for batch normalization, one computes the batch statistics only on a subset of the parallel training batches involved, which has even been shown to be advantageous over computing over exceptionally large total batches [24]. Collective communication can be accelerated by compressing the gradients before averaging [5,21,64]. The JUWELS Booster software stack provides Horovod [55] as a data-parallel framework with NCCL[2] as a communication framework that works with the supported deep learning frameworks TensorFlow and PyTorch, and comes with built-in FP16 gradient compression. Horovod is applied for the parallel training results shown in this paper. JSC also supports HeAT [26], a general distributed tensor framework for high-performance data analytics. The communication framework of HeAT provides the full MPI [42] functionality and shows a significantly speedup to the comparable library Dask [50]. Large deep learning models may not fit on a single computational device, requiring an extension of the purely data-parallel approach to model parallelism [43] or pipelining [20], which in turn requires automatic differentiation (AD) across different computational devices. AD is a critical feature of modern deep learning libraries, but most libraries[3] support AD only on a single node, and no deep learning library supports AD with MPI requiring extensions. JSC supports DeepSpeed [49], a cutting-edge deep learning optimisation library that supports data and model parallelisation as well as pipelining schemes or all in combination by a lightweight wrapper around

---

[2] https://docs.nvidia.com/deeplearning/nccl/index.html.

[3] PyTorch allows AD for distributing tensors across computational devices based on the remote procedure call (RPC) protocol [9]. However, the RPC framework does not compete with communication frameworks like NCCL or MPI with respect to performance.

PyTorch. In addition JSC supports MPI4Torch[4] allowing to write PyTorch code directly in distributed environments. The last level of parallelization considers the parallelization of the training procedure, which includes ensemble learning [38], model averaging [71], but also hyperparameter search [40], as well as model architecture search [39]. JSC supports training parallelization with the framework L2L [60].

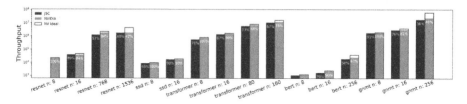

Fig. 1. Benchmark results of a subset of MLPerf training v0.7 runs for different tasks and different number of GPUs (n). Our results shown in blue, NVIDIA's in green. Empty bars indicate the throughput for ideal scaling conditions on NVIDIA's results. For each run the efficiency normalized by NVIDIA's single-node result is indicated in percent. (Color figure online)

2.4   Benchmark Results

We investigate the capability of JUWELS Booster to achieve nominal performance under practical machine learning conditions by running the MLPerf training benchmark following the v0.7 submission conditions [41]. As our machine shares key features with NVIDIA's Selene machine, we also run their submission code. To enable comparison, the number of nodes is doubled, as Selene features eight GPUs per node over JUWELS Booster's four. Containers are updated as well. The MLPerf training benchmark measures the time-to-accuracy. This was carefully optimized by NVIDIA by hyperparameter optimization. As we only re-run their benchmarks and do not optimize the hyperparameters, we instead report the throughput in images/second for the tasks *resnet* and *ssd*, words per second for the tasks *transformer* and *gnmt*, and in sequences per second for "bert". As indicated in Fig. 1, we are able to closely reproduce NVIDIA's results. Details of our implementation are published on our GitLab server[5].

3   Large Scale AI Research at JSC

3.1   Large-Scale Deep Learning for Efficient Cross-Domain Transfer

Transfer learning was successfully employed already at the very rise of deep neural networks. Early architectures like AlexNet, OverFeat, or VGG-16 were

---

[4] https://github.com/helmholtz-analytics/mpi4torch.

[5] https://gitlab.version.fz-juelich.de/kesselheim1/mlperf_juwelsbooster.

pre-trained on ImageNet-1k, a large natural image dataset which serves as a gold standard in the visual image understanding community [19,51]. Importantly, after fine-tuning on various other target datasets, pre-trained models showed better performance compared to models just trained on target datasets from scratch [47]. The combination of pre-training on a large generic dataset and transferring in an efficient way the pre-trained model to a specific target dataset, often much smaller in size than the one used during pre-training, has since proven itself as a viable strategy to create powerful models also for those scenarios where data is scarce [33].

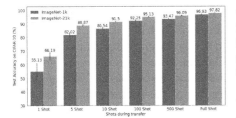

Fig. 2. Fine-tuning results of ResNet-152x4 on CIFAR-10 using pipeline of [33]. The model is pre-trained either on ImageNet-1k or ImageNet-21k, and we show few-shot (e.g. 1-shot means we use 1 example per class, thus a total of 10 examples for CIFAR-10) results as well as full fine-tuning results (the whole training set is used for fine-tuning).

Table 1. Fine-tuning results of ResNet-152x4 on the COVIDx dataset (we use the COVIDx V7A version) from [65]. In this setup, we pre-train on ImageNet-1k and follow the fine-tuning pipeline of [33].

	Precision	Recall	F1-score
COVID-19	0.88	0.84	0.86
Normal	0.96	0.92	0.94
Pneumonia	0.87	0.93	0.90

Recently, strong evidence was obtained that increasing the model size while at the same time increasing the amount of data and compute for pre-training results in very large models that have even stronger generalization and transfer capabilities [8,10,27,32,33]. Pre-training of large transferable models requires larger datasets, like for instance ImageNet-21k [19], and is computationally very expensive. Therefore, to obtain such large models and benefit from their improved transferability and generalization, machines like JUWELS Booster are required to perform distributed training efficiently across multiple nodes using a large amount of GPUs.

Here, we demonstrate the merits of such a large-scale distributed pre-training for transfer on different target datasets following [33]. We show that pre-training on ImageNet-21k ($\approx$ 10 times larger than the standard ImageNet-1k) provides a clear performance benefit in terms of accuracy achieved when transferring and fine-tuning the pre-trained model to smaller natural image datasets like CIFAR-10. Especially in the very low data regime using few-shot transfer, where only few examples per class are shown, the benefit of pre-training on large ImageNet-21k is striking (see Fig. 2). JUWELS Booster shows good scaling behavior during distributed training across a vast number of compute nodes using Horovod (Fig. 1), which allows us to execute large-scale pre-training procedures in a fraction of the time for single-node training and shorten experimental cycles. Still, a full pre-training of a large ResNet-152x4 network on ImageNet-21k for 90 epochs takes ca. 81 h when using 256 GPUs. Distributed training also performs without loss of accuracy [56] when compared to single-node training.

Following the goals of our initiative for large-scale transfer learning applied to medical imaging for COVID-19 diagnostics (COVIDNetX[6]), we also envisage application of large-scale generic model pre-training, for efficient and robust transfer to specific domains, like medical images. Motivated by the urgency to provide robust and widely available tools for predictive diagnostics of a patient's current and future state from medical imaging data with regard to a SARS-CoV-2 infection and its disease course [58,66], we have chosen a small publicly available dataset containing X-ray lung images of COVID-19, non-COVID, and healthy control patients (COVIDx) as a use case example for transfer [16,65]. First preliminary results for transfer performance are available for the large ResNet-152x4 model pre-trained on ImageNet-1k (see Table 1). Further investigations are necessary to quantify the benefits of pre-training on much larger datasets, like ImageNet-21k, when attempting to transfer to such small, domain-specific datasets like COVIDx (see e.g. [14] for a follow-up study).

In summary, we have prepared the grounds for advanced transfer learning techniques, which should allow us to efficiently transfer models pre-trained on large amounts of generic data, in a highly-performant, distributed manner, to various specific target datasets of much smaller size, with low computational cost for transfer [33]. Transfer efficiency also paves the road for energy efficient deep learning that is both data-sample and compute efficient, requiring only a small energy budget for each transfer. As follow-up work, we aim to demonstrate that the postulated benefits of better generalization and transfer attributed to large-scale models [8,10,27,32,33] hold across a very broad range of specialized domains and conditions used as transfer targets.

3.2   Deep Learning-Driven Weather Forecast

Weather can have an enormous effect on human lives. Improving weather forecasting can minimize the adverse effects of extreme weather and assist in planning economic activities. Numerical weather prediction (NWP) models are among the earliest and most demanding applications for supercomputers [7]. Recently, modern deep learning (DL) approaches are considered to potentially play an important role in every step of the NWP workflow, from data assimilation, to replacing numerical model parameterizations, to statistical output post-processing [7,48]. Because of the huge size of meteorological datasets from observations and numerical simulations, high-throughput supercomputing systems and parallel DL approaches are necessary.

In this study, we explore the use of state-of-the-art video prediction methods to forecast meteorological variables utilizing the global ERA5 reanalysis

---

[6] https://tinyurl.com/CovidNetXHelmholtz.

dataset [28]. The goal is to forecast the 2-metre temperature over Europe for 12 h in a data-driven way. The geographic domain consists of 56×92 grid points in meridional and zonal direction. Input variables are the 2-metre temperature, cloud cover, and 850hPa temperatures of the preceding 12 h. The first DL model selected is the convLSTM architecture [57]. Input and output tensors of our convLSTM model have a dimension of $12 \times 56 \times 92 \times 3$ each. The model has 429 251 parameters and was trained on 11 years of ERA5 reanalysis data in hourly resolution. The total volume of pre-processed data in TFRecords format amounts to 153 GB. An example of a 12-hour forecast is shown in Fig. 3.

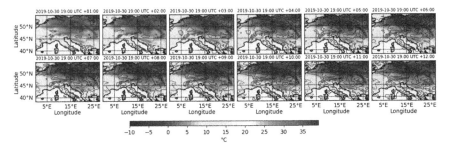

Fig. 3. Example of a 2-metre temperature (°C) prediction with convLSTM (see text for details). Solid (dotted) contours denote positive (negative) temperature differences between forecast and ground truth with an interval of 1K (starting from 0.5K).

Training on a single A100 GPU takes about 50 min/epoch. Given that a typical DL experiment typically requires up to 100 epochs to converge, such training times are prohibitive for any serious application, so training is parallelized using Horovod. Figure 4 shows that the model training achieves 90% scaling efficiency in terms of time comparing 1 GPU against 16 GPUs for 10 epochs. However, it is observed that time variances for all iterations increase significantly beyond 32 GPUs. This could be caused by data loading inefficiency, communication, or lack of enough GPU utilization. These issues are currently being investigated.

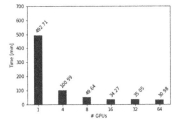
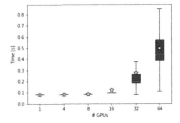

Fig. 4. Total training time in minutes (left) and box whisker plot of iteration time in seconds (right). The star in the box whisker plot denotes the averaged iteration time, while its median is highlighted by an orange line. (Color figure online)

After solving these issues, we plan to test more complex video prediction models (e.g. the stochastic adversarial video prediction architecture [37]) to improve prediction accuracy and push JUWELS Booster to its limits.

3.3   Multispectral Remote Sensing Image Classification

Among other application areas, spaceborne Remote Sensing (RS) can detect and observe the characteristics of the Earth's surface by measuring its reflected and emitted radiation at a distance. Applications from RS use multispectral RS images to classify different physical features that occupy the surface of the Earth (i.e. land-cover classes), as well as to describe the use of the land surface by humans (i.e. land-use classes) [12]. The RS community has started to produce several labeled RS datasets with large spatial coverage and variety of classes (e.g. BigEarthNet [61], SEN12MS [52], etc.). These datasets provide a high number of reliably labeled samples that can be used to train deep neural networks with supervised learning.

BigEarthNet-S2[7] is a large RS archive consisting of 590 326 patches (an example is shown in Fig. 5) extracted from tiles acquired by the Sentinel-2 satellites [62]. We train the models on the version of the dataset with 19 labels. Each patch can be associated with multiple labels, making this a multi-label classification problem. For the experiments we use the following spectral bands: 3 RGB bands and band 8 at 10m resolution, bands 5, 6, 7, 8a, 11, and 12 at 20 m resolution, and bands 1 and 9 at 60 m resolution. The bands at lower resolution are upsampled to 10 m resolution using bilinear interpolation.

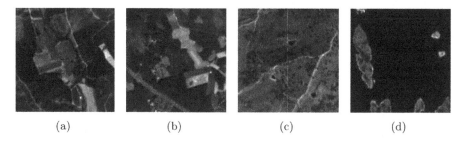

| (a) | (b) | (c) | (d) |

Fig. 5. Example of patches extracted from Sentinel-2 tiles [62]. The corresponding classes are: (**a**) "Permanent crops", "Broad-leaved forest", "Transitional woodland/shrub", (**b**) "Land principally occupied by agriculture, with significant areas of natural vegetation", "Broad-leaved forest", "Mixed forest", (**c**) "Pastures", "Agroforestry areas", (**d**) "Mixed forest", "Marine waters".

A multispectral ResNet-152 is trained from scratch on the training subset (60% of the entire dataset) and evaluated on the test subset (20% of the dataset). We run the experiments with the NovoGrad optimizer. The values of the learning

---

rate and weight decay follow the choices of [23]. Data augmentations with random flips, rotation of the patches, and mix-up are applied to reduce overfitting. The experiments are carried out for 100 epochs, on 1, 4, 16, and 64 nodes (4, 16, 64 and, 256 GPUs respectively). Horovod is employed to distribute the training on multiple compute nodes and GPUs [55]. The batch size per GPU selected for the experiments is 16, with a global batch size that ranges from 64 for 1-node to 4096 for the 64-node configurations respectively.

The results of the classification are evaluated using the macro F1 score, which remains stable among the experiments (0.73), and is in line with [62]. Using a data-parallel approach allows us to scale up a DL model on a large remote sensing dataset and consequently cut the training time down significantly, with an 80% efficiency comparing 1 node (ca. 2550 s per epoch) against 64 nodes (ca. 50 s per epoch). Various research questions remain open, and one salient point is understanding the feasibility of training with larger global batch sizes, which are known to pose optimization difficulties [25]. A comparison between different training strategies, such as the choice of the learning rate and optimizer, is also in the future plans of the authors. More effort is also needed to enhance the pre-processing and data loading pipeline to feed the model and possibly increase efficiency when using a large number of nodes.

3.4 RNA Structure with ML

On a fundamental level, all life as we know it is orchestrated by interactions between biomolecules, such as proteins, DNA, and RNA. Due to a direct structure-function relationship, it is important to structurally resolve biomolecules, even though this is experimentally challenging. A complementary approach is using statistical tools to mine the rich existing protein databases. Physics-based co-evolutionary models such as direct coupling analysis (DCA) [53,67,68] have in the last decade lead to the prediction of protein structures and complexes with astonishing accuracy [18,63] by a combination of bioinformatics tools with molecular simulations. Considering the aforementioned large, public databases with 100 000+ biomolecular structures and even larger sequence databases, the combination of these methods with machine learning (ML) approaches appears natural and has further improved their accuracy [54].

Another class of biomolecules, Ribonucleic acids (RNA), is critical for biological activities such as coding, regulation and expressions of genes. This critical importance also leads to RNA's application in pharmacology, as some of the most effective drugs in the current COVID epidemic are RNA-based. As for proteins, RNA function is closely related to its three-dimensional structure. It is, however, more challenging to gain structural information on RNA, as reflected by the small number of RNA 3-D structures in databases with many crucial RNA being still structurally unresolved – akin to dark matter of the biomolecular universe [3]. Unfortunately, while DCA still works well on RNA [3,17,22], ML methods so successful for proteins cannot be easily applied for RNA structure prediction, given that existing databases are considerably smaller [31]. Still, even the small amount of existing data can be used to significantly improve prediction of RNA by shallow neural networks by over 70% using simple convolutional neural networks [69]. Future work will therefore focus on using the massive computing resources of JUWELS to enhance these simple CNNs by, e.g. using knowledge gained from proteins by transfer learning approaches. Similarly, we plan to run complex molecular dynamics simulations (MD) on RNA, to gain more structural insight. As these simulations needs to simulate all atoms of the RNA and the surrounding solvent, they can quickly require $\mathcal{O}(10)+$ million core hours on highly parallel systems.

4   Summary and Outlook

In this paper we have demonstrated the hardware configuration of JUWELS Booster, currently not only the fastest supercomputer in Europe but also the most energy-efficient large-scale machine in the world. We have elucidated the key parallelization techniques that unlock this computational power for machine learning, and have shown that JUWELS Booster reaches its potential also in practical machine learning settings.

We have indicated how the availability of such a machine can foster developments in various research fields. We have shown that large-scale pre-training can render CV applications much more data-efficient, including medical imaging for COVID-19 detection. We demonstrated that DL video prediction methods are an option for computing weather forecasts. We have seen that large-scale data parallel training enables us to train models on large corpora of multispectral satellite images and the ML-based structure predictions can help us understanding the role of RNA for biology.

All applications not only rely on raw computational power, but also on a system design and infrastructure that allows for fast parallel implementations, and a software ecosystem that gives users the possibility for rapid development, employing groundbreaking methods. The Jülich Supercomputing Centre, hosting JUWELS Booster, brings all these ingredients together, creating a state-of-the art AI landscape.

Acknowledgements. This work was funded by Helmholtz Association's Initiative and Networking Fund under project number ZT-I-0003 and HelmholtzAI computing resources (HAICORE) Funding has been obtained through grants ERC-2017-ADG 787576 (IntelliAQ) and BMBF 01 IS 18O47A (DeepRain). This work was performed in the CoE RAISE and DEEP-EST projects receiving funding from EU's Horizon 2020 Research and Innovation Framework Programme under the grant agreement no. 951733 and no. 754304 respectively. We thank ECMWF for providing ERA-5 data. The authors gratefully acknowledge the Gauss Centre for Supercomputing e.V. (www.gauss-centre.eu) for funding this work by providing computing time through the John von Neumann Institute for Computing (NIC) on the GCS Supercomputers JUWELS, JUWELS Booster at Jülich Supercomputing Centre (JSC) and we acknowledge computing resources from the Helmholtz Data Federation. Further computing time was provided on supercomputer JUSUF in frame of offer for epidemiology research on COVID-19 by JSC.

References

1. Intel Math Kernel Library. Reference Manual. Intel Corporation (2009)
2. NVIDIA CUBLAS Library Documentation (2017). https://docs.nvidia.com/cuda/cublas/. Accessed 14 Apr 2021
3. Pucci, F., Schug, A.: Shedding light on the dark matter of the biomolecular structural universe: Progress in RNA 3D structure prediction. Methods **162–163**, 68–73 (2019). https://doi.org/10.1016/j.ymeth.2019.04.012
4. Abadi, M., et al.: TensorFlow: Large-Scale Machine Learning on Heterogeneous Systems (2015). http://tensorflow.org/, Software available from tensorflow.org
5. Agarwal, S., Wang, H., Venkataraman, S., Papailiopoulos, D.: On the utility of gradient compression in distributed training systems. ArXiv abs/2103.00543 (2021)
6. Amodei, D., Hernandez, D., Sastry, G., Clark, J., Brockman, G., Sutskever, I.: AI and compute. Technical report, OpenAI Blog (2018)
7. Bauer, P., Thorpe, A., Brunet, G.: Nature. https://doi.org/10.1038/nature14956
8. Belkin, M., Hsu, D., Ma, S., Mandal, S.: Reconciling modern machine-learning practice and the classical bias-variance trade-off. Proc. Natl. Acad. Sci. U.S.A. **116**, 15849–15854 (2019). https://doi.org/10.1073/pnas.1903070116
9. Birrell, A.D., Nelson, B.J.: Implementing remote procedure calls. ACM Trans. Comput. Syst. **2**(1), 39–59 (1984)
10. Brown, T., et al.: Language models are few-shot learners. In: Larochelle, H., Ranzato, M., Hadsell, R., Balcan, M.F., Lin, H. (eds.) Advances in Neural Information Processing Systems, vol. 33, pp. 1877–1901. Curran Associates, Inc. (2020)
11. Brown, T.B., et al.: Language models are few-shot learners. arXiv preprint arXiv:2005.14165 (2020)
12. Canty, M.: Image Analysis, Classification and Change Detection in Remote Sensing: With Algorithms for ENVI/IDL and Python, 3rd edn. Taylor & Francis, New York (2014). ISBN: 9781466570375
13. Chen, T., Kornblith, S., Swersky, K., Norouzi, M., Hinton, G.: Big self-supervised models are strong semi-supervised learners. arXiv preprint arXiv:2006.10029 (2020)
14. Cherti, M., Jitsev, J.: Effect of large-scale pre-training on full and few-shot transfer learning for natural and medical images. arXiv preprint arXiv:2106.00116 (2021)
15. Chetlur, S., et al.: cuDNN: efficient primitives for deep learning (2014)
16. Cohen, J.P., Morrison, P., Dao, L., Roth, K., Duong, T.Q., Ghassemi, M.: Covid-19 image data collection: Prospective predictions are the future. J. Mach. Learn. Biomed. Imaging (2020)
17. Cuturello, F., Tiana, G., Bussi, G.: Assessing the accuracy of direct-coupling analysis for RNA contact prediction (2020). https://doi.org/10.1261/rna.074179.119
18. Dago, A.E., Schug, A., Procaccini, A., Hoch, J.A., Weigt, M., Szurmant, H.: Structural basis of histidine kinase autophosphorylation deduced by integrating genomics, molecular dynamics, and mutagenesis. Proc. Natl. Acad. Sci. **109**(26), E1733–E1742 (2012)
19. Deng, J., Dong, W., Socher, R., Li, L., Li, K., Fei-Fei, L.: Imagenet: a large-scale hierarchical image database. In: Proceedings of IEEE Conference on Computer Vision and Pattern Recognition, pp. 248–255, June 2009. https://doi.org/10.1109/CVPR.2009.5206848
20. Deng, L., Yu, D., Platt, J.: Scalable stacking and learning for building deep architectures. In: 2012 IEEE International Conference on Acoustics, Speech and Signal Processing (ICASSP), pp. 2133–2136 (2012). https://doi.org/10.1109/ICASSP.2012.6288333

21. Dettmers, T.: 8-bit approximations for parallelism in deep learning (2015). arxiv:1511.04561

22. De Leonardis, E., et al.: Direct-Coupling Analysis of nucleotide coevolution facilitates RNA secondary and tertiary structure prediction. Nucl. Acids Res. **43**(21), 10444–10455 (2015). https://doi.org/10.1093/nar/gkv932

23. Ginsburg, B., et al.: Stochastic gradient methods with layer-wise adaptive moments for training of deep networks (2020)

24. Goyal, P., et al.: Accurate, large minibatch SGD: training Imagenet in 1 hour. CoRR abs/1706.02677 (2017). http://arxiv.org/abs/1706.02677

25. Goyal, P., et al.: Accurate, large minibatch SGD: training ImageNet in 1 hour (2018)

26. Götz, M., et al.: HeAT - a distributed and GPU-accelerated tensor framework for data analytics. In: Proceedings of the 19th IEEE International Conference on Big Data, pp. 276–288. IEEE, December 2020

27. Hernandez, D., Kaplan, J., Henighan, T., McCandlish, S.: Scaling laws for transfer. arXiv preprint arXiv:2102.01293 (2021)

28. Hersbach, H., et al.: The ERA5 global reanalysis. Q. J. R. Meteorol. Soc. **146**(730), 1999–2049 (2020). https://doi.org/10.1002/qj.3803

29. Ioffe, S., Szegedy, C.: Batch normalization: accelerating deep network training by reducing internal covariate shift. In: Bach, F., Blei, D. (eds.) Proceedings of the 32nd International Conference on Machine Learning. Proceedings of Machine Learning Research, vol. 37, pp. 448–456. PMLR, Lille, France, 7–9 July 2015. http://proceedings.mlr.press/v37/ioffe15.html

30. Jülich Supercomputing Centre: JUWELS: Modular Tier-0/1 Supercomputer at the Jülich Supercomputing Centre. J. Large-Scale Res. Facil. **5**(A171) (2019). http://dx.doi.org/10.17815/jlsrf-5-171

31. Kalvari, I., et al.: RFAM 13.0: shifting to a genome-centric resource for non-coding RNA families. Nucleic Acids Res. **46**(D1), D335–D342 (2017). https://doi.org/10.1093/nar/gkx1038

32. Kaplan, J., et al.: Scaling laws for neural language models. arXiv preprint arXiv:2001.08361 (2020)

33. Kolesnikov, A., et al.: Big transfer (bit): general visual representation learning. In: Vedaldi, A., Bischof, H., Brox, T., Frahm, J.M. (eds.) Computer Vision - ECCV 2020, pp. 491–507. Springer, Cham (2020)

34. Krizhevsky, A., Sutskever, I., Hinton, G.E.: ImageNet classification with deep convolutional neural networks. Adv. Neural. Inf. Process. Syst. **25**, 1097–1105 (2012)

35. Kurth, T., et al.: Exascale deep learning for climate analytics. In: SC18: International Conference for High Performance Computing, Networking, Storage and Analysis, pp. 649–660. IEEE (2018)

36. Laanait, N., et al.: Exascale deep learning for scientific inverse problems. arXiv preprint arXiv:1909.11150 (2019)

37. Lee, A.X., Zhang, R., Ebert, F., Abbeel, P., Finn, C., Levine, S.: Stochastic adversarial video prediction. arXiv preprint arXiv:1804.01523 (2018)

38. Lee, S., Purushwalkam, S., Cogswell, M., Crandall, D.J., Batra, D.: Why M heads are better than one: Training a diverse ensemble of deep networks. CoRR abs/1511.06314 (2015). http://arxiv.org/abs/1511.06314

39. Liu, H., Simonyan, K., Vinyals, O., Fernando, C., Kavukcuoglu, K.: Hierarchical representations for efficient architecture search. arXiv e-prints arXiv:1711.00436, November 2017

40. Lorenzo, P.R., Nalepa, J., Ramos, L., Ranilla, J.: Hyper-parameter selection in deep neural networks using parallel particle swarm optimization. In: Proceedings of the Genetic and Evolutionary Computation Conference Companion (2017)
41. Mattson, P., et al.: MLPerf: an industry standard benchmark suite for machine learning performance. IEEE Micro **40**(2), 8–16 (2020)
42. Message Passing Interface Forum: MPI: A Message-Passing Interface Standard, Version 3.1. High Performance Computing Center Stuttgart (HLRS) (2015). https://fs.hlrs.de/projects/par/mpi//mpi31/
43. Muller, U.A., Gunzinger, A.: Neural net simulation on parallel computers. In: Proceedings of 1994 IEEE International Conference on Neural Networks (ICNN 1994), vol. 6, pp. 3961–3966 (1994). https://doi.org/10.1109/ICNN.1994.374845
44. Orhan, E., Gupta, V., Lake, B.M.: Self-supervised learning through the eyes of a child. In: Advances in Neural Information Processing Systems, vol. 33 (2020)
45. Paszke, A., et al.: PyTorch: an imperative style, high-performance deep learning library. In: Advances in Neural Information Processing Systems, vol. 32, pp. 8024–8035. Curran Associates, Inc. (2019). http://papers.neurips.cc/paper/9015-pytorch-an-imperative-style-high-performance-deep-learning-library.pdf
46. Patton, R.M., et al.: Exascale deep learning to accelerate cancer research. In: 2019 IEEE International Conference on Big Data (Big Data), pp. 1488–1496. IEEE (2019)
47. Razavian, A.S., Azizpour, H., Sullivan, J., Carlsson, S.: CNN features off-the-shelf: an astounding baseline for recognition. In: Proceedings of IEEE Conference on Computer Vision and Pattern Recognition Workshops, pp. 512–519, June 2014. https://doi.org/10.1109/CVPRW.2014.131
48. Reichstein, M., Camps-Valls, G., Stevens, B., Jung, M., Denzler, J., Carvalhais, N.: Prabhat: deep learning and process understanding for data-driven Earth system science. Nature (2019). https://doi.org/10.1038/s41586-019-0912-1
49. Ren, J., et al.: Zero-offload: Democratizing billion-scale model training (2021)
50. Rocklin, M.: Dask: parallel computation with blocked algorithms and task scheduling. In: Huff, K., Bergstra, J. (eds.) Proceedings of the 14th Python in Science Conference (SciPy 2015), pp. 130–136 (2015)
51. Russakovsky, O., et al.: Imagenet large scale visual recognition challenge. Int. J. Comput. Vision **115**(3), 211–252 (2015)
52. Schmitt, M., Hughes, L.: Sen12ms
53. Schug, A., Weigt, M., Onuchic, J.N., Hwa, T., Szurmant, H.: High-resolution protein complexes from integrating genomic information with molecular simulation. Proc. Natl. Acad. Sci. **106**(52), 22124–22129 (2009)
54. Senior, A.W., et al.: Improved protein structure prediction using potentials from deep learning. Nature **577**(7792), 706–710 (2020). https://doi.org/10.1038/s41586-019-1923-7
55. Sergeev, A., Balso, M.D.: Horovod: Fast and Easy Distributed Deep Learning in TensorFlow. arXiv preprint arXiv:1802.05799 (2018)
56. Shallue, C.J., Lee, J., Antognini, J., Sohl-Dickstein, J., Frostig, R., Dahl, G.E.: Measuring the effects of data parallelism on neural network training. J. Mach. Learn. Res. **20**, 1–49 (2019)
57. Shi, X., et al.: Convolutional lstm network: A machine learning approach for precipitation nowcasting. In: Advances in Neural Information Processing Systems (2015)
58. Sriram, A., et al.: Covid-19 deterioration prediction via self-supervised representation learning and multi-image prediction. arXiv preprint arXiv:2101.04909 (2021)
59. Stodden, V., et al.: Enhancing reproducibility for computational methods. Science **354**(6317), 1240–1241 (2016)

60. Subramoney, A., et al.: Igitugraz/l2l: v1.0.0-beta, March 2019. https://doi.org/10.5281/zenodo.2590760
61. Sumbul, G., Charfuelan, M., Demir, B., Markl, V.: BigEarthNet: a large-scale benchmark archive for remote sensing image understanding. In: Proceedings of the IEEE International Geoscience and Remote Sensing Symposium (IGARSS) (2019). https://doi.org/10.1109/igarss.2019.8900532
62. Sumbul, G., Kang, J., Kreuziger, T., Marcelino, F., Costa, H., et al.: BigEarthNet dataset with a new class-nomenclature for remote sensing image understanding (2020). http://arxiv.org/abs/2001.06372
63. Uguzzoni, G., Lovis, S.J., Oteri, F., Schug, A., Szurmant, H., Weigt, M.: Large-scale identification of coevolution signals across homo-oligomeric protein interfaces by direct coupling analysis. Proc. Natl. Acad. Sci. **114**(13), E2662–E2671 (2017)
64. Vogels, T., Karimireddy, S.P., Jaggi, M.: PowerSGD: practical low-rank gradient compression for distributed optimization. In: Wallach, H., Larochelle, H., Beygelzimer, A., d' Alché-Buc, F., Fox, E., Garnett, R. (eds.) Advances in Neural Information Processing Systems, vol. 32. Curran Associates, Inc. (2019). https://proceedings.neurips.cc/paper/2019/file/d9fbed9da256e344c1fa46bb46c34c5f-Paper.pdf
65. Wang, L., Lin, Z.Q., Wong, A.: COVID-net: a tailored deep convolutional neural network design for detection of COVID-19 cases from chest x-ray images. Sci. Rep. **10**, 19549 (2020). https://doi.org/10.1038/s41598-020-76550-z
66. Wehbe, R.M., et al.: DeepCOVID-XR: an artificial intelligence algorithm to detect COVID-19 on chest radiographs trained and tested on a large U.S. clinical data set. Radiology **299**, E167–E176 (2021). https://doi.org/10.1148/radiol.2020203511
67. Weigt, M., White, R.A., Szurmant, H., Hoch, J.A., Hwa, T.: Identification of direct residue contacts in protein-protein interaction by message passing. Proc. Nat. Acad. Sci. **106**(1), 67–72 (2009)
68. Zerihun, M.B., Pucci, F., Peter, E.K., Schug, A.: pydca v1.0: a comprehensive software for direct coupling analysis of RNA and protein sequences. Bioinformatics **36**(7), 2264–2265 (2020)
69. Zerihun, M.B., Pucci, F., Schug, A.: Coconet: boosting RNA contact prediction by convolutional neural networks. bioRxiv (2020)
70. Zhang, D., et al.: The AI index 2021 annual report, Technical report. AI Index Steering Committee, Human-Centered AI Institute, Stanford University, Stanford, CA (2021)
71. Zhang, S., Choromanska, A.E., LeCun, Y.: Deep learning with elastic averaging SGD. In: Cortes, C., Lawrence, N., Lee, D., Sugiyama, M., Garnett, R. (eds.) Advances in Neural Information Processing Systems, vol. 28. Curran Associates, Inc. (2015). https://proceedings.neurips.cc/paper/2015/file/d18f655c3fce66ca401d5f38b48c89af-Paper.pdf

Fifth International Workshop on in Situ Visualization

5th International Workshop on In Situ Visualization (WOIV'21)

1 Background and Description

Large-scale HPC simulations with their inherent I/O bottleneck have made *in situ* an essential approach for data analysis. In situ coupling of analysis and visualization to a live simulation circumvents writing raw data to disk. Instead, data abstracts are generated that capture much more information than otherwise possible.

The "Workshop on In Situ Visualization" series provides a venue for speakers to share practical expertise and experience with in situ visualization approaches. This 5th edition of the workshop, WOIV'21, took place as a virtual half-day workshop on July 2nd, 2021, co-located with ISC High Performance Digital, after two half-day workshops in 2016 and 2017 and two full-day workshops in 2018 and 2019. In 2020 we had to cancel the workshop due to the COVID-19 crisis. The goal of the workshop, in general, is to appeal to a wide-ranging audience of visualization scientists, computational scientists, and simulation developers, who have to collaborate to develop, deploy, and maintain in situ visualization approaches on HPC infrastructures.

For WOIV'21, we again also encouraged submissions on approaches that did not live up to their expectations. With this, we expected to get first-hand reports on lessons learned. Speakers should detail if and how the application drove abstractions or other kinds of data reductions and how these interacted with the expressiveness and flexibility of the visualization for exploratory analysis or why the approach failed.

Newly encouraged this year at WOIV'21 were submissions describing new developments for in situ software. These include both the creation of new in situ software as well as additions to existing in situ software. These submissions with a greater focus of "development" over "research" encourage the primary goal of WOIV to connect in situ techniques with science practitioners.

In addition to an invited keynote, presentations at WOIV'21 were selected from submitted abstracts. The abstracts were reviewed by the workshop chairs and organizers for appropriateness to WOIV. Accepted abstracts were invited to present at WOIV and to submit a full paper. (Not all presenters chose to submit a full paper.) Full papers underwent a peer review process by a program committee comprising diverse members from academia, government, and industry and many nationalities. Each submitted paper received two reviews, and those with sufficient scores were selected for publication. For presentations at WOIV that do not have an accepted full paper, the associated abstract is provided in these proceedings. We have separated abstracts from full papers in these proceedings for clarity.

2   Workshop Summary

2.1   Keynote

Andrew Bauer gave the keynote speech. He shared his thoughts on "In situ and time". Andrew is a Research Mechanical Engineer at the United States Army Corps of Engineers. He works primarily on developing algorithms and interfaces for software that numerically discretizes partial differential equations (PDE). His focus has been on the finite element method (FEM) for spatial discretizations of the PDE using adaptive techniques and parallel computing to ensure efficient use of available computing resources. Previously, Andrew was a Staff R&D Engineer at Kitware, where he has worked on the Visualization Toolkit (VTK) and ParaView open source projects focusing on ParaView Catalyst.

2.2   Abstracts

Loring et al., in their abstract "The SENSEI Generic In Situ Interface's Use of Ascent as an Endpoint", describe engineering enhancements to SENSEI, a generic in situ interface that makes it possible for a simulation code to be instrumented once, then connected to any number of different endpoints in an in situ or in transit processing configuration. The new enhancements enable SENSEI-instrumented data producers to take advantage of Ascent-based endpoints in either in situ or in transit processing configurations. They conclude by presenting examples that demonstrate this new capability.

Zavala-Ake et al., in their abstract "PAAKAT: an HPC in-situ analysis tool", present an HPC analysis tool that allows a straightforward, real-time handling of data from visualization algorithms as implemented in the Visualization Toolkit (VTK). They present results demonstrating flexibility and scalability of their modular design and conclude by presenting two use cases in detail.

Witzler et al., in their abstract "Including in-situ visualization and analysis in PDI", integrate in-situ possibilities into the general purpose code-coupling library PDI. They use the simulation code Alya as an example but the design provides possibilities to extend this to other simulation codes that are using PDI. ADIOS2 is used for the data transport and SENSEI is interposed between simulation code and ADIOS2 as well as in the in-transit endpoint between ADIOS2 and the visualization software.

2.3   Full Papers

Esposito and Holst, in their paper "In Situ Visualization of WRF Data using Universal Data Junction", present an in situ co-processing visualization pipeline based on the Universal Data Junction (UDJ) library and Inshimtu used for processing data from Weather Research and Forecasting (WRF) simulations. They show that, for the common case of analyzing just a number of fields during simulation, UDJ transfers and redistributes the data in approximately 6% of the time needed by WRF for a MPI-IO output of all variables upon which a previous method with Inshimtu is based. Further, the relative cost of transport and redistribution compared to IO remains approximately constant up to the highest considered node count without obvious impediments to scale further.

Pugmire et al. argue in their paper "Fides: A General Purpose Data Model Library for Streaming Data" that data models are required to provide the semantics of the underlying data stream for in situ visualization. They describe a set of metrics for such a data model that are useful in meeting the needs of the scientific community for visualization. They then present Fides, a library that provides a schema for the VTK-m data model, and uses the ADIOS middleware library for access to streaming data. To evaluate their model, they present four use cases of Fides in different scientific workflows, and provide an evaluation of each use case against the proposed metrics.

Ayachit el. in their paper "Catalyst Revised: Rethinking the ParaView In Situ Analysis and Visualization API" discussed the design and implementation of Catalyst, an API for in situ analysis using ParaView, which has been refactored with respect to ease of development, deployment, and maintenance. They argue that, as in situ analysis goes mainstream, these objectives become essential, perhaps more so than raw capabilities. In their paper, they present their implementation combining design ideas from in situ frameworks and HPC tools, like Ascent and MPICH.

3   Organizing Committee

Workshop Chairs

Thomas Theußl	KAUST, Saudi Arabia
Tom Vierjahn	Westphalian University of Applied Sciences, Germany

Workshop Co-organizers

Steffen Frey	University of Groningen, The Netherlands
Kenneth Moreland	Oak Ridge National Laboratory, USA
Guido Reina	University of Stuttgart, Germany

Programm Committee

Wes Bethel	Lawrence Berkeley National Laboratory, USA
Hank Childs	University of Oregon, USA
James Kress	University of Oregon, USA
Shaomeng Li	National Center for Atmospheric Research, USA
Kwan-Liu Ma	University of California, Davis, USA
Benson Muite	University of Tartu, Estonia

Ingrid Hotz   Linköping University, Sweden
Silvio Rizzi   Argonne National Laboratory, USA
Niklas Röber   DKRZ, Germany
Gunther Weber   Lawrence Berkeley National Laboratory, USA

In Situ Visualization of WRF Data Using Universal Data Junction

Aniello Esposito[1]([⊠])[iD] and Glendon Holst[2]

[1] Hewlett Packard Enterprise, Basel, Switzerland
aniello.esposito@hpe.com
[2] King Abdullah University of Science and Technology, Thuwal, Saudi Arabia
glendon.holst@kaust.edu.sa

Abstract. An in situ co-processing visualization pipeline based on the Universal Data Junction (UDJ) library and Inshimtu is presented and used for processing data from Weather Research and Forecasting (WRF) simulations. For the common case of analyzing just a number of fields during simulation, UDJ transfers and redistributes the data in approximately 6% of the time needed by WRF for a MPI-IO output of all variables upon which a previous method with Inshimtu is based. The relative cost of transport and redistribution compared to IO remains approximately constant up to the highest considered node count without obvious impediments to scale further.

Keywords: In situ · Co-processing · Universal data junction · Inshimtu

1 Introduction

The output data of scientific simulations are not end-goals in themselves. Rather, it is the scientific story which the data contains that is the real value proposition of interest for scientists. Extracting this "scientific story" from simulation data involves a variety of techniques from scientific visualizations to statistical analysis. Typically, these visualization/analytic processes are described as sequences of function applications (called the pipeline) applied to the source data. Because exploration is iterative and often either curiosity driven or research domain dependent, these pipelines need to be easy to create and modify. These pipelines also need to process the entire dataset (or large portions of it); but, in exchange, they produce significantly more compact representations of the phenomenon of interest (even movies and meshes can be orders of magnitude smaller than the original data).

Post-processing is the traditional approach to analyzing large simulation outputs. Typically, simulation data is written to a filesystem and then processed independently by dedicated tools. This straightforward approach only requires the user to manage a single program at a time, e.g., there is no need to consider resource contention issues. Furthermore, it safely composes multiple programs,

H. Jagode et al. (Eds.): ISC High Performance 2021 Workshops, LNCS 12761, pp. 475–483, 2021.
https://doi.org/10.1007/978-3-030-90539-2_32

because a crash in a visualization tool doesn't affect the simulation. It also alleviates the need to pre-plan the analysis and visualization phases prior to running the simulation. However, this approach also comes with an inherent inefficiency that heavily depends upon plentiful persistent storage and fast IO (because large files must be written out just to be read back into memory). This inefficiency is accentuated when pipeline processing is overlapped with simulation. And finally, since IO performance (generation-to-generation) does not improve at the same pace as compute performance, the inefficiencies of the post-processing approach will only get worse.

There are a variety of data processing strategies, such as In-situ and co-processing, to mitigate these issues [2,7]; each with their own trade-offs. The key to these approaches is that they bypass the round-trip write/read to slow filesystems, and either avoid data movement altogether, or transfer data directly using fast networks. This can enable analysis and visualization at significantly higher spatial and temporal resolutions. To do this, they induce a coupling between simulation and visualization. In-situ processing adds visualization and analytic capabilities to the simulation codes directly. This requires developer support to implement, but promises efficiencies by potentially using data in-place (provided the data is stored in a way the visualization codes support). ParaView Catalyst [1] is an example of this approach. This tight coupling can have downsides. If the visualization pipeline crashes, so does the simulation. The number of nodes, and the way that data is split between them, may also not be an ideal configuration for the visualization pipeline. Co-processing, by contrast, loosely-couples visualization pipelines to the simulation since the process space for visualization codes are separate from those of the simulation. Simulation codes must still be modified by the developer to make the data in memory available; but, instead of directly processing the data in a pipeline, it is transferred to the processes that will run the pipeline. This requires an efficient 'data bus' between simulation and visualization processes to communicate data requests and efficiently transfer data. Data transfer may also involve restructuring of the data (i.e., when copying a dataset split over M simulation nodes, to N visualization nodes). Examples of co-processing enabling libraries include ADIOS [3] and UDJ (Universal Data Junction).

The various components of the presented pipeline are explained in the following section together with the WRF use case for the experiments. Results are shown in a dedicated section followed by conclusions.

2 Materials and Methods

2.1 Universal Data Junction

The UDJ is a communication library implemented in C by the EMEA research lab at HPE for transporting distributed data between parallel high performance computing applications. UDJ provides the capability for an application to concisely describe a set of distributed data, and communicate that data to another

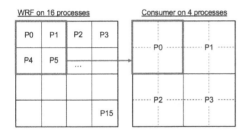

Fig. 1. Example of two-dimensional processor grid used by WRF and the mapping to a reduced grid employed by UDJ.

Table 1. Processor grid. UDJ uses a single node.

Nodes		8	16	32	64
WRF	px	16	32	32	64
	py	16	16	32	32
	Total	256	512	1024	2048
UDJ	px	8	8	8	8
	py	4	4	4	4
	Total	32	32	32	32

concurrently running application using one of a set of available transport substrates. UDJ allows the user to avoid the typical performance bottleneck of filesystem-based data transport for coupled applications, whilst also providing optimized and implicit data redistribution for coupling applications with differing parallel distribution schemes. In this work, UDJ transports data generated by WRF on Cartesian grids and distributed on a two-dimensional Cartesian processor grid to a smaller compatible processor grid which is then passed to the visualization pipeline. An illustration of a processor mapping in two dimensions is given in Fig. 1. The two-dimensional mapping is also used to transport three-dimensional data while one- and zero-dimensional data is packed in the metadata transported separately. Minimal intervention is needed in `module_dm.F` and `module_io.F` of WRF to enable transport over UDJ. These calls can be straight-forwardly summarized in an API which can be used in other applications. The embedding of UDJ in the pipeline is shown in Fig. 3(b).

2.2 Inshimtu

Inshimtu is a `C++` MPI application with built-in Python scripting capability that functions as a 'shim' between the simulation and the in-situ/co-processing visualization. It works with the existing simulation output file, does not require changes to simulation codes, can use the Cray DataWarp based burst-buffer to speed up data transfers, and uses the VTK toolkit (part of ParaView) and ParaView Catalyst [1] for visualizations. It works by watching the filesystem for new simulation output files, notifying the visualization ranks to read in their slice of data from these files, and then processing them with the specified visualization pipeline scripts. The much smaller visualization artifacts are then written to the permanent storage. The high-level architecture of Inshimtu is illustrated in Fig. 2. The first application [5] of Inshimtu was WRF [8], which utilized a workflow that was saving many large data files to a Lustre filesystem for storage. Inshimtu enabled higher spatio-temporal resolution of the simulation without significantly impacting storage requirements. This workflow is illustrated in Fig. 3(a). In the following, the application generating the data is referred to as the producer.

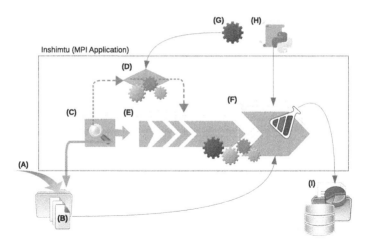

Fig. 2. High-level architecture and data flow for Inshimtu MPI application. An external simulation (e.g., WRF) writes (A) files (B) to temporary burst-buffer scratch. Inshimtu sentinels (C) notify controller (D) of file writes/closes across nodes. The controller (D) instigates pipeline(s) (E) which includes inporter (F). The inporter (F) reads files (B) and provides variables specified by their Catalyst-pipeline (H). The Catalyst-pipeline generates output visualization artifacts (I) onto persistent storage. The Inshimtu and Catalyst pipelines are specified by configurations (G) and Python scripts (H).

2.3   Inshimtu+UDJ

Even with burst-buffers, the reliance on filesystem-based data-transfer is a significant performance bottleneck for Inshimtu. What is needed, is a way to bypass the filesystem and communicate directly between the simulation and Inshimtu. UDJ provides this with minimal dependencies (UDJ, Protobuf, MPI). While UDJ provides high-performance data-transfer and redistribution, Protobuf encapsulates meta-information and MPI supports communication between producer and consumer nodes, where Inshimtu functions as a consumer. In the current prototype, the meta-data exchange between producers and consumers is ad-hoc (and not part of UDJ proper). Inshimtu re-implemented the meta-data exchange in C++ to better fit its architecture (a challenge to track changes made to the producer and to correctly match the expect MPI synchronization points). The critical mismatch between the data-pull request model of Catalyst/Inshimtu and the data-push model used in the prototype will be discussed later. Several changes were made to enable UDJ support in Inshimtu. CMake build specification were updated to add UDJ and C++ Protobuf. UDJ requires including a few headers and linking against the library. Protobuf is already used by VTK and ParaView, so Inshimtu utilizes the executable, and includes the headers from this version. UDJ requires calls to `udj_init` and `udj_finalize` for initialization and cleanup respectively. These were added to the application class constructor and destructor (similarly to MPI init and finalize). In the producer/consumer model of UDJ, when used with MPMD (Multiple Program Multiple Data), a side-channel

MPI communicators for participant ranks (essentially the 'producer' + 'inporter' ranks) has to be established. This requires coordination and synchronization with the producer ranks. This handshake code was rewritten in Inshimtu to preserve its architecture and code flow. Inshimtu needs to identify new communicator groups, and pass these along to those inporters needing to communicate via them. A dummy UDJ notifier as added to Inshimtu to signal the availability of the next UDJ data exchange and a UDJ inporter was added to Inshimtu, triggered by the UDJ notifier. The inporter processing begins with a meta-data exchange with the producer ranks. This meta-data includes a protobuf with the variable name and dimensions, followed by an exchange of per-producer rank extents. From these extents, the UDJ transfer distribution (mapping sub-extents of the data between producer and consumer) is established and the data synchronized. The transferred buffer is copied into a VTK image data-structure with the halos removed. This data is then passed to the Catalyst co-processor. Because of limitations of the data-push model, the Catalyst-pipeline can only process a single variable, and must process it every time step. As mentioned, Catalyst-pipelines are queried to determine which variables it needs. The inporter, a data importer that is backed by a Catalyst adaptor, must then provide the variables requested. This pull-based approach is important both for efficiency and flexibility. Only the consumer pipeline knows what it needs and when it needs it (for efficiency, Catalyst-pipelines can process some variables at a reduced rate). In the ad-hoc approach of the prototype, environment variables tell the producer which variables to push. So, the producer pushes out each variable, every simulation frame, and consumers must read the data, even if they don't need it (because failing to read the data would introduce synchronization issues). Additionally, this impedance mismatch between pull and push-data means that multi-variable visualization pipelines cannot be supported (because inporters don't know what data they'll receive until after the producer indicates via the meta-data). One possible solution, might be to embed UDJ, into another publish-subscribe capable framework, like ADIOS2 [4], that could enable consumers to request which data they want to transfer. The interplay of Inshimtu and UDJ is illustrated in Fig. 3(b).

2.4 Test Case

A simulation of the cyclonic storm Chapala is considered which moved over the Arabic Sea from October 23rd to November 3rd 2015 which was also used in Ref. [5]. Two domains are simulated with the WRF model version 4.0.3 [9] at the same time. One produces three-dimensional fields of resolution $(1599, 1599, 29)$ and the other $(3045, 2421, 29)$. The corresponding sizes of two-dimensional fields is given by the first two dimensions. In the following, the latter and the former are denoted as the large and the small domain, respectively. A two-dimensional processor grid is employed by WRF also for three-dimensional data. More details about the processor grids and time intervals are given in Sect. 2.5.

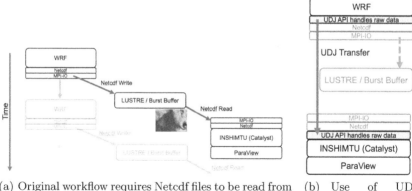

(a) Original workflow requires Netcdf files to be read from LUSTRE for post-processing. Relies on IO performance (shared). Is portable but still requires programming work on consumer side (Netcdf)

(b) Use of UDJ instead of LUS-TRE/Burst Buffers.

Fig. 3. Workflows for in situ visualization of WRF data based on LUSTRE/Burst Buffers and UDJ.

2.5   Simulation Environment and Setup

WRF is compiled with `intel/19.1.3.304` while UDJ is built with `gcc/8.3.0` to allow optimal compatibility with Inshimtu. The testbed consists of a Cray XC system featuring Intel Cascade Lake CPUs with 48 cores and 192 GB of memory per node which is accessed only by a single user for the experiments. The nodes are underpopulated with 32 MPI ranks per node. Data is written by WRF to LUSTRE file system using 4 OSTs. Separate experiments have been performed to measure the UDJ overhead.

3   Results and Discussion

The time spent in the WRF routine `ext_pnc_write_field` in `module_io.F` includes the generation of a NETCDF file in memory containing all variables and the MPI output to the filesystem. This time is compared to the UDJ transport of two two-dimensional and two three-dimensional fields using customized timers. The total sizes of these fields are 495 MB and 1.69 GB while the sizes of NETCDF files for the full dataset are 6.9 GB and 20 GB for the small and large domain, respectively. Every domain is written once per time step and time averages and standard deviations are computed over time steps. For the given test case, a strong scaling series with processor grids `[px,py]` for WRF and UDJ given in Table 1 is considered, where UDJ uses a single node. More details on the simulation setup and test case are given in Sects. 2.5 and 2.4. The absolute times for WRF output and UDJ transport are shown in Fig. 4(a) while the relative UDJ time is shown in Fig. 4(b). The standard deviation is very small because the machine was used only by a single user. The UDJ transport time is roughly

6% of the regular NETCDF output and does not increase for larger numbers of nodes. As a second criterion, the `Timing for Writing` reported by WRF is compared without and with UDJ transport enabled in addition to regular NETCDF writes and the absolute and relative overhead is shown in Figs. 5(a) and 5(b), respectively. The impact of UDJ transport on the regular write routine does not increase for larger number of nodes and is roughly 10% for 64 nodes. Finally, a visualization example of data captured from WRF over UDJ by Inshimtu+UDJ and rendered in ParaView is shown in Fig. 6.

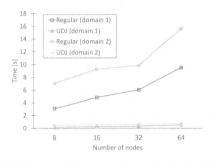
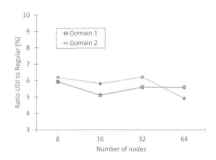

(a) Average time per step and standard deviation of regular WRF output and UDJ transport.

(b) Average and standard deviation of relative UDJ transport time.

Fig. 4. Comparison of regular WRF output and UDJ transport time for both domains and different number of nodes. Average and standard deviation are taken over time steps.

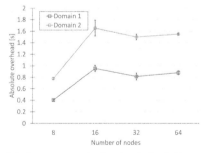
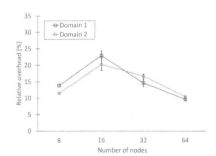

(a) Average and standard deviation of absolute UDJ overhead.

(b) Average and standard deviation of relative UDJ overhead.

Fig. 5. Comparison of total write time per step as reported by WRF for both domains and different number of nodes. Average and standard deviation are taken over time steps.

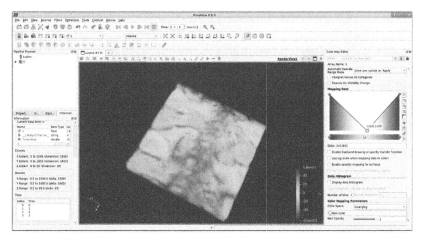

Fig. 6. Example visualization artifact captured from WRF by Inshimtu+UDJ and rendered in ParaView.

4   Related Work

Redistribution of data between applications as it is generated has been studied recently by Loring et al. [6] which provides more references to similar efforts and preceding work. The focus of Ref. [6] is on optimized extraction and partitioning of lower dimensional data such as iso-surfaces and slices for data transfer to a consumer running on a variable number of ranks which is similar to the present work. However, while the optimized extraction and partitioning causes a small overhead compared to simulation time in the case of a realistic application, the default processing for bulk data, which is closer to present work, adds more than 10% to simulation time. The focus of the current work is on the efficient transport and redistribution of raw bulk data with minimal intervention on the consumer side and UDJ achieves this goal with a scalable 6% of overhead compared to the default IO time and not the total simulation time. Classical approaches to real-time WRF data visualization, where one visualization process matches one simulation process in a tightly coupled WRF/Catalyst workflow either with copying the data in memory or referencing pointers, have been reported elsewhere with promising results on several hundred nodes. However, this has a minor overlap with the present work which preserves the flexibility of having consumer and producer running on different processor grids and moves all the post-processing burden away from the producer space.

5   Conclusion and Future Work

Using an in-network transport and redistribution method for an in situ co-working visualization pipeline turns out to be an important ingredient for an efficient scaling of the pipeline up to a considerable number of nodes. In particular, using Inshimtu+UDJ for the visualization of WRF data up to 64 nodes on a Cray XC system causes an approximately constant overhead. The current implementation is tailored to WRF but the minor interventions by UDJ can be summarized as an API similar to state-of-the-art interfaces and straightforwardly applied to other applications. The choice of a single node for the consumer seemed appropriate for the current test case but there is interest to follow up in a future work with much larger simulations requiring multiple consumer nodes to further test the scalability of the method and using an dedicated API to experiment with other applications.

Acknowledgment. This work is part of the HPE/Cray center of excellence collaboration at KAUST. UDJ development has received funding from the European Union's Horizon 2020 research and innovation programme under grant agreement No 773897. We want to thank Hari Dasari colleagues for helping with the test case as well as Tim Dykes and Utz Uwe Haus from the HPE EMEA research lab for support with UDJ.

References

1. Ayachit, U., et al.: Paraview catalyst: enabling in situ data analysis and visualization. In: ISAV2015: Proceedings of the First Workshop on In Situ Infrastructures for Enabling Extreme-Scale Analysis and Visualization, vol. 1, no. (1), pp. 25–29, November 2015. https://doi.org/10.1145/2828612.2828624. https://dl.acm.org/doi/10.1145/2828612.2828624
2. Bauer, A.C., et al.: In situ methods, infrastructures, and applications on high performance computing platforms. Comput. Graph. Forum **35**(3), 577–597 (2016)
3. Boyuka, D.A., et al.: Transparent in situ data transformations in adios. In: Proceedings of the 14th IEEE/ACM International Symposium on Cluster, Cloud, and Grid Computing, CCGRID 2014, pp. 256–266. IEEE Press (2014). https://doi.org/10.1109/CCGrid.2014.73
4. Godoy, W.F., et al.: ADIOS 2: the adaptable input output system. A framework for high-performance data management. SoftwareX **12**, 100561 (2020). https://doi.org/10.1016/j.softx.2020.100561. https://www.sciencedirect.com/science/article/pii/S2352711019302560
5. Holst, G., Dasari, H.P., Markomanolis, G., Hoteit, I., Theussl, T.: Inshimtu - a lightweight in-situ visualization "shim" (2017). https://woiv.gitlab.io/woiv17/ISC_WOIV_Holst.pdf
6. Loring, B., et al.: Improving performance of m-to-n processing and data redistribution in in transit analysis and visualization. Technical report, Lawrence Berkeley National Lab. (LBNL), Berkeley, CA (United States) (2020)
7. Moreland, K.: The tensions of in situ visualization. IEEE Comput. Graphics Appl. **36**(2), 5–9 (2016). https://doi.org/10.1109/MCG.2016.35
8. Skamarock, W.C., et al.: A description of the advanced research WRF version 3. National Center for Atmospheric Research: Boulder, CO, USA, June 2008. https://doi.org/10.5065/D68S4MVH
9. Skamarock, W.C., et al.: A description of the advanced research WRF model version 4. National Center for Atmospheric Research: Boulder, CO, USA, p. 145 (2019). https://doi.org/10.5065/1dfh-6p97

Catalyst Revised: Rethinking the ParaView in Situ Analysis and Visualization API

Utkarsh Ayachit[1]([✉]), Andrew C. Bauer[3], Ben Boeckel[1], Berk Geveci[1],
Kenneth Moreland[2], Patrick O'Leary[1], and Tom Osika[1]

[1] Kitware, Inc., Clifton Park, NY, USA
utkarsh.ayachit@kitware.com
[2] Oak Ridge National Lab, Oak Ridge, TN, USA
[3] U.S. Army Engineer Research and Development Center, Vicksburg, MS, USA

Abstract. As in situ analysis goes mainstream, ease of development, deployment, and maintenance becomes essential, perhaps more so than raw capabilities. In this paper, we present the design and implementation of *Catalyst*, an API for in situ analysis using ParaView, which we refactored with these objectives in mind. Our implementation combines design ideas from in situ frameworks and HPC tools, like Ascent and MPICH.

Keywords: In situ analysis and visualization · High-performance computing · Software engineering

1 Introduction

Since the first release of ParaView Catalyst [4,6], the in situ data analysis landscape has evolved considerably. A wide array of libraries and frameworks are now available, each targeting different use-cases or environments [1,5,11,18]. Leveraging these in situ frameworks for data analysis typically involves modifying the simulation code to pass and convert the simulation data structures to something that the in situ data analysis frameworks can interpret and then request processing. This development step is called instrumentation. With Para-View Catalyst, this instrumentation process has involved developing an adaptor that converts simulation data structures to VTK data objects. The VTK data model defines various ways of representing computation meshes and variables. The VTK data objects are then passed to the ParaView Catalyst engine for processing using the provided API. Except for a few Python-based simulations, i.e., simulations that use Python as the primary programming language or those that use Python to pass data (and control) to ParaView Catalyst, this adaptor is invariably a C++ codebase that requires a ParaView software-development-kit (SDK) to build. The simulation build and deployment workflow thus involves building the adaptor with a ParaView SDK and linking that with the simulation.

H. Jagode et al. (Eds.): ISC High Performance 2021 Workshops, LNCS 12761, pp. 484–494, 2021.
https://doi.org/10.1007/978-3-030-90539-2_33

This workflow, which seemed fairly reasonable in the early years, exposed significant maintenance challenges as the simulation codes and ParaView progressed through multiple versions.

Challenges Developing the Adaptor: Writing a new adaptor requires an intimate understanding of the VTK data model. The choice of the type of data object often has implications on both memory overhead and performance. Furthermore, VTK data APIs often support multiple ways of initialization. We expect developers to be aware of which APIs result in deep-copies and which ones do not. It is not uncommon for developers to pick an incorrect variant without realizing that it results in deep copies. The VTK data model itself keeps evolving. Since the first release of ParaView Catalyst, there have been changes to array layouts (array-of-structures and structure-of-arrays) [17], ghost-cell definitions [14], unstructured grid cell connectivity layout, and even addition of new data types for better representing composite datasets and AMR datasets. Several of these changes were motivated by the need to support various standard simulation memory layouts to avoid deep copies. Leveraging these changes, however, requires updating the adaptors to use the new APIs. This update adds another burden on the adaptor developers – to stay up-to-date with such data model changes and then update the adaptor to leverage them.

Challenges with Build and Deployment: For Fortran, C, and C++ simulators, the standard adaptor is written in C++ and uses ParaView and VTK C++ APIs. This process requires the adaptor is built using a ParaView software-development-kit (SDK). The SDK provides all the necessary ParaView headers and libraries needed to compile the adaptor. These are not available in standard ParaView package. Thus, developers have to build ParaView and all its dependencies from source and cannot use readily available binary distributions. The large set of dependencies and the diversity of supported compilers and platforms make providing a redistributable universal SDK challenging. Building ParaView and all its dependencies from source can be quite challenging, too.

There are several ways to build ParaView and its dependencies, including superbuild [16] and Spack [8]; however, with each release, there are inevitable new issues since the platforms, the dependencies, and the ParaView codebase are continually changing. Furthermore, the adaptor's build-system often needs to be updated to reflect changes to ParaView's build system. Over the years, ParaView library names have changed as have the ways of linking against them. These changes require that in addition to keeping abreast with the API changes, adaptor maintainers need to update the build system with each ParaView release. Since the adaptor links with the simulation executable, the simulation has a transitive dependency on the ParaView build. Thus, for every new release of ParaView, the maintainer needs to update and build the adaptor and rebuild the simulation. Each simulation build is tightly coupled with a specific ParaView build. Short of having multiple builds, it is not easy to switch between different adaptor or ParaView versions. Consequently, if there is a regression in a newer version of ParaView, the users cannot quickly test with an older version without having a separate complete build for the simulation.

These challenges apply to all of the in situ frameworks mentioned earlier to varying degrees, primarily based on the complexity, capability, and flexibility of the codebase and its dependencies.

In this paper, we propose an approach to the in situ API design that alleviates these maintenance difficulties for production in situ analysis and visualization. Our proposal defines a stable API that we call the Catalyst API and the mechanisms to provide ABI-compatible API implementation. ParaView-Catalyst is simply implementation of the Catalyst API that uses ParaView for data processing and visualization and is ABI-compatible with any other Catalyst API implementations. ABI-compatibility implies that a simulation built using any Catalyst API implementation can swap the implementation at runtime without rebuilding the simulation code.

2   Design

Our design takes a multi-pronged approach to address the challenges we encountered as we started using ParaView for in situ data analysis and visualization in production workflows. We liberally leverage design ideas and implementation from other in situ frameworks and HPC tools during the design process whenever possible.

2.1   Simplifying the Adaptor

One of the challenges with the original Catalyst adaptor design is that it requires the developer to have a reasonable understanding of the VTK data model. Our original thinking was that it would be VTK and ParaView developers who would be the ones developing such adaptors – which, it turns out, does not reflect the reality. More often than not, it is the members of the simulation development community taking on the adaptor's development. This development requires a deep understanding of the VTK data model to make critical design choices when mapping simulation data structures to the VTK data model. The requirement is unreasonable and burdensome, impeding adoption and potentially resulting in implementations that leave room for memory and performance improvements.

Strawman [10], which later evolved into Ascent [12], presents an unique solution to this challenge. Instead of making the adaptor developers do the mapping to the target data model, it provides an API for describing and passing arrays of data. This API is called Conduit [10], which allows simulation developers to describe the simulation data, such as computational meshes and fields. By standardizing one (or several) schemas that support a diverse collection of computational meshes and field arrays encountered, we can provide standard implementations for converting a Conduit mesh description to an appropriate VTK data object. These converter implementations can be part of the ParaView distribution and hence evolve as the ParaView/VTK APIs evolve to represent the data optimally without requiring any effort on the part of simulation developers. Thus, the adaptor no longer requires converting simulation data structures to VTK data structures, but rather simply describes what they are using Conduit.

2.2 Simplifying Build and Deployment

Our design takes inspiration from the MPICH ABI compatibility initiative [15] to simplify the build and deployment process. The initiative aims to enable developers to build their code using any compatible MPI implementation and swap with another compatible implementation at runtime. This makes it easier to distribute executables (or libraries) without binding to a specific MPI implementation. We extend this concept for in situ APIs. We explicitly define functions that form the in situ API, which includes the API to describe simulation data structures (Sect. 2.1) and a few other function calls to initialize, update and finalize the in situ analysis. This API specification is what we now refer to as *Catalyst*. By enabling implementations of this API that are runtime compatible with one another, simulations can be compiled with one implementation and executed with a different implementation. This decoupling has several advantages.

First, developers no longer need a ParaView SDK to compile instrumented simulation codes. They can use any Catalyst API implementation, including the *stub* implementation that we provide. This stub implementation is lightweight, minimal-capability, easy-to-build, and has insignificant overhead at runtime. Developers can use this implementation during the compilation stage to compile the adaptor. At execution time, they can easily swap the Catalyst implementation using environment modules or other platform-specific loader configuration mechanisms. The ParaView distribution includes an implementation of the Catalyst API that we now refer to as *ParaView-Catalyst*. Thus, ParaView-Catalyst is simply one specific implementation of the Catalyst API that uses ParaView for data processing.

Second, switching between multiple versions of Catalyst API implementations does not require any recompilation. The Catalyst API version and the ParaView versions are independent. Thus, several versions of ParaView can provide Catalyst implementations that are runtime compatible with each other.

Third, if, in the future, non-backward compatible API changes are introduced to the Catalyst API causing its version number to change, implementations can continue to support earlier versions. Thus, ParaView distributions can continue to provide multiple versions of the ParaView-Catalyst library, each compatible with a particular version of the Catalyst API.

3 Implementation

The Catalyst API, together with the *stub* implementation, is now a separate project [7]. The project intentionally does not have any external dependencies. This separation keeps the project simple to build and easy to deploy on any platform with a C++ compiler and standard build tools. Simulation developers can use this *stub* implementation of the API when instrumenting simulations and do not need a full ParaView SDK.

```
# Catalyst install directory contents
..[install prefix]/
|-- include/
|    |-- catalyst-2.0/
|         |-- catalyst.h
|         |-- (other headers)
|    |-- lib/
|         |-- libcatalyst.so -> libcatalyst.so.2
|         |-- libcatalyst.so.2
|         |-- ...
```

Fig. 1. Contents of a Catalyst install

Figure 1 shows the directory structure and relevant files in a Catalyst install on a Linux-based system. The Catalyst API's current version number is 2.0 to help distinguish it from the earlier implementation of ParaView Catalyst. catalyst.h is the header with all function declarations that are part of the public API. It internally includes other headers installed under the include/ directory. The libcatalyst.so, which is a symbolic link to libcatalyst.so.2, is the single shared library for the *stub* implementation. The library name includes the Catalyst API version number. Whenever the API changes in a non-ABI compatible fashion, the number will be incremented. libcatalyst.so does not have any runtime dependencies except C and C++ language runtimes.

The Catalyst API comprises C functions and data-structures alone. We do not expose any C++ interface as part of this public API to avoid ABI compatibility issues when using different C++ compilers for compiling the simulation and the Catalyst implementation. Using C also makes interfacing with other languages such as Python and FORTRAN trivial. The API comprises four catalyst_.. functions that act as entry points to the Catalyst framework (Fig. 2) and several conduit_.... functions that are part of the Conduit C API used to communicate data and other parameters.

```
1  /** initialize catalyst */
2  void catalyst_initialize(const conduit_node* params);
3
4  /** execute catalyst per cycle */
5  void catalyst_execute(const conduit_node* params);
6
7  /** finalize catalyst **/
8  void catalyst_finalize(const conduit_node* params);
9
10 /** query information about catalyst implementation and capabilities **/
11 void catalyst_about(conduit_node* params);
```

Fig. 2. Catalyst API

The `conduit_node` object provides a JSON-inspired hierarchical description of parameters and in-core data, which communicates both the control parameters to configure the Catalyst implementation and the simulation meshes. A Catalyst implementation is free to define an arbitrary schema for exchanging data and control parameters with the simulation through this API. Simulations targeting a particular implementation use the appropriate schema when generating the hierarchical description. ParaView-Catalyst, which is now a ParaView-based implementation of the Catalyst API, supports the schema described in Fig. 3. The schema borrows heavily from the schema supported by Ascent [12] with simple extensions to support ParaView-Catalyst concepts such as channels and scripts.

```
1
2  { /* schema for 'catalyst_initialize' */
3    "catalyst": {
4      // all catalyst params/data are under this root
5      "scripts": {
6        // collection of Python scripts for analysis pipelines
7        "name0": "path/scriptname.py",
8        ...
9      }
10   }
11 }
12
13 { /* schema for 'catalyst_execute' */
14   "catalyst": {
15     "state": {
16       "cycle": [integer] /* cycle/timestep number */,
17       "time" : [number]  /* time */
18     },
19     "channels": {
20       // named data channels.
21       "channel-name0" : {
22         "type": [string] /* type of the channel data */
23         "data": {} /* data description node based on chosen 'type' */
24       }
25     }
26   }
27 }
```

Fig. 3. Schema supported by ParaView-Catalyst

The *channels* can be used to pass multiple meshes for in situ analysis. The "type" attribute selects the mesh schema. Currently, ParaView-Catalyst supports the Conduit Mesh Blueprint [13], which covers a wide range of computation meshes and memory layouts. The "type" attribute lets us support additional mesh description schema in future releases.

Instrumenting a simulation involves populating the `conduit_node` object with appropriate values based on the schema and invoking the `catalyst_...` functions at appropriate times. There is no explicit mapping of simulation data structures to VTK data objects anymore. Instead, developers simply provide the data description. Converting that to VTK data objects is handled by the ParaView-Catalyst library itself. The following snippet highlights modifications necessary to a typical simulation to use Catalyst.

```
1  // this header is needed for all the conduit_ and catalyst_ functions
2  #include <catalyst.h>
3
4  // ** initialize catalyst **
5  conduit_node* catalyst_init_params = conduit_node_create();
6  // pass initialization parameters e.g. scripts to load.
7  conduit_node_set_path_char8_str(catalyst_init_params,
8    "catalyst/scripts/script0", ".../script0.py");
9  ...
10 catalyst_initialize(catalyst_init_params);
11 conduit_node_destroy(catalyst_init_params);
12
13 ...
14 for (cycle=0; ..., ++cycle) // simulation loop
15 {
16   // ..... advance simulation ...
17
18   // ** execute catalyst per timestep/cycle**
19   conduit_node* catalyst_exec_params = conduit_node_create();
20   // 'state' is used to pass time/cycle information.
21   conduit_node_set_path_int64(catalyst_exec_params, "catalyst/state/cycle"
        , cycle);
22   conduit_node_set_path_float64(catalyst_exec_params, "catalyst/state/time
        ", time);
23
24   // the data must be provided on a named channel. the name is determined
        by the
25   // simulation. for this one, we're calling it "grid".
26
27   // declare the type of the channel; we're using Conduit Mesh Blueprint
28   // to describe the mesh and fields, chosen using the type "mesh"; in
        future
29   // other types can be supported.
30   conduit_node_set_path_char8_str(catalyst_exec_params,
31     "catalyst/channels/grid/type", "mesh");
32
33   // now, create the mesh;
34   conduit_node* mesh = conduit_node_create();
35
36   // The 'mesh' node is populated as per Conduit Mesh Blueprint applicable
37   // for the specific simulation. For example. a uniform grid is defined
        as follows
38   conduit_node_set_path_char8_str(mesh, "coordsets/coords/type", "uniform"
        );
39   conduit_node_set_path_int64(mesh, "coordsets/coords/dims/i", i_dim);
40   conduit_node_set_path_int64(mesh, "coordsets/coords/dims/j", j_dim);
41   conduit_node_set_path_int64(mesh, "coordsets/coords/dims/k", k_dim);
42   // .. and so on. Refer to Conduit Mesh Blueprint for details.
43
44   ...
45   // the mesh is passed on the named channel as "../data"
46   conduit_node_set_path_external_node(catalyst_exec_params,
47     "catalyst/channels/grid/data", mesh);
48   catalyst_execute(catalyst_exec_params);
49   conduit_node_destroy(catalyst_exec_params);
50   conduit_node_destroy(mesh);
51 }
52 ...
53
54 // ** finalize catalyst**
55 conduit_node* catalyst_fini_params = conduit_node_create();
56 catalyst_finalize(catalyst_fini_params);
57 conduit_node_destroy(catalyst_fini_params);
```

The instrumented simulation can be compiled with any implementation of the Catalyst API. The *stub* implementation is preferred since it is easy to build and has no dependencies. To compile this adaptor, one only needs to add the path to the `catalyst.h` header to the include path and link with the single catalyst shared library. With gcc, for example, this can be done as follows:

```
$ gcc -I<catalyst-install-prefix>/include/catalyst-2.0
      -L<catalyst-install-prefix>/lib
      -lcatalyst
      [source files] -o [output]
```

At execution time, the operating system loader will look to load the library `libcatalyst.so.2`. Since all Catalyst implementations for a specific version are compatible with one another, the end-user can make the loader load a different Catalyst implementation than the one compiled using standard mechanisms. On Linux systems, one can set the `LD_LIBRARY_PATH` environment variable to point to the `libcatalyst.so.2` in a ParaView binary distribution to use that ParaView-Catalyst implementation. Switching to another version solely requires changing the environment and re-executing, no need to recompile or require a ParaView SDK. On most HPC systems, this can be easily handled by environment modules.

4   Evaluation

To evaluate the design, we instrumented LULESH [9] – a mini-application (mini-app) that represents a typical hydrodynamics code, like ALE3D – to use the Catalyst API. Incidentally, LULESH was previously instrumented with the legacy ParaView/Catalyst framework [2], which allowed us to compare and contrast the two implementations.

Build System: LULESH uses a simple Makefile to build the code. The first thing that the legacy adaptor implementation did was convert the build-system to use CMake instead because adding a build dependency to the legacy ParaView/Catalyst implementation was much easier in a CMake-based system; the library dependency chain can be quite long and cumbersome to resolve outside of CMake. The new implementation [3] did not require us to perform similar work. We simply extended the Makefile to define two new variables, **CATALYST_CXXFLAGS** and **CATALYST_LDFLAGS**, and subsequently add them to the compile and link lines, respectively.

```
# for Catalyst
CATALYST_ROOT=...
CATALYST_CXXFLAGS = -DVIZ_CATALYST=1 -I$(CATALYST_ROOT)/include/catalyst
    -2.0/
CATALYST_LDFLAGS = -L$(CATALYST_ROOT)/lib -lcatalyst

.cc.o: lulesh.h
    @echo "Building $<"
    $(CXX) -c $(CXXFLAGS) $(CATALYST_CXXFLAGS) -o $@   $<

lulesh2.0: $(OBJECTS2.0)
    @echo "Linking"
    $(CXX) $(OBJECTS2.0) $(LDFLAGS) $(CATALYST_LDFLAGS) -lm -o $@
```

Adaptor Complexity: The legacy adaptor included approximately 13 header files. While this by itself is not necessarily a detriment, it is a good indication of the number of different classes the adaptor used and the different building blocks that the developer had to be aware of when developing the adaptor. In contrast, the new adaptor code only includes one header, `catalyst.h`. The bulk of the new adaptor code is simply populating the `conduit_node` object according to the schema described in Sect. 3. When deciding on the VTK dataset type to use, the legacy adaptor implementation for LULESH used a `vtkUnstructuredGrid`. While that is acceptable, in retrospect, that is not the best choice in this case since it requires that the cell connectivity is explicitly specified when the grid is actually topologically regular. Not only does that result in memory overhead, but it also impacts the performance of in situ analysis pipelines. This poor design choice underscores one of the primary motivations for this effort to revise the API. Without in-depth knowledge of the VTK data model, it was not easy to make the best choice of which VTK dataset type to use, and the choice often has a significant impact on the performance of the processing pipelines. The new Catalyst API does not suffer from the same issue since the VTK dataset choice is deferred to the Catalyst implementation, specifically, ParaView-Catalyst.

Code Changes: Comparing the code changes between the two implementations of the Catalyst Adaptor using git, we get the following:

```
 1  # legacy version
 2  git diff --stat master..catalyst_adaptor
 3    CMakeLists.txt        |  38
 4    lulesh-catalyst.cc  | 209
 5    lulesh-catalyst.h    |  17
 6    lulesh-util.cc        |  13
 7    lulesh.cc              |  18
 8    lulesh.h              |  33
 9    6 files changed, 325 insertions(+), 3 deletions(-)
10
11  # new version
12  git diff --compact-summary master..catalyst-2.0
13    Makefile              |  13
14    lulesh-catalyst.cc (new) | 52
15    lulesh-init.cc        |  56
16    lulesh-util.cc        |  10
17    lulesh.cc              |   5
18    lulesh.h              |  22
19    6 files changed, 155 insertions(+), 3 deletions(-)
```

As expected, the new code is more compact with only 155 lines of implementation compared to 325 lines of implementation with the legacy API. This reduction is mainly due to not including any code to create VTK datasets.

4.1 Debugging and Regression Testing

To make it easier to develop and debug, the Catalyst stub implementation supports generating binary data dumps for the conduit nodes passed to each `catalyst_` call. For each API call, it can write the `conduit_node` argument out to disk. Using another executable, `catalyst_replay`, these dumps can be read back in and each API call invoked again in the same order. This avoids the need for rerunning the simulation for debugging. To generate the data dumps, one uses the stub implementation with an environment variable `CATALYST_DATA_DUMP_DIRECTORY` set to point a directory where the node data for each API invocation should be saved. `catalyst_replay` can then be used to read these data dumps while using any Catalyst implementation.

Besides assisting in development and debugging, this also helps avoid regressions. Data dumps can be generated for validation and verification setups for codes of interest and then used by Catalyst implementations for regression testing to ensure newer versions continue to work for supported codes.

5   Conclusion and Future Work

As in situ analysis and visualization become widely adopted in production, ease of development, deployment, and maintenance become just as important as the framework capabilities.

The Catalyst API enables the development of implementations that use different libraries underneath for the actual in situ data processing instead of ParaView. It is conceivable that frameworks like SENSEI [1] and Ascent themselves can be provided as implementations of the Catalyst API. Thus, a simulation, once instrumented, can switch between any framework at runtime by merely switching runtime modules.

Our current design relies on shared libraries for runtime swapping of implementations. There may be cases where a fully static build is required. Our ongoing work is to ensure that such cases can be supported, albeit with limited runtime flexibility.

Our implementation currently only supports C/C++ codes. Fortran compatibility and Python simulation support is pending development.

Acknowledgments. This work was supported by the following funding sources.

This material is based in part upon work supported by the US Army's Engineer Research And Development Center.

This work was partially supported by the Exascale Computing Project (17-SC-20-SC), a collaborative effort of the U.S. Department of Energy Office of Science and the National Nuclear Security Administration.

This material is based in part upon work supported by the US Department of Energy, Office of Science, Office of Advanced Scientific Computing Research under contract DE-AC05-00OR22725.

This material is based upon work supported by the U.S. Department of Energy, Office of Science, ASCR program under Award Number DE-SC-0021343.

References

1. Ayachit, U., et al.: The sensei generic in situ interface. In: 2016 Second Workshop on In Situ Infrastructures for Enabling Extreme-Scale Analysis and Visualization (ISAV), pp. 40–44 (2016)

2. Ayachit, U.: ParaView catalyst enabled LULESH, February 2018. https://doi.org/10.5281/zenodo.4013875
3. Ayachit, U.: Catalyst2.0-enabled LULESH, July 2021. https://doi.org/10.5281/zenodo.5143793
4. Ayachit, U., et al.: ParaView catalyst: enabling in situ data analysis and visualization. In: Proceedings of the First Workshop on In Situ Infrastructures for Enabling Extreme-Scale Analysis and Visualization, ISAV2015, pp. 25–29. Association for Computing Machinery, New York (2015). https://doi.org/10.1145/2828612.2828624
5. Bauer, A.C., et al.: In situ methods, infrastructures, and applications on high performance computing platforms, a State-of-the-art (STAR) report. Computer Graphics Forum (Special Issue: Proceedings of EuroVis 2016), vol. 35, no. 3, June 2016. lBNL-1005709
6. Bauer, A.C., Geveci, B., Schroeder, W.: The ParaView Catalyst Users Guide. Kitware, Clifton Park (2013)
7. Catalyst Developers: Catalyst (2020). https://gitlab.kitware.com/paraview/catalyst/
8. Gamblin, T., et al.: The Spack Package Manager: Bringing order to HPC software chaos. In: Supercomputing 2015 (SC 2015), Austin, Texas, 15–20 November 2015. http://tgamblin.github.io/pubs/spack-sc15.pdf
9. Karlin, I., Keasler, J., Neely, R.: LULESH 2.0 updates and changes. Tech. Rep. LLNL-TR-641973, August 2013
10. Larsen, M., Harrison, C., Brugger, E., Griffin, K., Elliot, J.: Strawman: a batch in situ visualization and analysis infrastructure for multi-physics simulation codes (2016). https://doi.org/10.1145/2828612.2828625
11. Larsen, M., et al.: The alpine in situ infrastructure: ascending from the ashes of strawman. In: Proceedings of the In Situ Infrastructures on Enabling Extreme-Scale Analysis and Visualization, ISAV 2017, pp. 42–46. Association for Computing Machinery, New York (2017). https://doi.org/10.1145/3144769.3144778
12. Larsen, M., et al.: The ALPINE in situ infrastructure: ascending from the ashes of strawman, pp. 42–46 (2017). https://doi.org/10.1145/3144769.3144778
13. Lawrence Livermore National Laboratory: Conduit: Simplified Data Exchange for HPC Simulations - Conduit Blueprint (2019). https://llnl-conduit.readthedocs.io/en/v0.5.1/blueprint_mesh.html
14. Lipsa, D., Geveci, B.: Ghost and blanking (visibility) changes (2015). https://blog.kitware.com/ghost-and-blanking-visibility-changes/
15. MPICH Developers: MPICH ABI Compatibility Initiative (2014). https://wiki.mpich.org/mpich/index.php/ABI_Compatibility_Initiative
16. ParaView Developers: ParaView-Superbuild (2020). https://gitlab.kitware.com/paraview/paraview-superbuild/
17. Vacanti, A., Rose, L.: New Data Array Layouts in VTK 7.1 (2016). https://blog.kitware.com/new-data-array-layouts-in-vtk-7-1
18. Whitlock, B., Favre, J.M., Meredith, J.S.: Parallel in situ coupling of simulation with a fully featured visualization system. In: Proceedings of the 11th Eurographics Conference on Parallel Graphics and Visualization, EGPGV 2011, Goslar, DEU, pp. 101–109. Eurographics Association (2011)

Fides: A General Purpose Data Model Library for Streaming Data

David Pugmire[1(✉)] , Caitlin Ross[2] , Nicholas Thompson[1] ,
James Kress[1] , Chuck Atkins[2], Scott Klasky[1] , and Berk Geveci[2]

[1] Oak Ridge National Laboratory, Oak Ridge, TN, USA
{pugmire,4nt,kressjm,klasky}@ornl.gov
[2] Kitware, Albany, NY, USA
{caitlin.ross,chuck.atkins,berk.geveci}@kitware.com

Abstract. Data models are required to provide the semantics of the underlying data stream for in situ visualization. In this paper we describe a set of metrics for such a data model that are useful in meeting the needs of the scientific community for visualization. We then present Fides, a library that provides a schema for the VTK-m data model, and uses the ADIOS middleware library for access to streaming data. We present four use cases of Fides in different scientific workflows, and provide an evaluation of each use case against our metrics.

1 Introduction

Extracting understanding from large scientific data sets has always been challenging. In the past the process was nonetheless tractable because data was written to files in well defined formats. This file-centric process empowered collaboration and flexibility for analysis and visualization.

When simulations generate data faster than it can be written to disk, more complicated in situ analysis and visualization is required. Standardization is much more difficult as data may come from a number of different sources including from the memory of a GPU, over a socket in a node, over the network from another node, or from a remote experimental resource. In addition, scientists are moving towards the use of workflows to manage the complexity of data movement. These workflows are not always static as the processes used, and their connections can change between runs, or even dynamically during a run. Forthcoming supercomputing ecosystems, where experimental facilities, supercomputing centers, and edge computing are being linked with high speed networks and must function together in harmony, will significantly increase the complexity of in situ processing.

Addressing the complexity of in situ visualization is an active area of research [5]. In a recent publication [21], a service-based framework for visualization and analysis is presented and includes a set of abstractions to support such a framework [21]. One of the fundamental abstraction is a schema layer

© Springer Nature Switzerland AG 2021
H. Jagode et al. (Eds.): ISC High Performance 2021 Workshops, LNCS 12761, pp. 495–507, 2021.
https://doi.org/10.1007/978-3-030-90539-2_34

which provides a mechanism for producers and consumers to agree on the interpretation of the data. Schemas (data models which provide the semantics of the underlying data) are a standard way of communicating interpretation. Data models specify the mesh type (e.g., uniform, rectilinear, or explicit grids), the fields that exist on the mesh (such as pressure and/or density) and their associations (e.g., node, cell, edge), and other labels associated with the data, such as units. This allows the data consumer to understand and properly process the bulk data.

The effectiveness of a schema or data model can be enhanced if it provides the following desirable properties:

– **Rich data model.** A schema must be able to represent a large number of common layouts for scientific data. It must support simulation, experimental, and observational data. The schema also needs to provide a representation that is compatible with visualization and analysis tools. VTK provides a very expressive language for describing mesh types and data layouts. However, simulations often require bespoke data representations to be efficient, and the schema must be flexible enough to support these codes.
– **Usability.** Ease of use spans a wide range of topics, and includes ease of integration and deployment, development costs and the reliance on dependencies.
– **Support for data transformations.** A schema library should serve as a bridge between the data model and the underlying representation used by the visualization service. Zero-copy transformations are preferred, but in some cases, other transformations are required (e.g., resampling data onto a uniform grid).
– **Minimal performance impact.** Use of a schema should have a minimal impact on performance. This includes the time it takes to learn to use the library, as well as the memory efficiency. The schema should be able to describe the data as it is in memory, e.g., zero copy.
– **Interoperability.** A schema should make it possible for codes to be composed within a scientific workflow. This allows for different types of analysis and visualization to be connected together as needed to provide custom solutions. This also allows for different modes of interaction. A schema should allow for a range of uses cases, from files to in situ. The ability to use the same set of analysis and visualization tools for both post hoc and in situ use cases is very useful.
– **N × M processing.** It is common for the producer and consumer of data to run on different numbers of resources. As an example, a simulation will run on N nodes, and an analysis code will run M nodes. N and M may vary dynamically. The schema should provide a way to support these complex data layouts.

In this paper we describe a new library, Fides, which is targeted to address these requirements. In Sect. 3 we describe the design and implementation, as well as the underlying technologies used by Fides. In Sect. 4 we present examples of Fides being used for visualization and analysis tasks using different types of data access. We also discuss the performance of Fides with respect to the metrics described above. Finally, in Sect. 5 we present a summary and provide some thoughts on future directions.

2   Previous Work

Several projects have created schemas specifically targeting HPC simulation codes. Each of these efforts has worked to both provide a schema for identifying simulation output, as well as methods for efficiently storing and moving the actual output of the simulation itself. One example is the Open Standard for Particle-Mesh Data Files (openPMD) [10] which is a schema for describing mesh- and particle-based data. A second example is the eXtensible Data Model and Format (XDMF) [7] which is a schema for the standardized exchange of scientific data between HPC codes and analysis tools. It stores schema data in XML files and simulation output in the HDF5 file format. Finally there is the ADIOS Visualization Schema [23] which is an XML based markup schema for data written in ADIOS [9]. ADIOS is a middleware library that provides a publish/subscribe view of data access using several different data transport mechanisms, including files and several types of in situ processing. Conduit [15] is a library that provides a data model for scientific data using Blueprint [14] and is used for I/O, serialization and code coupling.

In situ visualization is a rich space that provides a number of tools that implement a variety of methodologies [5]. Tools such as VisIt Libsim [26], ParaView Catalyst [3], Ascent [13] and SENSEI [4] provide an API that can be embedded into a simulation code to perform in situ visualization. Both SENSEI and Ascent make use of the ADIOS middleware library to provide publish/subscribe capabilities. In contrast to these in situ visualization tools, as long as an application is using ADIOS, no other code changes are needed to use Fides.

Several data models for visualization exist, but the most commonly used is VTK [22]. Both ParaView and VisIt, the two most commonly used production tools, are based on VTK. Recently, DAX [18] and EAVL [17] were created to address the challenges of execution and memory layouts for many-core architectures. These projects were merged into a single project, VTK-m [19]. VTK-m provides a flexible data model that is suitable for in situ processing and execution on emerging many-core architectures.

3   Design and Implementation of Fides

The goal of Fides is to provide a general purpose data model for a wide range of different simulations that can be used for both post-hoc and in situ visualization. Fides builds on existing technologies for data movement and visualization, which are described below.

3.1 Enabling Technologies

Fides makes use of two underlying technologies, ADIOS and VTK-m. It uses ADIOS for flexible access to data, and uses VTK-m to take advantage of its flexible data model and portable performance across emerging processor architectures. Combining the capabilities of ADIOS and VTK-m enables scalable visualization and I/O while supporting inter-operable simulation tools that can be readily integrated into efficient workflows.

ADIOS. To address large-scale IO challenges, ADIOS was created to provide a simple, flexible way for scientists to describe the data in their code that is to be written, read, or processed within a running simulation [11]. ADIOS contains a number of engines that can perform file or streaming (whether that be interprocess communication using MPI or streaming over a wide area network) I/O. At run-time, ADIOS can ingest an XML file that describes the I/O objects used in the simulation and which engine should be used for each I/O object. Thus data can be treated differently without having to either change the source code or even recompile and relink the system.

ADIOS also provides an array-oriented data interface, resulting in simple APIs and high-performance data transfer. The flexibility in using ADIOS is that the same API provides access to all of the ADIOS engines, whether post hoc processing or an in situ processing engine is chosen. Because Fides requires *only* the ADIOS API, no additional changes are needed in the simulation or the visualization code to support post hoc or in situ processing.

VTK-m. VTK-m was created to leverage emerging processors and to provide high-performance, abstract data models [19]. It provides a flexible data model, where datasets are composed of cell sets and coordinate systems. The cell set defines the topological connection of the cells, what point each cell uses, and how these points connect to form cells, while the coordinate system defines the physical location of the points in a dataset. In VTK-m, the cell sets and coordinate systems are built upon an `ArrayHandle` infrastructure [2], which is a generic storage object which can represent arrays, array of structs, implicit, and functionally generated data. Because of this, new cell sets and coordinate systems can be implemented that work with existing visualization algorithms. Thus, the VTK-m data model allows for custom datasets that are tailored to a specific simulation or domain, which Fides leverages to support a wide range of simulations.

3.2 Data Description Schema

Many simulations already use ADIOS, but some simulations have developed their own custom schemas. In order to support a wide variety of simulation codes, this requires a flexible data description schema. Fides uses JSON for describing data models and an example for a triangle mesh is shown in Fig. 1. The user needs to specify one or more data sources, each of which corresponds to an ADIOS I/O object used in the application. In the example, the data will be read from

```
 1  { "VTK_Unstr_2": {                        13   "cell_set": {
 2    "data_sources": [                       14     "cell_set_type" : "single_type",
 3      { "name": "source",                   15     "cell_type" : "triangle",
 4      "filename_mode": "input" }],          16     "data_source": "source",
 5    "step_information" : {                   17     "variable" : "connectivity",
 6      "data_source" : "source" },           18     "static" : true },
 7    "coordinate_system" : {                 19   "fields": [
 8      "array" : {                           20     { "name": "dpot",
 9        "array_type" : "basic",             21       "association": "points",
10        "data_source": "source",            22       "array" : {
11        "variable" : "points",              23         "array_type" : "basic",
12        "static" : true } },                24         "data_source": "source",
                                              25         "variable" : "dpot" } } ] }}
```

Fig. 1. An example of a data model specifying an explicit grid with a single cell type.

a single source (named `source` on line 3 in Fig. 1), but in the case of multiple data sources, each source could use a different ADIOS engine. For instance, a mesh could be written to a file on disk, while the fields are streamed using one of the ADIOS in situ engines. Fides also has support for accessing time steps in either random access mode or streaming, depending on the ADIOS engine in use. When multiple data sources are being used, the source that contains the step information can be described as shown in the `step_information` object (see line 5 in Fig. 1) in the example.

The arrays that are used to create the coordinate system and cell set are then described in the `coordinate_system` and `cell_set` JSON objects in the data model. The required information for each array can vary depending on the type of mesh being described, but some general attributes that need to be provided include the `data_source`, `variable` (i.e., the name of the array in the ADIOS file/stream), and `array_type`. In most cases, `array_type` should be set to `basic`, but there are some specialized types depending on the mesh being used, which is described further in Sects. 3.3 and 3.4. In addition, the arrays can specify the attribute `static` to be true or false (with false being the default). When set to true, Fides will cache the data read on the initial read.

Fields are specified similarly in a Fides data model description, with added `association` to specify whether the data is located on cells or points. Fides also supports a "wildcard" field, where basic information such as array type and data source are specified in the JSON in a single field element. The JSON then also describes ADIOS attributes that will contain the variable names and their respective associations.

3.3 Mesh Support

Fides supports all of the standard meshes provided by VTK-m: uniform, rectilinear, curvilinear, explicit single type, and fully explicit. It supports node, zone and whole-mesh centered fields of arbitrary dimension.

Uniform. A uniform grid has a regular topology and geometry that can both be represented implicitly. The coordinate system requires describing the origin, spacing, and the dimensions. The cell set is created using VTK-m's structured cell set, which simply requires the dimensions to generate.

Rectilinear. Rectilinear grids are similar to uniform grids, except that the spacing between points can be irregular. In this case, Fides requires specifying separate arrays for the x, y, and z axes for the coordinate system, while the cell set requires only specifying the dimensions for a structured cell set.

Curvilinear. A curvilinear grid has an irregular geometry, so in a Fides data model, an array of the point coordinates should be described. The topology is regular and uses the same structured cell set used for uniform and rectilinear grids.

Explicit. Explicit grids have irregular topology and geometry, so for the coordinate system, the array of point coordinates must be described in the data model. For the cell set, three arrays are required that give information on the connectivity, types of cells, and number of vertices for each cell. In the case of datasets that only use a single cell type, this can be simplified to pointing to a single array for the connectivity and providing the cell type directly in the JSON.

3.4 Code-Specific Support

Fides also provides support for a number of code-specific data models, such as XGC [12] and GTC [25]. XGC is a plasma fusion code that uses a toroidal mesh. The coordinates of the mesh are represented as explicit in 2D (r-z dimensions) and implicit in the toroidal direction. Because of VTK-m's extensible data model, we were able to add cell set and coordinate system classes for XGC that work with the same data layout as it is stored in ADIOS. This is more efficient than transforming the XGC data to an unstructured grid with full explicit connectivity and mesh coordinates.

GTC, another plasma fusion code has explicit coordinates, but uses a complicated cell set which follows the magnetic field-lines. GTC stores the coordinates of the explicit mesh and an array of indices that are used to compute the connectivity along magnetic field-lines around the mesh. Fides uses this array of indices to create the explicit cell set in VTK-m.

3.5 Data Set Writer

Fides also supports writing VTK-m datasets with ADIOS. Given a set of VTK-m datasets, the JSON schema is generated automatically and stored as an attribute in the ADIOS data stream. The dataset writer supports uniform, rectilinear, curvilinear, single cell type explicit, fully explicit dataset types and works with all of the ADIOS writing engines. The data set writer makes it easy to create visualization services that can be connected together in arbitrary ways.

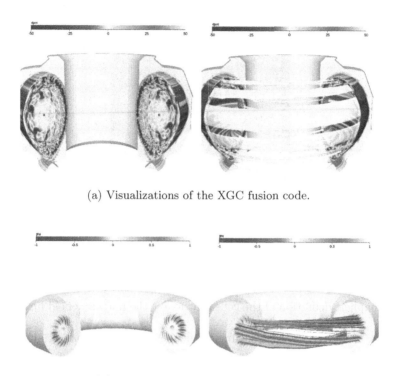

(a) Visualizations of the XGC fusion code.

(b) Visualization of the GTC fusion code.

Fig. 2. Visualizations from fusion codes showing cut-aways of the plasma on the left, and cutaways with features of interest on the right.

4 Results

In this section we describe four different visualization case studies that make use of the functionality of Fides described in Sect. 3. The case studies, and the Fides functionality used, are described in Sect. 4.1. We then evaluate the functionality of Fides in these cases against the metrics presented in Sect. 1.

4.1 Use Cases

Fusion Codes. Many fusion codes take advantage of the inherent symmetry of toroidal tokamaks to provide an efficient representation of the mesh. XGC is a gyrokinetic particle-in-cell code for the simulation of fusion plasma. The XGC mesh is a hybrid, explicit in 2D, and implicit in the third dimension. The mesh is represented by a set of triangles on a 2D plane. This plane is rotated around the central axis of the torus to create a 3D mesh, which consists of prism elements. GTC is also a gyrokinetic particle-in-cell code for simulation of fusion plasma. GTC uses an explicit representation for the 3D coordinates in the mesh, and

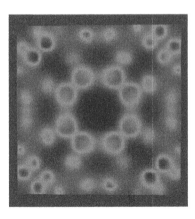

Fig. 3. Visualization of chemical concentrations from the Gray-Scott mini-app. The visualization was generated using in situ using the SST engine in ADIOS using the Fides/ParaView integration.

uses an implicit definition of the cells that follow the magnetic field lines around the torus.

Figure 2a shows two different images of the electrostatic potential that were rendered in situ during a run of the XGC simulation code. The image on the left shows a cross section of the electrostatic potential and the image on the right shows semi-transparent contours of high energy regions near the outside of the mesh. The in situ rendering service was part of a workflow system that is used to run XGC and the connections between the simulation and the in situ rendering service were specified at runtime. The rendering service used Fides to read in the XGC data for visualization. Fides used the code-specific support for the XGC data model to provide a zero-copy representation of the data, and was then rendered using VTK-m. Similarly, Fig. 2b shows two different images from the GTC simulation code. The image on the left shows a cutaway of the mesh to show the potential within the plasma. The image on the right shows isosurfaces of high potential. The rendering service used Fides to read in the GTC data. Fides used the code-specific support for GTC to create the coordinates for the explicit grid. Fides then used additional information saved in the ADIOS stream to calculate the field-line following cells.

Reaction Diffusion Code. The Gray-Scott equations are used to model the reaction and diffusion of two different chemical species. We modified a mini-app that solves the Gray-Scott equations [20] to write the simulation output data using ADIOS. We then created a JSON file to describe the rectilinear mesh used by the application. The visualization of these outputs was performed using the Fides/ParaView integration described in the next subsection. An image of an intermediate step in the simulation is shown in Fig. 3.

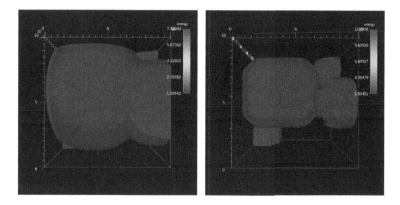

Fig. 4. In situ visualizations of data from two timesteps from the Cloverleaf3D mini-app.

Production Visualization Tool. Fides has recently been integrated into VTK [22] as a data reader. This makes it possible for any application that uses VTK to access ADIOS data using Fides. Using ADIOS to access data allows any of the file- or streaming-based engines to be used. This allows for a seamless way to visualize data files or data streams in a way that is decoupled from the simulation generating the code.

When using the Fides reader in ParaView, the data model will be generated on the fly based on the metadata contained either in the ADIOS data stream, or pulled from a JSON file describing the semantics of the ADIOS file. Currently, there is support for a number of common data models (e.g., uniform, rectilinear, explicit, etc.) as well as fusion data models like XGC. With the Fides/ParaView integration, the Simple Python module in ParaView can be used to quickly create a visualization pipeline using the Fides reader using any of the various ADIOS engines, be it file- or streaming-based engines. The Gray-Scott visualization in Fig. 3 was rendered in situ using this approach.

Hydrodynamics Code. CloverLeaf3D [1,16] is a hydrodynamics proxy-application that solves the compressible Euler equations on a Cartesian grid. We leveraged an existing integration of Cloverleaf3D with Ascent, which is a light-weight in situ analysis and visualization package. Ascent also has a mechanism to write data using ADIOS and HDF5. We integrated Fides into the ADIOS writer in Ascent. We then created a stand-alone visualization service that uses Fides to read VTK-m data from the ADIOS stream. In the example shown in Fig. 4, CloverLeaf3D was run with 6 nodes using 126 ranks on the Summit Supercomputer at the Oak Ridge Leadership Computing Facility [24]. A separate visualization service was run on 6 nodes using 66 ranks that used Fides to read data from the ADIOS stream, generate an isocontour of one of the variables from the simulation and then render the resulting geometry. This example was run using the SST writer in ADIOS to stream the data between the producer and consumer.

4.2   Metric Evaluation

In this section we evaluate the four use cases against the metrics described in Sect. 1 which can help quantify the utility of a schema for scientific visualization and analysis.

Data Model. Each of the four uses cases above took advantage of the data model provided by Fides. The diffusion-reaction and hydrodynamics codes utilized a uniform or rectilinear mesh. The use of simple metadata was sufficient to describe the mesh and the associated field data to perform a variety of visualization tasks. Visualization of the fusion data, which uses a specialized mesh type, made particular use of the Fides library. When specifying the XGC data model, Fides will provide a zero-copy representation of the mesh used by the simulation so that visualization tasks can be performed without the need to copy the data into a different format. The Paraview use case provides an example of using both standard and specialized data models in unison. The data model provided by Fides supports the standard set of mesh types used in ParaView. This allows the full set of capabilities in ParaView to be used via a direct mapping of the underlying ADIOS data arrays onto ParaView structures.

Usability. Again, each of the four uses cases took advantage of the usability provided by Fides. The barrier to entry for both file and in situ based visualization is significantly lowered by using the data movement abstractions provided by ADIOS. One of the major benefits of using ADIOS is that it doesn't require additional dependencies, or the adoption of an in situ API in order to be used. In situ processing uses the same mechanism that simulations and visualization programs already use; namely, I/O. This also allows the data transport (e.g., files, in situ) to be modified without changing the code.

Data Transforms. Basic mesh types such as uniform, rectilinear and explicit, generally do not require transformations. However, the representation of the XGC toroidal mesh would require that it be converted to a fully explicit mesh of prisms, which results in increased memory requirements. Fides is able to represent this 3D mesh using a small set of metadata and a zero-copy version of the 2D simulation mesh. This transformation makes it possible for the visualization to be performed on the mesh as-is. This is especially important for in situ uses cases where memory may be constrained, and the costs of transformations to a different form might be high.

Interoperability. They hydrodynamics and ParaView uses cases both require a high degree of interoperability. Both of these uses cases are examples of a scientific workflow where a number of components are connected together. Here, a scientist will design an experiment along with a workflow to manage the flow of data. The hydrodynamic code provides an example of how a number of services can be deployed at arbitrary locations in the workflow to visualize quantities of interest for the scientist. The ParaView example highlights how a production tool can connect to the real-time data being generated by a simulation and visualize the results. The tool can connect and disconnect as needed by the scientists for monitoring and analysis of the simulation. Fides provides the semantics so that different tools can be connected together and ensure that they understand the data that they consume.

N × M Processing. The hydrodynamics use cases demonstrates how easily the N × M processing can be done. The metadata provided by Fides also describes the number of blocks in the data stream, and provides a way to arbitrarily assign blocks to ranks. In the use case above, 126 blocks were generated by the simulation running on a total of 126 ranks. These blocks were consumed by a visualization program running on 66 ranks. Fides was used to provide the mapping, and transport of the 126 blocks from the simulation onto the 66 ranks of the consumer.

Performance. To quantify the performance impact of using Fides, we used the code profiling tool `perf` [8] on a variety of workflows and found that the overhead is generally less than 0.2%. When reading and rendering data from XGC, 96% of the time is spent in VTK-m filters and rendering, and 3.4% of the time is spent reading data via ADIOS2. Time spent in Fides only accounted for 0.18% of the total time. We also tested an example where Fides is used to write a number of VTK-m datasets to an ADIOS file, and then read it back as VTK-m datasets. We observed 97% of the time being consumed by filesystem reads and writes via ADIOS2, and 0.019% of the time being spent in Fides overhead, consistent with our other observations.

The use of a code-specific data model for the XGC code allows a zero-copy representation of the mesh. Fides constructs a VTK-m dataset that represents the XGC mesh using only a small amount of metadata.

5   Conclusion and Future Work

The problem of succinct description of the metadata for scientific data is not traditionally at the forefront of a scientist's mind. However, advancing science requires building teams of teams, and somehow, simulation, experimental and observational data must find a way into visualization tools. We presented a set of metrics that we feel are required to bridge this gap. We then described Fides, which solves this problem using an intuitive and low overhead JSON schema to describe scientific data in a way that can be interpreted by high performance visualization tools. Not only does Fides allow teams to integrate capabilities, but it also gives scientists an easy way to access in situ visualization, an increasingly necessary task as the compute to disk bandwidth ratio continues to increase. Finally, we demonstrated the usage of Fides in several different scientific workflows and evaluated these against the our metrics.

In the future, we would like to extend the data model in Fides to support a broader set of use cases. This includes support for high-dimensional data and a more general support for unstructured data (e.g., for Artificial Intelligence and Machine Learning). We will also provide additional code-specific data models in Fides. Plans are also in place to add Fides to additional visualization tools, such as Ascent and VisIt [6].

Acknowledgements. This work was supported by the U.S. Department of Energy, Office of Science, Office of Fusion Energy Sciences under Award Number DE-SC0018054 and the Scientific Discovery through Advanced Computing (SciDAC) program in U.S. Department of Energy. This work also used resources of the Oak Ridge Leadership Computing Facility, which is a U.S. Department of Energy, Office of Science User Facility.

References

1. Cloverleaf3D. http://uk-mac.github.io/CloverLeaf3D/. Accessed 19 Dec 2018
2. VTK-m users guide. https://m.vtk.org/images/c/c8/VTKmUsersGuide.pdf. Accessed 17 June 2021
3. Ayachit, U., et al.: ParaView catalyst: enabling in situ data analysis and visualization. In: Proceedings of the First Workshop on In Situ Infrastructures for Enabling Extreme-Scale Analysis and Visualization, pp. 25–29. ACM (2015)
4. Ayachit, U., et al.: Performance analysis, design considerations, and applications of extreme-scale in situ infrastructures. In: ACM/IEEE International Conference for High Performance Computing, Networking, Storage and Analysis (SC16), Salt Lake City, UT, USA, November 2016. https://doi.org/10.1109/SC.2016.78. lBNL-1007264
5. Childs, H., Bennett, J., Garth, C., Hentschel, B.: In situ visualization for computational science. IEEE Comput. Graph. Appl. **39**(6), 76–85 (2019)
6. Childs, H., et al.: VisIt: an end-user tool for visualizing and analyzing very large data. In: Bethel, E.W., Childs, H., Hansen, C. (eds.) High Performance Visualization-Enabling Extreme-Scale Scientific Insight, pp. 357–372. Chapman & Hall, CRC Computational Science, CRC Press/Francis-Taylor Group, Boca Raton, November 2012. http://www.crcpress.com/product/isbn/9781439875728. LBNL-6320E
7. Clarke, l.J., Mark, E.: Enhancements to the extensible data model and format (XDMF). In: 2007 DoD High Performance Computing Modernization Program Users Group Conference, pp. 322–327 (2007). https://doi.org/10.1109/HPCMP-UGC.2007.30
8. De Melo, A.C.: The new Linux 'perf' tools. In: Slides from Linux Kongress, vol. 18, pp. 1–42 (2010)
9. Godoy, W., et al.: Adios 2: The adaptable input output system. a framework for high-performance data management. SoftwareX **12**, 100561 (2020). https://doi.org/10.1016/j.softx.2020.100561
10. Huebl, A., et al.: openPMD: a meta data standard for particle and mesh based data (2015). https://doi.org/10.5281/zenodo.591699
11. Klasky, S., et al.: A view from ORNL: scientific data research opportunities in the big data age. In: 38th IEEE International Conference on Distributed Computing Systems, ICDCS 2018, Vienna, Austria, 2–6 July 2018, pp. 1357–1368. IEEE Computer Society (2018). https://doi.org/10.1109/ICDCS.2018.00136
12. Ku, S., et al.: A fast low-to-high confinement mode bifurcation dynamics in the boundary-plasma gyrokinetic code XGC1. Phys. Plasmas **25**(5), 056107 (2018). https://doi.org/10.1063/1.5020792
13. Larsen, M., et al.: The ALPINE in situ infrastructure: ascending from the ashes of strawman. In: Proceedings of the In Situ Infrastructures on Enabling Extreme-Scale Analysis and Visualization, pp. 42–46. ACM (2017)

14. Lawrence Livermore National Laboratory: Blueprint. https://llnl-conduit. readthedocs.io/en/latest/index.html. Accessed 18 June 2020
15. Lawrence Livermore National Laboratory: Conduit. https://llnl-conduit. readthedocs.io/en/latest/blueprint.html. Accessed 9 June 2020
16. Mallinson, A., et al.: CloverLeaf: preparing hydrodynamics codes for exascale. The Cray User Group 2013 (2013)
17. Meredith, J.S., Ahern, S., Pugmire, D., Sisneros, R.: EAVL: the extreme-scale analysis and visualization library. In: Childs, H., Kuhlen, T., Marton, F. (eds.) Eurographics Symposium on Parallel Graphics and Visualization. The Eurographics Association (2012). https://doi.org/10.2312/EGPGV/EGPGV12/021-030
18. Moreland, K., Ayachit, U., Geveci, B., Ma, K.: Dax toolkit: a proposed framework for data analysis and visualization at extreme scale. In: Rogers, D.H., Silva, C.T. (eds.) IEEE Symposium on Large Data Analysis and Visualization, LDAV 2011, Providence, Rhode Island, USA, 23–24 October 2011, pp. 97–104. IEEE Computer Society (2011). https://doi.org/10.1109/LDAV.2011.6092323
19. Moreland, K., et al.: VTK-m: accelerating the visualization toolkit for massively threaded architectures. IEEE Comput. Graph. Appl. **36**(3), 48–58 (2016). https:// doi.org/10.1109/MCG.2016.48
20. ORNL: Grey-Scott simulation code (2018). https://github.com/suchyta1/ adiosvm/blob/cpp/Tutorial/gray-scott/simulation/gray-scott.cpp. Accessed 9 Apr 2021
21. Pugmire, D., et al.: Visualization as a service for scientific data. In: Nichols, J., Verastegui, B., Maccabe, A.B., Hernandez, O., Parete-Koon, S., Ahearn, T. (eds.) SMC 2020. CCIS, vol. 1315, pp. 157–174. Springer, Cham (2020). https://doi.org/ 10.1007/978-3-030-63393-6_11
22. Schroeder, W.J., Lorensen, B., Martin, K.: The visualization toolkit: an object-oriented approach to 3D graphics. Kitware (2004)
23. Tchoua, R., et al.: Adios visualization schema: a first step towards improving interdisciplinary collaboration in high performance computing. In: 2013 IEEE 9th International Conference on e-Science, pp. 27–34 (2013). https://doi.org/10.1109/ eScience.2013.24
24. Vazhkudai, S.S., et al.: The design, deployment, and evaluation of the coral pre-exascale systems. In: SC18: International Conference for High Performance Computing, Networking, Storage and Analysis, pp. 661–672 (2018)
25. Wang, B., et al.: Kinetic turbulence simulations at extreme scale on leadership-class systems. In: Proceedings of the International Conference on High Performance Computing, Networking, Storage and Analysis, pp. 1–12 (2013)
26. Whitlock, B., Favre, J.M., Meredith, J.S.: Parallel in situ coupling of simulation with a fully featured visualization system. In: Kuhlen, T., et al. (eds.) Eurographics Symposium on Parallel Graphics and Visualization. The Eurographics Association (2011). https://doi.org/10.2312/EGPGV/EGPGV11/101-109

Including in Situ Visualization and Analysis in PDI

Christian Witzler[1](✉) , J. Miguel Zavala-Aké[2], Karol Sierociński[3] ,
and Herbert Owen[4]

[1] Jülich Supercomputing Centre, Forschungszentrum Jülich GmbH, Jülich, Germany
c.witzler@fz-juelich.de
http://www.fz-juelich.de/jsc
[2] Meteorologiska Institutionen, Stockholm, Sweden
miguelza@kth.se
[3] Poznan Supercomputing and Networking Center, Poznan, Poland
ksiero@man.poznan.pl
[4] Barcelona Supercomputing Center, Barcelona, Spain
herbert.owen@bsc.es

Abstract. The goal of this work was to integrate in situ possibilities into the general-purpose code-coupling library PDI [1]. This is done using the simulation code Alya as an example. Here, an open design is taken into account to later create possibilities to extend this to other simulation codes, that are using PDI.

Here, an in transit solution was chosen to separate the simulation as much as possible from the analysis and visualization. To implement this, ADIOS2 is used for data transport. However, to prevent too strong a commitment to one tool, SENSEI is interposed between simulation and ADIOS2 as well as in the in-transit endpoint between ADIOS2 and the visualization software. This allows a user who wants a different solution to easily implement it. However, the visualization with ParaView Catalyst was chosen as default for the time being.

Keywords: In transit · SENSEI · ADIOS2 · High-performance computing (HPC)

1 Motivation

The goal of this work was to integrate in situ possibilities into the general-purpose code-coupling library PDI [1]. This is done using the simulation code Alya as an example. Here, an open design is taken into account to later create possibilities to extend this to other simulation codes, that are using PDI.

The use of in situ procedures has many advantages. It allows to see first results faster, to analyze more intermediate steps and reduce the required I/O resources because fewer or even no complete data sets have to be stored. Despite

Supported by EoCoE-II and CoEC.

H. Jagode et al. (Eds.): ISC High Performance 2021 Workshops, LNCS 12761, pp. 508–512, 2021.
https://doi.org/10.1007/978-3-030-90539-2_35

these advantages, the use of in situ methods is fraught with problems. For example, there are further dependencies when programming simulations, as well as when compiling and running the simulation. These dependencies can also change with version changes of the used in situ library, which requires additional work on the simulation code to be able to use current versions with new features. In addition, there is also a competition for resources on the individual compute nodes, as additional code must now be run for the in situ procedures. This requires CPU time, network bandwidth, and most importantly for some simulations, working memory, depending on the chosen in-situ method. Especially in the case of an in situ visualization running on the same compute nodes as the simulation, there is a risk that small changes to the visualization pipeline can dramatically increase the amount of memory required. This then has the risk of crashing the simulation and the complete progress of the simulation could be lost.

2   pdi2sensei

Here we use different solutions that are already available in the in situ area and combine them in a way to make it as easy and as error-free as possible for the end-user. For this, we first use PDI [2] (PDI data interface), which allows reducing the dependencies of the simulation to a library. PDI allows users to customize the data output of the simulation via a configuration file without recompiling the simulation. PDI enables different methods of data output to be configured, such as traditional I/O with the use of HDF5. PDI requires only a library agnostic annotation of the simulation code and then allows the use of libraries from a specification tree [1].

The further problem of changes in version jumps of in situ libraries is solved by using SENSEI [7], which provides a common interface to use different in situ libraries with one interface. This allows to support various libraries at once and permits to change the visualization backend later if there are new or different requirements for the in situ analysis or visualization.

To minimize the conflict over resources and impact on the simulation, we use the in-transit specialization of the in situ solutions. Therefore, we use different computational nodes for the actual analysis and visualization work. This reduces the impact on the simulation nodes to only the data traffic to the in-transit nodes. It also allows us to use appropriate nodes (for example use nodes with GPU for your visualization) and node counts for both visualization and simulation. For the data transport, we use ADIOS2 [8,9], which transports the data for us. ADIOS2 also allows the use of M2N communication, so the number of simulation nodes can be different from the number of in-transit nodes, and ADIOS2 distributes the data. ADIOS2 has several transport mechanisms [9] (called engine in ADIOS2), currently, we use SST, which in our case uses a shared file system to exchange network information via a file and then transport the user data via the network. In the future, the different engines that are possible with ADIOS2 will also allow testing with new hardware such as burst buffers by writing to the burst buffer for data transfer and retrieving this data from other nodes. This would then make the simulation code even more independent from the analysis and visualization code.

ADIOS2 then passes the data on the in-transit node to SENSEI, where it can then be flexibly transferred to various in situ solutions. Here we use the solution developed by ParaView [10] called Catalyst [11]. Using Catalyst, a predefined visualization pipeline can be used to store rendered images and pre-analyzed data. In addition, there is the possibility to use a live interactive visualization, where you can send selected data to ParaView and adjust your visualization with ongoing updates.

Here we started with the development of pdi2sensei, which makes it possible to easily transfer the data passed by PDI from the simulation to SENSEI while making the conversion to the VTK data needed by SENSEI as simple as possible. As a base configuration, this SENSEI component is configured to use ADIOS2 to send the data directly to the in-transit nodes. Here we use SENSEI again to pass the data from ADIOS2 flexibly to different in situ solutions, here Catalyst. Using SENSEI in both places allows adapting both transport and in situ solutions to new requirements. As the first simulation using this setup, we have chosen Alya, for the purpose of simulating the airflow over complex terrain.

3   Example

Alya is a parallel multi-physics/multi-scale simulation code developed at the Barcelona Super-computing Center to run efficiently on high-performance computing environments. It can solve a wide range of problems, including solid mechanics, compressible and incompressible flow, flows with interfaces using the level set method, combustion, and thermal problems. The case presented in this work is an incompressible flow simulation using wall-modeled Large Eddy Simulation. The convective term is discretized using a recently proposed Galerkin finite element (FEM) scheme, which conserves linear and angular momentum, and kinetic energy at the discrete level described in [13]. Neither upwinding nor any equivalent momentum stabilization is employed. To use equal-order elements for both velocity and pressure, numerical dissipation is introduced only for pressure stabilization via a fractional step scheme. The set of equations is integrated in time using a third-order Runge-Kutta explicit scheme. Due to the high Reynolds number of Atmospheric Boundary Layer flows, wall modeling is required at the ground. A novel wall modeling finite element implementation is used [14] in this work.

The Bolund experiment is a classical benchmark for microscale atmospheric flow models over complex terrain [15–17]. It has been the basis for a unique blind comparison of flow models. Despite its relatively small size, its shape induces complex 3D flow. The wind comes from the sea, and thus the inflow profile is relatively simple to impose. The flow collides against a 10m height cliff, and a complex recirculation is formed at the region of interest located at the top of the cliff. For the results presented in this work, an unstructured grid with 31M elements has been used. The number of Elements can be scaled up by Alya as well, by passing on a subdivision command in the configuration file, splitting each cell into eight cells [18]. As this can be done multiple times the simulation's cell numbers can be increased by powers of eight, increasing the resolution of the simulation data.

4   Conclusion

To be able to use this in such a way some steps were necessary. First of all, PDI must be integrated to be able to transfer the data to PDI. Here it was very helpful that there is already a previous possibility to do in situ visualization in Alya, so the access to all needed data was already possible in one place in the code. However, the previous solution is not as flexible as the new solution, which is why this update was made. Next, a simple way had to be created in pdi2sensei to start the previously described setup with in-transit as easy as possible and with as little setup as necessary as a base configuration. Then, functions were implemented in pdi2sensei that allows for the user of pdi2sensei to connect data provided by the simulation through PDI to the data expected by SENSEI. This allows using the setup with few lines of code. You only have to pass your data to PDI in the simulation code and specify in the configuration file of PDI which values you want to pass to pdi2sensei.

Acknowledgment. This work was supported by the European Council under the Horizon 2020 Project Energy oriented Center of Excellence for computing applications - EoCoE II, grant agreement No 824158 and the Center of Excellence for combustion - CoEC, 952181.

References

1. PDI concepts. https://pdi.julien-bigot.fr/master/Concepts.html. Accessed 18 Jun 2021
2. PDI documentation. https://pdi.julien-bigot.fr/master/. Accessed 18 Jun 2021
3. Roussel, C., Keller, K., Gaalich, M., Gomez, L.B., Bigot, J.: PDI, an approach to decouple I/O concerns from high-performance simulation codes (2017)
4. YAML specification. https://yaml.org/spec/. Accessed 18 Jun 2021
5. HDF5 specification. https://support.hdfgroup.org/HDF5/doc/H5.format.html. Accessed 18 Jun 2021
6. pybind11 repository. https://github.com/pybind/pybind11. Accessed 18 Jun 2021
7. Sensei homepage. https://sensei-insitu.org/. Accessed 24 Apr 2021
8. ADIOS2 documentation. https://adios2.readthedocs.io/en/latest/. Accessed 24 Apr 2021
9. Godoy, W.F., et al.: ADIOS 2: the adaptable input output system. A framework for high-performance data management. SoftwareX **12**, 100561 (2020). https://doi.org/10.1016/j.softx.2020.100561
10. ParaView homepage, Kiteware. https://www.paraview.org/. Accessed 24 Apr 2021
11. Catalyst homepage, Kiteware. https://www.paraview.org/in-situ/. Accessed 24 Apr 2021

12. Usage introduction to PDI. https://pdi.julien-bigot.fr/1.2/First_steps.html. Accessed 18 Jun 2021
13. Lehmkuhl, O., Houzeaux, G., Owen, H., Chrysokentis, G., Rodriguez, I.: A low-dissipation finite element scheme for scale resolving simulations of turbulent flows. J. Comput. Phys. **390**, 51–65 (2019)
14. Owen, H., et al.: Wall-modeled large-eddy simulation in a finite element framework. Int. J. Numer. Methods Fluids **92**(1), 20–37 (2019)
15. Berg, J., Mann, J., Bechmann, A., Courtney, M., Jorgensen, H.: The Bolund experiment, part I: flow over a steep, three-dimensional hill. Bound Layer Meteorol. **141**(2), 219–243 (2011)
16. Bechmann, A., Sørensen, N., Berg, J., Mann, J., Rethore, P.E.: The Bolund experiment, part II: flow over a steep, three-dimensional hill. Bound Layer Meteorol. **141**(2), 245–271 (2011)
17. DTU Wind Energy. https://www.bolund.vindenergi.dtu.dk/the_bolund_experiment. Accessed 24 Apr 2021
18. Houzeaux, G., de la Cruz, R., Owen, H., Vázquez, M.: Parallel uniform mesh multiplication applied to a Navier-Stokes solver. Comput. Fluids **80**, 142–151 (2013)

Correction to: An Explainable Model for Fault Detection in HPC Systems

Martin Molan, Andrea Borghesi, Francesco Beneventi, Massimiliano Guarrasi, and Andrea Bartolini

Correction to:
Chapter "An Explainable Model for Fault Detection
in HPC Systems" in: H. Jagode et al. (Eds.):
High Performance Computing, **LNCS 12761,**
https://doi.org/10.1007/978-3-030-90539-2_25

The chapter was inadvertently published with the spelling error in the first author's name. It has been corrected to "Martin Molan".

The updated version of this chapter can be found at
https://doi.org/10.1007/978-3-030-90539-2_25

© Springer Nature Switzerland AG 2021
H. Jagode et al. (Eds.): ISC High Performance 2021 Workshops, LNCS 12761, p. C1, 2021.
https://doi.org/10.1007/978-3-030-90539-2_36

Correction to: Machine-Learning-Based Control of Perturbed and Heated Channel Flows

Mario Rüttgers⑩, Moritz Waldmann⑩, Wolfgang Schröder⑩,
and Andreas Lintermann⑩

Correction to:
Chapter "Machine-Learning-Based Control of Perturbed and Heated Channel Flows" in: H. Jagode et al. (Eds.):
High Performance Computing, **LNCS 12761,**
https://doi.org/10.1007/978-3-030-90539-2_1

Chapter "Machine-Learning-Based Control of Perturbed and Heated Channel Flows" was previously published non-open access. It has now been changed to open access under a CC BY 4.0 license and the copyright holder updated to 'The Author(s)'.

The updated version of this chapter can be found at
https://doi.org/10.1007/978-3-030-90539-2_1

Author Index

Printed in the United States
by Baker & Taylor Publisher Services